Lecture Notes in Computer Science 8739

Commenced Publication in 1973
Founding and Former Series Editors:
Gerhard Goos, Juris Hartmanis, and Jan van Leeuwen

Elvira Albert   Emil Sekerinski (Eds.)

Integrated Formal Methods

11th International Conference, IFM 2014
Bertinoro, Italy, September 9-11, 2014
Proceedings

 Springer

Volume Editors

Elvira Albert
Complutense University of Madrid
Departamento de Sistemas Informáticos y Programación
C/ Profesor José García Santesmases, s/n, 28040 Madrid, Spain
E-mail: elvira@sip.ucm.es

Emil Sekerinski
McMaster University
Department of Computing and Software
1280 Main Street West, Hamilton, ON, L8S 4K1, Canada
E-mail: emil@mcmaster.ca

ISSN 0302-9743   e-ISSN 1611-3349
ISBN 978-3-319-10180-4   e-ISBN 978-3-319-10181-1
DOI 10.1007/978-3-319-10181-1
Springer Cham Heidelberg New York Dordrecht London

Library of Congress Control Number: 2014945667

LNCS Sublibrary: SL 2 – Programming and Software Engineering

Typesetting: Camera-ready by author, data conversion by Scientific Publishing Services, Chennai, India

Printed on acid-free paper

Springer is part of Springer Science+Business Media (www.springer.com)

Preface

Mathematical software development techniques promise to facilitate *impeccable* software, which, given the reliance of society on computing devices, is undoubtedly a worthwhile ideal. The iFM conference series grew out of the observation that formal methods of software development and their associated tools historically tend to focus on a single aspect of software quality, are not integrated into the software development process, and thus their value is not widely appreciated. For formal methods to have a wide impact, correctness of programs, modelling of the environment, multiple representations of models, quantitative analysis, code generation, and code efficiency (with a recent emphasis on multi-core concurrency), security, distribution (with a recent emphasis on clouds), automation of analysis, systematic development steps, and involvement of multiple stakeholders in the software all need to be integrated. These proceedings document the outcome of the 11th International Conference on Integrated Formal Methods, iFM 2014, on recent developments toward this goal. The conference was held in Bertinoro, Italy, during September 9-11, 2014, and hosted by the University of Bologna. Previous editions of iFM were held in York, UK (1999), Schloss Dagstuhl, Germany (2000), Turku, Finland (2002), Kent, UK (2004), Eindhoven, The Netherlands (2005), Oxford, UK (2007), Düsseldorf, Germany (2009), Nancy, France (2010), Pisa, Italy (2012), and Turku, Finland (2013).

The conference received 43 submissions of authors from 22 countries. All full papers were reviewed by at least three members of the Program Committee. After careful deliberations, the Program Committee selected 21 papers for presentation. In addition to these papers, this volume contains papers of two invited speakers, Sophia Drossopoulou, Imperial College, UK and Helmut Veith, TU Wien, Austria:

- Sophia Drossopoulou, James Noble: "How to Break the Bank: Semantics of Capability Policies"
- Diego Calvanese, Tomer Kotek, Mantas Simkus, Helmut Veith, Florian Zuleger: "Shape and Content: A Database-theoretic Perspective on the Analysis of Data Structures"

Invited presentations are always the highlights of a conference; these contributions are, therefore, gratefully acknowledged.

This edition of iFM was co-located with the 11th International Conference on Formal Aspects of Component Software, FACS 2014. The programs of FACS and iFM were overlapping, and the invited speakers were shared, fostering exchange of ideas between the two communities. FACS and iFM were accompanied by following workshops, under the organization of the workshop chair, Elena Giachino, University of Bologna:

- Harnessing Theories for Tool Support in Software (TTSS)

- Logics and Model-checking for Self-* Systems (MOD*)
- Tools and Methods for Cyber-Physical Systems of Systems
- Workshop on Contracts for Efficient and Reliable Services
- Formal Methods: Business Impact of Application to Security-Relevant Devices (FM-BIASED)

The conference would not have been possible without the enthusiasm and dedication of the FACS and iFM general chair, Gianluigi Zavattaro, the Organization Committee with Gianluigi Zavattaro (chair), Saverio Giallorenzo (logistics) and Jacopo Mauro (web master), and the support of the Department of Computer Science and Engineering - DISI, University of Bologna, Italy. Additional organizational support was provided by the University Residential Center of Bertinoto - CeUB, Bertinoro. For the work of the Program Committee and the compilation of the proceedings, Andrei Voronkov's EasyChair system was employed; it freed us from many technical matters and allowed us to focus on the program, for which we are grateful. Conferences like iFM rely on the willingness of experts to serve on the Program Committee; their professionalism and their helpfulness was exemplary. Finally, we would like to thank all the authors for their submissions, their willingness to continue improving their papers, and their presentations!

July 2014

Elvira Albert
Emil Sekerinski

Organization

Program Committee

Erika Abraham	RWTH Aachen University, Germany
Elvira Albert	Complutense University of Madrid, Spain
Clara Benac Earle	Technical University of Madrid, Spain
Eerke Boiten	University of Kent, UK
Michael Butler	University of Southampton, UK
Ana Cavalcanti	University of York, UK
Frank De Boer	CWI Amsterdam, The Netherlands
David Deharbe	Federal University of Rio Grande do Norte, Brazil
John Derrick	Unversity of Sheffield, UK
Marc Frappier	University of Sherbrooke, Canada
Elena Giachino	University of Bologna, Italy
Susanne Graf	Verimag, France
John Hatcliff	Kansas State University, USA
Einar Broch Johnsen	University of Oslo, Norway
Rajeev Joshi	NASA Jet Propulsion Laboratory, USA
Laura Kovacs	Chalmers University of Technology, Sweden
Diego Latella	National Research Council, Pisa, Italy
Stefan Leue	University of Konstanz, Germany
Shaoying Liu	Hosei University, Japan
Dominique Mery	LORIA and University of Lorraine, France
Antoine Miné	Ecole Normale Supérieur, France
Luigia Petre	Åbo Akademi University, Finland
Guillermo Román-Díez	Technical University of Madrid, Spain
Fernando Rosa-Velardo	Complutense University of Madrid, Spain
Augusto Sampaio	University of Pernambuco, Brazil
Thomas Santen	European Microsoft Innovation Center, Germany
Steve Schneider	University of Surrey, UK
Emil Sekerinski	McMaster University, Canada
Graeme Smith	University of Queensland, Australia
Kenji Taguchi	AIST, Japan
Tayssir Touili	University Paris Diderot, France
Helen Treharne	University of Surrey, UK
Juri Vain	Tallinn University of Technology, Estonia
Heike Wehrheim	University of Paderborn, Germany
Peter Wong	Fredhopper B. V., The Netherlands

Additional Reviewers

Azadbakht, Keyvan
Beer, Adrian
Bey, Alina
Blanchet, Bruno
Blanchette, Jasmin Christian
Ciancia, Vincenzo
Corzilius, Florian
Dalla Preda, Mila
de Gouw, Stijn
Garoche, Pierre-Loic
Jansen, Nils
Kamali, Maryam
Kanter, Gert
Kawamoto, Yusuke
Kokash, Natallia
Kremer, Gereon
Leitner-Fischer, Florian
Li, Qin
Lienhardt, Michael

Miyazawa, Alvaro
Montenegro, Manuel
Mota, Alexandre
Nellen, Johanna
Neri Alborodo, Raul Nestor
Nobakht, Behrooz
Pérez, Jorge A.
Riesco, Adrian
Rodríguez, Ricardo J.
Romero, Daniel
Said, Mar Yah
Sandvik, Petter
Savicks, Vitaly
Serbanescu, Vlad Nicolae
Snook, Colin
Tammet, Tanel
Ter Beek, Maurice H.
Zunino, Roberto

Table of Contents

Invited Talks

Tool Integration

Model Verification

Program Development

Security Analysis

Analysis and Transformation

Concurrency and Control

Invited Talks

Shape and Content[*]

A Database-Theoretic Perspective
on the Analysis of Data Structures

Diego Calvanese[1], Tomer Kotek[2], Mantas Šimkus[2],
Helmut Veith[2], and Florian Zuleger[2]

[1] Free University of Bozen-Bolzano
[2] Vienna University of Technology

Abstract. The verification community has studied dynamic data structures primarily in a bottom-up way by analyzing pointers and the shapes induced by them. Recent work in fields such as separation logic has made significant progress in extracting shapes from program source code. Many real world programs however manipulate complex data whose structure and content is most naturally described by formalisms from object oriented programming and databases. In this paper, we look at the verification of programs with dynamic data structures from the perspective of content representation. Our approach is based on description logic, a widely used knowledge representation paradigm which gives a logical underpinning for diverse modeling frameworks such as UML and ER. Technically, we assume that we have separation logic shape invariants obtained from a shape analysis tool, and requirements on the program data in terms of description logic. We show that the two-variable fragment of first order logic with counting and trees can be used as a joint framework to embed suitable fragments of description logic and separation logic.

1   Introduction

The manipulation and storage of complex information in imperative programming languages is often achieved by dynamic data structures. The verification of programs with dynamic data structures, however, is notoriously difficult, and is a highly active area of current research. While much progress has been made recently in analyzing and verifying the *shape* of dynamic data structures, most notably by separation logic (SL) [24,17], the *content* of dynamic data structures has not received the same attention.

In contrast, disciplines as databases, modeling and knowledge representation have developed highly-successful theories for *content representation and verification*. These research communities typically model reality by classes and binary

[*] Kotek, Veith and Zuleger were supported by the Austrian National Research Network S11403-N23 (RiSE) of the Austrian Science Fund (FWF) and by the Vienna Science and Technology Fund (WWTF) through grants PROSEED and ICT12-059. Simkus was supported by the FWF grant P25518 and the WWTF grant ICT12-15.

E. Albert and E. Sekerinski (Eds.): IFM 2014, LNCS 8739, pp. 3–17, 2014.
© Springer International Publishing Switzerland 2014

relationships between these classes. For example, the database community uses *entity-relationship (ER)* diagrams, and *UML* diagrams have been studied in requirements engineering. Content representation in the form of UML and ER has become a central pillar of *industrial software engineering*. In complex software projects, the source code is usually accompanied by *design documents* which provide extensive documentation and models of data structure content. This documentation is both an opportunity and a challenge for program verification. Recent hardware verification papers have demonstrated how design diagrams can be integrated into an industrial verification workflow [18].

In this paper, we propose the use of *Description Logics* (DLs) for the formulation of content specifications. DLs are a well established and highly popular family of logics for representing knowledge in artificial intelligence [3]. In particular, DLs allow to precisely model and reason about UML and ER diagrams [6,2]. DLs are mature and well understood, they have good algorithmic properties and have efficient reasoners. DLs are very readable and form a natural base for developing specification languages. For example, they are the logical backbone of the Web Ontology Language (OWL) for the Semantic Web [22]. DLs vary in expressivity and complexity, and are usually selected according to the expressivity needed to formalize the given target domain.

Unfortunately, the existing content representation technology cannot be applied directly for the verification of content specifications of pointer-manipulating programs. This is to due the strict separation between high-level content descriptions such as UML/ER and the way data is actually stored. For example, query languages such as SQL and Datalog provide a convenient abstraction layer for formulating data queries while ignoring how the database is stored on the disk. In contrast, programs with dynamic data structures manipulate their data structures directly. Moreover, database schemes are usually static while a program may change the content of its data structures over time.

The main goal of this paper is to develop a verification methodology that allows to employ DLs for formulating and verifying content specifications of pointer-manipulating programs. We propose a two-step Hoare-style verification methodology: First, existing shape-analysis techniques are used to derive shape invariants. Second, the user strengthens the derived shape invariants with content annotations; the resulting verification conditions are then checked automatically. Technically, we employ a very expressive DL (henceforth called $\mathcal{L}$), based on the so called $\mathcal{ALCHOIF}$, which we specifically tailor to better support reasoning about complex pointer structures. For shape analysis we rely on the SL fragment from [7]. In order to reason automatically about the verification conditions involving DL as well as SL formulae, we identify a powerful decidable logic CT^2 which incorporates both logics [10]. We believe that our main contribution is conceptual, integrating these different formalisms for the first time. While the current approach is semi-manual, our long term goal is to increase the automatization of the method.

Overview and Contributions

- In Section 2, we introduce our formalism. In particular, we formally define *memory structures* for representing the heap and we study the DL $\mathcal{L}$ as a formalism for expressing *content properties* of memory structures.
- In Section 2, we further present the building blocks for our verification methodology: We give an embedding of $\mathcal{L}$ and an embedding of a fragment of the SL from [7] into CT^2 (Lemmata 2 and 3). Moreover, we give a complexity-preserving reduction of satisfiability of CT^2 over memory structures to finite satisfiability of CT^2 (Lemma 1).
- In Section 3, we describe a program model for sequential imperative heap-manipulating programs without procedures. Our main contribution is a Hoare-style proof system for verifying content properties on top of (already verified) shape properties stated in SL.
- Our main technical result is a precise backward-translation of content properties along loop-less code (Lemma 5). This backward-translation allows us to reduce the inductiveness of the Hoare-annotations to satisfiability in CT^2. Theorem 1 states the soundness and completeness of this reduction.

1.1   Running Example: Information System of a Company

Our running example will be a simple information system for a company with the following UML diagram:. The UML gives the relationships between entities in the informa-

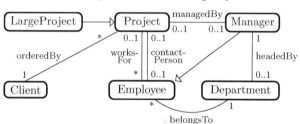

tion system, but says nothing regarding the implementations of the data structures that hold the data. We focus mostly on projects, and on the employees and managers which work on them. Here is an informal description of the programmers' intention. The employees and projects are stored in two lists, both using the *next* pointer. The heads of the two lists are pHd and eHd respectively. Here are some properties of our information system. (i)-(iii) extends the UML somewhat. (iv)-(vi) do not appear in the UML, but can be expressed in DL:

(i) Each employee in the list of employees has a pointer $wrkFor$ to a project on the list of projects, indicating the project that the employee is working on (or to null, in case no project is assigned to that employee).

(ii) Each project in the list has a pointer $mngBy$ to the employee list, indicating the manager of the project (or to null, if the project doesn't have one).

(iii) Employees have a Boolean field $isMngr$ marking them as managers, and only they can manage projects.

(iv) The manager of a project works for the project.

(v) At least 10 employees work on each large project.

(vi) The contact person for a large-scale project is a manager.

We will refer to these properties as the *system invariants*.

The programmer has written a program S (stated below) for verification. The programmer has the following intuition about her program: The code S adds a new project *proj* to the project list, and assigns to it all employees in the employee list which are not assigned to any project.

The programmer wants to verify that the system invariants are true after the execution of S, if they were true in the beginning (1). Note that *during* the execution of the code, they might not be true! Additionally the programmer wants to verify that after executing S, the project list has been extended by *proj*, the employee list still contains the same employees and indeed all employees who did not work for a project before now work for project *proj* (2). We will formally prove the correctness of S following our verification methodology discussed in the introduction. In Section 2.3 we describe how our DL can be used for specifying the verification goals (1) and (2). In Section 3.4 we state verification conditions that allow to conclude the correctness of (1) and (2) for S.

```
ℓ_b : proj := new ;
      proj . next := pHd ;
      pHd := proj ;
      e := eHd ;
ℓ_l : while ~( e = null )  do
        if ( e . wrkFor = null )
        then  e . wrkFor := proj ;
        e := e . next ;
      od
ℓ_e : end ;
```

2   Logics for Invariant Specification

2.1   Memory Structures

We use ordinary first order structures to represent memory in a precise way. A *structure* (or, *interpretation*) is a tuple $\mathcal{M} = (M, \tau, \cdot)$, where (i) M is an infinite set (the *universe*), (ii) τ is a set of *constants* and *relation symbols* with an associated non-negative arity, and (iii) $\cdot$ is an *interpretation function*, which assigns to each constant $c \in \tau$ an element $c^{\mathcal{M}} \in M$, and to each n-ary relation symbol $R \in \tau$ an n-ary relation $R^{\mathcal{M}}$ over M. Each relation is either unary or binary (i.e. $n \in \{1, 2\}$). Given $A \subseteq M$, a binary $R^{\mathcal{M}}$, $R^{\mathcal{M}}$ and $e \in A^{\mathcal{M}}$, we may use the notation $R^{\mathcal{M}}(e)$ if $R^{\mathcal{M}}$ is known to be a function over $A^{\mathcal{M}}$.

A *Memory structure* describes a snapshot of the heap and the local variables. We assume sets $\tau_{\mathrm{var}} \subseteq \tau$ of constants $\tau_{\mathrm{fields}} \subseteq \tau$ of binary relation symbols. We will later employ these symbols for variables and fields in programs. A *memory structure* is a structure $\mathcal{M} = (M, \tau, \cdot)$ that satisfies the following conditions:

(1) τ includes the constants $o_{\mathrm{null}}, o_{\mathbf{T}}, o_{\mathbf{F}}$.
(2) τ has the unary relations *Addresses*, *Alloc*, *PossibleTargets*, *MemPool*, and *Aux*.
(3) $Aux^{\mathcal{M}} = \{o_{\mathrm{null}}^{\mathcal{M}}, o_{\mathbf{T}}^{\mathcal{M}}, o_{\mathbf{F}}^{\mathcal{M}}\}$ and $|Aux^{\mathcal{M}}| = 3$.
(4) $Addresses^{\mathcal{M}} \cap Aux^{\mathcal{M}} = \emptyset$ and $Addresses^{\mathcal{M}} \cup Aux^{\mathcal{M}} = M$.
(5) $Alloc^{\mathcal{M}}$, $PossibleTargets^{\mathcal{M}}$ and $MemPool^{\mathcal{M}}$ form a partition of $Addresses^{\mathcal{M}}$.

(6) $c^{\mathcal{M}} \in M \backslash MemPool^{\mathcal{M}}$ for every constant c of τ.

(7) For all $f \in \tau_{\text{fields}}$, $f^{\mathcal{M}}$ is a function from $Addresses^{\mathcal{M}}$ to $M \backslash MemPool^{\mathcal{M}}$.

(8) If $e \in MemPool^{\mathcal{M}}$, then $f^{\mathcal{M}}(e) \in \{o_{\text{null}}^{\mathcal{M}}, o_{\mathbf{F}}^{\mathcal{M}}\}$.

(9) $R^{\mathcal{M}} \subseteq (M \backslash MemPool^{\mathcal{M}})^n$ for every[1] n-ary $R \in \tau \setminus (\{MemPool\} \cup \tau_{\text{fields}})$.

(10) $Alloc^{\mathcal{M}}$ and $PossibleTargets^{\mathcal{M}}$ are finite. $MemPool^{\mathcal{M}}$ is infinite.

We explain the intuition behind memory structures. Variables in programs will either have a Boolean value or be pointers. Thus, to represent null and the Boolean values $\mathbf{T}$ and $\mathbf{F}$, we employ the auxiliary relation $Aux^{\mathcal{M}}$ storing 3 elements corresponding to the 3 values. $Addresses^{\mathcal{M}}$ represents the memory cells. The relation $Alloc^{\mathcal{M}}$ is the set of allocated cells, $PossibleTargets^{\mathcal{M}}$ contains all cells which are not allocated, but are pointed to by allocated cells (for technical reasons it possibly contains some other unallocated cells). $MemPool^{\mathcal{M}}$ contains the cells which are not allocated, do not have any field values other than null and $\mathbf{F}$, are not pointed to by any field, do not participate in any other relation and do not interpret any constant (see (6-9)). The memory cells in $MemPool$ are the candidates for allocation during the run of a program. Since the allocated memory should by finite at any point of the execution of a program, we require that $Alloc^{\mathcal{M}}$ and $PossibleTargets^{\mathcal{M}}$ are finite (see (10)), while the available memory $Addresses^{\mathcal{M}}$ and the memory pool $MemPool^{\mathcal{M}}$ are infinite. Finally, each cell is seen as a record with the fields of τ_{fields}.

2.2   The Description Logic $\mathcal{L}$

$\mathcal{L}$ is defined w.r.t. a vocabulary τ consisting of relation and constant symbols.[2]

Definition 1 (Syntax of $\mathcal{L}$). *The sets of* roles *and* concepts *of $\mathcal{L}$ is defined inductively: (1) every unary relation symbol is a concept (atomic concept); (2) every constant symbol is a concept; (3) every binary relation symbol is a role (atomic role); (4) if r, s are roles, then $r \cup s$, $r \cap s$, $r \backslash s$ and r^- are roles; (5) if C, D are concepts, then so are $C \sqcap D$, $C \sqcup D$, and $\neg C$; (6) if r is a role and C is a concept, then $\exists r.C$ is also a concept; (7) if C, D are concepts, then $C \times D$ is a role (product role).*

The set of formulae *of $\mathcal{L}$ is the closure under $\wedge, \vee, \neg, \rightarrow$ of the atomic formulae: $C \sqsubseteq D$ (concept inclusion), where C, D are concepts; $r \sqsubseteq s$ (role inclusion), where r, s are roles; and $func(r)$ (functionality assertion), where r is a role.*

Definition 2 (Semantics of $\mathcal{L}$). *The semantics is given in terms of structures $\mathcal{M} = (M, \tau, \cdot)$. The extension of $\cdot^{\mathcal{M}}$ from the atomic relations and constants in M and the satisfaction relation $\models$ are given below. If $\mathcal{M} \models \varphi$, then $\mathcal{M}$ is a model of φ. We write $\psi \models \varphi$ if every model of ψ is also a model of φ.*

---

[1] Here $n \in \{1, 2\}$.

[2] In DL terms, $\mathcal{L}$ corresponds to Boolean $\mathcal{ALCHOIF}$ knowledge bases with the additional support for role intersection, role union, role difference and product roles.

$$(C \sqcap D)^{\mathcal{M}} \quad = C^{\mathcal{M}} \cap D^{\mathcal{M}} \qquad\qquad (r \sqcap s)^{\mathcal{M}} \quad = r^{\mathcal{M}} \cap s^{\mathcal{M}}$$
$$(C \sqcup D)^{\mathcal{M}} \quad = C^{\mathcal{M}} \cup D^{\mathcal{M}} \qquad\qquad (r \sqcup s)^{\mathcal{M}} \quad = r^{\mathcal{M}} \cup s^{\mathcal{M}}$$
$$(\neg C)^{\mathcal{M}} \quad = M \setminus C^{\mathcal{M}} \qquad\qquad (r \setminus s)^{\mathcal{M}} \quad = r^{\mathcal{M}} \setminus s^{\mathcal{M}}$$
$$(C \times D)^{\mathcal{M}} \quad = C^{\mathcal{M}} \times D^{\mathcal{M}} \qquad\qquad (r^{-})^{\mathcal{M}} \quad = \{(e, e') \mid (e', e) \in r^{\mathcal{M}}\}$$
$$(\exists r.C)^{\mathcal{M}} \quad = \{e \mid \exists e' : (e, e') \in r^{\mathcal{M}}\}$$
$$\mathcal{M} \models C \sqsubseteq D \text{ if } C^{\mathcal{M}} \subseteq D^{\mathcal{M}} \qquad\qquad \mathcal{M} \models r \sqsubseteq s \text{ if } r^{\mathcal{M}} \subseteq s^{\mathcal{M}}$$
$$\mathcal{M} \models func(r) \text{ if} \{(e, e_1), (e, e_2)\} \subseteq r^{\mathcal{M}} \text{ implies } e_1 = e_2$$

The closure of $\models$ under $\wedge \vee, \neg, \rightarrow$ is defined in the natural way. We abbreviate: $\top = C \sqcup \neg C$, where C is an arbitrary atomic concept and $\bot = \neg \top$; $\alpha \equiv \beta$ for the formula $\alpha \sqsubseteq \beta \wedge \beta \sqsubseteq \alpha$; and $\exists r$ for the concept $\exists r.\top$; (o, o') for the role $o \times o'$. Note that $\top^{\mathcal{M}} = M$ and $\bot^{\mathcal{M}} = \emptyset$ for any structure $\mathcal{M} = (M, \tau, \cdot)$.

2.3   Running Example: Content Invariants in $\mathcal{L}$

Now we make the example from Section 1.1 more precise. The concepts $ELst$ and $PLst$ are interpreted as the sets of elements in the employee list resp. the project list. $mngBy$, $isMngr$ and $wrkFor$ are roles. o_{eHd} and o_{pHd} are the constants which correspond to the heads of the two lists. The invariants of the systems are:

The emploee and project lists are allocated:	$PLst \sqcup ELst \quad \sqsubseteq$	$Alloc$
Projects and employees are distinct:	$PLst \sqcap ELst \quad \sqsubseteq$	$\bot$
$wrkFor$ is set to null for projects:	$PLst \quad \sqsubseteq \exists wrkFor.o_{\mathrm{null}}$	
$mngBy$ is set to null for employees:	$ELst \quad \sqsubseteq \exists mngBy.o_{\mathrm{null}}$	
$wrkFor$ of employees in the list point to projects in the list or to null:	$\exists wrkFor^{-}.ELst \sqsubseteq \quad PLst \sqcup o_{\mathrm{null}}$	
$isMngr$ is a Boolean field:	$\exists isMngr^{-}.ELst \sqsubseteq$	$Boolean$
$mngBy$ of projects point to managers or null:	$\exists mngBy^{-}.PLst \sqsubseteq$ $(ELst \sqcap \exists isMngr.o_{\mathbf{T}}) \sqcup o_{\mathrm{null}}$	
The manager of a project must work for the project:	$mngBy \cap (\top \times ELst) \sqsubseteq wrkFor^{-}$	

Let the conjunction of the invariants be given by $\varphi_{invariants}$.

Consider S from Section 1. The states of the heap before and after the execution of S can be related by the following $\mathcal{L}$ formulae. $\varphi_{lists-updt}$ and $\varphi_{p-assgn}$. $\varphi_{lists-updt}$ states that the employee list at the end of the program ($ELst$) is equal to the employee list at the beginning of the program ($ELst_{gho}$), and that the project list at the end of the program ($PLst$) is the same as the project list at the beginning of the program ($PLst_{gho}$), except that $PLst$ also contains the new project o_{proj}. $ELst_{gho}$ and $wrkFor_{gho}$ are ghost relation symbols, whose interpretations hold the corresponding values at the beginning of S.

$$\varphi_{lists-updt} = ELst_{gho} \equiv ELst \wedge PLst_{gho} \sqcup o_{proj} \equiv PLst$$
$$\varphi_{p-assgn} = ELst_{gho} \sqcap \exists wrkFor_{gho}.o_{\mathrm{null}} \equiv ELst \sqcap \exists wrkFor.o_{proj}$$

Ghost Symbols. As discussed in Section 2.3, in order to allow invariants of the form $\varphi_{lists-updt} = ELst_{gho} \equiv ELst \wedge PLst_{gho} \sqcup o_{proj} \equiv PLst$ we need ghost symbols. We assume τ contains, for every symbol e.g. $s \in \tau$, the symbol s_{gho}. Therefore, memory structures actually contain *two* snapshots of the memory: one is the *current* snapshot, on which the program operates, and the other is a *ghost* snapshot, which is a snapshot of the memory at the beginning of the program, and which the program does not change or interact with. We denote the two underlying memory structures of $\mathcal{M}$ by $\mathcal{M}_{cur}$ and $\mathcal{M}_{gho}$. Since the interpretations of ghost symbols should not change throughout the run of a program, they will sometime require special treatment.

2.4 The Separation Logic Fragment SLls

The SL that we use is denoted **SLls**, and is the logic from [7] with lists and multiple pointer fields, but without trees. It can express that the heap is partitioned into lists and individual cells. For example, to express that the heap contains only the two lists $ELst$ and $PLst$ we can write the **SLls** formula $\mathrm{ls}(pHd, \text{null}) * \mathrm{ls}(eHd, \text{null})$.

We denote by $var_i \in Var$ and $f_i \in Fields$ the sets of variables respectively fields to be used in **SLls**-formulae. var_i are constant symbols. f_i are binary relation symbols always interpreted as functions. An **SLls**-formula $\Pi \mid \Sigma$ is the conjunction of a *pure part* Π and a *spatial part* Σ. Π is a conjunction of equalities and inequalities of variables and o_{null}. Σ is a *spatial conjunction* $\Sigma = \beta_1 * \cdots * \beta_r$ of formulae of the form $\mathrm{ls}(E_1, E_2)$ and $var \mapsto [f_1 : E_1, \ldots, f_k : E_k]$, where each E_i is a variable or o_{null}. Additionally, Σ can be emp and Π can be **T**. When $\Pi = \mathbf{T}$ we write $\Pi \mid \Sigma$ simply as Σ.

The memory model of [7] is very similar to ours. We give the semantics of **SLls** in memory structures directly due to space constraints. See the full paper [19] for a discussion of the standard semantics of **SLls**. Π is interpreted in the natural way. Σ indicates that $Alloc^{\mathcal{M}}$ is the disjoint union of r parts $P_1^{\mathcal{M}}, \ldots, P_r^{\mathcal{M}}$. If β_i is of the form $var \mapsto [f_1 : E_1, \ldots, f_k : E_k]$ then $|P_i^{\mathcal{M}}| = 1$ and, denoting $v \in P_i^{\mathcal{M}}$, $f_j^{\mathcal{M}}(v) = E_j^{\mathcal{M}}$. If β_i is of the form $\mathrm{ls}(E_1, E_2)]$, then $|P_i^{\mathcal{M}}|$ is a list from $E_1^{\mathcal{M}}$ to $E_2^{\mathcal{M}}$. $E_2^{\mathcal{M}}$ might not belong to $P_i^{\mathcal{M}}$. If $\Sigma = emp$ then $Alloc^{\mathcal{M}} = \emptyset$.

2.5 The Two-Variable Fragment with Counting and Trees CT^2

C^2 is the subset of first-order logic whose formulae contain at most two variables, extended with counting quantifiers $\exists^{\leq k}$, $\exists^{\geq k}$ and $\exists^{=k}$ for all $k \in \mathbb{N}$. W. Charatonik and P. Witkowski [10] recently studied an extension of C^2 which trees which, as we will see, contains both our DL and our SL. CT^2 is the subset of second-order logic of the form $\exists F_1 \, \varphi(F_1) \wedge \varphi_{forest}(F_1)$ where $\varphi \in C^2$ and $\varphi_{forest}(F_1)$ says that F_1 is a forest. Note that CT^2 is not closed under negation, conjunction or disjunction. However, CT^2 is closed under conjunction or disjunction with C^2-formulae.

A CT^2-formula φ is *satisfiable in a memory structure* if there is a memory structure $\mathcal{M}$ such that $\mathcal{M} \models \varphi$. We write $\psi \models_m \varphi$ if $\mathcal{M} \models \psi$ implies $\mathcal{M} \models \varphi$ for every memory structure $\mathcal{M}$. Lemma 1 states the crucial property of CT^2 that we use. It follows from [10], by reducing the memory structures to closely related finite structures.[3] (see full version [19]).

Lemma 1. *Satisfiability of CT^2 by memory structures is in NEXPTIME.*

2.6 Embedding $\mathcal{L}$ and **SL**ls in CT^2

$\mathcal{L}$ has a fairly standard reduction (see e.g. [8]) to C^2:

Lemma 2. *For every vocabulary, there exists $tr : \mathcal{L}(\tau) \to C^2(\tau)$ such that for every $\varphi \in \mathcal{L}(\tau)$, φ and $tr(\varphi)$ agree on the truth value of all τ-structures.*

E.g., $tr(C_1 \sqsubseteq C_2) = \forall x\, C_1(x) \to C_2(x)$. The details of tr are given in the full version [19].

The translation of **SL**ls requires more work. Later we need the following related translations: $\alpha : \mathbf{SL}\mathrm{ls} \to \mathcal{L}$ extracts from the **SL**ls properties whatever can be expressed in $\mathcal{L}$. $\beta : \mathbf{SL}\mathrm{ls} \to CT^2$ captures **SL**ls precisely.

Given a structure $\mathcal{M}$, $L^{\mathcal{M}}$ is a *singly linked list from $o^{\mathcal{M}}_{var_1}$ to $o^{\mathcal{M}}_{var_2}$ w.r.t. the field $next^{\mathcal{M}}$* if $\mathcal{M}$ satisfies the following five conditions, or it is empty. Except for (5), the conditions are expressed fully in $\mathcal{L}$ below:
(1) $o^{\mathcal{M}}_{var_1}$ belongs to $L^{\mathcal{M}}$; (2) $o^{\mathcal{M}}_{var_2}$ is pointed to by an $L^{\mathcal{M}}$ element; (3) $o^{\mathcal{M}}_{var_2}$ does not belong to $L^{\mathcal{M}}$; (4) Every $L^{\mathcal{M}}$ element is pointed to from an $L^{\mathcal{M}}$ element, except possibly for $o^{\mathcal{M}}_{var_1}$; (5) all elements of $L^{\mathcal{M}}$ are reachable from $o^{\mathcal{M}}_{var_1}$ via $next^{\mathcal{M}}$. Let

$$
\begin{aligned}
\alpha^1(\mathrm{ls}) &= (o_{var_1} \sqsubseteq L) & \alpha^3(\mathrm{ls}) &= (o_{var_2} \sqsubseteq \neg L) \\
\alpha^2(\mathrm{ls}) &= (o_{var_2} \sqsubseteq \exists next^-.L) & \alpha^4(\mathrm{ls}) &= (L \sqsubseteq o_{var_1} \sqcup \exists next^-.L) \\
\alpha_{emp-ls}(\mathrm{ls}) &= (L \sqsubseteq \bot) \wedge (o_{var_1} = o_{var_2}) \\
\alpha(\mathrm{ls}) &= \alpha^1(\mathrm{ls}) \wedge \cdots \wedge \alpha^4(\mathrm{ls}) \vee \alpha_{emp-ls}(\mathrm{ls})
\end{aligned}
$$

In memory structures $\mathcal{M}$ satisfying $\alpha(\mathrm{ls})$, if $L^{\mathcal{M}}$ is not empty, then it contains a list segment from $o^{\mathcal{M}}_{var_1}$ to $o^{\mathcal{M}}_{var_2}$, but additionally $L^{\mathcal{M}}$ may contain additional simple $next^{\mathcal{M}}$-cycles, which are disjoint from the list segment. Here we use the finiteness of $Alloc^{\mathcal{M}}$ (which contains $L^{\mathcal{M}}$) and the functionality of $next^{\mathcal{M}}$. A connectivity condition is all that is lacking to express ls precisely. $\alpha(\mathrm{ls})$ can be extended to $\alpha : \mathbf{SL}\mathrm{ls} \to \mathcal{L}$ in a natural way (see the full version [19]) such that:

Lemma 3. *For every $\varphi \in \mathbf{SL}\mathrm{ls}$, φ implies $\alpha(\varphi)$ over memory structures.*

To rule out the superfluous cycles we turn to CT^2. Let $\beta^5(\mathrm{ls}) = \forall x \forall y\, \big[(L(x) \wedge L(y)) \to (F_1(x,y) \leftrightarrow next(x,y))\big] \wedge \forall x \big[(L(x) \wedge \forall y\,(L(y) \to \neg F_1(y,x))) \to (x \approx o_{var_1})\big]$. $\beta^5(\mathrm{ls})$ states that the forest F_1 coincides with $next$ inside L and that the forest induced by F_1 on L is a tree. Let $\beta(\mathrm{ls}) = \exists F_1\, tr(\alpha(\mathrm{ls})) \wedge \beta^5(\mathrm{ls}) \wedge \varphi_{forest}(F_1)$. $\beta(\mathrm{ls}) \in CT^2$ and it expresses that $L^{\mathcal{M}}$ is a list. The extension of $\beta(\mathrm{ls})$ to the translation function $\beta : \mathbf{SL}\mathrm{ls} \to CT^2$ is natural and discussed in the full version [19]. The full version [19] also discusses the translation of *cyclic data structures* under β.

---

[3] In fact [10] allows existential quantification over two forests, but will only need one.

Lemma 4. *For every $\varphi \in$ **SL**ls: φ and $\beta(\varphi)$ agree on all memory structures.*

CT^2's flexibility allows to easily express variations of singly-linked lists, such as doubly-linked lists, or lists in which every element points to a special head element via a pointer *head*, and analogue variants of trees.

2.7 Running Example: Shape Invariants

At the loop header of the program S from the introduction, the memory contains two distinct lists, namely $PLst$ and $ELst$. $ELst$ is partitioned into two parts: the employees who have been visited in the loop so far, and those that have not. This can be expressed in **SL**ls by the formula: $\varphi_{\ell_l} = \mathbf{T} \mid ls(eHd, e) *$ $ls(e, nil) * ls(pHd, nil)$. The translation $\alpha(\varphi_{\ell_l})$ is given by $P_1 \sqcup P_2 \sqcup P_3 \equiv Alloc \wedge$ $\alpha(ls(eHd, e, next, P_1)) \wedge \alpha(ls(e, null, next, P_2)) \wedge \alpha(ls(pHd, null, next, P_3)) \wedge P_1 \sqcap$ $P_2 \equiv \bot \wedge P_1 \sqcap P_3 \equiv \bot \wedge P_2 \sqcap P_3 \equiv \bot \wedge \alpha_{\mathbf{T}}$ The translation from SL assigns concepts P_i to each of the lists. $\alpha_{\mathbf{T}}$ which occurs in $\alpha(\varphi_{\ell_l})$ is the translation of $\Pi = \mathbf{T}$ in φ_{ℓ_l}. In order to clarify the meaning of $\alpha(\varphi_{\ell_l})$ we relate the P_i to the concept names from Section 2.3 and simplify the formula somewhat. Let $\psi_l = P_1 \sqcup P_2 \equiv ELst \wedge P_3 \equiv PLst$. P_1 contains the elements of $ELst$ visited in the loop so far. $\alpha(\varphi_{\ell_l})$ is equivalent to: $\alpha'(\varphi_{\ell_l}) = \psi_l \wedge ELst \sqcup PLst \equiv$ $Alloc \wedge ELst \sqcap PLst \equiv \bot \wedge \alpha(ls(eHd, e, next, P_1)) \wedge \alpha(ls(e, null, next, ELst \sqcap$ $\neg P_1)) \wedge \alpha(ls(pHd, null, next, PLst))$. We have $\beta^5(\Sigma) = \beta^5(ls(eHd, e, next, P_1)) \wedge$ $\beta^5(ls(e, null, next, ELst \sqcap \neg P_1)) \wedge \beta^5(ls(pHd, null, next, PLst))$ and $\beta(\varphi_{\ell_l}) =$ $\exists F_1 \, tr(\alpha(\varphi) \wedge \beta^5(\Sigma) \wedge \varphi_{forest}(F_1)$.

3 Content Analysis

3.1 Syntax and Semantics of the Programming Language

Loopless Programs are generated by the following syntax:

$$e :: var.f \mid var \mid \text{null} \qquad (f \in \tau_{\text{fields}}, o_{var} \in \tau_{var})$$
$$b :: (e_1 = e_2) \mid \sim b \mid (b_1 \, and \, b_2) \mid (b_1 \, or \, b_2) \mid \mathbf{T} \mid \mathbf{F}$$
$$S :: var_1 := e_2 \mid var_1.f := e_2 \mid skip \mid S_1; S_2 \mid var := new \mid dispose(var) \mid$$
$$\quad\quad if \, b \, then \, S_1 \, fi \mid if \, b \, then \, S_1 \, else \, S_2 \, fi \mid assume(b)$$

Let Exp denote the set of expressions e and $Bool$ denote the set of Boolean expressions b. To define the semantics of pointer and Boolean expressions, we extend $f^{\mathcal{M}}$ by $f^{\mathcal{M}}(\text{err}) = \text{err}$ for every $f \in \tau_{\text{fields}}$. We define $\mathcal{E}_e(\mathcal{M}) : Exp \rightarrow$ $Addresses^{\mathcal{M}} \cup \{\text{null}, \text{err}\}$ and $\mathcal{B}_b(\mathcal{M}) : Bool \rightarrow \{o_{\mathbf{T}}, o_{\mathbf{F}}, \text{err}\}$ (with $\text{err} \notin \mathcal{M}$):

$$\mathcal{E}_{var}(\mathcal{M}) = o_{var}^{\mathcal{M}}, \text{ if } o_{var}^{\mathcal{M}} \in Alloc^{\mathcal{M}} \quad \mathcal{B}_{e_1 = e_2}(\mathcal{M}) = \text{err if } \mathcal{E}_{e_i}(\mathcal{M}) = \text{err}, i \in \{1, 2\}$$
$$\mathcal{E}_{var}(\mathcal{M}) = \text{err, if } o_{var}^{\mathcal{M}} \notin Alloc^{\mathcal{M}} \quad \mathcal{B}_{e_1 = e_2}(\mathcal{M}) = o_{\mathbf{T}}, \text{ if } \mathcal{E}_{e_1}(\mathcal{M}) = \mathcal{E}_{e_2}(\mathcal{M})$$
$$\mathcal{E}_{ar.f}(\mathcal{M}) = f^{\mathcal{M}}(\mathcal{E}_{var}(\mathcal{M})) \quad\quad \mathcal{B}_{e_1 = e_2}(\mathcal{M}) = o_{\mathbf{F}}, \text{ if } \mathcal{E}_{e_1}(\mathcal{M}) \neq \mathcal{E}_{e_2}(\mathcal{M})$$

$\mathcal{B}$ extends naturally w.r.t. the Boolean connectives.

The operational semantics of the programming language is: For any command S, if $\mathcal{E}$ or $\mathcal{B}$ give the value err, then $\langle S, \mathcal{M} \rangle \rightsquigarrow$ abort. Otherwise, the semantics is as listed below. First we assume that in the memory structures involved all relation symbols either belong to τ_{fields}, are ghost symbols or are the required symbols of memory structures (*Alloc*, *Aux*, etc.).

1. $\langle skip, \mathcal{M} \rangle \rightsquigarrow \mathcal{M}$.
2. $\langle var_1 := e_2, \mathcal{M} \rangle \rightsquigarrow [\mathcal{M} \mid o_{var_1}^{\mathcal{M}}$ is set to $\mathcal{E}_{e_2}(\mathcal{M})]$.
3. $\langle var := new, \mathcal{M} \rangle \rightsquigarrow [\mathcal{M} \mid$ For some $t \in MemPool^{\mathcal{M}}$,
   t is moved to $Alloc^{\mathcal{M}}$ and $o_{var}^{\mathcal{M}}$ is set to $t]$,
4. If $o_{var}^{\mathcal{M}} \notin Alloc^{\mathcal{M}}$, $\langle dispose(var), \mathcal{M} \rangle \rightsquigarrow$ abort;
   otherwise $\langle dispose(var), \mathcal{M} \rangle \rightsquigarrow [\mathcal{M} \mid o_{var}^{\mathcal{M}}$ is removed from $Alloc^{\mathcal{M}}]$.
5. $\langle S_1; S_2, \mathcal{M} \rangle \rightsquigarrow \langle S_2, \langle S_1, \mathcal{M} \rangle \rangle$
6. $\langle if\ b\ then\ S_{\mathbf{T}}\ else\ S_{\mathbf{F}}, \mathcal{M} \rangle \rightsquigarrow \langle S_{tv}, \mathcal{M} \rangle$ where $tv = \mathcal{B}_b(\mathcal{M})$.
7. $\langle if\ b\ then\ S\ , \mathcal{M} \rangle \rightsquigarrow \langle if\ b\ then\ S\ else\ skip\ fi, \mathcal{M} \rangle$.
8. If $\mathcal{B}_b(\mathcal{M}) = \mathbf{T}$, then $\langle assume(b), \mathcal{M} \rangle \rightsquigarrow \mathcal{M}$;
   otherwise $\langle assume(b), \mathcal{M} \rangle \rightsquigarrow$ abort.

If $\mathcal{M}$ is a memory structure and $\langle S, \mathcal{M} \rangle \rightsquigarrow \mathcal{M}'$, then $\mathcal{M}'$ is a memory structure.

Now consider a relation symbol e.g. *ELst*. If $\langle S, \mathcal{M} \rangle \rightsquigarrow \mathcal{M}'$, then we want to think of $ELst^{\mathcal{M}}$ and $ELst^{\mathcal{M}'}$ as the employee list before and after the execution of S. However, the constraints that $ELst^{\mathcal{M}}$ and $ELst^{\mathcal{M}'}$ are lists and that $ELst^{\mathcal{M}'}$ is indeed obtained from from $ELst^{\mathcal{M}}$ by running S will be expressed as formulae. In the $\rightsquigarrow$ relation, we allow any values for $ELst^{\mathcal{M}}$ and $ELst^{\mathcal{M}'}$.

For any tuple $\bar{R}$ of relation symbols which do not belong to τ_{fields}, are not ghost symbols and are not the required symbols of memory structures (*Alloc*, *Aux*, etc.), we extend $\rightsquigarrow$ as follows: if $\langle S, \mathcal{M} \rangle \rightsquigarrow \mathcal{M}'$, then $\langle S, \langle \mathcal{M}, \bar{R}^{\mathcal{M}} \rangle \rangle \rightsquigarrow \left\langle \mathcal{M}', \bar{R}^{\mathcal{M}'} \right\rangle$, for any tuples $\bar{R}^{\mathcal{M}}$ and $\bar{R}^{\mathcal{M}'}$.

Programs with Loops are represented as hybrids of the programming language for loopless code and control flow graphs.

Definition 3 (Program). *A program is* $G = \langle V, E, \ell_{init}, shp, cnt, \lambda \rangle$ *such that* $G = (V, E)$ *is a directed graph with no multiple edge but possibly containing self-loops,* $\ell_{init} \in V$ *has in-degree 0,* $shp : V \rightarrow \mathbf{SLls}$, $cnt : V \rightarrow \mathcal{L}(\tau)$ *are functions, and* λ *is a function from* E *to the set of loopless programs.*

Here is the code S from the introduction:

$V = \{\ell_b, \ell_l, \ell_e\}$ $E = \{(\ell_b, \ell_l), (\ell_l, \ell_l), (\ell_l, \ell_e)\}$
$\lambda(\ell_b, \ell_l) = S_b$ $\ell_{init} = \ell_b$
$\lambda(\ell_l, \ell_l) = assume(\sim (e = null)); S_{\ell_l}$
$\lambda(\ell_l, \ell_e) = assume(e = null); S_e$

S_b, S_{ℓ_l} and S_e denote the three loopless code blocks which are respectively the code block before the loop, inside the loop and after the loop. The annotations shp and cnt are described in Section 3.4.

The semantics of programs derive from the semantics of loopless programs and is given in terms of program paths. Given a program G, a *path in* G is a finite sequence of directed edges $e_1, \ldots, e_t$ such that for all $1 \leq i \leq t-1$, the tail of e_i is the head of e_{i+1}. A path may contain cycles.

Definition 4 ($\leadsto^*$ for paths). *Given a program G, a path P in G, and memory structures $\mathcal{M}_1$ and $\mathcal{M}_2$ we define whether $\langle P, \mathcal{M}_1 \rangle \leadsto^* \mathcal{M}_2$ holds inductively. If P is empty, then $\langle P, \mathcal{M}_1 \rangle \leadsto^* \mathcal{M}_2$ iff $\mathcal{M}_1 = \mathcal{M}_2$. If e_t is the last edge of P, then $\langle P, \mathcal{M}_1 \rangle \leadsto^* \mathcal{M}_2$ iff there is $\mathcal{M}_3$ such that $\langle P \backslash \{e_t\}, \mathcal{M}_1 \rangle \leadsto^* \mathcal{M}_3$ and $\langle \lambda(e_t), \mathcal{M}_1 \rangle \leadsto^* \mathcal{M}_3$. $P \backslash \{e_t\}$ denotes the path obtained from P by removing the last edge e_t.*

3.2   Hoare-Style Proof System

Now we are ready to state our two-step verification methodology that we formulated in Section 1 precisely. Our methodology assumes a program P as in Definition 3 as input (ignoring the *shp* and *cnt* functions for the moment).

I. Shape Analysis. The user annotates the program locations with SL formulae from **SL**ls (stored in the *shp* function of P). Then the user proves the validity of the **SL**ls annotations, for example, by using techniques from [7].

II. Content Analysis. The user annotates the program locations with $\mathcal{L}$-formulae that she wants to verify (stored in the *cnt* function of P). We point out that an annotation $cnt(\ell)$ can use the concepts occurring in $\alpha(shp(\ell))$ (recall that $\alpha : \textbf{SL}_{\textbf{ls}} \to \mathcal{L}$ maps SL formulae to $\mathcal{L}$-formulae).

In the rest of the paper we discuss how to verify the *cnt* annotations. In Section 3.3 we describe how to derive a verification condition for every program edge. The verification conditions rely on the backwards propagation function Θ for $\mathcal{L}$-formulae which we introduce in Section 3.5. The key point of our methodology is that the validity of the verification conditions can be discharged automatically by a satisfiability solver for CT^2-formulae. We show that all the verification conditions are valid if and only if *cnt* is inductive. Intuitively, *cnt* being inductive ensures that the annotations *cnt* can be used in an inductive proof to show that all reachable memory structures indeed satisfy the annotations $cnt(\ell)$ at every program location ℓ (see Definition 6 below).

3.3   Content Verification

We want to prove that, for every initial memory structure $\mathcal{M}_1$ from which the computation satisfies *shp* and which satisfies the content pre-condition $cnt(\ell_{init})$, the computation satisfies *cnt*. Here are the corresponding verification conditions, which annotate the vertices of G:

Definition 5 (Verification conditions). *Given a program G, VC is the function from E to $\mathcal{L}$ given for $e = (\ell_0, \ell)$ by $VC(e) = \neg \big[\beta(shp(\ell_0)) \wedge tr(cnt(\ell_0)) \wedge tr\big(\Theta_{\lambda(e)}\big(\alpha(shp(\ell)) \wedge \neg cnt(\ell)\big)\big)\big]$ $VC(e)$ holds if $VC(e)$ is a tautology over memory structures ($\top \models_m VC(e)$).*

Θ is discussed in Section 3.5. As we will see, $VC(\ell_0, \ell)$ expresses that when running the loopless program $\lambda(e)$ when the memory satisfies the the annotations of ℓ_0, and when the shape annotation of ℓ is at least partly true (i.e., when $\alpha(shp(\ell))$), the content annotation of ℓ holds.

Let J be a set of memory structures. For a formula in CT^2 or $\mathcal{L}$, we write $J \models \varphi$ if, for every $\mathcal{M} \in J$, $\mathcal{M} \models \varphi$. Let *Init* be a set of memory structures.

Definition 6 (Inductive program annotation). *Let $f : V \to CT^2$. We say f is* inductive *for $Init$ if (i) $Init \models f(\ell_{init})$, and (ii) for every edge $e = (\ell_1, \ell_2) \in E$ and memory structures $\mathcal{M}_1$ and $\mathcal{M}_2$ such that $\mathcal{M}_1 \models f(\ell_1)$ and $\langle \lambda(e), \mathcal{M}_1 \rangle \leadsto \mathcal{M}_2$, we have $\mathcal{M}_2 \models f(\ell_2)$. We say shp is inductive for $Init$ if the composition $shp \circ \beta : V \to CT^2$ is inductive for $Init$. We say cnt is inductive for $Init$ relative to shp if shp is inductive for $Init$ and $g : V \to CT^2$ is inductive for $Init$, where $g(\ell) = tr(cnt(\ell)) \wedge \beta(shp(\ell))$.*

Theorem 1 (Soundness and Completeness of the Verification Conditions). *Let G be a program such that shp is inductive for $Init$ and $Init \models cnt(\ell_{init})$. The following statements are equivalent:*
(i) For all $e \in E$, $VC(e)$ holds.   (ii) cnt is inductive for $Init$ relative to shp.

Definition 7 ($Reach(\ell)$). *Given a program G, a node $\ell \in V$, and a set $Init$ of memory structures, $Reach(\ell)$ is the set of memory structures $\mathcal{M}$ for which there is $\mathcal{M}_{init} \in Init$ and a path P in G starting at ℓ_{init} such that $\langle P, \mathcal{M}_{init} \rangle \leadsto^* \mathcal{M}$.*

In particular, $Reach(\ell_{init}) = Init$. The proof of Theorem 1 and its consequence Theorem 2 below are given in the full version [19].

Theorem 2 (Soundness of the Verification Methodology). *Let G be a program such that shp is inductive for $Init$ and $Init \models cnt(\ell_{init})$. If for all $e \in E$, $VC(e)$ holds, then for $\ell \in V$, $Reach(\ell) \models cnt(\ell)$.*

3.4   Running Example: General Methodology

To verify the correctness of the code S, the shp and cnt annotations must be provided. The shape annotations of program S are: $shp(\ell_b) = \mathrm{ls}(eHd, \mathrm{null}) * \mathrm{ls}(pHd, \mathrm{null})$, $shp(\ell_e) = (proj = pHd) \mathbin{!} \mathrm{ls}(eHd, \mathrm{null}) * \mathrm{ls}(pHd, \mathrm{null})$, and $shp(\ell_l) = \varphi_{\ell_l}$, where φ_{ℓ_l} is from Section 2.7.

The three content annotations require that the system invariants $\varphi_{invariants}$ from Section 2.3 hold. The post-condition additionally requires that $\varphi_{p-assgn}$ and $\varphi_{lists-updts}$ hold. Recall $\varphi_{p-assgn}$ states that every employee which was not assigned a project, is assigned to o_{proj}. $\varphi_{lists-updts}$ states that the content of the two lists remain unchanged, except that the project o_{proj} is inserted to $PLst$.

In order to interact with the translations $\alpha(shp(\cdots))$ of the shape annotations, we need to related the P_i to the concepts $ELst$ and $PLst$. In Section 2.7 we defined ψ_l, which relates the P_i generated by α on $shp(\ell_l)$. We have $\psi_{\ell_b} = \psi_{\ell_e} = P_1 \equiv ELst \wedge P_2 \equiv PLst$. Then $cnt(\ell_b) = \psi_{\ell_b} \wedge \varphi_{invariants}$, $cnt(\ell_l) = \psi_{\ell_l} \wedge \varphi_{invariants} \wedge \varphi_{lists-updt} \wedge \varphi_{p-as-\ell_l}$, and $cnt(\ell_e) = \psi_{\ell_e} \wedge \varphi_{invariants} \wedge \varphi_{lists-updt} \wedge \varphi_{p-assgn}$, where $\varphi_{p-as-\ell_l} = P_1 \sqcap \exists wrkFor_{gho}.o_{\mathrm{null}} \equiv P_1 \sqcap \exists wrkFor.o_{proj}$. $\varphi_{p-as-\ell_l}$ states that, in the part of $ELst$ containing the employees visited so far in the loop, any employee which was not assigned to a project at the start of the program (i.e., in the ghost version of $wrkFor$) is assigned to the project $proj$. $\varphi_{p-as-\ell_l}$ makes no demands on elements of $ELst$ which have not been reach in the loop so far. The verification conditions of G are, for each $(\ell_1, \ell_2) \in E$, $VC(\ell_1, \ell_2) = \neg \big[\beta(shp(\ell_1)) \wedge tr(cnt(\ell_1)) \wedge tr(\Theta_{\lambda(l_1, l_2)}(\alpha(shp(\ell_2)) \wedge \neg cnt(\ell_2))) \big]$.

The verification conditions $VC(e)$ express that the loopless programs on the edges e of G satisfy their annotations. To prove the correctness of G w.r.t. $VC(e)$ using Theorem 2, we prove that $VC(e)$, $e \in E$, hold, in order to get as a conclusion that $Reach(\ell) \models cnt(\ell)$, for all $\ell \in V$.

3.5   Backwards Propagation and the Running Example

Here we shortly discuss the backwards propagation of a formula along a loopless program S. Let $\langle S, \mathcal{M}_1 \rangle \rightsquigarrow \mathcal{M}_2$ where $\mathcal{M}_1$ and $\mathcal{M}_2$ are memory structures over the same vocabulary τ. E.g., in our running example, for $i = 1, 2$, $\mathcal{M}_i$ is $\langle M,$ $ELst^{\mathcal{M}_i}, next^{\mathcal{M}_i}, mngBy^{\mathcal{M}_i}, \cdots, ELst^{\mathcal{M}_i}_{gho}, next^{\mathcal{M}_i}_{gho}, \cdots, Alloc^{\mathcal{M}_i}, Aux^{\mathcal{M}_i} \cdots \rangle$. We will show how to translate a formula for $\mathcal{M}_2$ to a formula for an extended $\mathcal{M}_1$. Fields and variables in $\mathcal{M}_2$ will be translated by the backwards propagation into expressions involving elements of $\mathcal{M}_1$. For ghost symbols s_{gho}, $s^{\mathcal{M}_1}_{gho}$ will be used instead of $s^{\mathcal{M}_2}_{gho}$ since they do not change during the run of the program. Let $\tau^{rem} \subseteq \tau$ be the set of the remaining symbols, i.e. the symbols of $\tau \setminus (\{PossibleTargets, MemPool\} \cup \tau_{\text{fields}})$ which are not ghost symbols, for example $ELst$, but not $ELst_{gho}$, $next$ or $mngBy$. We need the result of the backwards propagation to refer to the interpretations of symbols in τ^{rem} from $\mathcal{M}_2$ rather than $\mathcal{M}_1$. Therefore, these interpretations are copied as they are from $\mathcal{M}_2$ and added to $\mathcal{M}_1$ as follows. For every $R \in \tau^{rem}$, we add a symbol R^{ext} for the copied relation. We denote by $(\bar{R}^{ext})^{\mathcal{M}_1}$ the tuple $((R^{ext})^{\mathcal{M}_1} : (R^{ext})^{\mathcal{M}_1} = R^{\mathcal{M}_2}$ and $R \in \tau^{rem})$ Let τ^{ext} extend τ with R^{ext} for each $R \in \tau^{rem}$. The backwards propagation updates the fields and variables according to the loopless code. Afterwards, we substitute the symbols $R \in \tau^{rem}$ in φ with the corresponding R^{ext}. We present here a somewhat simplified version of the backwards propagation lemma. The precise version is similar in spirit and is in the full version [19]

Lemma 5 (Simplified). *Let S be a loopless program, let $\mathcal{M}_1$ and $\mathcal{M}_2$ be memory structures, and φ be an $\mathcal{L}$-formula over τ. (1) If $\langle S, \mathcal{M}_1 \rangle \rightsquigarrow \mathcal{M}_2$, then: $\mathcal{M}_2 \models \varphi$ iff $\langle \mathcal{M}_1, (\bar{R}^{ext})^{\mathcal{M}_1} \rangle \models \Theta_S(\varphi)$. (2) If $\langle S, \mathcal{M}_1 \rangle \rightsquigarrow abort$, then $\langle \mathcal{M}_1, (\bar{R}^{ext})^{\mathcal{M}_1}, \rangle \not\models \Theta_S(\varphi)$.*

As an example of the backwards propagation process, we consider a formula from Section 3.4, which is part of the content annotation of ℓ_l and perform the backwards propagation on the loopless program inside the loop: $\varphi_{p-as-\ell_l} = P_1 \sqcap \exists wrkFor_{gho}.o_{null} \equiv P_1 \sqcap \exists wrkFor.o_{proj}$ Since $next$ does not occur in $\varphi_{p-as-\ell_l}$, backwards propagation of $\varphi_{p-as-\ell_l}$ over $e := e.next$ does not change the formula (however $\alpha(shp(\ell_l))$ by this command). The backwards propagation of the if command gives $\Psi_{S_{\ell_l}}(\varphi_{p-as-\ell_l}) = \left(\neg(\exists wrkFor^-.o_e \equiv o_{null}) \wedge \varphi_{p-as-\ell_l} \right) \vee \exists wrkFor^-.o_e \equiv o_{null} \wedge \Psi_{e.wrkFor:=proj}(\varphi_{p-as-\ell_l})$ and $\Psi_{e.wrkFor:=proj}(\varphi_{p-as-\ell_l})$ $= P_1 \sqcap \exists wrkFor_{gho}.o_{null} \equiv P_1 \sqcap \exists((wrkFor\setminus(o_e \times \top)) \cup (o_e, o_{proj})).o_{proj}$. $\Psi_{e.wrkFor:=proj}(\varphi_{p-as-\ell_l})$ is obtained from $\varphi_{p-as-\ell_l}$ by substituting the $wrkFor$ role with the correction $((wrkFor\setminus(o_e \times \top)) \cup (o_e, o_{proj}))$ which updates the value of o_e in $wrkFor$ to $proj$. $\Phi_{S_{\ell_l}}(\varphi_{p-as-\ell_l})$ is obtained from

$\Psi_{S_{\ell_l}}(\varphi_{p-as-\ell_l})$ by substituting P_1 with $P_1{}^{ext}$. Θ is differs from Φ from technical reasons related to aborting computations (see the full version [19]).

4   Related Work

Shape Analysis attracted considerable attention in the literature. The classical introductory paper to SL [24] presents an expressive SL which turned out to be undecidable. We have restricted our attention to the better behaved fragment in [7]. The work on SL focuses mostly on shape rather than content in our sense. SL has been extended to object oriented languages, cf. e.g. [23,11], where shape properties similar to those studied in the non objected oriented case are the focus, and the main goal is to overcome difficulties introduced by the additional features of OO languages. Other shape analyses could be potential candidates for integration in our methodology. [25] use 3-valued logic to perform shape analysis. Regional logic is used to check correctness of program with shared dynamica memory areas [5]. [16] uses nested tree automata to represent the heap. [21] combines monadic second order logic with SMT solvers.

Description Logics have not been considerd for verification of programs with dynamically allocated memory, with the exception of [13] whose use (mostly undecidable) DLs to express shape-type invariants, ignoring content information. In [9] the authors consider verification of loopless code (transactions) in graph databases with integrity constraints expressed in DLs. Verification of temporal properties of dynamic systems in the presence of DL knowledge bases has received significant attention (see [4,14] and their references). *Temporal Description Logics*, which combine classic DLs with classic temporal logics, have also received significant attention in the last decade (see [20] for a survey).

Related Ideas. Some recent papers have studied verification strategies which use information beyond the semantics of the source code. E.g., [18] is using diagrams from design documentation to support verification. [12,1] infer the intended use of program variables to guide a program analysis. Instead of starting from code and verifying its correctness, [15] explores how to declaratively specify data structures with sharing and how to automatically generate code from this specification. Given the importance of both DL as a formalism of content representation and of program verification, and given that both are widely studied, we were surprised to find little related work. However, we believe this stems from large differences between the research in the two communities, and from the interdisciplinary nature of the work involved.

References

1. Apel, S., Beyer, D., Friedberger, K., Raimondi, F., von Rhein, A.: Domain types: Abstract-domain selection based on variable usage. In: Bertacco, V., Legay, A. (eds.) HVC 2013. LNCS, vol. 8244, pp. 262–278. Springer, Heidelberg (2013)
2. Artale, A., Calvanese, D., Kontchakov, R., Ryzhikov, V., Zakharyaschev, M.: Reasoning over extended ER models. In: Parent, C., Schewe, K.-D., Storey, V.C., Thalheim, B. (eds.) ER 2007. LNCS, vol. 4801, pp. 277–292. Springer, Heidelberg (2007)

3. Baader, F., Calvanese, D., McGuinness, D.L., Nardi, D., Patel-Schneider, P.F. (eds.): The Description Logic handbook: theory, implementation, and applications. Cambridge University Press (2003)

4. Baader, F., Zarrieß, B.: Verification of golog programs over description logic actions. In: Fontaine, P., Ringeissen, C., Schmidt, R.A. (eds.) FroCoS 2013. LNCS, vol. 8152, pp. 181–196. Springer, Heidelberg (2013)

5. Banerjee, A., Naumann, D.A., Rosenberg, S.: Local reasoning for global invariants, part I: Region logic. J. ACM 60(3), 18 (2013)

6. Berardi, D., Calvanese, D., De Giacomo, G.: Reasoning on UML class diagrams. Artificial Intelligence 168(1-2), 70–118 (2005)

7. Berdine, J., Calcagno, C., O'Hearn, P.W.: Symbolic Execution with Separation Logic. In: Yi, K. (ed.) APLAS 2005. LNCS, vol. 3780, pp. 52–68. Springer, Heidelberg (2005)

8. Borgida, A.: On the relative expressiveness of description logics and predicate logics. Artif. Intell. 82(1-2), 353–367 (1996)

9. Calvanese, D., Ortiz, M., Šimkus, M.: Evolving graph databases under description logic constraints. In: Proc. of DL, pp. 120–131 (2013)

10. Charatonik, W., Witkowski, P.: Two-variable logic with counting and trees. In: LICS, pp. 73–82 (2013)

11. Chin, W., David, C., Nguyen, H.H., Qin, S.: Enhancing modular oo verification with separation logic. In: POPL, pp. 87–99. ACM (2008)

12. Demyanova, Y., Veith, H., Zuleger, F.: On the concept of variable roles and its use in software analysis. In: FMCAD, pp. 226–230 (2013)

13. Georgieva, L., Maier, P.: Description Logics for shape analysis. In: SEFM, pp. 321–331 (2005)

14. De Giacomo, G., Lespérance, Y., Patrizi, F.: Bounded situation calculus action theories and decidable verification. In: Proc. of KR (2012)

15. Hawkins, P., Aiken, A., Fisher, K., Rinard, M., Sagiv, M.: Data structure fusion. In: Ueda, K. (ed.) APLAS 2010. LNCS, vol. 6461, pp. 204–221. Springer, Heidelberg (2010)

16. Holík, L., Lengál, O., Rogalewicz, A., Šimáček, J., Vojnar, T.: Fully automated shape analysis based on forest automata. In: Sharygina, N., Veith, H. (eds.) CAV 2013. LNCS, vol. 8044, pp. 740–755. Springer, Heidelberg (2013)

17. Ishtiaq, S.S., O'Hearn, P.W.: Bi as an assertion language for mutable data structures. In: POPL, pp. 14–26. ACM (2001)

18. James, D., Leonard, T., O'Leary, J., Talupur, M., Tuttle, M.R.: Extracting models from design documents with mapster. In: PODC (2008)

19. Kotek, T., Simkus, M., Veith, H., Zuleger, F.: Extending alcqio with reachability. CoRR, abs/1402.6804 (2014)

20. Lutz, C., Wolter, F., Zakharyaschev, M.: Temporal description logics: A survey. In: Proc. of TIME. IEEE Computer Society (2008)

21. Madhusudan, P., Parlato, G., Qiu, X.: Decidable logics combining heap structures and data. In: POPL, pp. 611–622. ACM, USA (2011)

22. W3C OWL Working Group. OWL 2 Web Ontology Language: Document Overview. W3C Recommendation (October 27, 2009)

23. Parkinson, M.J., Bierman, G.M.: Separation logic, abstraction and inheritance. SIGPLAN Not. 43(1), 75–86 (2008)

24. Reynolds, J.C.: Separation Logic: A logic for shared mutable data structures. In: Proc. of LICS, pp. 55–74. IEEE Computer Society, Washington, DC (2002)

25. Yorsh, G., Reps, T., Sagiv, M.: Symbolically computing most-precise abstract operations for shape analysis. In: Jensen, K., Podelski, A. (eds.) TACAS 2004. LNCS, vol. 2988, pp. 530–545. Springer, Heidelberg (2004)

How to Break the Bank: Semantics of Capability Policies

Sophia Drossopoulou[1] and James Noble[2]

[1] Imperial College London, UK
s.drossopoulou@imperial.ac.uk
[2] Victoria University of Wellington, NZ
kjx@ecs.vuw.ac.nz

Abstract. The object capability model is a de-facto industry standard widely adopted for the implementation of secure software. We call *capability policies* the policies enforced by programs using object capabilities. Such policies tend to restrict the objects and the circumstances which may access services. In this paper we argue that capability policies should be made explicit and written separately from the code implementing them. We also argue that the specification of capability policies requires concepts that go beyond the features of current specification languages. Moreover, we argue that we need methodologies with which to prove that programs adhere to their capability policies as specified.

To give precise semantics to capability policy specifications, we propose *execution observations*, which talk about various properties of a program's execution. We use execution observations to write the formal specification of five out of the six informal policies in the mint example, famous in the object capability literature. In these specifications, the conclusions but also the premises may relate to the state before as well as after execution, the code may be existentially or universally quantified, and interpretation quantifies over all modules extending the current module. In statically typed languages, adherence of code to the capability policies relies heavily on the guarantees provided by type system features such as final and private.

1 Introduction

Capabilities — unforgeable authentication tokens — have been used to provide security and task separation on multi-user machines since the 60s [5], *e.g.* PDP-1, operating systems *e.g.* CAL-TSS [13], and the CAP computer and operating system [38]. In capability-based security, resources can only be accessed via capabilities: possessing a capability gives the right to access the resource represented by that capability.

Object capabilities [22] apply capabilities to object-oriented programming. In an object capability system, an object is a capability for the services the object provides: any part of a program that has a reference to an object can always use all the services of that object. To restrict authority over an object, programmers must create an intermediate proxy object which offers only restricted services, delegating them back to the original object.

Object capabilities afford simpler and more fine-grained protection than privilege levels (as in Unix), static types, ad-hoc dynamic security managers (as in Java or JSand [1]), or state-machine-based event monitoring [2]. Object capabilities have been adopted

E. Albert and E. Sekerinski (Eds.): IFM 2014, LNCS 8739, pp. 18–35, 2014.

in several programming languages [24,19,36] and are increasingly used for the provision of security in web programming in industry [25,37,32].

Thus, object capabilities are employed to enforce policies which restrict access to services: which objects, and under what conditions, may activate these services. We call such policies, which regulate access to services, *capability policies*. Capability policies are *program centred, fine grained, open* in the sense that they specify aspects of the behaviour of all possible extensions of a program, and have *necessary* as well as *sufficient* parts; the latter require that certain effects may only take place if the originating code or the runtime context satisfy some conditions, [7].

The key problem with object capability programming as practiced today is that — because capabilities are just objects — code manipulating capabilities is tangled together with code supporting the functional behaviour of the program. The actual capability policies enforced by a program are *implicit* and scattered throughout the program's code, and the functionality concerns are tangled with those of the capability policy.

We argue that capability policies should be specified separately from the program implementing them. We also argue that the specification of capability policies requires features that go beyond what is available in current specification languages.

We propose that capability policies can be specified through *execution observations*, which are, essentially observations relating to program execution, accessibility, reachability and tracing. For example, execution observations can say things like "execution of a given code snippet in a given runtime context will access a certain field", or "it is possible to reach certain code through execution of some initial code".

We follow the Mint example [24] to illustrate our ideas; using execution observations we give precise meaning to five out of the six policies proposed informally in that paper. In these policies, the conclusions *but also the premises* may relate to the state before as well as after execution, the code may be existentially or universally quantified, and interpretation quantifies over all modules extending the current module. In the process of developing the mint specifications, we were surprised by the many different, and plausible interpretations we found for the policies.

The paper is organised as follows: Section 2 presents the Mint [19] as an example of object capability programming, implemented in Joe-E/Java. Based on that example, Section 3 distills the characteristics of capability policies. Section 4 then outlines executions observations, while section 5 uses them to express those policies, and discusses alternative interpretations. Section 6 discusses alternative meanings of these policies. Section 7 surveys related work, and Section 8 concludes.

2   The Mint: An Object Capability Example

We use as running example a system for electronic money proposed in [24]. This example allows for mints with electronic money, purses held within mints, and transfers of funds between purses. The *currency of a mint* is the sum of the balances of all purses created by that mint. The standard presentation of the mint example defines six capability policies, which we repeat here, as they were described in [24]:

Pol_1. With two purses of the same mint, one can transfer money between them.
Pol_2. Only someone with the mint of a given currency can violate conservation of that currency.

```
1  //  module MMint
2  public final class Mint {         }
3
4
5  //  module MPurse
6  public final class Purse {
7      private final Mint mint;
8      private long balance;
9      // INV: balance ≥ 0
10
11
12     // PRE: balance ≥ 0
13     // POST: result.mint=mint ∧ result.balance = 0
14     public Purse(Mint mint, long balance) {
15         if (balance<0){ throw new IllegalArgtException();  };
16         this.mint = mint;
17         this.balance = balance;
18     }
19
20     // PRE: true
21     // POST: result.mint=prs.mint ∧ result.balance = 0
22     public Purse(Purse prs ) {
23         this.mint = prs.mint;
24         this.balance = 0;
25     }
26
27     // PRE: this.mint=prs.mint ∧ amt≤prs.balance ∧
28     //        amt+this.balance≥0
29     // POST: this.balance=this.balancepre+amnt ∧
30     //         prs.balance=prs.balancepre- amnt
31     public void deposit(Purse prs, long amnt) {
32         if ( mint!=prs.mint
33              || amnt>prs.balance || amnt+balance<0 )
34                     { throw new IllegalArgtException(); };
35         prs.balance -= amnt;
36         balance += amnt;    }
37     }
38  }
```

Fig. 1. The Mint example, code taken from [19], specifications added by us

Pol_3. The mint can only inflate its own currency.

Pol_4. No one can affect the balance of a purse they don't have.

Pol_5. Balances are always non-negative integers.

Pol_6. A reported successful deposit can be trusted as much as one trusts the purse one is depositing into.

An immediate consequence of these policies is that the mint capability gives its holder the ability to subvert the currency system by "printing money", and that "printing money" is only possible, if one holds the mint. This means that while purse capabilities may safely be passed around the system, the mint capability must be carefully protected. This also means that protecting the mint suffices in order to protect the currency.

Several different implementations have been proposed for the mint. Fig.1 contains an implementation in Joe-E [19], a capability-oriented subset of Java, which restricts static variables and reflection.

In Fig.1, the policies are adhered to through the interplay of appropriate actions in the method bodies (*e.g.* the check in line 15), with the use of Java's *restrictive* language features (private members are visible to the same class only; final fields cannot be changed after initialisation; and final classes cannot be extended). The code concerned with the functional behaviour is tangled with the code implementing the policy (*e.g.* in deposit, lines 35-36 are concerned with the functionality, while lines 32-34 are concerned with **Pol_2**). The implementation of *one* policy is scattered throughout the code, and may use explicit runtime tests, as well as restrictive elements (*e.g.* **Pol_2** is implemented through a checks in line 32, the private and final annotations, and the initialisation in line 24). Note that an apparently innocuous change to this code — such as a public getMint accessor that returned a purse's mint — would be enough to leak the mint to untrusted code, destroying the security of the whole system, and thus break the bank!

An alternative implementation of the mint example appears in figure 2. Here, the Purse objects are used as indices into a map, which is held and administered by the Mint objects. A similar scattering and tangling of the policies and the functionality may be observed in this implementation. Policy **Pol_2** is implemented through the runtime tests in lines 17 and 19, though the transfer of moneys in lines 21 and 22, and through the use of the private modifier on the database field.

Comparison with Hoare-logic style specification. In the code from Fig. 1, we have given an specification in terms of PRE- and POST-conditions, in a style like that of JML. Note that except for **Pol_5**, this specification does not imply the capability policies.

No garbage collection of Purses. In all above, there is an implicit assumption that no purses are destroyed. This assumption is necessary because destruction of a purse would decrease the currency of a mint, in opposition to **Pol_3**.

```
1   //  module M_alt_Purse
2   public final class Purse {        }
3
4   //  module M_alt_Mint
5    public final class Mint {
6        private final HashMap<Purse,long> database
7                                = new HashMap<>();
8
9        public Purse makePurse(long balance) {
10           Purse p = new Purse();
11           database.put(p,balance);
12           return p;
13       }
14
15       public void deposit(Purse from, Purse into, long amnt) {
16           if ( (amount < 0)
17               || (!database.contains(from))
18               || (database.get(from) < amnt)
19               || (!database.contains(into)) )
20                       { throw new IllegalArgtException();
21                       };
22           database.put(from, database.get(from) - amnt);
23           database.put(into, database.get(into) + amnt);
24       }
25   }
```

Fig. 2. An alternative Mint implementation using a map as a database

3   Capability Policies

We use the term *capability policy* to describe policies which restrict the circumstances under which objects may have access to services. A range of such capability policies are discernible from the literature [22,24,23].

In the case of the Mint example, and apart from **Pol_6**, which requires separate studies [27], the policies from the previous section are concerned with the following services:

S_1 Transfer of money between purses.
S_2 Affecting the balance of a purse.
S_3 Affecting the currency of a mint.

Policy **Pol_1** expresses conditions for **S_1**: the service is protected by the respective purses. Policies **Pol_4** and **Pol_5** express conditions for **S_2**: the service is protectedby the purse, and the balance is always positive. Finally, **Pol_2** and **Pol_3** express conditions for **S_3**: the service is protected by the mint, and the currency can only increase.

Capability policies generally have the following characteristics:

- They are *program centered*: they talk about properties of programs rather than properties of specifications or protocols.
- They are *fine-grained*: they can talk about *individual objects*, while *coarse-grained* policies only talk about large components such as file servers or the DOM.
- They are *open*. *Open* requirements must be satisfied for any use of the code *extended in any possible manner* — e.g. through dynamic loading, inheritance, subclassing, mashups, mixins, reflection, interception, or any other extension mechanism supported by the programming language. This is in contrast to *closed* specifications that need only be satisfied for the actual code snippet itself.
- They have *necessary* as well as *sufficient* elements. Sufficient elements essentially promise that execution of a code snippet in a state satisfying a given pre-condition will reach another state which satisfies some post-condition [10]. Necessary elements promise that if execution of a code snippet reaches a certain state, or changes state in a certain way, or accesses some program entity, then the code snippet must satisfy some given properties.

4   Execution Observations for the Semantics of Capability Policies

In this section we introduce *execution observations*, the concepts necessary to give precise meaning to policies. In our yet unpublished report [8] we describe their manifestation in a "capability-safe" Java-subset and give precise definitions. We believe that such execution observations can easily be defined for a range of different programming languages and paradigms. In this paper, we bring out the most salient issues of execution observations.

Modules and Linking. To model the open nature of capability policies, we need to describe both the program we are checking, and potential extensions of that program (through subclasses, mashups, imports etc). For this we use *modules*, M, to denote programs, and $*$ to describe the combination of two programs into one larger program.

Adherence to policies often relies on the correct use of restrictive features. We support the method and class annotations private and final. The type rules of Java forbid access to private fields or methods outside their classes, forbid extensions of final classes, forbid redefinitions of final methods in subclasses, and forbid assignment to final fields outside their constructor [8].

The $*$ operator links modules together into new modules. Thus, $M_{Purse} * M_{Mint}$ is a module. Linking performs some compatibility checks, and therefore $*$ is only partially defined. For example, because the field balance is private, $M_{Purse} * M'$ would be undefined, if M' contained the expression newPurse.balance. The operation $*$ is only defined if it gives rise to a well-formed module.

Code. Modules are not directly executable, but are necessary for the execution of *code snippets*. We use the variables code, $code'$ to range over code snippets.

Runtime Configurations and Code Execution. Execution takes place in the context of runtime configurations $\kappa \in RTConf$. A configuration is a stack frame and heap. A stack frame is a tuple consisting of the following four components: the address of the receiver, a mapping giving values to the formal parameters, the class identifier, and the method identifier of the method being executed. A heap is a mapping from object addresses to objects.

Execution of a code snippet code for a module M takes a configuration κ and returns a value v and a new configuration κ'. We describe this through a large step semantics, of the shape M, κ, code $\leadsto \kappa'$, v'.

Reached and Arising Snapshots. When verifying adherence to policies, it is essential to consider only those snapshots (*i.e.,* configuration and code pairs) which may arise through the execution of the given modules. For example, if we considered *any* well-formed snapshots (well-formed in the sense of the type system), then we would be unable to show that **Pol_5** is obeyed by the mint example. Namely, **Pol_5** guarantees that balances are always positive: configurations where the balance is negative are well-formed, but will never actually arise in the execution of the program.

$\mathcal{R}each(M, \kappa, code)$ is the set of snapshots corresponding to the start of the execution of the body of any constructor or method called in the process of executing code in the context of M and κ. For example, $(\kappa_2, this.mint := prs.mint; this.balance := 0) \in \mathcal{R}each(M, \kappa_1, p1.deposit(p2); p3 = newPurse(p2))$. Note that $\mathcal{R}each(M, \kappa, code)$, corresponds to the *complete* body of a method; for example, $(\kappa_3, this.balance := 0) \notin \mathcal{R}each(M, \kappa_4, p3 = newPurse(p2))$ for any κ_3 and κ_4. $\mathcal{R}each(M, \kappa, code)$ is always defined, even though it may be infinite if execution of M, κ, code does not terminate.

$\mathcal{A}rising(M)$ is the set of snapshots which may be reached during execution of some initial snapshot, κ_0, $code_0$. Similarly to $\mathcal{R}each(M, \kappa, code)$, the function $\mathcal{A}rising(M)$ is always defined.

Accessible and Used Objects. As we have already discussed, objects protect services, *i.e.* some policies may require that services are only accessible through certain objects. Therefore, availability of a service is predicated on accessibility of the corresponding object. Therefore we need to model accessibility of objects.

We distinguish between $\mathcal{A}ccAll(\mathsf{M}, \kappa)$ — the set of all objects which are accessible from the frame in κ through *any* path — and $\mathcal{A}ccPub(\mathsf{M}, \kappa)$ — the set of all objects accessible through paths which include only public fields, and private fields of objects of the same class as this.

The notation $\mathsf{z} :_{\kappa} \mathsf{c}$ indicates that z is the name of an object which exists in the heap of κ and belongs to class c — with no requirement that there should be a path from the frame to this object.

The notation $\kappa \in \mathsf{c}$ expresses that the currently executing method in κ comes from class c, while $\kappa \in \mathsf{M}$ expresses that the class of the currently executing method is defined in module M.

$\mathcal{U}sed(\mathsf{M}, \kappa, \mathsf{code})$ is the set of all addresses used during execution of code in the configuration κ.

Paths, Pure Expressions, and Predicates. Capability policies are program-centered, therefore in order to express their semantics we need to be able to talk about all program entities, such as paths. For example, mint, prs.mint are paths.
Paths are interpreted in the context of runtime configurations,

$$\lceil \cdot \rfloor : Path \longrightarrow RTConf \longrightarrow Value$$

so that $\lceil \mathsf{p} \rfloor_{\kappa} = v$ if p is a path and $\emptyset, \kappa, \mathsf{p} \rightsquigarrow \kappa, v$.
Functions and predicates are interpreted in the expected manner

$$\lceil \cdot \rfloor : Func\_Id \times Var\_Id^* \longrightarrow RTConf \longrightarrow Value$$
$$\lceil \cdot \rfloor : Pred\_Id \longrightarrow \mathcal{P}(Value^*)$$

involving any necessary unfoldings of the definitions. Therefore, $\lceil f(\mathsf{p1}, ...\mathsf{pn}) \rfloor_{\kappa} = \lceil fFbody[\mathsf{p1}/x1, ...\mathsf{pn}/xn] \rfloor_{\kappa}$, where $fBody$ is the function definition of f, with free variables $x1,... xn$. Finally, $\lceil P(\mathsf{p1}, ...\mathsf{pn}) \rfloor_{\kappa} = \lceil P \rfloor (\lceil \mathsf{p1} \rfloor_{\kappa}, ...\lceil \mathsf{pn} \rfloor_{\kappa})$.

Defining the currency. In the Mint example, and using the code from Fig. 1, the function Currency is defined as follows

$$\mathsf{Currency}(\mathsf{mnt}) = \sum\nolimits_{\mathsf{p} \in Ps(\mathsf{mnt})} \mathsf{p.balance}$$
$$\text{where } Ps(\mathsf{mnt}) = \{\mathsf{p} \mid \mathsf{p} : \mathsf{Purse} \wedge \mathsf{p.mint} = \mathsf{mnt}\}$$

On the other hand, using the code from Fig. 2, the Currency is defined as follows

$$\mathsf{Currency}(\mathsf{mnt}) = \sum\nolimits_{\{ \mathsf{p} \mid \mathsf{mnt.database.contains(p)} \}} \mathsf{mnt.database.get(p)}$$

5   Semantics of the Mint Policies

We now turn our attention to the precise meaning of the first five policies from the Mint example. (We do not address the sixth policy as our formalisation does not yet incorporate trust). We discuss the policies in order of increasing complexity of their specification, rather than in numerical order.

Note that in the following we are specifying the policies regardless of whether the code is taken from Fig. 1, or from Fig. 2. We have already given definitions for Currency as defined in Fig. 1 and in Fig. 2. Wrt to the term prs.balance, when taking the Fig. 2 version, the term $\lceil$prs.balance$\rfloor_\kappa$ is a shorthand for $\lceil$mnt.database.get(prs)$\rfloor_\kappa$ where mnt is such that mnt.database.contains(prs).

The fifth policy. **Pol_5**, "Balances are always non-negative integers", is akin to a class invariant [20,28,33]. We can express the policy directly by requiring that a module M satisfies **Pol_5**, if for all M' legal extensions of M, and snapshots $(\kappa, \_)$ arising through execution of the augmented program M ∗ M', the balance is positive in κ.

$$M \models \textbf{Pol\_5}$$
$$\text{iff}$$
$$\forall M'. \forall (\kappa, \text{code}) \in \mathcal{Arising}(M * M'). \forall \text{prs} :_\kappa \text{Purse.}$$
$$\lceil \text{prs.balance} \rfloor_\kappa \geq 0$$

Note that the arising snapshots are considered in the context of the *extended* module M ∗ M', where M' is universally quantified. This reflects the open nature of capability policies, and allows calling methods and accessing fields defined in M but also in M' before reaching the snapshot (κ, code).

Note also that $\mathcal{Arising}(M * M')$ catches snapshots at the *beginning* of a method execution. Therefore, if a method were to temporarily set balance to a negative value, but restored it to a positive value before returning, would *not* violate **Pol_5**.

The third policy. **Pol_3**, stating "The mint can only inflate its own currency", could mean that the currency of a mint never decreases, or that the mint cannot affect the currency of a different mint. As we shall see later on, the second interpretation is a corollary of **Pol_2**; here we analyse the first interpretation:

$$M \models \textbf{Pol\_3}$$
$$\text{iff}$$
$$\forall M'. \forall (\kappa, \text{code}) \in \mathcal{Arising}(M * M'). \forall \text{mnt} :_\kappa \text{Mint.}$$
$$M * M', \kappa, \text{code} \rightsquigarrow \kappa', v$$
$$\Longrightarrow$$
$$\lceil \text{Currency(mnt)} \rfloor_\kappa \leq \lceil \text{Currency(mnt)} \rfloor_{\kappa'}$$

Namely, we require that for any arising snapshot (κ, code), and any execution originating from (κ, code) and leading to a new configuration κ', the Currency at the old configuration is less than or equal to the currency at the new configuration. Therefore, in the conclusion we talk about the values of functions in the old configuration (*i.e.* $\lceil \text{Currency}(\text{mnt}) \rfloor_\kappa$) as well as those in the new configuration (*i.e.* $\lceil \text{Currency}(\text{mnt}) \rfloor_{\kappa'}$). Conclusions which are in terms of the old as well as the new state are common in standard approaches to program specification. **Pol_3** describes a monotonic property, and is therefore related to history invariants [14].

The first policy. **Pol_1** states "With two purses of the same mint, one can transfer money between them". We can understand **Pol_1** to mean that if p1 and p2 are purses of the same mint, then the method call p1.deposit(p2, m) will transfer the money. In section 6, we shall present two other possible meanings for this policy. We write this first interpretation of **Pol_1** as:

$$M \models \textbf{Pol\_1A}$$
$$\text{iff}$$
$$\forall M'.\forall \, (\kappa, \text{p1.deposit}(\text{p2}, \text{m})) \in \mathcal{A}rising(M * M').$$
$$\forall \text{p1}, \text{p2} :_\kappa \text{Purse.} \lceil \text{p1.mint} \rfloor_\kappa = \lceil \text{p2.mint} \rfloor_\kappa \ \wedge \ \lceil \text{p2.balance} \rfloor_\kappa \geq m$$
$$\wedge \ M * M', \kappa, \text{p1.deposit}(\text{p2}, \text{m}) \rightsquigarrow \kappa', v$$
$$\implies$$
$$\lceil \text{p1.balance} \rfloor_{\kappa'} = \lceil \text{p1.balance} \rfloor_\kappa + m \quad \wedge \quad \lceil \text{p2.balance} \rfloor_{\kappa'} = \lceil \text{p2.balance} \rfloor_\kappa - m.$$

The specification **Pol_1A** again ranges over all module extensions, M'. This policy is stated as a sufficient condition, and is related to a Hoare triples,[1]. The quantification over modules M' requires that the code M' can do nothing to break the behaviour of the deposit method from M, thus either requiring the use of restrictive features (*e.g.* forcing the method deposit to be final, or the class Purse to be final, or package confined), or the use of contracts, where subclasses are implicitly expected to satisfy the superclass's contract,

The fourth policy. **Pol_4**, "No one can affect the balance of a purse they don't have", says that if some runtime configuration affects the balance of some purse prs, then the original runtime configuration must have had access to the prs itself.

---

[1] The corresponding Hoare triple would be

$$\{ \text{p1.mint} = \text{p2.mint} \ \wedge \ \text{p1.balance} = k1 \ \wedge \ \text{p2.balance} = k2 + m \}$$
$$\text{p1.deposit}(\text{p2}, \text{m})$$
$$\{ \text{p1.balance} = k1 + m \ \wedge \ \text{p2.balance} = k2 \}$$

$$M \models \mathbf{Pol\_4}$$
$$\text{iff}$$
$$\forall\, M',\, (\kappa, \text{code}) \in \mathcal{A}rising(M * M').\ \forall \text{prs} :_\kappa \text{Purse.}$$
$$M * M',\, \kappa \rightsquigarrow \kappa',\, v$$
$$\wedge\ \lceil \text{prs.balance} \rfloor_\kappa \neq \lceil \text{prs.balance} \rfloor_{\kappa'}$$
$$\Longrightarrow$$
$$\lceil \text{prs} \rfloor_\kappa \in \mathcal{U}sed(M * M',\, \kappa, \text{code})$$

Note that in contrast to the previous policies, and in contrast to the standard approach to program specification, the premise of the policy is in terms of both the old configuration (here $\lceil \text{prs.balance} \rfloor_\kappa$ and the new configuration (here $\lceil \text{prs.balance} \rfloor_{\kappa'}$).

The second policy. **Pol_2**, stating "Only someone with the mint of a given currency can violate conservation of that currency.", is similar to **Pol_4**, in that it mandates that a change (here a change in the currency) may only happen if the originating configuration had access to an entity (here access to the mint).

$$M \models \mathbf{Pol\_2}$$
$$\text{iff}$$
$$\forall\, M',\, (\kappa, \text{code}) \in \mathcal{A}rising(M * M').\ \forall \text{mnt} :_\kappa \text{Mint.}$$
$$M * M',\, \kappa, \text{code} \rightsquigarrow \kappa',\, v$$
$$\wedge\ \lceil \text{Currency(mnt)} \rfloor_\kappa \neq \lceil \text{Currency(mnt)} \rfloor_{\kappa'}$$
$$\Longrightarrow$$
$$\lceil \text{mnt} \rfloor_\kappa \in \mathcal{U}sed(M * M',\, \kappa, \text{code})$$

Policy Characteristics. The meanings of policies given in the previous section vary, but they share common characteristics:

– They refer to a fixed module M, and all its legal extensions M'.
– They specify that execution of some code, under some conditions, guarantees some conclusions.
– Both conditions *and* conclusions may refer to properties of the state *before* as well as *after* execution.
– The code may be universally or existentially quantified, or explicitly given.

6   Alternative interpretations of the Mint Policies

Because our policy descriptions have precise semantics — unlike the informal English policies from the original Mint example — a single English policy can have a number of plausible interpretations in our notation. We explore some of these alternatives here; we were surprised how many different interpretations we uncovered while analysing this example.

The first policy revisited. **Pol_1** states "With two purses of the same mint, one can transfer money between them". In section 4.2 we proposed as possible meaning that the call p1.deposit(p2) will transfer the money. This is perhaps an over-specification, as it prescribes *how* the transfer is to take place — by calling the p1.deposit(p2) method. Alternatively, we may want to require only that it is *possible* for the transfer to take place, without constraining the program design. We can define a second, more general version of the policy, which only requires the existence of a code snippet that performs the transaction, provided that purses p1 and p2 share the same mint, that p2 has sufficient funds, and that they are both accessible in κ without reading private fields ($AccPub(M, \kappa)$).

Module M satisfies policy **Pol_1B**

iff

$\forall (\kappa, \_) \in Arising(M). \forall p1, p2 :_\kappa$ Purse.

$\lceil p1.mint \rfloor_\kappa = \lceil p2.mint \rfloor_\kappa \ \wedge \ \lceil p2.balance \rfloor_\kappa \geq m$

$\wedge \ \lceil p1 \rfloor_\kappa, \lceil p2 \rfloor_\kappa \in AccPub(M, \kappa)$

$\Longrightarrow$

$\exists$ code. $\forall M'.$

$M * M', \kappa, code \rightsquigarrow \kappa', v$

$\wedge \ \lceil p1.balance \rfloor_{\kappa'} = \lceil p1.balance \rfloor_\kappa + m$

$\wedge \ \lceil p2.balance \rfloor_{\kappa'} = \lceil p2.balance \rfloor_\kappa - m.$

Note that this policy requires that execution of the code has the required properties for *all* extending modules M'.

A third possible meaning of **Pol_1** is that deposit can be called successfully only if the two purses belonged to the same mint:

Module M satisfies policy **Pol_1C**

iff

$\forall M'. \forall (\kappa, p1.deposit(p2)) \in Arising(M * M').$

$M * M', \kappa, p1.deposit(p2, m) \rightsquigarrow \kappa', v$

$\Longrightarrow$

$\lceil p1.mint \rfloor_\kappa = \lceil p2.mint \rfloor_\kappa$

The requirement $M * M', \kappa, \text{p1.deposit}(\text{p2}, m) \rightsquigarrow \kappa', v$ is crucial in the premise, in that it ensures that execution does not lead to an error (our current definition of the language $\mathcal{C}_j$ does not support exceptions). Note, also, that in this specification the conclusion is only concerned with properties observable in the original configuration, κ, while the premise is concerned with properties observable in κ as well as κ'. This reflects the deny nature of the policy.

Finally, a fourth, and more straightforward meaning of **Pol_1** would mandate that the balance of a purse p1 may change only if deposit was executed on p1 or with p1 as an argument. This can be expressed as follows:

Module M satisfies policy **Pol_1D**
iff
$$\forall M'. \, \forall (\kappa, \text{code}) \in \mathcal{A}rising(M * M'). \, \forall \text{p1} :_\kappa \text{Purse}.$$
$$M * M', \kappa, \text{code} \rightsquigarrow \kappa', v$$
$$\wedge \, \lceil \text{p1.balance} \rfloor_\kappa \neq \lceil \text{p1.balance} \rfloor_{\kappa'}$$
$$\Longrightarrow$$
$$\exists \kappa', \text{ s.t.}$$
$$(\kappa', \_) \in \mathcal{R}each(M * M', \kappa, \text{code})$$
$$\wedge \quad \kappa' = (\_, \_, \text{Purse}, \text{deposit})$$
$$\wedge \quad (\lceil \text{this} \rfloor_{\kappa'} = \lceil \text{p1} \rfloor_\kappa \vee \lceil \text{prs} \rfloor_{\kappa'} = \lceil \text{p1} \rfloor_\kappa)$$

The assertion $(\kappa', \_) \in \mathcal{R}each(M*M', \kappa, \text{code}) \wedge \kappa' = (\_, \_, \text{Purse}, \text{deposit})$ guarantees that execution of the snapshot (κ, code) will reach a point where it calls the method deposit from Purse. The assertion $(\lceil \text{this} \rfloor_{\kappa'} = \lceil \text{p1} \rfloor_\kappa \vee \lceil \text{prs} \rfloor_{\kappa'} = \lceil \text{p1} \rfloor_\kappa)$ guarantees that the receiver or the first argument of that method call will be $\lceil \text{p1} \rfloor_\kappa$.

The second policy revisited. **Pol_2**, "Only someone with the mint of a given currency can violate conservation of that currency." mandates that a change in the currency may only happen if the originating configuration had access to the mint. In section 4.2 we took "access to" to mean that the code executed eventually would read the mint object (i.e. that the mint was in the set $\mathcal{U}sed$). We see three alternative interpretations for the meaning of *having access to*:

1. $\lceil \text{mnt} \rfloor_\kappa \in \mathcal{U}sed(M, \kappa, \text{code})$, i.e. that execution of code in the context of κ will at some point use the object mnt.
2. $\lceil \text{mnt} \rfloor_\kappa \in \mathcal{A}ccAll(M, \kappa)$, i.e. that κ has a path from the stack frame to mnt which involves any fields.
3. $\lceil \text{mnt} \rfloor_\kappa \in \mathcal{A}ccPub(\kappa, \text{code})$, i.e. that κ has a path from the stack frame to mnt which involves only public fields, or private fields from the same class as the current receiver.

This means there are two further ways in which **Pol_2** may be understood:

$$M \models \textbf{Pol\_2B}$$
$$\text{iff}$$
$$\forall\, M'.\ \forall (\kappa, \text{code}) \in \mathcal{A}rising(M * M').\ \forall \text{mnt} :_\kappa \text{Mint}.$$
$$M * M', \kappa, \text{code} \rightsquigarrow \kappa', v$$
$$\wedge\ \lceil \text{Currency(mnt)} \rfloor_\kappa \neq \lceil \text{Currency(mnt)} \rfloor_{\kappa'}$$
$$\Longrightarrow$$
$$\lceil \text{mnt} \rfloor_\kappa \in \mathcal{A}cc\mathcal{A}ll(M * M', \kappa)$$

$$M \models \textbf{Pol\_2C}$$
$$\text{iff}$$
$$\forall\, M'.\ \forall (\kappa, \text{code}) \in \mathcal{A}rising(M * M').\ \forall \text{mnt} :_\kappa \text{Mint}.$$
$$M * M', \kappa, \text{code} \rightsquigarrow \kappa', v$$
$$\wedge\ \lceil \text{Currency(mnt)} \rfloor_\kappa \neq \lceil \text{Currency}_{\kappa'}(\text{mnt}) \rfloor_\kappa$$
$$\Longrightarrow$$
$$\lceil \text{mnt} \rfloor_\kappa \in \mathcal{A}cc\mathcal{P}ub(M * M', \kappa)$$

Our interpretation of **Pol_2** in section 4.2 uses the first choice. In [8], we prove that $M_{\text{Mint}} * M_{\text{Purse}} \models \textbf{Pol\_2A}$. Moreover, we prove lemmas which guarantee that mnt $:_\kappa$ Mint and $\lceil mnt \rfloor_\kappa \in \mathcal{U}sed(M, \kappa, \text{code})$ imply that $\lceil mnt \rfloor_\kappa \in \mathcal{A}cc\mathcal{A}ll(M, \kappa)$. Ttherefore any code which satisfies **Pol_2A** also adheres to **Pol_2B**. This gives that $M_{\text{Mint}} * M_{\text{Purse}} \models \textbf{Pol\_2A}$.

What about **Pol_2C**? It gives a stronger guarantee than **Pol_2B**, and therefore is to be preferred over **Pol_2B**, however, $M_{\text{Purse}} * M_{\text{Mint}}$ does *not* satisfy **Pol_2C**. More importantly, without the concept of package and package-local classes, or some concept of ownership, it is impossible to write an implementation for Purse so that it satisfies **Pol_2C**. The following example shows why:

```
class CentralBank {
    private final Mint myMint = new Mint();

    public void inflate() {
        Purse tmpPurse = new Purse(myMint,1000000000)
    }
}
```

A `CentralBank` has a mint. The `inflate` method creates a new temporary purse containing a billion dollars from thin air — perhaps this method should have been called `quantitativeEasing`. Now consider a client of a `CentralBank` object — the finance minister say. The finance minister does *not* have a public access to the mint (because the central bank is supposed to be independent!) so by **Pol_2C** she should not be able to inflate the currency. If, however, the finance minister calls `myCentralBank .inflate` then the currency will be inflated all the same.

Discussion. We leave the question as to the "correct" meaning of the policies open. Our contribution is the provision of the tools with which to give precise meaning to policies, and the clarification of the differences. However, the "correct" meaning is determined by the use of the policies in the wider setting, for example, in the application of the policies to prove properties of the use of the mint/purse system, e.g. in the escrow example [21].

7 Related Work

Object capabilities were first introduced [22] seven years ago, and many recent studies manage or verify safety or correctness of object capability programs.

Google's Caja [25] applies sandboxes, proxies, and wrappers to limit components' access to *ambient* capabilities. Sandboxing has been validated formally: Maffeis et al. [16] develop a model of JavaScript, demonstrate that it obeys two principles of object capability systems and show how untrusted applications can be prevented from interfering with the rest of the system. Alternatively, Taly et al. [35] model JavaScript APIs in Datalog, and then carry out a Datalog search for an "attacker" from the set of all valid API calls. This search is similar to the quantification over potential code snippets in our model. Murray and Lowe [26] model object capability programs in CSP, and use a model checker to ensure program executions do not leak information.

Karim et al. apply static analysis on Mozilla's JavaScript Jetpack extension framework [12], including pointer analyses. Bhargavan et al. [3] extend language-based sandboxing techniques to support "defensive" components that can execute successfully in otherwise untrusted environments. Meredith et al. [18] encode policies as types in higher order reflective π-calculus.. Politz et al. [29] use a JavaScript typechecker to check properties such as *"multiple widgets on the same page cannot communicate."* — somewhat similar in spirit to our **Pol_4**. Lerner et al. extend this system to ensure browser extensions observe *"private mode"* browsing conventions, such as that *"no private browsing history retained"* [15]. Dimoulas et al. [6] generalise the language and typechecker based approach to enforce explicit policies, that describe which components may access, or may influence the use of, particular capabilities.

The WebSand [4,17] and Jeeves [40] projects use dynamic techniques to monitor safe execution of information flow policies. Richards et al. [31] extended this approach by incorporating explicit dynamic ownership of objects (and thus of capabilities) and policies that may examine the history of objects' computations. While these dynamic techniques can restrict or terminate the execution of a component that breaches its security policies, they cannot guarantee in advance that such violations can never happen. While information flow policies are concerned with the flow of objects (and thus also capabilities) across the program code, our work is more concerned with the identification of the objects which protect the services.

A few formal verification frameworks address JavaScript's highly dynamic, prototype-based semantics. Gardner et al. [9] developed a formalisation of JavaScript based on separation logic and verified examples. Xiong and Qin et al. [39,30] worked on similar lines. Swamy et al. [34] recently developed a mechanised verification technique for JavaScript based on the Dijkstra Monad in the F* programming language. Finally, Jang et al. [11] developed a machine-checked proof of five important properties of a web browser — again similar to our simple deny policies — such as *"cookies may not be shared across domains"* by writing the minimal kernel of the browser in Coq.

8 Conclusions and Future Work

In this paper, we have advocated that capability policies are necessary for reasoning about programs using object capability security. We have argued that capability policies are program centred, fine grained, open, and contain necessary as well as sufficient conditions.

These novel features of the policies require novel features in specifications. We have proposed execution observations, and developed a capability specification style, which incorporates universal and existential quantification over program code, explicit naming of snapshots before, after and during execution, and their use in premises and in conclusions. We have used our approach to specify most of the Mint example.

We have shown how efforts at specifying policies precisely can uncover ambiguities in policies' interpretations, and can help find additional implicit policies that can be made explicit. We have proposed another five policies for the Mint, and formulated then in our language.

In further work, we want to refine the execution observations, to develop a programmer-friendly notation for specifications, to consider the specification of the further policies we uncovered as well as other policies from the literature, and to extend our toy language to encompass further salient programming language features. We also want to develop a formal logic to support reasoning about code's adherence to capability policies. We need to model trust (or the lack of it) between components, so we can model systems composed both trusted and untrusted code. Finally, inspired by the original Mint work, we want to consider the specification and verification of capabilities in other programming languages, in particular, languages without static types.

Acknowledgments. This work is partly supported by the Royal Society of New Zealand Marsden Fund and by the EU FP7 project Upscale.

References

1. Agten, P., Van Acker, S., Brondsema, Y., Phung, P.H., Desmet, L., Piessens, F.: JSand: complete client-side sandboxing of third-party JavaScript without browser modifications. In: ACSAC (2012)
2. Bauer, L., Ligatti, J., Walker, D.: Composing security policies with Polymer. In: PLDI (2005)
3. Bhargavan, K., Delignat-Lavaud, A., Maffeisp, S.: Language-based defenses against untrusted browser origins. In: USENIX Security (2013)
4. Birgisson, A., Russo, A., Sabelfeld, A.: Capabilities for information flow. In: Programming Languages and Analysis for Security (PLAS) (2011)

5. Dennis, J.B., Van Horn, E.C.: Programming Semantics for Multiprogrammed Computations. Comm. ACM 9(3) (1966)
6. Dimoulas, C., Moore, S., Askarov, A., Chong, S.: Declarative policies for capability control. In: Computer Security Foundations Symposium (CSF) (2014)
7. Drossopoulou, S., Noble, J.: The need for capability policies. In: (FTfJP) (2013)
8. Drossopoulou, S., Noble, J.: Towards Capability Policy Specification and Verification. Technical Report ECSTR-14-05, School of Engineering and Computer Science, Victoria University of Wellington (2014)
9. Gardner, P., Maffeis, S., Smith, G.D.: Towards a program logic for JavaScript. In: POPL (2012)
10. Hoare, C.A.R.: Proofs of correctness of data representation. Acta Informatica 1, 271–281 (1972)
11. Jang, D., Tatlock, Z., Lerner, S.: Establishing browser security guarantees through formal shim verification. In: USENIX Security (2012)
12. Karim, R., Dhawan, M., Ganapathy, V., Shan, C.-C.: An Analysis of the Mozilla Jetpack Extension Framework. In: Noble, J. (ed.) ECOOP 2012. LNCS, vol. 7313, pp. 333–355. Springer, Heidelberg (2012)
13. Lampson, B.W., Sturgis, H.E.: Reflection on an Operating System Design. Communications of the ACM 19(5) (1976)
14. Leino, K.R.M., Schulte, W.: Using history invariants to verify observers. In: De Nicola, R. (ed.) ESOP 2007. LNCS, vol. 4421, pp. 80–94. Springer, Heidelberg (2007)
15. Lerner, B.S., Elberty, L., Poole, N., Krishnamurthi, S.: Verifying web browser extensions' compliance with private-browsing mode. In: Crampton, J., Jajodia, S., Mayes, K. (eds.) ESORICS 2013. LNCS, vol. 8134, pp. 57–74. Springer, Heidelberg (2013)
16. Maffeis, S., Mitchell, J.C., Taly, A.: Object capabilities and isolation of untrusted web applications. In: Proc. of IEEE Security and Privacy (2010)
17. Magazinius, J., Russo, A., Sabelfeld, A.: On-the-fly inlining of dynamic security monitors. Computers & Security 31(7), 827–843 (2012)
18. Meredith, L.G., Stay, M., Drossopoulou, S.: Policy as types. arXiv:1307.7766 [cs.CR] (July 2013)
19. Mettler, A., Wagner, D., Close, T.: Joe-E a Security-Oriented Subset of Java. In: NDSS (2010)
20. Meyer, B.: Object-Oriented Software Construction. Prentice-Hall (1988)
21. Miller, M.S., Van Cutsem, T., Tulloh, B.: Distributed Electronic Rights in JavaScript. In: Felleisen, M., Gardner, P. (eds.) Programming Languages and Systems. LNCS, vol. 7792, pp. 1–20. Springer, Heidelberg (2013)
22. Miller, M.S.: Robust Composition: Towards a Unified Approach to Access Control and Concurrency Control. PhD thesis, Baltimore, Maryland (2006)
23. Miller, M.S.: Secure Distributed Programming with Object-capabilities in JavaScript. Talk at Vrije Universiteit Brussel (October 2011), http://mobicrant-talks.eventbrite.com
24. Miller, M.S., Morningstar, C., Frantz, B.: Capability-based Financial Instruments: From Object to Capabilities. In: Frankel, Y. (ed.) FC 2000. LNCS, vol. 1962, p. 349. Springer, Heidelberg (2001)
25. Miller, M.S., Samuel, M., Laurie, B., Awad, I., Stay, M.: Safe active content in sanitized JavaScript (2008), http://code.google.com/p/google-caja/
26. Murray, T., Lowe, G.: Analysing the information flow properties of object-capability patterns. In: Degano, P., Guttman, J.D. (eds.) FAST 2009. LNCS, vol. 5983, pp. 81–95. Springer, Heidelberg (2010)
27. Noble, J., Drossopoulou, S.: A rational reconstruction of the escrow example. In: (FTfJP) (2014)

28. Parkinson, M.: A rational reconstruction of the escrow example. In: IWACO (2007)
29. Politz, J.G., Eliopoulos, S.A., Guha, A., Krishnamurthi, S.: ADsafety: Type-based verification of JavaScript sandboxing. In: USENIX Security (2011)
30. Qin, S., Chawdhary, A., Xiong, W., Munro, M., Qiu, Z., Zhu, H.: Towards an axiomatic verification system for JavaScript. In: TASE, pp. 133–141 (2011)
31. Richards, G., Hammer, C., Nardelli, F.Z., Jagannathan, S., Vitek, J.: Flexible access control for JavaScript. In: OOPSLA, pp. 305–322 (2013)
32. Stiegler, M.: The lazy programmer's guide to security. HP Labs, http://www.object-oriented-security.org
33. Summers, A.J., Drossopoulou, S., Müller, P.: The need for Flexible Object Invariants. In: IWACO. ACM DL (July 2009)
34. Swamy, N., Weinberger, J., Schlesinger, C., Chen, J., Livshits, B.: Verifying higher-order programs with the dijkstra monad. In: PLDI, pp. 387–398 (2013)
35. Taly, A., Erlingsson, U., Mitchell, J.C., Miller, M.S., Nagra, J.: Automated Analysis of Security-Critical JavaScript APIs. In: IEEE Symposium on Security and Privacy (SP) (2011)
36. The Newspeak Team. Several Newspeak Documents (September 2012), http://newspeaklanguage.org/
37. Tom van Cutsem. Membranes in JavaScript (2012), http://prog.vub.ac.be/~tvcutsem/-invokedynamic/js-membranes
38. Wilkes, M.V., Needham, R.M.: The Cambridge CAP computer and its operating system (1979)
39. Xiong, W.: Verification and Validation of JavaScript. PhD thesis, Durham University (2013)
40. Yang, J., Yessenov, K., Solar-Lezama, A.: A language for automatically enforcing privacy policies. In: POPL (2012)

Tool Integration

Model-Checking *Circus* State-Rich Specifications

Marcel Vinicius Medeiros Oliveira[1,*], Augusto C.A. Sampaio[2],
and Madiel S. Conserva Filho[1]

[1] Departamento de Informática e Matemática Aplicada,
Universidade Federal do Rio Grande do Norte, Brazil
`marcel@dimap.ufrn.br`
[2] Centro de Informática, Universidade Federal de Pernambuco, Brazil

Abstract. Throughout the past decades two schools have been developing formal techniques for correct software development, taking complementary approaches: the model-based approach and the behavioural approach. Combinations of languages from both approaches have also been proposed. The lack of support for refinement of state-rich reactive systems in a calculational style has motivated the creation of *Circus*, a combination of Z, CSP, and Djikstra's commmand language. In this paper, we foster the reuse of theoretical results underpinned on CSP to *Circus* by providing a sound mapping for processes and refinement from *Circus* to CSP. This mapping is proved sound from an existing link between these languages, established in the Unifying Theories of Programming (UTP). Our results allow analysing *Circus* specifications with techniques and tools, like FDR2 and PAT, originally developed for CSP. We illustrate the overall approach with a running example.

Keywords: Formal methods integration, Model-checking, *Circus*, CSP.

1 Introduction

The existing formalisms for system modelling and verification are usually classified according to their focus on particular design aspects. Here, we emphasise two approaches: one of them focuses on data aspects, while the other one focuses on behavioural (control flow) aspects. Languages like Z [23] use a model-based approach, where mathematical objects from set theory form the basis of the specification. Although possible in a rather implicit fashion, specification of behavioural aspects such as choice, sequence, and parallel composition are not explicitly provided by any of these languages. Complementarily, CSP [19], among others, provide a rich set of constructs that can be used to describe the behaviour of a system in an abstract and structured way. However, they do not support concise description of data aspects. Notations that describe both aspects [9] have also been proposed. The combination of formalisms allows the reuse of notations to describe different modelling aspects. Some combinations have taken a syntactic approach [6] embedding one formalism into another, but

---

* Corresponding author.

E. Albert and E. Sekerinski (Eds.): IFM 2014, LNCS 8739, pp. 39–54, 2014.

imposing architectural restrictions. A semantic approach, in which formalisms are combined in a common semantic model, however, needs direct tool support.

Combinations of Z with CCS [8] and CSP [6,13], VDM with CSP (CML) [17], and B and CSP [21] are some examples. However, as far as we are aware, none of them supports refinement of state-rich reactive systems in a calculational style [12]. This has motivated the creation of *Circus* [5], which describes systems as processes grouping constructs that describe data (using Z) and control behaviour (using CSP), and has a support for formal stepwise development [5].

Mappings from one formalism into another are available in the literature. Some, like those presented in [6] and [13], take a syntactic approach and do not address the soundness of the translation in a common semantic framework. Furthermore, a partial mapping from *Circus* to CSP has been proposed in [2]. Our mapping, however, is proved sound and far more comprehensive including most of the *Circus* constructs and relating refinement notions.

In this paper, we foster the reuse of CSP theoretical results to *Circus* by providing a mapping (see Figure 1) for processes and refinement from *Circus* to CSP. Our mapping is limited to a subset of feasible divergence free *Circus* processes with a limited use of predicative specifications. This mapping is proved sound from a link [3,4] between these languages established in the UTP [10].

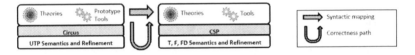

Fig. 1. Unification Path for Model-Checking *Circus*

Circus is supported by some academic tools like an animator [15], a refinement calculator [11], a translator to Java [1], and a prototype model-checker [22]. It, however, lacks more consolidated tool support. Our results allows one to analyse *Circus* specifications using well-established CSP tools like FDR2 [7] and PAT [20].

In Section 2, we introduce the relevant preliminary material. The mapping from *Circus* to CSP and its soundness are presented in Section 3. Section 4 describes the practical application of our theoretical results. In Section 5, we draw our conclusions and discuss related and future work.

2   Preliminaries

In this section, we introduce CSP, *Circus* and its semantical framework, the UTP.

2.1   CSP

CSP is a process algebra that can be used to describe systems composed by interacting components, which are independent self-contained processes with interfaces that are used to interact with the environment [19].

The two basic CSP processes are $STOP$ and $SKIP$; the former deadlocks, and the latter does nothing but terminates. The prefixing $a \rightarrow P$ is initially able to perform only the event a; afterwards it behaves like process P. A boolean guard may be associated with a process: g & P behaves like P if the predicate g is true; it deadlocks otherwise. The operator P_1; P_2 combines P_1 and P_2 in sequence. The external choice $P_1 \square P_2$ initially offers events of both processes. The performance of the first event or termination resolves the choice in favour of the process that performs either of them. The environment has no control over the internal choice $P_1 \sqcap P_2$, in which the choice is resolved internally. The sharing parallel composition $P_1 \llbracket cs \rrbracket P_2$ synchronises P_1 and P_2 on the events in the set cs; events that are not listed occur independently. The alphabetised parallel composition $P_1 \llbracket cs_1 \mid cs_2 \rrbracket P_2$ allows P_1 and P_2 to communicate in the sets cs_1 and cs_2, respectively; however, they must agree on events in $cs_1 \cap cs_2$. Processes composed in interleaving $P_1 \mid\mid\mid P_2$ run independently. The event hiding operator $P \setminus cs$ encapsulates the events that are in cs. Finally, $P \llbracket a \leftarrow b \rrbracket$ behaves like P except that all occurrences of a in P are replaced by b. CSP also provides finite iterated operators that can be used to generalise the binary operators of sequence, external and internal choice, parallel composition, and interleaving. For instance, $\mid\mid\mid\, i : S \bullet P(i)$ is the interleaving of all $P(i)$, with i taken from the set S. Further CSP operators are available, but omitted here for conciseness.

CSP has three classical semantic models [19]: traces, stable failures, and failures-divergences. The traces model ($\mathcal{T}$) describes processes as a set of all possible sequences of events (traces) it might perform. The stable-failures models ($\mathcal{F}$) describes processes as a set of failures: pairs containing the trace performed by the process and the set of events refused by the process after that trace. Finally, the failures-divergences model ($\mathcal{FD}$) extends $\mathcal{F}$ with the set of traces that lead the process to divergence. In this paper, we consider $\mathcal{F}$, which for the non-divergent processes considered in this paper, is equivalent to $\mathcal{FD}$.

2.2   *Circus*

Circus programs are declared as a sequence of paragraphs, which can either be a Z paragraph, a channel declaration, a channel set declaration, or a process declaration. Here, we illustrate the main constructs of *Circus* using the specification of a ring buffer (Figure 2), which is composed of a ring of cells with a central controller. Each single storage cell has its own identification and is able to store a value. The controller receives input and output requests from the environment and interacts accordingly with the ring of storage cells.

All the channels must be declared; we give their names and the types of the values they communicate. For example, the process $RingCell$ that represents a cell communicates through channels wrt and rrd. If a channel is used just for synchronisation, its declaration contains only its name. We also declare the channel set Ctr_I that contains all possible communications on rd_i and wrt_i; these channels are used to create indexed versions of the $RingCell$.

The declaration of a process is composed of its name and its body specification. A process may be explicitly defined or composed in terms of other processes, such

$maxbuff : 4$
$maxring = maxbuff - 1$
$Value = 0 .. 2$
$CellId = 1 .. maxring$

channel $input, output : Value$
channel $write, read, rd\_i, wrt\_i : CellId \times Value$
channel $rrd, wrt : Value$
chanset $Ctr_I = \{| rd\_i, wrt\_i |\}$

process $RingCell \;\hat{=}$
begin state $CellState \;\hat{=} [v : Value]$

$\quad InitCell \;\hat{=} \sqcap x : Value \bullet setV(x)$

$\quad setV \;\hat{=} \mathbf{val}\; newV : Value \bullet v := newV$
$\quad Cell \;\hat{=} wrt?x \rightarrow setV(x) \;\square\; rrd!v \rightarrow Skip$
$\quad \bullet InitCell; (\mu X \bullet Cell; X)$
end
$IRCell(i) \;\hat{=}$
$\quad RingCell[rrd, wrt := rd\_i.i, wrt\_i.i]$
$DRing \;\hat{=}\; \|\|\| \, i : CellId \bullet IRCell(i)$

process $Ctr \;\hat{=}$
begin
$\quad$**state** $CtrState \;\hat{=}$
$\quad\quad [cache : Value; size : \mathbb{N}; top, bot : CellId]$
$\quad InitCtr \;\hat{=} cache, size, top, bot := 0, 0, 1, 0$
$\quad Input \;\hat{=}\; (size < maxbuff) \;\&\; input?x \rightarrow$
$\quad\quad\quad (size = 0) \;\&\; cache := x; size := 1$
$\quad\quad\quad \square \; (size > 0) \;\&\;$
$\quad\quad\quad\quad write.top!x \rightarrow size := size + 1;$
$\quad\quad\quad\quad top := (top\; mod\; maxring) + 1$
$\quad Output \;\hat{=} (size > 0) \;\&\; output!cache \rightarrow$
$\quad\quad\quad (size > 1) \;\&\;$
$\quad\quad\quad\quad read.bot?x \rightarrow Skip;$
$\quad\quad\quad\quad size := size - 1;$
$\quad\quad\quad\quad bot := (bot\; mod\; maxring) + 1$
$\quad\quad\quad \square \; (size = 1) \;\&\; size := 0$
$\quad \bullet InitCtr; \mu X \bullet ((Input \;\square\; Output); X)$
end
$CtrR \;\hat{=}\; Ctr[read, write := rd\_i, wrt\_i]$
$RBuffer \;\hat{=}\; (CtrR \,[\![\,Ctr_I \,]\!]\, DRing) \setminus Ctr_I$

Fig. 2. A Distributed Ring Buffer

as the *RBuffer*, which is defined as the parallel composition of previously defined processes. An explicit process definition contains a sequence of paragraphs and a nameless main action that defines its behaviour. We use Z to define the state. For instance, *CellState* describes the state of the *RingCell*: a value v, which is initialised with an internally chosen value. The *RingCell* receives and outputs its value via *wrt* and *rrd*, respectively.

Process paragraphs include Z paragraphs and declarations of actions. An action can be a schema (a Z abstraction formed of variable declarations and an optional predicate that constrains the values these variables may assume), a primitive action like *Skip*, a guarded command, an invocation to another action, or a combination of these constructs using CSP operators. Actions may also be defined using assignment, guarded alternation, variable blocks, or a specification statement, which is not explained as it is not used in this paper, but see [12].

The CSP operators for sequence, external and internal choice, parallelism, interleaving and hiding may also be used to compose actions and processes. However, the parallelism and interleaving actions have a different declaration. In order to avoid conflict, they require the declaration of two sets that partition the variables in scope. In the parallel composition $A_1 \,[\![\, ns_1 \mid cs \mid ns_2 \,]\!]\, A_2$ the actions A_1 and A_2 synchronise on the channels in the set cs. Both actions, A_1 and A_2, have access to the initial values of all variables in scope. However, A_1 and A_2 may modify only the variables in ns_1 and ns_2, respectively. Interleaved actions $A_1 \,[\![ns_1 \mid ns_2]\!]\, A_2$ have the same behaviour regarding the state variables but they do not synchronise on any channels and run independently.

Communications and recursive definitions are also available for actions. The *RingCell* has a recursive behaviour: after its initialisation, it recursively behaves as action *Cell*, which represents the execution of a cycle of the *RingCell*. If it receives a request to write a value, it writes this value to the state: the operation *setV* sets the value v. The *RingCell* outputs its current value via channel *rrd*.

The renaming $P[o := c]$ replaces all references to o by references to c. For instance, $IRCell(i)$ parametrise $RingCell$ replacing references to rrd and wrt, to $rd\_i.i$ and $wrt\_i.i$, respectively, using the argument i. Similarly, $CtrR$ replaces $read$ and $write$ with rd_i and wrt_i, respectively.

Processes may also be defined in terms of existing processes using their names, CSP operators, or iterated CSP operators. The process $DRing$ is the iterated interleaving of ring cells. Furthermore, $RBuffer$ is the parallel composition of $CtrR$ and $DRing$ synchronising on rd_i and wrt_i, which are hidden from the environment. Interactions with $RBuffer$ is only through $input$ and $output$. The process $CtrR$ receives these requests and interacts with the $DRing$, updating its state according to the request and its *size*.

2.3   Unifying Theories of Programming

Every program, design, and specification in the UTP [10] is a relation between an initial observation and a single subsequent observation, which may be either an intermediate or a final observation of a program execution. The relations are defined as predicates over observational variables, which are names that describe all relevant aspects of a program behaviour. The initial observations of each variable are undecorated, and subsequent observations are dashed.

Here, four observational variables are important: the boolean *okay* indicates whether the process has been properly started in a stable state, in which case its value is *true*, or not; *okay'* means subsequent stabilisation in an observable state; the sequence of events tr records all the events in which a process has engaged; the boolean *wait* distinguishes the intermediate observations of waiting states from final observations on termination. In a stable intermediate state, *wait'* is *true*; a *false* value for *wait'* indicates that the process has reached a final state. Finally, the set of events *ref* describes the responsiveness of the process. All the events that may be refused before the process has started are members of *ref*, and possibly refused events at a later moment are members of *ref'*.

Healthiness conditions are used to test a program for feasibility, and reject it if it makes implementation impossible in the target language. They are expressed in terms of an idempotent function ϕ that makes a program healthy. Every healthy program P must be a fixed-point $P = \phi(P)$. Some healthiness conditions are used to identify the set of relations that are designs (**H1** and **H2**), reactive processes (**R1-R3**), and CSP processes (**CSP1-CSP2**) [10].

3   Mapping *Circus* into CSP

The major contribution of this paper is a sound mapping for a subset of *Circus* into CSP. This subset contains processes that obey the following restrictions: (1) feasible (no miracles); (2) divergence free; (3) limited use of predicative specifications; (4) external choices are only among prefixed actions [17], and; (5) actions do not write to input variables. The restrictions have impact on the specification style, but do not impose any relevant limitation in terms of expressiveness in practice. This is due to the fact that divergent and unfeasible processes (restrictions 1 and 2) have a theoretical importance but are not of practical interest. Furthermore, predicative specifications (restriction 3) may be further refined to a more concrete specification. Finally, processes may be easily rewritten to satisfy restrictions 4 and 5.

The lifting of theoretical results based on CSP to *Circus* requires us to take processes from a state-rich setting (processes with encapsulated states and local variables), in *Circus*, to a stateless one, in CSP. For this reason, our strategy for mapping *Circus* processes into CSP processes is twofold.

First, in Section 3.1, we transform state-rich *Circus* processes into stateless *Circus* processes using the memory model from [14], in which state components and local variables are detached from the processes and moved to memory cells that store their values. The function Ω transforms state-rich divergence-free *Circus* processes that obey the conditions previously stated into CSP processes. Its soundness is established using the *Circus* refinement calculus [5].

Next, in Section 3.2, we transform the resulting stateless *Circus* process into a CSP process using the function Υ. This function is total on the range of Ω, which contains all stateless processes whose main actions are defined only in terms of *Circus* behavioural actions that are directly available in CSP. This includes *Skip*, *Stop*, prefixing, external and internal choice, guarded actions, sequential composition, parallelism, interleaving, hiding, recursion and their iterated counterparts. This mapping allows us to safely reason about *Circus* specifications using the CSP notation, its semantic models and tools. The soundness of Υ is established for the traces and the failures models. For every *Circus* action A that is mapped into a CSP process P we prove that the $traces^{UTP}$ and the $failures^{UTP}$ of A (in the *Circus* semantics given in the UTP) are the same as the *traces* and *failures* of P (in the CSP traces and failures semantics), respectively. This is established based on the UTP link between *Circus* and CSP semantic models [4].

3.1   Rewriting State-rich *Circus* Processes

Stateless *Circus* processes can be directly mapped into their CSP behaviour using the function Υ presented in the next subsection. Stateful *Circus* processes, however, have state components and local variables in the main action, as in the general form of a process P below.

process $P \;\widehat{=}\;$ **begin state** $S \;\widehat{=}\; [v_0 : T_x; \; \ldots \; v_n : T_z \mid inv(v_0, \ldots, v_n)] \; PPArs$
    • **var** $l_0 : U_0; \; \ldots; \; l_m : U_m$ • $A(v_0, \ldots, v_n, l_0, \ldots, l_m)$
end

The rewriting function Ω moves the state components $v_0, \ldots, v_n$ and local variables $l_0, \ldots, l_m$ from P to a separate *Memory* action that encapsulates them. Each of them also has a corresponding member in $NAME ::= v_0 \mid \ldots \mid v_n \mid l_0 \mid \ldots \mid l_n$. The set of mappings from names to values is $BINDING \;\widehat{=}\; NAME \rightarrow \mathbb{U}$.

The main action of the rewritten process interacts with the memory either by requesting a variable value ($mget : NAME \times \mathbb{U}$) or by setting a variable's value ($mset : NAME \times \mathbb{U}$). The memory below has a recursive behaviour, but may also be required to *terminate*. These channels are the memory's interface ($MEM_I \; \hat{=} \; \{\!| \; mset, mget, terminate \; |\!\}$), which is hidden. The resulting transformation of P is a stateless process whose main action is the parallel composition of the memory with the rewritten main action A; if it terminates, the memory is also forced to terminate. The type of n is given by $\delta(n)$.

process $P \; \hat{=} \;$ **begin** $Memory \; \hat{=} \;$ **vres** $b : BINDING$ •
                   $(\square \, n : \text{dom } b \; \bullet \; mget.n!b(n) \rightarrow Memory(b))$
                   $\square \; (\square \, n : \text{dom } b \; \bullet \; mset.n?nv : (nv \in \delta(n)) \rightarrow Memory(b \oplus \{n \mapsto nv\}))$
                   $\square \; terminate \rightarrow Skip$
         • **var** $b : \{x : BINDING \mid x(v_0) \in T_0 \wedge \ldots \wedge inv(x(v_0), \ldots)\}$ •
                   $(\, (\Omega_A(A); \; terminate \rightarrow Skip) \, [\![\, \emptyset \mid MEM_I \mid \{b\} \,]\!] \, Memory(b) \,) \setminus MEM_I$
         end

Parallel and interleaved actions avoid conflicts in the access to variables in scope by partitioning them in two disjoint sets. In our example, the transformed action cannot write to any variable whilst the *Memory* has full access to b.

The use of a centralised memory considerably simplifies the proof of correctness because it uses no replicated operators, avoiding the need for induction on the number of memory cells in the proofs. Using the *Circus* refinement strategy we demonstrated that a distributed memory with independent memory cells for each variable is a refinement of the centralised memory [5]. The monotonicity of *Circus* refinement allows us to replace the latter by the former if needed.

The transformation Ω is justified by two iterations of the *Circus* refinement strategy [5]. The first one promotes all local variables to state components and guarantees that in the resulting process: (1) references to actions are replaced by their bodies; (2) recursive actions are written as fixed-point expressions; (3) there are no name clashes between processes or within the same process; (4) parametrised commands have been replaced by their definitions; (5) schemas are normalised, and (6) channels used by the memories are not referenced.

The first iteration uses an action refinement to adapt the process to the restrictions described above and to bring the scope of the variables to the main action. Finally, a process refinement promotes the local variables to state components and removes the process actions as they are no longer referenced in the main action. The result of this iteration is presented below.

process $RingCell =$ **begin state** $CellState \; \hat{=} \; [v : Value]$
         • $(\square \, x : Value \; \bullet \; v := x); \; (\mu X \; \bullet \; ((wrt?x \rightarrow v := x) \; \square \; (rrd!v \rightarrow Skip)); \; X)$
end

The final iteration removes the state of the process. First, a data refinement transforms a state with multiple components into a state with a single binding component b. Next, an action refinement transforms the main action into a stateless main action, in which the transformed main action $\Omega_A(A)$ interacts with a memory parametrised on b. Finally, a process refinement removes the process state as it not referenced in the main action. The resulting process is presented in Figure 3.

The function Ω_A yields actions that interact with the memory rather than accessing state components. We present its definition for some of the *Circus* actions. A full account can be found in [17].

$$
\begin{array}{l}
\textbf{process } RingCell \mathrel{\widehat=} \\
\textbf{begin } Memory \mathrel{\widehat=} \textbf{ vres } b : BINDING \bullet \\
\qquad (\Box\, n : \mathrm{dom}\, b \bullet mget.n!b(n) \to Memory(b)) \\
\qquad \Box\ (\Box\, n : \mathrm{dom}\, b \bullet mset.n?nv : (nv \in \delta(n)) \to Memory(b \oplus \{n \mapsto nv\})) \\
\qquad \Box\ terminate \to Skip \\
\quad \bullet \textbf{ var } b : \{x : BINDING \mid x(v) \in Value\} \bullet \\
\quad \left(\begin{array}{l}
\left(\begin{array}{l}
\Omega_A \left((\sqcap\, x : Value \bullet v := x); \left(\mu X \bullet \left(\begin{array}{l} wrt?x \to v := x \\ \Box\ rrd!v \to Skip \end{array} \right); X \right) \right); \\
terminate \to Skip
\end{array} \right) \\
[\![\emptyset \mid MEM_I \mid \{b\}]\!] \\
Memory(b)
\end{array} \right) \setminus MEM_I \\
\textbf{end}
\end{array}
$$

Fig. 3. Stateless *RingCell*

The main objective of Ω_A is to change only actions that access state components and local variables. Its definition uses an auxiliary function Ω'_A that is very similar to Ω_A, but does not retrieve any value ($mget$) and replaces references to x by its local copy vx, except when used as the identifier in memory access (*i.e.* $mset.x!e(x)$ becomes $mset.x!e(vx)$). For sequential composition, the difference is more substantial and discussed later in this section along with details on Ω'_A.

The transformation of prefixing differs according to the kind of the communication. Simple prefixing does not refer to memory components: $\Omega_A(c \to A)$ is defined as $c \to \Omega_A(A)$. Synchronisation ($c.e$) and output communications ($c!e$) might refer to memory components in e: before the communication, the rewritten action retrieves these values from the memory and replaces references to $v_0, \ldots, l_0, \ldots$ by the corresponding input variables $vv_0, \ldots, vl_0, \ldots$.

$$
\begin{array}{l}
\Omega_A(c.e(v_0, \ldots, l_0, \ldots) \to A) \mathrel{\widehat=} \\
\quad mget.v_0?vv_0 \to \cdots \to mget.l_0?vl_0 \to \cdots \to c.e(vv_0, \ldots, vl_0, \ldots) \to \Omega'_A(A)
\end{array}
$$

We omit the similar definition for output communication.

This approach is used to rewrite all *Circus* actions that need a read access to memory components like guarded actions, which use their values in the guards.

$$
\begin{array}{l}
\Omega_A(g(v_0, \ldots, l_0, \ldots)\ \&\ A) \mathrel{\widehat=} \\
\quad mget.v_0?vv_0 \to \cdots \to mget.l_0?vl_0 \to \cdots \to g(vv_0, \ldots, vl_0, \ldots)\ \&\ \Omega'_A(A)
\end{array}
$$

The input prefixing $c?x : P \to A(x)$ may be associated with a condition P that determines the set of communicated values that may be communicated: the rewritten action receives these values before the communication. As our strategy forbids actions to write to input variables, they are not part of the memory.

$$
\begin{array}{l}
\Omega_A(c?x : P(x, v_0, \ldots, l_0, \ldots) \to A) \mathrel{\widehat=} \\
\quad mget.v_0?vv_0 \to \cdots \to mget.l_0?vl_0 \to \cdots \to c?x : P(x, vv_0, \ldots, vl_0, \ldots) \to \Omega'_A(A)
\end{array}
$$

The rewriting of external choice requires the actions involved to be prefixed. The noise of the $mget$ events is avoided by performing them before the choice.

$$
\Omega_A(A_1 \Box A_2) \mathrel{\widehat=} mget.v_0?vv_0 \to \cdots \to mget.l_0?vl_0 \to \cdots \to (\Omega'_A(A_1) \Box \Omega'_A(A_2))
$$

Circus does not have shared variables: it uses a parallel-by-merge [10] approach in the semantics of parallel composition. For this reason, we use the initial values of the state variables while the choice is still waiting for one of the events, even if their values are updated by a parallel action.

In parallel composition (and interleaving), *Circus* avoids conflicts in the access to the variables with the declaration of two disjoint sets of variables. In $A_1 \,[\![\, ns_1 \mid cs \mid ns_2 \,]\!]\, A_2$, both A_1 and A_2 have access to the initial values of all variables, but A_1 may modify only the variables in ns_1, and A_2, the variables in ns_2. Furthermore, A_1 is not affected by variable updates of A_2, and vice-versa. Our rewriting function uses one copy of the memory for each parallel branch. A merge writes the final values to the main memory according to the state partition.

The local memory *MemoryMerge* behaves like *Memory*, but writes its final bindings either to *mleft* or to *mright* after termination, based on the side given as argument. Before termination, each parallel branch communicates with *Merge* using *mleft* and *mright*, which are hidden from the environment. The *Merge* receives the bindings and writes to the main memory based on the partitions.

$$
\begin{aligned}
&\Omega_A(A_1 \,[\![\, ns_1 \mid cs \mid ns_2 \,]\!]\, A_2) \;\widehat{=}\; \\
&\quad mget.v_0?vv_0 \to \cdots \to mget.l_0?vl_0 \to \cdots \to \\
&\qquad \left(\!\!\left(\!\!\left(\!\!\begin{pmatrix} (\Omega'_A(A_1);\; terminate \to Skip) \\ [\![\emptyset \mid MEM_I \mid \emptyset]\!] \\ MemoryMerge(\{v_0 \mapsto vv_0, \ldots\}, LEFT) \end{pmatrix} \setminus MEM_I \right) \right.\right. \\
&\qquad\qquad [\![\emptyset \mid cs \mid \emptyset]\!] \\
&\qquad\qquad \left.\left.\begin{pmatrix} (\Omega'_A(A_2);\; terminate \to Skip) \\ [\![\emptyset \mid MEM_I \mid \emptyset]\!] \\ MemoryMerge(\{v_0 \mapsto vv_0, \ldots\}, RIGHT) \end{pmatrix} \setminus MEM_I \right) [\![\emptyset \mid MRG_I \mid \emptyset]\!] \; Merge \right) \\
&\qquad \setminus \{\!|\; mleft, mright \;|\!\}
\end{aligned}
$$

where $Merge \;\widehat{=}\; (mleft?l \to (\overset{o}{\underset{9}{}}\; n : ns_1 \bullet mset.n!l(n) \to Skip))$
$\qquad\qquad\quad \;|\!|\!|\; (mright?r \to (\overset{o}{\underset{9}{}}\; n : ns_2 \bullet mset.n!r(n) \to Skip))$

Rewriting distributes over hiding, instantiation of parametrised actions, internal choice and iterated actions. Furthermore, our approach forbids input variables to be updated, yielding updates only to global variables. This allows the rewriting also to distribute over recursion.

The commands that change the state are completely rewritten like, for example, assignment. All the variables involved in the expressions (on the right-hand sides of assignments) must have their current values fetched from memory; then each expression e_i can be evaluated and the corresponding value is set as the current value of the variable x_i in the memory.

$$
\begin{aligned}
&\Omega_A(x_0, \ldots, x_n := e_0(v_0, \ldots, l_0, \ldots), \ldots, e_n(v_0, \ldots, l_0, \ldots)) \;\widehat{=}\; \\
&\quad mget.v_0?vv_0 \to \cdots \to mget.l_0?vl_0 \to \cdots \to \\
&\quad mset.x_0!e_0(vv_0, \ldots, vl_0, \ldots) \to \cdots \to mset.x_n!e_n(vv_0, \ldots, vl_0, \ldots) \to Skip
\end{aligned}
$$

Alternation might refer to memory components; its rewritten action reads their values from the memory before the rewritten alternation (using Ω'_A). The result of rewriting a specification statement first reads the values of the memory. If the precondition is not satisfied it diverges. Otherwise, the action internally chooses values that establish the postcondition and writes them to the memory. The variables that are not in the frame are left unchanged ($\mathrm{seq}(\overline{w}') = \mathrm{seq}(\overline{w})$) .

$$\Omega_A(w : [pre(v_0, \ldots, l_0, \ldots), post(v_0, \ldots, l_0, \ldots, v_0', \ldots, l_0', \ldots)]) \cong$$
$$mget.v_0?vv_0 \to \cdots \to mget.l_0?vl_0 \to \cdots \to$$
$$\neg\, pre(vv_0, \ldots, vl_0, \ldots) \,\&\, Chaos$$
$$\square\, pre(vv_0, \ldots, vl_0, \ldots) \,\&$$
$$\left(\sqcap vv : \left\{\begin{array}{l} x_0 : \delta(v_0); \ \ldots; \ x_m : \delta(l_0); \ \ldots \\ |\ post(vv_0, \ldots, vl_0, \ldots, x_0, \ldots, x_m, \ldots) \wedge \mathrm{seq}(\overline{w}') = \mathrm{seq}(\overline{w}) \\ \bullet\ (x_0, \ldots, x_m, \ldots) \end{array}\right\} \bullet \right.$$
$$\left. mset.v_0!(vv.0) \to \cdots \to mset.l_0!(vv.m) \to \cdots \to Skip \right)$$
where $\overline{w}' = \{v_0', \ldots, l_0', \ldots\} \setminus w'$ and $\overline{w} = \{v_0, \ldots, l_0, \ldots\} \setminus w$

The *Circus* semantics [16] assumes specifications that initially contain no command and, therefore, change the state using only Z operations, which explicitly include the state invariant and guarantee that it is maintained. We also assume that there is no additional centralised state invariant as is usual in Z state schemas. Considering them only in operations facilitates the refinement process.

Circus assertions, coercions and schema expressions are defined in terms of specification statements [16]. Furthermore, variable renaming is defined as variable substitution. This is reflected in the definition of Ω_A for these constructs.

The auxiliary function Ω_A' is similar to Ω_A. It, however, does not read values from the memory and replaces references to variables by references to their local copies. For this reason, Ω_A' is the same as Ω_A for actions in which no values are retrieved like in $\Omega_A'(c \to A)$. Here, we omit most of the definitions of Ω_A', and present only those that differ from Ω_A.

In $c.e \to A$, the expression e might refer to the memory components. The function Ω_A', however, does not read them from the memory.

$$\Omega_A'(c.e(v_0, \ldots, v_n, l_0, \ldots, l_m) \to A) \cong c.e(vv_0, \ldots, vv_n, vl_0, \ldots, vl_m) \to \Omega_A'(A)$$

The most important difference is for sequential compositions $A_1; A_2$: variables read in A_1 are not in the scope of A_2, which needs to access the memory again.

$$\Omega_A'(A_1; A_2) \cong \Omega_A'(A_1); \Omega_A(A_2)$$

Syntactically, state updates in *Circus* can only be achieved by actions that require any subsequent action to be sequentially composed. The definition above guarantees that the rewritten version of A_2 reads the updated values before any reference to memory components.

The result of the application of Ω_A to the main action of *RingCell* (Figure 3) is presented below.

$$(\sqcap x : Value \bullet mget.v?vv : (\delta(v)) \to mset.v!x \to Skip);$$
$$\mu X \bullet \left(mget.v?vv : (\delta(v)) \to \left(\begin{array}{l} rd!v \to Skip \\ \square\ wrt?x \to mset.v!x \to Skip \end{array} \right) \right); X$$

This action can be mapped into CSP using the mapping discussed in Section 3.2.

Soundness. The soundness of Ω is ensured by the following theorem.

Theorem 1. *Let P be a Circus process with state S and main action A in the domain of Ω ($P_S.A$). Then, $P_S.A = \Omega(P_S.A)$.*

The proof of this theorem is achieved by induction on the syntax of *Circus* using its refinement calculus [5]. A complete detailed proof, including those for more elaborated compositions like parallel composition, can be found in [17] (Appendix K – Page 402). Here, we informally discuss the proof for *Skip*.

Lemma 1. $P_S.Skip = \Omega(P_S.Skip)$

Proof Sketch. We start the proof from the right side of the theorem by using the definition of Ω and Ω_A. Next, since *Skip* is the sequence unit, we remove the *Skip* at the left branch of the parallel composition and the *Memory* is unfolded at the right branch of the parallel composition. We then apply the semantics of **vres** and, to avoid conflicts in variable names, we also rename the outermost b to sb. Here, the scope of the innermost b (in the right branch of the parallel composition) may be expanded because it is not in the left parallel branch. Next, we remove the first assignment ($b := sb$), replacing b for sb in the remaining action. The final and innocuous assignment $sb := sb$, placed at the end of the action can also be removed. At this point, the variable b is no longer referenced; we also remove its variable block. For consistency purposes, we rename the variable sb back to b. We are left with a parallel composition of a prefixing on *terminate* with an external choice. The only possible synchronisation in this parallel composition is on *terminate*, which is hidden from the environment. For this reason, we remove this communication, leaving a parallel composition on *Skip* that is equivalent to *Skip*, on which hiding has no effect. Finally, we promote the variable b to a state component of a stateless process.

3.2   Mapping *Circus* Stateless Actions into CSP Processes

The definition of the function that maps *Circus* processes into CSP processes, Υ, is direct for most of the cases. In [17], we present its full definition. Here, we focus on its most interesting parts. As a simple example, the restricted input prefixing $c?x : P \rightarrow A$ slightly differs from that of CSP because, in *Circus*, the restriction P is a predicate, whereas in CSP it is a set: Υ returns a CSP prefixing restricted by the set we build based on the *Circus* predicate.

$$\Upsilon(c?x : P \rightarrow A) \,\widehat{=}\, c?x : \{x \mid x \leftarrow \delta(c), \Upsilon(P)\} \rightarrow \Upsilon(A)$$

The mapping of alternation uses a special event *choose*. This approach maintains existing non-deterministic choices if more than one guard is valid. The rewritten action offers a choice among those actions whose guards are valid, prefixed by *choose*, which is hidden. In *Circus*, the alternation diverges if none of the guards is true: to ensure divergence freedom, which is one of the mapping requirements, at least one of the guards must be true.

$$\Upsilon(\textbf{if } g_0 \rightarrow A_0 \| \,\ldots\, \| \, g_n \rightarrow A_n \textbf{ fi}) \,\widehat{=}\,$$
$$(g_0 \,\&\, choose \rightarrow \Omega_A(A_0) \,\square\, \ldots\, \square\, g_n \,\&\, choose \rightarrow \Omega_A(A_n)) \setminus \{\!| \, choose \, |\!\}$$

Finally, we map recursive actions to local process definitions as CSP does not provide anonymous recursive actions.

$$\Upsilon(\mu X \bullet A(X)) \,\widehat{=}\, let \, A_{rec} = \Upsilon(A(A_{rec})) \, within \, A_{rec}$$

This illustrates the definition of the mapping Υ, which has been successfully applied to our example. By way of illustration, we present below part of the CSP model resulting from the application of Υ to the changed main action of the stateless *RingCell*.

```
...
MEM_I = {| mset, mget, terminate |}

Memory(b) = ([] n:dom(b) @ mget.n!(apply(b,n)) -> Memory(b))
             [] ([] n:dom(b) @ mset.n?x:type(n) -> Memory(over(b,n,x)))
             [] terminate -> SKIP
RingCellMain = (|~| v:Value @ mget.RingCell_v?vRingCell_v:(type(RingCell_v)) ->
                            ~mset.RingCell_v!((tag(RingCell_v)).v) -> SKIP);
               (let MuCellX = (mget.RingCell_v?vRingCell_v:(type(RingCell_v)) ->
                              ( rd!(value(vRingCell_v)) -> SKIP
                            [] wrt?x -> mset.RingCell_v!((tag(RingCell_v)).x) ->
                               SKIP)); MuCellX
               within MuCellX)
MemoryRingCell =
   |~| b:BINDINGS @ ((RingCellMain; terminate -> SKIP) [| MEM_I |] Memory(b)) \ MEM_I
```

Using FDR2's functional language, we have implemented some functions on bindings: dom(b) yields the domain of a given mapping b; apply(b,n) yields the value
$b(n)$, and over(b,n,x) overwrites b by mapping n to x (in languages like Z,
one would write $b \oplus \{n \mapsto x\}$). Finally, the functions type and tag deal with
the typing of the variables and their names[1].

Soundness. In [4], Cavalcanti *et al* provide a link between *Circus* and CSP
theories within the UTP. The predicate $A^n \; \hat{=} \; okay \wedge \neg \, wait \wedge A \wedge okay'$ gives
the behaviour of the action A when its preceding action has not diverged ($okay$)
and has terminated ($\neg \, wait$), and when A itself does not lead to divergence ($A \wedge
okay'$). This is the normal behaviour of A; behaviour in other situations is defined
by healthiness conditions. The terminating, non-diverging behaviour of A is $A^t \; \hat{=}
A^n \wedge \neg \, wait'$. Finally, the diverging behaviour of A is $A^d \; \hat{=} \; okay \wedge \neg \, wait \wedge
A \wedge \neg \, okay'$. The divergent behaviour is captured by the predicate $\neg \, okay'$.

The function $traces^{UTP}(A) = \{tr' - tr \mid A^n\} \cup \{(tr' - tr) \frown \langle \checkmark \rangle \mid A^t\}$ gives
the set of traces of a *Circus* action defined as a UTP predicate A. This gives a
traces model to A compatible with that adopted in the traces model of CSP.
The behaviour of the action itself is that prescribed when $okay$ and $\neg \, wait$.
The behaviour in the other cases is determined by healthiness conditions of
the UTP theory. For example, in the presence of divergence ($\neg \, okay$), every
action can only guarantee that the trace is only extended, so that past history is
not modified. This behaviour is not recorded by $traces^{UTP}(A)$. The variable tr
records the history of interactions before the start of the action; tr' carries this
history forward. Therefore, the traces in $traces^{UTP}(A)$ are sequences $tr' - tr$
obtained by removing from tr' its prefix tr. In addition, if $tr' - tr$ leads to
termination, then $traces^{UTP}(A)$ also includes $(tr' - tr) \frown \langle \checkmark \rangle$, since $\checkmark$ is used
in the CSP traces model to signal termination.

The function below gives the set of failures of a divergence-free action A.

$$failures^{UTP}(A) = \{(tr' - tr, ref') \mid A^n\} \cup \{(tr' - tr, ref' \cup \{\checkmark\}) \mid A^n \wedge wait'\}$$
$$\cup \{((tr' - tr) \frown \langle \checkmark \rangle, ref') \mid A^t\} \cup \{((tr' - tr) \frown \langle \checkmark \rangle, ref' \cup \{\checkmark\}) \mid A^t\}$$

In a state that is not terminating, for every refusal set ref', there is an extra set
$ref' \cup \{\checkmark\}$. This is because $\checkmark$ is not part of the UTP model and is not considered

---

[1] All the steps for the mapping from *Circus* to CSP of our example can be found in
   http://www.dimap.ufrn.br/~marcel/research/compass/ifm2014.rar

in the definition of ref', just as it is not considered in the definition of tr'. As before, for a terminating state, the extra trace $(tr' - tr)^\frown\langle\checkmark\rangle$ is recorded. Finally, after termination, $\checkmark$ is also refused, and so $ref' \cup \{\checkmark\}$ is included.

We demonstrate the soundness of Υ for the traces model by proving the following theorem, which states that for every *Circus* action A that have a mapping $\Upsilon(A)$ in CSP, the set of traces of A ($traces^{\mathcal{UTP}}(A)$) is equal to the set of traces, as defined in [19], of $\Upsilon(A)$ in CSP ($traces(\Upsilon(A))$). For the failures model, we use a similar approach based on a similarly defined linking function $failures^{\mathcal{UTP}}$.

Theorem 2. $\forall A : \mathrm{dom}(\Upsilon) \bullet traces^{\mathcal{UTP}}(A) = traces(\Upsilon(A)) \wedge failures^{\mathcal{UTP}}(A) = failures(\Upsilon(A))$

The detailed proof of this theorem for each of the *Circus* actions constructs is omitted here due to space restrictions; it can be found in [17].

3.3   Refinement and Verification

In [3,4], failures refinement is defined in the expected way: $P \sqsubseteq_{\mathcal{F}}^{\mathcal{UTP}} Q$ if, and only if, $traces^{\mathcal{UTP}}(Q) \subseteq traces^{\mathcal{UTP}}(P)$ and $failures^{\mathcal{UTP}}(Q) \subseteq failures^{\mathcal{UTP}}(P)$. Cavalcanti *et al* [3] provide a characterisation for refinement of divergent-free processes using traces refinement and conformance relations, which allows us to establish the equivalence of *Circus* process refinement ($\sqsubseteq_P$) and the failures refinement within the UTP defined above ($\sqsubseteq_{\mathcal{F}}^{\mathcal{UTP}}$). For non-divergent processes, failures refinement corresponds to failures-divergences refinement ($\sqsubseteq_{\mathcal{FD}}^{\mathcal{UTP}}$).

$$P_{St_P}.MA_p \sqsubseteq_P Q_{St_Q}.MA_q \Leftrightarrow main_p \sqsubseteq_{\mathcal{FD}}^{\mathcal{UTP}} main_q$$

Finally, based on the results of [3,4] and the results presented here, we are able to establish a connection between *Circus* process refinement and CSP's failures-divergence refinement ($\sqsubseteq_{\mathcal{FD}}$).

Theorem 3. *For every two Circus process $P_{St_P}.MA_p$ and $Q_{St_Q}.MA_q$ in the domain of Ω: $P_{St_P}.MA_p \sqsubseteq_P Q_{St_Q}.MA_q \Leftrightarrow \Upsilon(\Omega(MA_p)) \sqsubseteq_{\mathcal{FD}} \Upsilon(\Omega(MA_q))$*

The sound mapping for processes and refinement notions from *Circus* to CSP, presented here, fosters the reuse of CSP theoretical results in the context of Circus. From a more practical perspective, it provides a strategy for model-checking *Circus* specifications as we discuss in the next section.

4   Model-checking *Circus* Specifications

A first application of our results is the use of CSP tools like FDR to analyse *Circus* processes. In our experiments, we verified that the *RBuffer* (Figure 2) is deadlock-free and livelock-free by translating it into CSP using our mapping and model-checking the CSP specification in FDR (depicted in Figure 4). Such analyses could not be done automatically before the results presented here.

This strategy was also used to verify, using FDR, that the concrete distributed *RBuffer* is a refinement of an abstract specification of a centralised buffer [5].

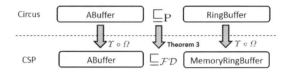

Fig. 4. Analysing the *Circus RBuffer* using FDR

At the theoretical perspective, in [18] we describe a CSP-based foundation for a correct-by-construction strategy to ensure the preservation of deadlock-freedom of a system (in terms of its components). The strategy can also be applied to predict other safety and liveness properties. Using our results, we lifted these results to provide a similar systematic approach to build trustworthy *Circus* systems [17]. The main principle for lifting the approach from CSP to *Circus* is to keep the main structure of the definitions and rules. Its soundness at the *Circus* level is assured using our results.

5   Conclusions

In this paper, we provide a mapping for processes and refinement notions from *Circus* to CSP, which fosters the reuse of theoretical results and tools (originally developed for CSP) to *Circus*. Our mapping was proved sound based on the existing UTP link between *Circus* and CSP. This proof allows us to freely migrate results from CSP to *Circus*, particularly concerning analysis that can be conducted using existing tools for CSP, like FDR and PAT.

We have applied our mapping as a theoretical foundation for benefitting from this potential reuse in two different perspectives. At the practical perspective, our results provide an alternative path for model-checking *Circus* using the established CSP tools. In our experiments, we have analysed properties of *Circus* processes (deadlock freedom, livelockfreedom, and refinement) using FDR by translating them into CSP using our mapping and model-checking the resulting specification in FDR. At the theoretical perspective, we used it to validate the lifting from CSP to *Circus* of a correct-by-construction strategy to ensure the preservation of properties of a system in terms of its components.

Some mappings from state rich processes into CSP have been presented as a means to provide combination of formalisms taking a syntactic approach [6,13]. To the best of our knowledge, however, they do not address the soundness of the translation in a common semantic framework. The work presented in [2] is the one that directly relates to ours as they aim at providing a mapping from *Circus* to CSP. Nevertheless, the "raw initial idea described in the paper" has not been further developed and a formal proof has not be presented. We, however, provide a far more comprehensive, concrete and detailed approach for this mapping that includes most of the *Circus* constructs, and a relation between the refinement notions. More importantly, the soundness of our approach has been demonstrated for both the mapping of constructs and the refinement relation.

Although our strategy allows model-checking *Circus* specifications, the practical application of the proposed mapping, however, requires tool support since its manual application is very error-prone. The implementation of a tool that translates *Circus* specifications into CSP specifications using our mapping is in our research agenda. This tool will also provide means for relating counter-examples provided by FDR to the original *Circus* specifications.

Finally, we will also investigate the resulting CSP models aiming at an optimisation of FDR's model-checking. For example, we have already reduced verification time by forcing the memory of a process to contain only those names used in it. For that, we use `Memory(dres(b,{RingCell_v}))` rather than `Memory(b)`, where `dres(f,ns)` implements the domain restriction (usually written as $ns \triangleleft f$) that removes from f all pairs whose first element are not in ns.

Acknowledgments. The EU FP7 Integrated Project COMPASS (Grant Agreement 287829) financed most of the work presented here. INES and CNPq supports the work of Marcel Oliveira: 573964/2008-4, 560014/2010-4 and 483329/2012-6. We thank Ana Cavalcanti and Jim Woodcock for suggestions on our work.

References

1. Barrocas, S.L.M., Oliveira, M.V.M.: JCircus 2.0: an extension of an automatic translator from Circus to Java. In: Welch, P., Barnes, F.R.M., Chalmers, K., Pedersen, J.B., Sampson, A.T. (eds.) Communicating Process Architectures 2012. WoTUG, vol. 34, pp. 15–36. Open Channel Publishing (August 2012)
2. Beg, A., Butterfield, A.: Linking a state-rich process algebra to a state-free algebra to verify software/hardware implementation. In: Proceedings of the 8th International Conference on Frontiers of Information Technology, pp. 47:1–47:5. ACM, New York (2010)
3. Cavalcanti, A.L.C., Gaudel, M.-C.: Testing for Refinement in CSP. In: Butler, M., Hinchey, M.G., Larrondo-Petrie, M.M. (eds.) ICFEM 2007. LNCS, vol. 4789, pp. 151–170. Springer, Heidelberg (2007)
4. Cavalcanti, A., Gaudel, M.-C.: A note on traces refinement and the *conf* relation in the Unifying Theories of Programming. In: Butterfield, A. (ed.) UTP 2008. LNCS, vol. 5713, pp. 42–61. Springer, Heidelberg (2010)
5. Cavalcanti, A.L.C., Sampaio, A.C.A., Woodcock, J.C.P.: A Refinement Strategy for Circus. Formal Aspects of Computing 15(2-3), 146–181 (2003)
6. Fischer, C.: How to Combine Z with a Process Algebra. In: Bowen, J.P., Fett, A., Hinchey, M.G. (eds.) ZUM 1998. LNCS, vol. 1493, pp. 5–25. Springer, Heidelberg (1998)
7. Formal Systems Ltd. FDR2: User Manual, version 2.94 (2012)
8. Galloway, A.: Integrated Formal Methods with Richer Methodological Profiles for the Development of Multi-perspective Systems. PhD thesis, School of Computing and Mathematics, University of Teeside (1996)
9. The RAISE Language Group. The RAISE Specification Language. Prentice-Hall (1992)
10. Hoare, C.A.R., Jifeng, H.: Unifying Theories of Programming. Prentice-Hall (1998)

11. Conserva Filho, M., Oliveira, M.V.M.: Implementing Tactics of Refinement in CRe-fine. In: Eleftherakis, G., Hinchey, M., Holcombe, M. (eds.) SEFM 2012. LNCS, vol. 7504, pp. 342–351. Springer, Heidelberg (2012)
12. Morgan, C.: Programming from Specifications. Prentice-Hall (1994)
13. Mota, A.C., Sampaio, A.C.A.: Model-checking CSP-Z: strategy, tool support and industrial application. Science of Computer Programming 40, 59–96 (2001)
14. Nogueira, S., Sampaio, A.C.A., Mota, A.C.: Test generation from state based use case models. In: Formal Aspects of Computing (online first), pp. 1–50 (2012)
15. Oliveira, D., Oliveira, M.V.M.: Joker: An Animation Framework for Formal Speci-cations. In: Simão, A., Morgan, C. (eds.) 14th Brazilian Symposium on Formal Methods - Short Papers, pp. 43–48. ICMC/USP (September 2011)
16. Oliveira, M.V.M., Cavalcanti, A.L.C., Woodcock, J.C.P.: A UTP Semantics for Circus. In: Formal Aspects of Computing (2008), doi:10.1007/s00165-007-0052-5
17. Oliveira, M.V.M., Sampaio, A.C.A., Antonino, P.R.G., Ramos, R.T., Cavancalti, A.L.C., Woodcock, J.C.P.: Compositional Analysis and Design of CML Models. Technical Report D24.1, COMPASS Deliverable (2013),
    http://www.compass-research.eu/
18. Ramos, R.T., Sampaio, A.C.A., Mota, A.C.: Systematic development of trustwor-thy component systems. In: Cavalcanti, A., Dams, D.R. (eds.) FM 2009. LNCS, vol. 5850, pp. 140–156. Springer, Heidelberg (2009)
19. Roscoe, A.W.: The Theory and Practice of Concurrency. Prentice-Hall Series in Computer Science. Prentice-Hall (1998)
20. Sun, J., Liu, Y., Dong, J.S., Pang, J.: Pat: Towards flexible verification under fairness. In: Bouajjani, A., Maler, O. (eds.) CAV 2009. LNCS, vol. 5643, pp. 709–714. Springer, Heidelberg (2009)
21. Treharne, H., Schneider, S.: Using a process algebra to control B operations. In: Araki, K., Galloway, A., Taguchi, K. (eds.) Proceedings of the 1st International Conference on Integrated Formal Methods, pp. 437–456. Springer (June 1999)
22. Woodcock, J., Cavalcanti, A., Freitas, L.: Operational semantics for model-checking Circus. In: Fitzgerald, J.S., Hayes, I.J., Tarlecki, A. (eds.) FM 2005. LNCS, vol. 3582, pp. 237–252. Springer, Heidelberg (2005)
23. Woodcock, J.C.P., Davies, J.: Using Z—Specification, Refinement, and Proof. Prentice-Hall (1996)

An Interactive Verification Tool Meets an IDE

Martin Hentschel, Stefan Käsdorf, Reiner Hähnle, and Richard Bubel

TU Darmstadt, Dept. of Computer Science, Darmstadt, Germany
{hentschel,haehnle,bubel}@cs.tu-darmstadt.de,
stefan.kaesdorf@stud.tu-darmstadt.de

Abstract. We present a general approach on how to integrate a semi-automatic verification tool into a state-of-the-art integrated development environment (IDE). The objective and challenge is to keep implementation, specification and proofs in sync. Following a change in one of the specifications or implementations, all proofs that could possibly be affected by that change are rescheduled. To improve performance we look at several optimizations. User feedback about proof results is provided within the IDE using standard markers and views. The approach has been implemented and realizes an integration of the interactive verification system KeY into the Eclipse IDE.

Keywords: Verification, Integration of formal methods into software engineering practice.

1 Introduction

A major challenge in software development is to keep the different artefacts such as source code, comments, test cases and manuals up-to-date. Changes in the source code are not reflected in comments and as soon as artefacts are not managed in a single source, which is often the case for manuals or other technical documents, the gap widens.

Adding static analyses, such as deductive verification, to a software development process, aggravates the problem of keeping artefacts synchronized. A systematic analysis of the dependencies and how they can be resolved becomes mandatory for practical formal verification. Hence, we need to analyze which additional tasks and artefacts software verification does add to the software development process? Obviously, there is the specification of the intended program behavior in a formal specification language like (Event-)B [1] or the Java Modeling Language (JML) [10]. Second, the proof that a program adheres to its specification. Conducting proofs is generally expensive. Depending on the complexity and expressivity of the specification language, program logic and precision of the underlying verification system, user interaction might be needed to complete the proofs. But also completely automatic approaches (which of course might fail to prove that a correct program is correct) for non-trivial properties take a long time. The artefacts produced are source code, specification and proofs.

To illustrate the dependencies between the artefacts we use the Java program shown in Listing 1.1. The source code is specified in JML, which follows the

E. Albert and E. Sekerinski (Eds.): IFM 2014, LNCS 8739, pp. 55–70, 2014.

design-by-contract paradigm [12]. It provides means to specify methods, instance invariants and framing properties.

In our example the specification consists of two method contracts encompassing three specification cases. The two **normal_behavior** cases require that if their respective precondition (**requires** clause) is satisfied at invocation time then the method terminates normally (without an exception) and in its final state the postconditon (**ensures** clause) holds. The **exceptional_behavior** case specifies the additional (**also**) method behavior in case of an uncaught exception. The **signals** clause is used to state the thrown exception and to provide a postcondition for the method's final state.

The verification argument that the two methods satisfy their respective contracts gives rise to three verification conditions (proof obligations), and hence proofs[1].

Listing 1.1. Example Java class specified with JML

```
 1 package banking;
 2
 3 public class Account {
 4     private /*@ spec_public @*/ int balance;
 5     private /*@ spec_public @*/ int overdraftLimit;
 6
 7     /*@ normal_behavior
 8       @ requires canUpdate(amount);
 9       @ ensures balance == \old(balance) + amount;
10       @ assignable balance;
11       @ also
12       @ exceptional_behavior
13       @ requires !canUpdate(amount);
14       @ signals (Exception) true;
15       @ assignable \nothing;
16       @*/
17     public void update(int amount) throws Exception {
18         if (canUpdate(amount)) { balance += amount; }
19         else { throw new Exception(); }
20     }
21
22     /*@ normal_behavior
23       @ ensures \result == balance+amount > overdraftLimit;
24       @*/
25     public /*@ pure @*/ boolean canUpdate(int amount) {
26         return balance + amount >= overdraftLimit;
27     }
28 }
```

---

[1] Depending on the verification system certain verification conditions might be combined into one proof or split up into several subproofs.

As it happens, the given specification is erroneous. The method contract for canUpdate() promises in its postcondition that the sum of the account balance and the amount argument is greater than the overdraft limit, whereas the implementation only guarantees greater-or-equal. Consequently, we have to change either the implementation or the specification. Changing the implementation requires to redo the proof that canUpdate() satisfies its contract (and preserves the invariants), but all other proofs remain valid provided that they use the method's contract and not its implementation. Changing the contract of canUpdate(), however, requires to redo not only the proof for canUpdate(), but also the proof for update() which uses the contract to represent the effect of the invocation of canUpdate() in its conditional statement (and in its contract).

The example has a rather simple structure regarding implementation and specification, so all proofs should close automatically. In more realistic examples it might be necessary to assist the prover by performing some proof steps interactively. More complex specifications make also use of invariants and advanced framing concepts (**assignable** clause) which introduce additional verification conditions and a higher degree of dependencies among different proofs. In such a context it becomes challenging to keep all artifacts synchronized. In particular, in the presence of continuous changes to implementation and specification, the whole process has to be efficient—otherwise the user will turn the feature off. Hence, to determine the smallest set of proofs that need to be redone as well as to communicate the failure to find proofs (and thus potential bugs) to the user is crucial for practical adoption of formal verification.

We make the following contributions: In Section 2 we present a novel approach to store proof dependencies (and introduce some general notions). Section 3 presents our main contribution, namely the concept on how to integrate an interactive verification tool into an IDE. In Section 4 we present a concrete implementation of our concept based on Eclipse and the verification system KeY [2]. Finally, we evaluate our approach and the proposed optimizations in Section 5.

2   Background

We introduce the concepts implemented by (almost) any integrated development environment (IDE) to manage development projects. Further, we introduce *proof dependencies*, a new concept, which allows to determine the (sub-)set of proofs that might become obsolete due to a change and need to be redone.

2.1   Basic IDE Concepts

A *project* has a unique name and is the root of a structured collection of resources. Resources are of different kinds: source code, libraries, or meta information such as the build path and settings. IDEs present the project structure usually as a tree resembling the standard rendering of file systems. Source code is usually displayed as a subtree of the project tree, where the inner nodes correspond to modules or packages and the leaves represent the actual classes or files.

A *marker* is a tag that can be attached to resources or content contained in a resource. Markers have a kind (e.g., *information, warning, error*), a position, and a description text. For instance, in case of a compilation error an error marker can be positioned at the statement or line of code causing the error. IDEs visualize markers in several ways: as a list of errors and warnings in a separate view or as an icon shown within an editor next to the marker's position.

2.2   Proof Dependencies

To determine efficiently which proofs must be redone in presence of a change, we introduce the concept of proof dependencies as one contribution of the paper. In the following definition we assume that a program annotated with specifications is given as the context.

Definition 1 (Proof dependency). *A proof dependency is a pair (proof obligation, target descriptor) linking a proof obligation to a target descriptor. A target descriptor represents a program or specification element used in the proof of the proof obligation. A proof dependency and a change to the context program is called*

- dangling, *if one of the program elements referred to by the target descriptor does no longer exist;*
- tainted, *if the change might effect the evaluation or execution of the program or specification element referred to by the target descriptor.*

Remark 1. Proof dependencies capture the dependencies of a particular proof to source code or specification elements and are thus proof dependent.

Depending on the kind of program element and its treatment by the calculus used as basis for the verification system, we distinguish different kinds of proof dependencies. For instance:

Method Invocation Proof Dependencies link a proof obligation to a method invocation descriptor $(m, ct, ctxt)$ where m denotes the signature of the called method, ct the static type of the callee and $ctxt$ the class where the method invocation occurred. Such a proof dependency is created when a proof contains an explicit case distinction over all possible implementations of a method to evaluate a given method invocation statement. A change causes a tainted (or even dangling) proof dependency if it removes and/or adds a new binding for the described method invocation.

Method Inlining Proof Dependencies link a proof obligation to a method implementation (m, ct) with ct the class containing an actual implementation of method m. Proof dependencies of this kind are created when the verification system inlines a method (instead of using a contract). Such a proof dependency becomes dangling when method m is removed and tainted if its implementation has been changed.

Use Contract Proof Dependencies link a proof obligation to a contract of a method and are created whenever the verification system uses a method contract instead of inlining the method. It becomes dangling if the contract has been removed and tainted in case the contract has been changed. The exact definition when a contract has been changed depends on the semantics of the specification language.

Field Access Proof Dependencies link a proof obligation to a field access descriptor (fd, ct) with fd denoting a field declaration fd and ct the static type of the reference prefix. They are created whenever a field is accessed in source code or specifications. A change taints a field access proof dependency if the field declaration has changed or if the parent hierarchy has changed. A dangling proof dependency is caused if the field has been removed altogether.

Use Invariant Proof Dependencies link a proof obligation to an instance or static invariant. They are created whenever a property assured by an invariant is used in a proof. They become dangling if the invariant has been removed and tainted in case the invariant has been changed.

3   Integrated Proof Management

We describe our approach to integrated proof (or analysis) management. The concept has been developed with semi-automatic verification systems in mind, but we want to emphasize that automatic or completely interactive verification or static analysis systems in general can profit as well. The approach is designed for modular verification which gives rise to a number of proof obligations.

The concept consists of an appropriate file structure (Section 3.1) and of an automatic update process (Section 3.2). Section 3.3 summarizes the requirements on verification tool and IDE needed to realize our approach.

3.1   Proof Storage and Proof Markers

Proofs are the central artefacts produced by software verification tools. To manage proofs we extend a project with an additional resource kind for proofs. Managing proofs as part of a project is advantageous in many ways: (i) the user has direct access to the proofs and can inspect or manipulate them; (ii) if a version control system is used, then source code, specifications *and* proofs are committed and updated together ensuring their synchronization. Further, it is possible to compare different versions of a proof.

For a concise representation of verification results we use markers as described in Section 2.1 to indicate the status of proof obligations. *Information markers* indicate successful (closed) proofs, possibly with a hint that not all used specifications (theorems) have yet been proven. *Warning markers* are created for open proofs and provide details of the reason why a proof was not successful (timeout or unclosable goal detected). *Error markers* with a failure description indicate syntax errors in specifications, failed global correctness checks (such as cyclic dependencies), or unexpected events like uncaught exceptions.

3.2   Update Process

The proof manager is responsible to keep (i) source code, specification and proofs synchronized as well as (ii) the verification status information (in the form of markers) up-to-date.

Changes to source code and/or specifications may invalidate existing proofs or give rise to additional proof obligations whose proofs (proof attempts) are stored as new proofs. The markers need then to be updated to reflect the correct status. This scenario is shown in Fig. 1a. The second source of change is a modified proof, for instance, after the user performed some interactive proof steps. In this case only the result markers need to be updated to reflect the new status (see Fig. 1b). Changing the status of one proof might trigger status changes of dependent proofs, for example: the proof that a method m adheres to its specification could be closed but uses the contract of method n. Hence, the overall correctness of the proof for m depends on the proof that method n adheres to its specification.

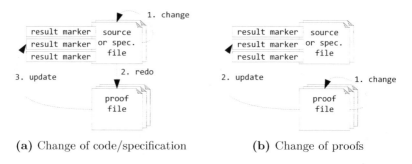

(a) Change of code/specification   (b) Change of proofs

Fig. 1. Change handling

We describe the update process for source code or specification changes (first scenario) in detail. It contains the process for proof changes (second scenario) as a subroutine. The update process is triggered whenever a change occurs, for instance, every time a file is saved. The naïve approach to simply redo *all* proofs upon each change turns out to be too inefficient and does not scale to larger projects. Instead we propose the algorithm shown in Algorithm 1 to reduce the overall verification time. The algorithm provides several anchor points in which different optimizations can be plugged in.

Upon a change the IDE informs the proof manager and provides the affected project as well as additional information about the change. The detail of the provided change information depends on the IDE and the nature of the change. It can range from detailed information like renaming of a method or field to a simple list of files that have been changed.

When the update process is triggered by a source code or specification change, it first retrieves all proof obligations available for the project (line 1). In a second step (line 2) the relevant proof obligations for which proofs have to be redone

---

input: A project p and a list of changes ci (change information) in p

1 allProofObligations ← listAllPO (p);
2 pendingProofObligations ← filter (allProofObligations, ci);
3 pendingProofObligations ← sort (pendingProofObligations);
4 **foreach** po **in** pendingProofObligations **do**
5 | proofResult ← doProof (po);
6 | showInfoOrWarning (proofResult);
7 **end**
8 cycles ← checkCycles (allProofObligations);
9 showError (cycles);

Algorithm 1. Update process (source code/specification change)

are determined and (line 3) prioritized. The proof obligations are then processed in order of their priority and proof attempts are initiated (line 5). The status of each performed and completed proof attempt is updated (line 6).

When all proof attempts have been completed (successful or not), a global correctness check (line 8) is performed to ensure that no cyclic proof dependencies exist (e.g., to avoid that when proving total correctness of a recursive method its own contract is used to eliminate the recursion). The global correctness check must look at *all* proof obligations and their respective proof dependencies. Finally, the result markers are updated again (line 9) to reflect the result of the global correctness check. In case of a proof change only the global correctness check and result update has to be performed.

For a naïve approach the implementation of the procedures filter (line 2) and sort (line 3) simply return the list of proof obligations given as their argument, while method doProof starts a new proof search for each proof obligation. In the following we present for each of these procedures an optimized implementation to achieve a significantly reduced proof effort and to provide faster feedback to the developer.

Optimization Selection. Proofs are modular in the sense that they rely only on specific parts of the implementation and specification. Hence, method filter can remove all proof obligations for which the related proof is known to not be affected by the change. To this extent method filter retrieves the stored proof dependencies for each proof obligation and checks whether the change caused a tainted or dangling proof dependency (see Section 2.2). Proof obligations with no tainted or dangling proof dependencies are filtered out. The achieved precision depends on granularity with which changes are recorded (changed files, code fragments, specification elements, ...). Proof obligations remaining from previous changes (e.g., if a previous change was not well-formed and caused compilation errors) have to be returned as well.

Optimization Prioritization. For usability reasons it is important to provide feedback about the status of the different proofs to the developer in a timely manner. This is achieved by (i) updating the proof status after each completed proof attempt (line 6) and by (ii) prioritizing the proof-obligations to be proven (line 3). Prioritization takes into account that the developer is not interested in all proofs to the same degree. A developer changing the specification of a method m has an immediate interest to know whether that method still satisfies the modified contract; once this is achieved, it is proven whether the modified contract is (still) sufficiently strong to prove the correctness of methods invoking m. A prioritization (in descending order) might be as follows: proof obligations (p.o.) for the currently selected element → p.o. for the currently selected type → p.o. for the currently selected file → p.o for other opened files → all other proof obligations.

Optimization Proof Replay. This optimisation concerns the implementation of doProof(). Proof replay is usually faster than proof search for two reasons:

- if closing a proof required user interaction, the interactive steps are saved and performed automatically during proof replay (if still applicable);
- if the proof format stores each performed step (and not only a script), proof replay avoids expensive proof search strategies completely.

To benefit from proof replay, doProof() proceeds as follows: if no saved proof exists then proof search is used. Otherwise, proof replay is attempted. Proof replay may complete with two outcomes: (i) either the saved proof can be replayed completely or (ii) the proof replay stops at some point, because some proof step is no longer applicable (due to the performed change). In the latter case, proof search is initiated to attempt to close the proof. Note that even in case (i) the replayed proof might not be closed in case the change did not affect that proof and a previous proof attempt was unsuccessful. In that case, we do not start automatic proof search, but ask the user to finish the proof interactively.

If the underlying verification system provides more intelligent proof reuse strategies [14,9] than simple proof replay, these can be used instead (or in combination) to reduce the verification effort.

Optimization Parallelization. The for-loop of Algorithm 1 can be parallelized to execute several proofs concurrently. The time required for proof search differs from proof to proof and thus it is not advisable to have a fixed assignment from proof obligations to threads, but to use pooling instead. We can even distribute the update process to other computers as long as it reduces the overall time.

3.3   Requirements

To implement the proposed proof management and update process, the IDE and verification tool need to satisfy some minimal requirements:

- The verification tool must be able to list all proof obligations for a project, to instantiate a proof and start the proof search. For proof replay, the verification system must be able to save and replay proofs. For the optimized

selection, the proof format of the verification tool must be proof producing and the proof format must contain enough information to extract proof dependencies.
- The IDE must be extensible to add support for managing proofs inside a project and to listen for project changes to trigger the update process. Native support for markers is advantageous for seamless integration, but not a necessity.

4 Implementation

We realized our concept by integrating the verification system KeY into Eclipse (the tool is available at www.key-project.org). Fig. 2 shows a screenshot of our Eclipse integration called KeY Resources.

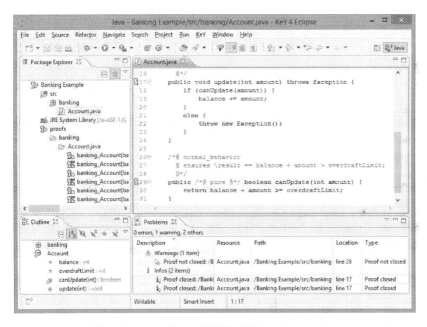

Fig. 2. Screenshot of KeY's Eclipse integration

The *Package Explorer* view provides access to all files organized in a *KeY project* which extends the original Java project with the features of the integrated proof management as described in Sect. 3. The project structure is extended by a proof folder *proofs* which stores the proofs together with meta files that contain in particular the proof dependencies. For ease of navigation the proof folder reflects the hierarchy of the source folder.

The editor shows the file *Account.java* with the program from Listing 1.1. The *Outline* view lists basic code members for navigation purposes. The information marker in front of line 17 indicates that both proofs of method `update` are closed while the warning marker in front of line 29 indicates that the proof of `canUpdate` is still open. The user can directly open a proof in KeY to inspect or continue the proof interactively by using Eclipse's *quick fix* functionality. In addition to the markers, view *Problems* is used to summarize the proof results together with other detected issues.

Eclipse satisfies all requirements on the IDE side. Projects, folders and files are represented as a *resource* within Eclipse. A resource can be annotated with *resource markers* which are used to present proof results to the user. *Integrated project builders* are triggered when the project content has changed. We implemented a builder which executes our update process.

Our implementation determines proof dependencies by analyzing the applied calculus rules. The dependencies can be then directly extracted from their introducing rules. Hence, the computation complexity is linear to the proof size. Note, the dependencies have to be computed only once and are then stored in a meta file.

Our implementation realizes all optimizations suggested in Sect. 3.2 except prioritization. Eclipse provides change information by default only on the file level which restricts the precision of the selection optimization. As a consequence, we need to consider proof dependencies as tainted or dangling whenever the file containing the element referenced by the target descriptor has changed (or a file containing a subtype or supertype has changed). Proofs are performed in parallel in a user-defined number of threads. If a stored proof is available, proof replay is attempted.

5   Evaluation

We compare the impact of the proposed optimizations for the reduction of the overall proof time based on our implementation. To this end, we simulate a development process on a small Java project where the source code and its specifications are modified several times.

We use the PayCard case study of the KeY Quicktour[2] as a starting point. Initially, the PayCard case study consists of 4 classes, 18 methods and 22 contracts but has no inheritance relations. We perform 25 modifications (see Table 1) which add new elements, modify or remove existing ones. By performing these modifications the project grows intermittently to 10 classes, 27 methods, 61 contracts and 6 inheritance relations. Hence, we consider the performed changes as the independent variable. For the dependent variable we focus on the overall proof time. We measured the total time required to perform the verification process without the parsing time for the source code to achieve comparable results not obfuscated by technical issues. The system used for the evaluation is powered by an Intel Core i7-2600K CPU, 8 GB RAM and Windows 7 64 Bit. For the Java Virtual Machine the initial heap size is 128 MB and the maximum memory allocation is set to 1024 MB.

---

[2] http://www.key-project.org/download/quicktour/quicktour-2.0.zip

Table 1. Performed modifications

Modification	Description	Classes	Proofs
1	Populate the project with initial classes	4	22
2	Delete a proof file	4	22
3	Delete a meta file	4	22
4	Modify a proof file	4	22
5–8	Modify an initial class	4	22
9	Add two new subclasses	6	34
10	Add two new subclasses	8	49
11	Add two new subclasses	10	61
12	Modify an initial class	10	61
13–18	Modify an added class	10	61
19–21	Modify an initial class	10	61
22	Delete two added classes	8	46
23	Delete four added classes	4	22
24	Remove a method from initial class	4	21
25	Remove a constructor from initial class	4	20

Impact of Optimization Selection. Fig. 3 shows that the selection optimization reduces the number of proofs in some cases significantly, while in others most proofs need to be redone. The reason is that some modifications invalidate almost all proofs while others have only a local effect. The initial population (modification 1) requires all proofs to be redone as no previous proofs exist. Starting with modification 2 the optimization was always successful in filtering out some proofs. This is also reflected by the overall proof times shown in Fig. 4.

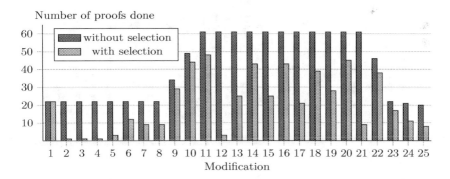

Fig. 3. Proof count of optimization selection

As mentioned in Sect. 4, the decision whether a proof has to be performed is based on changed files and not on the changed content within a file. We expect even better results by taking more information about the modification into account.

Overall proof time in seconds

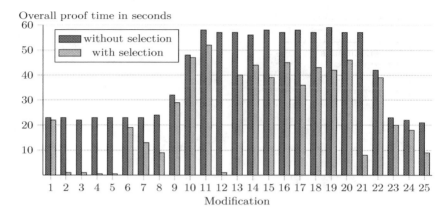

Fig. 4. Proof times of optimization selection

Impact of Proof Replay. Fig. 5 compares the overall proof times per modification with and without replay. Parallelization and filtering are not performed. We observe that the proof time is almost identical across different modifications as long as the number of performed proofs is the same. The overall proof time with replay is always less than the proof time without proof replay.

Overall proof time in seconds

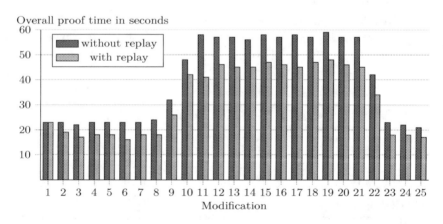

Fig. 5. Proof times of optimization proof replay

Impact of Optimization Parallelization. Fig. 6 shows the results comparing the use of 1, 2, 4 and 8 threads without replaying and selecting proofs. We can see that with a growing number of threads the proof time is reduced until a certain threshold is reached. Beyond that threshold additional threads increase the overall proof time because of increased synchronization overhead. This overhead is implementation- and hardware-specific and cannot be generalized.

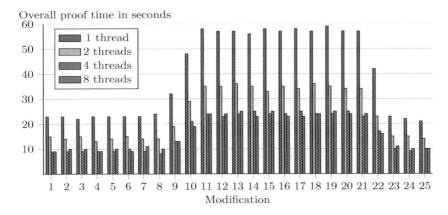

Fig. 6. Proof times of optimization parallelization

Combined Optimizations. As we described above each optimization on its own reduces the overall proof time. Now we combine all optimizations such that the number of performed proofs is reduced, replay is used and proofs are performed in parallel. The result is shown in Fig. 7.

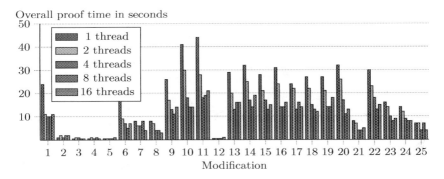

Fig. 7. Proof times of combined optimizations

Table 2 summarizes the results. The first column specifies which optimizations are used. The next three columns show first the sum of all proof times per modification, the resulting average value and the percent compared to the worst scenario without optimizations. The last three columns list the total number of done proofs of all modifications, the resulting average value and again percent comparison to the worst case.

Each optimization on its own reduces the overall proof time. The best value is achieved by combining all optimizations and using 8 threads, which reduces the overall proof time by 77% from 40.1 seconds to 9.1 seconds.

The achieved improvement is significant but not yet sufficient. A developer may save a file every few seconds triggering the proof process each time. For

Table 2. Analysis of proof times and number of performed proofs

Description	Proof time			# of proofs		
	Σ in s	$\varnothing$ in s	%	Σ	$\varnothing$	%
1 Thread no replay and no selection	1003	40.1	100	1039	41.6	100
1 Thread with no replay and selection	624	25.0	62	534	21.4	51
4 Threads no replay and selection	417	16.7	42	1039	41.6	100
8 Threads no replay and selection	421	16.8	42	1039	41.6	100
1 Thread with replay	803	32.1	80	1039	41.6	100
1 Thread with replay and selection	476	19.0	47	534	21.4	51
4 Threads with replay and selection	245	9.8	24	534	21.4	51
8 Threads with replay and selection	**227**	**9.1**	**23**	**534**	**21.4**	**51**
16 Threads with replay and selection	243	9.7	24	534	21.4	51

this reason it is required that the user can continue working while the update process is running. To achieve this, the project builder should only be concerned with determining and prioritizing the proof obligations. Everything else has to be performed outside the builder.

Threats to Validity. We measured the total proof time which strongly depends on the number and the complexity of the proofs. The chosen example is well known in the KeY community and covers different verification scenarios. We designed the applied changes carefully to simulate realistic modifications and to cover all scenarios which can influence the implemented selection optimization. However, the achieved improvement depends in the end on the source code and its specifications as well as on the used verification tool.

6   Related Work

In [13] development graphs (DG) are suggested for proof management. DGs constitute a more general structure than proof dependencies, but are tailored to algebraic specification languages such as CASL. DGs capture dependencies among specifications and can be used to compute the effect of a specification change. Proofs seem not to be analyzed which might result in more proofs being redone than necessary. Instantiating DGs to a design-by-contract setting for a real-world programming language is not straightforward concerning the representation of source code. DGs are implemented in the tool Maya, which seems not be integrated with a mainstream IDE. Proof dependencies provide a lightweight approach that can be implemented for most combinations of verification system and IDE.

Dafny [11], VCC [3], SPEEDY [5] and OpenJML with ESC [4] provide an integration into an IDE. To the best of our knowledge they do neither manage proofs nor use change information to restrict the amount of verification effort. In case of interactive or semi-automatic verification tools the user is also interested in the proofs and to maintain them along the source code.

Rodin is the main IDE used for modeling in Event-B [1]. It features a semi-automatic verification system for Event-B models and stores proofs within the project similar to our approach. The detection of invalidated proofs is based on the name of proof obligations which change when the model is changed. Invalid proofs are neither redone nor removed automatically.

Other static analyses like FindBugs [8] use also common IDE concepts to organize the work and to present results, but do not manage their results within the IDE and have to be run again from scratch when the source code is modified.

7   Conclusion and Future Work

We presented a lightweight approach to integrate an interactive verification tool into an IDE and implemented it on the basis of KeY and Eclipse. The integration achieves that source code, specifications and proofs are always in sync without placing that responsibility on the user. Proof results are presented as early as possible and user interaction is only required when a proof cannot be closed automatically. Several optimizations can be added in a modular manner. With them we could reduce overall proof time on average by 77% in our case study.

In state-of-art software development nearly all tasks are done within an IDE to achieve a consistent software development process. Verification should aim to become part of that process and integrate seamlessly into the existing infrastructure. Our approach is a step toward this goal and can be realized without any changes on the verification tool.

We plan to increase the precision of the selection optimization by identifying changed elements within a file and to implement the prioritization optimization. We will also investigate whether and how proof reuse [9] and abstract contracts [7] may help to reduce the overall proof time. In addition we will formalize proof dependencies to obtain a formal proof of the correctness of our approach.

References

1. Abrial, J.-R.: Modeling in Event-B - System and Software Engineering. Cambridge University Press (2010)
2. Beckert, B., Hähnle, R., Schmitt, P.H. (eds.): Verification of Object-Oriented Software. LNCS (LNAI), vol. 4334. Springer, Heidelberg (2007)
3. Cohen, E., Dahlweid, M., Hillebrand, M., Leinenbach, D., Moskal, M., Santen, T., Schulte, W., Tobies, S.: VCC: A practical system for verifying concurrent C. In: Berghofer, S., Nipkow, T., Urban, C., Wenzel, M. (eds.) TPHOLs 2009. LNCS, vol. 5674, pp. 23–42. Springer, Heidelberg (2009)
4. Cok, D.R.: OpenJML: Software verification for Java 7 using JML, OpenJDK, and Eclipse. In: Dubois, et al. (eds.) [6], pp. 79–92
5. Cok, D.R., Johnson, S.C.: Speedy: An eclipse-based ide for invariant inference. In: Dubois, et al. (eds.) [6], pp. 44–57

6. Dubois, C., Giannakopoulou, D., Méry, D.: Proc. 1st Workshop on Formal Integrated Development Environment, F-IDE 2014, Grenoble, France. EPTCS, vol. 149 (2014)
7. Hähnle, R., Schaefer, I., Bubel, R.: Reuse in Software Verification by Abstract Method Calls. In: Bonacina, M.P. (ed.) CADE 2013. LNCS, vol. 7898, pp. 300–314. Springer, Heidelberg (2013)
8. Hovemeyer, D., Pugh, W.: Finding bugs is easy. SIGPLAN Not. 39(12), 92–106 (2004)
9. Klebanov, V.: Proof reuse. In: Beckert, et al. (eds.) [2]
10. Leavens, G.T., Poll, E., Clifton, C., Cheon, Y., Ruby, C., Cok, D., Müller, P., Kiniry, J., Chalin, P., Zimmerman, D.M.: JML Reference Manual (September 2009)
11. Leino, K.R.M.: Dafny: An automatic program verifier for functional correctness. In: Clarke, E.M., Voronkov, A. (eds.) LPAR-16 2010. LNCS, vol. 6355, pp. 348–370. Springer, Heidelberg (2010)
12. Meyer, B.: Applying "design by contract". IEEE Computer 25(10), 40–51 (1992)
13. Mossakowski, T., Autexier, S., Hutter, D.: Development graphs—proof management for structured specifications. J. Logic & Alg. Progr. 67(1-2), 114–145 (2006)
14. Reif, W., Stenzel, K.: Reuse of proofs in software verification. In: Shyamasundar, R.K. (ed.) FSTTCS 1993. LNCS, vol. 761, pp. 284–293. Springer, Heidelberg (1993)

An Analysis Pathway for the Quantitative Evaluation of Public Transport Systems

Stephen Gilmore[2], Mirco Tribastone[1], and Andrea Vandin[1]

[1] Electronics and Computer Science, University of Southampton, Southampton, UK
[2] Laboratory for Foundations of Computer Science, University of Edinburgh, Edinburgh, UK

Abstract. We consider the problem of evaluating quantitative service-level agreements in public services such as transportation systems. We describe the integration of quantitative analysis tools for data fitting, model generation, simulation, and statistical model-checking, creating an analysis pathway leading from system measurement data to verification results. We apply our pathway to the problem of determining whether public bus systems are delivering an appropriate quality of service as required by regulators. We exercise the pathway on service data obtained from Lothian Buses about the arrival and departure times of their buses on key bus routes through the city of Edinburgh. Although we include only that example in the present paper, our methods are sufficiently general to apply to other transport systems and other cities.

1 Introduction

Modern public transport systems are richly instrumented. The vehicles in a modern bus fleet are equipped with accurate GPS receivers, Wi-Fi, and on-board communications, allowing them to report their location for purposes such as fleet management and arrival-time prediction. High-frequency, high-resolution location data streams back from the vehicles in the fleet to be consumed by the predictive models used in real-time *bus tracking systems*.

We live in a data-hungry world. Users of public transport systems now expect to be able to access live data about arrival times, transit connections, service disruptions, and many other types of status updates and reports at almost every stage of their journey. Studies suggest that providing real-time information on bus journeys and arrival times in this way encourages greater use of buses [1] with beneficial effects for the bus service. In contrast, when use of buses decreases, transport experts suggest that this aggravates existing problems such as outdated routes, bunching of vehicles, and insufficient provision of greenways or bus priority lanes. Each of these problems makes operating the bus service more difficult. Bus timetables become less dependable, new passengers are discouraged from using the bus service due to bad publicity, which leads inevitably to budget cuts that further accelerate the decline of the service.

Service regulators are no less data-hungry than passengers, requiring transport operators to report service-level statistics and key performance indicators which are used to assess the service delivered in practice against regulatory requirements on the quality of service expected. Many of these regulatory requirements relate to *punctuality* of buses,

E. Albert and E. Sekerinski (Eds.): IFM 2014, LNCS 8739, pp. 71–86, 2014.

defined in terms of the percentage of buses which depart within the window of tolerance around the timetabled departure time; and *reliability* of buses, defined in terms of
the number of miles planned and the number of miles operated. The terms *schedule
adherence* or *on-time performance* are also used to refer to the degree of success of a
transportation service running to the published timetable.

With the aim of helping service providers to be able to work with models which
can be used to analyse and predict on-time performance, we have connected a set
of modelling and analysis tools into an analysis pathway, starting from system measurement data, going through data fitting, model generation, simulation and statistical
model-checking to compute verification results which are of significance both to service
providers and to regulatory authorities.

The steps of the analysis pathway, depicted in Figure 1, are as follows:

1. Data is harvested from a bus tracking system to compile an empirical cumulative distribution function data set of recorded journey times for each stage of the
   bus journey. In this paper, we generate inputs to the system using the BusTracker
   automatic vehicle tracking system developed by the City of Edinburgh council and
   Lothian Buses [2].
2. The software tool HyperStar [3] is used to fit phase-type distributions to the data
   sets.
3. A phase-type distribution enables a Markovian representation of journey times
   which can be encoded in high-level formalisms such as stochastic process algebras.
   In particular, we use the Bus Kernel model generator (BusKer), a Java application which consumes the phase-type distribution parameters computed by Hyper-
   Star and generates a formal model of the bus journey expressed in the Bio-PEPA
   stochastic process algebra [4]. In addition, the BusKer tool generates an expression in MultiQuaTEx, the query language supported by the MultiVeStA statistical
   model-checker [5]. This is used to formally express queries on service-level agreements about the bus route under study.
4. The Bio-PEPA Eclipse Plugin [6] is used to perform stochastic simulations of the
   Bio-PEPA model.
5. MultiVeStA is hooked to the simulation engine of the Bio-PEPA Eclipse Plugin,
   consuming individual simulation events to evaluate the automatically generated
   MultiQuaTEx expressions. It produces as its results plots of the related quantitative properties.

We are devoting more than the usual amount of effort to ensuring that our tools are
user-friendly and easy-to-use. This is because we want our software tools to be used "in-
house" by service providers because only then can service providers retain control over
access to their own proprietary data about their service provision. With respect to ease-
of-use in particular, making model parameterisation simpler is a crucial step in making
models re-usable. Because vehicle occupancy fluctuates according to the seasons, with
the consequence that buses spend more or less time at bus stops boarding passengers, it
is essential to be able to re-parameterise and re-run models for different data sets from
different months of the year.

It is also necessary to be able to re-run an analysis based on historical measurement
data if timetables change, or the key definitions used in the evaluation of regulatory

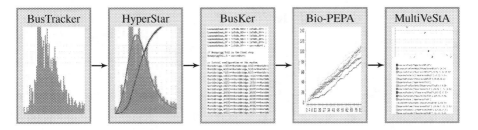

Fig. 1. The analysis pathway

requirements change. Evidently, a high degree of automation in the process is essential, hence our interest in an analysis pathway.

Related work. We are not aware of other toolchains based on formal methods for the quantitative analysis of public transportation systems. The same bus system is studied in [7], from which we inherited the data-set acquisition and its fitting to phase-type distributions. Differently from our approach, in [7] different software tools are individually used to perform distinct analyses of the scenario. For example, the Traviando [8] post-mortem simulation trace analyser is fed with precomputed simulation traces of a Bio-PEPA model similar to ours, and the probabilistic model checker PRISM [9] is used to analyse a corresponding model defined in the PRISM's input language.

More generally, our approach takes inspiration from generative programming techniques [10], in that we aim at automatic generation of possibly large stochastic process algebra models (our target language) from more compact higher-level descriptions (i.e., the timetable representation and the model parameters).

The generation of MultiQuaTEx expressions fits well with the literature on higher-level specification patterns for temporal logic formulae [11]. Temporal logics, the common property specification languages of model checkers, are not in widespread use in industry, as they require a high degree of mathematical maturity and experience in formal language theory. Furthermore, most system requirements are written in natural language, and often contain ambiguities which make it difficult to accurately formalise them in any temporal logic. In an attempt to ease the use of temporal logic, [11] gives a pattern-based classification for capturing requirements, paving the way for semi-automated methodologies for the generation of inputs to model checking tools. From a general perspective, in this work we fix the property patterns of interest, and completely hide property generation and evaluation to the end user.

Paper structure. Section 2 motivates our reasons for constructing a stochastic model of the problem. Section 3 describes the analysis problem in greater detail and presents the key definitions used in the paper. Section 4 describes how measurement data is transformed into model parameters to initiate the analysis which is undertaken. Section 5 describes the software tools in the analysis pathway. Section 6 presents the software analyser which combines these disparate tools. Section 7 presents our analysis in terms of the key definitions of the paper. Conclusions are presented in Section 8.

2   The Importance of Modelling

We are working in a context where we have an existing operational instrumented system which is gathering data on its service provision. However, instead of working directly with the data we will construct a high-level stochastic model of the data, using Erlang distributions with a number of phases and an exponentially-distributed rate to describe a journey between two timing points. The timing points are those bus stops which are named in the published timetable for the route.

We work with a stochastic model instead of working with the data directly because, importantly, we are not concerned with detecting post-hoc violations of the regulations from measurement data. Rather, we are trying to estimate the likelihood of future violations of the regulations in journeys which are similar to those which we have seen, although not identical to them. For this reason we generalise from the data to a stochastic process which describes the data well in a precise sense statistically.

Measurement data only records particular historical events: it does not generalise. For example, if our collected observations tell us that a bus journey can take five, six, eight, or nine minutes it is reasonable to assume that it can also take seven minutes, although this is not actually recorded in the data. Generalising from data like this is the act of abstraction which is at the heart of modelling. Models have many other strengths.

- Models are intellectual tools for understanding systems. They can be understood by service operators and used to communicate with regulators or other stakeholders.
- Models impose order on data, shaping it to become information which can be used in making decisions about how systems are modified.
- Models are concise and can be easily compared. In contrast, data is verbose and difficult to compare.
- Models are high-level and structured. Data is low-level and unstructured.
- Models are scalable. The number of phases in the stochastic description of the journey can be easily modified in order to explore the effect of different routes. Adding more phases corresponds to lengthening the route; removing phases corresponds to shortening it. Data is not scalable in this way.
- Models are tuneable. Rates can be easily adjusted in order to explore the effect of increased congestion on the routes or the effect of changes in the speed limit on parts of a route. Data is not tuneable in this way.
- Models are editable in a way which data is not. We can predict the effect of planned engineering works on journey times by using measurement data which incorporates the effect of previous engineering works and scaling it to fit if needed.

Because measurement data consists of a finite number of observations we know that there is additional possible behaviour which we have not seen. Stochastic modelling is a powerful reasoning tool allowing us to estimate the likelihood of values which we have not seen based on the frequency of occurrences of those values which we have seen. Conclusions drawn solely from the data would be misleading in that we would be led to believe that some combinations of events were impossible when in fact they are only relatively unlikely.

Finally, in moving from the data to the stochastic model we only need to ensure that we have identified a suitable stochastic process to represent the data. In Section 4 we will explain the use of the Kolmogorov-Smirnov statistical test to ensure this.

3   The Analysis Problem

The notion of punctuality which we are considering here is defined in terms of the concept of a "window of tolerance" around the departure times advertised in the timetable. Perhaps not very surprisingly, this notion differs between different operators and different countries, for instance:

- According to Transport for London, a bus is considered to be on time if it departs between two minutes and 30 seconds early and five minutes late [12].
- In England outside London, a bus is considered to be on time if it departs between one minute early and five minutes, 59 seconds late [13].
- In Scotland, according to the definitions reported in the Scottish Government's *Bus Punctuality Improvement Partnerships* report, a bus is considered to be on time if it departs between one minute early and five minutes late [14].

Each region has a definition of on-time in terms of the window of tolerance but clearly when comparing the quality of service in one region with the quality of service in another it is necessary to be able to re-evaluate the service delivered historically against the definitions used by another.

Our problem is to generate a mathematical model which allows us to analyse the following properties, for each bus stop advertised in a timetable.

P1. The average time of departure from the bus stop.
P2. The average distance of the departure time from the timetabled time.
P3. The probability that a bus departs on time.
P4. The probability of an early departure.
P5. The probability of a late departure.

Since the window of tolerance is asymmetric with respect to the timetable, property P2 is formally defined as the expected value of the absolute value of the difference between the time of departure and the respective timetabled time. Note that properties P3–P5 clearly depend on the notion of punctuality adopted.

In this paper we focus on a particular bus route. Specifically, we consider the Lothian Buses #31 bus on its journey from North Bridge in Edinburgh's city centre to Bonnyrigg Toll in the south, passing through the Cameron Toll and Lasswade Road timing points. The same bus route has been studied in [7], as discussed in Section 1. Table 1 shows its timetable, where the departure time from North Bridge is taken as the reference time 0.

Table 1. Timetable for the #31 bus operated by Lothian Buses in Edinburgh

Timing point	Code	Timetable (in minutes)
North Bridge	NB	0
Cameron Toll	CT	16
Lasswade Road	LR	24
Bonnyrigg Toll	BT	34

4   From Measurement Data to Model Parameters

We now turn our attention to how model parameters are found for a BusKer input.

4.1   The BusTracker Data

The raw data which is the input to the pathway is a dataset compiling measured journey times between timing points, forming an empirical distribution over the journey times. This data set incorporates the unpredictable effects of many different types of delays which the service can experience, due to traffic congestion and competition with other buses for access to bus stops. The data is obtained from the passenger waiting time website for Lothian Buses [2]. We collected raw data from this website by scripting, and wrote the data to a file for post-processing. This data is available from the QUANTICOL website at http://www.quanticol.eu. Post-processing identified departure events in the data, and computed journey times between timing points, compiling an empirical distribution of journey times.

4.2   HyperStar

Phase-type distributions are a class of probability distributions formally defined as the time to absorption of a continuous-time Markov chain (CTMC). They are very popular in the performance evaluation community because they can approximate, with arbitrary precision, generally-distributed events by means of appropriate *stages* (or *phases*) of independent exponential distributions [15]. Concretely, this allows a modeller to accurately describe general systems exhibiting nonexponential distributions using a Markov chain as the underlying mathematical formalism. An Erlang distribution, hereafter denoted by $Erl(k, \lambda)$, is a special case of a series of $k > 0$ exponential phases, each with mean duration given by $1/\lambda$, with $\lambda > 0$. The mean duration of the distribution is k/λ. It is particularly useful for modelling activities with low variance — in the limit $k \to \infty$ it behaves deterministically. It has been found in [7] to approximate bus journey times well. For this reason, our current implementation supports Erlang distributions only, although an extension to general phase-type distributions is possible.

Given a set of observed durations, the problem is to find the parameters of a phase-type distribution that fits them most appropriately (according to some criterion of optimality). For an Erlang distribution, this amounts to finding the values of the parameters k and λ that completely characterise it. For this, we use HyperStar, a new software tool released in 2013 [3] to convert our empirical distribution to an analytic one.

4.3   The Kolmogorov-Smirnov Test

The Kolmogorov-Smirnov test can be used to quantify the distance between an empirical distribution function and a cumulative distribution function. The test can be used to answer the question whether the data would be thought to have come from the specified distribution. We applied this test to the empirical data and the Erlang distributions returned by HyperStar. The null hypothesis was accepted with credible test statistics and critical values in all three cases meaning that the Erlang distributions are suitable stochastic process descriptions of the data.

5 The Analysis Pathway

In this section we describe in more detail the modelling tools and formal languages of our analysis pathway, as well as their integration.

5.1 BusKer

The Bus Kernel model generator (BusKer) is a Java command-line application that takes as input the specification of the window of tolerance (parameters `maxAdvance` and `maxDelay`, respectively) and a *BusKer specification*, i.e. a comma-separated representation of the timetable and the Erlang distribution for the time to reach the next timetabled bus stop. For instance, in this paper we will consider the parameter fitting used in [7] for the route in Table 1, which yields the following BusKer specification:

$$\# \textit{Timing point}, \textit{Code}, \textit{Timetable}, k, \lambda$$
$$\text{North Bridge}, NB, 0, 105, 6.47$$
$$\text{Cameron Toll}, CT, 16, 83, 8.79 \tag{1}$$
$$\text{Lasswade Road}, LR, 24, 98, 10.54$$
$$\text{Bonnyrigg Toll}, BT, 34, -, -$$

As a result, BusKer generates the inputs for the next two steps of our analysis pathway: a Bio-PEPA model of the bus service, and the MultiQuaTEx expression analysed by MultiVeStA to state the quality of the studied bus service with respect to the provided window of tolerance.

5.2 Bio-PEPA

Although designed for application to modelling problems in biological systems, Bio-PEPA has been effectively applied to problems as diverse as crowd dynamics [16], emergency egress [17] and swarm robotics [18]. Here, we use it because it is a stochastic process algebra with an underlying CTMC semantics; as such it is possible to encode phase-type distributions in Bio-PEPA. Furthermore, it is implemented by a software tool, the BioPEPA Eclipse Plugin, which supports stochastic simulation in a way that is easily consumable by MultiVeStA. Referring the reader to [4] for the complete formal account, we will use the following simplified BusKer specification to briefly overview the language:

$$\# \textit{Timing point}, \textit{Code}, \textit{Timetable}, k, \lambda$$
$$\text{North Bridge}, NB, 0, 3, 0.19 \tag{2}$$
$$\text{Cameron Toll}, CT, 16, -, -$$

BusKer will generate the specification shown in Listing 1.1. The model concerns the five *species* NB_1, NB_2, NB_3, CT_1 and DepsFromNB, representing the number of buses in North Bridge (NB_1), those in the first (NB_2) and second (NB_3) part of the journey from North Bridge to Cameron Toll, and the number of buses at Cameron Toll

```
 1    // Definitions of rate functions
 2      // Functions for North Bridge -> Cameron Toll (3 phases)
 3      NBtoCT_1 = [0.19 * NB_1];
 4      NBtoCT_2 = [0.19 * NB_2];
 5      NBtoCT_ARRIVED = [0.19 * NB_3];
 6    // Definitions of processes
 7      // Processes for North Bridge -> Cameron Toll (3 phases)
 8      NB_1 = NBtoCT_1<< ;
 9      NB_2 = NBtoCT_1>> + NBtoCT_2<< ;
10      NB_3 = NBtoCT_2>> + NBtoCT_ARRIVED<< ;
11      // Cameron Toll is the final stop.
12      CT_1 = NBtoCT_ARRIVED>> ;
13    // State observations
14      DepsFromNB = NBtoCT_1>> ;
15    // Initial configuration of the system (one bus in North Bridge)
16      NB_1[1] <*> NB_2[0] <*> NB_3[0] <*>
17      CT_1[0] <*>
18      DepsFromNB[0]
```

Listing 1.1. The Bio-PEPA model generated by BusKer for the scenario of (2)

(CT_1). Finally, DepsFromNB is an observer process used to count the number of departures from North Bridge. Lines 16–18 provide the initial system configuration: one bus is in North Bridge, while all the other populations are set to 0. A reaction prefix such as NBtoCT_1<< in a species definition (e.g. NB_1 = NBtoCT_1<< at line 8) causes the population count of that species (NB_1) to decrease by one when the reaction NBtoCT_1 occurs. In particular, line 3 specifies that the reaction NBtoCT_1 occurs with a rate obtained by multiplying the constant 0.19 with the population count of the species NB_1. In our model we follow the journey of a single prototypical bus, so this product in the rate expression acts as a switch, allowing the reaction to fire when a bus is present and preventing it from firing at other times (because the rate evaluates to 0 when a bus is not present). Similar to this is the case of the reaction prefix NBtoCT_1>>, the only difference being that in this case the involved population counts increase by one. For example, line 14 specifies that the population of the species DepsFromNB increases by one whenever the reaction NBtoCT_1 occurs, making DepsFromNB a *de facto* counter for the departures of buses from North Bridge. In contrast, line 10 specifies that the population of the species NB_3, i.e. the buses in the second part of the journey from North Bridge to Cameron Toll, increases by one whenever a bus moves from the first to the second part of the journey (NBtoCT_2>>), and decreases by one whenever a bus arrives at Cameron Toll (NBtoCT_ARRIVED<<).

The Bio-PEPA model built from the input to BusKer is a statistically-plausible stochastic model of the journey of a prototypical bus travelling from the first to the last specified bus stops, using the Erlang parameters learnt from the measurement data which has been processed by HyperStar. Clearly, the predictive power of this model depends crucially on the quality and scope of the data supplied to HyperStar. Because it is ultimately learnt from data, the model will incorporate the effects of contention for bus stops with other buses serving the same route, and, for good or ill, it will incorporate the influence of any atypical events (e.g. unusually long delays) which occurred during the measurement period.

```
1  DepartureTime ( depsFromBusStop ) =
2    if { s.rval ( depsFromBusStop ) == 1.0 } then s.rval ( "time" )
3                      else # DepartureTime ( depsFromBusStop )
4    fi ;
5  eval E[ DepartureTime ( "DepsFromNB" ) ]; eval E[ DepartureTime ( "DepsFromCT" ) ];
6  eval E[ DepartureTime ( "DepsFromLR" ) ];
```

Listing 1.2. A MultiQuaTEx expression to query expected departure times

5.3 MultiVeStA

MultiVeStA [5] is a recently-developed Java-based distributed statistical model checker which allows its users to enrich existing discrete event simulators with automated and statistical analysis capabilities. The analysis algorithms of MultiVeStA do not depend on the underlying simulation engine: MultiVeStA only makes the assumption that multiple discrete event simulations can be performed on the input model. The tool has been used to reason about collision-avoidance robots [19], volunteer clouds [20] and crowd-steering [21] scenarios.

MultiVeStA comes with a property specification language, MultiQuaTEx, which makes it possible for users to express and evaluate many properties over the same simulated path. In contrast to Continuous Stochastic Logic [22,23] and Probabilistic Computation Tree Logic [24] commonly used in probabilistic and statistical model checking, MultiQuaTEx allows users to define their own parametric recursive temporal operators within the logic itself, and to query real-typed properties, rather than just probabilities. In particular, with MultiQuaTEx we can express all the properties listed in Section 3.

A MultiQuaTEx expression is evaluated statistically. Given a statistical estimate $\bar{x}$, then with probability $(1 - \alpha)$ its true value lies within the interval $[\bar{x} - \delta/2, \bar{x} + \delta/2]$, where (α, δ) is a user-specified confidence interval. An in-depth presentation of Multi-QuaTEx is out of the scope of this paper, but can be found in [5].

Listing 1.2 provides a MultiQuaTEx expression to estimate the expected departure times from each bus stop of interest (property P1) using the BusKer specification (1). Lines 5–6 specify the three expected values to be estimated, i.e. the departure times from North Bridge, Cameron Toll and Lasswade Road. Lines 1–4 specify a *parametric recursive temporal operator* which returns, for each simulation, the departure time of the bus from the bus stop specified as the parameter. This is iteratively evaluated by performing steps of simulations (triggered by the operator #) until the guard of the if statement is satisfied, i.e. until a departure occurs from the selected bus stop. Intuitively, as discussed in Section 5.2, the Bio-PEPA model generated by BusKer counts the departures from each bus stop by defining observer processes DepsFromNB, DepsFromCT and DepsFromLR whose populations are incremented every time the corresponding event happens. Finally, we note that MultiVeStA can access information about the current state of the simulation with s.rval(observation), where observation can be the current simulated time (i.e. time), or the current population of a species (e.g. "DepsFromNB").

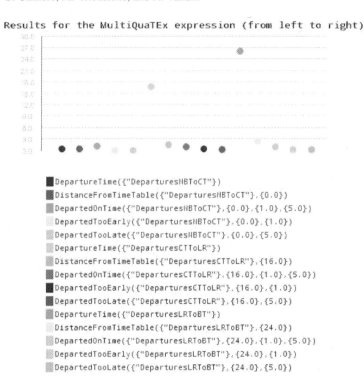

Fig. 2. Plot generated by TBA for the specification presented in Equation (1), and the (1,5) window of tolerance

6   Tool Chaining: The Bus Analyzer

The last three tools of our analysis pathway, highlighted in Figure 1, have been integrated in a single tool called *TBA: The Bus Analyzer*. TBA hides from the user the steps involved in the generation of the Bio-PEPA model and of the MultiQuaTEx expression, as well as the invocation of MultiVeStA. TBA can be downloaded, together with our BusKer specification (1), from the Tools section of the QUANTICOL web-site at http://www.quanticol.eu/.

A first clear advantage brought by TBA is the automation of the analysis phase, as the user only has to execute the command

$$\text{java -jar TBA.jar busker scenario.busker maxAdv maxDelay } [servers] \qquad (3)$$

where *scenario.busker* is a file containing a BusKer specification, and *maxAdv* and *maxDelay* specify the required window of tolerance (in minutes). The optional parameter *servers* gives the degree of parallelism to automatically distribute independent simulations across CPU cores.

TBA evaluates properties P1–P5. The results are provided to the user via a GUI consisting of an interactive scatter plot containing a point for each studied property, and

```
1   // Definitions of rate functions
2     // Functions for North Bridge -> Cameron Toll (105 phases)
3     NBtoCT_1 = [6.47 * NB_1];
4     ...
5     NBtoCT_104 = [6.47 * NB_104];
6     NBtoCT_ARRIVED = [6.47 * NB_105];
7     // Functions for Cameron Toll -> Lasswade Road (83 phases)
8     CTtoLR_1 = [8.79 * CT_1];
9     ...
10    CTtoLR_82 = [8.79 * CT_82];
11    CTtoLR_ARRIVED = [8.79 * CT_83];
12    // Functions for Lasswade Road -> Bonnyrigg Toll (98 phases)
13    LRtoBT_1 = [10.54 * LR_1];
14    ...
15    LRtoBT_97 = [10.54 * LR_97];
16    LRtoBT_ARRIVED = [10.54 * LR_98];
17  // Definitions of processes
18    // Processes for North Bridge -> Cameron Toll (105 phases)
19    NB_1 = NBtoCT_1 <<;
20    NB_2 = NBtoCT_1 >> + NBtoCT_2 <<;
21    ...
22    NB_104 = NBtoCT_103 >> + NBtoCT_104 <<;
23    NB_105 = NBtoCT_104 >> + NBtoCT_ARRIVED <<;
24    // Processes for Cameron Toll -> Lasswade Road (83 phases)
25    CT_1 = NBtoCT_ARRIVED >> + CTtoLR_1 <<;
26    CT_2 = CTtoLR_1 >> + CTtoLR_2 <<;
27    ...
28    CT_82 = CTtoLR_81 >> + CTtoLR_82 <<;
29    CT_83 = CTtoLR_82 >> + CTtoLR_ARRIVED <<;
30    // Processes for Lasswade Road -> Bonnyrigg Toll (98 phases)
31    LR_1 = CTtoLR_ARRIVED >> + LRtoBT_1 <<;
32    LR_2 = LRtoBT_1 >> + LRtoBT_2 <<;
33    ...
34    LR_97 = LRtoBT_96 >> + LRtoBT_97 <<;
35    LR_98 = LRtoBT_97 >> + LRtoBT_ARRIVED <<;
36    // Bonnyrigg Toll is the final stop.
37    BT_1 = LRtoBT_ARRIVED >>;
38  // State observations
39    DepsFromNB = NBtoCT_1 >>; DepsFromCT = CTtoLR_1 >>; DepsFromLR = LRtoBT_1 >>;
40  // Initial configuration of the system (one bus in North Bridge)
41    NB_1 [1] <*> ... <*> NB_105 [0] <*>
42    CT_1 [0] <*> ... <*> CT_83 [0]  <*>
43    LR_1 [0] <*> ... <*> LR_98 [0]  <*> BT_1 [0] <*>
44    DepsFromNB [0] <*> DepsFromCT [0] <*> DepsFromLR [0]
```

Listing 1.3. The Bio-PEPA model generated by BusKer for input Equation (1)

are also stored on disk. For example, the interactive plot allows the modeller to hide some properties, to apply zooming or rescaling operations, to change the considered boundaries, and to save the plot as a picture. Figure 2 depicts the plot obtained for the BusKer specification (1) when considering the Scottish window of tolerance, i.e., maxAdv=1 and maxDelay=5. A discussion of the analysis is provided in Section 7. In the remainder of this section we focus on the usability and accessibility advantages provided by chaining the three tools.

Clearly, given that TBA hides the generation of the model and of the property, as well as their analysis, the user is not required to learn the two formal languages, nor to use their related tools. Furthermore, for realistic bus scenarios the generated Bio-PEPA models and MultiQuaTEx expressions tend to be large and thus error-prone to write down manually. For example, the Bio-PEPA model generated by TBA for our scenario

```
1   //Static part of the expression: the parametric temporal operators
2   //Probabilities of departing on time, too early or too late
3   DepartedOnTime(depsFromBusStop,timeTabledDep,maxAdv,maxDelay) =
4    if { s.rval(depsFromBusStop) == 1.0 }
5        then CheckIfDepOnTime(depsFromBusStop,timeTabledDep,maxAdv,maxDelay)
6        else # DepartedOnTime(depsFromBusStop,timeTabledDep,maxAdv,maxDelay)
7    fi;
8   CheckIfDepOnTime(depsFromBusStop,timeTabledDep,maxAdv,maxDelay) =
9    if { timeTabledDep - s.rval("time") > maxAdv }
10       then 0.0
11       else if { s.rval("time") - timeTabledDep > maxDelay }
12               then 0.0 else 1.0
13          fi
14   fi;
15  DepartedTooEarly(depsFromBusStop,timeTabledDep,maxAdv) =//like DepartedOnTime
16  DepartedTooLate(depsFromBusStop,timeTabledDep,maxDelay)=//like DepartedOnTime
17  //Expected departure time
18  DepartureTime(depsFromBusStop) = //as in Listing 1.2
19  //Expected deviation from the timetabled departure time
20  DistanceFromTimeTable(depsFromBusStop,timeTabledDep) =
21   if { s.rval(depsFromBusStop) == 1.0 }
22       then ComputeDistanceFromTimeTable(depsFromBusStop,timeTabledDep)
23       else # DistanceFromTimeTable(depsFromBusStop,timeTabledDep)
24   fi;
25  ComputeDistanceFromTimeTable(depsFromBusStop,timeTabledDep) =
26   if { timeTabledDep > s.rval("time") }
27       then timeTabledDep - s.rval("time") else s.rval("time") - timeTabledDep
28   fi;
29  //Static part of the expression: the 15 properties to be estimated
30   eval E[ DepartureTime("DepsFromNB") ];
31   eval E[ DistanceFromTimeTable("DepsFromNB",0.0) ];
32   eval E[ DepartedOnTime("DepsFromNB",0.0,1.0,5.0) ];
33   eval E[ DepartedTooEarly("DepsFromNB",0.0,1.0) ];
34   eval E[ DepartedTooLate("DepsFromNB",0.0,5.0) ];
35  //same eval clauses for "DepsFromCT", and "16.0" rather than 0.0
36  //same eval clauses for "DepsFromLR", and "24.0" rather than 0.0
```

Listing 1.4. The MultiQuaTEx expression generated by BusKer

is almost 900 lines long, as sketched in Listing 1.3. This is due to the the fact that the journeys between bus stops are modelled using Erlang distributions with many phases, and each phase is associated with a distinct species (hence at least a line in the source code). More specifically, Listing 1.3 can be divided in four parts: lines 1–16 define the rates with which the modelled prototypical bus moves, lines 17–36 define the processes specifying the bus's stochastic behaviour, lines 37–38 define the state observations of interest, while lines 39–44 specify the initial configuration of the system. The third section only depends on the number of considered bus stops, while, as depicted by the ellipsis, the other ones also depend on the number of phases of the provided BusKer specification.

The MultiQuaTEx expression generated by BusKer for our scenario is a fixed length for any window of tolerance. It is sketched in Listing 1.4 for the Scottish window of tolerance. Overall it evaluates fifteen properties, i.e., P1–P5 for each of the three bus stops. Lines 1–28 define the parametric recursive temporal operators which specify how to compute such properties, whereas lines 29–36 list the fifteen properties to be estimated.

Table 2. Analysis results for the #31 bus operated by Lothian Buses in Edinburgh

	North Bridge	Cameron Toll	Lasswade Road
P1	0.32	16.42	25.84
P2	0.32	1.28	2.13
P3	1.00	0.81	0.88
P4	0.00	0.19	0.04
P5	0.00	0.00	0.06

For each simulation, each temporal operator observes the bus stop provided as a parameter, specifically: `DepartedOnTime`, `DepartedTooEarly` and `DepartedTooLate` return 1 if the bus departed on time, too early, or too late, respectively. `DepartureTime` returns the departure time of the bus, while `DistanceFromTimeTable` returns the absolute value of the difference between the actual departure time and the timetabled one. That expression does not depend on the number of phases of the BusKer specification, but only on the number of timetabled bus stops. In particular, the expression can be divided in a *static* part, which is given once, for any possible input specification, and a dynamic one, which instead depends on the input specification. Thanks to their parametrisation, the temporal operators (lines 1–27) do not depend on the input specification, and are thus the static part of the expression. Lines 28–35 are the dynamic part of the expression, as five `eval` clauses instantiated with the timetabled departures and the window of tolerance are needed for each bus stop considered.

7   Analysis of the Scenario

In this section we present the analysis of our scenario using TBA. The results for the Scottish window of tolerance [14] are summarised in Table 2. We fixed $\alpha = 0.05$ for all properties, $\delta = 0.2$ for those regarding the expected departure times and deviations from the timetable, and $\delta = 0.05$ for the probabilities. It was necessary to perform 1860 simulations to attain this confidence interval for all the 15 studied properties, requiring less than 10 seconds in total, thus without requiring to resort to MultiVeStA's capability of distributing simulations.

These results suggest that buses tend to lose adherence with respect to the timetable while performing the route. This effect is also observed in practice: the variance of departure times is seen to increase along the route. However, this does not necessarily correspond to a degradation of the quality of service, as a greater deviation from the timetable generated by delayed departures may correspond to a better quality of service than a smaller deviation generated by *anticipated* departures.

In order to have further insights into the quality of the studied #31 bus service, the last three rows of Table 2 provide the probabilities that a bus departs on time, too early, or too late from each bus stop. Consistent with the slight deviation found from the timetable, we have that buses always depart on time from the North Bridge stop. Then, buses tend to perform the route from North Bridge to Cameron Toll too quickly, causing early departures in 20% of cases. The quality of service improves at Lasswade Road, where only 12% of departures are outside the window of tolerance. This may seem to

Table 3. The quality of the #31 bus service for the Scottish (SC) and English (EN) window of tolerance

	North Bridge		Cameron Toll		Lasswade Road	
	SC	EN	SC	EN	SC	EN
P3	1.00	1.00	0.81	0.82	0.88	0.92
P4	0.00	0.00	0.19	0.18	0.04	0.05
P5	0.00	0.00	0.00	0.00	0.06	0.03

contradict the results about the deviation from the timetable, as we found that at the Lasswade Roll time point there is a greater deviation from the timetable with respect to that at Cameron Toll. However, this is explained by noticing that our analysis tells us that the deviations from the timetable are mainly caused by *anticipated* departures at Cameron Toll, and by delayed departures at Lasswade Road. In fact, we first of all notice that the expected departure time is 0.42 minutes greater than the timetabled one at Cameron Toll, and 1.84 at Lasswade Road.

Furthermore, we have early departures in 20% of cases and no late departures at Cameron Toll. Instead, at Lasswade Road we have early departures in only 4% of cases, and late departures in 6% of cases. In conclusion, we find that buses tend to spend more time than is scheduled in performing the journey from Cameron Toll to Lasswade Road, thus absorbing the effect of earlier departures from Cameron Toll, leading to a halved percentage of departures there outside the window of tolerance with respect to Cameron Toll.

It is worthwhile to note that analysing the quality of service with respect to other windows of tolerance only requires launching the command (3) with different parameters. For example, Table 3 compares the results using the Scottish window of tolerance (SC), and the English one (EN), the latter obtained by setting parameters `maxAdv=1` and `maxDelay=5.59`. Not surprisingly, the table depicts a slightly better quality of service for the same data when considering the looser English window of tolerance rather than the stricter Scottish one.

8   Conclusions

In this paper we have presented an analysis pathway for the quantitative evaluation of service-level agreements for public transportation systems. Although we discussed a concrete application focussing on a specific bus route in a specific city, our approach is more general and it can in principle be applied to other transportation systems publishing timetabled departure times.

The methodology which we have proposed here requires the availability of the raw data from a bus tracking system. At first sight, it might have seemed that the properties of interest could have been calculated directly from measurement data. However, data sets are necessarily incomplete and working from the data provides less coverage of the full range of the system behaviour and hence delivers fewer insights than are obtained when working with a stochastic process abstraction of the data.

In addition, only (automatically generated) models can assist service providers and regulatory authorities in evaluating *what-if scenarios*, e.g., understanding the impact of changes along a route on the offered quality of service. In this respect, the measurements are crucial to calibrate the model with realistic parameters, which can be changed by the modeller (by simply manipulating the compact BusKer specification) in order to study how the properties would be affected. For instance, regulators could determine how proposals to amend the notion of punctuality might impact on a provider's capability to satisfy the regulations on services.

As discussed, the model involves a single route only, hence the measurements already incorporate effects of contention such as those due to multiple buses sharing the same route, and multiple routes sharing segments of the road. Developing a model where such effects are captured explicitly is an interesting line of future work, as is extending our analysis pathway to such a scenario.

Acknowledgements. This work is supported by the EU project QUANTICOL, 600708. The Bio-PEPA Eclipse Plugin software can be obtained from www.biopepa.org. The MultiVeStA statistical analysis tool is available from code.google.com/p/ multivesta/. The authors thank Allan Clark and Ludovica Luisa Vissat for the work in [7] which provided the model parameters for the present paper. The authors thank the anonymous reviewers for suggestions which helped us to improve the paper.

References

1. Tang, L., (Vonu) Thakuriah, P.: Ridership effects of real-time bus information system: A case study in the city of Chicago. Transportation Research Part C: Emerging Technologies 22, 146–161 (2012)
2. The City of Edinburgh Council. Bus Tracker Edinburgh real-time bus information website (2014), http://www.mybustracker.co.uk
3. Reinecke, P., Krauß, T., Wolter, K.: Phase-type fitting using HyperStar. In: Balsamo, M.S., Knottenbelt, W.J., Marin, A. (eds.) EPEW 2013. LNCS, vol. 8168, pp. 164–175. Springer, Heidelberg (2013)
4. Ciocchetta, F., Hillston, J.: Bio-PEPA: A framework for the modelling and analysis of biological systems. Theoretical Computer Science 410(33-34), 3065–3084 (2009)
5. Sebastio, S., Vandin, A.: MultiVeStA: Statistical model checking for discrete event simulators. In: 7th International Conference on Performance Evaluation Methodologies and Tools, VALUETOOLS, Torino, Italy (December 2013)
6. Duguid, A., Gilmore, S., Guerriero, M.L., Hillston, J., Loewe, L.: Design and development of software tools for Bio-PEPA. In: Dunkin, A., Ingalls, R.G., Yücesan, E., Rossetti, M.D., Hill, R., Johansson, B. (eds.) Winter Simulation Conference, WSC, pp. 956–967 (2009)
7. Vissat, L.L., Clark, A., Gilmore, S.: Finding optimal timetables for Edinburgh bus routes. In: Proceedings of the Seventh International Workshop on Practical Applications of Stochastic Modelling (PASM 2014), Newcastle, England (May 2014)
8. Kemper, P., Tepperp, C.: Automated trace analysis of discrete-event system models. IEEE Trans. Software Eng. 35(2), 195–208 (2009)
9. Kwiatkowska, M., Norman, G., Parker, D.: PRISM 4.0: Verification of probabilistic real-time systems. In: Gopalakrishnan, G., Qadeer, S. (eds.) CAV 2011. LNCS, vol. 6806, pp. 585–591. Springer, Heidelberg (2011)
10. Czarnecki, K., Eiseneckerp, U.W.: Generative Programming: Methods, Tools, and Applications. Addison-Wesley (2000)

11. Dwyer, M.B., Avrunin, G.S., Corbett, J.C.: Patterns in property specifications for finite-state verification. In: Boehm, B.W., Garlan, D., Kramer, J. (eds.) ICSE, pp. 411–420. ACM (1999)

12. Reed, S.: Transport for London—Using tools, analytics and data to inform passengers. Journeys, 96–104 (September 2013)

13. Tranter, M.: Department for Transport—annual bus statistics: England 2012/2013 (September 2013)

14. Smarter Scotland: Scottish Government. Bus Punctuality Improvement Partnerships (BPIP) (March 2009)

15. Stewart, W.J.: Probability, Markov Chains, Queues, and Simulation. Princeton University Press (2009)

16. Massink, M., Latella, D., Bracciali, A., Hillston, J.: Modelling non-linear crowd dynamics in Bio-PEPA. In: Giannakopoulou, D., Orejas, F. (eds.) FASE 2011. LNCS, vol. 6603, pp. 96–110. Springer, Heidelberg (2011)

17. Massink, M., Latella, D., Bracciali, A., Harrison, M.D., Hillston, J.: Scalable context-dependent analysis of emergency egress models. Formal Aspects of Computing 24(2), 267–302 (2012)

18. Massink, M., Brambilla, M., Latella, D., Dorigo, M., Birattari, M.: On the use of Bio-PEPA for modelling and analysing collective behaviours in swarm robotics. Swarm Intelligence 7(2-3), 201–228 (2013)

19. Belzner, L., De Nicola, R., Vandin, A., Wirsing, M.: Reasoning (on) service component ensembles in rewriting logic. In: Iida, S., Meseguer, J., Ogata, K. (eds.) Specification, Algebra, and Software. LNCS, vol. 8373, pp. 188–211. Springer, Heidelberg (2014)

20. Sebastio, S., Amoretti, M., Lluch-Lafuente, A.: A computational field framework for collaborative task execution in volunteer clouds. In: Proceedings of the 9th International Symposium on Software Engineering for Adaptive and Self-Managing Systems (SEAMS 2014) (2014)

21. Pianini, D., Sebastio, S., Vandin, A.: Distributed statistical analysis of complex systems modeled through a chemical metaphor. In: 5th International Workshop on Modeling and Simulation of Peer-to-Peer and Autonomic Systems (MOSPAS 2014) (2014)

22. Aziz, A., Singhal, V., Balarin, F., Brayton, R., Sangiovanni-Vincentelli, A.L.: It usually works: The temporal logic of stochastic systems. In: Wolper, P. (ed.) CAV 1995. LNCS, vol. 939, pp. 155–165. Springer, Heidelberg (1995)

23. Baier, C., Katoen, J.-P., Hermanns, H.: Approximate Symbolic Model Checking of Continuous-Time Markov Chains (Extended Abstract). In: Baeten, J.C.M., Mauw, S. (eds.) CONCUR 1999. LNCS, vol. 1664, pp. 146–161. Springer, Heidelberg (1999)

24. Hansson, H., Jonsson, B.: A logic for reasoning about time and reliability. Formal Asp. Comput. 6(5), 512–535 (1994)

Modeling UML Template Classes with FoCaLiZe

Messaoud Abbas[1,3,4], Choukri-Bey Ben-Yelles[2], and Renaud Rioboo[1]

[1] CPR CEDRIC ENSIIE Square de la Résistance F-91025 Evry
Renaud.Rioboo@ensiie.fr
[2] Univ. Grenoble Alpes, LCIS, Rue Barthélémy de Laffemas F-26901 Valence
choukri.ben-yelles@iut-valence.fr
[3] USTHB. LSI, BP32 EL-Alia, Bab Ezzouar, Algiers, Algeria
[4] College of Sciences and Technology, El-Oued University, El-Oued, Algeria
abbasmessaoud@gmail.com

Abstract. UML is the defacto standard language to graphically describe systems in an object oriented way. Once an application has been specified, Model Driven Architecture (MDA) techniques can be applied to generate code from such specifications. Because UML lacks formal basis to analyze and check model consistency, it is pertinent to choose a formal target language (in the MDA process) to enable proofs and verification techniques. To achieve this goal, we have associated to UML the FoCaLiZe language, an object-oriented development environment using a proof-based formal approach. This paper focuses on a subset of UML constructors, the template classes. These latter allow developers to create generic models that can be instantiated for actual models through a binding relationship. Specifically, we propose a formal transformation of UML template classes annotated with OCL constraints into FoCaLiZe specification. The proposed mapping directly supports most of UML template features.

Keywords: UML, OCL, template, FoCaLiZe, proof, semantics.

1 Introduction

In the last few years, UML templates have been largely used for application development such as in Design Pattern modeling [1], aspect-oriented modeling (AOM) [2] or in the modeling of generic classes (as in C++ templates) [3]. But using UML and OCL, we can only describe UML templates and specify constraints upon them: no formal proof is available to check whether OCL properties hold in an UML template.

In this context, several studies have focused on the transformation of UML/ OCL models into formal methods. Such transformations produce an abstract formal specification in the target language where it is possible to verify and prove the original UML/OCL properties using proof techniques available in the formal language. The most used formal tools are the B language [4], the Alloy formal tool [5], the Maude system [6] and the Isabelle/HOL [7] among several others. However, they do not provide similar mechanisms.

E. Albert and E. Sekerinski (Eds.): IFM 2014, LNCS 8739, pp. 87–102, 2014.
© Springer International Publishing Switzerland 2014

To address this need, we propose a formal transformation from UML template classes annotated with OCL constraints into the FoCaLiZe environment [8]. To achieve this goal, we adopt a compiling approach (by translation). The choice of FoCaLiZe does not solely rely on its formal aspects. FoCaLiZe supports most of the requirements mandated by standards upon the assessment of a software development life cycle [9]. More precisely, our choice is motivated by the three following arguments.

First, FoCaLiZe supports most of UML conceptual and architectural features such as encapsulation, inheritance (generalization/specialization) and multiple inheritance, function redefinition, late-binding, dependency. In particular, FoCaLiZe supports both UML template classes and template bindings through its own constructs without additional structures or invariants. These features enable us to keep a similar logic of development.

The second motivation of FoCaLiZe lies in the paradigm of its language. The FoCaLiZe language is based on the functional aspect of the Ocaml[1] language, this avoids side effects during program execution.

Finally, the use of the FoCaLiZe environment is also motivated by the availability of its automated theorem prover Zenon [10] and its proof checker Coq [11]. Realizing proofs with Zenon makes the user intervention much easier since it manages to fulfill most of the proof obligations automatically. In addition, whenever such a proof fails, Zenon helps the user to locate the source of the inconsistency. At the last step, Coq validates the proof.

This document is organized as follows: sections 2 and 3 present FoCaLiZe and UML template concepts, sections 4 and 5 describe our transformation approach. In section 6 we develop the framework that integrates UML template classes annotated with OCL constraints and the FoCaLiZe environment to check model consistency. Before concluding, section 7 proposes a comparison with related works.

2   FoCaLiZe Concepts

The FoCaLiZe [8] environment, initiated by T. Hardin and R. Rioboo, is an integrated development environment with formal features. A FoCaLiZe development is organized as a hierarchy of species that may have several roots. This hierarchy is built step by step (incremental approach), starting with abstract specifications and heading to concrete implementations using object oriented features such as inheritance and parameterization.

A species groups together methods using ML-like types and expressions:

- The carrier type (representation), describes the data structure of the species. The representation of a species can depend on the representation of other species. It is mandatory and can either be explicitly given or obtained by inheritance.
- Function declarations (signature), specify functional types that will be defined later through inheritance (no computational body is provided at this stage).

---

[1] The Ocaml home site : http://caml.inria.fr/

- Function definitions (`let`), consist of optional functional types together with computational bodies.
- Properties (`property`), statements expressed by a first-order formula specifying requirements to be satisfied in the context of the species.
- Properties together with their proofs (`theorem`).

The general syntax of a species is given as follows:

species *species_name* =
[**representation** = *rep_type*;]
signature *function_name* : *function_type*;
[**local** / **logical**] **let** [**rec**] *function_name* = *function_body*;
property *property_name* : *property_specification* ;
theorem *theorem_name* : *theorem_specification* **proof** = *theorem_proof* ;
end ;;

As we mentioned above, species have object-oriented flavors [12]. We can create a species from scratch or from other species using (multiple) inheritance. Through inheritance, it is possible to associate a definition of function to a signature or a proof to a property. Similarly, it is possible to redefine a method even if it is already used by an existing method. The late-binding mechanism ensures that the selected method is always the latest defined along the inheritance tree.

A species is said to be `complete` if all declarations have received definitions and all properties have received proofs. The representations of complete species are encapsulated through species `interfaces`. The interface of a complete species is the list of its function types and its logical statements. It corresponds to the end user point of view, who needs only to know which functions he can use, and which properties these functions have, but doesn't care about the details of the implementation. When complete, a species can be implemented through the creation of collections. A collection can hence be seen as an abstract data type, only usable through the methods of its interface.

The following example presents the widely used species `Setoid`. It models any non-empty set with an equivalence relation on the equality (=) method:

```
species Setoid = inherit Basic_object;
 signature equal: Self-> Self-> bool;
 signature element: Self;
 property equal_reflexive: all x: Self, equal (x, x) ;
 property equal_symmetric: all x y: Self, equal(x, y) -> equal (y, x) ;
 property equal_transitive:all x y z: Self,
                           equal(x, y)-> equal(y, z) -> equal(x, z);
 end;;
```

A species can also be parameterized either by collections or by entities of a collection. Table 1 presents the species `Circle` parameterized by the species `Point`. We note that the representation of the species `Point` is abstract (not defined yet).

The representation of the species `Circle` has form P * float, where P is a variable type. It models the type of the center of a circle. The type float

Table 1. Example of Parameterization

```
species Point =
 signature getX : Self -> int;      signature getY : Self -> int;
 signature move : Self -> int -> int -> Self;
(* distance: calculates the distance between two given points *)
 let distance (a:Self,  b: Self):float = if (a = b) then 0.0 else
       sqrt( float_of_int( ((getX(a) - getX(b))*(getX(a) - getX(b)) ) +
                           ((getY(a) - getY(b))*(getY(a) - getY(b)) )));
(* distanceSpecification: specifies the method distance *)
 property distanceSpecification: all p :Self, distance(p, p) = 0.0;
 end;;
species Circle (P is Point) =
 representation = P * float ;
 let newCircle(centre:P, rayon:float):Self = (centre, rayon);
 let getCenter(c:Self):P = fst(c);
 let getRadius(c:Self):float = snd(c);
 let belongs(p:P, c:Self):bool =
                     ( P!distance(p, getCenter(c)) = getRadius(c));
 end;;
```

represents the radius type of a circle. As we can notice here, the species `Circle` can use all methods of the species `Point` through the formal parameter P, even if they are only declared. The method `belongs` is a logical method (returns boolean results) deciding whether a given point `p:P` belongs to a given circle `c:Self`.

Before implementing a species, all logical statements must be proven. Currently, FoCaLiZe uses the automated theorem prover Zenon [10], [13].

Compilation of FoCaLiZe sources gives rise to both OCaml code and Coq code. The generated OCaml code provides the executable form of the development. When Zenon succeeds, it provides automatically a Coq code which will be checked by the Coq theorem prover. Coq will act as an assessor, not only on all the proofs contained in the development but also on the whole consistency of the model [9], [14].

3   UML Templates

The two main types of UML templates are template classes and template packages. For reason of simplicity and clarity, we only focus on template classes in this paper, nevertheless template packages can be handled the same way. In order to provide a formal framework for the transformation of templates into FoCaLiZe specifications, we propose an abstract syntax for the subset of UML template constructs that we consider, using mostly UML Metamodel syntax [15]:

class-template ::= *option* **class** *class-name* [*param-signature*] [**binds** *bind* {, *bind*}*]
      [**inherits** *class-name* {, *class-name* }*] = *attr** *opr** **end**

An UML template class is an UML class that is characterized by its name and is composed of attributes and operations. A template class can also have a list of generalization relationships, which indicates the parent classes it specializes.

Each attribute (instance or state variable) of a template class has a name and a specification which is either a primitive type or another class of the model. Specifications may describe multiple values of a type ($[multiplicity]$):

$attr$ $::= visibility[/]attr\text{-}name[:type\text{-}exp][[multiplicity]][=default]$ [$attr\text{-}modifiers$]
$type\text{-}exp ::=$ **Integer** | **Boolean** | **String** | **Real** | **UnlimitedNatural** | $class\text{-}name$
opr $::= [visibility][\ll op\text{-}stereotype\gg]op\text{-}name([op\text{-}param\{,op\text{-}param\}*])$
            $[:return\text{-}type]\ [[multiplicity]]$
$op\text{-}param ::= [direction]\ param\text{-}name\ :\ type\text{-}exp\ [[multiplicity]]\ [=\ default]$

Each template class has a signature that specifies its formal parameters:

$param\text{-}signature ::= (formal\text{-}param\ \{,\ formal\text{-}param\}*)$
$formal\text{-}param$ $::= formal\text{-}param\text{-}name\ [\ :\ parameter\text{-}kind\ ]\ [=\ default]$
$parameter\text{-}kind$ $::= type\text{-}exp\ |$ **Class**
$default$ $::= class\text{-}name$

The *parameter-kind* is an UML parameterable element (ParameterableElement in UML Template Metamodel, see [15] page 634). Only parametrable elements can be used as formal template parameters of a template. For brevity, we only consider classifiers (in particular, UML classes) and UML primitive types as parametrable elements.

Bound models can be derived from template classes through substitutions of formal parameters. These substitutions are described in a dedicated **binding relationship** that links the bound model to the template class (from which it was obtained). The binding relationship specifies a set of template parameter substitutions that associates actual elements (of the bound model) to formal parameters (of the template):

$bind$ $::= class\text{-}template\text{-}name\ <\ subs\ [,\ subs*]\ >$
$subs$ $::= formal\text{-}param\text{-}name\ \text{->}\ actual\text{-}param$
$actual\text{-}param$ $::= class\text{-}name\ |\ value\text{-}specification$

Standard constraints impose that the type of each actual parameter (in the bound model) must be a sub-type of the corresponding formal parameter. The structure of the bound model is based on the structure of the template, where any element used as a formal parameter is substituted by the actual element specified in the binding relationship [15].

Templates have also a specific graphical notation which consists in superimposing a small dashed rectangle containing the signature on the top right-hand corner of the corresponding symbol (see Fig.1). This class, CStack, is graphically represented as a standard UML class with a dashed rectangle containing its parameter signature. Here, the signature is composed of two formal parameters: T of type Class (the type of the stack elements) and I of type Integer (the maximum length of the stack). The operations head, push, pop, isFull, isEmpty and length are the usual operations over stacks.

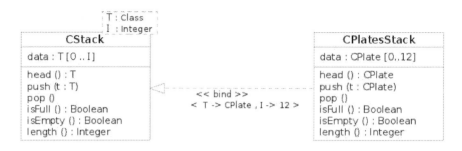

Fig. 1. Template Class

The right side of this figure shows the class `CPlatesStack` which is bound to the `CStack` template through a binding relationship. This class is the result of the substitution of the template formal parameters `T` and `I` respectively to actual values `CPlate` (the class that models plates) and the integer value 12.

4   From Template Classes to FoCaLiZe

During the transformation of template classes into FoCaLiZe, we will maintain two contexts, Γ_U for UML and Γ_F for FoCaLiZe. For a given template class named c_n, $\Gamma_U(c\_n)$ is its local context. In a symmetrical way, the FoCaLiZe typing context of a given species s_n, is denoted $\Gamma_F(s\_n)$. For an UML element U we will denote[2] $[\![U]\!]_{\Gamma_U, \Gamma_F}$ its translation into FoCaLiZe. The general definition of a template class is given as follows:

$< class\_template\_def > =$ [**public** | **private** | **protected**] [**final** | **abstract**]
class c_n $(\mathbb{P})$ **inherits** $\mathbb{H} = \mathbb{A}$; $\mathbb{O}$ **end**

where
- c_n is the name of the template class,
- $\mathbb{P}$ is a list of formal parameter declarations,
- $\mathbb{H}$ designates the list of classes from which the current class inherits,
- $\mathbb{A}$ is the attribute list of the class,
- $\mathbb{O}$ is its operations list.

Since most of the UML design features can seamlessly be represented in FoCaLiZe (following [12] and [16]) we transform an UML template class into a FoCaLiZe parameterized species. For brevity, we do not describe here such elements as visibility, inheritance and instantiation.

The carrier type (`representation`) of the derived species is a cartesian product type grouping all types of the instance variables. Each attribute is also modeled with a getter function in the corresponding species. The template class operations will be converted into functional signatures of a species. The general

---

[2] We may use super-indexes to distinguish between the different transformation rules, for example $[\![\ ]\!]_{\Gamma_U, \Gamma_F}^{param}$ (in Fig. 2) represents parameter transformation.

transformation rule is presented as follows:

$$[\![< class\text{-}template\text{-}def >]\!]_{\Gamma_U,\Gamma_F} = \textsf{species} \quad s\_n \ (\ [\![\mathbb{P}]\!]_{\Gamma_U,\Gamma_F})=$$
$$\textsf{inherit Setoid},\ [\![\mathbb{H}]\!]_{\Gamma_U,\Gamma_F}\ ;\ [\![\mathbb{A}]\!]_{\Gamma_U,\Gamma_F}\ [\![\mathbb{O}]\!]_{\Gamma_U,\Gamma_F}$$
$$\textsf{end} \ ;;$$

4.1 Transformation of Template Signatures

Let $\mathbb{P} = \mathbb{P}_1, \mathbb{P}_2, \ldots \mathbb{P}_m$ be the list of parameters of the template class named c_n. Each $\mathbb{P}_i$ has form: $\mathbb{P}_i = p\_n_i : typeExp_i$,
where p_n_i is the parameter name and $typeExp_i$ its type.

These parameters are transformed into parameters of the species s_n derived from the template class c_n as described in Fig. 2. Table 2 illustrates the transformation of the template class CStack given above.

$$[\![\mathbb{P}]\!]_{\Gamma_U,\Gamma_F} = [\![p\_n_1 : typeExp_1]\!]^{param}_{\Gamma_{U_1},\Gamma_F}, \quad \ldots, \quad [\![p\_n_m : typeExp_m]\!]^{param}_{\Gamma_{U_m},\Gamma_F}$$

where each $[\![p\_n_i : typeExp_i]\!]^{param}_{\Gamma_{U_i},\Gamma_F} =$

$lower(p\_n_i)$ in IntCollection	if $typeExp_i = $ Integer
$lower(p\_n_i)$ in FloatCollection	if $typeExp_i = $ Float
$lower(p\_n_i)$ in StringCollection	if $typeExp_i = $ String
$lower(p\_n_i)$ in BooleanCollection	if $typeExp_i = $ Boolean
$lower(p\_n_i)$ in UnlimitedNaturalCollection	if $typeExp_i = $ UnlimitedNatural
$upper(p\_n_i)$ is Setoid	if $typeExp_i = $ Class
$\Gamma_{s\_n_i}(\mathbb{P}_{s\_n_i}),\ upper(p\_n_i)$ is $s\_n_i(\Gamma_{s\_n}(\mathbb{P}_{s\_n_i}))$	if $typeExp_i$ is a class name c_n_i
	and s_n_i its transformation.

with:
- $upper(p\_n_i)$ returns p_n_i with its first character capitalized and $lower(p\_n_i)$ returns p_n_i with its first character in lowercase,
- $\Gamma_{U_i} = \Gamma_U$ enriched with E_i, such that $E_1 = \emptyset$, $E_2 = \{p\_n_1 : typeExp_1\}$, $E_m = \{p\_n_1 : typeExp_1, \ldots, p\_n_{m-1} : typeExp_{m-1}\}$,
- $\Gamma_{s\_n_i}(\mathbb{P}_{s\_n_i})$: returns the list of parameters of the species s_n_i,
- $s\_n_i(\Gamma_{s\_n}(\mathbb{P}_{s\_n_i}))$ is the application of the species s_n_i on its parameters,
- IntCollection: the collection that models integers in FoCaLiZe,
- FloatCollection: the collection that models floats in FoCaLiZe and
- BooleanCollection: the collection that models booleans in FoCaLiZe.

Fig. 2. General transformation of template signatures

As described in Fig.2, the parameter T:Class of the template class CStack is converted into a parameter of type Setoid and the parameter I:Integer is converted into a parameter of type IntCollection (which models integers in FoCaLiZe). The carrier type of the species SStack (derived from the template

Table 2. Transformation of the template class `CStack`

UML Template Class	FoCaLiZe species

![CStack template class diagram: T : Class, I : Integer; CStack; data : T [0..I]; head () : T; push (t : T); pop (); isFull () : Boolean; isEmpty () : Boolean; length () : Integer]	`species SStack (Obj is Setoid,`
	 `            i   in IntCollection)=`
	 `      inherit Setoid ;`
	 `representation = list(Obj);`
	 `signature newStack : list(Obj) -> Self ;`
	 `signature get_data : Self -> list(Obj);`
	 `signature length : Self -> int;`
	 `signature push : Obj -> Self -> Self ;`
	 `signature pop :  Self -> Self ;`
	 `signature head : Self -> Obj ;`
	 `signature isFull : Self -> bool ;`
	 `signature isEmpty : Self -> bool ;`
	 `end;;`

class `CStack`) is `list(Obj)`, since the multiplicity (`[0..I]`) of the attribute `data` of the template `CStack` is different from 1. The function `newStack` corresponds to the template class constructor.

4.2   Transformation of Binding Relationships

To transform a binding relationship, we use both inheritance and parameterization mechanisms in FoCaLiZe. In FoCaLiZe, if a species `S1` inherits from a parameterized species `S0`, it must instantiate all the parameters of `S0`. The instances must be sub-types of the matching formal parameters. For example, a new species `ColoredCircle` may be created by inheritance from the species `Circle` (see Tab.1) as follows:

`species ColoredPoint = inherit Point;  ... end;;`

`species ColoredCircle(CP is ColoredPoint) = inherit Circle(CP); ... end;;`

The species `ColoredCircle` substitutes the formal parameter of the species `Circle` (`P is Point`) by the actual parameter (`CP is ColoredPoint`). FoCaLiZe imposes that the species `ColoredCircle` should be derived through inheritance from the species `Point` to enable such a substitution.

Considering a classifier named c_n created from a template class $c\_template$ through a binding relationship, its general definition is as follows:

$< binding\_relationship\_def > =$ **class** c_n **bind** $c\_template$ $< \mathbb{T} >$ **end**

where c_n is the name of the bound class, $\mathbb{T} = < \mathcal{T}_1 \ \dots \ \mathcal{T}_n >$ is a list of substitutions of formal parameters with actual parameters and

$\mathcal{T}_i = formal\text{-}param\text{-}name \rightarrow actual\text{-}param, for\ i : 1..n.$

The transformation of such a binding relationship is handled as follows :

1. We create a new species s_n by inheritance from the species $s\_template$ derived from the template class $c\_template$ (see Fig.3).
2. We provide actual parameters for the species s_n by substitutions of its formal parameters with actual ones, according to the substitution list $\mathbb{T}$.

$$< binding\_relationship\_def >_{\Gamma_U,\Gamma_F} = \quad \texttt{species} \quad s\_n \ (\ [\![\mathbb{P}]\!]_{\Gamma_U,\Gamma_F})=$$
$$\texttt{inherit} \quad s\_template \ ([\![\mathbb{T}]\!]_{\Gamma_U,\Gamma_F}) \ ; \ \texttt{end;;}$$

Fig. 3. General Transformation of a binding relationship

Table 3 shows a transformation example of a binding relationship.

Table 3. Transformation of a template binding

UML Template Binding	FoCaLiZe

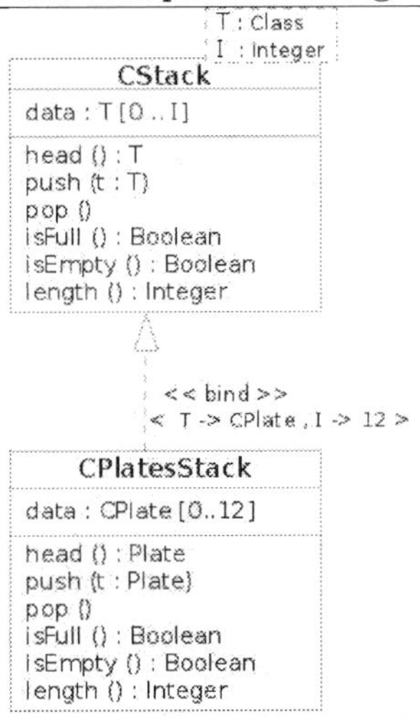 T : Class
I : Integer
CStack
data : T[0..I]
 	
head () : T
push {t : T}
pop ()
isFull () : Boolean
isEmpty () : Boolean
length () : Integer
 	
< < bind > >
< T -> CPlate , I -> 12 >
 	
CPlatesStack
data : CPlate [0..12]
 	
head () : Plate
push {t : Plate}
pop ()
isFull () : Boolean
isEmpty () : Boolean
length () : Integer
	`species SStack (Obj is Setoid,`
	`    i in IntCollection)= inherit Setoid ;`
	`representation = list(Obj);`
	`signature newStack : list(Obj) -> Self ;`
	`signature get_data : Self -> list(Obj);`
	`signature length : Self -> int;`
	`signature push : Obj -> Self -> Self ;`
	`signature pop :  Self -> Self ;`
	`signature head : Self -> Obj ;`
	`signature isFull : Self -> bool ;`
	`signature isEmpty : Self -> bool ;`
	`end;;`
	`species SPlate = inherit Setoid;  ...  end;;`
	`let e = IntCollection!createInt(12);;`
	`species SPlatesStack (T is SPlate,`
	`                     i in IntCollection)=`
	`             inherit SStack(T, e) ;`
	`...`
	`end;;`

5   From OCL Constraints to FoCaLiZe

An OCL constraint is an expression of the OCL language [17] which uses types and operations on types. We distinguish between primitive types (`Integer`, `Boolean`, `Real` and `String`), enumeration types, object types (classes of UML model) and collection types (`Collection(T)`).

To transform OCL expressions we have built an OCL framework library support. In this library we model primitive types using FoCaLiZe primitive types predefined in `basics` library (`int`, `bool`, `string` and `float`). For collection types, we have a species named `OCL_Collection(Obj is Setoid)` implementing OCL operations on collections (`forAll`, `isEmpty`, `size` ...). Other kinds of collection (`Set(T)`, `OrderedSet(T)`, `Bag(T)` and `Sequence(T)`) are also described by species which are inherited from `OCL_Collection`.

All OCL constraints are mapped into FoCaLiZe properties (`property` or `theorem`) in a particular species. For example, all the OCL constraints that have the template class `CStack` as context, will be transformed and proved in

a species that we call `SStack_constraints`. This latter, inherits the species
`SStack` derived from the class `CStack`.

The OCL expressions describing invariants, the pre-conditions and the post-
conditions are then converted into FoCaLiZe equivalent expressions. We have
proposed a formal transformation rule for each supported OCL construct.

During the transformation of OCL constraints into FoCaLiZe, we will main-
tain a typing context Γ_O in addition to our previous contexts Γ_U and Γ_F. For an
OCL element $\mathbb{S}$, we will denote $[\![\mathbb{S}]\!]_{\Gamma_U, \Gamma_F, \Gamma_O}$ its transformation into FoCaLiZe.
To be brief, we will only present the general transformation of OCL invariants
and pre and post-conditions.

Let $\mathbb{S}_i$ be an OCL invariant associated to the class named c_n. Its general
form is: $\mathbb{S}_i =$ `context` c_n `inv` : $\mathbb{E}_{inv}$
where $\mathbb{E}_{inv}$ is the OCL expression describing the invariant $\mathbb{S}_i$.

The invariant $\mathbb{S}_i$ is converted into a FoCaLiZe property as follows:

$[\![\mathbb{S}_i]\!]_{\Gamma_U, \Gamma_F, \Gamma_O}^{inv} =$ `property` inv_ident : `all` e : `Self` , $[\![\mathbb{E}_{inv}]\!]_{\Gamma_U, \Gamma_F, \Gamma_O}^{exp}$;

where,
- inv_ident is an identifier that we assign for the invariant $\mathbb{S}_i$ and
- $[\![\mathbb{E}_{inv}]\!]_{\Gamma_U, \Gamma_F, \Gamma_O}^{exp}$ is the transformation of the OCL expression describing the invariant into FoCaLiZe.

Let $\mathbb{S}_j$ be an OCL pre and post-condition associated to the operation OP of
the class named c_n. Its general form is
$\mathbb{S}_j =$ `context` c_n `::` OP_n (p_1 : $typeExp_1 \ldots p_m$: $typeExp_m$) : $returnType$
              `pre` : $\mathbb{E}_{pre}$ `post` : $\mathbb{E}_{post}$
where OP_n is the operation name, $p_1 \ldots p_m$ are the operation parameters,
$typeExp_1 \ldots typeExp_m$ their corresponding types and $\mathbb{E}_{pre}$ and $\mathbb{E}_{post}$ are the
OCL expressions describing the pre and the post conditions. An OCL pre and
post-condition is converted into a FoCaLiZe implication (*pre-condition* $\Rightarrow$ *postcondition*) as follows:

$[\![\mathbb{S}_j]\!]_{\Gamma_U, \Gamma_F, \Gamma_O}^{prepost} =$ `property` pre_post_ident :
   `all` e : `Self`,
   `all` x_1 : $[\![typeExp_1]\!]_{\Gamma_U, \Gamma_F}$, ... ,
   `all` x_m : $[\![typeExp_m]\!]_{\Gamma_U, \Gamma_F}$, $[\![\mathbb{E}_{pre}]\!]_{\Gamma_U, \Gamma_F, \Gamma_O}^{exp}$ -> $[\![\mathbb{E}_{post}]\!]_{\Gamma_U, \Gamma_F, \Gamma_O}^{exp}$;

where,
- pre_post_ident is an identifier that we assign for $\mathbb{S}_j$,
- $x_1 \ldots x_m$ are bound variables, $x_1 = lower(p_1)$, ..., $x_m = lower(p_m)$,
- $[\![typeExp_i]\!]_{\Gamma_U, \Gamma_F}$ is the transformation of variable types (similar to type expression
  transformation in Fig. 2) and
- $[\![\mathbb{E}_{pre}]\!]_{\Gamma_U, \Gamma_F, \Gamma_O}^{exp}$ ($[\![\mathbb{E}_{post}]\!]_{\Gamma_U, \Gamma_F, \Gamma_O}^{exp}$) is the transformation of the OCL expressions
  describing the pre (post) conditions into FoCaLiZe.

Table 4 presents the transformation of invariants stated on the template class
`CStack`. It also presents an example of transformation of pre and post-conditions

associated to the operation `push(t:T)` of our class `CStack`. This latter constraint expresses that if a stack is empty, then it remains empty when an element is pushed and then popped. The symbol ~~ indicates the negation in FoCaLiZe.

Table 4. Example of OCL constraints transformation

OCL	FoCaLiZe
context CStack	species SStack_constraints
inv : self.allInstances ->	(Obj is Setoid, i in IntCollection,
forAll(s|	S is SStack(Obj, i),
s.isEmpty() implies	C is Ocl_Collection(S))=
s.length() = 0)	inherit SStack(Obj, i)
	property inv_SStack_1 : all s : Self,
inv : self.isEmpty() implies	isEmpty(s) -> (length(s) = 0);
not(self.isFull())	property inv_SStack_2 : all s : Self,
	isEmpty(s) -> ~~(isFull(s));
-- pre and post condition	property pre_post_push_2: all e : Obj,
context CStack :: push(t:T)	all s : Self,
pre : self.isEmpty()	isEmpty (s) -> isEmpty(pop(push(e, s)));
Post: let s = self.pop() in	...
(s.isEmpty())	end ;;

6   A Framework for Formal Proofs

Our goal is to provide a framework that generates automatically a FoCaLiZe abstract specifications from an UML template class with OCL constraint. Then a FoCaLiZe user will be able to prove the derived properties using the automated theorem prover Zenon.

In general, we adopt the following proof process (see Fig.4):

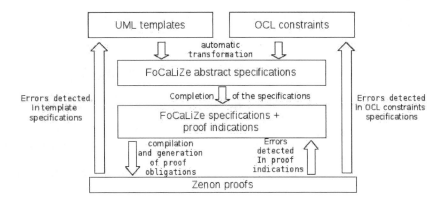

Fig. 4. Proof Framework

1. Complete the FoCaLiZe abstract specifications by implementing all related functions.
2. Introduce proof indications using the FoCaLiZe proof language.
3. Compile the FoCaLiZe source using the command *focalizec*. This latter invokes the command *zvtov* to achieve the proofs by Zenon (the automated theorem prover of FoCaLiZe).

From an UML/OCL model, an abstract FoCaLiZe specification is generated. Then, a FoCaLiZe user needs only to complete the specification by implementing all derived methods to obtain a complete specification. Finally, when compiling the FoCaLiZe source, proof obligations are generated.

If a proof fails, the FoCaLiZe compiler indicates the line of code responsible for the error. In this case, The FoCaLiZe developer analyses the source in order to correct and/or complete the UML model, and then restarts the development cycle.

There are two main kinds of errors: either Zenon could not find a proof automatically, or there are inconsistencies in the original UML/OCL model. In the first case the developer interaction is needed to give appropriate hints to prove the properties, while in the second case we must go back to the original UML/OCL model to correct and/or complete it.

To illustrate how UML errors are detected, let us study the transformation of the following binding relationship:

```
species C_spec =
  representation = int;   end ;;
species D_spec =
  representation = string;   end ;;
species A_spec (Q is C_spec) =   end;;
species B_spec (P is D_spec) = inherit A_spec(P);
  end;;
```

When compiling the FoCaLiZe source, we get the following error message: "`Collection 'P' is not a subspecies of 'Q'`". This error expresses that since D is not a sub-type of C, then the substitution `T -> D` is not correct.

To clarify the proof process, we present the proof of the property `pre_post_push_2` (see Tab.4) derived from the pre and post-condition associated to the operation `push(t:T)` of our template class `CStack`. First, we obtain the species `SStack` (Tab.2) and the species `SStack_constra- ints`. This latter inherits from the species `SStack` and transforms all OCL constraints specified on the template class `CStack`. For brevity, we focus on the property `pre_post_push_2`. Then, we provide definitions to all inherited signatures and we introduce proof scripts to prove theorems as follows:

```
species SStack_constraints(Obj is Setoid, i in IntCollection,
                  S is SStack(Obj, i),
                  C is Ocl_Collection(S) ) = inherit SStack(Obj, i);
let newStack(x: list(Obj)):Self = x; let get_data (x: Self):list(Obj)=x;
let equal(x:Self, y:Self): bool = (x = y);
let isFull(x:Self):bool = (length(x) = (IntCollection!to_int(i))) ;
let isEmpty(x:Self):bool = (length(x) = 0) ;
let push (o: Obj, y: Self):Self =
     if ~~(isFull(y)) then newStack(o::get_data(y))
     else focalize_error ("The stack is full");
let rec length(x: Self):int = match (x) with
     | [] -> 0   | y :: z -> 1 + length(z);
let head(x: Self):Obj = match get_data(x) with
     | [] -> focalize_error ("The stack is empty")
     | y :: z -> y;
let pop(x: Self):Self = match get_data(x) with
     | [] -> focalize_error ("The stack is empty")
     | y :: z -> newStack(z);
property inv_SStack_1 : all s : Self, isEmpty(s) -> (length(s) = 0);
property inv_SStack_2 : all s : Self , isEmpty (s) -> ~~(isFull(s)) ;
property pre_post_push_1 : all e : Obj, all s : Self,
                   ~~( isFull(s)) ->  equal(pop (push (e, s)), s);
property pre_post_push_2 : all e : Obj , all s : Self ,
  isEmpty(s) -> isEmpty(pop(push(e, s)));
proof of pre_post_push_2 =
   <1>1 assume e : Obj, s : Self,
   hypothesis H1 : isEmpty(s),
   prove isEmpty (pop(push(e, s)))
   <2>1 prove  equal( pop ( push (e, s ) ), s )
        by hypothesis H1  property inv_SStack_2 , pre_post_push_1
   <2>2 prove   isEmpty(pop (push (e, s ) ))
        by hypothesis H1 step <2>1
        definition of equal property equal_symmetric
   <2>3 qed by step <2>2
   <1>2 conclude ;
 end;;
```

The proof of the property `pre_post_push_2` is composed of several steps (`<1>1`, `<2>1` …) which are written in the FoCaLiZe proof language. At each step we ask Zenon to search for a proof using the hints we provide.

Finally, the compilation of the FoCaLiZe source (*stack.fcl*) ensures the correctness of the specification. If no error has occurred, this means that the compilation, code generation and Coq verification were successful.

7   Related Work

Several works are interested in the transformation from UML into B language based tools such as [18, 19], UML2B [20], UML-B [21]. However, they do not consider UML templates and template bindings since B language based tools do not provide such features. Formal parameters of an abstract machine may only be scalar parameters or set parameters [4]. The formal parameters of an abstract machine can not be an implementation (the ultimate step in B language refinements) or another abstract machine of the model. This limitation makes it difficult to model the UML templates with B constructs.

Alloy [5] is another formal tool which has been recently used to check the consistency of UML/OCL models. In works such as [22] and [23], an UML class is modeled by a signature (a set of atoms). At signature level, there is no kind of parameterization or binding relationships. The only architecture feature is the `extends` (simple inheritance in UML) relationship between signatures. At module level[3], Alloy enables to parameterize one module with signatures that must be instantiated during module importation. In this way, it is not possible to import abstract modules (at specification level). In Alloy, there is no mechanisms for binding module parameters to create a new module.

The Maude system [6] is also used in formalizing UML/OCL models such as in [24, 25]. To our knowledge, there is no particular work concerning the transformation from UML template and template binding into Maude. Nevertheless, Maude allows to specify a module parameterized with formal parameters. Then, a new module can be created by binding of actual parameters with formal ones. We think that this feature enables to formalize UML template and template binding. However, Maude lacks specification features such as function redefinition and late binding mechanisms which are often used in parallel with parameterization.

Other formal tools based on higher order logic (HOL) such as HOL-OCL [26] are concentrated in producing OCL evaluator tools. They provide a theorem proving environments for UML/OCL based on rewriting logic. But, they do not support such features as template classes or binding relationships.

One can notice that UML template and template binding are ignored in all the aforementioned works, while thanks to the specification power of the FoCaLiZe language, these features are naturally supported in our proposal. In fact, FoCaLiZe enables the use of a species as a parameter of another species, even at the specification level. Later on, the collection and late-binding mechanisms ensure that all methods appearing in a species (used as formal parameter) are indeed implemented and all properties are proved.

8   Conclusion and Perspectives

In this paper, we have proposed a formal transformation of UML template classes annotated with OCL constraints into FoCaLiZe, defined in the following way:

A parameterized species is associated to each template class: formal parameters of a template class are converted into formal parameters of the derived

---

[3] A module is a structure grouping some paragraphs, each paragraph may be a signature, fact, function, predicate, assertion, run command or check command.

species, and **bind** relationship is formalized through inheritance and parameter substitution mechanisms in FoCaLiZe. The representation of each associated species is a cartesian product type that represents the state of the object. Class operations are converted into functions of the derived species and OCL constraints (class invariants, pre-condition and post-condition) correspond to FoCaLiZe properties.

To implement the presented approach, we propose to use the XMI technology (XML Metadata Interchange) through an UML tool that supports the UML2 constructs such as the UML2 Eclipse plug-in. We parse the XMI document to translate it into the UML proposed syntax (using an XSLT stylesheet), so that it is possible to apply the transformation rules that we have proposed for each UML construct. The correctness of the transformation is ensured by the proposed formal rules.

The presented work support most of UML template class specification features. In addition to the **bind** relationship, it supports encapsulation, inheritance and late-binding which permit to derive a formal specification expressed through a species hierarchy that matches the original UML model. To our knowledge, there is no formal tool that supports the UML template classes features the way they are taken care of in the FoCaLiZe environment.

This approach suggest as a direct application, the collaboration of UML template classes and FoCaLiZe in the same framework (see Fig.4). It consists in using an UML template class annotated with OCL constraints as a starting point for a FoCaLiZe development to benefit from both formalisms.

As future works, first we plan to extend our mapping to deal with UML template packages, UML packages specified with formal parameters. Second, we will consider larger subsets of OCL. In particular, we want to deal with the sub-types of the gene-ral collection type `Collection(T)` which are `Set(T)`, `OrderedSet(T)`, `Bag(T)` and `Sequence(T)`.

References

1. Sunyé, G., Le Guennec, A., Jézéquel, J.-M.: Design Patterns Application in UML. In: Bertino, E. (ed.) ECOOP 2000. LNCS, vol. 1850, pp. 44–62. Springer, Heidelberg (2000)
2. Kienzle, J., Al Abed, W., Fleurey, F., Jézéquel, J.-M., Klein, J.: Aspect-Oriented Design with Reusable Aspect Models. In: Katz, S., Mezini, M., Kienzle, J. (eds.) Transactions on AOSD VII. LNCS, vol. 6210, pp. 272–320. Springer, Heidelberg (2010)
3. Cuccuru, A., Radermacher, A., Gérard, S., Terrier, F.: Constraining Type Parameters of UML 2 Templates with Substitutable Classifiers. In: Schürr, A., Selic, B. (eds.) MODELS 2009. LNCS, vol. 5795, pp. 644–649. Springer, Heidelberg (2009)
4. Abrial, J.R.: The B-Book: Assigning Programs to Meanings. Cambridge University Press (2005)
5. Jackson, D.: Software Abstractions: Logic, Language and Anlysis. MIT Press (2012)
6. Clavel, M., Durán, F., Eker, S., Lincoln, P., Martí-Oliet, N., Meseguer, J., Talcott, C.: All About Maude - A High-Performance Logical Framework. LNCS, vol. 4350. Springer, Heidelberg (2007)

7. Nipkow, T., Paulson, L.C., Wenzel, M.: Isabelle/HOL. LNCS, vol. 2283. Springer, Heidelberg (2002)
8. Hardin, T., Francois, P., Pierre, W., Damien, D.: FoCaLiZe: Tutorial and Reference Manual, version 0.8.0. CNAM/INRIA/LIP6 (2012), http://focalize.inria.fr
9. Ayrault, P., Hardin, T., Pessaux, F.: Development Life-Cycle of Critical Software under FoCal. Electronic Notes in Theoretical Computer Science 243, 15–31 (2009)
10. Doligez, D.: The Zenon Tool. Software and Documentations freely available at http://focal.inria.fr/zenon/
11. Coq: The Coq Proof Assistant, Tutorial and Reference Manual, version 8.4. INRIA – LIP – LRI – LIX – PPS (2012), Distribution available at http://coq.inria.fr/
12. Fechter, S.: Sémantique des Traits Orientés Objet de Focal. PhD thesis, Paris 6 (2005)
13. François, P.: Another Tutorial for FoCaLize: Playing with Proofs (2013)
14. Dubois, C., Hardin, T., Donzeau-Gouge, V.: Building Certified Components within FOCAL. Trends in Functional Programming 5, 33–48 (2006)
15. OMG: UML: Superstructure, version 2.4 (January 2011), http://www.omg.org/spec/UML/2.4/Infrastructure
16. Delahaye, D., Étienne, J., Donzeau-Gouge, V.: Producing UML Models from Focal Specifications: An Application to Airport Security Regulations. In: 2nd IFIP/IEEE International Symposium on Theoretical Aspects of Software Engineering, pp. 121–124 (2008)
17. OMG: OCL: Object Constraint Language 2.3.1 (January 2012), http://www.omg.org/spec/{OCL}
18. Snook, C., Savicks, V., Butler, M.: Verification of UML Models by Translation to UML-B. In: Aichernig, B.K., de Boer, F.S., Bonsangue, M.M. (eds.) Formal Methods for Components and Objects. LNCS, vol. 6957, pp. 251–266. Springer, Heidelberg (2011)
19. Ledang, H., Souquières, J., Charles, S., et al.: Argouml+ B: Un Outil de Transformation Systématique de Spécifications UML en B. In: Approches Formelles dans l'Assistance au Développement de Logiciels (2003)
20. Hazem, L., Levy, N., Marcano-Kamenoff, R.: UML2B: Un Outil pour la Génération de Mod'eles Formels. In: AFADL (2004)
21. Snook, C., Butler, M.: UML-B: Formal Modeling and Design Aided by UML. ACM Transactions on Software Engineering and Methodology (TOSEM) 15(1), 92–122 (2006)
22. Cunha, A., Garis, A., Riesco, D.: Translating between Alloy Specifications and UML Class Diagrams Annotated with OCL Constraints. Software & Systems Modeling, 1–21 (2013)
23. Anastasakis, K., Bordbar, B., Georg, G., Ray, I.: UML2Alloy: A Challenging Model Transformation. In: Engels, G., Opdyke, B., Schmidt, D.C., Weil, F. (eds.) MODELS 2007. LNCS, vol. 4735, pp. 436–450. Springer, Heidelberg (2007)
24. Durán, F., Gogolla, M., Roldán, M.: Tracing Properties of UML and OCL Models with Maude. arXiv preprint arXiv:1107.0068 (2011)
25. Mokhati, F., Sahraoui, B., Bouzaher, S., Kimour, M.T.: A Tool for Specifying and Validating Agents' Interaction Protocols: From Agent UML to Maude. Object Technology 9(3) (2010)
26. Brucker, A.D., Wolff, B.: HOL-OCL: A Formal Proof Environment for UML/OCL. In: Fiadeiro, J.L., Inverardi, P. (eds.) FASE 2008. LNCS, vol. 4961, pp. 97–100. Springer, Heidelberg (2008)

Integrating Event-B Modelling and Discrete-Event Simulation to Analyse Resilience of Data Stores in the Cloud

Linas Laibinis[1], Benjamin Byholm[1], Inna Pereverzeva[1,2], Elena Troubitsyna[1], Kuan Eeik Tan[3], and Ivan Porres[1]

[1] Åbo Akademi University, Turku, Finland
[2] Turku Centre for Computer Science, Turku, Finland
[3] F-Secure Corporation, Helsinki, Finland
{linas.laibinis,benjamin.byholm,inna.pereverzeva}@abo.fi,
{elena.troubitsyna,ivan.porres}@abo.fi,
kuan.eeik.tan@f-secure.com

Abstract. Ensuring resilience of large data stores in the cloud is a challenging engineering issue. It requires the development techniques that allow the designers to predict the main resilience characteristics — fault tolerance and performance — at the early design stages. In this paper, we experiment with integrating Event-B modelling with discrete-event simulation. Event-B allows us to reason about correctness and data integrity properties of data stores, while discrete-event simulation in SimPy enables quantitative assessment of performance and reliability. Since testing in a real cloud environment is expensive and time-consuming, the proposed approach offers several benefits in industrial settings.

Keywords: Formal modelling, Event-B, discrete-event simulation.

1 Introduction

Development and verification of cloud-based data stores constitutes a challenging engineering task. To guarantee resilience and satisfy Service Level Agreement (SLA) that regulates service behaviour with respect to its customers, the developers should ensure two main properties – data integrity and performance. To achieve this goal, F-Secure Corporation – a company providing secure data storage solutions – relies on massive replication and the non-transactional approach.

In our previous work [10], we have undertaken formal modelling of resilient data store and logically defined data integrity properties of different architectural solutions. To analyse performance/fault tolerance ratio of architectural alternatives, we have attempted to integrate quantitative verification. However, complexity of the system turned out to be prohibitive for probabilistic model checkers and the quantitative analysis, which is essential for engineering resilient cloud data stores, has not been performed.

To address this issue, in this paper we propose an approach to integrating formal modelling in Event-B with discrete-event simulation in SimPy [14] – a

E. Albert and E. Sekerinski (Eds.): IFM 2014, LNCS 8739, pp. 103–119, 2014.

library and development framework in Python. Event-B [2] is a state-based approach to correct-by-construction system development. A powerful tool support – the Rodin platform [11] – automates the development and provides us with a scalable proof-based verification. In this paper, we rely on Event-B to formally represent and verify system-level logical properties, while simulation in SimPy is used for the quantitative analysis. SimPy [14] is a popular discrete-event simulation framework offering versatility and attractive visualisation features.

To facilitate an integration with SimPy and discussions with the industrial engineers, we have created a simple graphical notation – a process-oriented model. The notation is light-weight and introduces only the core concepts of the domain together with the key artefacts required for formal modelling and simulation. Such a graphical model defines the component interactions, representation of statistical parameters as well as reactions on faults. The process-oriented model plays the role of a unifying blue-print of the system and allows us to define the structure of the Event-B and simulation models as well as provide an easy-to-comprehend visual representation to the engineers. Once the initial models are derived from the process-oriented model, the Event-B model is refined to represent and verify data integrity properties, while the simulation model is executed to analyse performance/reliability ratio, e.g., under different service and failure rates.

We believe that the proposed approach constitutes a promising direction in the development of complex resilient systems. A combination of formal modelling and simulation amplifies the benefits of both approaches. Reliance on formal modelling not only guarantees system correctness but also increases confidence in the created simulation models, while simulation supports quantitative assessment of various design alternatives.

The paper is structured as follows. Section 2 briefly presents our case study, resilient cloud data storage, which serves as a motivation of this work. Section 3 overviews the approaches we aim to integrate – Event-B and Discrete-Event Simulation. Our integration proposal is described in detail and illustrated by a small example in Section 4. In Section 5, we demonstrate how to apply the proposed approach to perform quantitative assessment of our case study. Finally, Section 6 overviews the related work and gives some concluding remarks.

2   Resilient Data Storage in the Cloud

Our work is motivated by an industrial case study – a resilient cloud data storage [10]. The system is developed by F-Secure to provide highly performant and secure storage of client data on the cloud. Essentially, a cloud data storage can be seen as a networked online data storage available for its clients as a cloud service. Cloud data storage providers should ensure that their customers can safely and easily store their content and access it from their devices. Therefore, there is a clear demand to achieve both resilience and high performance in handling data.

Write-ahead logging (WAL) is a standard data base technique for ensuring data integrity. The main principle of WAL is to apply the requested changes to data files only after they have been logged, i.e., after the log has been stored in the persistent storage. The WAL mechanism ensures fault tolerance because, in case of a crash, the system can recover using the log. The WAL mechanism also helps to optimise performance, since only the log file should be written to the permanent storage to guarantee that a transaction is (eventually) committed.

The WAL mechanism has been studied under the reliable persistent storage assumption, i.e., if the disk containing the log never crashes. However, implementing such a highly-reliable data store in the cloud is rather unfeasible. Therefore, to ensure resilience, F-Secure has chosen a solution that combines WAL with replication. The resulting system – distributed data store (DDS) – consists of a number of nodes distributed across different physical locations. One of the nodes, called *master*, is appointed to serve incoming data requests from DDS clients and report on success or failure of such requests. The remaining nodes, called *standby* or *worker nodes*, contain replicas of the stored data.

Each request received by the master is recorded in the *master log* and then applied to the stored data. After this, an acknowledgement is sent to the client. The standby nodes are constantly monitoring and streaming the master log records into their own logs, before applying them to their persistent data. If the master crashes, one of the standby nodes becomes a new master in its stead.

DDS can implement different models of logging. In the *asynchronous model*, the client request is acknowledged after the master node has performed the required modifications in its persistent storage. In the *synchronous* model, the transaction is committed only after all the replica nodes have written into their persistent storage, i.e., synchronised with the master node. Obviously, such logging models deliver different resilience guarantees in cases of component crashes.

In our previous work [10], we have formally defined and verified data integrity properties for each described architecture using the Event-B framework. Our development provided the designers with a *qualitative* assessment of system resilience. However, while developing cloud software, it is also vital to obtain a *quantitative* assessment of resilience to optimise the choice of a resource management strategy. Usually such an assessment is achieved via testing. However, testing in the cloud requires the same usage of the resources as the real system operation, and hence is expensive. Moreover, it is often hard to reproduce the conditions of the peak load and hence obtain the insights on system resilience during the stress conditions. Therefore, there is a strong demand on the integrated approaches that enable both qualitative and quantitative analysis of resilience.

The earlier in the development process such an analysis can be performed, the better architecture can be build. To address this issue, in this paper we propose an approach to integrating formal modelling in Event-B and discrete-event simulation. Next we give a short background overview of both techniques.

3   Background

Event-B. Event-B is a state-based formal approach that promotes the correct-by-construction development paradigm and formal verification by theorem proving. In Event-B, a system model is specified using the notion of an *abstract state machine* [2]. An abstract state machine encapsulates the model state, represented as a collection of variables, and defines operations on the state, i.e., it describes the dynamic behaviour of a modelled system. The important system properties to be preserved are defined as model *invariants*. A machine usually has the accompanying component, called *context*. A context may include user-defined carrier sets, constants and their properties (defined as model *axioms*).

The dynamic behaviour of the system is defined by a collection of atomic *events*. Generally, an event has the following form:

$$e \;\widehat{=}\; \textbf{any } a \textbf{ where } G_e \textbf{ then } R_e \textbf{ end},$$

where e is the event's name, a is the list of local variables, and (the event *guard*) G_e is a predicate over the model state. The body of an event is defined by a *multiple* (possibly nondeterministic) assignment to the system variables. In Event-B, this assignment is semantically defined as the next-state relation R_e. The event guard defines the conditions under which the event is *enabled*, i.e., its body can be executed. If several events are enabled at the same time, any of them can be chosen for execution nondeterministically.

Event-B employs a top-down refinement-based approach to system development. A development starts from an abstract system specification. In a sequence of refinement steps we gradually reduce system nondeterminism and introduce detailed design decisions. The consistency of Event-B models, i.e., invariant preservation, correctness of refinement steps, is demonstrated by discharging the relevant proof obligations. The Rodin platform [11] provides an automated support for modelling and verification.

Discrete-Event Simulation. Simulation is the act of imitating how an actual system behaves over time [3]. To achieve this goal, a simulation generates an artificial system history, thereby enabling analysis of its general behaviour. It also allows sensitivity analysis, which can be highly beneficial in the system design.

Table 1 shows an ad-hoc simulation of a bank with a single teller and 5 customers. Customers arrive at a uniformly distributed rate between 1 and 10 minutes. A customer requires a dedicated service from the teller in between 1 to 6 minutes. Each row represents a customer, with an identifier in column (1). Next columns show the generated random inter-arrival times, (2), specific computed arrival time for each customer, (3), and generated random service times, (4). From this information, we can derive a system history and study its performance. The conducted simulation allows us to obtain the following system estimates:

Average time in system $\frac{18}{5} = 3.6$ min
The clerk is idle $\frac{9}{25} = 36$ % of the time
Average queuing time $\frac{2}{5} = 0.4$ min
Ratio of customers having to queue $\frac{1}{5} = 20$ %
Average queuing time for those that queued $\frac{2}{1} = 2$ min

One type of simulation is known as discrete-event simulation (DES). In a DES, system state remains constant over an interval of time between two consecutive

Table 1. Ad-hoc simulation of a bank system with one teller

(1)	(2)	(3)	(4)	(5)	(6)	(7)	(8)	(9)
Client Count	Arrival Interim	Arrival Time	Service Time	Service Begins	Service Ends	System Time	Idle Time	Queue Time
1	—	0	5	0	5	5	0	0
2	3	3	2	5	7	4	0	2
3	6	9	5	9	14	5	2	0
4	10	19	3	19	22	3	5	0
5	5	24	1	24	25	1	2	0
						18	9	2

events. Thus events signify occurrences that change the system state. Events can be classified as either internal or external. *Internal events*, e.g., the bank teller has finished serving a customer, occur within the modelled system. *External events*, like customer arrivals, occur outside the system, but still affect it. A simulation is run by a mechanism that repeatedly moves simulated time forward to the starting time of the next scheduled event, until there are no more events [13].

Architecturally, a DES system consists of a number of *entities* (e.g., components, processes, agents, etc.), which are either producers or recipients of discrete events. Entities can have *attributes*, e.g., the busy status of the bank teller. There are two kinds of entities: *dynamic entities*, moving into or out of the system, like the bank customer, and *static entities*, serving other entities, like the bank teller. Static entities can often be represented as *resources*. Waiting for a particular event to occur can lead to a *delay*, lasting for an indefinite amount of time. In other cases, the time estimate may be known apriori, e.g., when bank customers receive service by the teller. Events can be also *interrupted* and pre-empted, e.g., in reaction to component failures or pre-defined high-priority events.

There are four primary simulation paradigms [3]: process-interaction, event-scheduling, activity scanning, and the three-phase method. Our simulation model uses SimPy [14], a simulation framework based on process-interaction in Python.

Motivation and Plan for Integration. DES constitutes an attractive technology for quantitative assessment of various characteristics of cloud applications. Firstly, it allows the designers to perform various "what-if" type of analysis that demonstrates sensitivity of the service architecture to changes of its parameters. For instance, it gives an insight on how the system reacts on peak-loads, how adding new resources affects its performance, what is the relationships between the degree of redundancy and fault tolerance, etc. Secondly, while simulating the service behaviour, the designers also obtain the insights on which parameters should be monitored at run-time to optimise a resource allocation strategy. However, to obtain all the above-mentioned benefits, we have to ensure that the simulation models are correct and indeed representative of the actual system. This is achievable via integration of simulation with formal modelling.

To adequately model complex cloud services, we need a framework with a good automated tool support and scalability. We have chosen Event-B because it satisfies these criteria and has been successfully applied to model data stores in the cloud [10]. However, the fine granularity of Event-B models made it cumbersome to communicate the modelling decisions across a diverse team of experts. Therefore, we needed an easy-to-understand light-weight graphical notation that would allow us to generate both Event-B and simulation models in a compatible way.

One alternative to creating a visual system model would be to choose one of the existing architectural languages. However, to achieve simplicity and comprehensibility, we decided against it. The introduced graphical notation, called a *process-oriented model*, is domain-specific and minimal in a sense that each element is introduced only if it is required either in our formal modelling or a DES representation. It captures only the key concepts of the domain and hence alleviates the burden of customising a general-purpose architectural language. The proposed approach also gives us a full control over defining the interpretation of all elements of the introduced graphical notation in Event-B and SimPy models, thus ensuring a mutually-compatible derivation of these models. Once the models are derived from the common process-oriented model, each of them is used independently. The Event-B model is refined to reason about the logical system properties, while the simulation model is exercised to perform the quantitative analysis. Obviously, if the simulation indicates that the chosen architecture is unable to fulfil the target SLA, the architecture should be amended together with its process-oriented model. This inevitably leads to redesign of the corresponding Event-B and SimPy models to faithfully represent the changed architecture.

As a result of such integration, we gain more flexibility and control over the simulation models. We can experiment more freely with different service configurations and perform sensitivity analysis in a more efficient way. The formal backbone gives us more confidence in the simulation models and we can clearly see the entire effect of model changes, thus alleviating the verification burden.

4   Process-Oriented Model

In this section we will present a process-oriented system model that serves as a "common ground" for both formal modelling in Event-B and simulation in SimPy. The model has the associated graphical notation for representing system architecture in terms of its units (components and processes) and interaction mechanisms between these units.

In general, we are interested in modelling, simulating, and analysing the systems that have the following characteristics:

- A system consists of a number of parallel processes, interacting asynchronously by means of discrete events;
- System processes can be grouped together into a number of components. The discrete events triggering interactions between the component processes then become *internal process events*, while the remaining discrete events can be considered as the *external component interface* for its interaction with other components or the environment;
- Within a process, execution follows the pre-defined scenario expressed in terms of functional blocks (activities) and transitions between them. Each such functional block is typically associated with particular incoming events the process reacts to and/or outgoing events it produces;

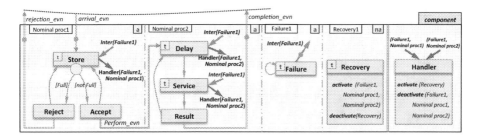

Fig. 1. Example of a system component

- A system component can fail and (in some cases) recover. In other words, component failures and recovery mechanisms are a part of the component description. They can be described as the special component processes simulating different types of failures and recovery procedures of the component;
- Some events (e.g., component failures) should be reacted on immediately upon their occurrence, thus interrupting the process current activities. Such special events (*interrupts*) are explicitly described in the component description and associated with dedicated functional blocks (interruption handlers).

An example of such a component is graphically presented on Fig.1. The component interface consists of one incoming event (*arrival_evn*) and two outgoing events (*rejection_evn* and *completion_evn*). The component itself contains two processes describing its "nominal" behaviour: the first one stores requests to perform a certain service, and the second one performs a requested service and returns the produced results. The internal event *perform_evn* triggers the request execution by the second process. In addition, the component includes the *Failure* and *Recovery* processes to simulate possible component failures and its recovery. More specifically, the *Failure* process generates an internal interrupt event for both nominal processes, which is then handled by the *Handler* block. In general, a component can have several such processes and handler blocks.

In our process-oriented model, time progress is associated with either waiting for an incoming event or an internal activity requiring time (e.g., data processing of a received service request, see Service in Fig.1). Only such functional blocks (marked by "t" in a diagram) can be interrupted.

Some functional blocks may indicate activities related to accessing the underlying storage resource (e.g., putting the received data into a buffer). Such blocks are decorated by a circle from below, for example, see Store in Fig.1.

The component state is mostly hidden in a process-oriented model, focusing instead on the required control flow and interaction between the processes. However, sometimes we need to reveal a part of this state to be able to constrain incoming or outgoing events as well as internal transitions between functional blocks. For this purpose, we use the following pre-defined component attributes:

- (for each component) the component unique identifier id;
- (for each process) the process activity status PAS, which can be either *Active* or *Inactive*. Changing this attribute to *Inactive* allows us to explicitly block

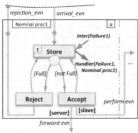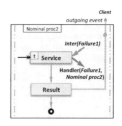

Fig. 2. Using component's attributes   **Fig. 3.** Dynamic creation of processes

a particular process. The process will remain blocked and thus irresponsive to any events until the attribute is not changed to Active again;

- (for each storage-related functional block) the storage availability status SAS, which can be either *Full* or *NotFull*. The attribute value reflects whether the operation of adding data into the storage can be successfully completed;

- (for each component) the component operational mode Mode, which can be one of pre-defined values for this type of a component. For instance, the component on Fig.1 can be used in two different modes, either as a "server" or a "slave". This assumption allows us to redefine the description of the Nominal proc1, see Fig.2. If the mode is "server", it forwards the request to another (slave) component by generating the outgoing event *forward_evn*.

If the attribute we are referring to is clear from the context, we will use a shorthand notation [attribute_value] to stand for the condition *attribute_name* = *attribute_value*. For instance, in Fig.2 the transitions of *Nominal_proc1* from its Store to either Reject or Accept are dependant on whether the used storage is currently full or not. We specify this by the added conditions [Full] and [not Full] on the corresponding process transitions. Similarly, the outgoing events *perform_evn* and *forward_evn* for Accept are created depending on the component role, which is reflected by the conditions [server] and [slave] on the corresponding arrows. We also assume that all the events and internal transitions have implicit conditions [Active], checking that the process in question is not currently blocked.

If we need to change the attribute value, we again use the notation [attribute_value], however within a functional block. In addition, for quickly changing the process activity status for a number of processes, we employ another shorthand notation: **activate(Proc1, ..., ProcN)** and **deactivate(Proc1, ..., ProcN)**.

By default, we assume that the processes are created and terminated together with their encompassing component. However, sometimes we need to dynamically create and terminate component processes. Let us consider an alternative version of *Nominal_proc2*, presented in Fig.3. Here the process *Nominal_proc2* is created each time a request from *Nominal_proc1* is ready to be served. Moreover, once the outgoing event for successful service completion is created, the process is terminated (depicted as a black circle).

To collect the quantitative information about the considered system, we assume the implicit presence of a monitor component. The information is collected about the occurrence of particular events of interest. The arrows representing the events of a component to be monitored by such a component are decorated with small circles in a process-oriented model. If the system contains other components, they should be explicitly composed by matching their external interfaces.

"**Common ground**". A process-oriented model serves as a basis for both Event-B development and system simulation in SimPy. Translating a process-oriented model into Event-B gives us the starting point of our formal development with the already fixed system architecture and control flow between main system components. The corresponding system properties are explicitly formulated and proved as system invariants. Additional properties (e.g., the relationships between processes being active or inactive) can be verified too. By the definition of Event-B refinement, the following refined models preserve these properties, elaborating only on the newly introduced data structures and intermediate system transitions.

While translating a process-oriented model to SimPy, we augment the resulting code with concrete values for its basic quantitative characteristics, such as data arrival, service, and failure rates. This allows us to compare system performance and reliability for different system parameter configurations. If a satisfactory configuration values can be found and thus re-design of the base process-oriented model is not needed, the simulation results does not affect the Event-B formal development and can be considered completely complementary to it.

Translating to Event-B. Here we present general guidelines how to proceed from a process-oriented model of a system component to the corresponding Event-B specification. From now on, we refer to Event-B events as operations to avoid confusion with DES events. During the translation, the respective elements of a process-oriented model may become one or several Event-B operations, the corresponding guard or action expressions within a particular operation, or the invariant predicates to be verified for the resulting Event-B model. Moreover, a number of Event-B variables standing for component attributes, incoming or outgoing events, as well as the variables ensuring the required control flow have to be introduced. The translation guidelines are summarised in Fig.4.

We will demonstrate the use of these guidelines on the component example from the previous section (Fig.1). Each functional block of the process-oriented model is translated to one or two Event-B operations. Two operations are needed in the cases when the block in question is interruptible. Then the first operation specifies a possible start of the block, while the second one models its completion. For instance, the block Store will be represented as two Event-B operations:

$Store\_step1 \;\hat{=}$
when $Nominal\_proc1 = Active$
$\qquad Arrived\_env = FALSE$
then $Arrived\_env :\in BOOL$
end

$Store\_step2 \;\hat{=}$
any j
when $Nominal\_proc1 = Active$
$\qquad failure\_interrupt = TRUE$
$\qquad Arrived\_evn = TRUE$
$\qquad j \in JOBS \setminus \{NILL\}$
then $ArrivedJob := j$
$\qquad Arrived\_evn := FALSE$
$\qquad Storage\_status :\in \{Full, NotFull\}$
end

Here the boolean variables *Arrived_evn* and *failure_interrupt* model occurrence of the corresponding system events. Moreover, the process activity attributes (e.g., *Nominal_proc1*) are represented as eponymous variables that can take values from the set {*Active,Inactive*}. Similarly, the storage availability attribute is introduced as a separate variable *Storage_status* taking values from {*Full,NotFull*}. The other functional blocks (Reject, Service, Delay, Result) are modelled in a similar way.

During the system execution a failure of the component might happen at any time. In that case, the component halts its nominal processes and is only involved in its recovery process. Upon successful recovery, the component reactivates its nominal processes. The corresponding blocks Failure and Handler are as follows:

Failure $\widehat{=}$

 when $Failure\_proc = Active$
  $failure\_interrupt = FALSE$
 then $failure\_interrupt :\in BOOL$
end

Handler $\widehat{=}$

 when $failure\_interrupt = TRUE$
 then $Failure\_proc := Inactive$
  $failure\_interrupt := FALSE$
  $Nominal\_proc1 := Inactive$
  $Nominal\_proc2 := Inactive$
  $Recovery := Active$

end

The Failure operation models non-deterministic occurrence of a system failure, which leads to a creation of the *failure_interrupt* event. The Handler operation models handling of this interrupt by blocking the nominal and *Failure* processes, while activating the *Recovery* process.

In this simple system, the *Recovery* process is active only when all the rest processes are inactive. This is formulated as the following invariant to be verified:

$$Recovery = Active \Leftrightarrow Nominal\_proc1 = Inactive \wedge Nominal\_proc2 = Inactive \wedge ...$$

Similarly, the invariants ensuring the required control flow and component interaction order can be added and verified in the resulting Event-B model.

Translating to SimPy. This section describes how to represent the system in Fig. 1 using SimPy. In SimPy, we represent components as classes. Component processes become SimPy processes, which are based on Python's generators. Functional blocks are represented as sequences of instructions that alter the system state and wait for events. Events are used for inter-process communication and can take optional values as arguments (see Fig. 4 for a detailed guide).

A partial code listing corresponding to the system in Fig. 1 is shown in Listing 1.1. This component has four processes. Lines 3–6 in Listing1.1 create these processes upon initialisation of the component object, using a method for process creation provided by the SimPy simulation environment. Process creation requires a Python generator as its argument, which will become the body of the process. On Lines 8–9 we initialise two shared events which will be used to activate and deactivate the processes.

Lines 11–26 constitute the generator for Nominal_proc1. A sub-generator used for interrupt handling is defined in Lines 12–15. Upon invocation, this generator will activate the recovery process and wait until the `activation_event` is triggered, which makes Nominal_proc1 inactive while recovery is in progress.

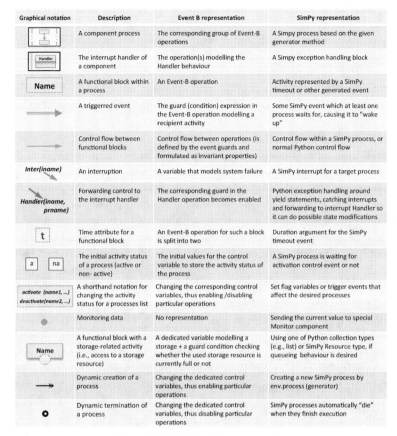

Graphical notation	Description	Event B representation	SimPy representation
	A component process	The corresponding group of Event-B operations	A Simpy process based on the given generator method
Handler	The interrupt handler of a component	The operation(s) modelling the Handler behaviour	A Simpy exception handling block
Name	A functional block within a process	An Event-B operation	Activity represented by a SimPy timeout or other generated event
⟶	A triggerred event	The guard (condition) expression in the Event-B operation modelling a recipient activity	Some SimPy event which at least one process waits for, causing it to "wake up"
⟶	Control flow between functional blocks	Control flow between operations (is defined by the event guards and formulated as invariant properties)	Control flow within a SimPy process, or normal Python control flow
Inter(iname)	An interruption	A variable that models system failure	A SimPy interrupt for a target process
Handler(iname, prname)	Forwarding control to the interrupt handler	The corresponding guard in the Handler operation becomes enabled	Python exception handling around yield statements, catching interrupts and forwarding to interrupt Handler so it can do possible state modifications
t	Time attribute for a functional block	An Event-B operation for such a block is split into two	Duration argument for the SimPy timeout event
a na	The initial activity status of a process (active or non- active)	The initial values for the control variable to store the activity status of the process	A SimPy process is waiting for activation control event or not
activate (name1, ...) deactivate(name2, ...)	A shorthand notation for changing the activity status for a processes list	Changing the corresponding control variables, thus enabling /disabling particular operations	Set flag variables or trigger events that affect the desired processes
◉	Monitoring data	No representation	Sending the current value to special Monitor component
Name	A functional block with a storage-related activity (i.e., access to a storage resource)	A dedicated variable modelling a storage + a guard condition checking whether the used storage resource is currently full or not	Using one of Python collection types (e.g., list) or SimPy Resource type, if queueing behaviour is desired
⟶	Dynamic creation of a process	Changing the dedicated control variables, thus enabling particular operations	Creating a new SimPy process by env.process (generator)
○	Dynamic termination of a process	Changing the dedicated control variables, thus disabling particular operations	SimPy processes automatically "die" when they finish execution

Fig. 4. Guidelines for integration

Because all processes in this example are non-terminating, every process generator contains an infinite loop, as in Lines 17–27.

Since Nominal_proc1 is interruptible, we need to surround the yield statement with exception handling (Lines 18–27), which will catch possible interrupts. Interrupts can only occur at yield statements, because an interrupt must come from another process and other processes cannot run until the active process has yielded execution, similarly to cooperative multitasking. Line 19 corresponds to the store activity, which uses a discrete resource, a store, as a pipe for interprocess communication. Execution of the process is halted until a job is put in the pipe. When a job arrives through the pipe, the status of the buffer is checked and the requested is either rejected or accepted and put in the pipe connecting Nominal_proc1 and Nominal_proc2.

Similarly to Nominal_proc1, Nominal_proc2 waits until a job arrives in its incoming pipe (Line 35). Thereafter, Line 36 simulates time required for serving the job. An interrupt may occur at either of these two yield statements.

The generator for the failure process spans Lines 44–50. The process waits for an exponentially distributed amount of time (46), the time between failures. Upon failure, the two nominal processes are interrupted (48–49) and the failure process becomes inactive until the recovery process triggers the `activation_event`.

Contrary to the other processes, the recovery process starts in an inactive state. We achieve this by waiting until the `recovery_activation_event` is triggered (Line 54). When activated, the recovery process waits for some time (Line 55) before activating the other processes (Lines 56–57) and becoming inactive again.

5   Applying the Integrated Approach

In this section, we will demonstrate the proposed approach on our case study – a replicated data storage in the cloud. As explained in Section 2, we consider two different system architectures: asynchronous and synchronous models.

In Fig. 5 and Fig. 6, we present the process-oriented models for the node components of these architectures. The component has a similar structure to the example we considered in the previous section. Additionally, there is a separate process *FailureDet_proc* that models reaction to a new master notification. The node components can be also employed either in the master or standby (worker) modes. In addition, each system also contains the (implicit) Monitor component as well as the Failure Detector component, responsible for detecting a failed master and then assigning a new one. The *Failure* and *Recovery* processes are similar to the ones from Fig.1 and are not presented here.

Listing 1.1. SimPy representation of the Component class

```
1   class Component:
2       def __init__(self, env, ...):
3           self.p1 = self.env.process(self.proc1())
4           self.p2 = self.env.process(self.proc2())
5           self.failure_proc = self.env.process(self.fail())
6           self.recovery_proc = self.env.process(self.recover())
7
8           self.activation_event = self.env.event()
9           self.recovery_activation_event = self.env.event()
10
11      def proc1(self):
12          def handle_interrupt():
13              self.recovery_activation_event.succeed()
14              self.recovery_activation_event = self.env.event()
15              yield self.activation_event
16
17          while True:
18              try:
19                  rq = yield self.arrival_pipe.get()
20                  if len(self.buffer) < self.capacity:
21                      self.buffer.append(rq)
22                      yield self.interproc_pipe.put(rq)
23                  else:
24                      self.rejected += 1
25              except Interrupt as interrupt:
26                  yield from handle_interrupt()
27                  continue
28
29      def proc2(self):
30          def handle_interrupt():
31              yield self.activation_event
32
```

```
33          while True:
34              try:
35                  yield self.interproc_pipe.get()
36                  yield self.env.timeout(expovariate(self.service_rate))
37                  self.buffer.pop()
38                  self.completed += 1
39
40              except Interrupt as interrupt:
41                  yield from handle_interrupt()
42                  continue
43
44      def fail(self):
45          while True:
46              yield self.env.timeout(expovariate(self.failure_rate))
47              self.failures += 1
48              self.p1.interrupt('failure1')
49              self.p2.interrupt('failure1')
50              yield self.activation_event
51
52      def recover(self):
53          while True:
54              yield self.recovery_activation_event
55              yield self.env.timeout(expovariate(self.repair_rate))
56              self.activation_event.succeed()
57              self.activation_event = self.env.event()
```

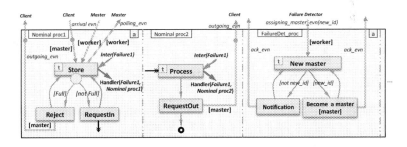

Fig. 5. Asynchronous model

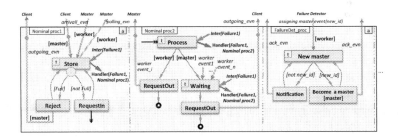

Fig. 6. Synchronous model

Event-B Modelling. The resulting Event-B models become starting points of our formal development, with main architectural system elements and their communication already in place. In the following refinement steps, we extend the abstract models by elaborating on the WAL mechanism and explicitly expressing the required data interdependencies between the master and standby logs.

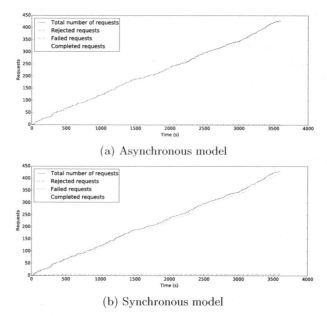

(a) Asynchronous model

(b) Synchronous model

Fig. 7. Comparison of the two models. Mean arrival rate is 7.5/min, service time is 5s, buffer capacity is 5 and mean failure rate is 1.8/h

Table 2. Results from model comparison

	Completed (%)	Rejected (%)	Failed (%)
Asynchronous	99.3	0	0.2
Synchronous	97.2	1.6	0.7

For instance, for the *asynchronous* model, we formulate and prove the data consistency property. Specifically, it states that all the requests that are now handled by a standby node should have been already completed by the master before. Moreover, we explicitly formulate and prove (as a model invariant) the log data integrity property stating that the corresponding log elements of any two storage nodes are always the same. In other words, all logs are consistent with respect to the log records of the master node. For more details, see [10].

Simulation in SimPy. Creating simulations for the models in Fig.5 and Fig.6 allows us to compare the two architectures as well as evaluate how different parameters affect the results within an architecture. Let us consider the system operating with the master and 3 workers. The workers poll the master 30 times per minute. The buffer capacity is set to 5. The arrival rate is exponentially distributed with mean 7.5/min. Each component requires 5s to process a request. Components randomly fail at an exponentially distributed rate of 1.8/h, rendering them inoperable until they have been repaired, which takes 4 seconds.

Fig.7 shows the results of a simulation involving the two models. With identical operating conditions and parameters, the *asynchronous* model has higher throughput, completing 99.3 % of requests in 1 hour. This is expected, because the *asynchronous* model involves less delay than the *synchronous* one, which completes 97.2 % of requests in 1 hour. Table 2 summarises the results.

Let us take a closer look at the asynchronous architecture. What happens if the buffer capacity was lowered from 5 to 2? What if the mean failure rate then was increased to 18/h? These questions are easy to answer with DES. According to Fig. 8, reducing the buffer capacity has a large negative impact on the throughput of the system, which only manages to complete 87.4% of requests within an hour. Contrary to the previous experiment, a substantial amount of arriving requests, 11.9%, are rejected. Additionally increasing the mean failure rate by a factor of 10 has less impact on the system than the previous change, with 83.4% of requests completed. Table 3 summarises the results.

Further experiments can reveal more information about the system. For example, changing the number of workers does not have great impact on the performance of the *asynchronous* model, because its primary work-flow only involves the master. For the *synchronous* model, the number of workers does not affect performance much by itself, as processing on the workers occurs in parallel, but if the repair rate is very low, increasing the number of workers actually results in worse performance. This is because each request requires processing on each component and, whenever a component fails, the system has to wait for it to be repaired before pending requests can be completed. Increasing the number of workers in the synchronous model then results in an effective increase in the mean failure rate of the system.

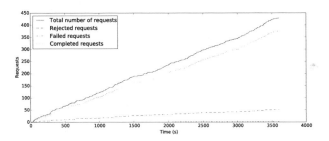

(a) Buffer capacity is down to 2, the mean failure rate stays 1.8/h.

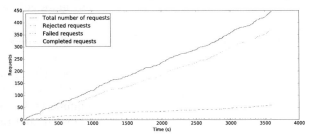

(b) Buffer capacity is down to 2, the mean failure rate is up to 18/h.

Fig. 8. Sensitivity analysis (Async. model). Arrival rate is 7.5/min, service time is 5 s.

Table 3. Results from sensitivity analysis with the asynchronous model

	Completed (%)	Rejected (%)	Failed (%)
Less Capacity	87.4	11.9	0.2
Less Capacity and More Failures	83.4	13.3	0.9

6   Related Work and Conclusions

This work augments with formal modelling our previous research [5] on using DES to analyse reliability and cost of different session management policies in the cloud. The problem of inadequate support for development of cloud services has also been identified by Boer et al [4]. Similarly to us, they aim at integrating reasoning about correctness with simulation. In our case, Event-B allows us to formally represent and verify system-level properties, while in [4] the stress is put on creating executable specifications and analysis of corresponding traces.

Our proposed process-oriented model is similar to Activity Cycle Diagrams (ACD) [6,9] – a graphical notation to model discrete events and interactions. In particular, [6] presents an extension of ACS to enable automatic translation to Java programs, while [9] proposes extended ACD to represent the relationship between conditions and events in a discrete event system that are not covered by the classical ACD. In contrast, our process-oriented models allow us to represent a high level system architecture in terms of components, processes and their interactions. Moreover, our proposed models can be both used as a basis to formal modelling and simulation at the same time.

The WAL mechanism has been investigated in [8,7], where the authors analyse the performance aspects of this technique. They distinguish four types of the delays that the WAL mechanism can impose on transaction handling and propose an approach to increase log scalability. In our work, we focus on integrating formal verification and DES to evaluate the system both qualitatively and quantitatively.

The problem of a formal verification and simulation-based validation is addressed in the ADVANCE project [1]. However, the focus of the proposed methodologies is related to cyber-physical systems, which are characterised by a mixture of discrete-event and continuous-time components. The proposed simulation-based approach combines the Event-B development and co-simulation with tool-independent physical components via the FMI interface [12]. In our work we deal with discrete-event systems and focus on integrating separate approaches for qualitative and quantitative reasoning about such systems.

In this paper, we have proposed a pragmatic approach to integrating formal modelling in Event-B and discrete-event simulation in SimPy. Our aim was to find a scalable solution to integrated engineering of resilient data stores in the cloud. We have succeeded in overcoming the scalability problems experienced while attempting to apply probabilistic model checking and achieved the desired goal – quantitative assessment of system resilience. Since testing cloud services in general is expensive and time consuming, we believe that the proposed approach offers benefits for the designers of cloud services.

Proof of concept integration of formal modelling and DES presented in this paper can be seen as an initial step towards creating an automated tool support for an integrated engineering environment of cloud services. Our future work will continue in two directions: one the one hand, we will create a tool for automatic translation of Event-B models in SimPy as well as work on visualisation of formal and simulation models. On other hand, we will experiment with deriving resilience monitors from system models to enable proactive resilience at run-time.

Acknowledgements. The authors would like to thank the reviewers for their valuable comments. This work is partly supported by the Need for Speed (N4S) Program (http://www.n4s.fi).

References

1. FP7 ADVANCE Project, http://www.advance-ict.eu/
2. Abrial, J.R.: Modeling in Event-B. Cambridge University Press (2010)
3. Banks, J.: Principles of simulation. In: Banks, J. (ed.) Handbook of Simulation, pp. 3–30. John Wiley & Sons, Inc. (2007)
4. de Boer, F.S., Hähnle, R., Johnsen, E.B., Schlatte, R., Wong, P.Y.H.: Formal modeling of resource management for cloud architectures: An industrial case study. In: De Paoli, F., Pimentel, E., Zavattaro, G. (eds.) ESOCC 2012. LNCS, vol. 7592, pp. 91–106. Springer, Heidelberg (2012)
5. Byholm, B., Porres, I.: Cost-Efficient, Reliable, Utility-Based Session Management in the Cloud. In: 14th IEEE/ACM International Symposium on Cluster, Cloud, and Grid Computing, pp. 102–111. IEEE Computer Society (2014)
6. De Lara Araújo Filho, W., Hirata, C.M.: Translating Activity Cycle Diagrams to Java Simulation Programs. In: ANSS 2004, pp. 157–164. IEEE (2004)
7. Johnson, R., Pandis, I., Stoica, R., Athanassoulis, M., Ailamaki, A.: Scalability of Write-Ahead Logging on Multicore and Multisocket Hardware. The VLDB Journal 21(2), 239–263
8. Johnson, R., Pandis, I., Stoica, R., Athanassoulis, M., Ailamaki, A.: Aether: A Scalable Approach to Logging. VLDB Endowment 3, 681–692 (2010)
9. Kang, D., Choi, B.K.: The extended activity cycle diagram and its generality. Simulation Modelling Practice and Theory 19(2), 785–800 (2011)
10. Pereverzeva, I., Laibinis, L., Troubitsyna, E., Holmberg, M., Pöri, M.: Formal Modelling of Resilient Data Storage in Cloud. In: Groves, L., Sun, J. (eds.) ICFEM 2013. LNCS, vol. 8144, pp. 363–379. Springer, Heidelberg (2013)
11. Rodin: Event-B Platform, http://www.event-b.org/
12. Savicks, V., Butler, M., Colley, J., Bendisposto, J.: Rodin Multi-Simulation Plugin. In: 5th Rodin User and Developer Workshop (2014)
13. Schriber, T.J., Brunner, D.T.: How Discrete-Event Simulation Software Works. In: Banks, J. (ed.) Handbook of Simulation, pp. 765–812. John Wiley & Sons (2007)
14. SimPy: Simulation framework in Python, http://simpy.readthedocs.org/

Applying an Integrated Modelling Process to Run-time Management of Many-Core Systems

Asieh Salehi Fathabadi, Colin Snook, and Michael Butler

University of Southampton, Southampton, UK
{asf08r,cfs,mjb}@ecs.soton.ac.uk

Abstract. A *Run-Time Management* system for many-core architecture is aware of application requirements and able to save energy by sacrificing performance when it will have negligible impact on user experience. This paper outlines the application of a process for development of a run-time management system that integrates a range of modelling, validation, verification and generation tools at appropriate stages. We outline the models, process and tools we used to develop a temperature aware run-time management system for *Dynamic Voltage and Frequency Scaling* (DVFS) of a media display application. The *Event Refinement Structure* (ERS) approach is used to visualise the abstract level of the DVFS control. The *Model Decomposition* technique is used to tackle the complexity of the model. To model the process-oriented aspects of the system we used *iUML-B Statemachines*. We use several different visual animation tools, running them synchronously to exploit their different strengths, in order to demonstrate the model to stakeholders. In addition, a continuous model of the physical properties of the cores is simulated in conjunction with discrete simulation of the Event-B run-time management system. Finally executable code is generated automatically using the *Code Generation* plug-in. The main contribution of this paper is to demonstrate the complementarity of the tools and the ease of their integrated use through the Rodin platform.

Keywords: Many-core, Event-B, Formal methods, Run-time management, DVFS, Task allocation.

1 Introduction

As electronic fabrication techniques approach the limit of atomic dimension, increases in performance can no longer be obtained from a single core with relative ease. Transistorised electronic devices gradually wear out due to physical phenomena such as electromigration and hot-carrier injection [1]. This effect is becoming more significant now that fabrication techniques are approaching the level of a few atoms. Interest in recent years, therefore, has increasingly focused on many core devices. Managing the use of a large collection of cores to achieve a given computing task with adequate performance in an energy efficient manner while minimising wear-out is a challenging problem, which is being tackled by the PRiME project [2]. A *Run-Time Management* system that is aware of application requirements and able to save energy by sacrificing performance when it will

E. Albert and E. Sekerinski (Eds.): IFM 2014, LNCS 8739, pp. 120–135, 2014.
© Springer International Publishing Switzerland 2014

have negligible impact on user experience is required. The run-time management system is also required to be aware of wear-out effects and minimise situations that accelerate them where possible. Furthermore we require such a system for disparate operating systems and hardware platforms.

Our approach is to developed formal models in Event-B [3] using the Rodin modelling platform [4] and plug-ins in an integrated formal development process, from requirements analysis through to code generation, so that we obtain a precise and correct specification from which we can generate variants and subsequently code for different platforms. Here we describe the models and modelling techniques we used as part of the formal development process to specify a temperature aware run-time management system for *Dynamic Voltage and Frequency Scaling* (DVFS) of a media display application. The run-time management system learns from the application when it can scale back voltage and frequency to save energy without missing too many frame deadlines. The run-time management system is also aware of core temperatures and controls thread scheduling of the operating system by setting thread-core affinity in order to avoid wear-out due to heating effects in the cores.

Figure 1 shows the complete formal development process indicating where different tools and methods are used. This figure should be referred to throughout the paper as different stages are discussed. The requirements are analysed using the *MCC* (Monitored, Controlled, Commanded) [5,6] set of guidelines for creating an initial abstract Event-B model. The model is defined and refined using the *Event Refinement Structure* (ERS) approach [7,8] and *iUML-B*

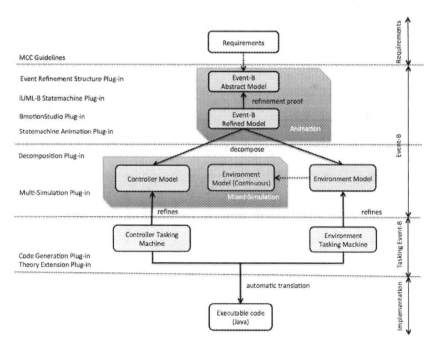

Fig. 1. Formal Design Towards Implementation

Statemachines [9,10] wherever appropriate. As well as formal refinement verification proof, the models are demonstrated to be valid using BMotionStudio [11] and iUML-B State-machine animation in tandem. The models are decomposed into controller and environment using *Model Decomposition* [12,13]. To demonstrate the validity of the control of continuous environmental phenomena, a continuous model of the environment is created and co-simulated with the discrete Event-B controller using the multi-simulation plug-in [14]. Code can then be generated using the *Code Generation* plug-in [15] plug-in which has been enhanced for our purposes using the theory plug-in [16].

The contribution of this paper is to show how all of these different techniques and tools complement each other in a complete formal modelling process for a multi-core runtime management system. In section 2 we briefly describe the techniques and tools used. In section 3 we introduce the media decoder case study and the run-time management control of DVFS and temperature. In section 4 we describe the method of requirements analysis using the MCC guideline to obtain an initial abstract model. In section 5 we described our use of diagrammatic modelling notations. In section 6 we describe how we model the environment by decomposing the complete system model and/or by modelling in a continuous domain modelling tool. In section 7 we describe our use of visual animation and simulation tools to validate the models. In section 8 we describe how we generate an implementation from the refined models.

2   Background

Event-B [3] is a formal method for system-level modelling and analysis. Key features of Event-B are the use of set theory and first order logic as a modelling notation, the use of refinement to represent systems at different abstraction levels and the use of mathematical proof to verify correctness of models and consistency between refinement levels. The *Rodin* [4] platform is an Eclipse-based IDE for Event-B that provides effective support for modelling and mathematical proof.

We use Monitored, Controlled and Commanded phenomena (*MCC*) guideline [5,6] to structure requirements. The MCC guideline facilitates formal modelling of a control system and help to formalising a set of informal requirements. Details are presented in section 4.

We use the *Event Refinement Structure* (ERS) approach [7,8] to visualise and build the abstract and refined levels of the DVFS control as an Event-B model. ERS augments Event-B methodology with a diagrammatic notation for explicit representation of control flows and refinement relationships. Providing such diagrams aids understanding and analysing the control flow requirements and refinements without getting involved with the complexity of the mathematical formal language notation. Details are presented in section 5.2.

We use *Model Decomposition* [12,13] to divide the DVFS control model into two sub-models: Controller and Environment. The controller sub-model consists of variables/events describing the softwaree layer properties whereas the environment sub-model consists of variables/events describing the properties of the user and the hardware layer. Details are presented in section 6.1.

We use *iUML-B Statemachines* [9,10] to model the thread scheduling process of the operating system under the influence of the run-time management system. State-machines provide excellent visualisation of mode-oriented problems and are animated for validation in synchronisation with BMotionStudio [11] visualisations of other parts of the model. Details are presented in section 5.3 (modelling) and 7.1 (animation).

We developed a continuous model of the thermal properties of a core depending on voltage and frequency using the Modellica [17] language. The continuous model is simulated in conjunction with ProB [18] simulation of the Event-B run-time management system. This is achieved via tools for mixed-simulation [14] which are under development in the ADVANCE project [19] . Details are presented in section 6.2 (modelling) and 7.2 (simulation).

Executable code was generated using the *Code Generation* plug-in [15]. The code generation feature provides support for the generation of code from refined Event-B models. To this end a multi-tasking approach has been added to the Event-B methodology. Tasks are modelled by an extension to Event-B, called *tasking machines* which are an extension of the existing Event-B machine component. The code generation plug-in provides the ability to translate to C and Java in addition to Ada source code. We adapted the code generation plug-in and used it to generate a Java implementation of the DVFS system. Details are presented in section 8.

3   The Case Study

Multimedia applications are expected to form a large portion of workload in general purpose PC and portable devices. The ever-increasing computation intensity of multimedia applications elevates the processor temperature and consequently impairs the reliability and performance of the system [20]. The run-time management system of the media decoder system scales the value of Voltage and Frequency (*VF*) for each frame of the media file. The VF value is scaled based on the speed of playing media requested by the operator and the type of the decoding frame. The run-time management system also learns from the number of CPU clock cycles taken to decode previous frames. The run-time management system aims to select an optimally minimal scaled VF value that provides adequate performance at minimal power consumption. The run-time management system also minimises thermal wear-out by selecting CPU cores that are well within the temperature thresholds for such effects. Unnecessary thermal cycling, which may also contribute to wear-out, is also avoided by selecting cores that are already warm when available.

The run-time management system operates in conjunction with an operating system by constraining or instructing the operating system in order to achieve the additional management features. Although we focus, here, on one type of multimedia application, the run-time management system should eventually be more generic and handle multiple types of application running simultaneously on a many-core platform. This is reflected in our modelling of the more generic layers of run-time management system and operating system.

4   Requirements and Analysis of the Case Study

Guidelines can be used to facilitate the transition between an informal requirements and its formal representation. Influenced by Parnas four-variable [21], a
guideline to model a control system using its monitored, commanded and controlled (*MCC*) phenomena is proposed in [5,6]. A phenomenon can be of type
variable or event. The definitions of MCC variable and event phenomena are
given below:

- *Monitored phenomena*: Monitored variables whose values are determined by
  the environment. Environment events update monitored variables.
- *Controlled phenomena*: Controlled variables representing phenomena in the
  environment whose values are set by the controller. Control events update
  controlled variables.
- *Commanded phenomena*: Commanded variables whose values are determined
  by the user and that influence controlled phenomena. Commanded events are
  user requests to modify commanded variables.

We have used the MCC guideline to structure requirements of the media decoder case study. The PRiME architecture structures a many core system into
four layers: user, application, system software and hardware (Fig. 2). Fig. 3 and
Fig. 4 illustrate how the MCC phenomena map to the PRiME layers. In Fig. 2,
from top to bottom, the interaction between the user layer and the application
layer is categorised as commanded phenomena. We propose a new phenomena,
called *task characterization*. Task characterization phenomena are determined
by the application layer and are fixed during run time. The controlled phenomena values are set by the software layer, and finally the monitored values are
determined by the hardware.

Fig. 3 presents the PRiME layers and corresponding requirements phenomena
for the media decoder DVFS aspects of the case study. Here the user of the
system is an operator who attempts to open the media file and request the speed

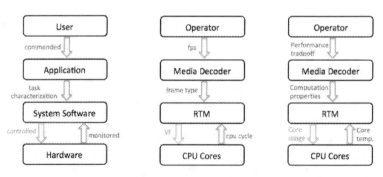

Fig. 2. PRiME Layers
Illustration

Fig. 3. DVFS As-
pects of Case Study

Fig. 4.   Thermal
Aspects   of   Case
Study

of playing media. The application is the decoder. The software layer corresponds to the run-time management, and the hardware layer corresponds to the CPU cores. The definition of the MCC phenomena are as below:

- *Commanded*: Frame Per Second (*fps*) property whose value is determined by the operator.
- *Task Characterization*: Frame type property whose value is determined by the decoder application.
- *Controlled*: Voltage and Frequency (*VF*) property representing the value of VF to be set in the hardware; VF value is set by the run-time management system.
- *Monitored*: CPU cycles number whose value is determined by the core.

These phenomena are specified as variables and events in the Event-B model. For example *fps* property is modelled as a variable and an event (*set_fps* introduced in Section 5.2) to set its value. The ordering between these phenomena (from top to bottom) are specified as invariants and event guards in the Event-B model (details in Section 5.2).

Fig. 4 presents the PRiME layers and corresponding requirements phenomena for the temperature control aspects of the case study. The definition of the MCC phenomena are as below:

- *Commanded*: Performance tradeoff is a property which the operator can adjust to control the balance between performance and wear-out
- *Task Characterization*: Computation properties (multi-threading) whose value is determined by the decoder application.
- *Controlled*: Core usage property representing the allocation of threads to CPU cores controlled by the run-time management system.
- *Monitored*: Core temperature measured for each CPU core.

5   Modelling

5.1   The Event-B Formal Method

Event-B [3] evolved from the B-Method [22] and adopts the more flexible systems-oriented refinement of Action systems [23]. New events can be introduced in refinements or old ones split into different cases as more complex data structures reveal more detailed behaviour. Event-B modelling and verification proof is supported by the Rodin platform [4]. Different design and modelling techniques, such as UML-B, model decomposition, ERS etc., have been developed and integrated into the Rodin platform as plug-in extensions which enrich the Event-B modelling process. The primary aim of Event-B is to validate that we are building the right system. Since validation is inherently a human decision it is important to build models which clearly show the important properties of a system. Event-B's method of verified refinement allows us to make abstractions so that important properties can be modelled and validated without being obscured by detail. Verified refinement allows us to then add more details in simple stages in the knowledge that the validated properties are maintained. We use visual animation tools to validate abstract levels of the model and mixed-simulation at more refined levels.

5.2   Event Refinement Structure Approach

The Event Refinement Structure (ERS) approach [7,8] is used to visualise and build the control flows of the abstract level and refinement levels of the DVFS control Event-B model. In Event-B, control flows are implicitly modelled by laboriously adding control variables, and corresponding guards and actions in order to specify the sequencing of events. ERS provides an explicit visual representation of control flows which is used to automatically generate these control variables, guards and actions. In addition, ERS provides explicit representation of the refinement relationships between an abstract event and the refining concrete events. ERS augments Event-B with a diagrammatic notation that is capable of explicit representation of control flow requirements and the corresponding refinement structure. The rest of the requirements are modelled directly in Event-B which allows full expressiveness. Providing such diagrams aids understanding and analysing the control flow requirements in a more direct way than the plain Event-B representation. The ERS diagram of the DVFS control is illustrated in Fig. 5.

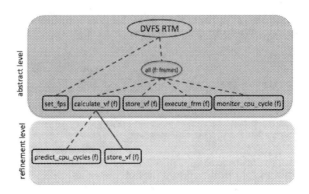

Fig. 5. ERS Diagram, Abstract Level of DVFS Model

The root oval contains the name of the system, DVFS RTM, Dynamic Voltage and Frequency System Run Time Management. Considering the abstract layer (blue region), the leaves are read from left to right, indicating the ordering between them. First the *set_fps* event executes followed by execution of four events for all of the frames of the decoding media file. The *"all"* replicator, appearing in the oval, indicates (potentially parallel) execution of its children for all of the instances of parameter *"f"* of type *"frames"* . For each frame, first the optimal value of the value of the VF is calculated (*calculate_vf* event), second the VF value is stored (*store_vf* event), then the frame is executed in the core (*execute_frm* event) and finally the number of taken CPU cycles is monitored (*monitor_cpu_cycle* event). In the refinement level (green region), *calculate_vf* is decomposed into two sub-events, *predict_cpu_cycles* and *select_vf*. The ERS diagram explicitly illustrates that the effect achieved by *calculate_vf* at the abstract level is realised at the refined level by occurrence of *predict_cpu_cycles* followed by *select_vf*. The solid line indicates that *select_vf* event refines *calculate_vf* event while the dashed line indicates that *predict_cpu_cycles* event is a new event which refines skip.

5.3   iUML-B State-Machines

iUML-B State-machines provide a mode-oriented control over a sequence of events. Hierarchical State-machines are added to the Event-B model and contribute (i.e. automatically generate) guards and actions to existing events in order to represent the transition source and target. Additional guards and actions may be added to transitions and invariants may be placed within states. We used state-machines to visualise the affinity-restricted thread scheduling of the temperature control operating system (Fig. 6). The state-machine shows that a thread is initially *PREMPTED* and may then *start* with a new time-slot (time-slot is modelled in the underlying Event-B and not shown in the diagram). While *RUNNING*, the thread can *progress* which consumes time-slot until it runs out (*timeup*) and becomes *EXPIRED*. If it has completed it will then *exit*. If not it returns to *PREMPTED* via *prempt* and must then *resume* (or *resumeCold*) with a new time-slot when a core is available. When resuming, the scheduler chooses a hot core (*resume*) in preference to a cold one (*resumeCold*) in order to avoid thermal cycling which increases wear-out. The alternative *suspend-SUSPENDED-activate* path represents a thread becoming blocked while waiting for resources to become available. The superstate *CURRENT*, consisting of *RUNNING* and *EXPIRED*, represents the conditions when the thread is allocated to a cpu core. The state-machine is 'lifted' to the set of current threads so that each thread has an independent state. During animation, (section 7) example instances are used to illustrate the behaviour of the model and appear as tokens indicating the current mode of each thread. The affinity restrictions are in the form of additional transition guards that restrict the selection of a CPU core when the *start*, *resume* or *resumeCold* transitions are taken. Refinement is performed by adding new state-machines inside old states. For example the states *RUNNING* and *EXPIRED* and transitions *timeup* and *progress* would not have existed in the abstract version of Fig 6.

5.4   ERS versus State-Machines

ERS and State-machines both provide visual modelling tools for adding event sequence restrictions to Event-B. We use ERS for explicit representation of iterative flow (e.g., all) and for representing *event* decomposition in refinement.

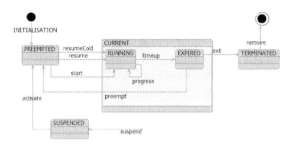

Fig. 6. iUML-B State-machine model of Thread Scheduling

We choose state-machines for modelling cyclical modal behaviour and for representing *state* decomposition. Since these visual models are alternatives for representing the same thing (i.e. event sequencing) they are not both used for the same events but can be used for different sets of events within the same Event-B model. This is achieved by simply referring to different events in the respective diagrams. In our case study, we have used ERS to show the progressive event refinement of the DFVS processes and state-machines for the hierarchical modal behaviour of the thread scheduling. Another approach would be to use activity diagrams as explored by Dygham et al. [24], however, there is currently no tool support for activity diagrams in Rodin.

6   Modelling the Environment

6.1   Model Decomposition

Model decomposition pre-dated Event-B and is found in action systems [25]. Model decomposition in Event-B [12,13], is used to manage the complexity and increase the modularity of an Event-B model. The idea of model decomposition is to divide it into components that can be refined independently while ensuring that if the components were re-composed they would constitute a valid refinement of the original model. The components interact through synchronisation over shared events. We applied the model decomposition technique to the DVFS control model dividing it into two sub-models: Controller and Environment. The controller sub-model consists of variables/events describing the SW layer properties whereas the environment sub-model consists of variables/events describing the properties of the user and HW layers. We have also used the definition of the model decomposition for code generation purpose. By using model decomposition, we introduce the controller and environment actions to the code generation process. Details of the code generation application are provided in section 8.

The *predict_cpu_cycles*, *select_vf*, *store_vf* and *monitor_cpu_cycle* events are the actions of the operating system (SW layer) and are included in the controller sub-model. There are two shared events between the controller and the environment which appear in both sub-models: *set_fps* and *execute_frm*. The *set_fps* event is the action of reading the fps value from the environment (user layer) and setting its value in a controller variable. The *execute_frm* event models execution of the frame in the core; it sets the environment variable recording the CPU cycle number taken for execution of the frames; this variable is read later by the controller (by execution of *monitor_cpu_cycle* event).

6.2   Continuous Models of the Environment

While Event-B is very suitable for modelling the discrete state-event based behaviour of a system, it is sometimes important to model the physical continuous behaviour of an environment. For the Temperature Control system we modelled the thermal characteristics of CPU cores in Modellica [17], Fig. 7. The left side of the model (blue connectors) calculates the amount of power being consumed. This is the sum of the static power which is proportional to the voltage and the dynamic power which is proportional to frequency and square of voltage. The power then determines the amount of heat flowing into the right side (red connectors). The thermal model consists of the heat capacitance of the core and a thermal conductor to the cooling system (which we assume is a fixed flow to ambient for now). The model has a boolean input *Active* which is controlled by the run-time management system (Event-B) model to represent when the core is running a thread (i.e. in state *RUNNING* of Fig. 6) on that core, and an output, *temp* which is returned to the run-time management system and used to influence decisions about which cores to use. Currently the model is an approximation which needs further development and more detailed comparison with empirical measurements. In particular, the cooling component is over simplified and the coefficients are chosen to give a typical response. However this is sufficient for our purpose which is to illustrate how the controller responds to and controls a typical environmental phenomena.

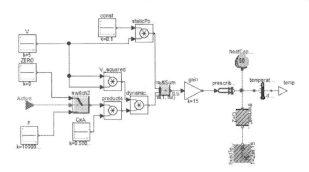

Fig. 7. Core Temperature modelled in Modellica

6.3   Decomposition versus Continuous Models

We started from an abstract model of the system that includes the application, run-time manager, operating system and the hardware. We refine this model in steps to add details and then, at a suitable point, decompose it into two subsystems representing the software and the hardware. We consider the hardware to be an environment for the software subsystem. Following this process, we obtain a discrete event model of the environment that is a verified refinement of the abstract system model. This is an advantage when the controlled and measured phenomena of the environment can be adequately modelled by discrete events. However, for continuous physical properties such as temperature, the verification relies on the validity of the discrete abstractions. Using a continuous model enables us to validate how the run-time management system works with these physical properties (as will be described in section 7.2) in order to improve our confidence in the discrete representation of them that the Event-B model uses. A further step would be to model the continuous properties in Event-B using recent extensions for continuous domain modelling [26] which would allow verifications of dynamic properties within Event-B. This would be beneficial when the validity of discrete approximations is less clear and can not be reliably determined simply by simulation.

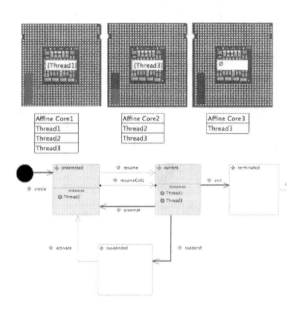

Fig. 8. Animating the model using BMotionStudio and State-machine Animation

7 Validation

7.1 BMotion Studio and Statemachine Animation

In order to validate our models we performed visual animations to demonstrate them to stakeholders. The ProB [18] model checker provides an animation facility which is the basis for two visual animation tools. BMotionStudio [11] is used to provide a graphical visualisation of three cores with threads being run on them and the resultant core temperatures increasing and decreasing. The iUML-B state-machine plug-in includes an animation tool to highlight active states and enabled transitions showing which threads are in each state at any point in time. The two visualisation work together on the same ProB animation, complementing each others view of the underlying model.

7.2   Mixed-Simulation

To validate the response of the system to the continuous model of core temperature, we linked the Event-B run-time management system model with the continuous Modellica model using the co-simulation plug-in [14] developed in the ADVANCE project [19]. Fig. 9 shows the temperature (red line) of a single core heating rapidly when a thread becomes active (blue line goes low) and cooling when no thread is active. Currently the model only supports co-simulation of a single core and we are unable to demonstrate the temperature response to thread-core allocation for multiple cores. However, we are currently addressing this and co-simulation has the potential to allow us to demonstrate the validity of the run-time management system model in a simulation that appears close to reality, before going on to generate the implementation.

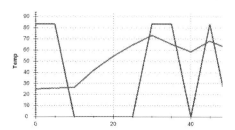

Fig. 9. Mixed-Simulation of Continuous Thermal Model and Event-B Discrete Run-time Management System

8   Code Generation

Code generation is an important part of the formal engineering tool chain that enables support for development from high-level models down to executable implementations. In the Event-B methodology, the code generation feature [15] provides support for the generation of code, for real-time embedded control systems, from refined Event-B models. To this end a multi-tasking approach, which is conceptually similar to that of the Ada tasking model, is designed and added to the Event-B methodology. Tasks are modelled by an extension to Event-B, called tasking machines which are an extension of the existing Event-B machine component. The code generation plug-in supports translation to C, Java or Ada source code. In the DVFS run-time management system are currently using the Java code generation option.

The theory plug-in [16] allows mathematical extensions to be added to an Event-B development. The code generation plug-in uses a theory component to define new data types, and their translation into target programming language data types [27]. In the DVFS run-time management system model, we specify the relation between a frame and the corresponding assigned VF as a function data type:

$frm\_vf \in FRAMES \rightarrow VF$

The function data type is not supported by the current release of the code generation plug-in. We extended the code generation plug-in to support functions by adding a new theory component to define a function data type and a translation rule to the target data type (a Java hash map). Fig. 10 presents the definition of the implementable function ($pfunImp$) with arguments for the types of the domain D and range R. $newpFunImp$ is a constructor for an empty $pfunImp$.

```
THEORY
   FunctionImpl
TYPE PARAMETERS
   D
   R
OPERATORS

   ·pfunImpl  :  pfunImpl(d : P(D), r : P(R))

   direct definition
     pfunImpl(d : P(D), r : P(R)) ≙ d↮r

   ·newpFunImpl  :  newpFunImpl(f : D ↠ R)

   direct definition
     newpFunImpl(f : D ↠ R) ≙ ø⦂P(D × R)
```

```
TRANSLATOR
   Java
   Metavariables
    · f ∈ P(D×R)
    · d ∈ D
    · r ∈ R
   Translator Rules
     newpFunImplRule   :
       newpFunImpl(ø⦂P(D×R)} ⤇
         new HashMapImpl<D,R>()
```

Fig. 10. Theory Extension for the New Function Data Type

Fig. 11. Translation of Function Data Type

In the controller refinement, we first refine the Event-B definition of frm_vf as a function, to instead use the new function data type:

$frm\_vf \in pfunImp(FRAMES, VF)$;

with initialisation:

$frm\_vf := newpFunImpl(\varnothing \; {⦂} \; \mathbb{P}(FRAMES \times VF))$

The translation of the function data-type to the target of the Java *HashMap* data type is presented in Fig. 11. Here is the generated Java code for the frm_vf variable:

```
HashMapImpl<FRAMES,VF>  frm_vf = new HashMapImpl<FRAMES,VF>();
```

In the controller tasking machine, we specify the task body, where we define the flow of control in the controller sub-model as below; and the control flow in the Java codes is managed using threads.

set_fps;

$calculate\_vf$;

$store\_vf$;

$execute\_frm$;

$monitor\_cpu\_cycle$

To date, we have executed the generated code on a simulation of the hardware. We are currently working on porting the code to run on real hardware in order to evaluate the performance of the generated code.

9   Conclusion and Future Work

We have shown how various Rodin plug-ins can be used with the basic Event-B modelling and verification platform to form a complete formal development process including requirements analysis, model development using diagrammatic modelling editors, model refinement, decomposition, validation, mixed-simulation and code generation. Several authors have discussed using formal methods within an existing development process (e.g. [28],[29]). However these works are quite dated and did not have the benefit of extensive tool support. As far as we know there is no comparable work on how all of the various Rodin centred tools and plug-ins can be utilised to form a new development process.

We have not stressed verification in this paper. It is an inherent feature of the Event-B refinement method where proof obligations are automatically generated and discharged within the Rodin platform ensuring that the models are well-formed and consistent. All of our refinements were fully verified using the Atelier-B automatic provers available for Rodin. Here we focus on the use of diagrammatic modelling aids which make models easier to construct and understand and visual validation tools which allow us to observe the behaviour of the model so that we can demonstrate that it behaves as we desire. Having produced a correct and useful model we use code generation to obtain a high-quality implementation from it. In summary, we use the following Rodin plug-ins to provide tool-support for a useable model-based formal development process.

- MCC provides a systematic way of structuring the requirements and of constructing a formal model from the requirements for a control system.
- ERS provides explicit representation of replication of flow (e.g., all) and for representing event decomposition.
- iUML-B state-machines provide explicit representation of cyclical modal behaviour and for representing state decomposition.
- Animation with BMotionStudio and iUML-B state-machines allow for easy validation by stakeholders who do not have Event-B expertise.
- Co-simulation supports validation the the discrete controller model behaves correctly in conjunction with a continuous model of the environment.
- Code generation provides an automated way of generating multi-tasking code with the potential for easy targeting of different languages and architectures.
- Rodin provers support formal verification of correctness of design with respect to a (discrete) model of the system.

The temperature control model contains of 4 levels of refinement, including 9 variables in total and 13 events in the last refinement. All of the proof obligation (118 in total) are discharged automatically by the Rodin prover. The DVFS control model contains 2 levels of refinement, including 9 variables and 7 events in the last refinement. 13 out of 38 proof obligations are discharged automatically; the rest are discharged manually due to introducing the mathematical extension using the theory plugin. The new defined operators cause manual effort to discharge proof obligation generated for the sub-component after the model decomposition.

We think our process of formal design and integrated modelling can be scaled and promoted in industry. MCC provides guidance to overcome the difficult task of constructing an abstract model from the requirements. Diagrammatic editors like iUML-B and ERS provide a high-level visualisation of the models and automate some of the lower-level Event-B infrastructure making the construction of models more intuitive for engineers. Visual animation and simulation techniques bridge the semantic gap between mathematical models and real-world problem domains making the models accessible to stakeholders for validation. Generating code from a verified model reduces code and testing effort to offset the resources put into the modelling process. One self-criticism is that, although they can be used along side each other, in some areas the plug-in tools would benefit from better integration. For example, the ERS and iUML-B diagramming plugins could be integrated so that they use the same common diagram framework and generation mechanisms. Similarly, the animation tools could be integrated into a common visualisation.

One of the motivations for our approach is that we can produce model variants at the lower levels of refinement so that we can generate different implementations for different platforms. For example, we could provide alternative thread scheduling for different operating systems. In future work we will investigate these variants. Further work is also needed in order to use code generation to different target languages such as C. In future work, we will also perform experiments running the generated code on different many-core hardware platforms such as XEON Phi etc. in order to fully evaluate the benefits of the run-time management system.

Acknowledgement. This work is funded by the FP7 ADVANCE Project, www.advance-ict.eu, and the EPSRC PRiME Project, www.prime-project.org.

References

1. Oboril, F., Tahoori, M.: Extratime: Modeling and analysis of wearout due to transistor aging at microarchitecture-level. In: 2012 42nd Annual IEEE/IFIP International Conference on Dependable Systems and Networks (DSN), pp. 1–12 (June 2012)
2. PRiME: Power-efficient, Reliable, Many-core Embedded systems,
   http://www.prime-project.org
3. Abrial, J.R.: Modeling in Event-B - System and Software Engineering. Cambridge University Press (2010)
4. Abrial, J.R., Butler, M., Hallerstede, S., Hoang, T., Mehta, F., Voisin, L.: Rodin: an open toolset for modelling and reasoning in Event-B. International Journal on Software Tools for Technology Transfer 12(6), 447–466 (2010)
5. Yeganefard, S., Butler, M.: Structuring Functional Requirements of Control Systems to Facilitate Refinement-based Formalisation. ECEASST 46 (2011)
6. Yeganefard, S., Butler, M.: Control Systems: Phenomena and Structuring Functional Requirement Documents. In: ICECCS, pp. 39–48 (2012)
7. Butler, M.: Decomposition Structures for Event-B. In: Leuschel, M., Wehrheim, H. (eds.) IFM 2009. LNCS, vol. 5423, pp. 20–38. Springer, Heidelberg (2009)

8. Salehi Fathabadi, A., Butler, M., Rezazadeh, A.: A Systematic Approach to Atomicity Decomposition in Event-B. In: Eleftherakis, G., Hinchey, M., Holcombe, M. (eds.) SEFM 2012. LNCS, vol. 7504, pp. 78–93. Springer, Heidelberg (2012)
9. Snook, C.: Modelling Control Process and Control Mode with Synchronising Orthogonal Statemachines. In: B2011. Limerick (2011)
10. Savicks, V., Snook, C.: A Framework for Diagrammatic Modelling Extensions in Rodin. In: Rodin Workshop 2012, Fontainbleau (2012)
11. Ladenberger, L., Bendisposto, J., Leuschel, M.: Visualising Event-B Models with B-Motion Studio. In: Alpuente, M., Cook, B., Joubert, C. (eds.) FMICS 2009. LNCS, vol. 5825, pp. 202–204. Springer, Heidelberg (2009)
12. Silva, R., Pascal, C., Hoang, T.S., Butler, M.: Decomposition tool for Event-B. Softw.; Pract. Exper. 41(2), 199–208 (2011)
13. Hoang, T.S., Iliasov, A., Silva, R., Wei, W.: A Survey on Event-B Decomposition. ECEASST 46 (2011)
14. Savicks, V., Butler, M., Bendisposto, J., Colley, J.: Co-simulation of Event-B and Continuous Models in Rodin. In: Rodin Workshop 2013, Turku (2012)
15. Edmunds, A., Butler, M.: Tasking Event-B: An Extension to Event-B for Generating Concurrent Code. In: PLACES (2011)
16. Butler, M., Maamria, I.: Practical Theory Extension in Event-B. In: Liu, Z., Woodcock, J., Zhu, H. (eds.) Theories of Programming and Formal Methods. LNCS, vol. 8051, pp. 67–81. Springer, Heidelberg (2013)
17. Fritzson, P., Engelson, V.: ModelicaA unified object-oriented language for system modeling and simulation. In: Jul, E. (ed.) ECOOP 1998. LNCS, vol. 1445, pp. 67–90. Springer, Heidelberg (1998)
18. Leuschel, M., Butler, M.: ProB: A Model Checker for B. In: Araki, K., Gnesi, S., Mandrioli, D. (eds.) FME 2003. LNCS, vol. 2805, pp. 855–874. Springer, Heidelberg (2003)
19. ADVANCE: Advanced Design and Verification Environment for Cyber-physical System Engineering, http://www.advance-ict.eu/
20. Ge, Y., Qiu, Q.: Dynamic thermal management for multimedia applications using machine learning. In: DAC, pp. 95–100 (2011)
21. Parnas, D.L., Madey, J.: Functional Documents for Computer Systems. Science of Computer Programming 25, 41–61 (1995)
22. Abrial, J.R.: The B-book - assigning programs to meanings. Cambridge University Press (2005)
23. Back, R.J., Kurki-Suonio, R.: Distributed cooperation with action systems. ACM Trans. Program. Lang. Syst. 10(4), 513–554 (1988)
24. Dghaym, D., Butler, M., Fathabadi, A.S.: Evaluation of Graphical Control Flow Management Approaches for Event-B Modelling. ECEASST 66 (2013)
25. Back, R.J.: Refinement calculus, part ii: Parallel and reactive programs. In: REX Workshop, pp. 67–93 (1989)
26. Abrial, J.-R., Su, W., Zhu, H.: Formalizing Hybrid Systems with Event-B. In: Derrick, J., Fitzgerald, J., Gnesi, S., Khurshid, S., Leuschel, M., Reeves, S., Riccobene, E. (eds.) ABZ 2012. LNCS, vol. 7316, pp. 178–193. Springer, Heidelberg (2012)
27. Edmunds, A., Butler, M., Maamria, I., Silva, R., Lovell, C.: Event-B Code Generation: Type Extension with Theories. In: Derrick, J., Fitzgerald, J., Gnesi, S., Khurshid, S., Leuschel, M., Reeves, S., Riccobene, E. (eds.) ABZ 2012. LNCS, vol. 7316, pp. 365–368. Springer, Heidelberg (2012)
28. Fraser, M.D., Kumar, K., Vaishnavi, V.K.: Strategies for incorporating formal specifications in software development. Commun. ACM 37(10), 74–86 (1994)
29. Kemmerer, R.: Integrating formal methods into the development process. IEEE Software 7(5), 37–50 (1990)

Model Verification

Verifying Behavioral UML Systems via CEGAR

Yael Meller[1], Orna Grumberg[1], and Karen Yorav[2]

[1] CS Department, Technion, Israel
[2] IBM Research, Haifa, Israel
{ymeller,orna}@cs.technion.ac.il, yorav@il.ibm.com

Abstract. This work presents a novel approach for applying abstraction and refinement in the verification of behavioral UML models.

The *Unified Modeling Language* (UML) is a widely accepted modeling language for embedded and safety critical systems. As such the correct behavior of systems represented as UML models is crucial. *Model checking* is a successful automated verification technique for checking whether a system satisfies a desired property. Nevertheless, its applicability is often impeded by its high time and memory requirements. A successful approach to avoiding this limitation is *CounterExample-Guided Abstraction-Refinement (CEGAR)*. We propose a CEGAR-like approach for UML systems. We present a model-to-model transformation that generates an *abstract UML system* from a given concrete one, and formally prove that our transformation creates an *over-approximation*.

The abstract system is often much smaller, thus model checking is easier. Because the abstraction creates an over-approximation we are guaranteed that if the abstract model satisfies the property then so does the concrete one. If not, we check whether the resulting abstract counterexample is *spurious*. In case it is, we automatically *refine* the abstract system, in order to obtain a more precise abstraction.

1 Introduction

This work presents a novel approach for applying abstraction and refinement for the verification of behavioral UML models. The *Unified Modeling Language* (UML) [2] is a widely accepted modeling language that can be used to specify and construct systems. It provides means to represent a system in terms of classes and their relationships, and to describe the systems' internal structure and behavior. UML has been developed as a standard object-oriented modeling language by the Object Management Group (OMG) [11]. It is becoming the dominant modeling language for embedded and safety critical systems. As such, the correct behavior of systems represented as UML models is crucial and verification techniques applicable to such models are required.

Model checking [6] is a successful automated verification technique for checking whether a given system satisfies a desired property. It traverses *all* of the system behaviors, and either confirms that the system is correct w.r.t. the checked property, or provides a *counterexample (CEX)* that demonstrates an erroneous behavior. Model checking is widely recognized as an important approach to increasing reliability of hardware and software systems and is vastly used in industry.

E. Albert and E. Sekerinski (Eds.): IFM 2014, LNCS 8739, pp. 139–154, 2014.

Unfortunately, the applicability of model checking is impeded by its high time and memory requirements. One of the most successful approaches for fighting these problems is *abstraction*, where some of the system details are hidden. This results in an *over-approximated* system that has *more behaviors and less states* than the concrete (original) system. The abstract system has the feature that if a property holds on the abstract system, then it also holds on the concrete system. However, if the property does not hold, then nothing can be concluded of the concrete system. *CounterExample-Guided Abstraction Refinement (CEGAR)* approach [4] provides an automatic and iterative framework for abstraction and refinement, where the refinement is based on a spurious CEX. When model checking returns an abstract CEX, a matching concrete CEX is searched. If there exists one, then a real bug on the concrete system is found. Otherwise, the CEX is *spurious* and a refinement is needed. During refinement, more details are added to the abstract system, in order to eliminate the spurious CEX.

In this paper we focus on behavioral systems that rely on *UML state machines*. UML state machines are a standard graphical language for modeling the behavior of event-driven software components. We propose a CEGAR-like framework for verifying such systems. We present a model-to-model transformation that generates an *abstract system* from a given concrete one. Our transformation is done on the UML level, thus resulting in a *new UML behavioral system* which is an *over-approximation* of the original system. We adapt the CEGAR approach to our UML framework, and apply refinement if needed. Our refinement is also performed as a model-to-model transformation. It is important to note that by defining abstraction and refinement in terms of model-to-model transformation, we avoid the translation to lower level representation (such as Kripke structures). This is highly beneficial to the user, since both the property, the abstraction, and the abstract CEX are given on the UML level and are therefore more meaningful.

Our abstraction is obtained by abstracting some (or all) of the state machines in the concrete system. When abstracting a state machine, we over-approximate its *interface behavior* w.r.t. the rest of the system. In the context of behavioral UML systems, the interface includes the events generated/consumed and the (non-private) variables. We thus abstract part of the system's variables, and maintain an *abstract view* of the events generated by the abstracted state machines. In particular, the abstract state machines may change the number and order of the generated events. Further, abstracted variables are assigned the "don't-know" value. Our abstraction does not necessarily replace an *entire* state machine. Rather, it enables abstracting *different parts* of a state machine whose behavior is irrelevant to the checked property. We present our abstraction construction in section 4.

We show that the abstract system is an over-approximation by proving that for every concrete system computation there exists an abstract system computation that "behaves similarly". This is formally defined and proved in section 5. To formalize the notion of *system computation*, we present in section 3 a formal semantics for behavioral UML systems that rely on state machines. Works such as [7,10,15] also give formal semantics to state machines, however they all differ from our semantics: e.g. [7] defines the semantics on flat state machines and present a translation from hierarchical to flat state machines, whereas we maintain the hierarchical structure of the state machines. [10] define the semantics of a *single* state machine. Thus it neither addresses the semantics of the full system, nor the communication between state machines. [15] addresses the communication of state machines, however their notion of run-to-completion step does not enable context switches during a run-to-completion step. Our formal semantics is defined for a *system*, possibly multi-threaded, where the atomicity level is a transition execution (formally defined later).

Our CEGAR framework is suitable for verifying LTL_x, which is the Linear-time Temporal Logic (LTL)[22] without the next-time operator. Also, we assume the existence of a model checker for behavioral UML systems. Extensive work has been done in the last years to provide such model checkers by translating the system into an input language of some model checker. [3,5] present translation of state machines to SMV. Several works [18,14,21,1,8] translate state machines to PROMELA, which is the input language of the model checker SPIN. A verification environment for UML behavioral models was developed in the context of the European research project OMEGA [20], and works such as [25,19] apply different methods for model checking these models. [12,16] translate a UML behavioral model to C code, and apply bounded model checking via CBMC. We add the special value "don't-know" to the domain of the variables. This results in a 3-valued semantics for UML systems, as shown in section 4. To model check abstract systems we need a 3-valued model checker. Extending a model checker to support the 3-valued semantics (e.g., [27,13]) is straightforward.

Many works such as [26,28,24,9,23] address *semantic refinement* of state machines, which is adding details to a partially defined state machine while preserving behavior of the original (abstracted) model. Though we also address an abstraction-refinement relation between state machines, these works are very different from ours. These works look at manual refinement as part of the modeling process, whereas we are suggesting an *automatic* abstraction and refinement, and our goal is improving scalability of the verification tool. Moreover, these works handle a single state machine level, where we consider a system which includes possibly many state machines that interact with each other. To the best of our knowledge, this is the first work that addresses the abstraction for a behavioral UML system at the UML level.

2   Preliminaries - UML Behavioral Systems

Behavioral UML systems include objects (instances of classes) that process events. Event processing is defined by state machines, which include complex features such as hierarchy, concurrency and communication. UML objects communicate by sending each other events (asynchronous messages) that are kept in *event queues* (EQs). Every object is associated with a single EQ, and several objects can be associated with the same EQ. In a multi-threaded system there are several EQs, one for each thread. Each thread executes a never-ending loop, taking an event from its EQ, and dispatching it to the target object. The target object makes a *run-to-completion (RTC)* step, where it processes the event and continues execution until it cannot continue anymore. RTCs are composed of a series of *steps*, formally defined later. Only when the target object finishes its RTC, the thread dispatches the next event available in its EQ. Steps of different threads are interleaved. Next we formally define state machines, UML systems, and the set of behaviors associated with them. The following definitions closely follow the UML2 standard.

2.1   UML State Machines

We first define the following notions: $EV = EV_{env} \cup EV_{sys}$ is a fixed set of events, where EV_{sys} includes events sent by a state machine in the system. EV_{env} includes events which are considered to be sent by the "environment" of the system. An event e is a pair $(type(e), trgt(e))$, where $type(e)$ denotes the event name (or type), and $trgt(e)$ denotes the state machine to which the event was sent (formally defined later). V is a fixed set of variables over finite domains.

We use a running example to present state machines and behavioral UML systems. Fig. 1 describes the state machine of class DB. A *state machine* is a tuple $SM = (S, R, \Omega, init, TR, L)$ where S and R are sets of states and regions respectively. We assume $TOP \in R$. States are graphically represented as squares. $\Omega : S \cup R \to S \cup R \cup \{\epsilon\}$ represents the hierarchical structure of states and regions: for every $s \in S$, $\Omega(s) \in R$, $\Omega(TOP) = \epsilon$ and for every other $r \in R$, $\Omega(r) \in S$. E.g., in Fig 1, $\Omega(Working) = \Omega(Vacation) = TOP$. The transitive closure of Ω is irreflexive and induces a partial order. $u' \in \Omega^+(u)$ if u' *contains* u (possibly transitively). This is denoted $u \triangleleft u'$. Two different regions $r_1, r_2 \in R$ are *orthogonal*, denoted $ORTH(r_1, r_2)$, if $\Omega(r_1) = \Omega(r_2)$. Regions are graphically represented only if they are orthogonal. Orthogonal regions are denoted by a dashed line. E.g., state $Working$ contains two orthogonal regions. $init \subseteq S$ is a set of initial states, s.t. there is one initial state in each region. Initial states are marked with a transition with no source state. TR is a set of transitions. Each $t \in TR$ connects a single source state, denoted $src(t)$, with a single target state, denoted $trgt(t)$. L is a function that labels each transition t with a trigger $(trig(t))$, a guard $(grd(t))$, and an action $(act(t))$. A trigger is a type of an event from EV. $\epsilon \in EV$ represents no trigger. A guard is a Boolean expression over V. An action is a sequence of statements in some programming language where $skip$ is an empty statement. Actions can include "GEN(e)" statements, representing a generation of an event. In the graphical representation, a transition t is labeled with $tr[g]/a$ where $tr = trig(t)$, $g = grd(t)$ and $a = act(t)$. If $tr = \epsilon$, $g = true$ or $a = skip$ they are omitted from the representation. We assume there exists a macro $GEN(\{e_1, ..., e_h\})$, representing a generation of *one of the events* from $\{e_1, ..., e_h\}$ non-deterministically. Given an action act, by abuse of notation we write $GEN(e) \in act$ iff $GEN(e)$ is one of the statements in act. $modif(act)$ denotes the set of variables that may be modified on act (are in the left hand side of an assignment statement). By abuse of notation, $modif(t)$ denotes the set of variables that may be modified by $act(t)$.

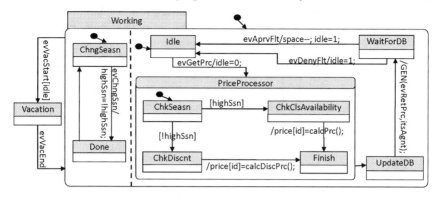

Fig. 1. DB State Machine

Let SM be a state machine, a *state machine configuration (SM-conf)* is a tuple $c = (\omega, \rho)$ where $\rho \in type(EV) \cup \{\epsilon\}$ holds the type of an event currently *dispatched* to SM and not yet consumed, and $\omega \subseteq S$ is the set of currently active states. ω always contains a single state s s.t. $\Omega(s) = TOP$. It also has the property that for every $s \in \omega$ and for every $r \in R$ s.t. $\Omega(r) = s$ there exists a *single* $s' \in S$ s.t. $\Omega(s') = r$ and $s' \in \omega$.

From here on, we assume the following restrictions on SM:
(1) An action includes at most one "$GEN(e)$". In addition, an action that includes "$GEN(e)$" is a non-branching sequence of statements. If either one of these restrictions does not hold, then SM can be preprocessed s.t. the transition is replaced with a series of states and transitions, each executing part of the original action.
(2) SM does not include the following complex UML syntactic features: history, cross-hierarchy transitions, fork, join, entry and exit actions. It is straightforward to eliminate these features, at the expense of additional states, transitions and variables. Note that the hierarchical structure of the state machines is maintained, thus avoiding the exponential blow-up incurred by flattening.

2.2   Systems

Next we define UML systems and their behavior. UML2 places no restrictions on the implementation of the EQ and neither do we. A finite sequence $q = (e_1, ..., e_l)$ of events $e_i \in EV$ represents the EQ at a particular point in time. We assume functions $top(q)$, $pop(q)$ and $push(q, e)$ are defined in the usual way.

A *system* is a tuple $\Gamma = (SM_1, ..., SM_n, Q_1, ..., Q_m, thrd, V)$ s.t. $SM_1, ..., SM_n$ are state machines, $Q_1, ..., Q_m$ ($m \leq n$) are EQs (one for each thread), $thrd : \{1, ..., n\} \rightarrow \{1, ..., m\}$ assigns each SM_i to a thread, and V is a collection of variables over finite domains. A *system configuration (Γ-conf)* is a tuple $C = (c_1, ..., c_n, q_1, ..., q_m, id_1, ..., id_m, \sigma)$ s.t. c_i is a SM-conf of SM_i, q_j is the contents of Q_j, $id_j \in \{0, ..., n\}$ is the id of the SM associated with thread j that is currently executing a RTC ($id_j = 0$ means that all SMs of thread j are *inactive*), and σ is a legal assignment to all variables in V.

From now on we fix a given system $\Gamma = (SM_1, ..., SM_n, Q_1, ..., Q_m, thrd, V)$. We use c for SM-confs and C for Γ-confs. We use k as a superscript to range over steps in time, making c_i^k the SM-conf of SM_i at time k. For every $e \in EV$, we define $trgt(e) \in \{0, ..., n\}$ to give the index of the SM that is the target of e. $trgt(e) = 0$ means the event is sent to the environment of Γ.

A transition $t \in TR_i$ can be executed in C if SM_i is currently executing a RTC, and t is *enabled* in C, denoted $enabled(t, C)$. t is enabled in C if the source state is active ($src(t) \in \omega_i$), the trigger is the currently dispatched event ($\rho_i = trig(t)$) or no trigger on t if $\rho_i = \epsilon$, the guard is satisfied under the current variable assignment, and all transitions from states s s.t. $s \lhd src(t)$ are not enabled. When t executes, SM_i moves to $c_i' = (\omega_i', \rho_i')$, denoted $dest(c_i, t)$, where $\rho_i' = \epsilon$ (an event is consumed once). ω' is obtained by removing from ω $src(t)$ and states contained in it and then adding $trgt(t)$ and states contained in it, based on $init$.

Let C be a Γ-conf, SM_i be a state machine in Γ, and let $s_1, s_2 \in S_i$ and $t, t_1, ..., t_y \in TR_i$. We use the following notations. $Qpush(t, (q_1, ..., q_m)) = (q_1', ..., q_m')$ denotes the effect of executing t on the different EQs of the system: if for some event e, $GEN(e) \in act(t)$, then executing t pushes e to the relevant EQ (to $Q_{thrd(trgt(e))}$). The rest of the EQs remain unchanged. $act(t)(\sigma, C) = \sigma'$ represents the effect of executing the assignments in $act(t)$ on the valuation σ of C, which results in a new assignment, σ'. States are *orthogonal* iff they are contained (possibly transitively) in orthogonal regions. $maxORTH((t_1, ..., t_y), C) = true$ iff $(t_1, ..., t_y)$ is a *maximal set* of *enabled* orthogonal transitions. $t_1, ..., t_y$ are *orthogonal* iff their sources are pairwise orthogonal. In Fig 1, the transition from $ChkSeasn$ to $ChkDiscnt$ is orthogonal to the transition from $ChngSeasn$ to $Done$.

The function *apply* defines the effect of executing a sequence of transitions on a Γ-conf C. $apply((t_1, ..., t_y), C) = C'$ represents the effect of executing t_1 on C followed by t_2 on the result etc. until executing t_y, which results in $C' = (c_1, ..., c_i', ..., c_n, q_1', ..., q_m', id_1, ..., id_m, \sigma')$ where: $c_i' = dest(...dest(c_i, t_1)..., t_y)$, $q_1', ..., q_m' = Qpush(t_y, ...Qpush(t_1, (q_1, ..., q_m)))$, $\sigma' = act(t_y)(...act(t_1)(\sigma, C), C)$.

3   System Computations

Def. 1 (System Computations). *A computation of a system Γ is a maximal sequence $\pi = C^0, step^0, C^1, step^1, ...$ s.t.: (1) each C^k is a Γ-conf, (2) each step $C^k \xrightarrow{step^k} C^{k+1}$ can be generated by one of the inference rules detailed below, and (3) each $step^k$ is a pair $(thid^k, t^k)$ where $thid^k \in \{1, ..., m\}$ represents the id of the thread executing the step (t^k is described in the inference rules).*

We now define the set of inference rules describing $C \xrightarrow{step} C'$. We specify only the parts of C' that change w.r.t. C due to $step$.

Initialization. In the initial configuration C^0 all EQs are empty, and each SM_i is inactive (for every j, $id_j^0 = 0$) and is in its initial state (for every c_i^0, $\rho_i^0 = \epsilon$ and $\omega_i^0 = \{s \in S_i | s \in init_i \wedge \forall s' \in S_i.s \lhd s' \to s' \in init_i\}$).

Dispatch. An event can be dispatched from thread j's EQ only if the previous RTC on thread j ended and the EQ is not empty.

$$DISP(j, e) : \quad \frac{id_j = 0 \quad q_j \neq \phi \quad top(q_j) = e \quad trgt(e) = l}{id'_j = l \quad q'_j = pop(q_j) \quad c'_l = (\omega_l, type(e))}$$

Transition. UML2 defines a single case where transitions are executed simultaneously, when the transitions are in orthogonal regions and all simultaneously consume an event (on the first step of a RTC). Since it is not clear how to define simultaneous execution, we define an interleaved execution of these transitions. Only after all transitions have executed, the next step is enabled.

$$TRANS(j, (t_1, ..., t_y)) : \quad \frac{\begin{array}{c} id_j = l > 0 \quad t_1, ..., t_y \in TR_l \\ \rho_l \neq \epsilon \rightarrow (maxORTH((t_1, ..., t_y), C) = true) \\ \rho_l = \epsilon \rightarrow (y = 1 \wedge enabled(t_1, C)) \end{array}}{C' = apply((t_1, ..., t_y), C)}$$

EndRTC. If the currently running state machine on thread j has no enabled transitions, then the RTC is complete.

$$EndRTC(j, \epsilon) : \quad \frac{id_j = l > 0 \quad \forall t \in TR_l.enabled(t, C) = false}{id'_j = 0 \quad c'_l = (\omega_l, \epsilon)}$$

ENV. The behavior of the environment is not precisely described in the UML standard. We assume the most general definition, where the environment may insert events into the EQs at any step.

$$ENV(j, e) : \quad \frac{e \in EV_{env} \quad thrd(trgt(e)) = j}{q'_j = push(q_j, e)}$$

Intuitively, a computation is a series of steps that follow the RTC semantics per-thread, where RTCs of different threads are interleaved.

4 Abstracting a Behavioral UML System

4.1 Abstracting a State Machine

Let SM be a concrete state machine. The abstraction of SM is defined w.r.t. a *collection* $A = \{A^1, ..., A^k\}$, where for every i, the *abstraction set* A^i is a set of states from S s.t. for every $s, s' \in A^i$, $\Omega(s) = \Omega(s')$. Intuitively, our abstraction replaces every A^i (and all states contained in A^i) with a *different construct* that ignores the details of A^i and maintains an over-approximated behavior of the events generated by A^i. For simplicity, from here on we assume the collection contains a single abstraction set A. A description of the framework for any collection size is available in [17].

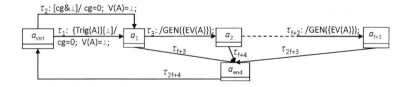

Fig. 2. $\Delta(A)$: The abstraction construct created for A

We add the value $don't - know$, denoted $\perp$, to the domain of all variables in V, where $\perp$ represents any value in the domain. The semantics of boolean operations is extended to 3-valued logic in the usual way: $\perp \wedge false = false$, $\perp \wedge true = \perp$ and $\neg \perp = \perp$. An expression is evaluated to $\perp$ if one of its arguments is $\perp$. For simplicity of presentation, we enable $trig(t)$ to be a *set of triggers*. I.e. $trig(t) = \{e_1, ..., e_q\} \cup \epsilon$, and $enabled(t, C) = true$ if *one of the events* from $trig(t)$ matches ρ.

Next, we define several notions that are concrete and are defined w.r.t. A:

- $S(A) = \{s \in S | \exists s' \in A.(s \lhd s')\}$ are the *abstracted states*.
- $R(A) = \{r \in R | \exists s \in A.(r \lhd s)\}$ are the *abstracted regions*.
- $TR(A) = \{t \in TR | src(t), trgt(t) \in S(A)\}$ are the *abstracted transitions*.
- $EV(A) = \{e \in EV | \exists t \in TR(A).(GEN(e) \in act(t))\}$
- $Trig(A) = \{tr | \exists t \in TR(A).(trig(t) = tr)\} \setminus \{\epsilon\}$
- $V(A) = \{v \in V | \exists t \in TR(A).(v \in modif(t))\}$
- $GRDV(A) = \{v \in V | \exists t \in TR(A).(trig(t) = \epsilon \wedge v \in grd(t))\}$

We require the following restrictions on A of SM_i:
(1) For every $v \in GRDV(A)$, if v can be modified by several SMs in Γ, then all these SMs are assigned to the same thread. This is needed for correctness of the construction (details in [17]).
(2) There are no loops without triggers within $S(A)$. Further, there are no self loops without a trigger on states containing $S(A)$. This is needed to enable static analysis described next.

In order to explain our abstraction we introduce the notion of an *A-round*. Let π be a computation on the concrete system Γ, an A-round is a maximal, possibly non-consecutive, sequence of steps, $step_{i_1}, ..., step_{i_d}$ from π, s.t. all the steps are part of a single RTC, every step executes a transition from $TR(A)$, and the SM remains in an abstracted state throughout the A-round. I.e., for every $j \in \{i_1, i_1 + 1, ..., i_d\}$: $\omega^j \cap S(A) \neq \phi$. Due to the above requirement (2), we can easily apply static analysis in order to determine the maximal number of events that can be generated by any single A-round. We denote this number by f.

Given an abstraction set A, our abstraction replaces $S(A)$, $R(A)$ and $TR(A)$ with *a new construct*, referred to as $\Delta(A)$, demonstrated in Fig. 2. $\Delta(A)$ includes an initial state a_{strt} and a final state a_{end}. Every A-round over states from $S(A)$ is represented by a computation from a_{strt} to a_{end}. $\Delta(A)$ includes computations that can generate any sequence of size 0 to f events from $EV(A)$. Also, all the variables that *can* be modified in the A-round are given the value $\perp$.

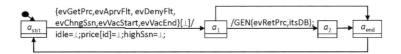

Fig. 3. Abstract DB State Machine

An A-round whose first transition consumes an event, is represented by a computation that starts with transition τ_1 from a_{strt} to a_1, which can consume any single event from $Trig(A)$. The guard $\bot$ on τ_1 and τ_2 represents a non-deterministic choice between "true" or "false". If the first transition on an A-round does not consume an event, it will be represented by transition τ_2, which is not marked with a trigger. Since $\Delta(A)$ contains a loop of transitions without triggers we must ensure that all RTCs through $\Delta(A)$ are finite. We introduce a new Boolean variable cg. A trace on $\Delta(A)$ can be initiated without a trigger only if cg is 1. $\Delta(A)$ then sets cg to 0 on the transitions exiting a_{strt}.

When cg is set to 1 it signals that it is possible to execute an A-round that does not consume an event. Such a situation abstracts a concrete execution in which the RTC that includes the A-round starts at a state that is not abstracted and continues within the abstraction. The situation can also occur if an abstracted transition becomes enabled due to some variable change. I.e., execution of some transition t, which is either orthogonal to A or is in a different state machine, and t modifies a variable $v \in GRDV(A)$.

If by static analysis we can conclude that the first transition of every A-round *consumes an event*, then cg is redundant (and τ_2 can be removed). All the A-rounds are then represented by computations that start by traversing τ_1.

We now formally define our abstract state machines. Given $SM = (S, R, \Omega, init, TR, L)$ and an abstraction set $A \subseteq S$, $SM(A) = (S^A, R^A, \Omega^A, init^A, TR^A, L^A)$ is the abstraction of SM w.r.t. A. We denote functions over the abstraction (src, $trgt$, $trig$, grd, and act) with a superscript A.

- $S^A = (S \setminus S(A)) \cup \{a_{strt}, a_1, ..., a_{f+1}, a_{end}\}$ and $R^A = (R \setminus R(A))$
- For every $s \in (S^A \cap S) \cup R^A$: $\Omega^A(s) = \Omega(s)$.
  For every $s \in \{a_{strt}, a_1, ..., a_{f+1}, a_{end}\}$: $\Omega^A(s) = \Omega(s')$ for some $s' \in A$.
- $init^A = init \cap S^A$ or $init^A = (init \cap S^A) \cup \{a_{strt}\}$ if $\exists s \in A$ s.t. $s \in init$
- $TR^A = (TR \setminus TR(A)) \cup \{\tau_1, ..., \tau_{2f+4}\}$.

The src^A, $trgt^A$, $trig^A$, grd^A and act^A functions are redefined as follows:

Transitions $\tau_1, ..., \tau_{2f+4}$ are defined according to Fig. 2. Every transition $t \in TR \setminus TR(A)$ has a representation (*matching transition*) in $SM(A)$. Note that for every such transition, at least one of $src(t)$ and $trgt(t)$ are not abstracted. If $src(t)$ or $trgt(t)$ are abstracted, then $src^A(t)$ or $trgt^A(t)$ respectively are in $\Delta(A)$. The handling of cg is added to the relevant actions, as discussed above. In the following we present only the values of src^A, $trgt^A$, $trig^A$ grd^A and act^A that change in $SM(A)$ w.r.t. SM. For every $t \in TR \setminus TR(A)$:

1. $trgt(t) \in S(A)$ (the target of t is abstracted): we define $trgt^A(t) = a_{strt}$.
   If there exists an abstracted transition from $trgt(t)$ whose trigger is ϵ then $act^A(t) = act(t); cg = 1$ (otherwise, $act^A(t) = act(t)$).

2. $src(t) \in S(A)$ (the source of t is abstracted): we define $src^A(t) = a_{strt}$, $act^A(t) = cg = 0; act(t)$ and $grd^A(t) = grd(t)\&\bot$. We add $\bot$ to the guard in order to ensure that executions of possibly enabled transitions from states containing the abstraction remain (possibly) enabled.

3. Otherwise (neither $src(t)$ nor $trgt(t)$ are abstracted):

   Case a: $A \lhd trgt(t)$. If an execution of t results in a new ω that includes an abstracted state $s \in S(A)$, and there exists an abstracted transition from s whose trigger is ϵ. Then: $act^A(t) = act(t); cg = 1$ (otherwise, $act^A(t) = act(t)$).

   Case b: $src(t)$ and a_{strt} are contained in orthogonal regions (t can be executed orthogonally to the abstraction). Then: $act^A(t) = act(t)$ with the following modifications: If $\exists v \in GRDV(A)$ s.t. $v \in modif(t)$ then $cg = 1$ is added to $act^A(t)$. In addition, if SM is in an abstracted state, then variables that *can* be modified by abstracted transitions should remain $\bot$. For that, every assignment $x = e$ in $act(t)$, if $x \in V(A)$ then $x = e$ is replaced with: "if $(isIn(A))$ $x = \bot$; else $x = e$;" in $act^A(t)$. The current state is checked using the macro $isIn(U)$, that checks whether a certain state from U is active.

Fig. 3 shows the state machine created by abstracting the DB state machine (Fig. 1) with $A = \{Working, Vacation\}$. Note that in this state machine, by static analysis we can conclude that every A-round first consumes an event, and therefore we do not need the cg flag and transition τ_2. Also, on every A-round no more than one event can be generated, therefore $f = 1$.

4.2   Abstracting a System

Next we define an abstract system. This is a system in which some of the state machines are abstract. For SM_i and an abstraction set A_i, SM_i^A denotes the abstraction of SM_i w.r.t. A_i. We denote the cg variable in SM_i^A as cg_i.

Def. 2. *Let Γ and Γ' be two systems, each with n SMs and m EQs. We say that Γ' is an abstraction of Γ, denoted Γ^A, if the following holds. (1) For $i \in \{1, ..., n\}$, $SM_i' = SM_i$ or $SM_i' = SM_i^A$, (2) $thrd = thrd'$, (3) $V' = V \cup \{cg_i | SM_i' = SM_i^A\}$, and (4) for every $i, j \in \{1, ..., n\}$ s.t. $i \neq j$, and for every $t \in TR_j'$: if there exists a variable $v \in GRDV(A_i)$ and $v \in modif(t)$ then $cg_i = 1$ is added to $act'(t)$.*

Recall that setting cg_i to 1 on SM_i^A signals that it is possible to execute an A-round on SM_i without consuming an event. Req. (4) in Def. 2 handles the case where a guard of an abstracted transition of SM_i may change by a transition t of SM_j. It ensures that cg_i is set to 1 on such transitions of TR_j'.

Adding the value $\bot$ to the domain of all variables in V affects the cases when a transition is enabled, since now $grd(t)(\sigma) \in \{true, false, \bot\}$. Intuitively, if $grd(t)(\sigma) = \bot$ then we assume it *can* be either *true* or *false*. We thus consider both cases in the analysis. Therefore, $enabled(t, C) = true$ iff t *can* be enabled w.r.t. C ($grd(t)(\sigma) \in \{true, \bot\}$) and all transitions t' from states contained in $src(t)$ *can* be not enabled ($grd(t')(\sigma) \in \{false, \bot\}$). Note that when enabling

3-valued semantics, a transition may be enabled, even though lower level transitions may be enabled as well.

5   Correctness of the Abstraction

In this section we prove that Γ^A is an over-approximation of Γ by showing that every computation of Γ has a "matching" computation in Γ^A.

Def. 3 (Abstraction of SM-conf). *Let $c = (\omega, \rho)$ and $c^A = (\omega^A, \rho^A)$ be SM-confs of SM and SM^A respectively. c^A abstracts c, denoted $c \preceq c^A$, if $\rho = \rho^A$, and c, c^A agree on the joint states: $\omega \neq \omega^A$ iff $\omega \setminus \omega^A \subseteq S(A)$ and $\omega^A \setminus \omega \subseteq \Delta(A)$.*

Def. 4 (Abstraction of Γ-conf). *Let C and C' be two Γ-confs of Γ and Γ^A respectively. We say that C' abstracts C, denoted $C \preceq C'$, if the Γ-confs agree on the EQs and id elements, and the SM-confs and σ' of Γ^A are abstraction of the matching elements in Γ: for $j \in \{1, ..., m\}$, $q_j = q'_j$ and $id_j = id'_j$, for $i \in \{1, ..., n\}$, $c_i \preceq c'_i$, and for every $v \in V$ either $\sigma(v) = \sigma'(v)$ or $\sigma'(v) = \bot$.*

We now define *stuttering computation inclusion*, which is an extension of stuttering-trace inclusion ([6]) to system computations. For simplicity of presentation, we assume that computations are infinite. However, all the results presented hold for finite computations as well. Intuitively, there exists stuttering inclusion between π and π' if they can be partitioned into infinitely many finite intervals, s.t. *every* configuration in the kth interval of π' abstracts *every* configuration in the kth interval of π.

Def. 5 (Stuttering Computation Inclusion). *Let $\pi = C^0, step^0, C^1, step^1, ...$ and $\pi' = C'^0, step'^0, C'^1, step'^1, ...$ be two computations over Γ and Γ^A respectively. There exists a stuttering computation inclusion between π and π', denoted $\pi \preceq_s \pi'$, if there are two infinite sequences of integers $0 = i_0 < i_1 < ...$ and $0 = i'_0 < i'_1 < ...$ s.t. for every $k \geq 0$:*
For every $j \in \{i_k, ..., (i_{k+1}) - 1\}$ and for every $j' \in \{i'_k, ..., (i'_{k+1}) - 1\}$: $C^j \preceq C'^{j'}$.

Fig. 4 illustrates two computations where $\pi \preceq_s \pi'$. Def. 4 implies that steps of type $DISP$, ENV and $EndRTC$ cannot be steps within an interval, due to the effect of these steps on Γ-conf. For example, in Fig. 4, $C^6 \preceq C'^5$. Assume $step^6 = EndRTC(j, \epsilon)$, then by the definition of $EndRTC$ step, the value of id_j changes from C^6 to C^7. Since Γ-conf abstraction requires equality of the id elements, then clearly $C^7 \npreceq C'^5$. Thus C^6 and C^7 cannot be in the same interval. For a similar reason, a step of type $DISP$, ENV or $EndRTC$ on π implies a step of the same type on π', and vice versa. Steps of type $TRANS$ that are either the first step in a RTC or a step that generates events are also steps that cannot be part of an interval, due to the effect of these steps on the ρ elements and the EQs.

An immediate consequence of the above is that an interval can be of size greater than one only if the steps in the interval are $TRANS$ steps that are neither a first step in a RTC nor a step generating an event. Recall that Def. 4 requires a correlation between the current states of the state machines. It can

Fig. 4. Stuttering Computation Inclusion

therefore be shown that if $step^i = TRANS(j,(t))$ is a step between two configurations in the same interval, then one the following holds: (1) If $step^i \in \pi$ then t is an abstracted transition, (2) If $step^i \in \pi'$ then $t \in \Delta(A)$.

We extend the notion of stuttering inclusion to systems, and say that there exists a *stuttering inclusion* between Γ and Γ^A, denoted $\Gamma \preceq_s \Gamma^A$, if for each computation π of Γ from an initial configuration C_{init}, there exists a computation π' of Γ^A from an initial configuration C'_{init} s.t. $\pi \preceq_s \pi'$.

The following theorem captures the relation between Γ and Γ^A, stating that there *exists* stuttering inclusion between Γ and Γ^A.

Theorem 6. *If Γ^A is an abstraction of Γ then $\Gamma \preceq_s \Gamma^A$.*

Every system Γ can be viewed as a Kripke structure K, where the K-states are the set of Γ-confs, and there exists a K-transition (C, C') iff C' is reachable from C within a single *step*. Thus, every computation of Γ corresponds to a trace in K. Let Γ be a system, and let $A\psi$ be an LTL formula, where the atomic propositions are predicates over Γ. Then $\Gamma \models A\psi$ iff for every computation π of Γ from an initial configuration, $\pi \models \psi$. By preservation of LTL_x over stuttering-traces inclusion we conclude:

Corollary 7. *Let Γ and Γ^A be two systems, s.t. $\Gamma \preceq_s \Gamma^A$, and let $A\psi$ be an LTL_x formula over joint elements of Γ and Γ^A. If $\Gamma^A \models A\psi$ then $\Gamma \models A\psi$.*

Due to the stuttering-inclusion, Γ^A preserves LTL_x and not LTL. It is important to note that since Γ itself is a multi-threaded system, properties of interest are commonly defined without the next-time operator.

The proof of Theorem 6 is available in [17]. We give here an intuitive explanation to why for every π of Γ from C_{init}, there exists π' of Γ^A from C'_{init} s.t. $\pi \preceq_s \pi'$. For every step executed on Γ that does not include execution of an abstracted transition it is possible to execute the same step on Γ^A. More specifically, for every transition t executed on Γ, if t has a matching transition t_a in Γ^A, then t_a can be executed on π'. For every step of type ENV, $DISP$ and $EndRTC$ on π it is possible to execute the same step on π'. This holds since matching configurations C^r and C'^p of π and π' respectively agree on their joint elements, and σ'^p might assign $\perp$ to variables. Thus, if a transition t is enabled, then its matching transition t_a *can* be enabled.

For execution of abstracted transitions on Γ, every A-round χ on some concrete state machine SM_i can be matched to a trace from a_{strt} to a_{end} on SM_i^A. The matching is as follows: every transition t that is traversed on χ and where t generates an event $(GEN(e) \in act(t))$ matches a transition from a_i to a_{i+1} (for some i). Every transition t that is traversed on χ and where t does not generate or consume an event, matches an interval of length one on π' (Γ^A does not execute a matching step). Since χ can generate at most f events, then indeed we can match the transitions as described. All variables that *can* be modified on χ are given the value $\bot$ upon execution of the first transition in $\Delta(A)$ (transitions from a_{strt} to a_1). This value is maintained in the variables throughout the traversal on $\Delta(A)$.

6 Using Abstraction

We now present the applicability of our abstraction framework by an example. Consider a system Γ describing a travel agent (of class $Agent$) that books flights and communicates with both airline databases (of class DB) and clients. Assume Γ includes n different DB objects, where the behavior of each DB is defined in Fig. 1. The single $Agent$ object in Γ communicates with clients (modeled as the environment) and with all of the DBs. The $Agent$ behavior is as follows: upon receiving a flight request from a client, it requests a price offer from all DBs by sending them event $evGetPrc$. After getting an answer from the DBs (via $evRetPrc$), it chooses an offer, reserves the flight from the relevant DB (via $evAprvFlt$) and rejects the offers from the rest of the DB (via $evDenyFlt$).

Assume now we create an abstract system Γ^A, where the DBs are abstracted as in Fig. 3 (the $Agent$ remains concrete). If $Agent$ state machine includes x states, then Γ has $(12*n+x)$ states, whereas Γ^A has $(4*n+x)$ states. Moreover, Γ^A does not include the pieces of code in the actions of the transitions of DBs, which may be complicated. E.g., the method $calcPrc()$ is not part of the abstract state machine of DB, and this method might include complex computations.

Assume we want to verify the property describing that on all computations of Γ, if $Agent$ orders a flight from some DB, then all the DBs returned an answer to the $Agent$ before the $Agent$ chooses an offer. For this property it is enough to consider only the *interface* of the DBs. The property is not affected, for example, by the calculation of a price by the DBs. It is an outcome only of the information that every DB can consume an event $evGetPrc$, and can send an event $evRetPrc$. We can therefore verify the property on Γ^A. If the property holds, then we can conclude that Γ also satisfies the property.

Consider another property: we want to verify that due to a single request from the client, *space* decreases by at most 1. Clearly, when verifying the property on Γ^A, the result is $\bot$, since Γ^A abstracts the variable *space*. This means that we cannot conclude whether or not the property holds on Γ by model checking Γ^A. However, it might be possible to *refine* Γ^A, and create a different abstraction Γ'^A for which this property can be verified. Following, in section 7 we present how to refine an abstract system when the verification does not succeed.

7 Refinement

Once we have an abstract system Γ^A, we model check our LTL_x property $A\psi$ over the abstract system. Since variables in Γ^A can have the value $\bot$, then $(\Gamma^A \models A\psi) \in \{true, false, \bot\}$. If $(\Gamma^A \models A\psi) = true$, then from Theorem 6 the property holds on Γ as well. If $(\Gamma^A \models A\psi) \in \{false, \bot\}$ then due to Γ^A being an over-approximation we cannot determine whether or not the property holds on Γ. Typical model checkers provide the user with a CEX in case verification does not succeed. A CEX π^A on Γ^A is either a finite computation or a lasso computation s.t. either $(\pi^A \models \psi) = false$ or $(\pi^A \models \psi) = \bot$.

Next we present a CEGAR-like algorithm for refining Γ^A based on π^A. The refinement step suggests how to create a new abstract system Γ'^A, where one or more of the abstracted states of Γ are removed from the abstraction sets. Since the concrete system Γ is finite, the $CEGAR$ algorithm ultimately terminates and returns a correct result.

If $(\pi^A \models \psi) = \bot$ then we cannot determine the value of the property. If $(\pi^A \models \psi) = false$, then this CEX might be spurious. In both cases we search for a computation π on Γ s.t. $\pi \preceq_s \pi^A$. Given π^A, we inductively construct π w.r.t. π^A. Note that if the concrete model enables non-determinism, then there might be more than one matching concrete CEXs. In this case, all the matching concrete CEXs are simultaneously constructed. Intuitively, the construction of π follows the steps of π^A, maintaining the stuttering inclusion. During the construction, if for some prefix of π^A: $C'^0, step'^0, ..., step'^{p-1}, C'^p$ it is not possible to extend any of the matching concrete computations based on $step'^p$, then π^A is a spurious CEX and we should refine the system. Detailed description of the construction of π is presented in [17]. There are three cases where we cannot extend a concrete computation $\pi = C^0, step^0, ..., C^r$ ($C^r \preceq C'^p$) based on $step'^p$: (1) $step'^p$ is an $EndRTC$ step on SM_l' but there exists an enabled transition in TR_l w.r.t. C^r. (2) $step'^p$ is a $TRANS$ step on SM_l' that executes a transition $t_a \notin \Delta(A)$, and the concrete transition t that matches t_a is not enabled. (3) $step'^p$ is a $TRANS$ step on SM_l' that executes a transition $t_a \in \Delta(A)$ that generates an event e, and there is no enabled concrete transition $t \in TR(A)$ where $GEN(e) \in act(t)$.

We call the configuration $C'^p \in \pi^A$ from which we cannot extend a matching concrete computation *failure-conf*. Following, we distinguish between two reasons that can cause a failure-conf, and show how to refine the system in each case.

Case 1: $step'^p$ executes a transition that does not have a matching behavior in Γ. E.g., when $step'^p = TRANS(j, (t^a))$, $id_j'^p = l$, and the concrete t that matches t_a is not enabled since $src(t) \notin \omega_l^r$. This is possible only if $src(t) \in S(A)$ and $trgt(t) \notin S(A)$. Another example for such a failure is when Γ^A generates an event e as part of the action of t_a, but e cannot be generated from C^r on any possible *step*. This can happen only if $t_a \in \Delta(A)$. In both cases we refine by removing a state $s \in S(A)$ s.t. $s \in \omega_l^r$ from the abstraction.

Case 2: There exists $v \in V$ for which $\sigma'^p(v) = \bot$ and the value of $\sigma^r(v)$ causes the failure-conf. For example, when $step'^p = TRANS(j, (t_a))$ and the concrete t that matches t_a is not enabled since $grd(t)(\sigma^r) = false$. Since $C^r \preceq C'^p$ and $grd(t_a) = grd(t)$, then clearly $grd(t_a)(\sigma'^p) = \bot$ and for some v, $\sigma'^p(v) = \bot$ and v affects the value of $grd(t_a)$. We refine Γ^A to obtain a concrete value on v: We trace π^A back to find the variable that gave v the value $\bot$. The only place where a variable is initially assigned the value $\bot$ is a transition from a_{strt} to a_1

in some $\Delta(A_i)$. Thus, the tracing back of π^A terminates at C'^α s.t. $a_{strt} \in \omega_i^\alpha$. We find the matching Γ-conf C^β in π s.t. $C^\beta \preceq C'^\alpha$, and refine the model by removing from the abstraction a state $s \in S(A_i)$ s.t. $s \in \omega_i^\beta$.

If we are able to construct π s.t. $\pi \preceq \pi^A$, then one of the following holds: (a) If $(\pi^A \models \psi) = false$ then no need to check π. By construction, $\pi \not\models \psi$, and we can conclude that $\Gamma \not\models A\psi$, (b) If $(\pi^A \models \psi) = \bot$ then we check π w.r.t. ψ. If $\pi \not\models \psi$ then again π is a concrete CEX and we conclude that $\Gamma \not\models A\psi$. Otherwise $(\pi \models \psi)$, the abstraction is too coarse and we need to refine. Notice that in the latter case, since $(\pi^A \models \psi) = \bot$ then there exists $v \in V$ which affects the value of ψ, and v has the value $\bot$. We then refine Γ^A in order to have a concrete value on v, as described above (Case 2).

Consider the example system presented in section 6, and consider a property that addresses the variable *space*. Recall that under the abstraction presented for this example, such a property is evaluated to $\bot$, since the variable *space* is abstracted. During the refinement, state $WaitForDB$ is suggested for refinement, and is removed from the abstraction. We can then create a *refined* system Γ'^A, where DB objects are abstracted w.r.t. a new abstraction set $A' = \{Idle, PriceProcessor, UpdateDB\}$. The property can then be verified on Γ'^A, and we can conclude that it holds on the concrete system.

8   Conclusion

In this work we presented a CEGAR-like method for abstraction and refinement of behavioral UML systems. It is important to note that our framework is completely automatic. An initial abstraction can be one that abstracts entire state machines, based on the given property. We presented a basic and automatic refinement method. Heuristics can be applied during the refinement stage in order to converge in less iterations. For example, when refining due to a variable v whose value is $\bot$, we can refine by adding all abstracted transitions that modify v (or v's cone-of-influence). Note, however, that there always exists a tradeoff between quick convergence and the growth in size of the abstract system.

References

1. Majzik, I., Darvas, A., Beny, B.: Verification of UML statechart models of embedded systems. In: DDECS 2002 (2002)
2. Booch, G., Rumbaugh, J.E., Jacobson, I.: The unified modeling language user guide. J. Database Manag. 10(4), 51–52 (1999)
3. Chan, W., Anderson, R.J., Beame, P., Burns, S., Modugno, F., Notkin, D., Reese, J.D.: Model checking large software specifications. IEEE Trans. Software Eng. 24(7), 498–520 (1998)
4. Clarke, E.M., Grumberg, O., Jha, S., Lu, Y., Veith, H.: Counterexample-guided abstraction refinement. Journal of the ACM 50(5), 752–794 (2003)
5. Clarke, E.M., Heinle, W.: Modular translation of statecharts to SMV. Tr, CMU (2000)
6. Clarke, E.M., Grumberg, O., Peled, D.A.: Model Checking. MIT Press (1999)

7. Damm, W., Josko, B., Pnueli, A., Votintseva, A.: Understanding UML: A formal semantics of concurrency and communication in real-time UML. In: de Boer, F.S., Bonsangue, M.M., Graf, S., de Roever, W.-P. (eds.) FMCO 2002. LNCS, vol. 2852, pp. 71–98. Springer, Heidelberg (2003)
8. Dubrovin, J., Junttila, T.A.: Symbolic model checking of hierarchical UML state machines. In: ACSD 2008 (2008)
9. Fecher, H., Huth, M., Schmidt, H., Schönborn, J.: Refinement sensitive formal semantics of state machines with persistent choice. Electron. Notes Theor. Comput. Sci. 250(1), 71–86 (2009)
10. Fecher, H., Schönborn, J.: UML 2.0 state machines: Complete formal semantics via core state machine. In: Brim, L., Haverkort, B.R., Leucker, M., van de Pol, J. (eds.) FMICS 2006 and PDMC 2006. LNCS, vol. 4346, pp. 244–260. Springer, Heidelberg (2007)
11. Object Management Group. OMG Unified Modeling Language (UML) Infrastructure, version 2.4. ptc/2010-11-16 (2010)
12. Grumberg, O., Meller, Y., Yorav, K.: Applying software model checking techniques for behavioral UML models. In: Giannakopoulou, D., Méry, D. (eds.) FM 2012. LNCS, vol. 7436, pp. 277–292. Springer, Heidelberg (2012)
13. Gurfinkel, A., Chechik, M.: Why waste a perfectly good abstraction? In: Hermanns, H., Palsberg, J. (eds.) TACAS 2006. LNCS, vol. 3920, pp. 212–226. Springer, Heidelberg (2006)
14. Latella, D., Majzik, I., Massink, M.: Automatic verification of a behavioural subset of UML statechart diagrams using the spin model-checker. Formal Asp. Comput. 11(6), 637–664 (1999)
15. Liu, S., Liu, Y., André, É., Choppy, C., Sun, J., Wadhwa, B., Dong, J.S.: A formal semantics for complete UML state machines with communications. In: Johnsen, E.B., Petre, L. (eds.) IFM 2013. LNCS, vol. 7940, pp. 331–346. Springer, Heidelberg (2013)
16. Madhukar, K., Metta, R., Singh, P., Venkatesh, R.: Reachability verification of rhapsody statecharts. In: ICSTW 2013 (2013)
17. Meller, Y., Grumberg, O., Yorav, K.: Verifying behavioral UML systems via CEGAR. TR CS-2014-01, Dept. of Computer Science. Technion - Israel Institute of Technology (2014)
18. Mikk, E., Lakhnech, Y., Siegel, M., Holzmann, G.J.: Implementing statecharts in promela/spin. In: WIFT 1998 (1998)
19. Ober, I., Graf, S., Ober, I.: Validating timed UML models by simulation and verification. STTT 8(2), 128–145 (2006)
20. IST-2001-33522 OMEGA (2001), http://www-omega.imag.fr
21. Lilius, J., Paltor, I.P.: Formalising UML state machines for model checking. In: France, R.B. (ed.) UML 1999. LNCS, vol. 1723, pp. 430–444. Springer, Heidelberg (1999)
22. Pnueli, A.: The temporal logic of programs. In: FOCS 1977 (1977)
23. Prehofer, C.: Behavioral refinement and compatibility of statechart extensions. Electron. Notes Theor. Comput. Sci. 295(5), 65–78 (2013)
24. Reeve, G., Reeves, S.: Logic and refinement for charts. In: ACSC 2006 (2006)
25. Schinz, I., Toben, T., Mrugalla, C., Westphal, B.: The rhapsody UML verification environment. In: SEFM 2004 (2004)
26. Scholz, P.: Incremental design of statechart specifications. Sci. Comput. Program. 40(1), 119–145 (2001)
27. Seger, C.H., Bryant, R.E.: Formal verification by symbolic evaluation of partially-ordered trajectories. Form. Methods Syst. Des. 6(2), 147–189 (1995)
28. Simons, A.J.H., Stannett, M.P., Bogdanov, K.E., Holcombe, W.M.L.: Plug and play safely: Rules for behavioural compatibility. In: SEA 2002 (2002)

Formal Refinement in SysML

Alvaro Miyazawa and Ana Cavalcanti

Department of Computer Science, The University of York, UK
{alvaro.miyazawa,ana.cavalcanti}@york.ac.uk

Abstract. SysML is a UML-based graphical notation for systems engineering that is becoming a *de facto* standard. Whilst it reuses a number of UML diagrams, it introduces new diagrams, and maintains the loose UML semantics. Refinement is a formal technique that supports the validation and verification of models by capturing a notion of correctness based on observable behaviour. In this paper, we analyse the issue of formal refinement in the context of SysML. First, we identify the requirements for supporting refinement in SysML, next we propose extensions to SysML that satisfy these requirements, and finally we present a few refinement laws and discuss their validity.

1 Introduction

SysML [1] is a profile of UML 2.0 for systems engineering. SysML retains a number of UML 2.0 diagrams, modifies others (like the block definition, internal block, and state-machine diagrams) and adds a new type of diagram. It supports modelling of a variety of aspects of a system, including software and hardware components, and socio-technical aspects. SysML includes a notion of refinement, but it is informal and there is no universally accepted understanding of its meaning. Whilst it is difficult to gauge adoption of SysML in industry, its current support by tool vendors such as IBM [2], Atego [3] and Sparx Systems [4] indicates that adoption is at least perceived as wide.

In [5,6,7] a denotational semantics for a subset of SysML has been proposed; it is based on the state-rich refinement process algebra CML, which is a combination of VDM [8], CSP [9,10] and the refinement calculus [11]. CML is related to the *Circus* family of refinement languages, and its semantics is specified in Hoare and He's Unifying Theories of Programming (UTP) [12], which is a relational refinement framework. *Circus* has a refinement strategy [13] with associated notions of refinement that can be directly adopted in the context of CML.

In this paper we lift the notion of refinement of CML to SysML, propose extensions to SysML that enable reasoning based on refinement at the level of the diagrammatic notation rather than CML, and present refinement laws both for diagrams written using only standard SysML and for diagrams that use our extensions. Our objective is to support stepwise refinement, and we also explain how the *Circus* refinement strategy can be lifted to SysML; the laws that we present are useful in the context of that strategy.

There have been several studies of refinement in UML. They either do not consider formal refinement [14], take refinement as a syntactic notion based

E. Albert and E. Sekerinski (Eds.): IFM 2014, LNCS 8739, pp. 155–170, 2014.

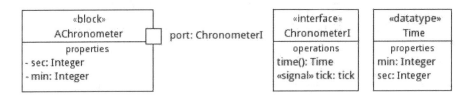

Fig. 1. Block definition diagram of abstract model

directly on UML components [15,16,17], or do not focus on laws of refinement for model transformations as we do here [18,19,20,21,22]. Our objective is to support sound model transformation at the diagrammatic level.

The structure of this paper is as follows. Section 2 introduces SysML and its formal model [7]. Section 3 presents our notions of refinement. Section 4 discusses the limitations of SysML in supporting refinement and proposes extensions to overcome these limitations. Section 5 presents refinement laws. Finally, Section 6 summarises our results and discusses related and future work.

2   SysML and Its Formal Model

Although our definition of refinement applies to models involving an arbitrary set of diagrams, in this paper, we focus on block definition, internal block and state-machine diagrams. Block definition diagrams allow the declaration of blocks, which are the main modelling units in SysML used to define systems and their components, and their relationships (composition, aggregation, generalisation and association), internal block diagrams support the specification of the internal connections of a composite block, and state machines provide the means of specifying the behaviour of a block. Activities play a similar role to state machines, and are omitted here to simplify the exposition.

To illustrate refinement in SysML, we introduce a simple example of a chronometer that records seconds and minutes, and accepts a `tick` signal that increments the chronometer and a `time` operation that queries the recorded time. The example consists of two distinct models, one abstract, depicted in Figure 1 and one concrete, shown in Figure 2, related by refinement. Whilst the abstract model is centralised, the concrete one has two components, one recording the seconds and the other recording the minutes. The components of the concrete model cooperate to realise the behaviour specified in the abstract model.

Figure 1 shows the block definition diagram of the abstract model; it declares a single block `AChronometer` with two private properties `sec` and `min`, both of type `Integer`, and a port `port` that provides the operations and signals in the interface `ChronometerI`. This interface is also defined by a block and contains an operation `time` that returns a value of type `Time`, and a signal `tick` that models the passing of time. The type `Time` is a datatype with two components, `min` and `sec`, that encode a time instant in minutes and seconds.

Since the block `AChronometer` is simple, there is no internal block diagram specifying its internal structure. The remaining diagram in the abstract model

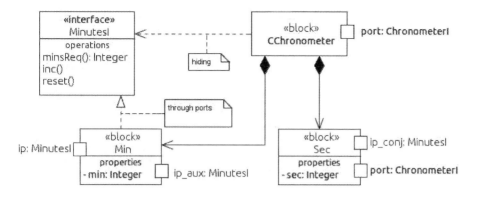

Fig. 2. Block definition diagram of concrete model

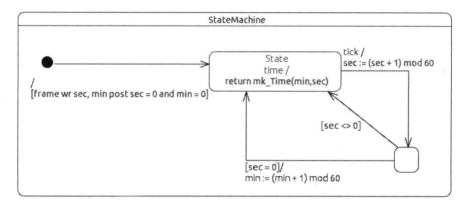

Fig. 3. State machine diagram of the abstract model

is the state-machine diagram shown in Figure 3; it contains two simple states. When the state machine is started, the properties `min` and `sec` are initialised to 0, and the state `State` is entered. When the state is active, either the internal transition triggered by `time` is executed, or the transition triggered by `tick` is executed. The first models the treatment of a call to the operation `time` and returns a value of type `Time` built from `min` and `sec`, whilst the second models the passing of time and increments the block's properties. The second transition leads to a state that is exited as soon as it is entered due to the fact that its outgoing transitions do not have triggers.

The concrete model is formed by four diagrams: one block definition diagram, one internal block diagram and two state-machine diagrams. The first is shown in Figure 2; it declares three blocks `CChronometer`, `Min` and `Sec`. The first is composed of the other two as indicated by the composition relation (arrow with a black diamond). The block `CChronometer` is similar to the block of the abstract model except that it has no properties. These are distributed in the components `Min` and `Sec`. The block `Min` has a single private property and two ports, `ip`

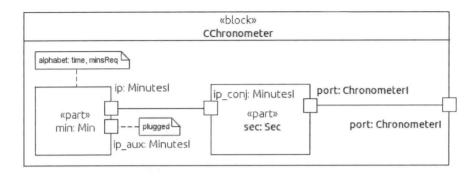

Fig. 4. Internal block diagram of concrete model

and ip_aux, that both provide the operations in the interface MinutesI. The provided and required interfaces of a port are the sets of operation calls and signals that the block, respectively, receives and sends through the port.

The block Sec also has a single property, but two ports, port and ip_conj. The first is identical to the port of the block CChronometer, whilst the second is complementary to the port ip of Min and requires the operations in the interface MinutesI. The block definition diagram has some extra annotations (hiding and through port), which support refinement and are explained in Section 4.

The internal block diagram of the concrete model (Figure 4) shows the composite block CChronometer and its components (marked with ≪part≫); it specifies that the port port of Sec is connected to the port of CChronometer, and that the ports ip and ip_conj are connected to each other. Finally, the blocks Sec and Min have each one state machine (Figure 5). The state machine of Sec is called SecMain and is similar to the state machine of the abstract model, except that it delegates the operations involving minutes to the block Min. These operations are treated by the state machine MinMain that contains a single state with two internal transitions that react to a call to the operations minsReq and inc. The first returns the value stored in min, and the second increments it. Next, we describe the main elements of SysML that are covered in this paper.

Block. A block may declare properties, which are typed named elements (sec and min in Figure 1), receptions (tick), which specify the signals that can be treated by the block, and operations (time()). Additionally, it may generalise other blocks, use and realise interfaces, and declare ports (ip, ip_conj and port in Figure 4), parts (min and sec in Figure 4) and references.

State machine. State machines contain states (State in Figure 3), which may be simple or composite, regions, transitions (the four arrows in Figure 3), junctions (the small black circle in Figure 3), joins, forks, history junctions, initial junctions (the larger black circle in Figure 3) and final states. States may declare entry actions (executed when a state is entered), do activities (executed after the state is entered), and exit actions (executed when the state is exited). Composite states have one or more regions, which are entered, executed and exited in parallel. Regions may contain states, both simple and composite, initial junctions

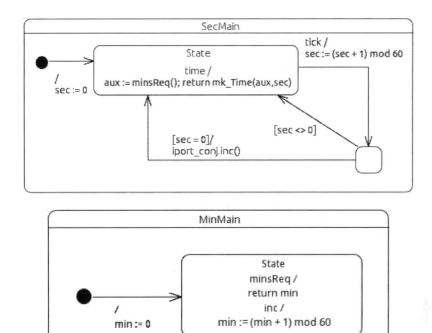

Fig. 5. State machine diagrams of the concrete model

and final states. Initial junctions specify which state of a region is entered first, and final states indicate when the behaviour of a region has terminated.

Transitions allow the deactivation of one or more states, and the activation of others. Whilst two states may be connected directly by a transition, the connection may be extended by the use of junctions that allow the specification of more complex flows; for instance, the three transitions connected to the junction in Figure 3 specify that after `sec` is incremented, if its value is zero, nothing is done and `State` is re-entered, otherwise, `min` is incremented and `State` is re-entered Transitions may be triggered by events (`tick` in Figure 3) and guarded by conditions (`[sec <> 0]` in Figure 3). Additionally, they may specify an action that is executed when the transition is taken (`[frame wr sec, min post sec = 0 and min = 0]` in Figure 3). Joins and forks allow transitions to link one state to multiple parallel states (contained in regions).

CML. A CML specification is a sequence of paragraphs that declare types, constants, functions, channels, channel sets and processes. Figure 6 illustrates the specification of a message buffer in CML.

First, the type of identifiers (`ID`) is defined as the type `token`, which is a universal type in CML, and the type of messages is defined as a record type with three components that record the origin of the message, its destination and the text of the message. An invariant requires that the origin and destination

```
types
   ID = token
   MSG :: origin: ID dest: ID msg: seq of char
      inv mk_MSG(o,d,-) == o <> d
values MAX = 5
channels read, write: MSG
process Buffer =  begin
   state b: seq of MSG inv len b <= MAX
   operations
      Init: () ==> ()
      Init() == b := []
   actions
      Read = [len b > 0] & read!(hd b) -> b := tl b
      Write = [len b < MAX] & write?x -> b := b^[x]
   @ Init(); mu X @ ((Read [] Write); X)
end
```

Fig. 6. A CML specification of a message buffer

must be different. Next, the maximum size of the buffer is declared as a constant
MAX, and two channels as specified: read and write. They each communicate a
message, and are used to add and remove values from the buffer.

Finally, the process Buffer is declared. It encapsulates a single state component b that holds sequences of messages of size at most MAX. A data operation
Init is declared to initialise the state component with an empty sequence, and
two actions, Read and Write, specify how the channels read and write are used
to interact with the buffer. In the first case, it is only possible to obtain a value
through the channel read, if there is at least one value in the buffer. In the
second case, the action specifies that it is only possible to send a value through
the channel write if there is space on the buffer (len b < MAX). Finally, the data
operation and actions are combined to specify the behaviour of the process (after @): it initialises the state and starts a recursive action (mu X @ ...) that at
each step offer a choice between the actions Read and Write.

Central to CML is the notion of refinement that supports the comparison of
processes with respect to their external communications. Calculational stepwise
refinement is supported in CML by a rich catalogue of refinement laws that cover
both data and process refinement.

Formalising SysML. Our formal model of SysML is a CML specification that
declares a number of types, values, channels, channel sets and processes. The
semantics of a block is given by a CML process; it offers interactions through a
number of channels:

- set and get channels for each property of a block to allow properties to be
  read and written to;
- op and sig channels that allow the receipt of operations and signals; and
- ext_op and ext_sig channels for each port that also allow the receipt of
  operations and signals.

The model of the system defined by the SysML diagrams is captured in CML by the process that defines the block that characterises that system. The process defines the system interface in terms of the above channels, and interacts with other processes that capture other diagrams of the SysML model and restrict the interface of the system as indicated in those diagrams.

The structure of the processes that model blocks differs according to the nature of the block: simple or composite. The process that models a composite block is formed by the parallel composition of the processes that model the blocks that type its parts; the parallel composition is determined by the internal blocks diagram that describes the composite block. For instance, the block CChronometer in Figure 5 is modelled by a process that is defined by the parallel composition of the processes that model the blocks Min and Sec with their channels appropriately renamed to allow the communication between ports ip and ip_conj, and ports port of Sec and port of CChronometer.

Simple blocks, on the other hand, are modelled by processes that describe which operations and signals can be received by the block and may interact with a state machine process to treat them. These processes are formed by the parallel composition of processes that model the block's interface, the state machine that describes the behaviour of the block, and the block's ports. State machines are modelled by CML processes that are prepared to receive SysML events and react according to the behaviour specified in the state machines. Whilst communication in CML is synchronous, it is asynchronous in SysML, and, therefore, cannot be specified directly in CML. In our semantics, SysML communications are modelled in terms of buffers and CML communications.

The semantics of SysML is specified by inductive functions over the meta-model of SysML. The semantics of a SysML model is given by the function t_model, which takes a model as argument and characterises its corresponding CML specification. The formalisation of the semantics of SysML is in [7].

3   Refinement in SysML

Informally, our notion of refinement for SysML models compares the two blocks that define the systems with respect to their operations and signals. Essentially, if a block A is refined by a block B, the following properties must hold:

1. A and B must accept exactly the same public signals;
2. A and B must accept exactly the same public operations;
3. A and B must have exactly the same public properties;
4. for each public operation of A, if its return value is nondeterministically chosen from a set S, the same operation on block B must return a value that is nondeterministically chosen from a subset of S;
5. for each property of A, if its value is nondeterministically chosen from a set S, the same property on the block B must have a value nondeterministically chosen from a subset of S.

This refinement relation is induced by the CML semantics of SysML and corresponds to the refinement relation of CML process.

First of all, since process refinement is compositional in CML, and the main SysML elements (blocks, state machines and activities) map to processes used to define the CML process that defines the system model, we can refine the models of the individual diagrams to refine the SysML model as whole.

Next, we formalise the notion of refinement for blocks and state machines.

Definition 1 (Block refinement). *Let $\mathfrak{M}$ be a SysML model, and let $\mathfrak{B}_1$ and $\mathfrak{B}_2$ be blocks of $\mathfrak{M}$, then*

$$\mathfrak{B}_1 \sqsubseteq_{Block}^{\mathfrak{M}} \mathfrak{B}_2 \Leftrightarrow t\_model\,(\mathfrak{M}).B_1 \sqsubseteq_P t\_model\,(\mathfrak{M}).B_2$$

That is, block $\mathfrak{B}_1$ is refined by block $\mathfrak{B}_2$ (written $\mathfrak{B}_1 \sqsubseteq_{Block}^{\mathfrak{M}} \mathfrak{B}_2$) if, and only if, the CML process B_1 that models the block $\mathfrak{B}_1$ is refined by the process B_2 that models $\mathfrak{B}_2$. With the view that a system is specified by a block in a SysML model, block refinement as formalised in Definition 1 is the main relation that must be verified to establish refinement between systems.

Data-refinement in SysML is defined similarly to behavioural refinement by lifting CML data-refinement, which is based on forward simulation.

Definition 2 (Forward Simulation). *A forward simulation $(\preccurlyeq_R^{\mathfrak{M}})$ between blocks $\mathfrak{B}_1$ and $\mathfrak{B}_2$ of a SysML model $\mathfrak{M}$ is a relation R between $\mathfrak{B}_1.PrivateProps$ and $\mathfrak{B}_2.PrivateProps$ if, and only if, R is a forward simulation between the processes $t\_model\,(\mathfrak{M}).B_1$ and $t\_model\,(\mathfrak{M}).B_2$.*

Unlike state components of CML processes, properties of blocks are not necessarily encapsulated (private). For this reason, forward simulation in SysML is defined with respect to private properties of the blocks. This is an extension of a calculational approach to data refinement presented in [11] to allow (private) variables in local blocks to have their types data refined.

Definition 3 (State machine refinement). *Let $\mathfrak{M}$ be a SysML model, and let $\mathfrak{S}_1$ and $\mathfrak{S}_2$ be state machines of $\mathfrak{M}$, then*

$$\mathfrak{S}_1 \sqsubseteq_{Stm}^{\mathfrak{M}} \mathfrak{S}_2 \Leftrightarrow t\_model\,(\mathfrak{M}).S_1 \sqsubseteq_P t\_model\,(\mathfrak{M}).S_2$$

That is, a state machine $\mathfrak{S}_1$ is refined by another state machine $\mathfrak{S}_2$ (written $\mathfrak{S}_1 \sqsubseteq_{Stm}^{\mathfrak{M}} \mathfrak{S}_2$) if, and only if, the CML process S_1 that models the state machine $\mathfrak{S}_1$ is refined by the process S_2 that models $\mathfrak{S}_2$.

Notions of refinement for states (written $\sqsubseteq_{State}^{\mathfrak{M}}$), regions, transitions and actions are similarly defined. For states, the observations that are preserved by refinement are the activation and deactivation of the top state (that is, the substates are not observable), and the signals and operation calls performed inside the state. The observations of regions are the activation and deactivation of the region and the signals and operation calls performed inside the region. Transition refinement preserves the observation of activation and deactivation of states as well as the signals and operation calls performed by the transition.

As indicated in the previous section and further explained in Section 4, a subset of CML is used as action language for SysML. This subset excluding signals, operation calls and return statements retains the original CML semantics (except that they are enclosed in a variable block that models a local copy of the shared state). For this reason, CML refinement laws for such statements can be reused in the refinement of SysML models.

4   SysML Extensions

In general, we wish to prove that an abstract model, where possibly no particular design has been chosen, is refined by a more concrete model in which some design decisions have been taken. In SysML, the more concrete model often adds new operations to the abstract model in order to implement particular designs. This, however, makes the refinement invalid as new operations are now observable in the concrete model. The extra operations should in fact be internal, and used solely to implement behaviour specified in the abstract model. An alternative notion of refinement could allow addition of operations and use hiding to lift the CML notion of refinement. Here, we adopt the standard notion of refinement in process algebra directly.

In our example, we wish to show that the block `AChronometer` is refined by `CChronometer`. However, based solely on the pure SysML model, it is not possible to verify this refinement since block `CChronometer` clearly offers more operations than `AChronometer`: `inc`, `minsReq` and `reset` from block `Min` in Figure 2. These operations are used to implement the operation `time`, and are not meant to be visible outside the block `CChronometer`, that is, they are meant to be internal.

Moreover, since some of the ports of internal parts can be left unconnected, the operations and signals they offer are not called by another part, and simply making them internal, could lead them to occur spontaneously. For this reason, there needs to be a way of making them unavailable when hidden.

Finally, SysML does not provide adequate support for specifying abstract behaviours: both state machines and activities define very concrete models, and the fact that their action language is undefined is also a hindrance. The use of a programming language to define the action does not address this issue; as it does not provide support for abstract specifications.

We address the problems above through five extensions to SysML: hiding, restrictions, alphabets, plugs and the definition of an action language. The first extension supports the specification of internal signals and operations, the next three can be used to make certain signals and operations unavailable, and the fifth adds support for abstract specifications.

In order to specify that certain operations and signals are internal to a block, we propose the use of the hiding extension. A set of operations and signals represented by a SysML interface is hidden in a block by creating a dependency between the block and the interface, and adding a `hiding` comment to the dependency as shown in Figure 2. The semantics of this extension is given by the hiding operator of CML, which makes a set of channels internal to a process, and therefore, independent from external influences.

As already mentioned, any internal operation or signal that is offered but not used can occur spontaneously, which in turn leads to an infinite loop of internal behaviours. Therefore, only operations and signals that are used as specified by the internal block diagram can be made internal.

This restriction, however, is too strong as unused operations are often assumed to be unavailable. In fact, in our example, none of the extra operations of CChronometer can be hidden due to this restriction: some of them (reset) are not used at all, and the others are used only through a particular port of Min. The next three extensions provide mechanisms to indicate that an operation or signal is unavailable under certain situations (and can, therefore, be hidden).

Operations and signals of a block can be called by referring directly to an instance of the block, or through the ports that provide them. In order to support the specification of operations and signals that are only used through ports or (directly) through the block, we propose the use of restrictions.

Restrictions are represented by a through ports or through block comment linked to an operation, signal or interface to indicate that it is offered only through ports or only through the block. If there is no comment, it remains available through both. Figure 2 illustrates the use of restrictions in the realisation between the block Min and the interface MinutesI. The semantics of a restriction that declares an operation O only available through ports is given by a reduction of the alphabet of the process that models the block. This reduction removes all communications that allow calls to the operation directly to the block.

Alphabets specify which operations and signals of a block are available when it is used as a part of another block. This extension is represented by a SysML comment that lists the used operations and signals and is associated with particular instances of blocks (parts). Alphabets must be connected to part (and not blocks) because they specify restrictions over the use of a block as a part. A block may be used in different contexts with different alphabets. In our example, to prevent the part min shown in Figure 4 from offering the operation reset, it is annotated with an alphabet containing minsReq and inc.

At this point, the operation reset can be hidden because it is not offered by the block CChronometer or its parts, but the remaining operations of Min cannot. They are offered on ports ip and ip_aux, but only used on ip as indicated by the connector between ip and ip_conj in Figure 4. Before these operations are made internal, the unused port ip_aux must be disabled. This is achieved by means of the plug extension, which allows us to mark a port as unused (plugged). A plug is specified by a comment linked to the port that is unavailable. Similarly to alphabets, this annotation must be placed on a port of a part since it does not affect a block in general, but only a particular use of a block. In our example, the port ip_aux is plugged as shown in Figure 4.

Finally, the problem of supporting abstract specifications is addressed by the use of a subset of CML as action language in state machines (and activities). This subset includes the CML statements (like the specification statement for instance), as well as sequential composition, external and internal choice, interleaving and guarded statements. These are the basic CML action constructors, except for those that involve communication (prefixing and parallel composition) since the communication paradigm of SysML (asynchronous) is different from that of CML (synchronous) and is already supported by signals and operation calls. In our example, the only statements that are used are assignments. specification statement and and sequential compositions as shown in Figures 3 and 5. The complete syntax of CML statements is in [23]

5   Refinement Laws in SysML

In this section, we describe how the *Circus* refinement strategy can be applied to SysML models and present a few laws that support the strategy. These laws fall into two main groups: refinement laws that rely solely on existing SysML constructs, and laws that use alphabets, restrictions, plugs or hiding.

The *Circus* refinement strategy is an iterative process. In each iteration, initially, a centralised abstract process is data refined to introduce concrete data models, next the actions of the process are refined to introduce parallelism, and finally the process is partitioned into one or more processes that interact with each other to implement the abstract process. Each of the new processes may become the object of a subsequent iteration of the strategy.

We illustrate the use of this refinement strategy for SysML and the new laws through a simple example that verifies that the distributed concrete model shown in Figure 2 is a refinement of the centralised abstract model in Figure 1.

The first phase of the refinement strategy is supported in SysML by simulation laws that distribute a forward simulation (see Definition 2) through a SysML model. Since the data model of our concrete specification is the same as that of the abstract specification, this phase is not required in this simple example. Simulation laws can be found in [24].

In the second phase, we start by introducing local auxiliary behaviours in the abstract model that are initially not used via state machine refinement laws. Namely, the local hidden operations `minsReq` and `inc` are introduced by the Law *Local operation introduction* presented below.

This law takes a block and an operation, introduces the operation in the block as a private operation, and hides it. The resulting block is identical to the original because the new operation is only available internally and is not used. Whilst this seems useless, further laws can take advantage of the availability of the local operation to replace behaviours by calls to it.

Still as part of the second phase of the strategy, we introduce some of the structure of the design. In our example, the single state in the abstract state machine is refined into a composite state with two regions using the Law *Region introduction* shown below – the first region corresponds to `SecMain` in Figure 5, and the second contains a state that offers the behaviours associated with the local operations. This does not modify the behaviour of the state machine because the newly introduced behaviours are triggered by unused local operations.

This law takes a composite state with a single region containing any number of substates and transitions, and refines it into a composite state with two regions: the first is the original region, and the second is an empty region. This is possible because the two regions are executed in parallel, and the empty region does not introduce new behaviours observable outside the composite state.

Law 1. Local operation introduction.

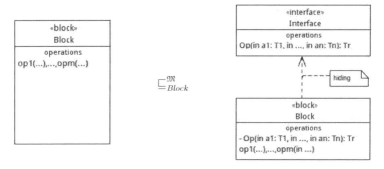

provided

1. $Op \notin used(Block.behaviour) \cup triggers(Block.behaviour)$

Law 2. Region introduction.

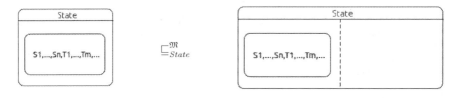

In the third phase, the block `AChronometer` is partitioned in two using Law *Block decomposition*. This law is a block refinement law that takes a simple block with two ports, `p1` and `p2`, and a state machine that at the top level has two regions, `R1` and `R2`. It refines the simple block into a composite block with the same two ports, but whose parts are two new blocks, `Block1` and `Block2`, each with two ports (e.g., `p1` and `ip1`), and each with its own state machine derived from one of the regions `R1` and `R2`. In this law, `I1` and `I2` represent both the provided and required interfaces of the port.

The provisos of this law guarantee that no new operations or signals are introduced and that their treatments (in the state machine) are independent and, therefore, can be separated. That is, this law can be applied as long as the a subset of the operations and signals (the external ones) of the original block are partitioned in the interfaces `I1` and `I2` (proviso 1), the transitions of the two top regions of the state machine have no triggers in common and the two regions do not share block properties (proviso 2), the provided items (operations and signals) of `I1` are not used in the triggers of the transitions of region `R2` and the required items of `I1` are not used in the actions of the states and transitions in `R2` (proviso 3), and the provided items of `I2` are not used in the triggers of the

Law 3. Block decomposition.

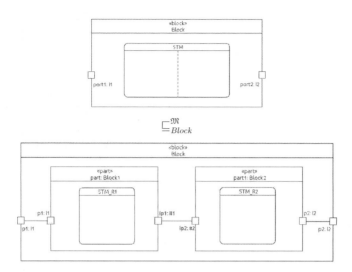

provided

1. $I1 \cap I2 = \varnothing \wedge I1 \cup I2 \subseteq Block$
2. $triggers(R1) \cap triggers(R2) = \varnothing \wedge usedV(R1) \cap usedV R2 = \varnothing$
3. $provided(I1) \cap trigger(R2) = \varnothing \wedge required(I1) \cap used(R2) = \varnothing$
4. $provided(I2) \cap trigger(R2) = \varnothing \wedge required(I2) \cap used(R2) = \varnothing$

where

1. $Block1 \cap Block2 = \varnothing \wedge Block1 \cup Block2 = Block$
2. $provided(II1) = Block1 \cap used(R2) \wedge required(II1) = Block2 \cap used(R1)$
3. $provided(II2) = Block2 \cap used(R1) \wedge required(II2) = Block1 \cap used(R2)$

transitions of region `R1` and the required items of `I2` are not used in the actions of the states and transitions in `R1` (proviso 4).

Each block has an event pool where received events (operation calls and signals) are stored for processing. The proviso 2 of Law 3 guarantees that it is possible to partition the event pool of the block into two parts: one containing only events that may be consumed by the first region, and the other containing the events that may be consumed by the second region. Since the order in which events are sent to the state machine is non-deterministic (see [7,25]), it is not possible to distinguish the two pairs of event pools and state machines from the original pair, thus allowing the block to be decomposed in two.

The two new blocks produced by the Law *Block decomposition* partition the operations and signals of the original block, and each has two ports; for instance, in `Block1` they are `p1` and `ip1`. The ports `p1` and `p2` are identical to those of the original block and are linked by a connector to the corresponding ports of the composite block. The connected ports ip1 and ip2 are introduced to allow one part to call operations of the other, which accounts for the use of block operations in the original state machine. The interfaces II1 and II2 of these internal ports are such that they contain as provided items those operations and signals of the associated block (Block1 or Block2) that are used by the region associated with the other block, and contain as required items those that are used by its associated region. Both of these interfaces are hidden.

In a second iteration of the refinement strategy, standard CML refinement laws are used to (1) introduce a local variable aux initialised with min in the behaviour of the transition triggered by time (see Figure 3), and (2) replace min in the record constructor mk_Time by the local variable. Finally, Law *Operation call introduction* [24] is applied twice, once to replace aux := min by a call to minsReq via port ip_conj, and again to replace min := (min + 1) mod 60 by a call to inc through the same port.

The soundness of these laws can be verified using the CML models induced by our semantics, and our notions of refinement. The soundness of the refinement laws presented in this paper is further discussed in [24].

6   Conclusions

In this paper we have presented our initial results regarding the use of refinement in SysML models. We have identified limitations of the diagrammatic notation that restrict, if not disallow, the use of refinement for all but the most trivial examples where concrete models add no extra operations, signals and components. To address these limitations, we have proposed extensions to SysML that address those limitations, and described a number of laws that support the development and verification of SysML models by stepwise refinement.

Current work on refinement in UML tends to follow three main directions First, [14] provides some extensions for structuring refinements, but does not present a formal notion of refinement.

Second, the notion of refinement in UML is analysed and contrasted with the notion of generalisation in [15], whilst in [16], it is related (informally) to a formal notion of refinement as inspiration for transformation patterns. Bergner et al. [17] use an extension of the informal notion of refinement available in UML to record evolution of models across different levels of abstraction. Our notion of refinement is induced by our semantics of SysML, whilst the above results use a notion of refinement based directly on components of UML models.

A third line of work is pursued [18,19,20,21,22]; our work differs from those most noticeably in our support for stepwise refinement at the level of SysML rather than of the model adopted. Hnatkowska et al. [18] formalise in a description logic refinement between models at different levels of abstraction and semantic levels, but it is not clear what properties are preserved by such notions of refinement. A similar approach is taken in [20], where the notion of refinement is based on the observation of operation calls.

Liu et al. [19] formalise a subset of UML in an object-oriented specification language that supports refinement. Similarly to our work, refinement patterns are proposed and their soundness is argued based on the formalisation. However, complicating aspects such as concurrency are not explored. Furthermore, it is not clear if compositional refinement patterns for state machines are supported as the formalisation of state machines is based on a preprocessing phase that flattens the state machine eliminating the hierarchical structure.

In [21], refinement is explored in a formal variant of UML based on Event-B [26]. This work differs from our mainly in that the Event-B approach is based on the guess-and-verify paradigm, where a new model is created and the refinement is verified rather than on refinement laws.

Finally, [22] explores refinement in UML by formalising a subset of UML in CSP. The notions of refinement are those of CSP, and the preserved properties are similar to ours, interaction between blocks via operations and signals. In that work, however, refinement supports verification via model checking.

The soundness of the refinement laws is based on the formal semantics of SysML published in [7,5,6] and the CML refinement calculus. As future work, we will extend the catalogue of refinement laws for SysML models and apply it to more examples. Furthermore, we plan to extend the SysML profile in [27] to include our extensions and to use the CML theorem prover [28] to formalise and mechanically verify our refinement laws, as well as to automate as much as possible the verification of the provisos generated by a refinement.

References

1. OMG: OMG Systems Modeling Language (OMG SysML^{TM}). Technical report, OMG Document Number: formal/2010-06-02 (2010)
2. Rational Rhapsody Architect for Systems Engineers, http://tinyurl.com/rrafse (accessed April 11, 2013)
3. Artisan Studio, http://atego.com/products/artisan-studio/ (accessed April 11, 2013)
4. Sparx Systems' Enterprise Architect supports the Systems Modeling Language, http://www.sparxsystems.com/products/mdg/tech/sysml (accessed April 11, 2013)
5. Miyazawa, A., Lima, L., Cavalcanti, A.: Formal models of sysml blocks. In: Groves, L., Sun, J. (eds.) ICFEM 2013. LNCS, vol. 8144, pp. 249–264. Springer, Heidelberg (2013)
6. Lima, L., Didier, A., Cornélio, M.: A Formal Semantics for SysML Activity Diagrams. In: Iyoda, J., de Moura, L. (eds.) SBMF 2013. LNCS, vol. 8195, pp. 179–194. Springer, Heidelberg (2013)
7. Albertins, L., Cavalcanti, A., Cornélio, M., Iyoda, J., Miyazawa, A., Payne, R.: Final Report on Combining SysML and CML. Technical Report D22.4, COMPASS Deliverable (March 2013)
8. Fitzgerald, J., Larsen, P.G.: Modelling Systems – Practical Tools and Techniques in Software Development, 2nd edn. Cambridge University Press (2009)
9. Hoare, C.A.R.: Communicating sequential processes. Prentice-Hall, Inc. (1985)
10. Roscoe, A.W.: The Theory and Practice of Concurrency. Prentice-Hall Series in Computer Science. Prentice-Hall, New York (1998)

11. Morgan, C.C.: Programming from Specifications, 2nd edn. Prentice Hall International Series in Computer Science (1994)
12. Hoare, T., Jifeng, H.: Unifying Theories of Programming. Prentice Hall (1998)
13. Cavalcanti, A.L.C., Sampaio, A.C.A., Woodcock, J.C.P.: A Refinement Strategy for Circus. Formal Aspects of Computing 15(2-3), 146–181 (2003)
14. Correa, N., Giandini, R.: A UML extension to specify model refinements. In: XXXII Latin American Conference on Informatics (2006)
15. Pons, C., Perez, G., Giandini, R., Kutsche, R.D., TU-Berlin, F.: Understanding Refinement and Specialization in the UML. In: 2nd International Workshop on MAnaging SPEcialization/Generalization Hierarchies (MASPEGHI) (2003)
16. Pons, C.: On the definition of UML refinement patterns. In: 2nd MoDeVa Workshop, Model Design and Validation. ACM/IEEE (2005)
17. Bergner, K., Rausch, A., Sihling, M., Vilbig, A.: Structuring and refinement of class diagrams. In: Proc. of the 32nd Annual Hawaii International Conference on Systems Sciences. IEEE (1999)
18. Hnatkowska, B., Huzar, Z., Kuźniarz, L., Tuzinkiewicz, L.: On understanding of refinement relationship. In: Consistency Problems in UML-based Software Development: Understanding and Usage of Dependency (2004)
19. Liu, Z., Li, X., Liu, J., Jifeng, H.: Consistency and refinement of UML models. In: Consistency Problems in UML-based Software Development: Understanding and Usage of Dependency (2004)
20. Van Der Straeten, R.: Formalizing Behaviour Preserving Dependencies in UML. In: Consistency Problems in UML-Based Software Development: Understanding and Usage of Dependency (2004)
21. Said, M.Y., Butler, M., Snook, C.: Class and state machine refinement in UML-B. In: Proc. of Workshop on Integration of Model-Based Formal Methods and Tools (2009)
22. Davies, J., Crichton, C.: Concurrency and refinement in the unified modeling language. Formal Aspects of Computing 15(2-3), 118–145 (2003)
23. Woodcock, J., Cavalcanti, A., Coleman, J., Didier, A., Larsen, P.G., Miyazawa, A., Oliveira, M.: CML Definition 0. Technical Report D23.1, COMPASS Deliverable (June 2012)
24. Miyazawa, A., Cavalcanti, A., Foster, S.: Refinement in SysML and CML. Technical report, Department of Computer Science, The University of York (2014), http://cs.york.ac.uk/~alvarohm/report2014a.pdf
25. OMG: OMG Unified Modeling Language (OMG UML), superstructure, version 2.4.1. Technical report (2011)
26. Abrial, J.R.: The Event-B Modelling Notation (October 2007)
27. Bryans, J., Fitzgerald, J., Payne, R., Miyazawa, A., Kristensen, K.: SysML Contracts for Systems of Systems. In: Proc. of the 9th International Conference on Systems of Systems Enginering (2014)
28. Foster, S., Payne, R., Couto, L.D.: Towards Verification of Constituent Systems through Automated Proof. In: Proc. of the Workshop on Engineering Dependable Systems of Systems (EDSoS) (2014)

Verifying Modal Workflow Specifications Using Constraint Solving

Hadrien Bride[1,2], Olga Kouchnarenko[1,2], and Fabien Peureux[1]

[1] Institut FEMTO-ST – UMR CNRS 6174, University of Franche-Comté
16, route de Gray, 25030 Besançon, France
{hbride,okouchna,fpeureux}@femto-st.fr
[2] Inria Nancy Grand Est – CASSIS Project
Campus Scientifique, BP 239, 54506 Vandœuvre-lès-Nancy cedex
{hadrien.bride,olga.kouchnarenko}@inria.fr

Abstract. Nowadays workflows are extensively used by companies to improve organizational efficiency and productivity. This paper focuses on the verification of modal workflow specifications using constraint solving as a computational tool. Its main contribution consists in developing an innovative formal framework based on constraint systems to model executions of workflow Petri nets and their structural properties, as well as to verify their modal specifications. Finally, an implementation and promising experimental results constitute a practical contribution.

Keywords: Modal specifications, Workflow Petri nets, Verification of Business Processes, Constraint Logic Programming.

1 Introduction

Nowadays workflows are extensively used by companies in order to improve organizational efficiency and productivity by managing the tasks and steps of business processes. Intuitively, a workflow system describes the set of possible runs of a particular system/process. Among modelling languages for workflow systems [1, 2], workflow Petri nets (WF-nets for short) are well suited for modelling and analysing discrete event systems exhibiting behaviours such as concurrency, conflict, and causal dependency between events as shown in [3, 4]. They represent finite or infinite-state processes in a readable graphical and/or a formal manner, and several important verification problems, like reachability or soundness, are known to be decidable. With the increasing use of workflows for modelling crucial business processes, the verification of specifications, i.e. of desired properties of WF-nets, becomes mandatory. To accompany engineers in their specification and validation activities, modal specifications [5] have been designed to allow, e.g., *loose* specifications with restrictions on transitions. Those specifications are notably used within refinement approaches for software development. Modal specifications impose restrictions on the possible refinements by indicating whether activities (transitions in the case of WF-nets) are *necessary*

E. Albert and E. Sekerinski (Eds.): IFM 2014, LNCS 8739, pp. 171–186, 2014.

or *admissible*. Modalities provide a flexible tool for workflow development as decisions can be delayed to later steps (refinements) of the development life cycle.

This paper focuses on the verification of modal WF-net specifications using constraint solving as a computational tool. More precisely, given a modal WF-net, a constraint system modelling its correct executions is built and then computed to verify modal properties of interest over this workflow specification. After introducing a motivating example in Sect. 2 and defining preliminaries on WF-nets with their modal specifications in Sect. 3, the paper describes its main contribution in Sect. 4. It consists in developing a formal framework based on constraint systems to model executions of WF-nets and their structural properties, as well as to verify their modal specifications. An implementation supporting the proposed approach and promising experimental results constitute a practical contribution in Sect. 5. Finally, a discussion on related work is provided before concluding.

2   Motivating Example

Our approach for verifying modal specifications is motivated by the increasing criticity of business processes, which define the core of many industrial companies and require therefore to be carefully designed. In this context, we choose a real-life example of an industrial business workflow, which is directly driven by the need to verify some behavioural properties possibly at the early stage of development life cycle, before going to implementation. This example concerns a proprietary issue tracking system used to manage bugs and issues requested by the customers of a tool provider company[1]. Basically, this system enables the provider to create, update and drop tickets reporting on customer's issues, and thus provides knowledge base containing problem definition, improvements and solutions to common problems, request status, and other relevant data needed to efficiently manage all the company projects. It must also be compliant with respect to several rules ensuring that business processes are suitable as well as streamlined, and implement best practices to increase management effectiveness.

Figure 1 depicts an excerpt of the corresponding business process—specified from textual requirements by a business analyst team of the company—modelled using a Petri net workflow (WF-net). The main process, in the top left model, is defined by two possible distinct scenarii (SubA and SubB), which are described by two other workflows. In the figure, big rectangles (as for SubA and SubB) define other workflows. Some of them are not presented here: this example is indeed deliberately simplified and abstracted to allow its small and easily understandable presentation in this paper; its complete WF-net contains 91 places and 113 transitions. For this business process, the goal is to verify, at the specification or design stage of the development, some required behavioural properties (denoted p_i for later references) derived from textual requirements and business analyst expertise such as: during a session, either the scenario SubA or the scenario SubB (and not both of them) must be executed (p_1); when the scenario SubB

---

[1] For confidentiality reasons, the details about this case-study are not given.

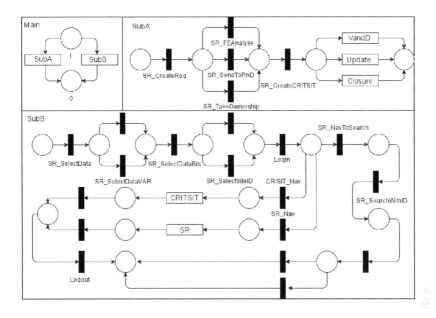

Fig. 1. Excerpt of issue tracking system WF-net

is considered then the user must login (p_2); once a critical situation request is pending, it can either be updated, validated and dispatched, or closed (p_3); once a critical situation is created, it can be updated and closed (p_4); at any time, a service request can be upgraded to a critical situation request (p_5); a logged user must logout to exit the current session (p_6).

To ensure the specified business process model verifies this kind of business rules, there is a need to express and assess them using modal specifications. However, usual modal specifications are relevant to express properties on single transition by specifying that a transition shall be a (*necessary*) *must*-transition or a (*admissible*) *may*-transition, but they do not allow to express requirements on several transitions. For instance, expressing the property p_1 using usual modal specifications allows to specify that transitions of SubA and SubB shall be *may*-transitions. Nevertheless, such formula does not ensure that SubA or SubB has to occur in a exclusive manner, and specifying some transitions as *must*-transition cannot tackle this imprecision. That is why we propose in this paper to extend the expressiveness of usual modal specifications by using modalities over a set of transitions, and to define dedicated algorithms to automate their verification.

3   Preliminaries

This section reminds background definitions and the notations used throughout this article. It briefly describes workflow Petri nets as well as some of their behavioural properties. Modal specifications are also introduced.

3.1   Workflow Petri Nets

As mentioned above, workflows can be
modelled using a class of Petri nets,
called the workflow nets (WF-nets).
Figure 2 provides an example of a
Petri net where the places are represented by circles, the transitions by
rectangles, and the arcs by arrows.

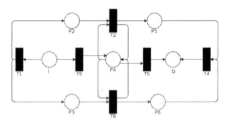

Fig. 2. Basic example of a WF-net (ex1)

Definition 1 (Petri net). *A Petri net is a tuple (P, T, F) where P is a finite
set of places, T is a finite set of transitions ($P \cap T = \emptyset$), and $F \subseteq (P \times T) \cup (T \times P)$
is a set of arcs.*

Let $g \in P \cup T$ and $G \subseteq P \cup T$. We use the following notations: $g^\bullet = \{g' | (g, g') \in F\}$, $^\bullet g = \{g' | (g', g) \in F\}$, $G^\bullet = \cup_{g \in G} \, g^\bullet$, and $^\bullet G = \cup_{g \in G} \, ^\bullet g$.
A *marking* of Petri net is a function $M : P \to \mathbb{N}$. The marking represents the
number of token(s) on each place. The marking of a Petri net evolves during
its execution. Transitions change the marking of a Petri net according to the
following *firing rules*. A transition t is *enabled* if and only if $\forall p \in {}^\bullet t, M(p) \geq 1$.
When an *enabled* transition t is *fired*, it *consumes* one token from each place of
$^\bullet t$ and *produces* one token for each place of $t^\bullet$. With respect to these rules, a
transition t is *dead* at marking M if it is not *enabled* in any marking M' reachable
from M. A transition t is *live* if it is not *dead* in any marking reachable from
the initial marking. A Petri net system is *live* if each transition is *live*.

Definition 2 (WF-net). *A Petri net $PN = (P, T, F)$ is a WF-net (Workflow
net) if and only if PN have two special places i and o, where $^\bullet i = \emptyset$ and $o^\bullet = \emptyset$,
and for each node $n \in (P \cup T)$ there exists a path from i to o passing through n.*

For example, the Petri net in Fig. 2 is a WF-net. Let us notice that in the context
of *workflow*, specifiers are used to consider *ordinary* Petri nets [6], i.e. Petri nets
with arcs of weight 1. In the rest of the paper, the following notations are used:

- $M_\emptyset$: the marking defined by $\forall p \in P, M(p) = 0$,
- $M_a \xrightarrow{t} M_b$: the transition t is *enabled* in marking M_a, and *firing* it results in
  the marking M_b,
- $M_a \to M_b$: there exists t such that $M_a \xrightarrow{t} M_b$,
- $M_1 \xrightarrow{\sigma} M_n$: the sequence of transitions $\sigma = t_1, t_2, ..., t_{n-1}$ leads from the
  marking M_1 to the marking M_n (i.e. $M_1 \xrightarrow{t_1} M_2 \xrightarrow{t_2} ... \xrightarrow{t_{n-1}} M_n$),
- $M_a \xrightarrow{*} M_b$: the marking M_b is reachable from marking M_a (i.e. there exists
  σ such that $M_a \xrightarrow{\sigma} M_b$).

We denote $M_{i(k)}$ the initial marking (i.e. $M_i(n) = k$ if $n = i$, and 0 otherwise)
and $M_{o(k)}$ the final marking (i.e. $M_o(n) = k$ if $n = o$, and 0 otherwise). When
k is not specified, it equals 1. A sequence σ of transitions of a Petri net is an
execution if there are M_a, M_b such that $M_a \xrightarrow{\sigma} M_b$. A *correct* execution of a

WF-net is an execution σ such that $M_i \xrightarrow{\sigma} M_o$. For example, $M_i \xrightarrow{\sigma} M_o$ where $\sigma = T6,T5$ is a *correct* execution of the WF-net in Fig. 2. The behaviour of a WF-net is defined as the set Σ of all its correct executions. For the transition t and the execution σ, the function $O_t(\sigma)$ is the number of occurrences of t in σ.

Definition 3 (Siphon/Trap). *Let $N \subseteq P$ such that $N \neq \emptyset$:*

- *N is a trap if and only if $N^\bullet \subseteq {}^\bullet N$.*
- *N is a siphon if and only if ${}^\bullet N \subseteq N^\bullet$.*

Figure 2 displays an example of a Petri net with a siphon. Let $N = \{P4\}$, since ${}^\bullet N = \{T1, T2\} \subseteq N^\bullet = \{T1, T2\}$, the set of places $N = \{P4\}$ is a siphon.

Theorem 1 (from [7]). *An ordinary Petri net without siphons is live.*

3.2   WF-Nets with Modalities

Modal specifications have been designed to allow *loose* specifications to be expressed by imposing restrictions on transitions [5]. They allow specifiers to indicate that a transition is *necessary* or just *admissible*. In the framework of WF-nets, this concept provides two kinds of transitions: the *must*-transitions and the *may*-transitions. A *may*-transition (resp. *must*-transition) is a transition fired by at least one execution (resp. all the executions) of the procedure modelled by a WF-net.

While basic modal specifications are useful, they usually lack expressiveness for real-life applications, as only individual transitions are concerned with. We propose to extend modal specifications to express requirements on several transitions and on their causalities. To this end, the language S of well-formed *modal* specification formulae is inductively defined by : $\forall t \in T, t$ is a well-formed *modal* formula, and given $A_1, A_2 \in S$, $A_1 \wedge A_2$, $A_1 \vee A_2$, and $\neg A_1$ are well-formed *modal* formulae. These formulae allow specifiers to express modal properties about WF-nets' correct executions. Any modal specification formula $m \in S$ can be interpreted as a *may*-formula or a *must*-formula. A *may*-formula describes a behaviour that has to be ensured by at least one correct execution of the WF-net. The set of *may*-formulae forms a subset of CTL formulae where only the *possibly* operator (i.e. along at least one path) is used. On the other hand, a *must*-formula describes a behaviour that has to be ensured by all the correct executions of the WF-net. The set of *must*-formulae forms a subset of CTL formulae where only the *inevitably* operator (i.e. along all paths) is used. For example, for the WF-net ex2 of 3(b), the *may*-formula $T9$ means that there exists a correct execution firing transition $T9$ at least once (i.e. $T9$ is a *may*-transition). More complex behaviours can be expressed. For example, the *must*-formula $(T8 \wedge T9) \wedge (\neg T6 \vee T5)$ means that $T8$ and $T9$ must be fired by every correct execution, and if an execution fires $T6$ then $T5$ is also fired at least once. Formally, given $t \in T$:

- $PN \models_{may} t$ if and only if $\exists \, \sigma \in \Sigma.\, O_t(\sigma) > 0$, and
- $PN \models_{must} t$ if and only if $\forall \, \sigma \in \Sigma.\, O_t(\sigma) > 0$.

Further, given a well-formed *may*-formula (resp. *must*-formula) $m \in S$, a WF-net PN satisfies m, written $PN \models_{may} m$ (resp. $PN \models_{must} m$), when at least one (resp. all) correct execution(s) of PN satisfies (resp. satisfy) m. The semantics of $\neg, \vee$ and $\wedge$ is standard.

Definition 4 (Modal Petri net). *A modal Petri net* $MPN = (P, T, F, m, M)$ *is a Petri net* $PN = (P, T, F)$ *together with a modal specification* (m, M) *where:*
- $m \in S$ *is a well-formed* modal *must-formula[2], and*
- $M \subset S$ *is a set of well-formed* modal *may-formulae.*

We say that a WF-net PN satisfies a modal specification (m, M) if and only if $PN \models_{must} m$ and $\forall m' \in M, PN \models_{may} m'$.

3.3   Hierarchical Petri Nets

Modelling large and intricate WF-nets can be a difficult task. Fortunately, similarly to modular programming, WF-nets can be designed using other WF-nets as building blocks. One of the simple methods used to construct composed WF-nets is by transitions substitution. A composed WF-net built using this method has special transitions that represent several whole (composed or not) WF-nets. The composed WF-nets can then be viewed as WF-nets with multiple layers of details; they are called hierarchical WF-nets. While this does not add any expressiveness to WF-nets, it greatly simplifies the modelling work, allowing to model small parts of the whole process that are combined into a composed WF-net.

3.4   Constraint System

A constraint system is defined by a set of constraints (properties), which must be satisfied by the solution of the problem it models. Such a system can be represented as a Constraint Satisfaction Problem (CSP) [8]. It is such that each variable appearing in a constraint should take its value from its domain. Formally, a CSP is a tuple $\Omega =< X, D, C >$ where X is a set of variables $\{x_1, \ldots, x_n\}$, D is a set of domains $\{d_1, \ldots, d_n\}$, where d_i is the domain associated with the variable x_i, and C is a set of constraints $\{c_1(X_1), \ldots, c_m(X_m)\}$, where a constraint c_j involves a subset X_j of the variables of X. A CSP thus models NP-complete problems as search problems where the corresponding search space is the Cartesian product space $d_1 \times \ldots \times d_n$. The solution of a CSP Ω is computed by a labelling function $\mathcal{L}$, which provides a set v (called valuation function) of tuples assigning each variable x_i of X to one value from its domain d_i such that all the constraints C are satisfied. More formally, v is consistent—or satisfies a constraint $c(X)$ of C—if the projection of v on X is in $c(X)$. If v satisfies all the constraints of C, then Ω is a consistent or satisfiable CSP. In the rest of the paper, the predicate $SAT(C, v)$ is true if the corresponding CSP Ω is made satisfiable by v, and the predicate $UNSAT(C)$ is true if there exists no such v.

---

[2] We only need a single *must*-formula because $PN \models_{must} m_1 \wedge PN \models_{must} m_2$ if and only if $PN \models_{must} (m_1 \wedge m_2)$, for any two *must*-formulae m_1 and m_2.

Using Logic Programming for solving a CSP has been investigated for many years, especially using Constraint Logic Programming over Finite Domains, written CLP(FD) [9]. This approach basically consists in embedding consistency techniques into Logic Programming by extending the concept of logical variables to the one of the domain-variables taking their value in a finite discrete set of integers. In this paper, we propose to use CLP(FD) to solve the CSP that represent the modal specifications to be verified.

4   Verification of Modal Specifications

To verify a modal specification of a WF-net, we model the executions of a WF-net by a constraint system, which is then solved to validate or invalidate the modal specifications of interest.

4.1   Modelling Executions of WF-Nets

Considering a WF-net $PN = (P, T, F)$, we start by modelling all the executions leading from a marking M_a to a marking M_b, i.e. all σ such that $M_a \xrightarrow{\sigma} M_b$.

Definition 5 (Minimum places potential constraint system). *Let* $PN = (P, T, F)$ *be a WF-net and* M_a, M_b *two markings of* PN, *the minimum places potential constraint system* $\varphi(PN, M_a, M_b)$ *associated with it is:*

$$\forall p \in P. \nu(p) = \sum_{t \in p^\bullet} \nu(t) + M_b(p) = \sum_{t \in {}^\bullet p} \nu(t) + M_a(p) \tag{1}$$

where $\nu : P \times T \to \mathbb{N}$ *is a valuation function.*

Equation (1) expresses the fact that for each place, the number of token(s) entering it plus the number of token(s) in M_a is equal to the number of tokens leaving it plus the number of token(s) in M_b. This constraint system is equivalent with respect to solution space to the state equation, aka the fundamental equation, of Petri nets, the only difference is that (1) explicitly gives information about the places involved in the modelled execution.

Theorem 2. *If* $M_a \xrightarrow{*} M_b$ *then a valuation satisfying* $\varphi(PN, M_a, M_b)$ *exists.*

Proof. Let $\sigma = t_1, t_2, ..., t_n$ and $M_a \xrightarrow{t_1} M_1 \xrightarrow{t_2} M_2...M_{n-1} \xrightarrow{t_n} M_b$. We define:

- $\forall t \in T. \nu(t) = O_t(\sigma)$
- $\forall p \in P. \nu(p) = \sum_{j \in \{1,2,...,n-1\} \cup \{a,b\}} M_j(p)$

Then $\forall p \in P$:

- $\sum_{j \in \{1,2,...,n-1\} \cup \{a,b\}} M_j(p) = \sum_{t \in p^\bullet} O_t(\sigma) + M_b(p) = \sum_{t \in {}^\bullet p} O_t(\sigma) + M_a(p)$. Indeed, as the WF-net is an ordinary Petri net, the sum of tokens in all markings of a place is equal to the sum of the occurrences of transitions producing (resp. consuming) a token at this place plus the number of token(s) in marking M_b (resp. M_a).

– $\nu(p) = \sum_{t \in p^\bullet} \nu(t) + M_b(p) = \sum_{t \in {}^\bullet p} \nu(t) + M_a(p)$.

Consequently, ν is a valuation satisfying $\varphi(PN, M_a, M_b)$.

For example, $M_i \xrightarrow{\sigma} M_o$ where $\sigma = T6, T5$ is a correct execution of the WF-net in Fig. 2, therefore we can find a valuation $\nu(n) = 1$ if $n \in \{T6, T5, i, o\}$, and $\nu(n) = 0$ otherwise. By Th. 2, this valuation ν satisfies the constraints system $\varphi(ex1, M_i, M_o)$.

Theorem 2 allows to conclude that a WF-net PN does not have any correct executions if $\varphi(PN, M_i, M_o)$ does not have a valuation satisfying it. However, even if there is a valuation satisfying $\varphi(PN, M_i, M_o)$, it does not necessary correspond to a correct execution. For example, the valuation $\nu(n) = 1$ if $n \in \{T1, T2, T8, T4, i, P2, P3, P5, P6, o\}$, $\nu(n) = 2$ if $n \in \{P4\}$, and $\nu(n) = 0$ otherwise, satisfies $\varphi(ex1, M_i, M_o)$ but it does not correspond to any correct execution. This is due to the fact that transitions $T2$ and $T8$ cannot fire simultaneously using as an input token an output token of each other. Consequently, the set of solutions of $\varphi(PN, M_i, M_o)$ constitutes an over-approximation of the set of correct executions of PN. In the rest of the paper, the solutions of $\varphi(PN, M_i, M_o)$ that do not correspond to correct executions of PN are called spurious solutions. Hence our goal is to refine this over-approximation in order to be able to conclude on properties relative to all correct executions of a WF-net.

4.2   Verifying Structural Properties over Executions

While considering the modelling of WF-net executions, siphons and traps have interesting structural features. Indeed, an unmarked siphon will always be unmarked, and a marked trap will always be marked. Therefore a WF-net can only have siphons composed of at least the place i and traps composed of at least place o. Theorem 3 allows to conclude on the existence of a siphon in a WF-net.

Theorem 3. *Let $\theta(PN)$ be the following constraint system associated with a WF-net $PN = (P, T, F)$:*

– $\forall p \in P, \forall t \in {}^\bullet p. \sum_{p' \in {}^\bullet t} \xi(p') \geq \xi(p)$
– $\sum_{p \in P} \xi(p) > 0$

where $\xi : P \to \{0, 1\}$ is a valuation function. PN contains a siphon if and only if there is a valuation satisfying $\theta(PN)$.

Proof. ($\Leftarrow$) Let ξ be a valuation satisfying $\theta(PN)$, and $N \subseteq P$ such that $\xi(p) = 1 \Leftrightarrow p \in N$. Then $\forall p \in N, \forall t \in {}^\bullet p. \sum_{p' \in {}^\bullet t} \xi(p') \geq 1$, which implies ${}^\bullet N \subseteq N^\bullet$. Consequently, N is a siphon.
($\Rightarrow$) Suppose that N is a siphon then obviously the valuation $\xi(p)$ defined as: $\xi(p) = 1$ if $p \in N$, and 0 otherwise, satisfies $\theta(PN)$.

For example, for the WF-net of Fig. 2 where the set of places $N = \{P4\}$ is a siphon, $\xi(p) = 1$ *if* $p \in N$, *else* 0 is a valuation satisfying $\theta(ex1)$.

The places (excluding places i and o) and transitions composing a correct execution of a WF-net cannot form a trap or a siphon. Using this propriety we refine the over-approximation made using $\varphi(PN, M_i, M_o)$. Theorem 4 states that for any solution of $\varphi(PN, M_a, M_b)$, the subnet, composed of places (excluding place i and o) and of the transitions of the modelled execution, contains a trap if and only if it has also a siphon. Therefore we only need to check the presence of a siphon (or, respectively, of a trap).

Theorem 4. *Let $PN = (P, T, F)$ a WF-net, M_a, M_b two markings of PN, and $\nu : P \times T \to \mathbb{N}$ a valuation satisfying $\varphi(PN, M_a, M_b)$. We define the subnet $sPN(\nu) = (sP, sT, sF)$ where:*
- *$sP = \{p \in P \setminus \{i, o\} \mid \nu(p) > 0\}$*
- *$sT = \{t \in T \mid \nu(t) > 0\}$*
- *$sF = \{(a, b) \in F \mid a \in (sP \cup sT) \wedge b \in (sP \cup sT)\}$*

If $sPN(\nu)$ contains a trap (resp. siphon) N then N is also a siphon (resp. trap).

Proof. ($\Rightarrow$) Let $N \subseteq sP$ such that $N \neq \emptyset$, so $\sum_{p \in N} \nu(p) = \sum_{p \in N} \sum_{t \in p^\bullet} \nu(t)$ $= \sum_{p \in N} \sum_{t \in {}^\bullet p} \nu(t)$. It implies $\sum_{p \in N} \sum_{t \in p^\bullet \cap N^\bullet} \nu(t) + \sum_{p \in N} \sum_{t \in p^\bullet \cap sT / N^\bullet} \nu(t)$ $= \sum_{p \in N} \sum_{t \in {}^\bullet p \cap N^\bullet} \nu(t) + \sum_{p \in N} \sum_{t \in {}^\bullet p \cap sT / N^\bullet} \nu(t)$ that can be simplified as $\sum_{p \in N} \sum_{t \in p^\bullet} \nu(t) = \sum_{p \in N} \sum_{t \in {}^\bullet p \cap N^\bullet} \nu(t) + \sum_{p \in N} \sum_{t \in {}^\bullet p \cap sT / N^\bullet} \nu(t)$ because $\forall p \in N.p^\bullet \cap sT / N^\bullet = \emptyset$. Let N be a trap ($N^\bullet \subseteq {}^\bullet N$) such that N is not a siphon (${}^\bullet N \not\subseteq N^\bullet$). Thus, one has $\sum_{p \in N} \sum_{t \in p^\bullet} \nu(t) = \sum_{p \in N} \sum_{t \in {}^\bullet p \cap N^\bullet} \nu(t)$ implying $\sum_{p \in N} \sum_{t \in p^\bullet} \nu(t) = \sum_{p \in N} \sum_{t \in p^\bullet} \nu(t) + \sum_{p \in N} \sum_{t \in {}^\bullet p \cap sT / N^\bullet} \nu(t)$. We finally have $\forall p \in N.{}^\bullet p \cap sT / N^\bullet = \emptyset$ because $\forall t \in sT.\nu(t) > 0$. This implies ${}^\bullet N \subseteq N^\bullet$, a contradiction.

($\Leftarrow$) The proof that if N is a siphon then N is a trap, is similar.

Theorem 5. *The Petri net $sPN(\nu)$ contains no siphon and no trap if and only if $\theta(sPN(\nu))$ does not have a valuation satisfying it.*

Proof. Follows from Th. 3 and 4.

Using Th. 5 allows defining the constraint system in Th. 6, which refines $\varphi(PN, M_a, M_b)$. Thanks to this new system, the spurious solutions of $\varphi(PN, M_a, M_b)$ corresponding to an execution with siphon/trap are no more considered.

Theorem 6. *Let $PN = (P, T, F)$ be a WF-net and M_a, M_b two marking of PN. There exists $\nu : P \times T \to \mathbb{N}$ a valuation satisfying $\varphi(PN, M_a, M_b)$ such that $\theta(sPN(\nu))$ does not have a satisfying valuation if and only if there exist σ and $k \in \mathbb{N}$ such that $\forall p \in P \setminus \{i\}. M_{a'}(p) = M_a(p), M_{a'}(i) = k, \forall p \in P \setminus \{o\}.M_{b'}(p) = M_b(p), M_{b'}(o) = k, M_{a'} \xrightarrow{\sigma} M_{b'}$ and $\forall t \in T. O_t(\sigma) \geq \nu(t)$.*

Proof. ($\Rightarrow$) Suppose $\nu : P \times T \to \mathbb{N}$ is a valuation satisfying $\varphi(PN, M_a, M_b)$ such that $\theta(sPN(\nu))$ does not have a satisfying valuation. By Th. 5, $sPN(\nu)$ contains no siphon and therefore is live (cf. Th. 1). It implies that there is σ such that $M_a \xrightarrow{\sigma} M_b$ in $sPN(\nu)$ where $\forall t \in sT. O_t(\sigma) \geq \nu(t)$. Using the fact that a transition of σ is in $i^\bullet$, and a transition of σ is in ${}^\bullet o$, we can conclude that $M_{a'} \xrightarrow{\sigma} M_{b'}$ such that $\forall t \in T. O_t(\sigma) \geq \nu(t)$.

($\Leftarrow$) Suppose σ such that $M_a \xrightarrow{\sigma} M_b$ and $\forall t \in T.\ O_t(\sigma) = \nu(t)$. By Th. 2 we can complete the definition of ν to make ν a satisfying valuation of $\varphi(PN, M_a, M_b)$. In addition, $sPN(\nu)$ contains no siphon and no trap because it would contradict $M_a \xrightarrow{\sigma} M_b$. By Th. 5, $\theta(sPN(\nu))$ does not have a satisfying valuation.

For example, let us consider the WF-net of Fig. 2, the valuation $\nu(n) = 1$ if $n \in \{T1, T2, T8, T4, i, P2, P3, P5, P6, o\}$, $\nu(n) = 2$ if $n \in \{P4\}$, otherwise $\nu(n) = 0$, is a satisfying valuation of $\varphi(ex1, M_i, M_o)$. The set of places $N = \{P4\}$ is a trap/siphon. Figure 3(a) displays $sPN(\nu)$. Therefore by Th. 3 there is a valuation satisfying $\theta(sPN(\nu))$. By Th. 6, ν does not correspond to a correct execution of the WF-net of Fig. 2.

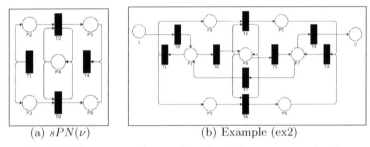

(a) $sPN(\nu)$ (b) Example (ex2)

Fig. 3. WF-net examples used to illustrate over-approximation

The constraint system of Th. 6 can be used to over-approximate the correct executions of a WF-net. Indeed, for the WF-net in Fig. 3(b), the valuation $\nu(n) = 1$ if $n \in \{T1, T8, T6, T2, T7, T8, T5, T9, T4, i, P2, P3, P5, P6, o\}$, $\nu(n) = 2$ if $n \in \{P1, P7\}$, and $\nu(n) = 3$ if $n \in \{P4\}$, is a valuation satisfying $\varphi(ex3, M_i, M_o)$ such that $\theta(sPN(\nu))$ does not have a satisfying valuation.

By Th. 6 there exist σ and k such that $M_{i(k)} \xrightarrow{\sigma} M_{o(k)}$ and $\forall t \in T.\ O_t(\sigma) \geq \nu(t)$. In this case there is no σ such that $k = 1$. Indeed, $P4$ cannot be empty when either $T2$ or $T8$ is fired, and therefore a marking with at least one token in $P4$ and one in either $P2$ or $P3$ must be reachable. As there is no execution possible with only one token that leads to such marking, we have $k > 1$.

While defining an over-approximation might be useful for the verification of safety property, in our case, we want to be able to verify a modal specification. As the approximation is difficult to handle, we need to be able to model an execution that violates the modal specification if it exists.

Theorem 7. *Let $PN = (P, T, F)$ be a WF-net, and M_a, M_b its two markings. If there is $\nu : P \times T \to \mathbb{N}$ such that $SAT(\varphi(PN, M_a, M_b), \nu) \wedge UNSAT(\theta(sPN(\nu)))$ $\wedge \forall n \in P \times T.\ \nu(n) \leq 1$ then $M_a \xrightarrow{\sigma} M_b$ and $\forall t \in T.\ O_t(\sigma) = \nu(t)$.*

Proof. Any place is involved with at most one transition consuming one token, and at most one transition producing one token. By Th. 6 one has $M_{a'} \xrightarrow{\sigma} M_{b'}$. Since at most one transition can consume a token in i (resp. produce a token in o), we have $M_{a'} = M_a$ (resp. $M_{b'} = M_b$).

In the rest of the paper, a segment of an execution is defined as an execution modelled by the constraint system in Th. 7. In this way, we now propose to decompose an execution modelled by the constraint system of Th. 6 into segment(s) modelled by Th. 7. If such a decomposition exists then the execution is a correct execution. Otherwise, we can conclude that the found solution is a spurious one. Indeed, spurious solutions can appear because the order of transition firing is not taken into account in the modelled execution. Therefore, decomposing the execution into segments forces the ordering of transitions where order matters.

Theorem 8. *Let* $PN = (P, T, F)$ *be a WF-net, and* M_a, M_b *its two markings.* $M_a \xrightarrow{\sigma} M_b$ *if and only if there exists* $k \in \mathbb{N}$ *such that* $M_1 \xrightarrow{\sigma_1} M_2 \cdots M_k \xrightarrow{\sigma_{(k)}} M_{k+1}$, *where* $M_1 = M_a$, $M_{k+1} = M_b$ *and for every* i, $0 < i \leq k$, *there is* ν_i *s.t.* $SAT(\varphi(PN, M_i, M_{i+1}, \nu_i)) \wedge UNSAT(\theta(sPN(\nu_i))) \wedge \forall n \in P \times T. \ \nu_i(n) \leq 1$.

Proof. ($\Rightarrow$) Suppose $M_a \xrightarrow{\sigma} M_b$ where $\sigma = t_1, \ldots, t_k$ then by definition there exist $M_1 \xrightarrow{t_1} M_2 \cdots M_k \xrightarrow{t_{(k)}} M_{k+1}$, where $M_1 = M_a$, $M_{k+1} = M_b$. Moreover, for every i, $0 < i \leq k$, there is ν_i such that $SAT(\varphi(PN, M_i, M_{i+1}, \nu_i)) \wedge UNSAT(\theta(sPN(\nu_i))) \wedge \forall n \in P \times T. \ \nu_i(n) \leq 1$, as ν_i is a valuation modelling the execution of a single transition.
($\Leftarrow$) Follows from Th. 7.

In the rest of the paper, we denote $\phi(PN, M_a, M_b, k)$ the constraint system of Th. 8, where k is the number of segments composing the execution. As $\phi(PN, M_i, M_o, k)$ can be used to model any execution of PN composed of k or less segments, we propose to use it to determine the validity of a WF-net with regards to a given modal specification.

4.3   Verifying Modal Formulae

When determining whether or not a WF-net satisfies the modal properties of interest, we distinguish two decision problems. The first one, called the K-*bounded validity of a modal formula*, only considers executions formed by K segments, at most. The second one, called the *unbounded validity of a modal formula*, deals with executions formed by an arbitrary number of segments; it generalizes the first problem. To verify modalities over a single transition, constraint systems come very naturally into the play. Intuitively, for a *may*-transition t, determining one correct execution firing t at least once is enough to validate its *may*-specification. On the other hand, for a *must*-transition t, the lack of correct executions without firing it validates its *must*-specification.

In our approach, verifying modal specifications from Def. 4 relies on their expression by constraints. To build these constraints, for every transition $t \in T$, the corresponding terminal symbol of the formulae is replaced by $\nu(t) > 0$, where ν is the valuation of the constraint system. For example, for the modal formula $(T0 \wedge T5) \wedge (\neg T7 \vee T6)$, the corresponding constraint is $(\nu(T0) > 0 \wedge \nu(T5) > 0) \wedge (\neg \nu(T7) > 0 \vee \nu(T6) > 0)$. Given a modal formula $f \in S$, $C(f, \nu)$ denotes the constraint built from f, where ν is a the valuation of the constraint system. The following theorem extends the constraint systems to verify modal specifications.

Theorem 9. *Let $MPN = (P, T, F, m, M)$ a modal WF-net. The WF-net $PN = (P, T, F)$ satisfies the modal specification (m, M) if and only if:*

- *there is no $\nu, k \in \mathbb{N}$ such that $SAT(\phi(PN, M_i, M_o, k) \wedge \neg C(m, \nu), \nu)$, and*
- *for every $f \in M$, there exist $\nu, k \in \mathbb{N}$ such that $SAT(\phi(PN, M_i, M_o, k) \wedge C(f, \nu), \nu)$.*

Proof. By Th. 8, there exist $\nu, k \in \mathbb{N}$ such that $SAT(\phi(PN, M_i, M_o, k) \wedge \neg C(m, \nu), \nu)$ if and only if $PN \not\models_{must} m$. In addition, there are $\nu, k \in \mathbb{N}$ such that $SAT(\phi(PN, M_i, M_o, k) \wedge C(f, \nu), \nu)$ if and only if $PN \models_{may} f$.

Theorem 9 can be adapted to the case of hierarchical WF-nets. In this case, the modal formula has to be verified for the main WF-net, i.e. the highest level net, and also for the WF-nets substituting transitions at lower levels.

Theorem 10. *Let $PN = (P, T, F)$ be a WF-net, $\bar{R}_{must}$ the set of all well-formed must-formulae not satisfied by PN, and R_{may} the set of all well-formed may-formulae satisfied by PN. There exists K_{max} such that:*

- $\forall f \in \bar{R}_{must}, \exists\ \nu, k \leq K_{max}.\ SAT(\phi(PN, M_i, M_o, k) \wedge \neg C(f, \nu), \nu),$
- $\forall f \in R_{may}, \exists\ \nu, k \leq K_{max}.\ SAT(\phi(PN, M_i, M_o, k) \wedge C(f, \nu), \nu).$

Proof. Sketch. The set of correct executions of a WF-net is possibly infinite. This is due to the fact that T-invariants (i.e. sequence of transitions σ such that $M \xrightarrow{\sigma} M$) could be fired indefinitely. However, when considering the verification of modal formulae, we are only interested in the presence or absence of transitions in correct executions (i.e. the number of their firings does not matter). Therefore considering the set of correct executions where T-invariants are allowed to fire at most once is enough to check the validity of modal formulae. This restricted set of correct executions is finite. As a consequence, there exists K_{max} such that any execution of this set can be modelled by K_{max} segments, at most.

Theorem 10 implies that for any WF-net $PN = (P, T, F)$, there exists K_{max} such that any modal *may*-formula (resp. *must*-formula) f can be verified regarding the consistency of the constraint system $\phi(PN, M_i, M_o, K_{max}) \wedge C(f, \nu)$ (resp. $\phi(PN, M_i, M_o, K_{max}) \wedge \neg C(f, \nu)$). In other words, to verify any *may*-formula (resp. *must*-formula), it is not necessary to look for the existence (resp. non-existence) of correct execution respecting (resp. not respecting) the behaviour expressed by the *may*-formula (resp. *must*-formula) of this WF-net composed of more than K_{max} segments. However determining the K_{max} value of a WF-net from its structure is still an open problem. However, we can infer an upper-bound of $\sum_{j=1}^{|T|} j!$.

5   Implementation and Experiments

The proposed approach has been fully automated, allowing practitioners, at any stage of the workflow design, to verify modal formulae using an integrated tool chain. This section describes this tool chain developed to experimentally validate the proposed approach, and illustrates its use and obtained results on the case study introduced in Sect. 2.

5.1 Implementation Architecture

As a proof of concept, an implementation supporting the approach we propose has been developed to provide an integrated tool chain to design WF-nets and verify modal specifications. The architecture is shown in Fig. 4.

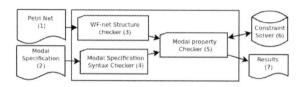

Fig. 4. Tool chain description

The tool chain takes as inputs a WF-net model (1) and the modal specifications (2) to be verified. WF-net model is exported from a third party software (e.g., Yasper [10], PIPE [11]) as an XML file, as well as the modal specifications that are expressed in a dedicated and proprietary XML format. From these inputs, the developed tool first checks the structure of the WF-net model (3) to exclude Petri nets that do not correspond to WF-nets definition (cf. Def. 2). It then checks the modal specifications regarding the syntax proposed in Sect. 4 (4). Once validated, these inputs are translated into a constraint system (5) that is handled using the CLP(FD) library of Sicstus Prolog [12] (6). Finally, a report about the validity of modal specifications of the WF-net is generated (7).

To verify a *may*-formula (resp. a *must*-formula) m (resp. M), the tool first checks if there exists a solution of the over-approximation, given by Th. 6, such that the modelled execution satisfies (resp. does not satisfy) m (resp. M). If such an execution exists, it then tries to find an execution of the under-approximation, given by Th. 8, which satisfies (resp. does not satisfy) m. As an illustration, Figure 5 gives the algorithm of the function checking the validity of a *must*-formula. It returns the K-bounded validity of a given modal formula m. To cope with the complexity raised by K_{max}, K can be fixed to a manageable value. Nevertheless, when fixing K to K_{max} (or greater than K_{max}), the algorithm enables to decide the unbounded validity of the *must*-formula m. The results in Sect. 4.1 ensure its soundness and completeness. Finally, solving a CSP over a finite domain being an NP-complete problem with respect to the domain size, this algorithm inherits this complexity.

5.2 Experimental Results

The approach and the corresponding implementation have been firstly validated on a set of models collected from the literature, especially from [4, 13, 14], and afterwards experimented in the field of issue tracking systems using the industrial example described in Sect. 2. Table 1 shows an extract of the experimental results obtained on this industrial example, focusing on the six properties (p_1 to p_6) and the WF-net model introduced in Sect. 2.

Inputs: PN - a WF-net, m - a *must*-formula, K a positive integer.
Results: $TRUE$ - $PN \models_{must} m$, $FALSE$ - $PN \not\models_{must} m$.
function IsMustValid(PN,m,K)
   if $SAT(\varphi(PN, M_i, M_o) \wedge \neg C(m, \nu), \nu) \wedge UNSAT(\theta(sPN(\nu)))$ **then**
      $k = max(\{v(n)|n \in T\})$
      if $k == 1$ **then return** $FALSE$
      else
         while $k \leq K$ **do**
            if $SAT(\phi(PN, M_i, M_o, k) \wedge \neg C(f, v), \nu)$ **then return** $FALSE$
            else $k = k + 1$
            end if
         end while
         return $TRUE$
      end if
   else return $TRUE$
   end if
end function

Fig. 5. Algorithm checking the validity of a *must*-formula

The properties p_1 to p_6 are representative of the kind of properties that have to be verified by engineers when they design the business process to be implemented. Moreover, These properties are sufficiently clear without a complete description of the workflow and enable to show all possible outcomes of our approach. The modal formula associated with each property is specified, and the result of the computation is given by its final result as well as the internal evaluation of φ. The input K and the corresponding computed value of $\phi(K)$ are also precised when it makes sense, i.e. when the algorithm cannot conclude without this bound.

When verifying *must*-formulae that are satisfied by the WF-net (see p_1, p_2 and p_3), or *may*-formulae that are not satisfied by the WF-net (see p_4), the overapproximation proposed in Th. 6 is usually enough to conclude. On the other hand, when verifying *may*-formulae that are satisfied by the WF-net (see p_5), or *must*-formulae that are not satisfied by the WF-net (see p_6), the decomposition into K segments is needed. We empirically demonstrate that this decomposition is very effective since values of K_{max} are usually moderate ($K_{max} = 6$ in the case of p_5, less than 10 with all the experimentations on this case-study). We can also notice the definitive invalidity of p_6 (a user can exit the current session without logout), which enabled to highlight an ambiguity in the textual requirements.

Thanks to the experiments, we can conclude that the proposed method is feasible and efficient. Moreover, the developed tool is able to conclude about the (in)validity of the studied properties in a very short time (less than a second).

Table 1. Experimentation results

#	Formula	φ	K	$\phi(K)$	Result
p_1	$PN \models_{must} (SubA \wedge \neg SubA) \vee (SubB \wedge \neg SubA)$	TRUE	-	-	TRUE
p_2	$PN \models_{must} SubB \Rightarrow Login$	TRUE	-	-	TRUE
p_3	$PN \models_{must} SR\_CreateCRITSIT \Rightarrow (VandD \vee Update \vee Closure)$	TRUE	-	-	TRUE
p_4	$PN \models_{may} SR\_CreateCRITSIT \Rightarrow (Update \wedge Closure)$	FALSE	-	-	FALSE
p_5	$PN \models_{may} SR\_UpgradeToCRITSIT$	TRUE	1	FALSE	FALSE
			6	TRUE	TRUE
p_6	$PN \models_{must} Login \Rightarrow Logout$	FALSE	1	FALSE	FALSE

6   Conclusion and Related Work

Modal specifications introduced in [15] allow loose or partial specifications in a process algebraic framework. Since, modal specifications have been ported to Petri nets, as in [16]. In this work, a relation between generated modal languages is used for deciding specifications' refinement and asynchronous composition. Instead of comparing modal languages, our approach deals with the correct executions of WF-nets modelled by constraint systems. A lot of work has been done [17–19] in order to model and to analyse the behaviour of Petri nets by using equational approaches. Among popular resolution techniques, the constraint programming framework has been successfully used to analyse properties of Petri net [20, 21]. But, like in [21], the state equation together with a trap equation are used in order to verify properties such as deadlock-freedom. Our approach also takes advantage of trap and siphon properties in pursuance of modelling correct executions. Constraint programming has also been used to tackle the reachability problem—one of central verification problems. Let us quote [22] where a decomposition into *step sequences* was modelled by a constraint system. Our approach is similar, the main difference is that the constraints we propose on step sequences, i.e. segments, are stronger. This is due to the fact that we are not only interested in the reachability of a marking, but also in the transitions involved in the sequences of transitions that reach it.

This paper hence presents an original and innovative formal framework based on constraint systems to model executions of WF-nets and their structural properties, as well as to verify their modal specifications. It also reports on encouraging experimental results obtained using a proof-of-concept tool chain. In particular, a business process example from the IT domain enables to successfully assess the reliability of our contributions. As a future work, we plan extensive experimentation to determine and improve the scalability of our verification approach based on constraint systems. We also need to improve its readiness level in order to foster its use by business analysts. For instance, we could propose a user-friendly patterns to express the modal properties. Finally, generalizing our approach by handling coloured Petri nets is another research direction.

Acknowledgment. This project is performed in cooperation with the Labex ACTION program (contract ANR-11-LABX-0001-01) – see http://www.labex-action.fr/en .

References

1. van der Aalst, W.M.P., ter Hofstede, A.H.M.: YAWL: Yet another workflow language. Journal of Information Systems 30(4), 245–275 (2005)
2. Dumas, M., ter Hofstede, A.H.M.: UML activity diagrams as a workflow specification language. In: Gogolla, M., Kobryn, C. (eds.) UML 2001. LNCS, vol. 2185, pp. 76–90. Springer, Heidelberg (2001)

3. van der Aalst, W.M.P.: The application of Petri nets to workflow management. Journal of Circuits, Systems, and Computers 8(1), 21–66 (1998)
4. van der Aalst, W.M.P.: Three good reasons for using a Petri-net-based workflow management system. Journal of Information and Process Integration in Enterprises 428, 161–182 (1997)
5. Larsen, K.G.: Modal specifications. In: Sifakis, J. (ed.) CAV 1989. LNCS, vol. 407, pp. 232–246. Springer, Heidelberg (1990)
6. van der Aalst, W.M.P.: Verification of workflow nets. In: Azéma, P., Balbo, G. (eds.) ICATPN 1997. LNCS, vol. 1248, pp. 407–426. Springer, Heidelberg (1997)
7. Heiner, M., Gilbert, D., Donaldson, R.: Petri nets for systems and synthetic biology. In: Bernardo, M., Degano, P., Zavattaro, G. (eds.) SFM 2008. LNCS, vol. 5016, pp. 215–264. Springer, Heidelberg (2008)
8. Macworth, A.K.: Consistency in networks of relations. Journal of Artificial Intelligence 8(1), 99–118 (1977)
9. Tsang, E.: Foundation of constraint satisfaction. Academic Press (1993)
10. van Hee, K., et al.: Yasper: a tool for workflow modeling and analysis. In: Proc. of the 6th Int. Conf. on Application of Concurrency to System Design (ACSD 2006), Turku, Finland, pp. 279–282. IEEE CS (June 2006)
11. Bonet, P., Lladó, C.M., Puijaner, R., Knottenbelt, W.J.: PIPE v2.5: A Petri net tool for performance modelling. In: Proc. of the 23rd Latin American Conference on Informatics (CLEI 2007), San Jose, Costa Rica (October 2007)
12. Carlsson, M., et al.: SICStus Prolog user's manual (Release 4.2.3). Swedish Institute of Computer Science, Kista, Sweden (October 2012)
13. Kouchnarenko, O., Sidorova, N., Trcka, N.: Petri nets with may/must semantics. In: Proc. of the Workshop on Concurrency, Specification, and Programming (CS&P 2009), Kraków-Przegorzaly, Poland, pp. 291–302 (September 2009)
14. van der Aalst, W.M.P.: Business process management demystified: A tutorial on models, systems and standards for workflow management. In: Desel, J., Reisig, W., Rozenberg, G. (eds.) ACPN 2003. LNCS, vol. 3098, pp. 1–65. Springer, Heidelberg (2004)
15. Larsen, K.G., Thomsen, B.: A modal process logic. In: Proc. of the 3rd Annual Symp. on Logic in Computer Science (LICS 1988), pp. 203–210. IEEE (July 1988)
16. Elhog-Benzina, D., Haddad, S., Hennicker, R.: Refinement and asynchronous composition of modal petri nets. In: Jensen, K., Donatelli, S., Kleijn, J. (eds.) ToPNoC V. LNCS, vol. 6900, pp. 96–120. Springer, Heidelberg (2012)
17. Desel, J.: Basic linear algebraic techniques for place/transition nets. In: Reisig, W., Rozenberg, G. (eds.) APN 1998. LNCS, vol. 1491, pp. 257–308. Springer, Heidelberg (1998)
18. Wimmel, H., Wolf, K.: Applying CEGAR to the Petri net state equation. In: Abdulla, P.A., Leino, K.R.M. (eds.) TACAS 2011. LNCS, vol. 6605, pp. 224–238. Springer, Heidelberg (2011)
19. Schmidt, K.: Narrowing Petri net state spaces using the state equation. Fundamenta Informaticae 47(3-4), 325–335 (2001)
20. Soliman, S.: Finding minimal P/T-invariants as a CSP. In: Proc. of the 4th Workshop on Constraint Based Methods for Bioinformatics (WCB 2008) (May 2008)
21. Melzer, S., Esparza, J.: Checking system properties via integer programming. In: Riis Nielson, H. (ed.) ESOP 1996. LNCS, vol. 1058, pp. 250–264. Springer, Heidelberg (1996)
22. Bourdeaud'huy, T., Hanafi, S., Yim, P.: Incremental integer linear programming models for Petri nets reachability problems. Petri Net: Theory and Applications, pp. 401–434 (February 2008)

Program Development

Proofs and Refutations in Invariant-Based Programming

Johannes Eriksson, Masoumeh Parsa, and Ralph-Johan Back

Department of Information Technologies, Åbo Akademi University
Joukahaisenkatu 3-5 A, Turku, FI-20520, Finland
{joheriks,mparsa,backrj}@abo.fi

Abstract. *Invariant-based programming* is a correct-by-construction approach to program development in which the invariants of a program are written before the actual code. Socos is an environment for graphically constructing invariant-based programs (as statechart-like diagrams) and verifying their correctness (by invoking an automatic theorem prover). It borrows the specification language, logical framework and proof tactics from the PVS system. In this paper, we describe an extension to Socos for animating invariant-based programs in the logical framework of PVS. An invariant-based program is represented as an abstract datatype encoding the program state coupled a small-step state transition function encoding the operational semantics of the program. Socos visualizes the execution, allowing the user to inspect the current state and identify invalid assertions through test cases. Since programs are executed within the theorem prover framework (rather than translated into another language or compiled to machine code), failed test cases are logically sound refutations of the verification conditions. Invariants not executable in the general (e.g., containing unbounded quantification) can be handled for bounded test cases by introducing custom evaluation functions. While such functions provide no correctness guarantees, they can increase the assurance of a correctness condition before doing the actual proof. We illustrate this workflow through a verification exercise with non-trivial verification conditions, arguing that animation of invariant diagrams serves as an important stepping stone towards a fully verified program.

1 Introduction

In the *correct-by-construction* approach to program verification, a program is constructed together with its correctness proof. A specification is refined into a collection of *contracts* (pre- and postconditions) for the individual program routines. In the next step, the routines are implemented and proved to satisfy their contracts. Loops are annotated with inductive *invariants* that must be maintained by the loop body. Traditionally, invariants are introduced just before the proofs are carried out. In *invariant-based programming* (IBP) the invariants are instead introduced even before the program code. Consequently, the program is structured around the invariants, rather than vice versa. This approach has the advantage that the proof closely follows the program structure, reducing the gap

E. Albert and E. Sekerinski (Eds.): IFM 2014, LNCS 8739, pp. 189–204, 2014.

between programming and verification. The idea was proposed in a number of different forms already in the late seventies [22,13,4], but has later been refined into a formal program calculus [5,8]. It has also been used as an educational device [6] for introducing formal methods to novices.

Socos [14] is a graphical environment[1] for drawing invariant diagrams and verifying their correctness using the theorem prover PVS [19]. While most conditions derived from typical programs are proved automatically, the specification language of Socos (PVS) allows higher-order predicates, rendering the proof tools incomplete in the general. Conditions not automatically discharged can be proved interactively using the PVS proof assistant. In practice, this requires considerable expertise, both in using an interactive theorem prover and in developing *background theories* (collections of functions and lemmas) to concisely express the specification and proofs in the domain at hand.

Verification is an iterative, feedback-driven workflow in which both unsuccessful proofs and refutations serve as stepping stones towards a fully correct program. While correctness cannot be achieved by testing alone, tests and proofs are complementary in practice. In early stages of development, exercising the behavior of the program with test cases is an expedient way of detecting errors. Visualization plays an important role here by providing fast feedback when something goes wrong. In later stages, when the background theories are sufficiently developed, invoking a fully automatic prover (such as an SMT solver) can discharge a large number of verification conditions. After this stage, correctness is achieved by proving the final remaining conditions interactively. This incremental workflow prevents proof building effort being spent on invalid assertions.

This paper describes an extension to *Socos* called "animator" that executes invariant diagrams within the theorem prover framework of PVS and visualizes the state transitions in Eclipse. The animator integrates into the verification workflow by providing refutations (failed tests) complementary to the feedback provided by the verifier (see Figure 1). An invariant diagram is translated into

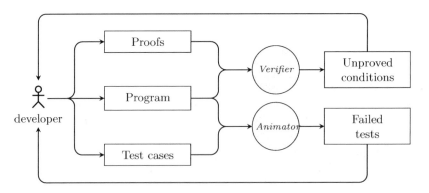

Fig. 1. Verification workflow

---

[1] Available at http://imped.abo.fi/socos

a state datatype with a constructor for each location in the diagram. A step function over the state type evaluates one statement using the built-in PVS ground evaluator [24,18]. The user view of the execution is an animated diagram accompanied by a state inspector. Non-executable specifications can be animated through custom functions and/or PVS semantic attachments (written in Lisp). Such functions are restricted to animation, and do not compromise the soundness of the verifier.

The rest of the paper is structured as follows. Section 2 introduces IBP and Socos. In Section 3, we describe our embedding of invariant diagrams in PVS. Section 4 walks through a case study in program verification using Socos, focusing on how animation integrates into the verification workflow. Section 5 discusses related work, while Section 6 concludes the paper and suggests future work.

2 Invariant-Based Programming in Socos

Figure 2 shows an invariant diagram representing a linear search procedure search taking three parameters: an integer vector a, the value x to search for, and the start index i. The keyword valres indicates that i is mutable with value-result semantics; upon termination, i points to the next occurrence of x following the initial value of i (denoted i__0). Boxes with round corners represent the internal *situations* of the procedure, respectively. The *initial situation* (situation without incoming transitions) describes the precondition of the procedure. In the example, the precondition constrains i to an index in vector a. *Final situations* (situations without outgoing transitions) describe the postconditions of the program. Invariant diagrams can have multiple final situations: search exits in either Found or NotFound. The *intermediate situation* Loop defines the loop invariant, constraining the index i and the values of elements a[i__0]...a[i-1].

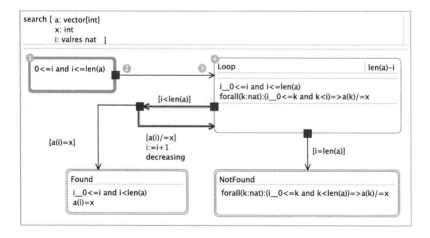

Fig. 2. Liner search starting from index i

Situations can additionally be *nested*, in which case the nested situations inherit the invariants of the enclosing situations. The *variant* (ranking function) of the loop is given in the top right hand corner of the situation; in this case, `len(a)-i` must be decreasing for each re-entry into the situation and must be bounded from below (implicitly, by 0).

A *transition* is an arrow labeled by an optional *guard* (within brackets) followed by zero or more assignments and procedure calls. Above, two transitions with guards `[i=len(a)]` and `[i<len(a)]` originate from `Loop` (the latter subsequently branches into two subtransitions). The guard defines the condition under which the assignments can be executed. The `decreasing` keyword on the transition back to `Loop` specifies that the variant should be proved to decrease in this transition.

Calls to procedures with multiple postconditions can map each postcondition to different outgoing transitions. The loop transition of the diagram in Figure 3 contains a call to `search`. Depending on which postcondition `search` terminates in (`Found` or `NotFound`), the program either goes into the next loop iteration or terminates in its final situation.

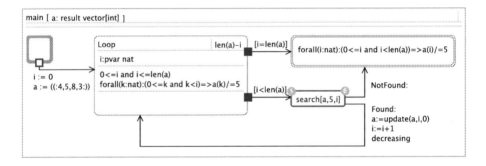

Fig. 3. Procedure call

2.1 Verifying Correctness

An invariant diagram gives rise to three kinds of verification conditions: *consistency*, *termination* and *liveness* conditions. Consistency means that the program preserves the invariants. To verify consistency, we must prove that each transition establishes its target situation. Termination means that the program has no infinite loops. To verify termination, we must associate each recurring situation with a variant that is decreased by all transitions back to the situation. Liveness means that at least one transition is enabled in all situations except for the final situations (i.e., the disjunction of all guards is true). If we prove consistency, termination and liveness for a program, we have proved that it is totally correct. The individual verification conditions associated with a transition depend only on the source and target situations, and the statements of the transition. For example, the consistency condition for the highlighted transition in Figure 2 is:

```
    i__0<=i AND i<=len(a)
 /\ (FORALL (k:nat): i__0<=k AND k<=i => a(k)/=x)
 /\ i<len(a) /\ a(i) /= x /\ i_1 = i+1
 => 0<=i_1 AND i_1<=len(a)
 /\ (FORALL (k:nat): i__0<=k AND k<=i_1 => a(k)/=x)
```

The antecedents derive from the source situation (Loop), the guards, and the assignment statements. The consequent is simply the target situation (again Loop).

2.2 Architecture

Socos consists of two subsystems: the front-end diagram editor and the back-end verifier and animator (Figure 4). The front-end is implemented as a plug-in to the Eclipse IDE and allows the user to draw invariant diagrams using drag-and-drop gestures. By the click of a button, the back-end verifier generates verification conditions from the diagram and sends them to PVS. The default strategy attempts to automatically prove them using a combination of PVS proof strategies and the Yices SMT solver [12]. Conditions that were not proved automatically are highlighted in the diagram editor. Alternatively, the animator executes the program until completion (as described in the sequel). Specifications and invariants are written in the PVS syntax, and program variables can have any PVS type. Socos programs can also import type and function definitions from PVS theories. While PVS is primarily an interactive theorem prover, it can also be used as a back-end through its so-called *raw mode*. In this mode, PVS acts as a read-eval-loop exposing its internal Lisp API to an external process [20]. When checking an invariant diagram, the Socos program checker generates a PVS theory containing the situation predicates and a lemma for each verification condition (consistency, liveness and termination). A proof script invoking Yices is generated for each lemma, and the result of running the proofs is obtained through the PVS API and visualized in the front-end. Socos interacts with PVS through this interface for both verification and animation of invariant diagrams.

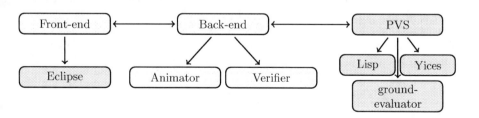

Fig. 4. Animator architecture

3   Animating Invariant Diagrams in PVS

An invariant diagram defines a set *Loc* of unique *locations* at which the diagram has an observable state—i.e., each scoped variable has a value. Socos supports local variables, meaning that locations can add or remove variables to the scope. A new variable is added to the scope when it first appears on the left-hand side of an assignment statement. A variable disappears from the scope at the end of a transition, unless it is declared in the target situation. The state can be represented as the dependent type $State = \langle l : Loc \times (V_l \rightarrow T_l)\rangle$, where $V_l \rightarrow T_l$ is the function mapping the variables V_l in scope at location l to their current values of types T_l. A statement from one program location to another is represented by a *step function* of type $State \rightarrow State$. Next, we describe how the state and the step function are implemented in PVS.

3.1   State Representation

PVS abstract data types [23] provide a flexible approach for defining data types with multiple constructors (since the variables that are in scope can vary for each location, a record type is not suitable for representing the state). We define the internal state type of one invariant diagram in PVS as the following datatype:

$$\texttt{state} = l_1(V_{l_1} : T_{l_1}) \mid l_2(V_{l_2} : T_{l_2}) \mid \cdots \mid l_n(V_{l_n} : T_{l_n})$$

Each $l_i \in Loc$ $(1 \leq i \leq n)$ is an internal location of the invariant diagram with the associated list of variables V_{l_i} along with their types T_{l_i}. In other words, the datatype $\texttt{state}$, defines the constructors $l_1, \ldots, l_n$ each taking variables $V_{l_1}, \ldots, V_{l_n}$ as parameters. The externally visible locations of the diagram (the pre- and postconditions) are represented by a smaller, but separate datatype:

$$\texttt{spec} = pre(V_{pre} : T_{pre}) \mid post_1(V_{post_1} : T_{post_1}) \mid \cdots \mid post_m(V_{post_m} : T_{post_m})$$

where $pre, post_1, \ldots, post_m \in Loc$. The reason behind this separation is that the actual parameters to a procedure call, as well as the results from the call, are handled as variables of the callee's $\texttt{spec}$ type in the caller's internal state. The caller cannot reference the callee's internal $\texttt{state}$ type, since this leads to cyclic imports if a procedure references itself either directly (through recursion) or indirectly (through mutual recursion).

To exemplify the above, we show the two datatypes generated for corresponding to the $\texttt{search}$ procedure (Figure 2) in the listing below. For brevity, only the constructors for the numbered locations in Figure 2 are shown (identifiers suffixed with '?' are the recognizer predicates associated with the datatype).

```
state__search: DATATYPE BEGIN
  ①  ini__(a:vector[int],x:int):  ini__?
  ②  ini__if(a:vector[int],x:int,i:nat):  ini__if?
  ③  ini__goto(a:vector[int],x:int,i:nat):  ini__goto?
```

```
  Loop(a:vector[int],x:int,i:nat): Loop?
    ⋮

END state__search

spec__search: DATATYPE BEGIN
    ini__(a:vector[int],x:int): ini__?
    NotFound(i:nat): NotFound?
    Found(i:nat): Found?
END spec__search
```

Procedure actual parameters and return values are represented in the caller as variables of the callee's spec type. For example, the procedure call ⬤-⬤ in Figure 3 is represented by the following constructors:

```
  state__main: DATATYPE BEGIN
    ⋮

  Loop__if__trs1__call1(a:vector[int],i:nat):
    Loop__if__trs1__call1?
  Loop__if__trs1__ret1(a:vector[int],i:nat,cs__:
    spec__search):Loop__if__trs1__ret1?
    ⋮

END state__main
```

3.2 Step Function

The function step for a procedure receives the current state of the invariant diagram and returns the next state by mapping each data type constructor to the statement at the corresponding location. For a diagram with locations $l_1, \ldots, l_n$ step is defined in a PVS theory as follows:

```
step(s:state): state =
    CASES s OF
        l₁(V_{l₁}): [[l₁]], ..., lₙ(V_{lₙ}): [[lₙ]]
    ENDCASES
```

where $[\![l_i]\!]$ is the operational definition of location l_i. It is defined over the structure of invariant diagrams as follows:

$$\left[\!\!\left[\begin{array}{|c|} \hline sit \\ \hline \end{array}\!\!-\!\!o\; trs \right]\!\!\right] \;=\; trs(V_{sit})$$

$$\left[\!\!\left[\; goto\; o\!\!\rightarrow\!\!\begin{array}{|c|} \hline sit \\ \hline inv \\ \hline \end{array}\!\!\right]\!\!\right] \;=\; \begin{array}{l} \text{IF}\;\; inv(V_{goto})\;\; \text{THEN}\;\; sit(V_{goto}) \\ \text{ELSE}\;\; goto(V_{goto}) \end{array}$$

$$\left[\!\!\left[\; if\blacksquare\!\!\begin{array}{l} ^{[grd_1]}\!\!-\!\!o\; trs_1 \\ ^{[grd_m]} \;\;\vdots \\ \;\;\;\;\;\;-\!\!o\; trs_m \end{array}\!\!\right]\!\!\right] \;=\; \begin{array}{l} \text{IF}\;\; grd_1(V_{if})\;\; \text{THEN}\;\; trs_1(V_{if}) \\ \cdots \\ \text{ELSE}\;\; \text{IF}\;\; grd_m(V_{if})\;\; \text{THEN}\;\; trs_m(V_{if}) \\ \text{ELSE}\;\; choice(V_{if}) \end{array}$$

$$\left[\!\!\left[\; ass\; o\!\!-\!\!\overset{X:=E}{-\!\!-\!\!-}\!\!-\!\!o\; trs \right]\!\!\right] \;=\; (\text{LAMBDA}\;\; X: trs(V_{ass}, X))(E)$$

There is no explicit error state; in the case of a failed invariant assertion, the program *gets stuck* at the current location. This is reported as an abnormal termination by the front-end.

For a call $p[E, X]$ to procedure p with precondition pre_p and mapped postconditions $post_{p,1} \ldots, post_{p,m}$, and expressions E passed for the formal value-parameters V and variables X passed for the formal result parameters R, we have:

$$\left[\!\!\left[\; call\; \langle p[E, X] \rangle\; ret \right]\!\!\right] \;=\; (\text{LAMBDA}\;\; \text{cs}\_\_: ret(V_{call}, \text{cs}\_\_))\,(pre_p(E, X))$$

$$\left[\!\!\left[\begin{array}{c} p[E, X]\; \langle ret \end{array}\!\!\begin{array}{l} ^{post_{p,1}:}\!\!-\!\!o\; trs_1 \\ \;\;\vdots \\ _{post_{p,m}:}\!\!-\!\!o\; trs_m \end{array}\!\!\right]\!\!\right] \;=\; \begin{array}{l} \text{CASES}\;\; \text{cs}\_\_\;\; \text{OF} \\ \quad post_{p,1}(R): (\text{LAMBDA}\;\; X: trs_1(V_{call}))\,(R) \\ \quad \cdots \\ \quad post_{p,m}(R): (\text{LAMBDA}\;\; X: trs_m(V_{call}))\,(R) \\ \quad \text{ELSE}: \;\; ret(V_{ret}) \\ \text{ENDCASES} \end{array}$$

Similarly to a failed assertion, an unmapped postcondition repeats the current location (the ELSE-clause above).

For example, the PVS translation of the procedure call ⦿—⦿ in Figure 3 is as follows:

```
exec__main: THEORY BEGIN
    IMPORTING state__main
    IMPORTING spec__search

    step(s:state__main): state =
        CASES s OF
```

$\vdots$

```
⊙ Loop__if__trs1__call1(a,i):
      Loop__if__trs1__ret1(a,i,spec__search.ini___
          (a,i)),
⊙ Loop__if__trs1__ret1(a,i,cs__):
      CASES cs__ OF
          Found(i): Loop__if__trs1__trs1__ass1(a,i
              ),
          NotFound(i): Loop__if__trs1__trs2__goto(
              a,i),
          ELSE: Loop__if__trs1__ret1(a,i,cs__)
      ENDCASES
```

$\vdots$

```
      ENDCASES
END exec__main
```

Note that since main is a caller of search, it imports the corresponding spec datatype (spec__search).

3.3 Animator Back-End

When a diagram is animated Socos generates, for each procedure, the spec and exec datatypes and a theory containing the step function. A thin run-to-completion shell (implemented in PVS Lisp) then executes the step function of the parameterless procedure main (maintaining a stack of exec and step functions for procedure invocations). Evaluation of invariants can optionally be turned off during animation. If active, the user can additionally specify *animation extensions* for invariants that cannot as such be evaluated (i.e., containing uninterpreted functions, unbounded quantification or non-ground terms). Importantly, such extensions are only used by the animator (the verifier ignores them). An example of an animation extension is given in Section 4.

3.4 Animator Front-End

Figure 5 shows the linear search program given in Figure 2 animated in the Socos environment. Execution is visualized in two Eclipse views: the current location is highlighted in the diagram editor tab, and the state of the call stack is shown in the "Inspector" tab. The user can start, break and single-step the execution using toolbar buttons. The debugger environment shows the current location, the values of the variables, and the user can optionally specify that situations should be evaluated (if enabled, each predicate in a situation is evaluated separately).

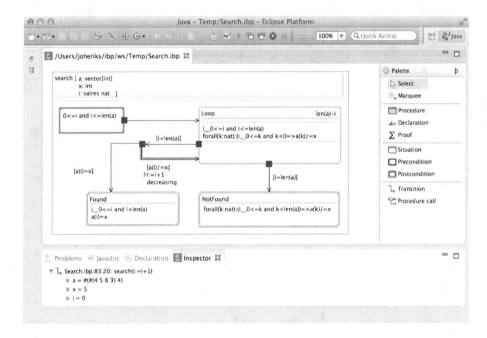

Fig. 5. Animating linear search

4   Example: Tree Reconstruction

In this case study, we will consider the problem of verifying an algorithm that reconstructs a binary tree given a list of leaf depths.[2] A binary tree can be encoded as a list of natural numbers giving the depth of the leaves in order. For example, the tree

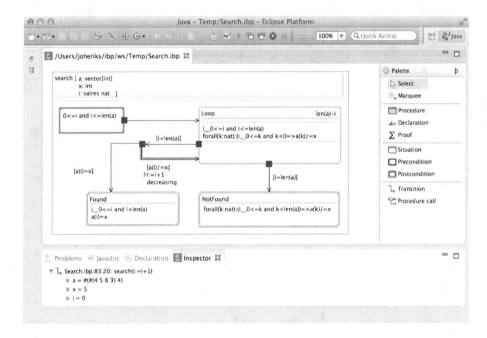

corresponds to the list $(1, 3, 3, 2)$. Given this list, the challenge is to reconstruct the above tree. For lists of natural numbers not corresponding to a binary tree, such as $(1, 3, 3, 1)$, the algorithm should return a constant indicating failure.

Algorithm 1 (`build`) is a recursive solution to this problem. The algorithm has two exits: it returns `Found(t)` where the tree `t` corresponds to the list `s`; or `Fail` if `s` is not a valid tree encoding. Each recursive invocation of the procedure `build_rec` either returns a subtree at depth `d` corresponding to a prefix of the list, or fails. The algorithm mutates the list `s` throughout the recursion: when

---

[2] A verification challenge in the 2012 VSTTE competition
(https://groups.google.com/forum/#!forum/
vstte-2012-verification-competition)

a leaf is produced, the head of the list is popped as a side effect. While the outermost call to build_rec may terminate leaving a non-empty list s, procedure build succeeds only if the whole list could be reduced.

Algorithm 1. Tree reconstruction algorithm

```
build(s:list): tree =              build_rec(d:int,s:list): tree =
    case build_rec(0,s) of             IF s=() THEN
        Fail -> RETURN Fail,               RETURN Fail;
        Found(t) ->                    h := head(0);
            IF s=() THEN               IF h<d THEN
                RETURN Fail                RETURN Fail;
            ELSE                       ELIF h=d THEN
                RETURN Found(t             s := tail(s);
                )                          RETURN Found(Leaf)
                                       ELSE
                                           l := build_rec(d+1, s)
                                           r := build_rec(d+1, s)
                                           RETURN Found(Node(l, r))
```

While verifying an implementation of this algorithm is not overly difficult, the verification conditions associated with the program are challenging enough to elude fully automatic proof. In addition to ensuring that the computed tree matches the given list, the program has a completeness condition: a tree is always returned if s is a valid tree encoding. Auxiliary lemmas need to be introduced and proved to discharge the verification conditions. Executing the program with invariant evaluation enables false hypotheses to be identified. Found condition can be tested by evaluating positive cases. The Fail condition cannot be executed as such, but a bounded evaluation can be specified through an *animation extension*. In the next, we will show how these steps are carried out in Socos.

4.1   Implementation in Socos

For the purpose of this example, we use the following list and tree datatypes:

```
list[T:TYPE]: DATATYPE BEGIN        tree: DATATYPE BEGIN
    null: null?                         Leaf: Leaf?
    cons(car:T,cdr:list):cons?          Node(l,r:tree): Node?
END list                            END tree
```

These datatypes are efficiently evaluated by the PVS ground evaluator.

To formalize the `Found` exit condition, we introduce the function `list_of` to denote the leaf-depth-list corresponding to a tree `t` and the auxiliary function `map_add`:

```
map_add(n:nat,s:list[nat]): list[nat] =
    map(LAMBDA (i:nat): n + i)(s)

list_of(t:tree): RECURSIVE list[nat] =
    CASES t OF
        Leaf: cons(0,null),
        Node(l,r): map_add(1,append(list_of(l),list_of(r)))
    ENDCASES
MEASURE t BY <<;
```

Figure 6 shows one possible invariant diagram implementation of Algorithm 1. The final situations `Fail` and `Found` correspond to the two exit conditions of the algorithm. The keyword `valres` declares that the parameter `s` is mutable with value-result semantics, and allows the constant `s__0` to be used in specifications to refer to the value of `s` upon entry to the procedure. If we ask Socos to check this program, the default catch-all strategy (`endgame`) (which invokes the SMT solver Yices) does not automatically discharge all verification conditions. This is because the proofs requires reasoning about non-trivial tree properties (in particular, the proof requires induction on `tree`). Hence, as a first step towards checking the proposed program we would like to execute the program on a number of test inputs to exercise the proposed invariants and postconditions.

4.2   Animation

To get a stronger assurance about the validity of the invariants and postconditions, we can run procedure `build` on a test case that is a valid encoding of a tree. As `list_of` and `map_add` are evaluable by PVS, so is the postcondition `Found` and all intermediate situations leading up to `Found`. An animation of the testcase (1,3,3,1) is shown in Figure 7 (a).

On the other hand, if we run the program on a test case that is not a valid tree encoding (e.g., (1,3,3,1)) to animate the `Fail` postcondition, the evaluator cannot validate the postcondition due to unbounded quantification over trees and lists. However, the postcondition becomes testable if we limit the quantification to trees with a fixed number of leaves (equal to the length of the list) and the remaining suffix of `s`. By introducing an animation extension for `Fail` that enumerates all trees with a given leaf depth, we can achieve a higher degree of assurance about the postcondition before attempting to prove the program. Attachments can either be written in Lisp (as so called *semantic attachments* [10]) or as executable PVS functions connected to specific situations. Taking the latter approach, we define the following evaluable attachment of postcondition `Found` in procedure `build_rec`:

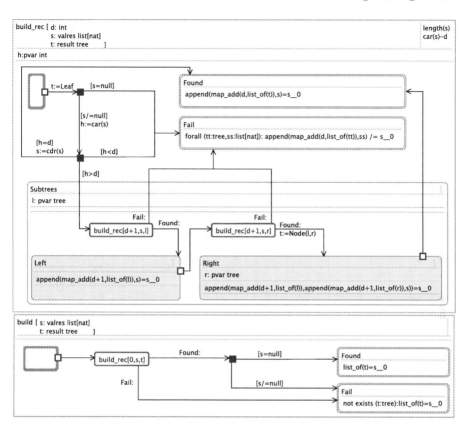

Fig. 6. Invariant-based implementation of Algorithm 1

```
FORALL (tt:trees(n)):
    append(map_add(d,list_of(tt)),
            sublist(s__0,length(s),length(s__0))) /= s__0
```

The function `trees` enumerates all trees of the given leaf count, whereas `sublist` returns a sublist as specified by its arguments (we omit the definition of these functions here). With the above semantic attachment in place, `Fail` is exhaustively evaluated for all trees with leaf count equal to the length of the processed list. Figure 7 (b) shows two scenarios, in which both `Found` and `Fail` are evaluated in the outermost call to `build_rec`. Such bounded evaluation allows small test cases to be carried out, increasing the assurance that the given invariants are true. Even though testing does not provide correctness guarantees, specification animation can improve the assurance that an intermediate assertion (e.g., an invariant) is valid. In particular, it can disprove a false hypothesis before undue proof effort is spent in vain. Hence, we find it a worthwhile step in the verification workflow. After this step, the programmer can start proving the remaining conditions with higher confidence.

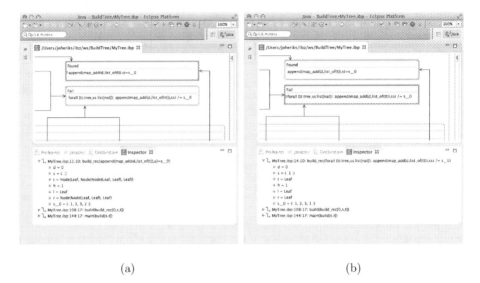

(a)   (b)

Fig. 7. Found (a) and Fail (b) evaluated for test cases (1,3,3,2) and (1,3,3,1), respectively

5   Related Work

State of the art examples of prover-backed verification tools for imperative languages include the Dafny language and verifier [16], the Spec# system for C# [9], the KeY tool [3] for Java, and Frama-C [11] for C. These tools target the verification of large object-oriented systems, and regard invariants as annotations to traditional program constructs (classes, for-loops) rather than as basic program building blocks.

Some verification tools support animation of specifications. *Rodin* [1] is an Eclipse-based IDE based on the Event-B formal method [2]. Event-B focuses on reactive systems, whereas our tool is concerned with verifying sequential programs. The *ProB animator* [17] is a model checker for Event-B. It provides a user interface for triggering events and evaluating invariants. Alloy [15] is a bounded model checker that generates all models of a specification up to a given size. Models are constructed by assistance of SAT solvers. However, Alloy does not address verification.

Ad hoc animation of invariant diagrams was supported in a predecessor of *Socos* [7]. This animation was based on translation into Python, rather than being carried out in the theorem prover framework. An embedding of invariant diagrams for the theorem prover Isabelle has been proposed [21]. An advantage of this approach over the one described here is an (automatic) proof that the operational definition (as a set of mutually recursive functions) is consistent with the verification conditions (as a set of lemmas proved by the programmer). However, no Isabelle support exists for invariant-based programming yet.

6   Conclusion and Future Work

Invariant-based programming is a graphical formalism for correct-by-construction development. The Socos environment allows the programmer to construct invariant diagrams and check their correctness using the PVS theorem prover and the Yices SMT solver. In this paper, we have described an extension to Socos that allows the user to inspect the runtime behavior of invariant diagrams. An invariant diagram is translated into a datatype representing the state space and a step function representing the transitions. The programmer can inspect the state and invariants visually during animation. While the underlying evaluation mechanism still relies on translation to Lisp, this approach requires a smaller trusted core (the PVS ground evaluator) compared to translating diagrams to a programming language or machine code. Animation integrates into the verification workflow, serving as a stepping stone to a fully verified program.

Several tool enhancements still remain to be done. We are currently investigating how to integrate automatic strategies (such as bounded model checking) to evaluate common classes of non-executable invariants (in particular, unbounded quantification). Modifying the program state (e.g., changing the values of individual variables) during animation, as well as standard debugging tools such as breakpoints and watches are currently not supported. Furthermore, support for editing the diagram during animation (cf. hot-swapping code in the Eclipse Java debugger) would likely enhance the user experience. Finally, the approach is yet to be tried out in a larger case study.

Acknowledgment. The authors would like to thank Viorel Preoteasa for suggesting the case study presented as well as developing its background theories.

References

1. Abrial, J.R., Butler, M., Hallerstede, S., Hoang, T.S., Mehta, F., Voisin, L.: Rodin: an open toolset for modelling and reasoning in Event-B. Int. J. Softw. Tools Technol. Transf. 12(6), 447–466 (2010)
2. Abrial, J.-R., Hoang, T.S.: Using design patterns in formal methods: An event-B approach. In: Fitzgerald, J.S., Haxthausen, A.E., Yenigun, H. (eds.) ICTAC 2008. LNCS, vol. 5160, pp. 1–2. Springer, Heidelberg (2008)
3. Ahrendt, W., Baar, T., Beckert, B., Bubel, R., Giese, M., Hähnle, R., Menzel, W., Mostowski, W., Roth, A., Schlager, S., Schmitt, P.H.: The KeY tool. Software and System Modeling 4, 32–54 (2005)
4. Back, R.J.: Invariant based programs and their correctness. In: Biermann, W., Guiho, G., Kodratoff, Y. (eds.) Automatic Program Construction Techniques, pp. 223–242. MacMillan Publishing Company (1983)
5. Back, R.J.: Invariant based programming: Basic approach and teaching experiences. Formal Aspects of Computing 21(3), 227–244 (2009)
6. Back, R.J., Eriksson, J., Mannila, L.: Teaching the construction of correct programs using invariant based programming. In: 3rd South-East European Workshop on Formal Methods (SEEFM 2007). South-East European Research Centre (2007)

7. Back, R.J., Eriksson, J., Myreen, M.: Testing and verifying invariant based programs in the SOCOS environment. In: Gurevich, Y., Meyer, B. (eds.) TAP 2007. LNCS, vol. 4454, pp. 61–78. Springer, Heidelberg (2007)

8. Back, R.J., Preoteasa, V.: Semantics and proof rules of invariant based programs. In: Proceedings of the 2011 ACM Symposium on Applied Computing. ACM (2011)

9. Barnett, M., Leino, K.R.M., Schulte, W.: The Spec# programming system: An overview. In: Barthe, G., Burdy, L., Huisman, M., Lanet, J.-L., Muntean, T. (eds.) CASSIS 2004. LNCS, vol. 3362, pp. 49–69. Springer, Heidelberg (2005)

10. Crow, J., Owre, S., Rushby, J., Shankar, N., Stringer-Calvert, D.: Evaluating, testing, and animating PVS specifications. Tech. rep., Computer Science Laboratory, SRI International (March 2001)

11. Cuoq, P., Kirchner, F., Kosmatov, N., Prevosto, V., Signoles, J., Yakobowski, B.: Frama-C: a software analysis perspective. In: Eleftherakis, G., Hinchey, M., Holcombe, M. (eds.) SEFM 2012. LNCS, vol. 7504, pp. 233–247. Springer, Heidelberg (2012)

12. Dutertre, B., de Moura, L.: The Yices SMT solver. Tech. rep., Computer Science Laboratory, SRI International, Menlo Park, CA (August 2006)

13. van Emden, M.H.: Programming with verification conditions. IEEE Transactions on Software Engineering 5(2), 148–159 (1979)

14. Eriksson, J.: Tool-Supported Invariant-Based Programming. Ph.d. thesis, Turku Centre for Computer Science, Finland (2010)

15. Jackson, D.: Alloy: A lightweight object modelling notation. ACM Trans. Softw. Eng. Methodol. 11(2), 256–290 (2002)

16. Leino, K.R.M.: Dafny: An automatic program verifier for functional correctness. In: Clarke, E.M., Voronkov, A. (eds.) LPAR-16 2010. LNCS, vol. 6355, pp. 348–370. Springer, Heidelberg (2010)

17. Leuschel, M., Butler, M.: ProB: A model checker for B. In: Araki, K., Gnesi, S., Mandrioli, D. (eds.) FME 2003. LNCS, vol. 2805, pp. 855–874. Springer, Heidelberg (2003)

18. Muñoz, C.: Rapid prototyping in PVS. Contractor Report NASA/CR-2003-212418, NASA, Langley Research Center, Hampton VA 23681-2199, USA (May 2003)

19. Owre, S., Rushby, J.M., Shankar, N.: PVS: A prototype verification system. In: Kapur, D. (ed.) CADE 1992. LNCS, vol. 607, pp. 748–752. Springer, Heidelberg (1992)

20. Owre, S.: A brief overview of the PVS user interface. In: 8th International Workshop User Interfaces for Theorem Provers (UITP 2008) (August 2008)

21. Preoteasa, V., Back, R.J., Eriksson, J.: Verification and code generation for invariant diagrams in Isabelle. The Journal of Logic and Algebraic Programming, http://www.sciencedirect.com/science/article/pii/S1567832613000441 (in press)

22. Reynolds, J.C.: Programming with transition diagrams. In: Gries, D. (ed.) Programming Methodology, pp. 153–165. Springer (1978)

23. Sam, O., Natarajan, S.: Abstract datatypes in PVS. Tech. rep., Computer Science Laboratory, SRI International (1997)

24. Shankar, N.: Efficiently executing PVS. Tech. rep., Computer Science Laboratory, SRI International (1999)

Automated Theorem Prover Assisted Program Calculations

Dipak L. Chaudhari and Om Damani

Indian Institute of Technology Bombay, India
{dipakc,damani}@cse.iitb.ac.in

Abstract. *Calculational Style of Programming*, while very appealing, has several practical difficulties when done manually. Due to the large number of proofs involved, the derivations can be cumbersome and error-prone. To address these issues, we have developed automated theorem provers assisted program and formula transformation rules, which when coupled with the ability to extract context of a subformula, help in shortening and simplifying the derivations. We have implemented this approach in a Calculational Assistant for Programming from Specifications (CAPS). With the help of simple examples, we show how the calculational assistant helps in taking the drudgery out of the derivation process while ensuring correctness.

Keywords: Calculational Style, Program Derivation, Correct by Construction, Program Correctness.

1 Introduction

Calculational Style of Programming [11], [18] is a programming methodology wherein programs are systematically derived from their formal specifications. At every step in the derivation process, a partially derived program/formula is transformed into another form, by following certain heuristic guidelines. The derived programs are correct-by-construction since correctness is implicit in the derivation. The calculational style is known for its readability and rigour. The calculational derivation helps in understanding the rationale behind the introduction of the program constructs and associated invariants thereby providing more opportunities to explore alternative solutions. This method often results in simple and elegant programs [18]. Although very appealing, there are several practical difficulties in effectively adopting this methodology. For many programming problems, the derivations are long and difficult to organize. As a result, the derivations, if done manually, are error-prone and cumbersome. To address these issues, the present work takes inspiration from various approaches from the fields of program verification, automated theorem proving, and interactive theorem proving to design and build a Calculational Assistant for Programming from Specifications (CAPS)[1]. Our aim has been to address the difficulties

---

[1] CAPS is available at http://www.cse.iitb.ac.in/~dipakc/CAPS

E. Albert and E. Sekerinski (Eds.): IFM 2014, LNCS 8739, pp. 205–220, 2014.

associated with the pen-and-paper calculational style while retaining the positive aspects.

Various tools exists to assist programmers in verifying the correctness of programs during the implementation phase itself. Tools like Dafny [19], Why3 [13], VCC [7] and VeriFast [17] generate the verification conditions and try to automatically prove these verification conditions. Dafny even has an extension called *poC* (program-oriented calculations) [20] which provides support for automatic verification of calculational proofs. However, the primary focus of such tools being the verification of programs, these tools provide limited guidance to the programmer in the actual task of deriving the programs.

There is a recent trend in program synthesis in which the programmer provides a syntactic template for the desired program in addition to the correctness specification [16], [23], [24]. These are automatic approaches which require a syntactic template to be provided by the user. Our focus, on the other hand, is on calculational derivation in an interactive setting.

Tools like Refinement Calculator [5] and PRT [6] provide tool support for the refinement based formal program derivation. Refinement Calculator uses HOL as an underlying proof engine. The PRT tool has similar goals; it extends the Ergo theorem prover and provides an Emacs based user interface. With these tools, the program constructs need to be encoded in the language of the underlying theorem prover. We chose not to tightly couple the system with any particular theorem prover. CAPS has built-in refinement rules and the system generates the required correctness proof obligations. We have tried to keep the notation and style of the derivation as close as possible to the pen-and-paper calculational style which is known for its readability. Our main emphasis has been on developing theorem prover assisted tactics to reduce the length of the derivations.

The main contributions of this work are as follows. (a) We have designed and implemented a calculational assistant for derivation of imperative programs. The tool provides a tactic based framework for carrying out program as well as formula transformations in a coherent way. (b) We have extended the *Structured Calculational Proof* format [2] by making the transformation relation explicit and by adding metavariable support. We have automated the mundane formula manipulation tasks and exploited the power of automated theorem proving to design powerful transformation rules (tactics) which help in shortening and simplifying the derivations without sacrificing the correctness. The automated theorem prover (ATP) assisted tactics also help in carrying out derivations that are not amenable to the calculational style. (c) By providing a unified framework for carrying out formula as well as program transformations, we have kept the derivation style in CAPS close to the calculational style.

With the help of simple examples, we show how the theorem prover assisted tactics help in shortening and simplifying the derivations thereby taking the drudgery out of the derivation process while ensuring correctness.

2   Motivating Example

In this section, we derive – without using any tool support – a simple program by following the calculational style of program derivation. This exercise highlights the complex user interactions usually involved in a typical program derivation session. We use this example in later sections to motivate and illustrate the main features of CAPS.

Consider the following programming problem specified in a natural language (adapted from exercise 4.3.4 in [18]).

Let $f[0..N)$ be an array of booleans where N is a natural number. Derive a program for the computation of a boolean variable r such that r is true iff all the true values in the array come before all the false values.

One of the several ways to formally specify this problem is shown in Fig. 1(a) where S denotes the program to be derived. For representing quantified expressions, we use the *Eindhoven* notation $(OP\,i : R : T)$ [18] where OP is the quantifier version of a symmetric and associative binary operator op, i is a list of quantified variables, R is the *Range* - a boolean expression typically involving the quantified variables, and T is the *Term* - an expression. This notation is usually used for arithmetic quantified terms $(\sum, \prod)$. By using the same notation for all the quantified terms – including the logical quantified terms $(\forall, \exists)$ – we can have generalized calculational rules.

We start by analysing the shape of the postcondition R and apply the *Replacing Constants by Variables* heuristics [18]. In particular, we introduce a fresh variable n, add bounds on n, and rewrite postcondition R as

$$\left(r \equiv \left(\exists p : 0 \le p \le n : \left(\begin{array}{l} (\forall i : 0 \le i < p : f[i]) \\ \land\, (\forall i : p \le i < n : \neg f[i]) \end{array} \right) \right) \right) \\ \land\, 0 \le n \le N \;\land\; n = N$$

We then apply the *Taking Conjuncts as Invariant* heuristics [18] to arrive at loop invariant $P_0 \land P_1$ and guard $\neg(n = N)$ where P_0 and P_1 are as follows.

$$P_0 : \left(r \equiv \left(\exists p : 0 \le p \le n : \left(\begin{array}{l} (\forall i : 0 \le i < p : f[i]) \\ \land\, (\forall i : p \le i < n : \neg f[i]) \end{array} \right) \right) \right) \\ P_1 : 0 \le n \le N$$

We observe that P_0 and P_1 can be established initially by $r, n := true, 0$. At this stage, we arrive at the program shown in Fig. 1(b) as the solution for S. We investigate an increase of n by 1 and envision the multiple assignment $r, n := r', n + 1$ for S_0 where r' is a placeholder for the unknown expression.

From the *Invariance Theorem* [18], the proof obligation for invariance of P_0 is $P_0 \land P_1 \land n \ne N \Rightarrow wp(r, n := r', n + 1; , P_0)$ where wp is the *weakest precondition predicate transformer* [12]. To calculate r', we assume P_0, P_1, and $n \ne N$ and simplify the consequent of this formula as shown in Fig. 1(c). Every step in the calculation is associated with the relation to be maintained ($\equiv$ in this case) and a hint justifying the step. For brevity, we skip the proof of preservation of P_1.

con N: int $\{N \geq 0\}$; **var** f: array $[0..N]$ of bool;

var r: bool;

S

$R : \left\{ r \equiv \left(\exists p : 0 \leq p \leq N : \left(\begin{array}{c} (\forall i : 0 \leq i < p : f[i]) \\ \wedge (\forall i : p \leq i < N : \neg f[i]) \end{array} \right) \right) \right\}$

(a)

$r, n := true, 0;$

$\left\{ \begin{array}{l} inv : P_0 \wedge P_1 \\ bound : N - n \end{array} \right\}$

do $n \neq N \rightarrow$

$\qquad S_0$

od

(b)

0	$wp(S_0, P_0)$
1	$\equiv \{$ envision $r, n := r', n + 1$ for $S_0 \}$
2	$wp(r, n := r', n + 1; , P_0)$
4	$\equiv \{$ definition of P_0 and assignment $\}$
5	$r' \equiv (\exists p : 0 \leq p \leq n + 1 : (\forall i : 0 \leq i < p : f[i]) \wedge (\forall i : p \leq i < n + 1 : \neg f[i]))$
6	$\equiv \{$ split off $p = n + 1; 0 \leq n + 1 \}$
7	$r' \equiv \left(\begin{array}{l} (\exists p : 0 \leq p \leq n : (\forall i : 0 \leq i < p : f[i]) \wedge (\forall i : p \leq i < n + 1 : \neg f[i])) \\ \vee (\forall i : 0 \leq i < n + 1 : f[i]) \wedge (\forall i : n + 1 \leq i < n + 1 : \neg f[i]) \end{array} \right)$
8	$\equiv \{$ empty range rule $\}$
9	$r' \equiv \left(\begin{array}{l} (\exists p : 0 \leq p \leq n : (\forall i : 0 \leq i < p : f[i]) \wedge (\forall i : p \leq i < n + 1 : \neg f[i])) \\ \vee (\forall i : 0 \leq i < n + 1 : f[i]) \end{array} \right)$
10	$\equiv \{$ split off $i = n \}$
11	$r' \equiv \left(\begin{array}{l} (\exists p : 0 \leq p \leq n : (\forall i : 0 \leq i < p : f[i]) \wedge (\forall i : p \leq i < n : \neg f[i]) \wedge \neg f[n]) \\ \vee (\forall i : 0 \leq i < n + 1 : f[i]) \end{array} \right)$
12	$\equiv \{$ distribute $\wedge$ over $\exists$ since $\neg f[n]$ does not have free occurrence of $p \}$
13	$r' \equiv \left(\begin{array}{l} ((\exists p : 0 \leq p \leq n : (\forall i : 0 \leq i < p : f[i]) \wedge (\forall i : p \leq i < n : \neg f[i])) \wedge \neg f[n]) \\ \vee (\forall i : 0 \leq i < n + 1 : f[i]) \end{array} \right)$
14	$\equiv \{$ invariant $P_0 \}$
15	$r' \equiv (r \wedge \neg f[n]) \vee (\forall i : 0 \leq i < n + 1 : f[i])$
16	$\equiv \{$ add invariant $P_2 : s \equiv (\forall i : 0 \leq i < n : f[i])$ and assume $P_2(n := n + 1).\}$
17	$r' \equiv (r \wedge \neg f[n]) \vee s$
18	$\equiv \{$ instantiating r' to $(r \wedge \neg f[n]) \vee s \}$
19	$true$

(c)

$r, n, s := true, 0, true;$

$\left\{ \begin{array}{l} inv : P_0 \wedge P_1 \wedge P_2 \\ bound : N - n \end{array} \right\}$

do $n \neq N \rightarrow$

$\qquad \{P_2\} S_1 \{P_2(n := n + 1)\};$

$\qquad r, n := (r \wedge \neg f[n]) \vee s, n + 1;$

od

(d)

$r, n, s := true, 0, true;$

$\left\{ \begin{array}{l} inv : P_0 \wedge P_1 \wedge P_2 \\ bound : N - n \end{array} \right\}$

do $n \neq N \rightarrow$

$\qquad s := s \wedge f[n];$

$\qquad \{P_2(n := n + 1)\}$

$\qquad r, n := (r \wedge \neg f[n]) \vee s, n + 1$

od

(e)

Fig. 1. Calculational derivation of the motivating example

In step 15 in Fig. 1(c), the expression under consideration is neither easily computable nor easily expressible in terms of the program variables. We, therefore, introduce a variable s and add an invariant $P_2 : s \equiv (\forall i : 0 \leq i < n : f[i])$. We now observe that P_2 can be established initially by $s := true$ since the universal quantification over an empty range equals *true*. With this we arrive at the program shown in Fig. 1(d).

Program S_1 has been added to ensure that $P_2(n := n + 1)$ is a precondition of the assignment to r. For S_1, we envision the assignment $s := s'$. By following the same procedure as before, we can calculate the value of s' to be $s \wedge f[n]$. The final derived program is presented in Fig. 1(e).

As this example shows, the final derived program, even when annotated with the invariants, may not be sufficient to provide the reader with the rationale behind the introduction of the program constructs and the invariants; whole derivation history is required.

3   Harnessing the Automated Theorem Provers

Readability of the calculational style comes from its ability to express all the important steps in the derivation, and at the same time being able to hide the secondary steps. By secondary steps, we mean the steps that are of secondary importance in deciding the direction of the derivation. For example, the steps involved in the proof for the justifications of the transformations do not change the course of the derivation. These justifications, when obvious, are often stated as hints without explicitly proving them. However, when the justifications are not obvious, it might take several steps to prove them. During the pen-and-paper calculational derivations, the transformation steps are kept small enough to be verifiable manually. Doing low level reasoning involving simple propositional reasoning, arithmetic reasoning, or equality reasoning (replacing equals by equals), can get very long and tedious if done in a completely formal way. Moreover, the lengthy derivations involving the secondary steps often hamper the readability. In such cases, there is a temptation to take long jumps while doing such derivations manually (without a tool support) resulting in correctness errors. With the help of automated theorem provers, however, we can afford to take long jumps in the derivation without sacrificing the correctness.

Many common proof paradigms like proof by contradiction, case analysis, induction, etc. are not easily expressed in a purely calculational style. Although, with some effort, these proofs can be handled by the structured calculational approach [2], employing automated theorem provers greatly simplifies the proof process. We use ATP assisted tactics to automate transformation steps that may not always be amenable to the calculational style.

The template based program synthesis approaches [16], [23], [24] take the specification and the syntactic template of the program as an input and automatically generate the whole program. In contrast, we are interested not just in the final program but also in the complete derivation as it helps in understanding the rationale behind the introduction of the program constructs and the associated invariants. Therefore, we employ the automated theorem provers at a much lower level in an interactive setting. This choice gives the user more control to explore alternative solutions since all the design decisions are manifest in the derivation.

Using the Why3 tool [13] as an interface, we have integrated automated theorem provers Alt-Ergo [8], CVC3 [4], SPASS [25] and Z3 [9] with CAPS. The Why3 platform provides two languages: a logic language (Why) and a ML-like programming language (WhyML). In CAPS, we use only the logic language since we are using Why3 only for the purpose of interacting with various theorem provers. The proof obligation formulas are transformed to Why3's logic language and Why3 is invoked in the background to prove these proof obligations with the help of various theorem provers. Using Why3 as an interface saves us from dealing with the different logical languages and predefined theories of various theorem provers.

We next describe the CAPS system and its specific features which play vital role in designing the theorem prover assisted tactics.

4   Calculational Assistant

CAPS is a calculational assistant for programming from specifications (precondition and postcondition) specified in first-order logic. The core component of CAPS is implemented in the Scala programming language. An interactive user interface is provided in the form of a web application. The web application uses AJAX to provide a responsive user interface.

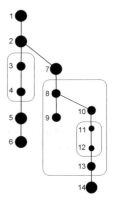

The derivation style in CAPS is very similar   to the calculational style explained in Section 2. Users start the derivation by providing the formal specification of the program and then incrementally transform it into a fully derived annotated program by applying predefined transformation rules called *Synthesis Tactics*. The complete derivation history is recorded in the form of a tree called *Synthesis Tree*. Fig. 2 shows a schematic representation of the *Synthesis Tree*. The portions of the tree enclosed by rectangles correspond to the transformations performed on the subprograms. This functionality is explained in Sec-

Fig. 2. A schematic representation of a Synthesis Tree

tion 5.1. Users have a facility to backtrack to any node in the Synthesis Tree and branch out to explore different derivation possibilities. The final output of the derivation is a fully synthesized *AnnotatedProgram* (explained in Section 4.1) along with the complete derivation history.

The GUI of the tool is shown in Fig. 3. The tactics panel shows the list of applied tactics (a path in the synthesis tree), the content panel shows the program/formula corresponding to the selected node, and the input panel is shows a input form used for a applying tactic. CAPS has in-built tactics for transforming partially derived annotated programs and proof obligations formulas.

While reasoning about a program fragment, it is natural to treat them as a formula (a Hoare triple) whose details needs to be worked out to make the formula valid. In CAPS, however, we treat programs and formulas differently as

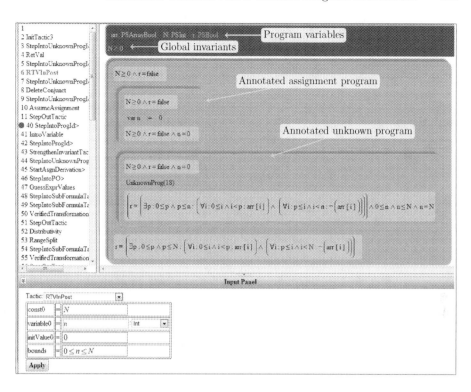

Fig. 3. CAPS GUI. There are three panels: *Tactics Panel* (left), *Content Panel*(center) and *Input Panel* (bottom). The input panel shows the input form for the *RTVInPost* (Replace term by variable) tactic.

they differ in many aspects: (a) Transformation rules for programs and formulas are quite different. (b) Program context consists of program variables whereas formula context consists of set of assumptions. (c) Visual representations of programs and formulas are quite different. By treating programs and formulas differently and keeping separate context management mechanisms for them, we are able to reason directly at the program level. This also helps in displaying programs and formulas in their natural form in the graphical user interface.

4.1   Program Transformations

For representing a program fragment and its specification, we introduce a data structure called *AnnotatedProgram*. It is obtained by augmenting each program construct in the Guarded Command Language (GCL) [10] with its precondition and postcondition. We also introduce a new program construct *UnknownProg* to represent an unsynthesized program fragment.

The program transformation tactics are based on the refinement rules from the refinement calculus [3], [21] and the high level program derivation heuristics from the literature on calculational program derivation [12], [18]. For example, consider the program transformation tactics shown in Fig. 4. The *Weaken the Precondition* tactic captures the rule "$\{R\} S \{Q\}$ and $P \Rightarrow R$ implies $\{P\} S \{Q\}$" whereas the *Take Conjuncts as Invariants* tactic captures the program derivation heuristics with the same name [18]. The main difference between the rules in the refinement calculus and the transformation tactics in CAPS is that the refinement rules gradually transform the specification to a program (without annotations) whereas our program transformation tactics transform a partially derived annotated program to a fully derived annotated program.

| Tactic:
  Weaken the Precondition.
Input:
  R
Applicability condition:
  $P \Rightarrow R$ | $\{P\}$
$UnknownProg\,(1)$
$\{Q\}$ $\rightarrow$ | $\{P\}$
  $\{P\}\ SkipProg$ $\{R\}$;
  $\{R\}\ UnknownProg(2)\ \{Q\}$
$\{Q\}$ |
| Tactic:
  Take Conjuncts as Invariants.
Inputs:
  Invariant conjuncts: R_1
  Variant: t
Applicability condition:
  $P \Rightarrow R_1$ | $\{P\}$
$UnknownProg\,(1)$
$\{R_1 \wedge R_2\}$ $\rightarrow$ | $\{P\}$
$\{inv : R_1\}\{variant : t\}$
While($\neg R_2$) {
  $\{R_1 \wedge \neg R_2\}$
    $UnknownProg\,(2)$
  $\{R_1\}$
}
$\{R_1 \wedge R_2\}$ |

Fig. 4. Program transformation tactics

4.2   Formula Transformations

As discussed in Section 2, program derivation often involves guessing the unknown program fragments in terms of placeholders and then deriving program expressions for the placeholders in order to discharge the correctness proof obligations. This functionality is implemented in CAPS by using metavariables to represent the placeholders.

Some steps in the derivations involve transformation of annotated programs whereas others involve transformation of proof obligation formulas. We call these two modes of the derivation as *program mode* and *formula mode* respectively. In order to emulate this functionality in a tactic based framework, we devised a tactic called *StepIntoPO*. On applying this tactic to an annotated program containing metavariables, a new formula node representing the proof obligations (verification conditions) is created in the synthesis tree. This formula is then incrementally transformed to a form, from which it is easier to instantiate the metavariables. After successfully discharging the proof obligation and instantiating all the metavariables, a tactic called *StepOut* is applied to get an annotated program with all the metavariables replaced by the corresponding instantiations.

Example. Fig. 5 shows a path in the synthesis tree corresponding to the derivation of the Integer Division program (compute the quotient (q) and the remainder (r) of the integer division of x by y where $x \geq 0$ and $y > 0$). Node *n1* in the synthesis

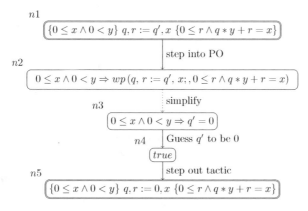

Fig. 5. A path in the synthesis tree for the Integer Division program. The *StepIntoPO* tactic is used to create a formula node corresponding to the proof obligation of the program node.

tree represents an assignment program which contains a metavariable q'. In order to discharge the corresponding proof obligation, the user applies a *StepIntoPO* tactic resulting in a formula node $n2$. The task for the user now is to derive an expression for q' that will make the formula valid. On further transformations, the user arrives at node $n3$ from which it is easier to instantiate q' as "0". Finally, the application of *StepOut* tactic results in a program node $n5$ where the metavariable q' is replaced with the instantiated expression "0".

Formula Transformations. We adopt a transformational style of inference wherein a formula F_0 is transformed step by step while preserving a reflexive and transitive relation R. Because of the transitivity of R, the sequence of transformations $F_0 R F_1 R, ... R F_n$ implies that $F_0 R F_n$ holds. This derivation is represented in the calculational notation as shown in Fig. 6.

$$
\begin{aligned}
&F_0 \\
R \quad &\{ \text{ hint justifying } F_0 \ R \ F_1 \ \} \\
&F_1 \\
R \quad &\{ \text{ hint justifying } F_1 \ R \ F_2 \ \} \\
&\cdots\cdots \\
R \quad &\{ \text{ hint justifying } F_{n-1} \ R \ F_n \ \} \\
&F_n
\end{aligned}
$$

Fig. 6. Calculation representation

Note that the relation maintained at an individual step can be stronger than the overall relation as the sequence of transformations $F_0 \ R_0 \ F_1 \ R_1, \ ... \ R_{n-1} \ F_n$ implies $F_0 \ R \ F_n$, provided relation R_i is at least as strong as the relation R for all i from 0 to $n-1$.

5   Theorem Prover Assisted Tactics

In order to integrate ATPs at local level, we first need to extract the context of the subprogram/subformula under consideration. The extracted context can then be used as assumptions while discharging the corresponding proof obligations.

5.1   Extracting Context of Subprograms

A partially derived program at some intermediate stage in the program derivation may contain multiple unsynthesized subprograms. Users may want to focus their attention on the derivation of one of these unknown subprograms. The derivation of a subprogram is, for the most part, independent of the rest of the program. Hence it is desirable to provide a mechanism wherein all the contextual information required for the derivation of a subprogram is extracted and presented to users so that they can carry out the derivation independently of the rest of the program. For example, in Fig. 1(b), user has focused on S_0 and derived it separately as shown in Fig. 1(c).

The activity of focusing on a subproblem is error-prone if carried out without tool support. In Fig. 1(d), subprogram S_1 is added to establish $P_2(n := n+1)$. We do not recalculate r' since the assumptions during the derivation of r' (invariant P_0 and P_1) still continue to hold provided S_1 does not modify variables r and n. User has to keep this fact in mind while deriving S_1 separately. Due care must be taken during manual derivation to ensure that after any modification, the earlier assumptions still continue to hold. In CAPS, every program fragment is associated with its full specification (precondition, postcondition) and the context, and the corresponding proof obligations are automatically generated.

Since the precondition and postcondition of each program construct are made explicit, user can focus on synthesizing a subprogram in isolation. Focusing on a subprogram is achieved by applying the *StepInTactic* which displays the subprogram under consideration along with the context and hides the rest of the program. User can then transform this subprogram to a desired form and apply the *StepOutTactic* when done. In Fig. 2, the portions of the tree enclosed by rectangles correspond to the transformations performed on the subprograms.

5.2   Extracting Context of Subformulas

CAPS also provides a functionality to focus on a subformula of the formula under consideration. Besides the obvious advantage of restricting attention to the subformula, this functionality also makes the additional contextual information available to the user which can be used for manipulating the subformula.

We adopt a style of reasoning similar to the window inference proof paradigm [14], [15], [22]. Our implementation differs from the stack based implementation in [15] since we maintain the history of all the transformations.

Extracting the Context. Let $F[f]$ be a formula with an identified subformula f and Γ be the set of current assumptions. Now, we want to transform the subformula f to f' (keeping the rest of the formula unchanged) such that $F[f] \, R \, F[f']$ holds where R is a reflexive and transitive relation to be preserved. The relationship to be preserved (r) and the contextual assumptions that can used (Γ') during the transformation of f to f' are governed by the following inference pattern [26].

Table 1. Contextual assumptions: The R-preserving transformation from $F[f]$ to $F[f']$ under the assumptions Γ can be achieved by r-preserving transformation from f to f' under the assumptions Γ'. (It is assumed that Γ does not contain a formula with i as a free variable. This is ensured during the derivation by appropriately renaming the bound variables.)

$F[f]$	R	r	Γ'
$\boxed{A} \wedge B$	$\equiv,\ \Rightarrow,\ \Leftarrow$	$\equiv,\ \Rightarrow,\ \Leftarrow$	$\Gamma \cup \{B\}$
$\boxed{A} \vee B$	$\equiv,\ \Rightarrow,\ \Leftarrow$	$\equiv,\ \Rightarrow,\ \Leftarrow$	$\Gamma \cup \{\neg B\}$
$\neg \boxed{A}$	$\equiv,\ \Rightarrow,\ \Leftarrow$	$\equiv,\ \Leftarrow,\ \Rightarrow$	Γ
$\boxed{A} \implies B$	$\equiv,\ \Rightarrow,\ \Leftarrow$	$\equiv,\ \Leftarrow,\ \Rightarrow$	$\Gamma \cup \{\neg B\}$
$B \implies \boxed{A}$	$\equiv,\ \Rightarrow,\ \Leftarrow$	$\equiv,\ \Rightarrow,\ \Leftarrow$	$\Gamma \cup \{B\}$

$F[f]$	R	r	Γ'
$\boxed{A} \equiv B$	$\equiv,\ \Rightarrow,\ \Leftarrow$	$\equiv,\ \equiv,\ \equiv$	Γ
$\left(\forall i : \boxed{R.i} : T.i\right)$	$\equiv,\ \Rightarrow,\ \Leftarrow$	$\equiv,\ \Leftarrow,\ \Rightarrow$	$\Gamma \cup \{\neg T.i\}$
$\left(\exists i : \boxed{R.i} : T.i\right)$	$\equiv,\ \Rightarrow,\ \Leftarrow$	$\equiv,\ \Rightarrow,\ \Leftarrow$	$\Gamma \cup \{T.i\}$
$\left(\forall i : R.i : \boxed{T.i}\right)$	$\equiv,\ \Rightarrow,\ \Leftarrow$	$\equiv,\ \Rightarrow,\ \Leftarrow$	$\Gamma \cup \{R.i\}$
$\left(\exists i : R.i : \boxed{T.i}\right)$	$\equiv,\ \Rightarrow,\ \Leftarrow$	$\equiv,\ \Rightarrow,\ \Leftarrow$	$\Gamma \cup \{R.i\}$

$$\frac{\Gamma' \vdash f\ r\ f'}{\Gamma \vdash F[f]\ R\ F[f']} \tag{1}$$

Table 1 lists the assumptions Γ' and the relation r for a few combinations of $F[f]$ and R. The *StepInTactic* applications can be chained together. For example, if we want to transform $A \wedge B \Rightarrow C$ while preserving implication ($\Rightarrow$) relation, we may focus on the subformula A and preserve reverse implication ($\Leftarrow$) assuming $\neg C$ and B.

Our representation is an extension of the *Structured Calculational Proof* format [2]. The transformations on the subformulas are indented and contextual information is stored in the top row of the indented derivation. Each indented derivation is called a *frame*. Besides the assumptions, a frame also stores the relation to be maintained by the transformations in the frame. Tactic applications ensure that the actual relation maintained is at least as strong as the frame relation. Fig. 7 shows two calculational derivations. In the first derivation, formula $F[f]$ is transformed into $F[f']$ by preserving relation R. The same outcome is achieved in the second derivation by focusing on the subformula f and transforming it to f' under the assumptions Γ' while preserving r provided $F[\_]$, Γ, R, Γ', and r are in accordance with Equation 1.

Fig. 8 shows application of this tactic in CAPS. The user focuses on a subformula and manipulates it further while preserving the equivalence ($\equiv$) relation (which is stronger than the frame relation $\Leftarrow$). The assumptions extracted from the context can be used during the transformation of the subformula.

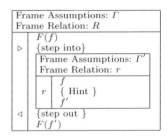

Fig. 7. Focusing on subformula

5.3 Automation at Tactic Level

We now describe the various functions of CAPS that are automated with the help of ATPs and the scenarios in which these automations are helpful.

Tactic Applicability Conditions. Some of the tactics are purely syntactic manipulations and are correct by construction whereas others have applicability conditions which need to be verified. For example, the *Split Range Tactic* and the *Empty Range Tactic* for the universal quantifier are shown below.

Split Range Tactic	**Empty Range Tactic**
$(\forall i : P.i \lor Q.i : T.i)$	$(\forall i : R.i : T.i)$
$\equiv \{$ Split Range $\}$	$\equiv \{$ Empty Range; $R.i \equiv false\}$
$(\forall i : P.i : T.i) \land (\forall i : Q.i : T.i)$	$true$

The *Split Range Tactic* does not have any applicability condition whereas the *Empty Range Tactic* has an additional applicability condition $(\forall i :: R.i \equiv false)$ (i.e. $R.i$ is unsatisfiable.). These conditions are automatically verified in CAPS using ATPs. Note that in the absence of this integration, the way to accomplish this transformation – at the risk of making the derivation lengthy – is to focus onto $R.i$ and transform it to $false$ and then step out and transform the whole formula to $true$.

Proofs involving no metavariables. Proofs that do not involve any metavariable are good candidates for full automation. In Section 2, we skipped the proof for preservation of the loop invariant $P_1 : 0 \leq n \leq N$. This invariant proof obligation does not involve any metavariable, and hence is not of interest from the synthesis point of view. We automatically prove such proof obligations with the help of ATPs. In case the automated provers fail to discharge the proof obligation or prove it invalid, we have to revert back to the step-by-step way of proving.

Verifying the transformations. During the calculational derivations, it is sometimes easier to directly specify the desired formula and verify it to be correct instead of deriving the formula in a purely interactive way. We have a *Verified-Transformation* tactic that serves this purpose. This tactic takes the formula corresponding to the next step and the relation to be maintained as an input and verifies if the relation holds. This functionality is similar in spirit to the

Fig. 8. Calculation of initialization assignment $(q, r := 0, x)$ to establish invariant $0 \leq r \wedge q * y + r = x$ in the derivation of *Integer Division* program

verified transformation functionality offered by the *poC* (program-oriented calculations) [21] extension of Dafny. The derivation in Fig. 8 has three instances of application of this tactic (labeled by a hint "Replace formula by an equivalent formula"). This tactic greatly reduces the length of the derivations.

The *VerifiedTransformation* tactic is also helpful in discharging proofs which are not amenable to the calculational style. Many common proof paradigms (like proof by contradiction, case analysis, induction, etc.) are not easily expressed in a purely calculational style [2]. Although, with some effort, these proofs can be discharged by using the functionality for focusing on subcomponents (which is based on the structured calculational approach in [2]), employing the automated theorem provers greatly simplifies the derivation. Note that this tactic is different from the earlier tactics; in all the other tactics a formula is transformed in a specific way and only the applicability condition is proved automatically, whereas in this tactic, the user directly specifies an arbitrary formula as the transformed form of a given formula and the tactic application just verifies the correctness of the transformation.

$$\left\langle \begin{array}{l} N \geq 1 \wedge f[0] \leq A < f[N] \wedge f[x] \leq A < f[y] \wedge \\ 0 \leq x < N \wedge x \leq y \leq N \wedge y \neq x + 1 \end{array} \right\rangle$$

Frame Relation: $\equiv$

$\quad f[x'] \leq A < f[y] \wedge 0 \leq x' < N \wedge x' < y \leq N$
$\equiv \{ A < f[y]; \text{ Simplify } \}$
$\quad f[x'] \leq A \wedge 0 \leq x' < N \wedge x' < y \leq N$
$\equiv \{ y \leq N; \text{ Simplify } \}$
$\quad f[x'] \leq A \wedge 0 \leq x' < N \wedge x' < y$
$\triangleright \{ \text{step into} \}$

$\qquad \left\langle \begin{array}{l} N \geq 1 \wedge f[0] \leq A < f[N] \wedge f[x] \leq A < f[y] \wedge \\ 0 \leq x < N \wedge x \leq y \leq N \wedge y \neq x + 1 \\ f[x'] \leq A \wedge 0 \leq x' \wedge x' < y \end{array} \right\rangle$

$\qquad$ Frame Relation: $\equiv$

$\qquad\quad x' < N$
$\qquad \equiv \{ x' < y \text{ and } y \leq N; \text{ Simplify } \}$
$\qquad\quad true$

$\triangleleft \{ \text{step out} \}$
$\quad f[x'] \leq A \wedge 0 \leq x' \wedge x' < y$

(a)

$$\left\langle \begin{array}{l} N \geq 1 \wedge f[0] \leq A < f[N] \wedge f[x] \leq A < f[y] \wedge \\ 0 \leq x < N \wedge x \leq y \leq N \wedge y \neq x + 1 \end{array} \right\rangle$$

Frame Relation: $\equiv$

$\quad f[x'] \leq A < f[y] \wedge 0 \leq x' < N \wedge x' < y \leq N$
$\equiv \{ \text{SimplifyAuto} \}$
$\quad f[x'] \leq A \wedge 0 \leq x' \wedge x' < y$

(b)

Fig. 9. (a) Excerpt from the derivation of the binary search program using multiple applications of the Simplify tactic, (b) The same derivation performed using the SimplifyAuto tactic

Simplification. The *Simplify* tactic simplifies the current formula by eliminating the *true/false* subformulas. For example, it transforms the formula $\varphi \wedge true$ to φ. The *SimplifyAuto* tactic takes this idea further by recursively focusing on the subformulas in bottom-up fashion and verifying – with the help of ATPs – if the subformulas are valid/invalid. The same effect can be achieved by interactively focusing on each subformula, proving/disproving the subformula under the modified assumptions, and then simplifying the formula. The *SimplifyAuto* tactic automates this process resulting in simpler derivations in many cases. Fig. 9(a) shows an excerpt from the derivation of the binary search program whereas Fig. 9(b) shows how the same outcome can be accomplished in a single step using the *SimplifyAuto* tactic.

6   Conclusions and Future Work

To address the problem of lengthy and tedious calculational program derivations, we have proposed an approach to integrate automated theorem provers at a tactic level and implemented it in a calculational assistant (CAPS) which we have built to assist users in deriving imperative programs from formal specifications. We have adapted various techniques from the fields of program verification and theorem proving for providing features like ability to step into proof obligations, metavariable support, and ability to extract context of a subformula, which help in realizing the tactic level automation. The introduced tactics help in shortening the derivations and also in carrying out derivations that are not amenable to the calculational style. We have managed to keep the derivation style close to the pen-and-paper calculational style thereby retaining the benefits of readability and rigour.

This tool will be used in the future offerings of the "Program Derivation" (CS420) class at IIT Bombay. To improve the usability, we plan to develop heuristics to rank the tactics in a given context so that at every stage in the derivation, users can be presented with a list of tactics sorted by descending likelihood of application. We also plan to develop high level program derivation tactics where the low level synthesis tasks (like synthesizing loop-free programs) are taken care of by the syntax-guided synthesis solvers [1].

Acknowledgements. The authors would like to thank the anonymous referees for their helpful comments. The work of the first author was supported by the Tata Consultancy Services (TCS) Research Fellowship.

References

1. Alur, R., Bodik, R., Juniwal, G., Martin, M.M.K., Raghothaman, M., Seshia, S.A., Singh, R., Solar-Lezama, A., Torlak, E., Udupa, A.: Syntax-guided synthesis. In: Proceedings of the IEEE International Conference on Formal Methods in Computer-Aided Design (FMCAD) (2013)
2. Back, R., Grundy, J., Von Wright, J.: Structured calculational proof. Formal Aspects of Computing 9(5-6), 469–483 (1997)
3. Back, R.J., von Wright, J.: Refinement Calculus: A Systematic Introduction. Graduate Texts in Computer Science. Springer, Berlin (1998)
4. Barrett, C., Tinelli, C.: CVC3. In: Damm, W., Hermanns, H. (eds.) CAV 2007. LNCS, vol. 4590, pp. 298–302. Springer, Heidelberg (2007)
5. Butler, M., Långbacka, T.: Program derivation using the refinement calculator. In: von Wright, J., Harrison, J., Grundy, J. (eds.) TPHOLs 1996. LNCS, vol. 1125, pp. 93–108. Springer, Heidelberg (1996)
6. Carrington, D., Hayes, I., Nickson, R., Watson, G.N., Welsh, J.: A tool for developing correct programs by refinement. Tech. rep. (1996),
   http://espace.library.uq.edu.au/view/UQ:10768
7. Cohen, E., Dahlweid, M., Hillebrand, M., Leinenbach, D., Moskal, M., Santen, T., Schulte, W., Tobies, S.: VCC: A practical system for verifying concurrent C. In: Berghofer, S., Nipkow, T., Urban, C., Wenzel, M. (eds.) TPHOLs 2009. LNCS, vol. 5674, pp. 23–42. Springer, Heidelberg (2009)
8. Conchon, S., Contejean, E.: The alt-ergo automatic theorem prover (2008),
   http://alt-ergo.lri.fr
9. De Moura, L., Bjørner, N.: Z3: An efficient SMT solver. In: Ramakrishnan, C.R., Rehof, J. (eds.) TACAS 2008. LNCS, vol. 4963, pp. 337–340. Springer, Heidelberg (2008)
10. Dijkstra, E.W.: Guarded commands, nondeterminacy and formal derivation of programs. Commun. ACM 18(8), 453–457 (1975)
11. Dijkstra, E.W., Feijen, W.H.: A Method of Programming. Addison-Wesley Longman Publishing Co., Inc., Boston (1988)

12. Dijkstra, E.W.: A Discipline of Programming. Prentice Hall, NJ (1997)
13. Filliâtre, J.-C., Paskevich, A.: Why3 — Where Programs Meet Provers. In: Felleisen, M., Gardner, P. (eds.) Programming Languages and Systems. LNCS, vol. 7792, pp. 125–128. Springer, Heidelberg (2013)
14. Grundy, J.: A window inference tool for refinement. In: 5th Refinement Workshop, pp. 230–254. Springer (1992)
15. Grundy, J.: A Method of Program Refinement. Ph.D. thesis, University of Cambridge Computer Laboratory, Cambridge, England (1993)
16. Gulwani, S., Jha, S., Tiwari, A., Venkatesan, R.: Synthesis of loop-free programs. In: Hall, M.W., Padua, D.A. (eds.) Proceedings of the 32nd ACM SIGPLAN Conference on Programming Language Design and Implementation, PLDI 2011, San Jose, CA, USA, June 4-8, pp. 62–73. ACM (2011)
17. Jacobs, B., Piessens, F.: The VeriFast program verifier. Technical Report CW-520, Dept. of Computer Science, Katholieke Universiteit Leuven (2008), http://www.cs.kuleuven.be/~bartj/verifast/verifast.pdf
18. Kaldewaij, A.: Programming: The Derivation of Algorithms. Prentice-Hall, Inc., NJ, USA (1990)
19. Leino, K.R.M.: Dafny: An automatic program verifier for functional correctness. In: Clarke, E.M., Voronkov, A. (eds.) LPAR-16 2010. LNCS, vol. 6355, pp. 348–370. Springer, Heidelberg (2010)
20. Leino, K.R.M., Polikarpova, N.: Verified calculations. In: Cohen, E., Rybalchenko, A. (eds.) VSTTE 2013. LNCS, vol. 8164, pp. 170–190. Springer, Heidelberg (2014)
21. Morgan, C.: Programming from Specifications. Prentice-Hall, Inc. (1990)
22. Robinson, P.J., Staples, J.: Formalizing a hierarchical structure of practical mathematical reasoning. Journal of Logic and Computation 3(1), 47–61 (1993)
23. Solar-Lezama, A., Tancau, L., Bodik, R., Seshia, S., Saraswat, V.: Combinatorial sketching for finite programs. ACM SIGARCH Computer Architecture News 34(5), 404–415 (2006)
24. Srivastava, S., Gulwani, S., Foster, J.S.: From program verification to program synthesis. In: POPL 2010, New York, NY, USA, pp. 313–326 (2010)
25. Weidenbach, C., Brahm, U., Hillenbrand, T., Keen, E., Theobald, C., Topic, D.: SPASS version 2.0. In: Voronkov, A. (ed.) CADE 2002. LNCS (LNAI), vol. 2392, pp. 275–279. Springer, Heidelberg (2002)
26. von Wright, J.: Extending window inference. In: Grundy, J., Newey, M. (eds.) TPHOLs 1998. LNCS, vol. 1479, pp. 17–32. Springer, Heidelberg (1998)

Managing LTL Properties in Event-B Refinement

Steve Schneider[1], Helen Treharne[1],
Heike Wehrheim[2], and David M. Williams[3]

[1] University of Surrey, England, UK
[2] University of Paderborn, Germany
[3] VU University Amsterdam

Abstract. Refinement in Event-B supports the development of systems via proof based step-wise refinement of events. This refinement approach ensures safety properties are preserved, but additional reasoning is required in order to establish liveness and fairness properties. In this paper we present results which allow a closer integration of two formal methods, Event-B and linear temporal logic. In particular we show how a class of temporal logic properties can carry through a refinement chain of machines. Refinement steps can include introduction of new events, event renaming and event splitting. We also identify a general liveness property that holds for the events of the initial system of a refinement chain. The approach will aid developers in enabling them to verify linear temporal logic properties at early stages of a development, knowing they will be preserved at later stages. We illustrate the results via a simple case study.

1 Introduction

Event-B [1] is a step-wise development method with excellent tools: Rodin platform [2] providing proof support and ProB [11] providing model checking. As Hoang and Abrial [10] clearly state the focus of verification within Event-B has been on the safety properties of a system to ensure that "something (bad) never happens". Typically, this has been done via the discharging of proof obligations. Nonetheless, the use of linear temporal logic (LTL) to specify temporal liveness properties has also been prevalent, for example in its application within the ProB tool [12]. The challenge is to identify more natural ways of integrating Event-B and LTL, so that LTL properties can be preserved by Event-B refinement, which is not currently the case in general.

Event-B describes systems in terms of *machines* with state, and *events* which are used to update the state. Events also have *guards*, which are conditions for the event to be enabled. One (abstract) machine may be refined by another (concrete) machine, using a *refinement step*. A *linking invariant* captures how the abstract and concrete states are related, and each abstract event must be refined by one or more concrete events whose state transformations match the abstract one in the sense of preserving the linking invariant. Refinement is transitive, so

E. Albert and E. Sekerinski (Eds.): IFM 2014, LNCS 8739, pp. 221–237, 2014.

a sequence of refinement steps, known as a *refinement chain*, will result in a concrete machine which is a refinement of the original abstract one.

A particular feature provided by Event-B is the introduction of *new* events in a refinement step—events which do not refine any abstract event. This allows for refinements to add finer levels of granularity and concretisation as the design develops; there are many examples in [1]. These new events are invisible at the abstract level (they correspond to the abstract state not changing), and we generally need to verify that they cannot occur forever. Event-B makes use of *labels* to keep track of the status of events as a refinement chain progresses. Event-B labels are *anticipated*, *convergent* and *ordinary*. The labelling of events in Event-B form part of the core of a system description but their inclusion is primarily to support the proof of safety properties and ensuring that events cannot occur forever: convergent events must decrease a variant and anticipated events cannot increase it. In this paper all newly introduced events must be convergent or anticipated, and anticipated events must become convergent at some stage. As an initial example, consider a *Lift* machine with two events *top* and *ground*, representing movement to the top and to the ground floor. This can be refined by a machine *Lift'* introducing two new anticipated events *openDoors* and *closeDoors*. The events *top* and *ground* are blocked when the doors are open, but enabled when the doors are closed.

Linear temporal logic provides a specification language for capturing properties of executions of systems, and is appropriate for reasoning about liveness and fairness. For example, we might verify for *Lift* that whenever *top* occurs, then eventually *ground* will occur. However, this is not guaranteed for its refinement *Lift'*: it may be that the doors open and close repeatedly forever following the *top* event, thus never reaching the next *ground* event. Alternatively it may be that the system deadlocks with the doors open, again preventing *ground* from occurring. Hence we see that LTL properties are not automatically preserved by Event-B refinement. In the first case we would require some assurance that *openDoors* and *closeDoors* cannot repeat forever without the lift moving; in the second case we require some liveness property on *closeDoors* to prevent termination with the doors open.

In this paper we present results for when temporal logic properties can be carried through Event-B refinement chains. The results generalise to events that are split—refined by several events—during a refinement chain. We also identify conditions on temporal logic properties that make them suitable for use in a refinement chain, since some properties are not preserved by Event-B refinement (for example, the property "*closeDoor* never occurs" holds for *Lift* but not for its refinement *Lift'*). The results are underpinned by our process algebra understanding of the Event-B semantics, in particular the traces, divergences and infinite traces semantics used for CSP and applied to Event-B in [15].

The paper is organised as follows: Section 2 provides the necessary Event-B refinement background and the refinement strategy we use in the paper. Section 3 introduces a running example. Section 4 defines the LTL we use. Sections 5 and 6 present and illustrate the main theoretical results. For reasons of space we do not include proofs, but they appear in the technical report available at [16]. We put our work into the context of related work in Section 7 and our future work in Section 8.

2   Event-B

2.1   Event-B Machines

An Event-B development is defined using *machines*. A machine M contains a vector of variables and a set of events. The *alphabet* of M, αM, is the set of events defined in M. Each event evt_i has the general form $evt_i \stackrel{\frown}{=}$ **any** x **where** $G_i(x, v)$ **then** $v :|\ BA_i(v, x, v')$ **end**, where x represents the parameters of the event, the guard $G_i(x, v)$ is the condition for the event to be enabled. The body is given by $v :|\ BA_i(v, x, v')$ whose execution assigns to v any value v' which makes the *before-after* predicate $BA_i(v, x, v')$ true. This simplifies to $evt_i \stackrel{\frown}{=}$ **when** $G_i(v)$ **then** $v :|\ BA_i(v, v')$ **end** when there are no parameters, since the guard and the *before-after* predicate does not refer to the parameters x.

Variables of a machine are initialised in an initialisation event *init* and are constrained by an invariant $I(v)$. The Event-B approach to semantics is to associate proof obligations with machines. The key proof obligation, INV, is that all events must preserve the invariant. There is also a proof obligation on a machine with respect to deadlock freedom which means that a guard of at least one event in M is always enabled. When this obligation holds M is *deadlock free*.

2.2   Event-B Refinement

An Event-B development is a sequence of B machines linked by a refinement relationship. In this paper we use M and M' when referring to a refinement between an *abstract* machine M and a *concrete* machine M' whereas a chain of refinements is referred to using numbered subscripts, i.e., M_0, M_i, ..., M_n, to represent the specific refinement levels.

A refinement machine can introduce new events and split existing events. We omit the treatment of merging events in this paper. New events are treated as refinements of *skip*, i.e., evt_i' does not refine an event in M. Note that when splitting events, M' has several events evt_i' refining a single event evt_i.

A machine M is considered to be refined by M' if the given *linking invariant* J on the variables between the two machines is established by their initialisation, and preserved by all events. This requirement is captured by the INV_REF proof obligation. Formally, we denote the refinement relation between two machines, written $M \preccurlyeq M'$, when all the following proof obligations hold: feasibility FIS_REF, guard strengthening GRD_REF and simulation INV_REF. Feasibility of an event is the property that, if the event is enabled (i.e., the guard is true), then there is some after-state. Guard strengthening requires that when a concrete event is enabled, then so is the abstract one. Finally, simulation ensure the occurrence of events in the concrete machine can be matched in the abstract one (including the initialization event). Further details of these proof obligations can be found in [1].

In Section 1 we introduced the three kinds of labelling of events in Event-B: *anticipated* (a), *convergent* (c) and *ordinary* (o) and noted that convergent events are those which must not execute forever whereas *anticipated* events provide a means of deferring consideration of divergence-freedom until later refinement steps. The proof obligation that deals with divergences is WFD_REF. It requires that the proposed variant V of a refinement machine satisfies the appropriate properties: that it is a natural number, that it decreases on occurrence of any convergent event, and that it does not increase on occurrence of any anticipated event. Therefore, we augment the previous refinement relation with WFD_REF such that $M \preccurlyeq_W M'$. Ordinary events can occur forever and therefore WFD_REF is not applicable for such events.

2.3   Event-B Development Strategies

Event-B has a strong but flexible refinement strategy which is described in [9]. In [15] we also discussed different Event-B refinement strategies and characterised them with respect to the approaches documented by Abrial in [1] and supported by the Rodin tool. In this paper we focus on the simplest strategy, and the one most commonly used. The strategy has the following set of restrictions on a refinement chain $M_0 \preccurlyeq_W M_1 \preccurlyeq_W \ldots \preccurlyeq_W M_n$:

1. all events in M_0 are labelled ordinary. This set of events is referred to as O_0.
2. each event of M_i is refined by at least one event of M_{i+1};
3. each new event in M_i is either anticipated or convergent, where $i > 0$;
4. each event in M_{i+1} which refines an anticipated event of M_i is itself either convergent or anticipated;
5. refinements of convergent or ordinary events of M_i are ordinary in M_{i+1}.
6. no anticipated events remain in the final machine.

Figure 1 illustrates our development strategy for a vending machine, detailed in Section 3, where C_i is the set of convergent events within M_i, and O_i is the set of ordinary events within M_i.

For example, $O_0 = \{selectBiscuit, selectChoc, dispenseBiscuit, dispenseChoc\}$ and $C_0 = \emptyset$ in VM_1. In VM_2 we note that $C_1 = \{refund\}$. In VM_3 we note that $C_2 = \{refill\}$ and in VM_4 we have $C_3 = \{pay\}$. Thus we denote $C_{all} = C_1 \cup C_2 \cup C_3$.

2.4   Event-B Semantics

In this paper we define a trace of M to be either an infinite sequences of events (a,c or o), i.e., $\langle e_0, e_1, \ldots \rangle$ or a finite sequence of events, i.e., $\langle e_0, \ldots, e_{k-1} \rangle$ where the machine M deadlocks after the occurrence of the final event. Traces correspond to maximal executions of machines. Plagge and Leuschel in [14] provided a definition of an infinite or finite path π of M in terms of a sequence of events

selectBiscuit (o)	selectBiscuit (o)	selectBiscuit (o)	selectBiscuit (o)
selectChoc (o)	selectChoc (o)	selectChoc (o)	selectChoc (o)
dispenseBiscuit (o)	dispenseBiscuit (o)	dispenseBiscuit (o)	dispenseBiscuit (o)
dispenseChoc (o)	dispenseChoc (o)	dispenseChoc (o)	dispenseChoc (o)
	pay (a)	pay (a)	pay (c)
	refund (c)	refund (o)	refund (o)
		refill (c)	refill (o)
VM_1	VM_2	VM_3	VM_4

Fig. 1. Events and their annotations in the Vending Machine development

and their intermediate states. In order to distinguish notation we use u to represent a trace without the intermediate states. We need not consider the particular states within a trace in our reasoning which is based on infinite traces. When a machine M is deadlock free all of its traces are infinite. We use the functions of concatenation ($^\frown$), projection ($\restriction$) and length ($\#$) on finite and infinite traces.

A more complex behavioural semantics for B machines was given by Schneider *et al.* in [15] based on the weakest precondition semantics of [13,6] for action systems and CSP. In [15] there are two key results that enable us to reason about infinite sequences of convergent and ordinary events in this paper. Firstly, the following predicate captures that if an infinite trace u performs infinitely many events from C then it has infinitely many events from O, where C and O are sets of events.

Definition 1. $CA(C, O)(u) \mathrel{\widehat{=}} (\#(u \restriction C) = \infty \Rightarrow \#(u \restriction O) = \infty)$

C and O will be used to capture convergent and ordinary events through a development. For an Event-B machine M the above means that it *does not diverge on its C events*. This is precisely what we get when we prove WFD_REF but the above definition describes the result on traces.

The second result from [15], restated as Theorem 1, allows us to conclude that there are no infinite sequences of convergent events in the final machine of a refinement chain M_n. The function $g_{1,n}$ defines a compositional mapping for all concrete events to abstract events in terms of a function mapping f at each refinement level where $f_{i+1} : \alpha M_{i+1} \twoheadrightarrow \alpha M_i$ and $f_{i+1}(evt_{i+1}) = evt_i \Leftrightarrow evt_{i+1}$ **refines** evt_i. (Note that $g_{1,0}$ is the identity function.)

Definition 2. $g_{i,j} = f_j; f_{j-1}; \ldots; f_i$

Theorem 1. *If* $M_0 \preccurlyeq_W M_1 \preccurlyeq_W \ldots \preccurlyeq_W M_n$ *then*

$$M_n \text{ sat } CA(g_{1,n}^{-1}(C_0) \cup \ldots \cup g_{i,n}^{-1}(C_i) \cup \ldots \cup C_n \,,\, g_{1,n}^{-1}(O_0))$$

The result for our example is simply VM_4 sat $CA(C_{all}, O_0)$ since there is no renaming: each function mapping f_i is the identity.

3   Example

In Section 2.3 we introduced a development strategy for a vending machine. Figures 2, 3, 4 and 5 illustrate a development chain from vending machine VM_1,

```
machine VM₁
variables chosen
invariant chosen ⊆ {choc, biscuit}
events
   init ≙ chosen := {}
   selectBiscuit ≙ status : ordinary
      when biscuit ∉ chosen then chosen := chosen ∪ {biscuit} end
   selectChoc ≙ status : ordinary
      when choc ∉ chosen then chosen := chosen ∪ {choc} end
   dispenseBiscuit ≙ status : ordinary
      when biscuit ∈ chosen then chosen := chosen − {biscuit} end
   dispenseChoc ≙ status : ordinary
      when choc ∈ chosen then chosen := chosen − {choc} end
end
```

Fig. 2. VM_1

VM_2, VM_3 to VM_4; there are no anticipated events in VM_4. Note the numbers of the vending machines start from one. We introduce VM_0 in Section 6. Thus M_0 in Theorem 1 corresponds to VM_1 etc.

VM_1 is a simple machine that supports the selection and dispensing of chocolates and biscuits via four events: *selectBiscuit*, *selectChoc*, *dispenseBiscuit* and *dispenseChoc*. We abbreviate their names in the narrative to *sb*, *sc*, *db* and *dc* respectively. The first refinement step introduces VM_2 and the notion of paying and refunding. The *pay* event in VM_2 is always enabled and allows positive credit to be input. The machine allows a biscuit to be chosen if it has not already been chosen and additionally provided a payment has been made; a chocolate selection is similar. Hence the guards of all four of the original events *sb*, *sc*, *db* and *db* are strengthened. The guard of the *refund* event means that credit cannot be refunded for selected items and cannot occur forever since it is convergent. Importantly, the *refundEnabled* flag is introduced so that it is only true after a dispense and prevents infinite loops of the *pay* followed by *refund*.

VM_3 introduces the notion of stocked items and a new *refill* event. We could have chosen many different guards for the *refill* event. For example, we could have labelled it *anticipated* with a guard of *true*. Instead we have made an underspecification where the stock can be restocked when there may be no biscuits or no chocolates, and established convergence. Again the guard of the four original events have been strengthened so that they are only enabled when the appropriate stocked item is in stock. But now *db* and *dc* also capture the non-deterministic notion of running out or not of their respective items. The guard of *refund* remains unchanged. The guard of *pay* has been strengthened so that it is only enabled when there is stock but this is not strong enough to prevent it happening infinitely often, hence it remains anticipated in VM_3.

The final machine, VM_4, is a straightforward data refinement which introduces the capacity of the machine. Apart from highlighting the refinement relationship

---

machine VM_2
variables $credit, chosen, refundEnabled$
invariant $credit \in \mathbb{N} \wedge chosen \subseteq \{choc, biscuit\} \wedge refundEnabled \in BOOL$
variant $if\ refundEnabled = FALSE\ then\ 0\ else\ 1$
events
  init $\widehat{=}$ $credit := 0\ ||\ chosen := \{\}\ ||\ refundEnabled := FALSE$
  pay $\widehat{=}$ **status** : anticipated
    any x **where** $x \in \mathbb{N}_1$
    then $credit := credit + x$ **end** $||\ refundEnabled := FALSE$ **end**
  selectBiscuit $\widehat{=}$ **status** : ordinary
    when $credit > 0 \wedge biscuit \notin chosen \wedge credit > card(chosen)$
    then $chosen := chosen \cup \{biscuit\}$ **end**
  selectChoc $\widehat{=}$ **status** : ordinary
    when $credit > 0 \wedge choc \notin chosen \wedge credit > card(chosen)$
    then $chosen := chosen \cup \{choc\}$ **end**
  dispenseBiscuit $\widehat{=}$ **status** : ordinary
    when $credit > 0 \wedge biscuit \in chosen$
    then $credit := credit - 1\ ||\ chosen := chosen - \{biscuit\}\ ||$
       $refundEnabled := TRUE$ **end**
  dispenseChoc $\widehat{=}$ **status** : ordinary
    when $credit > 0 \wedge choc \in chosen$
    then $credit := credit - 1\ ||\ chosen := chosen - \{choc\}\ ||$
       $refundEnabled := TRUE$ **end**
  refund $\widehat{=}$ **status** : convergent
    when $credit > card(chosen) \wedge refundEnabled := TRUE$
    then $credit := card(chosen)\ ||\ refundEnabled := FALSE$ **end**
end

Fig. 3. VM_2

between *stocked* and *chocStock* and *biscuitStock* note the strengthening of the guard of *refill* so that vending machine should only be refilled when there is no stock. Also the guard of *pay* is strengthened so that it becomes convergent.

4   LTL Notation

In this paper we use the grammar for the LTL operators presented by Plagge and Leuschel [14]:

$$\phi ::= true \mid [x] \mid \neg\phi \mid \phi_1 \vee \phi_2 \mid \phi_1\ U\ \phi_2$$

A machine M satifies ϕ, denoted $M \models \phi$, if all traces of M satisfy ϕ. The definition for u to satisfy ϕ is defined by induction over ϕ as follows:

$u \models true$
$u \models [x] \qquad \Leftrightarrow u = \langle x \rangle ^\frown u^1$
$u \models \neg\phi \qquad \Leftrightarrow$ it is not the case that $u \models \phi$
$u \models \phi_1 \vee \phi_2 \Leftrightarrow u \models \phi_1$ or $u \models \phi_2$
$u \models \phi_1 U \phi_2 \quad \Leftrightarrow \exists k \geq 0.\forall i < k.u^i \models \phi_1$ and $u^k \models \phi_2$

machine VM_3
variables $credit, chosen, refundEnabled, stocked$
invariant $credit \in \mathbb{N} \wedge chosen \subseteq \{choc, biscuit\} \wedge stocked \subseteq \{choc, biscuit\}$
       $(choc \in chosen \Rightarrow choc \in stocked) \wedge (biscuit \in chosen \Rightarrow biscuit \in stocked)$
variant $card\{choc, biscuit\} - stocked$
events
  init $\hat{=} \ldots \| stocked := \{choc, biscuit\}$
  pay $\hat{=}$ **status** : anticipated
    any x **where** $x \in \mathbb{N}_1 \wedge stocked \neq \emptyset$
    then $credit := credit + x$ **end** $\| refundEnabled := FALSE$ **end**
  selectBiscuit $\hat{=}$ **status** : ordinary
    when $\ldots \wedge biscuit \in stocked$
    then $chosen := chosen \cup \{biscuit\}$ **end**
  selectChoc $\hat{=}$ **status** : ordinary
    when $\ldots \wedge choc \in stocked$
    then $chosen := chosen \cup \{choc\}$ **end**
  dispenseBiscuit $\hat{=}$ **status** : ordinary
    when $credit > 0 \wedge biscuit \in chosen \wedge biscuit \in stocked$
    then $\ldots \|$ **any** x **where** $x \subseteq \{biscuit\}$ **then** $stocked := stocked - x$ **end end**
  dispenseChoc $\hat{=}$ **status** : ordinary
    when $credit > 0 \wedge choc \in chosen \wedge choc \in stocked$
    then $\ldots \|$ **any** x **where** $x \subseteq \{choc\}$ **then** $stocked := stocked - x$ **end end**
  refund $\hat{=}$ **status** : ordinary $\ldots$
  refill $\hat{=}$
    status : convergent
    when $choc \notin stocked \vee biscuit \notin stocked$
    then $stocked := \{choc, biscuit\}$ **end**
end

Fig. 4. VM_3

where u^n is u with the first n elements removed, i.e., $u = \langle x_0, \ldots, x_{n-1} \rangle \frown u^n$.

From these operators Plagge and Leuschel derived several additional operators, including: conjunction ($\phi_1 \wedge \phi_2$), finally (or eventually) ($F\phi$), and globally (or always) ($G\phi$), in the usual way; we also use these operators, and for explicitness we also provide direct definitions for them:

$$u \models \phi_1 \wedge \phi_2 \Leftrightarrow u \models \phi_1 \text{ and } u \models \phi_2$$
$$u \models F\phi \Leftrightarrow \exists i \geq 0.u^i \models \phi$$
$$u \models G\phi \Leftrightarrow \forall i \geq 0.u^i \models \phi$$

We omit atomic propositions on states since our traces are only dealing with events and not paths of states and transitions. We also omit the next operator, see Section 7. In this paper our running example uses globally, finally, or and implies.

---

machine VM_4
constants *capacity*
properties *capacity* > 0
variables *credit, chosen, refundEnabled, chocStock, biscuitStock*
invariant *credit* $\leq$ *capacity* $\wedge$ *chosen* $\subseteq$ {*choc, biscuit*} $\wedge$
    refundEnabled $\in BOOL \wedge$ *chocStock* $\leq$ *capacity* $\wedge$ *biscuitStock* $\leq$ *capacity* $\wedge$
    (*choc* $\notin$ *stocked* $\Rightarrow$ *chocStock* $= 0$) $\wedge$ (*choc* $\in$ *stocked* $\Rightarrow$ *chocStock* ≥ 0) $\wedge$
    (*biscuit* $\notin$ *stocked* $\Rightarrow$ *biscuitStock* $= 0$) $\wedge$ (*biscuit* $\in$ *stocked* $\Rightarrow$ *biscuitStock* ≥ 0)
variant $max\{(chocStock + biscuitStock) - credit, 0\}$
events
  init $\hat{=}$ ... $\|$ *chocStock* := *capacity* $\|$ *biscuitStock* := *capacity*
  pay $\hat{=}$ **status** : convergent
    any x **where** $x \in \mathbb{N}_1 \wedge$ (*chocStock* + *biscuitStock*) $>$ *credit*
    then *credit* := *credit* + x **end** $\|$ *refundEnabled* := *FALSE* **end**
  selectChoc $\hat{=}$ **status** : ordinary
    when ... $\wedge$ *chocStock* > 0
    then *chosen* := *chosen* $\cup$ {*choc*} **end**
  selectBiscuit $\hat{=}$ **status** : ordinary
    when ... $\wedge$ *biscuitStock* > 0
    then *chosen* := *chosen* $\cup$ {*biscuit*} **end**
  dispenseBiscuit $\hat{=}$ **status** : ordinary
    when *credit* $> 0 \wedge$ *biscuit* $\in$ *chosen* $\wedge$ *biscuitStock* > 0
    then ... $\|$ *chocStock* := *chocStock* $- 1$ **end**
  dispenseChoc $\hat{=}$ **status** : ordinary
    when *credit* $> 0 \wedge$ *choc* $\in$ *chosen* $\wedge$ *chockStock* > 0
    then ... $\|$ *chocStock* := *chocStock* $- 1$ **end**
  refund $\hat{=}$ **status** : ordinary ...
  refill $\hat{=}$ **status** : ordinary
    when *chocStock* $= 0 \wedge$ *biscuitStock* $= 0$
    then *chocStock* := *capacity* $\|$ *biscuitStock* := *capacity* **end**
end

Fig. 5. VM_4

For example, the informal specification for the *Lift* given in Section 1, that whenever *top* happens then eventually *ground* will happen, could be written as

$$G([top] \Rightarrow F[ground])$$

From our running *VM* example, the predicate $GF[selectBiscuit]$ expresses that *selectBiscuit* occurs infinitely often: at any point there is always some occurrence of *selectBiscuit* at some point in the future. We use this construction in the VM properties introduced in Section 5. For example, we have ϕ_2 given as

$$\phi_2 \;=\; (\neg GF[selectBiscuit]) \Rightarrow G([selectChoc] \Rightarrow F[dispenseChoc])$$

This states that provided *selectBiscuit* only occurs finitely often (i.e. eventually stops), then whenever *selectChoc* occurs then *dispenseChoc* will eventually occur.

It will also be useful to identify the events mentioned explicitly in an LTL formula ϕ. This set is called the alphabet of ϕ. This is written $\alpha(\phi)$, similar to the use of αM for the alphabet of machine M. For LTL formulae it is defined inductively as follows:

Definition 3

$$\alpha(true) = \{\}$$
$$\alpha([x]) = \{x\}$$
$$\alpha(\neg\phi) = \alpha(\phi)$$
$$\alpha(\phi_1 \vee \phi_2) = \alpha(\phi_1) \cup \alpha(\phi_2)$$
$$\alpha(\phi_1 \wedge \phi_2) = \alpha(\phi_1) \cup \alpha(\phi_2)$$
$$\alpha(\phi_1 \ U \ \phi_2) = \alpha(\phi_1) \ \cup \ \alpha(\phi_2)$$
$$\alpha(F\phi) = \alpha(\phi)$$
$$\alpha(G\phi) = \alpha(\phi)$$

For example, we have $\alpha(\phi_2) = \{selectBiscuit, selectChoc, dispenseChoc\}$ for ϕ_2 above.

5   Preserving LTL Properties

In this section we provide results to demonstrate when properties are preserved by refinement chains. Firstly, we consider chains which do not contain any renaming/splitting of events in a machine. Hence, each function mapping f_i for $M_i \ldots M_n$ is the identity. The first result is a general result identifying a particular temporal property that will always hold for all refinement chains which abide by the rules of the strategy presented in Section 2.3. The second result given in Lemma 2 concerns the preservation of temporal properties that would be proposed by a specifier. We have already observed from the vending machine example that new events can be introduced during a refinement, e.g., *pay*, *refill*, etc.. We aim for such properties to hold even though new anticipated and convergent events are being introduced.

Lemma 1 states that M_n at the end of the refinement chain will always eventually perform one of the events of the initial machine M_0. In other words, M_n will perform infinitely many of the initial events. This means that the events introduced along the refinement chain cannot occur forever at the expense of the original events. In our example, $\alpha M_0 = O_0$.

Lemma 1. *If $M_0 \preccurlyeq_W M_1 \preccurlyeq_W \ldots \preccurlyeq_W M_n$ and M_n is deadlock free and M_n does not contain any anticipated events then $M_n \models GF(\bigvee_{e \in \alpha M_0} [e])$*

Next we provide a definition which is used in Lemma 2 below and it enables us to gain insights into the kinds of temporal properties that are appropriate to be proposed and have the potential of being preserved through a refinement chain. Definition 4 describes a maximal execution satisfying a property ϕ. The execution may include some events which do not have an impact on whether the property holds or not therefore we can restrict the maximal execution to include only those events that impact on the property.

Definition 4. *Let β be a set of events. Then ϕ is β-dependent if $\alpha(\phi) \subseteq \beta$ and $u \models \phi \Leftrightarrow (u \restriction \beta) \models \phi$.*

An example of a β-dependent property is $GF(pay)$ where $\beta = \{pay\}$. If $u \models GF(pay)$ then $u \restriction pay \models GF(pay)$, and vice versa. Conversely, $\neg G(pay)$ is not $\{pay\}$-dependent. For example, if $u = \langle pay, refill, pay, pay, \ldots \rangle$ then $u \models \neg G(pay)$ but $u \restriction \{pay\} \not\models \neg G(pay)$.

As another example, define $\beta = \{sb, sc, db, dc\}$. Then $G(sb \vee sc \vee db \vee dc)$ is not β-dependent. This is exemplified by any trace u which contains events other than those in β. In this case $u \restriction \{sb, sc, db, sc\} \models G(sb \vee sc \vee db \vee dc)$ but $u \not\models G(sb \vee sc \vee db \vee dc)$. VM_4 exhibits such traces. Observe that this property holds for VM_1 but not for VM_4: it is not preserved by refinement. Since it is not β-dependent Lemma 2 below is not applicable for this property.

Our main result for this section identifies conditions under which an LTL property ϕ will be preserved in a refinement chain. The conditions are as follows:

- by the end of the refinement chain there should be no outstanding anticipated events (and so all newly introduced events have been shown to be convergent), as given by restriction 6 of the Development Strategy of Section 2.3;
- the final machine in the refinement chain must be deadlock-free; and
- all of the events that have an effect on whether or not ϕ is true are already present in M_i (ϕ is β-dependent for some $\beta \subseteq \alpha M_i$).

These conditions are enough to ensure that ϕ is preserved through refinement chains. This means that M_i can be checked for ϕ, and we can be sure that the resulting system M_n will also satisfy it.

The lemma is formally expressed as follows:

Lemma 2. *If $M_i \models \phi$ and $M_i \preccurlyeq_W \ldots \preccurlyeq_W M_n$ and $0 \leq i < n$ and M_n is deadlock free and M_n does not contain any anticipated events and ϕ is β-dependent and $\beta \subseteq \alpha M_i$ then $M_n \models \phi$.*

5.1   Preserving Vending Machine Properties

We consider the application of the above Lemmas to our running example on the refinement chain

$$VM_1 \preccurlyeq_W VM_2 \preccurlyeq_W VM_3 \preccurlyeq_W VM_4$$

In this case we obtain immediately from Lemma 1 that

$$VM_4 \models GF([selectBiscuit] \vee [selectChoc] \vee$$
$$[dispenseBiscuit] \vee [dispenseChoc])$$

Any execution of VM_4 will involve infinitely many occurrences of some of these events. The newly introduced events *pay*, *refund*, *refill* cannot be performed forever without the occurrence of the original events.

We consider some further properties to illustrate the applicability of Lemma 2. Taking VM_1 to be the first machine in the refinement chain, we can consider the following temporal properties ϕ for VM_1:

$$\phi_1 = G([selectChoc] \vee [selectBiscuit] \Rightarrow F([dispenseChoc] \vee [dispenseBiscuit]))$$
$$\phi_2 = (\neg GF[selectBiscuit]) \Rightarrow G([selectChoc] \Rightarrow F[dispenseChoc])$$
$$\phi_3 = (\neg GF[selectChoc]) \Rightarrow G([selectBiscuit] \Rightarrow F[dispenseBiscuit])$$
$$\phi_4 = G([selectChoc] \Rightarrow F[dispenseChoc])$$
$$\phi_5 = G([selectBiscuit] \Rightarrow F[dispenseBiscuit])$$

We note that each of the properties are β-dependent. Next we consider whether $VM_1 \models \phi_i$ for each $i \in 1..5$. Note that in fact $VM_1 \not\models \phi_4$ and $VM_1 \not\models \phi_5$ since there is a trace for which the properties fail, e.g., in the case of ϕ_4 the $\langle sc, sb, db, sb, db, \ldots \rangle$ we could have an infinite loop of sb, db events and never reach a dc event. Thus Lemma 2 is not applicable to these properties.

The properties ϕ_2 and ϕ_3 are the strongest; ϕ_2 states that if you do not always have an sb then you will be able to choose a chocolate and for it to be dispensed, and the dual applies in ϕ_3. Once we have also established the refinement chain $VM_1 \preccurlyeq_W VM_2 \preccurlyeq_W VM_3 \preccurlyeq_W VM_4$, and that VM_4 is deadlock free we can deduce using Lemma 2 that $VM_4 \models \phi_i$ for all $i \in 1..3$. Observe however that Lemma 2 does not establish that ϕ_i holds in all refinement machines, only those with no anticipated events. For example, VM_2 and VM_3 do not satisfy ϕ_1, ϕ_2 nor ϕ_3 since *pay* is anticipated and can be executed infinitely often.

Since VM_2 introduced the event *pay* we can also introduce new temporal properties that are required to hold from VM_2 onwards. In other words, we apply Lemma 2 on the chain $VM_2 \preccurlyeq_W VM_3 \preccurlyeq_W VM_4$. The properties to consider are:

$$\phi_6 = G([pay] \Rightarrow F([dispenseBiscuit] \vee [dispenseChoc]))$$
$$\phi_7 = GF[pay]$$

The infinite behaviour of *pay* means that ϕ_6 is not satisfied in VM_2. However, $VM_2 \models \phi_7$ thus we can again apply Lemma 2, and obtain that $VM_4 \models \phi_7$ since ϕ_7 is β-dependent. This exemplifies that new temporal properties can be added to the refinement verification chain.

We note that in fact $VM_4 \models \phi_6$. Thus ϕ_6 and ϕ_7 together imply that $GF([dispenseBiscuit] \vee [dispenseChoc])$ holds for VM_4.

6   Extending Preserving LTL Properties to Handle Splitting Events

In this section we generalise the results of Section 5 in order to deal with splitting events in Event-B, which occurs when abstract events are refined by several events in the concrete machine, corresponding to a set of alternatives. Consider as a motivating example VM_0 in Figure 6. This is refined by VM_1, with linking invariant $item = card(chosen)$, $selectItem$ refined by both $selectBiscuit$ and $selectChoc$, and $dispenseItem$ refined by both $dispenseBiscuit$ and $dispenseChoc$. Splitting events also involves their renaming to allow for several concrete events to map to the same abstract one. A refinement step will therefore be associated with a renaming function h from concrete events to the abstract events that they refine. In the general case h will be many-to-one, since many concrete events may map to a single abstract event; and it will also be partial, since new events in the concrete machine will not map to any abstract event.

In general, each step in a refinement chain $M_0 \preccurlyeq_W M_1 \preccurlyeq_W \ldots \preccurlyeq_W M_n$ will have an event renaming function h_i corresponding to the renaming and splitting step from M_i to M_{i-1}. We define $g_{i,n}$ to be the composition of these renaming function from h_n down to h_i. Observe that $g_{i,n}$ will be undefined on any event that does not map to M_{i-1}, in other words any event that corresponds to an event introduced at some point in the refinement chain. For example, for the chain $VM_0 \preccurlyeq_W VM_1 \preccurlyeq_W \ldots \preccurlyeq_W VM_4$, we obtain that $g_{1,4}(selectBiscuit) = g_{1,4}(selectChoc) = selectItem$, and $g_{1,4}(dispenseBiscuit) = g_{1,4}(dispenseChoc) = dispenseItem$, and $g_{1,4}$ is not defined on the remaining events of VM_4.

Lemma 1 generalises to state that the final machine in the refinement chain must always eventually perform some event relating to an event in the initial machine.

Lemma 3. *If $M_0 \preccurlyeq_W M_1 \preccurlyeq_W \ldots \preccurlyeq_W M_n$ and M_n is deadlock free and M_n does not contain any anticipated events then $M_n \models GF(\bigvee\limits_{e \in g_{1,n}^{-1}(\alpha M_0)} e)$.*

Observe that if there is no renaming or splitting, then $g_{1,n}$ is the identity function on the events in αM_0, yielding Lemma 1.

We are interested in how the LTL properties of an abstract machine becomes transformed through a refinement step such as VM_0 to VM_1. For example, the property $GF[selectItem]$ for VM_0 states that from any stage that is reached, $selectItem$ will eventually occur. This will translate to the property $GF([selectBiscuit] \vee [selectChoc])$ for VM_1. We now consider how LTL properties translate through a renaming function h.

For a given event renaming function h, we define $trans_h$ as the translation that maps LTL formulae by mapping abstract events to the disjunction of their corresponding concrete events, as follows:

> **machine** VM_0
> **variables** *item*
> **invariant** *item* $\in \mathbb{N}$
> **events**
>   init $\hat{=}$ *item* := 0
>   selectItem $\hat{=}$
>   **status** : ordinary
>   **when** *item* ≤ 2 **then** *item* := *item* + 1 **end**
>   dispenseItem $\hat{=}$
>   **status** : ordinary
>   **when** *item* > 0 **then** *item* := *item* − 1 **end**
> **end**

Fig. 6. VM_0

Definition 5

$$trans_h(true) = true$$
$$trans_h([x]) = \bigvee_{y|h(y)=x} [y]$$
$$trans_h(\neg\phi) = \neg trans_h(\phi)$$
$$trans_h(\phi_1 \vee \phi_2) = trans_h(\phi_1) \vee trans_h(\phi_2)$$
$$trans_h(\phi_1 \wedge \phi_2) = trans_h(\phi_1) \wedge trans_h(\phi_2)$$
$$trans_h(\phi_1 \ U \ \phi_2) = trans_h(\phi_1) \ U \ trans_h(\phi_2)$$
$$trans_h(G\phi) = G \ trans_h(\phi)$$
$$trans_h(F\phi) = F \ trans_h(\phi)$$

For example

$$trans_h(G([selectItem] \Rightarrow F[dispenseItem]))$$
$$= G(([selectBiscuit] \vee [selectChoc]) \Rightarrow F([dispenseBiscuit] \vee [dispenseChoc]))$$

Lemma 2 generalises to Lemma 4 below, to state that LTL properties are carried along the refinement chain by translating them. In particular, if a property ϕ is established for M_{i-1}, then $trans_{g_{i,n}}(\phi)$ will hold for M_n:

Lemma 4. *If $M_{i-1} \models \phi$ and $M_{i-1} \preccurlyeq_W \ \ldots \ \preccurlyeq_W M_n$ and $0 \leq i - 1 < n$, M_n is deadlock free and M_n does not contain any anticipated events and ϕ is β-dependent and $\beta \subseteq \alpha M_{i-1}$ then $M_n \models trans_{g_{i,n}}(\phi)$*

For example, from the result for VM_0 that whenever *selectItem* occurs then *dispenseItem* will eventually occur,

$$VM_0 \models G([selectItem] \Rightarrow F[dispenseItem])$$

we obtain from Lemma 4 that

$$VM_4 \models G(\ ([selectBiscuit] \lor [selectChoc])$$
$$\Rightarrow F([dispenseBiscuit] \lor [dispenseChoc])\ )$$

This states that whenever *selectBiscuit* or *selectChoc* occur, then *dispenseBiscuit* or *dispenseChoc* will eventually occur.

7   Discussion and Related Work

One of the few papers to discuss LTL preservation in Event-B refinement is Groslambert [8]. The LTL properties were defined in terms of predicates on system state rather than our paper's formulation in terms of the occurrence of events. His paper focused only on the introduction of new convergent events. It did not include a treatment of anticipated events but this is unsurprising since the paper was published before their inclusion in Event-B. Our results are more general in two ways. Firstly, the results support the treatment of anticipated events. Secondly, we allow more flexibility in the development methodology. A condition of Groslambert's results was that all the machines in the refinement chain needed to be deadlock free. The two main lemmas in our paper: Lemmas 2 and 4 do not require each machine in a refinement chain to be deadlock free, only the final machine. It is irrelevant if intermediate M_is deadlock as long as the deadlock is eventually refined away.

Groslambert deals with new events via stuttering and leaves them as visible events in a trace. This is why the LTL operators used by the author do not include the next operator (X). As new events may happen this may violate the X property to be checked. Plagge and Leuschel in [14] permit the use of the X operator since they treat the inclusion of new events as internal events which are not visible. Since we deal with new events as visible events we also lose the ability to reason about a temporal property using the typical X operator. Our reasoning is simpler than both Groslambert and Plagge and Leuschel since we only focus on events but this means we cannot have atomic propositions in our LTL, whereas they can.

The notion of verification of temporal properties of both classical and Event-B systems using proof obligations has been considered in many research papers. Abrial and Musat in an early paper, [3], introduced proof obligations to deal with dynamic constraints in classical B. In a more recent paper [10] Hoang and Abrial have also proposed new proof obligations for dealing with liveness properties in Event-B. They focus on three classes of properties: existence, progress and persistence, with a view to implementing them in Rodin. Bicarregui *et al.* in [5] introduced a temporal concept into events using the guard in the *when* clause and the additional labels of *within* and *next* so that the enabling conditions are captured clearly and separately. However, these concepts are not aligned with the standard Event-B labelling.

The interest of LTL preservation through refinement is wider than simply Event-B. Derrick and Smith [7] discuss the preservation of LTL properties in the context of Z refinement but the authors extend their results to other logics such as CTL and the μ calculus. They focus on discussing the restrictions that are needed on temporal-logic properties and retrieve relations to enable the model checking of such properties. Their refinements are restricted to data refinement and do not permit the introduction of new events in the refinement steps. Our paper does permit new events to be introduced during refinement steps; the contribution is in identifying conditions for LTL properties to hold even in the context of such new events.

8   Conclusions and Future Work

The paper has provided foundational results that justify when temporal properties hold at the end of an Event-B refinement chain for developments which contain anticipated, convergent and ordinary events, which goes beyond that presented in [8]. The paper has also provided restrictions on the temporal properties in terms of being β-dependent which help to determine when a temporal property of interest should be introduced into the development chain.

We could extend the results to deal with merging events. The inclusion of the X LTL operator and availability will require use to look at execution paths which include state transitions (π paths). The inclusion of availability will enable us to address more advanced and useful notions of fairness in the context of temporal properties. Our notion of weak fairness will be akin to that described in Barradas and Bert in [4]. It will draw on work by Williams $et\ al.$ [17]. We could also consider the impact on temporal property preservation in refinement chains which do not achieve convergence of all its new events by the end.

In ongoing work we are looking at event liveness via the proof obligation for strong deadlock freedom S_NDF. We have defined new labelling of events to so that liveness proofs are on particular events. This is analagous to proving WFD_REF for events that are labelled anticipated or convergent. We have recently defined the semantics of Event-B in terms of stable failures and detailed its relationship with S_NDF. We are currently combining these results with our work in [15] in order to provide a cohesive process algebra underpinning for Event-B.

Acknowledgments. Thanks to Thai Son Hoang and Thierry Lecomte for discussions about Event-B development strategies and the challenges of discharing liveness proofs. Thanks to Steve Wesemeyer for discussions on the example. Thanks to the reviewers for their constructive comments that helped to improve the paper.

References

1. Abrial, J.-R.: Modeling in Event-B: System and Software Engineering. Cambridge University Press (2010)
2. Abrial, J.-R., Butler, M.J., Hallerstede, S., Hoang, T.S., Mehta, F., Voisin, L.: Rodin: an open toolset for modelling and reasoning in Event-B. STTT 12(6), 447–466 (2010)
3. Abrial, J.-R., Mussat, L.: Introducing dynamic constraints in B. In: Bert, D. (ed.) B 1998. LNCS, vol. 1393, pp. 83–128. Springer, Heidelberg (1998)
4. Barradas, H., Bert, D.: Specification and proof of liveness properties under fairness assumptions in B event systems. In: Butler, M., Petre, L., Sere, K. (eds.) IFM 2002. LNCS, vol. 2335, pp. 360–379. Springer, Heidelberg (2002)
5. Feige, U., Arenas, A.E., Aziz, B., Massonet, P., Ponsard, C.: Towards modelling obligations in event-B. In: Börger, E., Butler, M., Bowen, J.P., Boca, P. (eds.) ABZ 2008. LNCS, vol. 5238, pp. 181–194. Springer, Heidelberg (2008)
6. Butler, M.J.: A CSP approach to Action Systems. DPhil thesis, Oxford U. (1992)
7. Derrick, J., Smith, G.: Temporal-logic property preservation under Z refinement. Formal Asp. Comput. 24(3), 393–416 (2012)
8. Groslambert, J.: Verification of LTL on B Event Systems. In: Julliand, J., Kouchnarenko, O. (eds.) B 2007. LNCS, vol. 4355, pp. 109–124. Springer, Heidelberg (2006)
9. Hallerstede, S., Leuschel, M., Plagge, D.: Validation of formal models by refinement animation. Science of Computer Programming 78(3), 272–292 (2013)
10. Hoang, T.S., Abrial, J.-R.: Reasoning about liveness properties in Event-B. In: Qin, S., Qiu, Z. (eds.) ICFEM 2011. LNCS, vol. 6991, pp. 456–471. Springer, Heidelberg (2011)
11. Leuschel, M., Butler, M.J.: ProB: an automated analysis toolset for the B method. STTT 10(2), 185–203 (2008)
12. Leuschel, M., Falampin, J., Fritz, F., Plagge, D.: Automated property verification for large scale B models. In: Cavalcanti, A., Dams, D.R. (eds.) FM 2009. LNCS, vol. 5850, pp. 708–723. Springer, Heidelberg (2009)
13. Morgan, C.: Of wp and CSP. Beauty is our business: a birthday salute to E. W. Dijkstra, pp. 319–326 (1990)
14. Plagge, D., Leuschel, M.: Seven at one stroke: LTL model checking for high-level specifications in B, Z, CSP, and more. STTT 12(1), 9–21 (2010)
15. Schneider, S., Treharne, H., Wehrheim, H.: The behavioural semantics of Event-B refinement. Formal Asp. Comput. 26(2), 251–280 (2014)
16. Schneider, S., Treharne, H., Wehrheim, H., Williams, D.: Managing LTL properties in Event-B refinement. arXiv:1406:6622 (June 2014)
17. Williams, D.M., de Ruiter, J., Fokkink, W.: Model checking under fairness in ProB and its application to fair exchange protocols. In: Roychoudhury, A., D'Souza, M. (eds.) ICTAC 2012. LNCS, vol. 7521, pp. 168–182. Springer, Heidelberg (2012)

Security Analysis

Formal Security Analysis of the MaCAN Protocol

Alessandro Bruni[1], Michal Sojka[2],
Flemming Nielson[1], and Hanne Riis Nielson[1]

[1] Technical University of Denmark
{albr,fnie,hrni}@dtu.dk
[2] Czech Technical University
sojkam1@fel.cvut.cz

Abstract. Embedded real-time network protocols such as the CAN bus cannot rely on off-the-shelf schemes for authentication, because of the bandwidth limitations imposed by the network. As a result, both academia and industry have proposed custom protocols that meet such constraints, with solutions that may be deemed insecure if considered out of context. MaCAN is one such compatible authentication protocol, proposed by Volkswagen Research and a strong candidate for being adopted by the automotive industry.

In this work we formally analyse MaCAN with ProVerif, an automated protocol verifier. Our formal analysis identifies two flaws in the original protocol: one creates unavailability concerns during key establishment, and the other allows re-using authenticated signals for different purposes. We propose and analyse a modification that improves its behaviour while fitting the constraints of CAN bus. Although the revised scheme improves the situation, it is still not completely secure. We argue that the modified protocol makes a good compromise between the desire to secure automotive systems and the limitations of CAN networks.

Keywords: protocol verification, embedded systems, Controller Area Network.

1 Introduction

The CAN Bus is a protocol for real-time broadcast communication introduced in 1983 by Bosch, and the current de facto standard for signal communication inside a modern vehicle. Its simplicity and long time of adoption have made it the most reasonable solution for building interoperable hardware in the automotive market. It is also a mandatory protocol for the OBD-II diagnostic interface in the United States and the similar EOBD standard for European countries. This also means that it is unlikely to be replaced by more powerful protocols in the foreseeable future (e.g. FlexRay [8]).

CAN is an unauthenticated broadcast protocol, therefore it offers no security-related features to system designers. As current vehicles get more interconnected

E. Albert and E. Sekerinski (Eds.): IFM 2014, LNCS 8739, pp. 241–255, 2014.

it is necessary to ensure that messages come from the right sources in order to secure car functionality that could result in safety hazards if compromised under an attack. Koscher et al. have shown [12,5] that current vehicles have practically no defence within their internal network. It is possible to perform an impressive array of attacks from interfaces like WiFi, Bluetooth and Cellular networks that are now available in modern vehicles.

In response to their study various groups have tried to secure the weak link in the chain, providing various flavours of authenticated CAN protocols: MaCAN [11], CANAuth [17], LiBrA-CAN [10] and Car2x [16]. Many of these schemes deviate from well-established communication protocols to meet the bandwidth and real-time constraints of the CAN network. Nevertheless, the authors of MaCAN and CANAuth, for example, only claim to guarantee certain security properties (e.g. authentication, freshness), without formally proving their correctness.

We analysed the MaCAN protocol as described in [11], with the assistance of the ProVerif protocol verifier [4]. Our analysis showed two flaws in the specification, one in the key distribution scheme, and another in signal authentication.

The first flaw allows the initiating principal to believe that a session has been established, while the other parties have not received a session key. Key distribution happens between three or more parties: an *initiator*, responsible for starting the procedure, the *key server*, responsible for delivering the session key, and one or more *responders*, which also need to obtain the session key.

The slightly asymmetric behaviour of the protocol allows an attacker to reuse the signature of the acknowledgement message sent by the initiator, in order to simulate an acknowledgement message coming from the responder, therefore completing authentication on one side. Furthermore, the attacker can manipulate the behaviour of the key server so that the responder never receives a request for authentication, and therefore the responder is never activated. This leads to an incomplete session establishment where one of the parties believes that it can communicate authenticated messages while the other will refuse such messages because it is not in possession of a valid session key.

Our proposed correction removes the asymmetry in the two phases of the protocol, and prevents the attack. We model our modification of the MaCAN protocol in ProVerif and discover another minor problem in the format of the acknowledgement message, that allows the attacker to successfully send acknowledgements with the signature of another principal in group sessions. Adding source information to the signature overcomes this annoyance, and allows us to prove the desired authentication property in the key establishment phase.

The second flaw allows repurposing an authenticated signal when a specific message format is used. An attacker can forge the signal number without this being detected, allowing, for example, the message with meaning "speed is 25" to be modified to "temperature is 25".

Our correction modifies the signature so that the signal number is considered, preventing that particular attack form happening. However the nature of the protocol allows replays within the validity time frame of a message, which can be rather long for its applications. Here we contribute with a discussion that clarifies which properties an application designer can expect from MaCAN, and needs to take into consideration when designing a system.

The paper proceeds as follows. Section 2 presents the applied π-calculus that we use in our models, Section 3 introduces the CAN bus protocol and its extensions, Section 4 describes the MaCAN protocol, Section 5 describes our formal analysis of the protocol, the discovered flaws and our proposed mitigations. We compare the result of our analysis with our implementation in Section 6 and present our conclusions in Section 7.

2   Modeling Protocols in ProVerif

ProVerif [4] is a protocol verifier that translates models in the applied π-calculus into a set of Prolog rules. Initially developed to verify secrecy properties [2], ProVerif uses a different resolution algorithm than Prolog's backward chaining to achieve better performance on the particular set of clauses that it generates.

ProVerif was later expanded to verify injective and non-injective agreements, by adding events to the applied π-calculus and extending the translation to verify non-injective and injective agreements, according to Lowe's [14] definitions. For a detailed presentation of the applied π-calculus with events and the analysis techniques used in this paper we refer to [3].

Figure 1 shows the language that we use in this paper. We have terms M, N which can be either variables, names, tuples or constructors applied to sub-terms. Patterns Π are used in inputs and let bindings and are either variable binders, patterns on tuples or equality checks on terms. Processes P, Q are either the stuck process, the infinite replication of a process, the parallel composition which runs two processes in parallel, the restriction which binds a in P to a fresh name, input which applies pattern Π to an input on channel M, output which outputs the term N on channel M, let which applies a rewrite rule of the form $g(M_1, \ldots, M_n) \rightarrow M$ — where $fv(M) \subseteq \bigcup_i fv(M_i)$ — and if it succeeds executes P after matching the result of the destruction to the pattern Π, otherwise executes Q, the if construct which checks equality between terms M and N and executes P if the two terms are equal, Q otherwise, and event, which signals an event in the execution of the process, marked with the term M.

3   CAN and Its Extensions

CAN [9] is a broadcast, prioritised, real-time protocol designed to work on a bus network topology of interconnected microcontrollers. At a high level, a CAN frame has two fields: *(i)* an identifier (CAN-ID) of either 11 or 29 bits, that is used for specifying which signal is being transmitted, and for arbitration purposes using Carrier Sense Multiple Access with Bitwise Arbitration (a multiple access scheme where lower ID values have priority on higher ID values and arbitration is resolved by sending the message IDs bit-by-bit), and *(ii)* a payload field of 1 to 8 bytes, that may contain information specific to the signal. Typical transmission

$$M, N ::= x, y, z \mid a, b, c \mid (M_1, \ldots, M_n) \mid f(M_1, \ldots, M_n) \qquad \text{terms}$$
$$\varPi ::= x \mid (\varPi_1, \ldots, \varPi_n) \mid {=}M \qquad\qquad\qquad\quad \text{patterns}$$
$$P, Q ::= 0 \qquad\qquad\qquad\qquad\qquad\qquad\qquad\quad \text{stuck process}$$
$$\mid\; !P \qquad\qquad\qquad\qquad\qquad\qquad\qquad\quad \text{replication}$$
$$\mid\; P|Q \qquad\qquad\qquad\qquad\qquad\qquad\qquad\; \text{parallel composition}$$
$$\mid\; (\nu\, a)\, P \qquad\qquad\qquad\qquad\qquad\qquad\quad \text{restriction}$$
$$\mid\; M(\varPi).P \qquad\qquad\qquad\qquad\qquad\qquad\; \text{input}$$
$$\mid\; \overline{M}\langle N\rangle.P \qquad\qquad\qquad\qquad\qquad\qquad\; \text{output}$$
$$\mid\; \text{let } \varPi = g(M_1, \ldots, M_n) \text{ in } P \text{ else } Q \qquad \text{destructor application}$$
$$\mid\; \text{if } M = N \text{ then } P \text{ else } Q \qquad\qquad\quad \text{conditional}$$
$$\mid\; \text{event}(M).P \qquad\qquad\qquad\qquad\qquad\quad \text{event}$$

Fig. 1. Applied π-calculus with events

speeds of the CAN bus are 125 KHz, 500 KHz and 1 MHz, and a single CAN frame occupies between 65 and 160 bits, depending on the length of the identifier field and of the payload. Other safety-related features of CAN include error detection using CRC codes and specific flags for signalling a failed transmission, and mechanisms for detecting and disabling malfunctioning devices.

Given the restricted size of CAN frames an authenticated network protocol must meet the tight space constraints. Splitting messages into more than one signal is rarely an acceptable solution, because most applications have real-time constraints and the bandwidth usage is approaching 80% [6].

To alleviate the payload limitation of CAN, two extensions have been proposed: CAN+ and CAN-FD. CAN+ [18] uses a clever encoding that allows to extend the payload by 15 times the original size, while being compatible with devices that use plain CAN, who see only the non-extended payload. This allows to use the extra bandwidth for authentication, as CANAuth [17] does. What hampers its adoption is the higher cost of required hardware, which has already been a compelling argument for industry to not switch to FlexRay.

CAN-FD [13] allows transmitting up to 64 bytes of payload by changing the data rate during payload transmission. This change is not transparent to standard CAN, but CAN and CAN-FD devices can coexist in the same network. CAN-FD is currently being integrated into ISO 11898, the standard defining CAN, so it is very likely to be adopted as a solution for extending the CAN payload. MaCAN has been designed to work on plain CAN networks, but it can be extended to use the extra payload offered by CAN-FD.

4 MaCAN

MaCAN [11] is an authenticated protocol specifically designed for the CAN bus. The authors argued that there was a need for a new authentication scheme that could fit into its small payload size. Other proposals such as CANAuth *rely* on

CAN-ID(SRC-ID)	Flags	DST-ID	Data	
CAN-ID		Data[0]	Data[1-7]	

Fig. 2. The Crypt Frame

the extra bits offered by CAN+ and *require* also switching to different hardware. MaCAN instead authenticates messages in 4 bytes of payload, leaving the other 4 bytes available for signal information. The signature length can also be extended when using CAN-FD in order to increase robustness and to allow more than 4 bytes of information to be transmitted.

The designers of MaCAN discarded the use of more traditional challenge-response protocols during message authentication, because of the real-time requirements that need to be met in the applications. They also considered problematic the use of counter values to ensure message freshness, since there is not enough space to transmit the counter and a hash together with a message, and synchronisation issues make it impossible to keep track of the current counter value. Instead, they chose to authenticate messages using a timestamp to ensure their freshness, and to synchronise the ECUs using a time server. Timestamps need not to be sent with every frame as all ECUs have a local clock, hence MaCAN saves precious bandwidth for communication.

4.1 The Crypt Frame

As depicted in Figure 2, the crypt frame is a specific interpretation of the traditional CAN frame where both CAN-ID and payload fields are used to encode authentication details.

The CAN ID in the crypt frame encodes a 6 bit source ID, which indicates the source Electronic Control Unit (ECU). The first byte of data is used to send a 2 bit flag field and a 6 bit destination ID, which could indicate a specific ECU or a group of ECUs, in order to make the protocol fully directional. This leaves available the remaining 7 bytes for signals and signatures.

In the following sections we are going to present the protocol using Alice&Bob notation for the messages, which leaves the field lengths unspecified. The reader may refer to the original paper [11] for the specific frame formats.

4.2 Key Establishment

The key establishment procedure in MaCAN establishes a session key between an initiator (ECU_i) and a responder (ECU_j) by communicating to a key server (KS). Figure 3 represents the authentication process in Alice&Bob notation. Both ECU_i and ECU_j have their own pre-shared key $K_{x,ks}$ registered with the key server, which the key server uses for sending session keys.

To establish a session key, the initiator ECU_i sends a challenge C_i to KS, signalling the ID of the requested partner id_j (4.2.1). KS encrypts (senc) with

$$ECU_i \rightarrow KS : \mathsf{CH}, C_i, id_j \tag{4.2.1}$$

$$KS \rightarrow ECU_i : \mathsf{SK}, \mathsf{senc}((C_i, id_j, id_i, SK_{i,j}), K_{i,ks}) \tag{4.2.2}$$

$$KS \rightarrow ECU_j : \mathsf{RC} \tag{4.2.3}$$

$$ECU_i \rightarrow ECU_j : \mathsf{ACK}, group\_field, \mathsf{cmac}((T, id_j, group\_field), SK_{i,j}) \tag{4.2.4}$$

$$ECU_j \rightarrow KS : \mathsf{CH}, C_j, id_i \tag{4.2.5}$$

$$KS \rightarrow ECU_j : \mathsf{SK}, \mathsf{senc}((C_j, id_i, id_j, SK_{i,j}), K_{j,ks}) \tag{4.2.6}$$

$$ECU_j \rightarrow ECU_i : \mathsf{ACK}, group\_field, \mathsf{cmac}((T, id_j, group\_field), SK_{i,j}) \tag{4.2.7}$$

$$ECU_i \rightarrow ECU_j : \mathsf{ACK}, group\_field, \mathsf{cmac}((T, id_j, group\_field), SK_{i,j}) \tag{4.2.8}$$

Fig. 3. MaCAN key establishment procedure

$K_{i,ks}$ a fresh session key $SK_{i,j}$, together with the challenge C_i and the IDs of ECU_i and ECU_j (4.2.2). KS then sends a request for challenge (RC) to ECU_j, in order to activate it (4.2.3).

ECU_i after decrypting the session key $SK_{i,j}$ received from the key server, sends an acknowledgement (ACK) to ECU_j, signing it with $SK_{i,j}$ and the current timestamp T. The *group_field* is a bit vector that represents the knowledge of ECU_i about which devices are authenticated[1]. After sending this message, ECU_i considers itself authenticated, and awaits ECU_j to conclude the protocol.

ECU_j then sends its own challenge C_j to KS (4.2.5), to which the key server replies with the encrypted session key, C_j, and the IDs of the two principals (4.2.6). Finally ECU_j sends a signed acknowledgement message to ECU_i, signalling that it received the session key and updating *group_field* (4.2.7).

In case of group authentication, when an authenticated ECU receives a *group_field* that does not mark itself as authenticated, it sends an acknowledgement message to inform the other ECUs in the group of its presence (4.2.8).

4.3   Message Authentication

Automotive CAN applications are based on the concept of "signals" (e.g. current vehicle speed is a signal) that are exchanged between cooperating ECUs by periodically transmitting messages with signal values. In MaCAN it is possible to require ECUs to authenticate a specific signal upon request. Then next, each or each n-th signal message will be additionally sent in the authenticated format. Figure 4 shows how authenticated messages can be requested (4.3.1) and provided (4.3.2, 4.3.3). *Sig#* specifies the signal number that needs to be authenticated. *Prescaler* specifies the signing behaviour, and is 0 to request the following message to be authenticated, 1 to request each following message to be

---

[1] MaCAN supports authentication of groups with more than two ECUs, but here we concentrate on the case where a session is established between two parties. Authenticating more than two ECUs requires the key server to interpret id_j as the ID of a group, which is statically defined, and to send requests for challenge to each ECU in the group.

$$ECU_i \rightarrow ECU_j : \text{SIG-AUTH-REQ}, Sig\#, Prescaler,$$

$$\text{cmac}((T, id_i, id_j, Sig\#, Prescaler), SK_{i,j}) \qquad (4.3.1)$$

$$ECU_j \rightarrow ECU_i : \text{SIG-AUTH}, Sig\#, Signal, \text{cmac}((T, id_i, id_j, Signal), SK_{i,j}) \quad (4.3.2)$$

$$ECU_j \rightarrow ECU_i : \text{SIG-AUTH}, Signal, \text{cmac}((T, id_i, id_j, Signal), SK_{i,j}) \qquad (4.3.3)$$

$$ECU_i \rightarrow TS : \text{CH}, C_i, fwd\_id = 0 \qquad (4.4.1)$$

$$TS \rightarrow ECU_i : T, \text{cmac}((C_i, T), SK_{ts,i}) \qquad (4.4.2)$$

Fig. 4. MaCAN signal authentication (4.3.1-3) and time requests (4.4.1-2)

authenticated, and any $n > 1$ to request each n-th message to be authenticated. The CMAC [7] signature uses the current timestamp T, the initiator and the responder IDs, to authenticate the request.

The responder to the authentication request replies with either (4.3.3) or (4.3.2), depending on whether the signal value ($Signal$) fits in 32 bits or not.

4.4 Serving Time

All signatures include a timestamp that is not sent in clear-text over the channel, and thus the communicating devices need to be synchronised, otherwise there is a risk that authenticated messages might not be recognised as valid. To mitigate unavailability concerns due to clock synchronisation, MaCAN introduces an authenticated time-serving protocol, shown in Figure 4.

Normally the current timestamp is broadcast periodically in an unauthenticated form. When ECU_i detects too big a mismatch between the internal clock and the received timestamp, it may send a request for an authentic time value from the time server. This is done by sending a challenge C_i to the time server (4.4.1), who will then reply with the last broadcasted timestamp T, signed using the challenge and a session key $SK_{ts,i}$ shared by the time server and the ECU.

5 Formal Analysis

5.1 Key Establishment

Figure 5 shows our model of the MaCAN authentication procedure in the applied π-calculus. All communication happens on a broadcast channel c, while we use a private channel psk for the key server to store the long term keys of the ECUs. The process KS represents the key server, ECU_i is the initiator process and ECU_j is the responder process.

Due to the abstractions introduced by ProVerif, we have to change some important aspects of the protocol in order to obtain a precise analysis. First and foremost, we remove timestamps from signatures, because ProVerif abstracts away the concept of state in its translation of processes to Horn clauses. Then

$$KS \triangleq c(i, =\mathsf{CH}, =ks, c_i, j).psk(=i, k_i).(\nu\ sk_{ij})\ \mathsf{event}(sessk_i(i, j, c_i, sk_{ij})).$$
$$\overline{c}\langle ks, \mathsf{SK}, i, \mathsf{senc}((c_i, j, i, sk_{ij}), k_i)\rangle.\overline{c}\langle ks, \mathsf{RC}, j\rangle.$$
$$c(=j, =\mathsf{CH}, =ks, c_j, =i).psk(=j, k_j).\mathsf{event}(sessk_j(j, i, c_i, sk_{ij})).$$
$$\overline{c}\langle ks, \mathsf{SK}, j, \mathsf{senc}((c_j, i, j, sk_{ij}), k_j)\rangle.c(=sk_{ij}).\overline{c}\langle error\rangle.0$$

$$ECU_i \triangleq (\nu\ c_i)\ \mathsf{event}(authStart_i(i, j, c_i)).\overline{c}\langle i, \mathsf{CH}, ks, c_i, j\rangle.$$
$$c(=ks, =\mathsf{SK}, =i, resp).\mathsf{let}\ (=c_i, =j, =i, sk_{ij}) = \mathsf{sdec}(resp, k_i)\ \mathsf{in}$$
$$\mathsf{event}(authAck_i(i, j, c_i, sk_{ij})).\overline{c}\langle i, \mathsf{ACK}, j, sign((j, AK), sk_{ij})\rangle.$$
$$c(=j, =\mathsf{ACK}, =i, =sign((j, \mathsf{ACK}), sk_{ij})).\mathsf{event}(authEnd_i(i, j, c_i, sk_{ij})).0$$

$$ECU_j \triangleq c(=ks, =\mathsf{RC}, =j)).c(i, =\mathsf{ACK}, =j, ack).(\nu\ c_j)$$
$$\mathsf{event}(authStart_j(j, i, c_j)).\overline{c}\langle j, \mathsf{CH}, ks, c_j, i\rangle.c(=ks, =\mathsf{SK}, =j, resp).$$
$$\mathsf{let}\ (=c_j, =i, =j, sk_{ij}) = \mathsf{sdec}(resp, k_j)\ \mathsf{in}$$
$$\mathsf{if}\ ack = sign((j, \mathsf{ACK}), sk_{ij})\ \mathsf{then}\ \mathsf{event}(authAck_j(j, i, c_j, sk_{ij})).$$
$$\overline{c}\langle j, AK, i, sign((j, \mathsf{ACK}), sk_{ij})\rangle.\mathsf{event}(authEnd_j(j, i, c_j, sk_{ij})).0$$

Fig. 5. MaCAN key establishment process in the applied π-calculus

we treat *group_field* as a name instead of a bit vector, in order to simplify the model. Finally we encode long encrypted messages that would be split into multiple frame as a single message. We take these changes into consideration when we interpret the results of our analysis and we argue to which extent they introduce overapproximations.

Current MaCAN configurations have clock rates of 1 second, so it is safe to assume that timestamps can be treated as constants, since the key establishment procedure can complete within a single clock tick. Note that it is undesirable to have high clock rates due to the following constraint: the receiving end of an authenticated signal needs to check a signature against all valid timestamps within the possible reception window of the message. Therefore, increasing the clock rate also requires more computation on the receiving end, which in turn increases the worst case response time for a signal transmission. The length of the reception window for a message can be obtained with schedulability analysis [6] and depends on the number of higher priority messages that can delay the transmission of the message in question.

In Figure 5, KS represent the key server process. It waits on the public channel for a challenge c_i to establish a session between ECU_i and ECU_j, retrieves k_i from its database, produces a fresh session key sk_{ij}, outputs the encoding of the session and sends a request for challenge to ECU_j. It then waits for a challenge c_j from ECU_j, retrieves its key k_j, and encodes the session key sk_{ij} in a message for ECU_j that includes the challenge c_j. Finally it waits for the session key to be sent in clear text on the channel to signal an error. If an error is not reachable then the secrecy of sk_{ij} is guaranteed.

$$authStart_i(id_i, id_j, C_i) \tag{5.1.1}$$

$$ECU_i \rightsquigarrow KS : \mathsf{CH}, C_i, id_j \tag{5.1.2}$$

$$\mathrm{M}[ECU_j] \rightarrow KS : \mathsf{CH}, a, id_i \tag{5.1.3}$$

$$sessk_i(id_j, id_i, a, SK_{i,j}) \tag{5.1.4}$$

$$KS \rightarrow ECU_j : \mathsf{SK}, \mathsf{senc}((a, id_i, id_j, SK_{i,j}), K_{ks,j}) \tag{5.1.5}$$

$$KS \rightsquigarrow ECU_i : \mathsf{RC} \tag{5.1.6}$$

$$\mathrm{M}[ECU_i] \rightarrow KS : \mathsf{CH}, C_i, id_j \tag{5.1.7}$$

$$sessk_j(id_i, id_j, C_i, SK_{i,j}) \tag{5.1.8}$$

$$KS \rightarrow ECU_i : \mathsf{SK}, \mathsf{senc}((C_i, id_j, id_i, SK_{i,j}), K_{ks,i}) \tag{5.1.9}$$

$$authAck_i(id_i, id_j, SK_{i,j}) \tag{5.1.10}$$

$$ECU_i \rightarrow ECU_j : \mathsf{ACK}, \mathsf{cmac}((T, id_j, group\_field), SK_{i,j}) \tag{5.1.11}$$

$$\mathrm{M}[ECU_j] \rightarrow ECU_i : \mathsf{ACK}, \mathsf{cmac}((T, id_j, group\_field), SK_{i,j}) \tag{5.1.12}$$

$$authEnd_i(id_i, id_j, SK_{i,j}) \tag{5.1.13}$$

Fig. 6. Attack trace

ECU_i creates a new challenge c_i sends the challenge to the key server, waits for the response of the key server and decodes the message to retrieve the session key sk_{ij}. ECU_i then sends an acknowledgement to ECU_j signed with sk_{ij}, and waits for a similar acknowledgement from ECU_j to conclude the key establishment procedure.

ECU_j waits for a request for challenge from the key server, reads the acknowledgement from ECU_i, sends its challenge to the key server, receives the session key sk_{ij}, verifies the validity of the acknowledgement from the other party and finally sends its own acknowledgement, concluding its part of the procedure.

Analysis results. We analysed the following five properties for key establishment:

(i) the secrecy of long term keys k_i, k_j,
(ii) the secrecy of session keys ks_{ij},
(iii) the agreement between the events $authStart_i(i, j, c_i)$, $sessk_i(i, j, c_i, sk_{ij})$, $authAck_i(i, j, c_i, sk_{ij})$, $authEnd_i(i, j, c_i, sk_{ij})$, and
(iv) the agreement between the events $authStart_j(j, i, c_j)$, $sessk_j(j, i, c_j, sk_{ij})$, $authAck_j(j, i, c_j, sk_{ij})$, $authEnd_j(j, i, c_j, sk_{ij})$.

Using ProVerif, we were able to verify the secrecy properties *(i,ii)*, but we found a counterexample for the event correspondence *(iii)*, where an attacker can run the protocol in such a way that ECU_i receives the proper session key from message (4.2.6) instead of (4.2.2), leaving the ECU_j unauthenticated. The correspondence *(iv)* for ECU_j is proven, therefore it can only authenticate as intended by the protocol.

Figure 6 shows our reconstruction of the attack trace produced by ProVerif for the query of events related to ECU_i (property *iii*), thereby providing feedback

$$ECU_i \rightarrow KS : \mathsf{CH}, C_i, id_j \tag{5.1.14}$$

$$KS \rightarrow ECU_i : \mathsf{SK}, \mathsf{senc}((C_i, id_j, id_i, SK_{i,j}), K_{i,ks}) \tag{5.1.15}$$

$$KS \rightarrow ECU_j : \mathsf{RC} \tag{5.1.16}$$

$$ECU_i \rightarrow ECU_j : \mathsf{ACK}, group\_field, \mathsf{cmac}((T, id_i, id_j, group\_field), SK_{i,j}) \tag{5.1.17}$$

$$ECU_j \rightarrow KS : \mathsf{CH}, C_j, id_i \tag{5.1.18}$$

$$KS \rightarrow ECU_j : \mathsf{SK}, \mathsf{senc}((C_j, id_i, id_j, SK_{i,j}), K_{j,ks}) \tag{5.1.19}$$

$$ECU_j \rightarrow ECU_i : \mathsf{ACK}, group\_field, \mathsf{cmac}((T, id_j, id_i, group\_field), SK_{i,j}) \tag{5.1.20}$$

Fig. 7. Modified MaCAN key establishment procedure

to the protocol designer about how to amend the protocol. In this trace "$\rightsquigarrow$" represents a message deleted by the attacker (this can be achieved by jamming the signal at the proper time or by making one of the participating nodes or an involved CAN gateway unavailable) and M[x] represent the malicious agent impersonating x (it can be done by sending a message with the proper CAN-ID).

This attack relies on the possibility to remove messages from the channel. The attacker learns the current challenge and the destination ID (5.1.2), while suppressing the message. It then impersonates ECU_j and starts sending a random challenge (5.1.3), initiating the communication with the key server in the opposite direction. The key server then sends a legitimate message to ECU_j (5.1.5), who will ignore it as it did not request a session key. Then the key server sends a request for challenge to ECU_i (5.1.6), which may be suppressed by the attacker. The attacker remembers the previous challenge from ECU_i and replays it on the key server (5.1.7), receiving the session key encrypted for ECU_i in return (5.1.9). Finally ECU_i sends its acknowledgement message (5.1.11), and since the form of the two acknowledgement messages is the same for ECU_i (4.2.4) and ECU_j (4.2.7), the attacker can impersonate ECU_j and send back the same signature (5.1.12) so that ECU_i believes that also ECU_j is authenticated.

Corrected model. We propose a correction of the model where the asymmetries that cause the improper authentication behaviour are removed. Figure 7 shows the corrected procedure.

To guarantee the agreement property we modify the form of the acknowledgement message. The CMAC signature is now using the current timestamp, the source and the destination of the message as content. Because CMAC is a hashed signature, adding more parameters to the function does not affect the final payload size, therefore the modified protocol still fits the space constraints of CAN. The two acknowledgement messages (5.1.17) and (5.1.20) are now symmetrical. We added the source information on the signed hashes, as well as the destination. This allows not only to prove the necessary correspondence for two-party sessions, but in case of group sessions it removes the chance for an intruder to reuse an acknowledgement message of another principal.

$$KS \triangleq c(i, =\mathsf{CH}, =ks, c_i, j).psk(=i, k_i).(\nu\ sk_{ij})\, \mathsf{event}(sessk_i(i, j, c_i, sk_{ij})).$$
$$\overline{c}\langle ks, \mathsf{SK}, i, \mathsf{senc}((c_i, j, i, sk_{ij}), k_i)\rangle.\overline{c}\langle ks, \mathsf{RC}, j, i\rangle.$$
$$c(=j, =\mathsf{CH}, =ks, c_j, =i).psk(=j, k_j).\mathsf{event}(sessk_j(j, i, c_i, sk_{ij})).$$
$$\overline{c}\langle ks, \mathsf{SK}, j, \mathsf{senc}((c_j, i, j, sk_{ij}), k_j)\rangle.c(=sk_{ij}).\overline{c}\langle error\rangle.0$$

$$ECU_i \triangleq (\nu\ c_i)\, \mathsf{event}(authStart_i(i, j, c_i)).\overline{c}\langle i, \mathsf{CH}, ks, c_i, j\rangle.$$
$$c(=ks, =\mathsf{SK}, =i, resp).\mathsf{let}\ (=c_i, =j, =i, sk_{ij}) = \mathsf{sdec}(resp, k_i)\ \mathsf{in}$$
$$\mathsf{event}(authAck_i(i, j, c_i, sk_{ij})).\overline{c}\langle i, \mathsf{ACK}, j, sign((i, j, AK), sk_{ij})\rangle.$$
$$c(=j, =\mathsf{ACK}, =i, =sign((j, i, \mathsf{ACK}), sk_{ij})).\mathsf{event}(authEnd_i(i, j, c_i, sk_{ij})).0$$

$$ECU_j \triangleq c(=ks, =\mathsf{RC}, =j, i).(\nu\ c_j)\, \mathsf{event}(authStart_j(j, i, c_j)).$$
$$\overline{c}\langle j, \mathsf{CH}, ks, c_j, i\rangle.c(i, =\mathsf{ACK}, =j, ack).c(=ks, =\mathsf{SK}, =j, resp).$$
$$\mathsf{let}\ (=c_j, =i, =j, sk_{ij}) = \mathsf{sdec}(resp, k_j)\ \mathsf{in}$$
$$\mathsf{if}\ ack = sign((i, j, \mathsf{ACK}), sk_{ij})\ \mathsf{then}\ \mathsf{event}(authAck_j(j, i, c_j, sk_{ij})).$$
$$\overline{c}\langle j, AK, i, sign((j, i, \mathsf{ACK}), sk_{ij})\rangle.\mathsf{event}(authEnd_j(j, i, c_j, sk_{ij})).0$$

Fig. 8. MaCAN key establishment process in the applied π-calculus

Figure 8 shows the corrected model in the applied π-calculus, where we applied the modified behaviour for the three processes. The properties *(i–iv)* that we defined in Section 5.1 have all been proved in this model.

5.2   MaCAN Message Authentication

During a session, authenticated parties can send authenticated signals. As described in Section 4.3 the transmission of an authenticated signal needs to follow a specific request (4.3.1). Depending on whether the authenticated signal fits in 32 bits — that is half of the available CAN payload size — the responding ECU uses either message format (4.3.3) or (4.3.2).

Figure 9 shows two communicating processes that exchange authenticated messages according to message format (4.3.2). ECU_i requests an authenticated signal with the first output according to (4.3.1). Then it keeps waiting for an authenticated signal and checks whether the signature corresponds to its own computation of it, marking with an *accept* the acceptance of an authenticated signal. On the other side ECU_j receives a request for authentication, checks its signature and starts sending signals, marking with a *send* event the transmission of a fresh signal.

The original paper [11] is not clear about whether the CMAC signature includes the signal number. The process in Figure 9 does not include the signal number as part of the signature for signals. Thus the correspondence between $send(sig\#, signal)$ and $accept(sig\#, signal)$ is not verified. An attacker can read

$$ECU_i \triangleq \overline{c}\langle i, \text{SIG-AUTH-REQ}, j, sig\#, n0, \text{cmac}((i, j, sig\#, n0), sk_{ij})\rangle.$$
$$!(c(=j, =\text{SIG-AUTH}, =i, sig\#, signal, x_{sig}).$$
$$\text{if } x_{sig} = \text{cmac}((i, j, signal), sk_{ij}) \text{ then}$$
$$\text{event}(accept(sig\#, signal)).0)$$

$$ECU_j \triangleq c(i, =\text{SIG-AUTH-REQ}, =j, sig\#, prescaler, x_s).$$
$$\text{if } x_s = \text{cmac}((i, j, sig\#, prescaler), k_{ij}) \text{ then}$$
$$!((\nu \; signal) \, \text{event}(send(sig\#, signal)).$$
$$\overline{c}\langle j, \text{SIG-AUTH}, i, sig\#, signal, \text{cmac}((i, j, signal), sk_{ij})\rangle.0)$$

Fig. 9. MaCAN message authentication processes in the applied π-calculus

a signed signal with a $sig\#$ value re-transmit the signal with a different $sig\#$ if multiple $sig\#$ have been requested within the same session.

A simple solution to this problem is to add $sig\#$ as part of the signature. With the modified process, which we omit for sake of brevity, we are able to verify the agreement between the events $send(sig\#, signal)$ and $accept(sig\#, signal)$.

Still we fail to verify an injective agreement between the two events. Given our specification it is possible to accept twice the same message, and this could constitute a freshness violation. Our abstraction removes all timestamps, as the modelling technology cannot efficiently deal with them, and we previously argued that they can be ignored and treated as constant within their validity window.

As current configurations have clock rates of one second, this constitutes a potentially serious flaw in the protocol. Imagine MaCAN authenticating messages for the brake control unit of a vehicle. In case of emergency braking at high speed, the driver might be tempted to go all the way down with the foot on the brake pedal, activating the ABS. The ABS control unit works by sending messages to the brake control unit, releasing the brakes at a fast interval, so that the wheels don't slide on the ground, reducing their grip. In this example an attacker could wait for a "release message" from the ABS control unit, and replay it for its whole validity, therefore effectively disabling the brake for an entire second in a dangerous situation.

Given the restrictions imposed by the CAN bus, we believe that MaCAN constitutes a good enough solution for authenticating signals. A better level of security can be achieved by incrementing the clock rate. This would reduce the time window available for replaying messages, and therefore reduce the potential effect of such replay. In case of fast control loops — where a specific signal needs to be sent every 50 ms, for example — a solution that completely prevents replay attacks would synchronise the clock with the message rate, and refuse any message signed with a timestamp that has been previously used. Specific care would then be required for synchronising the clock between the communicating devices, and to avoid any unavailability issues due to improper synchronisation.

In our work we also analysed CANAuth, an alternative proposal for an authenticated protocol on top of CAN, which appears to be immune from this kind of replay attacks. CANAuth uses counters as part of the signature for a message, and a receiving ECU accepts a message only if the counter is higher than any other counter value previously observed. This mechanism works, but relies on the extra bandwidth provided by CAN+ for transmitting both the signature and the current counter value. To our knowledge, MaCAN is the only protocol with authentication that is able to fit into the constrained frame of CAN bus.

6   Discussion

Abstraction gap. We developed our models of the MaCAN protocol in the applied π-calculus of ProVerif. We had to change some aspects of MaCAN, as described in Section 5, to be able to analyse it. One of such aspects is the use of timestamps to ensure freshness of messages. We were unsuccessful in modeling timestamps in ProVerif, as the tool abstracts away state information, and therefore we were not able to express freshness of timestamp values.

Other analysers such as StatVerif [1] have a global synchronised state, but in order to represent potentially infinite timestamps one needs more powerful abstractions that avoid exploring an infinite state-space. Explicitly inserting a fresh timestamp into a list and checking whether the current timestamp is in the list, for example, would generate terms of continuously increasing size, hanging the engine. The same behaviour we encountered in ProVerif, not surprisingly, as they share the same resolution engine.

A possible solution is the one offered by AIF [15], which abstracts values into the sets to which they belong: for example timestamps could be abstracted into current and expired ones by using two sets. We are currently working on implementing a similar abstraction on top of the applied π-calculus, in order to model more directly security protocols as communicating processes, reducing the distance between the model used for verification and the concrete program.

Implementation. We compared the result of our analysis with our implementation of MaCAN, developed independently from the analysis, which is available under an opensource license on Github[2]. We implemented the attacks to the key establishment and message authentication procedure, putting the attacker in control of a gateway as shown in Figure 10, which was demonstrated to be possible in practice by Checkoway et al. [5].

The attack on key establishment was possible only after aligning the implementation to the specification contained in the paper, as the necessary acknowledgement was already corrected in our implementation. We cannot trace back, however, whether this correction was due to explicit considerations by our skilled engineers, or it happened by chance by misinterpreting the flawed specification.

Our implementation also accepted authenticated acknowledgement messages replayed by the attacker impersonating another device in group authentication,

---

[2] https://github.com/CTU-IIG/macan

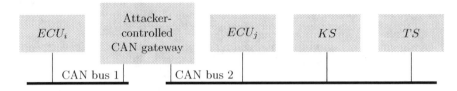

Fig. 10. Experimental setup

however with no practical consequences. We believe that this is a dangerous mistake to leave in a reference paper, which could lead to flawed implementations if left undetected. We could confirm the attack that allowed forging authenticated signals by changing signal number was present in our implementation. With it an attacker could forge potentially dangerous authenticated messages from legitimate ones. Comparing the models with the implementation also helped us to reveal some minor bugs that were introduced when coding it, and would have probably not been revealed by simple testing.

7   Conclusions

In this work we analysed MaCAN using the ProVerif protocol verifier, found a flaw in the key establishment procedure, experimentally verified the presence of an attack in our implementation, and proposed a modified version of the protocol that is immune from the problems that we discovered.

Resource constrained networks such as the CAN bus put a strong limit on the design of an authenticated protocol. The designers of MaCAN had to rely of custom schemes when designing its procedures, as previous literature did not consider such extreme bounds in terms of bandwidth as 8 bytes of payload per message. We contribute to the protocol with a formal and experimental analysis of its procedures and propose two changes that improve its behaviour.

During our analysis we also encountered some limitations in expressing the particular features of MaCAN with the languages and tools of our choice. We are currently working on an extension of the applied π-calculus that allows us to better model protocols with timestamps and counters.

Finally, protocols like MaCAN rely on relatively weak cryptography, so we would like to extend our analysis to cover possible attacks in the computational model, and be able to precisely evaluate the level of security of MaCAN.

Acknowledgments. This work is supported by the European project SESAMO. The authors would like to thank Roberto Vigo for valuable discussion on the models and the anonymous reviewers for helpful comments.

References

1. Arapinis, M., Ritter, E., Ryan, M.D.: StatVerif: Verification of Stateful Processes. In: 2011 IEEE 24th Computer Security Foundations, pp. 33–47 (2011)
2. Blanchet, B.: An efficient cryptographic protocol verifier based on prolog rules. In: Proceedings of the 14th IEEE workshop on Computer Security Foundations, pp. 82–96. IEEE Computer Society (2001)
3. Blanchet, B.: Automatic verification of correspondences for security protocols. Journal of Computer Security 17(4), 363–434 (2009)
4. Blanchet, B., Smyth, B.: Proverif 1.88: Automatic cryptographic protocol verifier, user manual and tutorial (2013)
5. Checkoway, S., McCoy, D., Kantor, B., Anderson, D., Shacham, H., Savage, S., Koscher, K., Czeskis, A., Roesner, F., Kohno, T.: Comprehensive experimental analyses of automotive attack surfaces. In: Proceedings of the 20th USENIX Conference on Security (2011)
6. Davis, R.I., Burns, A., Bril, R.J., Lukkien, J.J.: Controller area network (CAN) schedulability analysis: Refuted, revisited and revised. Real-Time Systems 35(3), 239–272 (2007)
7. Dworkin, M.J.: SP 800-38B. recommendation for block cipher modes of operation: the CMAC mode for authentication (2005)
8. FlexRay Consortium, et al.: FlexRay communications system-protocol specification. Version, 2(1):198–207 (2005)
9. Robert Bosch GmbH. Road vehicles – Controller area network (CAN) – Part 1: Data link layer and physical signalling (1991)
10. Groza, B., Murvay, S., Van Herrewege, A., Verbauwhede, I.: LiBrA-CAN: a Lightweight Broadcast Authentication protocol for Controller Area Networks (2012)
11. Hartkopp, O., Reuber, C., Schilling, R.: MaCAN - message authenticated CAN. In: Proceedings of the 10th Escar Conference on Embedded Security in Cars (2012)
12. Koscher, K., Czeskis, A., Roesner, F., Patel, S., Kohno, T., Checkoway, S., McCoy, D., Kantor, B., Anderson, D., Shacham, H., Savage, S.: Experimental Security Analysis of a Modern Automobile. In: 2010 IEEE Symposium on Security and Privacy, pp. 447–462 (2010)
13. Hartwich, F.: CAN with Flexible Data-Rate (2005)
14. Lowe, G.: A hierarchy of authentication specifications. In: Proceedings of the 10th Computer Security Foundations Workshop, pp. 31–43. IEEE (1997)
15. Mödersheim, S.A.: Abstraction by set-membership: verifying security protocols and web services with databases. In: Proceedings of the 17th ACM Conference on Computer and Communications Security, pp. 351–360. ACM (2010)
16. Schweppe, H., Roudier, Y., Weyl, B., Apvrille, L., Scheuermann, D.: Car2x communication: securing the last meter-a cost-effective approach for ensuring trust in car2x applications using in-vehicle symmetric cryptography. In: Vehicular Technology Conference (VTC Fall), pp. 1–5. IEEE (2011)
17. Van Herrewege, A., Singelee, D., Verbauwhede, I.: CANAuth — a simple, backward compatible broadcast authentication protocol for CAN bus. In: ECRYPT Workshop on Lightweight Cryptography 2011 (2011)
18. Ziermann, T., Wildermann, S., Teich, J.: CAN+: A new backward-compatible Controller Area Network (CAN) protocol with up to 16× higher data rates. In: Design, Automation & Test in Europe Conference & Exhibition, pp. 1088–1093. IEEE (2009)

A Probabilistic Framework for Security Scenarios with Dependent Actions

Barbara Kordy[1,2], Marc Pouly[3], and Patrick Schweitzer[1]

[1] University of Luxembourg, SnT, Luxembourg
[2] INSA/IRISA, Rennes, France
barbara.kordy,patrick.schweitzer@uni.lu
[3] Lucerne University of Applied Sciences and Arts, Switzerland
marc.pouly@hslu.ch

Abstract. This work addresses the growing need of performing meaningful probabilistic analysis of security. We propose a framework that integrates the graphical security modeling technique of attack–defense trees with probabilistic information expressed in terms of Bayesian networks. This allows us to perform probabilistic evaluation of attack–defense scenarios involving dependent actions. To improve the efficiency of our computations, we make use of inference algorithms from Bayesian networks and encoding techniques from constraint reasoning. We discuss the algebraic theory underlying our framework and point out several generalizations which are possible thanks to the use of semiring theory.

1 Introduction

Attack–defense trees [12] extend the well-known model of attack trees [26], by considering not only actions of an attacker, but also possible countermeasures of a defender. Since the augmented formalism models interactions between an attacker and a defender explicitly and is able to capture evolutionary aspects of attack–defense scenarios, it allows for a more accurate security assessment process compared to attack trees. In [16], we have proven that the analysis of attack–defense trees is computationally not more expensive than the analysis of attack trees. Furthermore, the usefulness of attack–defense trees for the analysis of real-world security problems has been validated in a large industrial case study [2]. These results show that attack–defense trees have the potential to become an efficient and practical security modeling and risk assessment tool.

Quantifying probabilistic aspects of attacks is one of the most important issues in security evaluation. Decisions concerning which defensive mechanisms should be implemented are based on the success probability of potential attacks. Furthermore, estimation of probability is necessary in order to evaluate risk related measures. Hence, a fully fledged methodology for security analysis needs to contain a mature framework for probabilistic computations. Unfortunately, the standard bottom-up approach for quantitative analysis of attack tree-based formalisms [18,13] can *only* be used for computing probabilities under

E. Albert and E. Sekerinski (Eds.): IFM 2014, LNCS 8739, pp. 256–271, 2014.

the assumption that *all considered actions are independent*. This is a very strong assumption which is unrealistic for real-life situations.

In this paper, we develop a *complete framework for probability computations on attack–defense trees*. Our approach combines the security methodology of attack–defense trees with the probabilistic framework of Bayesian networks. This allows us to overcome the mentioned limitation of the bottom-up approach and *perform probabilistic computations in the presence of dependent actions*. Since attack trees are formally a subclass of attack–defense trees, our framework *applies directly for the analysis of the former model*. Thus, the paper also contributes to the development of full-fledged analysis technique for attack trees which are widely accepted and commonly used by industry [15].

We give a brief overview of the attack–defense tree methodology in Section 2. After recalling basic concepts for Bayesian networks, we present our framework for dependent probability computations on attack–defense trees, in Section 3. Sections 4 and 5 are concerned with methods for improving the efficiency of the framework. We describe related work in Section 6 and conclude in Section 7.

2   Modeling of Security Scenarios

This section provides background knowledge about attack–defense trees, which is necessary to understand the framework developed in this paper. For a more detailed description of the formalism, we refer to [13] and [16].

2.1   Attack–Defense Trees

Attack–defense trees (ADTrees) allow to illustrate and quantify security scenarios that involve two opposing players: an attacker and a defender. The root of an ADTree represents the main goal of one of the players. When the root is an attack node, the tree represents how to attack a considered system. Conversely, when the root is a defense node, the tree is concerned with defending the system. In ADTrees, both types of nodes, attacks and defenses, can be conjunctively or disjunctively refined. A goal represented by a conjunctively refined node is reached when *all the subgoals* depicted by its child nodes are reached. A goal represented by a disjunctively refined node is reached when *at least one of the subgoals* depicted by its child nodes is reached. The refinement operation is applied until *basic actions* are obtained. Actions are considered to be basic if they can be easily understood and quantified. Basic actions are represented by the nodes which do not have any children of the same type. Each node of an ADTree can also have one child of the opposite type. Children of the opposite type represent countermeasures. These countermeasures can be refined and countered again. In ADTrees, attack nodes are modeled by circles, defense nodes by rectangles. A conjunctive refinement is depicted with an arc. Countermeasures are connected to the actions they counteract by a dotted line.

Example 1. Consider a scenario in which an attacker wants to infect a computer with a virus. In order to do this, the attacker needs to ensure that the virus

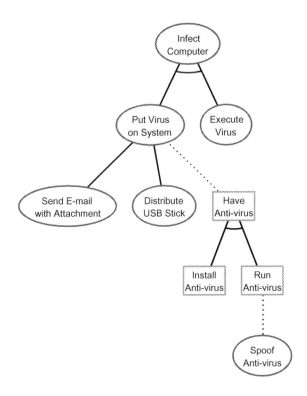

Fig. 1. ADTree for infecting a computer

file is accessible from the targeted computer and that it is executed. There are two possibilities to make the file accessible: an attacker can send the virus in an e-mail attachment or distribute an infected USB stick to the computer user. The computer user, on his part, can protect himself against a virus with an anti-virus program. For the anti-virus to be effective, it needs to be installed and it needs to be running. A resourceful attacker, in turn, could attack the anti-virus by using a fake version of an anti-virus, that disables the real anti-virus from running and only pretends that it is running. Fig. 1 depicts the described attack–defense scenario using an ADTree. In this tree, the basic actions are:

For the attacker
SE – "Send E-mail with Attachment"
DU – "Distribute USB Stick"
SA – "Spoof Anti-virus"
EV – "Execute Virus"

For the defender
IA – "Install Anti-virus"
RA – "Run Anti-virus"

The attack–defense scenario described above is used as the running example in this paper. Its main role is to illustrate how the introduced methodology works. We purposely keep the example simple (and incomplete) in order not to overwhelm the reader with too complex models.

Remark 1. Since the root of the ADTree in Fig. 1 represents an attack goal, the paper is concerned with the probability of attacking a system. In the case of an ADTree having a defensive root node, we would talk about the probability of defending a system.

2.2   The Propositional Semantics for ADTrees

In order to provide a broad spectrum of analysis methods, several formal semantics for ADTees have been defined in [13]. In this paper, we employ the *propositional semantics* which makes use of Boolean functions.

By r, we denote a countable set of propositional variables. A *configuration* with finite domain $u \subseteq r$ is a function $\mathbf{x} \colon u \to \{0,1\}$ that associates a value $\mathbf{x}(X) \in \{0,1\}$ with every variable $X \in u$. Thus, a configuration $\mathbf{x} \in \{0,1\}^u$ represents an assignment of Boolean values to the variables in u.

Definition 1. *A Boolean function f with domain u is a function $f \colon \{0,1\}^u \to \{0,1\}$ that assigns a value $f(\mathbf{x}) \in \{0,1\}$ to each configuration $\mathbf{x} \in \{0,1\}^u$.*

Given a configuration $\mathbf{x}$ with domain $u \subseteq r$, we denote by $\mathbf{x}^{\downarrow w}$ the projection of $\mathbf{x}$ to a subset $w \subseteq u$. Let f and g be two Boolean functions with domains u and w, respectively. The *disjunction* $(f \vee g)$ and the *conjunction* $(f \wedge g)$ of f and g are Boolean functions with domain $u \cup w$, defined for every $\mathbf{x} \in \{0,1\}^{u \cup w}$ by:

$$(f \vee g)(\mathbf{x}) = \max\{f(\mathbf{x}^{\downarrow u}), g(\mathbf{x}^{\downarrow w})\}, \qquad (f \wedge g)(\mathbf{x}) = f(\mathbf{x}^{\downarrow u}) \times g(\mathbf{x}^{\downarrow w}).$$

The *negation* of f (denoted by $\neg f$) is a Boolean function with domain u, defined for every $\mathbf{x} \in \{0,1\}^u$ by: $(\neg f)(\mathbf{x}) = 1 - f(\mathbf{x})$.

Now, we explain how the propositional semantics associates ADTrees with Boolean functions. Let $\mathbb{B}$ denote the set of all basic actions. First, for every $B \in \mathbb{B}$, a propositional variable $X_B \in r$ is constructed. We assume that for $B, B' \in \mathbb{B}$, $B \neq B' \implies X_B \neq X_{B'}$. Next, a Boolean function f_t is associated with every ADTree t, as follows.

- If $t = B \in \mathbb{B}$, then $f_B \colon \{0,1\}^{\{X_B\}} \to \{0,1\}$ is defined as $f_B(X_B) = X_B$. In other words, the Boolean function associated with B is an identity function. Thus, we often abuse notation and use X_B instead of f_B.
- If t is disjunctively refined into $t_1, \dots t_k$, then[1] $f_t = \bigvee_{i=1}^{k} f_{t_i}$,
- If t is conjunctively refined into $t_1, \dots t_k$, then $f_t = \bigwedge_{i=1}^{k} f_{t_i}$,
- If t is countered, then $f_t = f_{t_1} \wedge \neg f_{t_2}$, where t_1 corresponds to the refining subtree and t_2 represents the countering subtree.

---

[1] Here, $\bigwedge$ and $\bigvee$ stand for extensions of conjunction and disjunction of two Boolean functions to any finite number of Boolean functions. They are well-defined by associativity of $\times$ and max.

Example 2. Applying the introduced recursive construction results in the following Boolean function for the ADTree t from Figure 1:

$$f_t = \Big((X_{\mathrm{SE}} \vee X_{\mathrm{DU}}) \wedge \neg (X_{\mathrm{IA}} \wedge (X_{\mathrm{RA}} \wedge \neg X_{\mathrm{SA}})) \Big) \wedge X_{\mathrm{EV}}. \tag{1}$$

Given an ADTree t, we denote by var_t the domain of the Boolean function f_t. In other words, var_t is the set of propositional variables corresponding to the basic actions involved in t. A configuration $\mathbf{x} \in \{0,1\}^{\mathrm{var}_t}$ represents which actions succeed (the corresponding variables are set to 1) and which do not (the corresponding variables are set to 0). Following our terminology convention from Remark 1, if $f_t(\mathbf{x}) = 1$, then we say that $\mathbf{x}$ is an *attack with respect to t*.

3 Probabilistic Evaluation of ADTrees

The most often used computational procedure for quantitative assessment of ADTrees relies on a bottom-up procedure [26,18,13,14]. In this approach, values are assigned to the basic actions and the bottom-up algorithm is used to determine the values of the remaining nodes as a function of the values of their children. The computation stops when the value for the root node has been found. Since the value of a node only depends on the *values* of its children, and *not on their meaning*, the bottom-up procedure cannot take dependencies between actions into account. Thus, this technique implicitly assumes that all actions of an ADTree are independent. In the case of the probability parameter, such an assumption is unrealistic. For instance, the probability that the defender runs an anti-virus program depends on whether the anti-virus is installed or not.

In order to compute the probability of attacking a system, while taking dependencies between involved actions into account, we propose a framework which combines attack–defense trees with Bayesian networks.

3.1 Bayesian Network Associated with an ADTree

A *Bayesian network* [20] is a graphical representation of a *joint probability distribution* over a finite set of variables with finite domains. The network itself is a directed, acyclic graph that reflects the conditional interdependencies between the variables associated with the nodes of the network. A directed edge from the node associated with variable X_1 to the node associated with variable X_2 means that X_2 stochastically depends on X_1. Each node contains a *conditional probability table* that quantifies the influence between the variables. The joint probability distribution p of a Bayesian network over $\{X_1, \ldots, X_n\}$ is given by

$$p(X_1, \ldots, X_n) = \prod_{i=1}^{n} p(X_i \mid \mathrm{par}(X_i)), \tag{2}$$

where, $\mathrm{par}(X_i)$ denotes the set of nodes that have an outgoing edge that points into X_i. If the set $\mathrm{par}(X_i)$ is empty, the conditional probability becomes an ordinary probability distribution. Nodes (or subgraphs) of the Bayesian network that are unconnected represent stochastically independent (sets of) variables.

Our goal is to create a Bayesian network depicting stochastic dependencies between the actions involved in a security scenario given as an ADTree. In the ADTree methodology, refined nodes do not contain any additional information, other than how their children are connected (conjunctively or disjunctively). This means that refined nodes *do not* depict any additional actions. This is why, when constructing a Bayesian network for an ADTree, we take only basic actions into account.

A Bayesian network associated with an ADTree t, denoted by BN_t, is a Bayesian network over the set of propositional variables var_t, such that there exists a directed edge from X_A to X_B if and only if action B stochastically depends on action A. Bayesian network BN_t complements ADTree t with additional information which is not contained in t. The structure of the Bayesian network BN_t is usually constructed manually. This process can however be supported by numerous existing approaches for constructing Bayesian networks [8].

Example 3. A Bayesian network BN_t associated with our running ADTree t is shown in Fig. 2. The joint probability distribution for BN_t is

$$p(X_{\text{EV}}, X_{\text{SE}}, X_{\text{DU}}, X_{\text{SA}}, X_{\text{RA}}, X_{\text{IA}}) = p(X_{\text{RA}}|X_{\text{IA}}) \times p(X_{\text{IA}}) \times \qquad (3)$$
$$p(X_{\text{EV}}|X_{\text{SE}}, X_{\text{DU}}) \times p(X_{\text{SE}}|X_{\text{SA}}) \times p(X_{\text{DU}}|X_{\text{SA}}) \times p(X_{\text{SA}}).$$

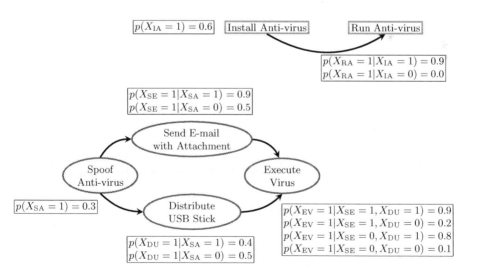

Fig. 2. Bayesian network BN_t associated with ADTree t from Figure 1

The conditional probability tables used in Figure 2 have been constructed on an intuitive basis. The accuracy of the input values, as well as the actual methods for their estimation are a research topic in itself and are outside the scope of this submission. In the rest of the paper, we assume that the conditional probability tables have been constructed and are available.

3.2   Probabilistic Computations in the Presence of Dependencies

We now present our framework for probability computations on an ADTree t, taking the dependencies between the involved actions into account. Our computation makes use of the Boolean function f_t and the Bayesian network BN_t.

Given configuration $\mathbf{x} \in \{0,1\}^{var_t}$, we define

$$\psi_t(\mathbf{x}) = f_t(\mathbf{x}) \times p(\mathbf{x}), \tag{4}$$

where p is the joint probability distribution of BN_t. If $\mathbf{x}$ is an attack with respect to t, then $f_t(\mathbf{x}) = 1$ and $\psi_t(\mathbf{x})$ returns the probability value for $\mathbf{x}$ from the Bayesian network, representing the success probability of attack $\mathbf{x}$. If $\mathbf{x}$ is not an attack with respect to t, then $f_t(\mathbf{x}) = 0$ and thus $\psi_t(\mathbf{x}) = 0$.

Example 4. Consider the situation where the attacker installs a virus file on the system by sending an e-mail with attachment ($X_{SE} = 1$ and $X_{DU} = 0$), executes the virus file ($X_{EV} = 1$), but does not use a fake anti-virus program ($X_{SA} = 0$). The defender, in turn, installs a real anti-virus ($X_{IA} = 1$) which however is not running ($X_{RA} = 0$). The corresponding configuration

$$\mathbf{x} = (X_{EV} = 1, X_{SE} = 1, X_{DU} = 0, X_{SA} = 0, X_{RA} = 0, X_{IA} = 1)$$

is an attack, because

$$f_t(\mathbf{x}) \overset{(1)}{=} \left(\Big((X_{SE} \vee X_{DU}) \wedge \neg(X_{IA} \wedge (X_{RA} \wedge \neg X_{SA})) \Big) \wedge X_{EV} \right)(\mathbf{x}) = 1.$$

By instantiating formula (3) with values from Fig. 2, we obtain that this attack will be successfully executed with the probability

$$\begin{aligned}
\psi_t(\mathbf{x}) = f_t(\mathbf{x}) \times p(\mathbf{x}) &= p(X_{EV} = 1 | X_{SE} = 1, X_{DU} = 0) \times p(X_{SE} = 1 | X_{SA} = 0) \\
&\times p(X_{DU} = 0 | X_{SA} = 0) \times p(X_{SA} = 0) \times p(X_{RA} = 0 | X_{IA} = 1) \times p(X_{IA} = 1) \\
&= 0.2 \times 0.5 \times (1 - 0.5) \times (1 - 0.3) \times (1 - 0.9) \times 0.6 = 0.0021.
\end{aligned}$$

Next, assume we are not interested in calculating the probability of successfully executing a specific set of basic actions, but more generally in the success probability of attacking a system according to the scenario represented with ADTree t. This corresponds to the sum of the probabilities of all possible attacks with respect to t. We thus have

$$P(t) = \sum_{\mathbf{x} \in \{0,1\}^{var_t}} \psi_t(\mathbf{x}) \overset{(4)}{=} \sum_{\mathbf{x} \in \{0,1\}^{var_t}} f_t(\mathbf{x}) \times p(\mathbf{x}). \tag{5}$$

We refer to the value $P(t)$ as *the probability related to ADTree t*. Finally, the success probability of the most probable attack with respect to t is computed as

$$P_{\max}(t) = \max_{\mathbf{x} \in \{0,1\}^{\mathrm{var}_t}} \psi_t(\mathbf{x}) \overset{(4)}{=} \max_{\mathbf{x} \in \{0,1\}^{\mathrm{var}_t}} f_t(\mathbf{x}) \times p(\mathbf{x}). \tag{6}$$

4   ADTrees as Constraint Systems

We know that the number of possible configurations is exponential with respect to the number of basic actions. Thus, for large systems, the brute force computation of $P(t)$ and $P_{\max}(t)$, as suggested by formulæ (5) and (6), is no longer possible. We now present methods allowing us to represent $P(t)$ and $P_{\max}(t)$ in a factorized form, in order to increase the efficiency of their computations.

4.1   Indicator Functions for ADTrees

We employ an encoding technique from constraint reasoning and construct a factorized *indicator function* ϕ_t for the Boolean function f_t. Indicator ϕ_t maps to 1 if and only if its arguments represent a valid assignment with respect to f_t. The construction of the global indicator ϕ_t relies on *local indicators* that make use of *inner variables* and are defined as follows.

1. If $f_t = \bigvee_{i=1}^{k} f_{t_i}$, then the propositional variables $Y, Y_1, \ldots, Y_k$ are associated with $f_t, f_{t_1}, \ldots, f_{t_k}$, respectively, and the local indicator function for f_t is defined as: $\phi(Y, Y_1, \ldots, Y_k) = 1$ if $Y = \max\{Y_1, \ldots, Y_k\}$ and 0 otherwise.
2. If $f_t = \bigwedge_{i=1}^{k} f_{t_i}$, then the propositional variables $Y, Y_1, \ldots, Y_k$ are associated with $f_t, f_{t_1}, \ldots, f_{t_k}$, respectively, and the local indicator function for f_t is defined as: $\phi(Y, Y_1, \ldots, Y_k) = 1$ if $Y = Y_1 \times \ldots \times Y_k$ and 0 otherwise.
3. If $f_t = f_{t_1} \wedge \neg f_{t_2}$, then the propositional variables Y, Y_1 and Y_2 are associated with f_t, f_{t_1} and f_{t_2}, respectively, and the local indicator function for f_t is defined as: $\phi(Y, Y_1, Y_2) = 1$ if $Y = Y_1 \times (1 - Y_2)$ and 0 otherwise.

Example 5. A step-wise construction of the local indicators for the Boolean function given in Example 2 proceeds as follows:

$$f_t = \Big(\underbrace{(X_{\mathrm{SE}} \vee X_{\mathrm{DU}})}_{Y_1} \wedge \neg \underbrace{(X_{\mathrm{IA}} \wedge \underbrace{(X_{\mathrm{RA}} \wedge \neg X_{\mathrm{SA}})}_{Y_2})}_{Y_3} \Big) \wedge X_{\mathrm{EV}}$$

In this case, the inner variables are Y_1, Y_2, Y_3, Y_4, Y_t and the local indicators are

$$\phi_1(Y_1, X_{\mathrm{SE}}, X_{\mathrm{DU}}) = 1 \quad \text{exactly if} \quad Y_1 = \max(X_{\mathrm{SE}}, X_{\mathrm{DU}}),$$
$$\phi_2(Y_2, X_{\mathrm{RA}}, X_{\mathrm{SA}}) = 1 \quad \text{exactly if} \quad Y_2 = X_{\mathrm{RA}} \times (1 - X_{\mathrm{SA}}),$$
$$\phi_3(Y_3, X_{\mathrm{IA}}, Y_2) = 1 \quad \text{exactly if} \quad Y_3 = X_{\mathrm{IA}} \times Y_2,$$
$$\phi_4(Y_4, Y_1, Y_3) = 1 \quad \text{exactly if} \quad Y_4 = Y_1 \times (1 - Y_3),$$
$$\phi_5(Y_t, Y_4, X_{\mathrm{EV}}) = 1 \quad \text{exactly if} \quad Y_t = Y_4 \times X_{\mathrm{EV}}.$$

Let t be an ADTree. Having constructed all local indicators, we can build the *global indicator function* ϕ_t. The domain of ϕ_t contains all variables used by the local indicators, i.e., the inner variables and the variables corresponding to basic actions of t. An assignment over all variables is valid if and only if each local assignment is valid. Hence, we may compute the global indicator function for f_t by multiplying all its local indicators. For the function from Example 5, we get:

$$\phi_t(Y_1, Y_2, Y_3, Y_4, Y_t, X_{\mathrm{SE}}, X_{\mathrm{DU}}, X_{\mathrm{RA}}, X_{\mathrm{SA}}, X_{\mathrm{IA}}, X_{\mathrm{EV}}) = \phi_1(Y_1, X_{\mathrm{SE}}, X_{\mathrm{DU}}) \times$$
$$\phi_2(Y_2, X_{\mathrm{RA}}, X_{\mathrm{SA}}) \times \phi_3(Y_3, X_{\mathrm{IA}}, Y_2) \times \phi_4(Y_4, Y_1, Y_3) \times \phi_5(Y_t, Y_4, X_{\mathrm{EV}}). \quad (7)$$

In this paper, we use the following notation: given the global indicator function ϕ_t for t, we denote by Y_t the inner variable corresponding to the entire tree t. The set of all inner variables of ϕ_t is denoted by d_t.

Consider an indicator function $\phi(Y, Y_1, \ldots, Y_k)$. Let $\mathbf{z}$ be an assignment of values to the variables $Y_1, \ldots, Y_k$. There is, by definition, exactly one value $y \in \{0, 1\}$ for Y, such that $\phi(y, \mathbf{z}) = 1$. Since the global indicator function is obtained by multiplication, we may directly conclude the following theorem.

Theorem 1. *Consider an ADTree t with basic actions $B_1, \ldots, B_n$ and its global indicator function ϕ_t. Given a specific assignment $\mathbf{x}$ of values to the variables $X_{B_1}, \ldots, X_{B_n}$ corresponding to basic actions, there is exactly one assignment $\mathbf{y}$ to the inner variables from d_t, such that $\phi_t(\mathbf{y}, \mathbf{x}) = 1$.*

An immediate consequence of Theorem 1 is that, for a specific assignment $\mathbf{x} \in \{0, 1\}^{\mathrm{var}_t}$ of values to the variables associated with basic actions, we have

$$\max_{\mathbf{y} \in \{0,1\}^{d_t}} \phi_t(\mathbf{y}, \mathbf{x}) = \sum_{\mathbf{y} \in \{0,1\}^{d_t}} \phi_t(\mathbf{y}, \mathbf{x}) = 1. \quad (8)$$

When performing probabilistic computations as specified by formulæ (4), (5) and (6), we are only interested in those combinations of basic actions that correspond to attacks. Thus, when reasoning in terms of global indicator functions, we need to restrict our considerations to those configurations where variable Y_t equals 1. This can be achieved by *conditioning* ϕ_t on $Y_t = 1$, which means that we invalidate all configurations with $Y_t = 0$. We therefore define a *filter* F_t for the ADTree t that satisfies $F_t(Y_t) = 1$ if and only if $Y_t = 1$. In other words, $F_t \colon \{0, 1\}^{\{Y_t\}} \to \{0, 1\}$ is the identity function for variable Y_t. Multiplying filter F_t and global indicator ϕ_t results in a function, denoted by $\phi_{t|Y_t=1}$, which maps to 1 if and only if the assignment of values to the variables is valid with respect to f_t *and* it represents an attack according to t. We thus have,

$$\forall \mathbf{z} \in \{0,1\}^{\text{var}_t \cup d_t} : \phi_{t|Y_t=1}(\mathbf{z}) = F_t(\mathbf{z}^{\downarrow\{Y_t\}}) \times \phi_t(\mathbf{z}). \tag{9}$$

Let t be an ADTree, ϕ_t be its global indicator function and F_t be the filter for t. Assume furthermore that we are given a specific configuration $\mathbf{x} \in \{0,1\}^{\text{var}_t}$. Configuration $\mathbf{x}$ is an attack with respect to t if and only if, there exists $\mathbf{y} \in \{0,1\}^{d_t}$, such that $\phi_{t|Y_t=1}(\mathbf{y}, \mathbf{x})$ maps to 1. Using formula (8), we obtain

$$\max_{\mathbf{y} \in \{0,1\}^{d_t}} \phi_{t|Y_t=1}(\mathbf{y}, \mathbf{x}) = \sum_{\mathbf{y} \in \{0,1\}^{d_t}} \phi_{t|Y_t=1}(\mathbf{y}, \mathbf{x}) = f_t(\mathbf{x}) = \begin{cases} 1 \text{ if } \mathbf{x} \text{ is an attack} \\ 0 \text{ otherwise.} \end{cases} \tag{10}$$

4.2   Indicators for Probability Computation

Making use of the property described by (10), the procedure for the probabilistic computations developed in Section 3.2 can be redefined as follows. Let t be an ADTree and $\mathbf{x} \in \{0,1\}^{\text{var}_t}$ be an assignment of Boolean values to the variables corresponding to the basic actions of t. If $\mathbf{x}$ is an attack with respect to t, then its probability is computed as

$$\psi_t(\mathbf{x}) \overset{(4)}{=} f_t(\mathbf{x}) \times p(\mathbf{x}) \overset{(10), \text{ distrib.}}{=} \sum_{\mathbf{y} \in \{0,1\}^{d_t}} \left(\phi_{t|Y_t=1}(\mathbf{y}, \mathbf{x}) \times p(\mathbf{x}) \right) \tag{11}$$

$$\overset{(10), \text{ distrib.}}{=} \max_{\mathbf{y} \in \{0,1\}^{d_t}} \left(\phi_{t|Y_t=1}(\mathbf{y}, \mathbf{x}) \times p(\mathbf{x}) \right). \tag{12}$$

The probability related to ADTree t is expressed as

$$P(t) \overset{(5)}{=} \sum_{\mathbf{x} \in \{0,1\}^{\text{var}_t}} \psi_t(\mathbf{x}) \overset{(11)}{=} \sum_{\mathbf{x} \in \{0,1\}^{\text{var}_t}} \sum_{\mathbf{y} \in \{0,1\}^{d_t}} \left(\phi_{t|Y_t=1}(\mathbf{y}, \mathbf{x}) \times p(\mathbf{x}) \right)$$

$$= \sum_{\mathbf{z} \in \{0,1\}^{\text{var}_t \cup d_t}} \left(\phi_{t|Y_t=1}(\mathbf{z}) \times p(\mathbf{z}^{\downarrow\text{var}_t}) \right). \tag{13}$$

Similarly, the probability of the most probable attack with respect to t is

$$P_{\max}(t) \overset{(6)}{=} \max_{\mathbf{x} \in \{0,1\}^{\text{var}_t}} \psi_t(\mathbf{x}) \overset{(12)}{=} \max_{\mathbf{z} \in \{0,1\}^{\text{var}_t \cup d_t}} \left(\phi_{t|Y_t=1}(\mathbf{z}) \times p(\mathbf{z}^{\downarrow\text{var}_t}) \right). \tag{14}$$

Example 6. Let $u = \{Y_1, Y_2, Y_3, Y_4, Y_t, X_{\text{SE}}, X_{\text{DU}}, X_{\text{RA}}, X_{\text{SA}}, X_{\text{IA}}, X_{\text{EV}}\}$. The factorized form for the probability related the ADTree from Figure 1 is

$$P(t) \overset{(13),(9),(7),(3)}{=} \tag{15}$$

$$\sum_{\mathbf{z} \in \{0,1\}^u} \Big(F_t(\mathbf{z}^{\downarrow\{Y_t\}}) \times \phi_1(\mathbf{z}^{\downarrow\{Y_1, X_{\text{SE}}, X_{\text{DU}}\}}) \times \phi_2(\mathbf{z}^{\downarrow\{Y_2, X_{\text{RA}}, X_{\text{SA}}\}}) \times \phi_3(\mathbf{z}^{\downarrow\{Y_3, X_{\text{IA}}, Y_2\}})$$

$$\times \phi_4(\mathbf{z}^{\downarrow\{Y_4, Y_1, Y_3\}}) \times \phi_5(\mathbf{z}^{\downarrow\{Y_t, Y_4, X_{\text{EV}}\}}) \times p(\mathbf{z}^{\downarrow\{X_{\text{EV}}, X_{\text{SE}}, X_{\text{DU}}\}}) \times p(\mathbf{z}^{\downarrow\{X_{\text{SE}}, X_{\text{SA}}\}})$$

$$\times p(\mathbf{z}^{\downarrow\{X_{\text{DU}}, X_{\text{SA}}\}}) \times p(\mathbf{z}^{\downarrow\{X_{\text{SA}}\}}) \times p(\mathbf{z}^{\downarrow\{X_{\text{RA}}, X_{\text{IA}}\}}) \times p(\mathbf{z}^{\downarrow\{X_{\text{IA}}\}}) \Big).$$

5 Efficiency Considerations

The factorization of the global indicator function, in terms of local indicators which are bounded in size, introduces additional structure that can be exploited for so-called *local computation* [22]. In this section, we show how the *fusion* algorithm allows us to improve the efficiency of evaluating formulas (13) and (14).

5.1 Semiring Valuations

An algebraic structure $\langle A, \oplus, \odot \rangle$ with binary operations $\oplus$ and $\odot$ is called *commutative semiring* if both operations are associative, commutative, and if $\odot$ distributes over $\oplus$, i.e., if for $a, b, c \in A$, we have $a \odot (b \oplus c) = (a \odot b) \oplus (a \odot c)$ and $(a \oplus b) \odot c = (a \odot c) \oplus (b \odot c)$. Typical examples of commutative semirings include the Boolean semiring $\langle \{0,1\}, \max, \times \rangle$, the tropical semiring $\langle \mathbb{N}, \min, + \rangle$, the product t-norm semiring $\langle [0,1], \max, \times \rangle$ and the arithmetic semiring $\langle \mathbb{R}, +, \times \rangle$.

Let $u \subseteq r$ be a finite set of propositional variables and $\langle A, \oplus, \odot \rangle$ be a commutative semiring. A *semiring valuation* over $\langle A, \oplus, \odot \rangle$ is a function $\phi : \{0,1\}^u \to A$ associating a value from A with each configuration from $\{0,1\}^u$. We denote by $\mathrm{dom}(\phi) = u$ the domain of valuation ϕ. The *combination* of two valuations ϕ and ψ over a semiring $\langle A, \oplus, \odot \rangle$ is defined, for all $\mathbf{x} \in \{0,1\}^{\mathrm{dom}(\phi) \cup \mathrm{dom}(\psi)}$, as:

$$(\phi \otimes \psi)(\mathbf{x}) = \phi(\mathbf{x}^{\downarrow \mathrm{dom}(\phi)}) \odot \psi(\mathbf{x}^{\downarrow \mathrm{dom}(\psi)}).$$

The *elimination* of variable $X \in \mathrm{dom}(\phi)$ is defined, for all $\mathbf{x} \in \{0,1\}^{\mathrm{dom}(\phi) \setminus \{X\}}$, as:

$$\phi^{-X}(\mathbf{x}) = \phi(\mathbf{x}, 0) \oplus \phi(\mathbf{x}, 1).$$

Due to associativity of semiring addition $\oplus$, we can eliminate variables in any order. For $\{X_1, \ldots, X_m\} \subseteq \mathrm{dom}(\phi)$, we may therefore write

$$\phi^{-\{X_1, \ldots, X_m\}} = \left(\ldots \left((\phi^{-X_1})^{-X_2} \right) \ldots \right)^{-X_m}.$$

Indicator functions are Boolean semiring valuations over $\langle \{0,1\}, \max, \times \rangle$. Arithmetic semiring valuations over $\langle \mathbb{R}, +, \times \rangle$ capture conditional probability tables from Bayesian networks, and product t-norm semiring valuations over $\langle [0,1], \max, \times \rangle$ compute maximum attack probabilities, as in formula (14).

It has been shown in [10] that semiring valuations over arbitrary commutative semirings always satisfy the axioms of a valuation algebra [9,22]. The computational interest in valuation algebras is stated by the *inference problem*. Given a set of (semiring) valuations $\{\phi_1, \ldots, \phi_n\}$, called *knowledgebase*, with domains $u_i = \mathrm{dom}(\phi_i)$, for $i = 1, \ldots, n$, and a set of variables $\{X_1, \ldots, X_m\} \subseteq u_1 \cup \ldots \cup u_n$, the inference problem consists of computing

$$\phi^{-\{X_1, \ldots, X_m\}} = (\phi_1 \otimes \ldots \otimes \phi_n)^{-\{X_1, \ldots, X_m\}}. \tag{16}$$

Example 7. Let $u = \{Y_1, Y_2, Y_3, Y_4, Y_t, X_{\mathrm{SE}}, X_{\mathrm{DU}}, X_{\mathrm{RA}}, X_{\mathrm{SA}}, X_{\mathrm{IA}}, X_{\mathrm{EV}}\}$. Computing the probability in Example 6 amounts to solving the inference problem

$$\left(F_t(\mathbf{z}^{\downarrow\{Y_t\}}) \times \phi_1(\mathbf{z}^{\downarrow\{Y_1, X_{\mathrm{SE}}, X_{\mathrm{DU}}\}}) \times \ldots \times p(\mathbf{z}^{\downarrow\{X_{\mathrm{IA}}\}})\right)^{-u} =$$

$$\sum_{\mathbf{z}\in\{0,1\}^u} \left(F_t(\mathbf{z}^{\downarrow\{Y_t\}}) \times \phi_1(\mathbf{z}^{\downarrow\{Y_1, X_{\mathrm{SE}}, X_{\mathrm{DU}}\}}) \times \ldots \times p(\mathbf{z}^{\downarrow\{X_{\mathrm{IA}}\}})\right).$$

Here, the knowledgebase consists of all local indicator functions, filter F_t and all conditional probability tables, which instantiate arithmetic semiring valuations. Likewise, computing maximum attack probability, expressed by formula (14), amounts to solving a similar inference problem over the product t-norm semiring.

5.2 Fusion

A direct evaluation of formulas (13), (14), and more generally of (16), is in most cases not possible, due to the exponential complexity of combination of semiring valuations. However, because the computational tasks are stated with respect to a factorization of the global indicator function and the joint probability distribution, we may exploit the additional structure inside the factorization and perform calculations locally on the domain of the factors. *Fusion* [27] (or *bucket-elimination* [5]) is one of the local computation algorithms that can be applied to factorizations of arbitrary valuation algebras. Thus, we may use it for processing inference problems obtained from ADTrees.

The elimination of a single variable $X \in \mathrm{dom}(\phi) = \mathrm{dom}(\phi_1) \cup \ldots \cup \mathrm{dom}(\phi_n)$ from a set $\{\phi_1, \ldots, \phi_n\}$ of valuations can be performed as follows:

$$\mathrm{Fus}_X(\{\phi_1, \ldots, \phi_n\}) = \{\psi^{-X}\} \cup \{\phi_i : X \notin \mathrm{dom}(\phi_i)\}, \tag{17}$$

where $\psi = \bigotimes_{i: X\in\mathrm{dom}(\phi_i)} \phi_i$. This means that we only need to eliminate X from the factors that have X in the domain. As described in [9], the fusion algorithm then follows by repeated application of this operation:

$$(\phi_1 \otimes \ldots \otimes \phi_n)^{-\{X_1,\ldots,X_m\}} = \bigotimes \mathrm{Fus}_{X_m}(\ldots (\mathrm{Fus}_{X_1}(\{\phi_1, \ldots, \phi_n\}))).$$

In every step $i = 1, \ldots, m$ of the fusion algorithm, the combination in (17) creates an intermediate factor ψ_i with domain $\mathrm{dom}(\psi_i)$. Then, variable X_i is eliminated only from ψ_i in (17). We define $\lambda(i) = \mathrm{dom}(\psi_i) \setminus \{X_i\}$ called *label* and observe that $\lambda(m) = (\mathrm{dom}(\phi_1) \cup \ldots \cup \mathrm{dom}(\phi_n)) \setminus \{X_1, \ldots, X_m\}$. The domains of all intermediate results of the fusion algorithm are therefore bounded by the size of the largest label plus one. The smaller the labels are, the more efficient fusion is. We further remark that the labels depend on the chosen elimination sequence for variables $X_1, \ldots, X_m$. Finding a sequence that leads to the smallest label is NP-complete [1], however, there are good heuristics that achieve reasonable execution time [6]. In summary, the complexity of computing (16) is not necessarily exponential in the number of variables involved in the problem, but only in the size of the largest label, also called *tree width* [25], that occurs during fusion.

We have applied fusion to the inference problem from Example 7. The results show that, when fusion is used, time and space complexity of the computation of $P(t)$ for our running ADTree are bounded by 2^5. To compare, a naive, direct computation, as in (15), is bounded by 2^{11}. We have also automated the computation of $P(t)$ with the help of the open-source tool Nenok [23] which provides an extensive library of generically implemented local computation algorithms. When applying fusion, Nenok outputs the value of $P(t)$ after 0.031 sec in contrast to 3.422 sec that the application requires to compute the same value in a naive way, i.e., by using expression (15) directly.

6   Related Work

ADTrees are only one of more than 30 graphical formalisms for security assessment, which are based on attack trees. A recent survey, by Kordy et al. [15] presents a complete state of the art in the field of DAG-based approaches for modeling of attacks and defenses. It summarizes existing formalisms, compares their features and proposes their taxonomy. The reader is referred to this survey for an overview of existing methods for quantitative, and in particular probabilistic, analysis of security. In the remainder of this section, we compare our framework with the most prominent, existing models that combine AND-OR graphs with Bayesian networks.

Qin and Lee are one of the pioneers in applying Bayesian networks for security analysis [24]. They propose a conversion of regular attack trees into Bayesian networks, in order to make use of probabilistic inference techniques to evaluate the likelihood of attack goals and predict potential upcoming attacks. Edges representing disjunctive refinements in the tree are also present in the corresponding Bayesian network, because they represent cause-consequence relations between components. Contrary to our interpretation, a conjunction in attack trees is assumed to have an explicit or implicit order in which the actions have to be executed. This allows to convert conjunctions into a directed path in the Bayesian network, starting from the first child, according to the given order, and ending with the parent node. The construction from [24] implies that the Bayesian network and the attack tree contain the same set of nodes. Furthermore the Bayesian network models cause-consequence relationships that correspond to the child-parent connections in the underlying attack tree. In our case, the Bayesian network depicts *additional* dependencies that represent how different basic actions are influenced by each other.

In [7], Frigault and Wang advance a model, called *Bayesian attack graphs*. They construct a Bayesian network starting from an attack graph which depicts how multiple vulnerabilities may be combined in an attack. The resulting directed acyclic graph contains all nodes of the original attack graph. Employing the CVSS mechanism [19], the nodes are then associated with the conditional probability tables. In [21], Poolsappasit et al. revisit the framework of Bayesian attack graphs to be able to deal with asset identification, system vulnerability and connectivity analysis, as well as mitigation strategies. In addition to the conditional probability tables that represent the probability with which an attack takes place, they consider edge probabilities expressing how likely a present attack succeeds. Furthermore, the authors of [21] augment Bayesian attack graphs with additional nodes and values representing defenses. This extended structure allows them to solve the multiobjective optimization problem of how to select optimal defenses. Even though this model is similar to ours, it does not cover interleaved attacks and defenses.

Yet another approach that makes use of Bayesian networks for security analysis was described by Sommestad et al. [28]. It transforms defense trees [3] (an extension of attack trees with defenses attached to leaf nodes) into extended influence diagrams [17] (an extension of Bayesian networks with conjunctive and disjunctive nodes as well as countermeasures). The relationships between the nodes are encoded in conditional probability tables assigned to each node. The authors state that with this setup, Bayesian inference can be used to derive values, however they do not provide detailed computation algorithms. Our paper specifies how the necessary computational steps could be performed.

Contrary to our design, none of the above approaches separate the logical structure (conjunctions and disjunctions) from the probabilistic structure. One advantage of our approach is that we are not transforming one model into another, but we are using them modularly. Merging the two methodologies is only implicitly done during fusion. Unlike our model, all related approaches assume a one-to-one correspondence between the nodes in the original graph and the Bayesian network. Since in our framework, the Bayesian network concerns only basic actions, its size is much smaller compared to the size of Bayesian networks used by the approaches described in this section.

7   Conclusion and Future Work

This paper proposes to combine the ADTree methodology with Bayesian networks in order to *evaluate probabilistic measures on attack–defense scenarios involving dependent actions*. The introduced approach improves upon the standard, bottom-up, computational routine for attack tree-based formalisms, which assumes that all actions involved in the model are independent. By lifting the independency assumption, we provide a pragmatic methodology for accurate probabilistic assessment of security scenarios modeled using attack trees or ADTrees.

In our framework, the Bayesian network *does not replace* the information represented by the structure of an ADTree, but complements it with *additional probabilistic dependencies* between attack steps, which cannot be depicted using AND-OR relations. Keeping the two models separated allows us to take advantage of the strengths of both formalisms. The propositional encoding of ADTrees is used to identify configurations which represent attacks. Bayesian networks together with the fusion algorithm and techniques based on semiring valuation algebras provide ways to improve the efficiency of probabilistic computations.

To support modeling and quantitative analysis of security using the ADTree methodology, a free software tool, called ADTool [11], has recently been developed. We are currently extending the functionality of ADTool by interfacing it with Nenok, so that it can handle the framework introduced in this paper. Since

Nenok implements generic algorithms for efficient processing of semiring-based computations, the extended tool will support efficient, automated probabilistic analysis of real-world, possibly large-scale, attack–defense scenarios.

Employing fusion implies that time and space complexity are bounded by a structural parameter of the problem rather than by the total number of variables involved. It thus cannot be predicted in general how well fusion can cope with large problems involving many variables. It all depends on whether a small tree width (or good elimination sequence) can be found by some heuristic. Prediction of the tree width is possible for specific families of graphs [4]. It is one of our future research directions to investigate whether combination of an ADTree with a Bayesian network, both produced by human security experts, would satisfy the definition of one such family.

The algorithmic technique based on semiring valuations that we have used in this paper also works in a broader context. From an algebraic perspective, the combination of indicator functions and probabilities is possible because the Boolean semiring for indicator functions is a sub-algebra of both semirings used for expressing probabilities, i.e., the arithmetic and product t-norm semiring. Consequently, we may directly apply the same construction to other semiring valuations under the additional condition that the corresponding semiring takes the Boolean semiring as sub-algebra. The large family of t-norm semirings [22] are important candidates used in possibility and fuzzy set theory [29].

Acknowledgments. We would like to thank Sjouke Mauw, Pieter Hartel, Jan-Willem Bullée, Lorena Montoya Morales, and the anonymous reviewers for their valuable comments that helped us to improve the paper. The research leading to these results has received funding from the European Union Seventh Framework Programme under grant agreement number 318003 (TRESPASS) and from the Fonds National de la Recherche Luxembourg under grants PHD-09-167 and C13/IS/5809105.

References

1. Arnborg, S., Corneil, D., Proskurowski, A.: Complexity of Finding Embeddings in a k-Tree. SIAM J. of Algebraic and Discrete Methods 8, 277–284 (1987)
2. Bagnato, A., Kordy, B., Meland, P.H., Schweitzer, P.: Attribute Decoration of Attack–Defense Trees. IJSSE 3(2), 1–35 (2012)
3. Bistarelli, S., Fioravanti, F., Peretti, P.: Defense Trees for Economic Evaluation of Security Investments. In: ARES, pp. 416–423. IEEE Computer Society (2006)
4. Bodlaender, H.L.: A Partial K-arboretum of Graphs with Bounded Treewidth. Theoretical Computer Science 209(1-2), 1–45 (1998)
5. Dechter, R.: Bucket Elimination: A Unifying Framework for Reasoning. Artif. Intell. 113, 41–85 (1999)
6. Dechter, R.: Constraint Processing. Morgan Kaufmann (2003)
7. Frigault, M., Wang, L.: Measuring Network Security Using Bayesian Network-Based Attack Graphs. In: COMPSAC, pp. 698–703 (2008)
8. van Harmelen, F., van Harmelen, F., Lifschitz, V., Porter, B.: Handbook of Knowledge Representation. Elsevier Science, San Diego (2007)

9. Kohlas, J.: Information Algebras: Generic Structures for Inference. Springer (2003)
10. Kohlas, J., Wilson, N.: Semiring induced Valuation Algebras: Exact and Approximate Local Computation algorithms. Artif. Intell. 172(11), 1360–1399 (2008)
11. Kordy, B., Kordy, P., Mauw, S., Schweitzer, P.: ADTool: Security Analysis with Attack–Defense Trees. In: Joshi, K., Siegle, M., Stoelinga, M., D'Argenio, P.R. (eds.) QEST 2013. LNCS, vol. 8054, pp. 173–176. Springer, Heidelberg (2013)
12. Kordy, B., Mauw, S., Radomirović, S., Schweitzer, P.: Foundations of Attack–Defense Trees. In: Degano, P., Etalle, S., Guttman, J. (eds.) FAST 2010. LNCS, vol. 6561, pp. 80–95. Springer, Heidelberg (2011)
13. Kordy, B., Mauw, S., Radomirović, S., Schweitzer, P.: Attack–Defense Trees. Journal of Logic and Computation 24(1), 55–87 (2014)
14. Kordy, B., Mauw, S., Schweitzer, P.: Quantitative Questions on Attack–Defense Trees. In: Kwon, T., Lee, M.-K., Kwon, D. (eds.) ICISC 2012. LNCS, vol. 7839, pp. 49–64. Springer, Heidelberg (2013)
15. Kordy, B., Piètre-Cambacédès, L., Schweitzer, P.: DAG-Based Attack and Defense Modeling: Don't Miss the Forest for the Attack Trees. CoRR 1303.7397 (2013), http://arxiv.org/abs/1303.7397 (under submission)
16. Kordy, B., Pouly, M., Schweitzer, P.: Computational Aspects of Attack–Defense Trees. In: Bouvry, P., Kłopotek, M.A., Leprévost, F., Marciniak, M., Mykowiecka, A., Rybiński, H. (eds.) SIIS 2011. LNCS, vol. 7053, pp. 103–116. Springer, Heidelberg (2012)
17. Lagerström, R., Johnson, P., Närman, P.: Extended Influence Diagram Generation. In: Jardim-Gonçalves, R., Müller, J.P., Mertins, K., Zelm, M. (eds.) IESA, pp. 599–602. Springer (2007)
18. Mauw, S., Oostdijk, M.: Foundations of Attack Trees. In: Won, D.H., Kim, S. (eds.) ICISC 2005. LNCS, vol. 3935, pp. 186–198. Springer, Heidelberg (2006)
19. Mell, P., Scarfone, K., Romanosky, S.: A Complete Guide to the Common Vulnerability Scoring System Version 2.0 (2007), http://www.first.org/cvss/cvss-guide.html
20. Pearl, J.: Probabilistic Reasoning in Intelligent Systems: Networks of Plausible Inference. Morgan Kaufmann (1988)
21. Poolsappasit, N., Dewri, R., Ray, I.: Dynamic Security Risk Management Using Bayesian Attack Graphs. IEEE Trans. Dep. Sec. Comp. 9(1), 61–74 (2012)
22. Pouly, M., Kohlas, J.: Generic Inference - A Unifying Theory for Automated Reasoning. John Wiley & Sons, Inc. (2011)
23. Pouly, M.: NENOK - A Software Architecture for Generic Inference. Int. J. on Artif. Intel. Tools 19, 65–99 (2010)
24. Qin, X., Lee, W.: Attack plan recognition and prediction using causal networks. In: ACSAC, pp. 370–379 (2004)
25. Robertson, N., Seymour, P.: Graph Minors I: Excluding a Forest. J. Comb. Theory, Ser. B 35(1), 39–61 (1983)
26. Schneier, B.: Attack Trees. Dr. Dobb's Journal of Software Tools 24(12), 21–29 (1999)
27. Shenoy, P.: Valuation-Based Systems: A Framework for Managing Uncertainty in Expert Systems. In: Zadeh, L., Kacprzyk, J. (eds.) Fuzzy Logic for the Management of Uncertainty, pp. 83–104. John Wiley & Sons, Inc. (1992)
28. Sommestad, T., Ekstedt, M., Nordström, L.: Modeling security of power communication systems using defense graphs and influence diagrams. IEEE Trans. Pow. Del. 24(4), 1801–1808 (2009)
29. Zadeh, L.: Fuzzy sets as a basis for a theory of possibility. Fuzzy Sets and Systems 1, 3–28 (1978)

A Hybrid Analysis
for Security Protocols with State*

John D. Ramsdell, Daniel J. Dougherty,
Joshua D. Guttman, and Paul D. Rowe

The MITRE Corporation and Worcester Polytechnic Institute
{guttman,prowe,ramsdell}@mitre.org, {dd,guttman}@wpi.edu

Abstract. Cryptographic protocols rely on message-passing to coordinate activity among principals. Many richly developed tools, based on well-understood foundations, are available for the design and analysis of pure message-passing protocols. However, in many protocols, a principal uses non-local, mutable state to coordinate its local sessions. Cross-session state poses difficulties for protocol analysis tools.

We provide a framework for modeling stateful protocols, and a hybrid analysis method. We leverage theorem-proving—specifically, PVS—for reasoning about computations over state. An "enrich-by-need" approach—embodied by CPSA—focuses on the message-passing part. The Envelope Protocol, due to Mark Ryan furnishes a case study.

Protocol analysis is largely about message-passing in a model in which every message transmitted is made available to the adversary. The adversary can deliver the messages transmitted by the regular (i.e. compliant) principals, if desired, or not. The adversary can also retain them indefinitely, so that in the future he can deliver them, or messages built from them, repeatedly.

However, some protocols also interact with long-term state. For instance, the Automated Teller Machine protocols interact with the long-term state stored in banks' account databases. Protocol actions are constrained by that long-term state; for instance, an ATM machine will be told not to dispense cash to a customer whose account has insufficient funds. Protocol actions cause updates to long-term state; for instance, a successful withdrawal reduces the funds in the customer's account. State-manipulating protocols are important to electronic finance and commerce. They are also important in trusted computing, i.e. in systems using Trusted Platform Modules for attestation and secrecy. Indeed, as software interacts with real-world resources in interoperable ways, cryptographic protocols that manipulate long-term state will be increasingly central.

Long-term state is fundamentally different from message passing. The adversary can always choose to redeliver an old message. But he cannot choose to redeliver an old state; for instance, the adversary in an ATM network cannot choose to replay a withdrawal, applying it to a state in which he has sufficient

* This work partially supported by the US National Security Agency, and partially supported by the National Science Foundation under grant CNS-1116557.

E. Albert and E. Sekerinski (Eds.): IFM 2014, LNCS 8739, pp. 272–287, 2014.

funds, in case he no longer does. Regular principals maintain long-term state across protocol executions in order to constrain subsequent executions, and ensure that future runs will behave differently from past runs.

The Cryptographic Protocol Shapes Analyzer [24] (CPSA) is our program for automatically characterizing the possible executions of a protocol compatible with a specified partial execution. It is grounded in strand space theory. There exists a mathematically rigorous theory [18] that backs up the implementation of CPSA in Haskell, and proves the algorithm produces characterizations that are complete, and that the algorithm enumerates these characterizations.

Part of state manipulation can be encoded by message-passing. In this "state-passing style," reception of a message bearing the state represents reading from the state, and transmission of an updated state as a message represents writing to the state. These conventions help CPSA analyze protocols with state. If a protocol interacts with the state, we add state-bearing receive/transmit event pairs to its roles, and CPSA attempts to find paths through state space as it generates executions. However, CPSA constructs some executions which are in fact not possible. In these executions, a state-bearing message is transmitted from one node and then received by two different state-receiving nodes.

CPSA does not recognize that this is not possible in a state-history, and thus provides only an approximate analysis. Showing the correctness of the protocol requires a more refined analysis.

Our contribution. We apply CPSA to a system that relies on state, coupling CPSA with the Prototype Verification System [21] (PVS) proof assistant.

We specified a version of strand space theory in PVS. On top of this theory, we encoded the result of a CPSA analysis run as a formula in the PVS logic. This formula is justified by the CPSA completeness result [23]. We then use this formula as an axiom in PVS. Proofs using this axiom may imply the existence of additional message transmission/receptions, leading to an enriched CPSA analysis. In this way the theorem-proving and execution-finding analysis activities cooperate, over the common semantic foundation of strand space theory. Hence, the combination is semantically sound.

Outline of the Analysis. Our paradigm is CPSA's enrich-by-need approach [15]. That is, we ask: What kinds of executions are possible, assuming that a particular pattern of events has occurred? To verify authentication properties, we observe that all executions contain certain required events. To verify confidentiality properties, we consider patterns that include a disclosure, and observing that no executions are possible.

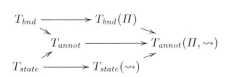

Fig. 1. Theory Inclusions

Our method involves a conversation (so to speak) between CPSA and PVS. The main steps are:

1. Within PVS we define theories (i) T_{bnd} of strand spaces and protocol executions ("bundles") and (ii) T_{state} of transition relations and their state

histories (see Fig. 1). T_{annot} is their union, a theory of protocol executions where some protocol steps are annotated with a state transition. Augmenting T_{bnd} with information about a protocol Π produces $T_{bnd}(\Pi)$. Augmenting T_{state} with information about a particular transition relation $\rightsquigarrow$ produces $T_{state}(\rightsquigarrow)$. The union of T_{annot}, $T_{bnd}(\Pi)$, and $T_{state}(\rightsquigarrow)$ is $T_{annot}(\Pi, \rightsquigarrow)$. Our PVS theories are in fact somewhat coarser than this.

2. Within the state transition theory $T_{state}(\rightsquigarrow)$, we prove lemmas in PVS such as Lemma 1 below. Some of their consequences in the annotated protocol theory $T_{annot}(\Pi, \rightsquigarrow)$ use only the limited vocabulary of $T_{bnd}(\Pi)$; we call them *bridge lemmas*. Lemma 3 is a bridge lemma. They bring information back from the state world to the protocol world.

3. Independently, CPSA analyzes the protocols, with state-manipulation modeled as message-passing, but without any special knowledge about state transition histories. A sentence, called a *shape analysis sentence* [22,15], summarizes its results in a sentence in the language of $T_{bnd}(\Pi)$. A shape analysis sentence, such as Lemma 2, is used as an axiom in proofs within PVS.

4. Using bridge lemmas and state analysis sentences jointly, we infer conclusions about protocol runs in $T_{bnd}(\Pi)$. If we prove a contradiction, that shows that the situation given to CPSA cannot in fact occur. Otherwise, we may prove that additional message transmissions and receptions occurred, as in Thm. 4.

5. We incorporate these additional nodes into a new CPSA starting point, and allow CPSA to draw conclusions. Additional round trips are possible.

1   The Envelope Protocol

The proof of an important security goal of the Envelope Protocol [2] was the focus of most of our effort. The protocol allows someone to package a secret such that another party can either reveal the secret or prove the secret never was and never will be revealed.

Protocol Motivation. The plight of a teenager motivates the protocol. The teenager is going out for the night, and her parents want to know her destination in case of emergency. Chafing at the loss of privacy, she agrees to the following protocol. Before leaving for the night, she writes her destination on a piece of paper and seals the note in an envelope. Upon her return, the parents can prove the secret was never revealed by returning the envelope unopened. Alternatively, they can open the envelope to learn her destination.

The parents would like to learn their daughter's destination while still pretending that they have respected her privacy. The parents are thus the adversary. The goal of the protocol is to prevent this deception.

Necessity of Long-Term State. The long-term state is the envelope. Once the envelope is torn open, the adversary no longer has access to a state in which the envelope is intact. A protocol based only on message passing is insufficient, because the ability of the adversary monotonically increases. At the beginning of the protocol the adversary can either return the envelope or tear it. In a purely message-based protocol the adversary will never lose these abilities.

Cryptographic Version. The cryptographic version of this protocol uses a TPM to achieve the security goal. Here we restrict our attention to a subset of the TPM's functionality. In particular we model the TPM as having a state consisting of a single Platform Configuration Register (PCR) and only responding to five commands. A `boot` command sets the PCR to a known value. The `extend` command takes a piece of data, d, and replaces the current value val of the PCR with the hash of d and val, i.e. $\#(d, val)$. In fact, the form of `extend` that we model, which is an `extend` within an encrypted session, also protects against replay. These are the only commands that alter the value in a PCR.

The TPM provides other services that do not alter the PCR. The `quote` command reports the value contained in the PCR and is signed in a way as to ensure its authenticity. The `create key` command causes the TPM can create an asymmetric key pair where the private part remains shielded within the TPM. However, it can only be used for decryption when the PCR has a specific value. The `decrypt` command causes the TPM to decrypt a message using this shielded private key, but only if the value in the PCR matches the constraint of the decryption key.

In what follows, Alice plays the role of the teenaged daughter packaging the secret. Alice calls the `extend` command with a fresh nonce n in an encrypted session. She uses the `create key` command constraining that new key to be used only when a specific value is present in the PCR. In particular, the constraining value cv she chooses is the following:

$$cv = \#(\text{``obtain''}, \#(n, val))$$

where val was the PCR value prior the extend command. She then encrypts her secret v with this newly created key.

Using typical message passing notation, Alice's part of the protocol might be represented as follows (where k' denotes the key created in the second line, and where we still ignore the replay protection):

$$
\begin{array}{rcl}
A \rightarrow \text{TPM} & : & \{\!|\,\text{``extend''}, n\,|\!\}_k \\
A \rightarrow \text{TPM} & : & \text{``create key''}, \#(\text{``obtain''}, \#(n, val)) \\
\text{TPM} \rightarrow A & : & k' \\
A \rightarrow \text{Parent} & : & \{\!|\,v\,|\!\}_{k'}
\end{array}
$$

The parent acts as the adversary in this protocol. We assume he can perform all the normal Dolev-Yao operations such as encrypting and decrypting messages when he has the relevant key, and interacting with honest protocol participants. Most importantly, the parent can use the TPM commands available in any order with any inputs he likes. Thus he can extend the PCR with the string `obtain` and use the key to decrypt the secret. Alternatively, he can extend the PCR with the string `refuse` and then generate a TPM quote as evidence the secret will never be exposed. The goal of the Envelope Protocol is to ensure that once Alice has prepared the TPM and encrypted her secret, the parent should not be able to both decrypt the secret and also generate a refusal quote, $\{\!|\,\text{``quote''}, \#(\text{``refuse''}, \#(n, val)), \{\!|\,v\,|\!\}_{k'}\,|\!\}_{aik}$.

Sorts: M, T, A, S, D, E
Subsorts: A < T, S < T, D < T, E < T
Operations: bt   : M   TPM boot
            ex   : T × M → M   TPM extend
            $(\cdot, \cdot)$: T × T → T   Pairing
            $\{\!|\cdot|\!\}_{(\cdot)}$: T × A → T   Asymmetric encryption
            $\{\!|\cdot|\!\}_{(\cdot)}$: T × S → T   Symmetric encryption
            $(\cdot)^{-1}$: A → A   Asymmetric key inverse
            $(\cdot)^{-1}$: S → S   Symmetric key inverse
            #   : T → S   Hashing
            a_i, b_i : A   Asymmetric key constants
            s_i : S   Symmetric key constants
            d_i : D   Data constants
            e_i : E   Text constants
            g_i : T   Tag constants
Equations: $a_i^{-1} = b_i \quad b_i^{-1} = a_i \ (i \in \mathbb{N})$
            $\forall k : A. (k^{-1})^{-1} = k \quad \forall k : S. k^{-1} = k$

Fig. 2. Crypto Algebra with State Signature

A crucial fact about the PCR role in this protocol is the injective nature of the hashing, ensuring that for every x

$$\#(\text{``obtain''}, \#(n, val)) \quad \neq \quad \#(\text{``refuse''}, x) \tag{1}$$

2   The TPM Model

In this section we introduce our TPM state theory $T_{state}(\leadsto)$ focusing on representing the value of the PCR and how the TPM commands may change it.

Fig. 2 shows the signature of the order-sorted algebra used in this paper. Sort M is the sort of TPM machine states and sort T is the top sort of messages. Messages of sort A (asymmetric keys), sort S (symmetric keys), sort D (data), and sort E (text) are called *atoms*. Messages are atoms, tag constants, or constructed using encryption $\{\!|\cdot|\!\}_{(\cdot)}$, hashing $\#(\cdot)$, and pairing $(\cdot, \cdot)$, where the comma operation is right associative and parentheses are omitted when the context permits.

The algebra is the initial quotient term algebra over the signature. It is easy to show that each term t of the algebra is equal to a unique term t' with no occurrences of the inverse operation $(\cdot)^{-1}$; we choose this t' to be the canonical representative of t.

We use the function pcr to coerce TPM states, which are of sort M, to messages, specifically to symmetric keys of sort S:

$$pcr(\text{bt}) = s_0 \qquad pcr(\text{ex}(t, m)) = \#(t, pcr(m))$$

where constant s_0 is known to all. Modeling the injectivity of the hash function (cf. Equation 1), we postulate that the function pcr is injective.

The definition of the TPM transition relation $\leadsto$ is

$$
\begin{aligned}
m_0 \leadsto m_1 \quad &\text{iff} & m_1 &= \mathsf{bt} & &\text{(boot)}\\
&\text{or } \exists t : \top. \; m_1 &= \mathsf{ex}(t, m_0) & &\text{(extend)}\\
&\text{or} & m_0 &= m_1 & &\text{(quote, decrypt)}
\end{aligned}
$$

The `create key` command does not interact with the state.

In this framework we prove a crucial property of all executions which we express in terms of the notion of a state *having* a message. A state *has* a message if an extend operation with it is part of the state. For example, $\mathsf{ex}(\text{"obtain"}, \mathsf{ex}(v, \mathsf{bt}))$ has "obtain" and v, but it does not have "refuse".

An infinite sequence of states π is a *path* if $\pi(0) = \mathsf{bt}$ and $\forall i \in \mathbb{N}. (\pi(i), \pi(i+1)) \in \leadsto$. Paths in this TPM model have several useful properties. For example, if a previous state is not a subterm of a state, there must have been an intervening boot. Also, if a state has a message, and a previous state is a boot state, there must have been an intervening transition that extends with the message. These two properties can be combined into the property used by the proof of the Envelope Protocol security goal: if a previous state is not a subterm of a state that has a message, there must have been an intervening transition that extends with the message. Lemma 1 formalizes this property in our state theory $T_{state}(\leadsto)$, and we proved it using PVS.

Lemma 1 (Prefix Boot Extend)

$$
\begin{aligned}
\forall \pi \in path, t : \top, i, k \in \mathbb{N}. \; &i \le k \wedge \pi(k) \text{ has } t\\
&\supset subterm(\pi(i), \pi(k))\\
&\quad \vee \exists j \in \mathbb{N}. \; i \le j < k \wedge \pi(j+1) = \mathsf{ex}(t, \pi(j))
\end{aligned}
$$

3 Strand Spaces

This section introduces our strand space theory of the envelope protocol, $T_{bnd}(\Pi)$. In strand space theory [25], a strand represents the local behavior of a principal in a single session. The *trace* of a strand is a linearly ordered sequence of events $e_0 \Rightarrow \cdots \Rightarrow e_{n-1}$, and an *event* is either a message transmission $+t$ or a reception $-t$, where t has sort $\top$. A *strand space* Θ is a map from a set of strands to a set of traces. In the PVS theory of strand spaces, the set of strands is a prefix of the natural numbers, so a strand space is a finite sequence of traces.

In a strand space, a node identifies an event. The *nodes* of strand space Θ are $\{(s, i) \mid s \in Dom(\Theta), 0 \le i < |\Theta(s)|\}$, and the event at a node is $evt_\Theta(s, i) = \Theta(s)(i)$.

A message t_0 is *carried by* t_1, written $t_0 \sqsubseteq t_1$ if t_0 can be extracted from a reception of t_1, assuming the necessary keys are available. In other words, $\sqsubseteq$ is the smallest reflexive, transitive relation such that $t_0 \sqsubseteq t_0$, $t_0 \sqsubseteq (t_0, t_1)$, $t_1 \sqsubseteq (t_0, t_1)$, and $t_0 \sqsubseteq \{\!|t_0|\!\}_{t_1}$. A message *originates* in trace c at index i if it is carried by $c(i)$, $c(i)$ is a transmission, and it is not carried by any event earlier in the trace. A message t is *non-originating* in a strand space Θ, written $non(\Theta, t)$, if it originates on no strand. A message t *uniquely originates* in a strand space Θ at node n, written $uniq(\Theta, t, n)$, if it originates in the trace of exactly one strand s at index i, and $n = (s, i)$.

The model of execution is a bundle. The pair $\Upsilon = (\Theta, \rightarrow)$ is a *bundle* if it defines a finite directed acyclic graph, where the vertices are the nodes of Θ, and an edge represents communication ($\rightarrow$) or strand succession ($\Rightarrow$) in Θ. For communication, if $n_0 \rightarrow n_1$, then there is a message t such that $evt_\Theta(n_0) = +t$ and $evt_\Theta(n_1) = -t$. For each reception node n_1, there is a unique transmission node n_0 with $n_0 \rightarrow n_1$. We use $\prec$ to denote the causal ordering of nodes in a bundle: the transitive closure of $\rightarrow \cup \Rightarrow$. The strand space associated with a bundle Υ will be denoted Θ_Υ unless the association is clear from the context.

When a bundle is a run of a protocol, the behavior of each strand is constrained by a role. Adversarial strands are constrained by roles as are non-adversarial strands. A *protocol* is a set of roles, and a *role* is a set of traces. A trace c is an *instance* of role r if c is a prefix of some member of r. More precisely, for protocol P, we say that bundle $\Upsilon = (\Theta, \rightarrow)$ is a *run of protocol* P if there exists a role assignment $ra \in Dom(\Theta) \rightarrow P$ such that for all $s \in Dom(\Theta)$, $\Theta(s)$ is an instance of $ra(s)$. In what follows, we fix the protocol P and only consider bundles that are runs of P.

The roles that constrain adversarial behavior are defined by the functions in Figure 3. The adversary can execute all instances of these patterns. For the encryption related roles, k:A|S asserts that k is either a symmetric or asymmetric key. For the create role, t : A|S|D|E asserts that t is an atom.

$$create(t : \mathsf{A|S|D|E}) = +t \qquad tag_i = +\mathsf{g}_i$$
$$pair(t_0 : \top, t_1 : \top) = -t_0 \Rightarrow -t_1 \Rightarrow +(t_0, t_1)$$
$$sep(t_0 : \top, t_1 : \top) = -(t_0, t_1) \Rightarrow +t_0 \Rightarrow +t_1$$
$$enc(t : \top, k : \mathsf{A|S}) = -t \Rightarrow -k \Rightarrow +\{\!|t|\!\}_k$$
$$dec(t : \top, k : \mathsf{A|S}) = -\{\!|t|\!\}_k \Rightarrow -k^{-1} \Rightarrow +t$$
$$hash(t : \top) = -t \Rightarrow +\#t$$

Fig. 3. Adversary Traces

Atoms, characteristically, are what the adversary can create out of thin air (modulo origination assumptions).

There is a role for each TPM operation. We represent them using a *state-passing style*. The state-passing style allows CPSA to do draw conclusions about where states could come from. Each role receives a message encoding the state at the time it occurs. It transmits a message encoding the state after any state change it causes. We do the encoding using a special tag g_0 and an encryption. For a transition $m_0 \rightsquigarrow m_1$, the role contains

$$\cdots \Rightarrow -\{\!|\, \mathsf{g}_0, pcr(m_0)|\!\}_{\#k} \Rightarrow +\{\!|\, \mathsf{g}_0, pcr(m_1)|\!\}_{\#k} \Rightarrow \cdots .$$

Here k is an uncompromised symmetric key used only in TPM operations. The states are encoded as encryptions using the hash $\#k$ of k. Tag g_0 is included to ensure that a state-bearing message is never confused with any other protocol message. State-passing style is less restrictive than actual state histories, since a state-bearing message may be received many times, even if it is sent only once.

Using these receive-transmit pairs of state-bearing messages the TPM roles are represented in Fig. 4, where tag g_1 is obtain and tag g_2 is refuse. In the *extend* role, we now show the two initial messages that provide replay prevention; the TPM supplies a fresh nonce as a session ID that must appear with the value to

$$boot(k : \mathsf{S}, p : \mathsf{T}) =$$
$$- \mathsf{g}_3 \Rightarrow -\{\!|\,\mathsf{g}_0, p\,|\!\}_{\#k} \Rightarrow +\{\!|\,\mathsf{g}_0, \mathsf{s}_0\,|\!\}_{\#k}$$

$$extend(sid : \mathsf{D}, tpmk : \mathsf{A}, esk, k : \mathsf{S}, p, t : \mathsf{T}) =$$
$$-(\mathsf{g}_4, tpmk, \{\!|\,esk\,|\!\}_{tpmk}) \Rightarrow +(\mathsf{g}_4, sid) \Rightarrow -\{\!|\,\mathsf{g}_5, t, sid\,|\!\}_{esk}$$
$$\Rightarrow -\{\!|\,\mathsf{g}_0, p\,|\!\}_{\#k} \Rightarrow +\{\!|\,\mathsf{g}_0, \#(t, p)\,|\!\}_{\#k}$$

$$quote(k : \mathsf{S}, aik : \mathsf{A}, p, n : \mathsf{T}) =$$
$$-(\mathsf{g}_6, n) \Rightarrow -\{\!|\,\mathsf{g}_0, p\,|\!\}_{\#k} \Rightarrow +\{\!|\,\mathsf{g}_0, p\,|\!\}_{\#k} \Rightarrow +\{\!|\,\mathsf{g}_6, p, n\,|\!\}_{aik}$$

$$decrypt(m, t : \mathsf{T}, k', aik : \mathsf{A}, k : \mathsf{S}) =$$
$$-(\mathsf{g}_7, \{\!|\,m\,|\!\}_{k'}) \Rightarrow -\{\!|\,\mathsf{g}_8, k', p\,|\!\}_{aik} \Rightarrow$$
$$-\{\!|\,\mathsf{g}_0, p\,|\!\}_{\#k} \Rightarrow +\{\!|\,\mathsf{g}_0, p\,|\!\}_{\#k} \Rightarrow +m$$

$$createkey(k, aik : \mathsf{A}, t : \mathsf{T}) =$$
$$-(\mathsf{g}_9, t) \Rightarrow +\{\!|\,\mathsf{g}_8, k, t\,|\!\}_{aik}$$

g_0	state
g_1	obtain
g_2	refuse
g_3	boot
g_4	session
g_5	extend
g_6	quote
g_7	decrypt
g_8	created
g_9	create key

Fig. 4. State-Bearing Traces

be extended into the PCR. The *createkey* role does not interact with the state. It simply creates a key that will be constrained by the state in the boot role.

Alice's role, including the messages to prevent replays, is:

$$alice(sid, v : \mathsf{D}, esk : \mathsf{S}, k, tpmk, aik : \mathsf{A}, n : \mathsf{E}, p : \mathsf{T}) =$$
$$+(\mathsf{g}_4, tpmk, \{\!|\,esk\,|\!\}_{tpmk}) \Rightarrow -(\mathsf{g}_4, sid)$$
$$\Rightarrow +\{\!|\,\mathsf{g}_5, n, sid\,|\!\}_{esk} \Rightarrow +(\mathsf{g}_9, \#(\mathsf{g}_1, \#(n, p)))$$
$$\Rightarrow -\{\!|\,\mathsf{g}_8, \#(\mathsf{g}_1, \#(n, p))\,|\!\}_{aik} \Rightarrow +\{\!|\,v\,|\!\}_k$$

The parameters *sid* and *tpmk* help prevent replays. To make formulas more comprehensible, we omit them.

4   CPSA

This section discusses how we use our analysis tool CPSA to infer results in the theory $T_{bnd}(\Pi)$. CPSA carries out enrich-by-need analysis, and characterizes the set of bundles consistent with a partial description of a bundle.

These partial descriptions are called *skeletons*. CPSA takes as input an initial skeleton $\mathbb{A}_0$, and when it terminates it outputs a set of more descriptive skeletons $\{\mathbb{B}_i\}_{i \in I}$. They have the property that any bundle containing the structure in the initial skeleton $\mathbb{A}_0$ also contains all the structure in one of the output skeletons $\mathbb{B}_i$. In particular, it infers all of the non-adversarial behavior that must be present in any bundle satisfying the initial description. Of course for some initial skeletons $\mathbb{A}_0$, there may be no bundles that are consistent with them. In this case, CPSA outputs the empty set.

The security goal for the Envelope Protocol is that a run of Alice's role should ensure that the secret and the refusal certificate are not both available:

Security Goal 1. *Consider the following events:*

- *An instance of the Alice role runs to completion, with secret v and nonce n both freshly chosen;*
- *v is observed unencrypted;*
- *the refusal certificate $\{| \text{ "quote"}, \#(\text{"refuse"}, \#(n, val)), \{|v|\}_{k'} |\}_{aik}$ is observed unencrypted.*

These events, which we call jointly $\mathbb{A}_0$, are not all present in any execution.

We can feed CPSA an input skeleton $\mathbb{A}_0$ representing this undesirable situation.

We would hope CPSA could determine that no bundles are consistent with this input $\mathbb{A}_0$ and return the empty set. However, our technique of using state-bearing messages to represent the TPM state transitions underconstrains the set of possible state paths. For this reason, CPSA actually produces one skeleton in its output. This skeleton represents some activity that must have occured within the TPM in any bundle conforming to the initial skeleton. It contains an instance of the decrypt role (to explain the secret leaking), an instance of the quote role (to explain the creation of the refusal token), and several instances of the extend role (to explain how the TPM state evolved in order to allow the other two operations).

Fig. 5 displays the relevant portion of CPSA's output displaying only the state-bearing nodes of the extend strands inferred by CPSA. Notice that two of the extend strands branch off from the third strand. This is a state split in which a single state evolves in two distinct ways. The technique of using state-bearing messages is not sufficient to preclude this possibility.

CPSA's enrich-by-need approach is a form of model finding, rather than theorem proving. In order to use CPSA's results to our advantage we need to express its conclusions in the logical theory $T_{bnd}(\Pi)$. For that purpose we transform our skeletons into formulas in order-sorted logic and define what it means for a bundle to satisfy these formulas. The sorts are the message algebra sorts augmented with a sort Z for strands and sort N for nodes. The atomic formula $\mathsf{htin}(z, h, c)$ asserts that strand z has a length of at least h, and its trace is a prefix of trace c. The formula $n_0 \ll n_1$ asserts node n_0 precedes node n_1. The formula $\mathsf{non}(t)$ asserts that message t is non-originating, and $\mathsf{uniq}(t, n)$ asserts that message t uniquely originates at node n. Finally, the formula $\mathsf{sends}(n, t)$ asserts that the event at node n is a transmission of message t. The roles of the protocol serve as function symbols. A skeleton $\mathbb{A}$ is represented by the conjunction of all facts true in the skeleton.

We encode an entire CPSA analysis by first encoding the input skeleton $\mathbb{A}_0$ and the output skeletons $\{\mathbb{B}_i\}_{i \in I}$. The analysis is then encoded as an implication. A formula Φ_0 describing the input $\mathbb{A}_0$, is the hypothesis of the conditional. The disjunction of the formulas Ψ_i describing the outputs $\{\mathbb{B}_i\}_{i \in I}$ form the conclusion. When CPSA discovers that there are no bundles compatible with the initial skeleton, the conclusion is encoded as the empty disjunction, $\bot$.

The satisfaction relation is defined using the clauses in Fig. 6. It relates a bundle, a variable assignment, and a formula: $\Upsilon, \alpha \models \Phi$. A bundle Υ is described by a skeleton iff the skeleton's sentence Φ satisfies Υ, written $\Upsilon \models \Phi$.

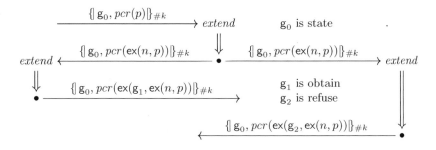

Fig. 5. State Splitting

$$\Upsilon, \alpha \models x = y \qquad \text{iff } \alpha(x) = \alpha(y);$$
$$\Upsilon, \alpha \models \mathsf{htin}(z, h, c) \quad \text{iff } |\Theta_\Upsilon(\alpha(z))| \geq \alpha(h) \text{ and}$$
$$\Theta_\Upsilon(\alpha(z)) \text{ is a prefix of } \alpha(c);$$
$$\Upsilon, \alpha \models n_0 \ll n_1 \qquad \text{iff } \alpha(n_0) \prec_\Upsilon \alpha(n_1);$$
$$\Upsilon, \alpha \models \mathsf{non}(t) \qquad \text{iff } non(\Theta_\Upsilon, \alpha(t));$$
$$\Upsilon, \alpha \models \mathsf{uniq}(t, n) \qquad \text{iff } uniq(\Theta_\Upsilon, \alpha(t), \alpha(n));$$
$$\Upsilon, \alpha \models \mathsf{sends}(n, t) \qquad \text{iff } evt_{\Theta_\Upsilon}(\alpha(n)) = +\alpha(t).$$

Fig. 6. Satisfaction

The formula Φ_0 that specifies the initial skeleton relevant to the Envelope Protocol security goal is

$$\begin{aligned}
&\mathsf{htin}(z, 4, alice(v, esk, k, aik, n, p)) \wedge \mathsf{sends}(n_1, v) \\
&\wedge \mathsf{sends}(n_2, \{\!| g_0, pcr(\mathsf{ex}(g_2, \mathsf{ex}(n, p))) |\!\}_{aik}) \\
&\wedge \mathsf{non}(aik) \wedge \mathsf{non}(esk) \\
&\wedge \mathsf{uniq}(n, (z, 1)) \wedge \mathsf{uniq}(v, (z, 4)),
\end{aligned} \tag{2}$$

where $v : \mathsf{D}, esk : \mathsf{S}, k, aik : \mathsf{A}, n : \mathsf{E}, p : \top, z : \mathsf{Z}, n_1, n_2 : \mathsf{N}$.

The output skeleton $\mathbb{B}_1$ is much larger and its formula Ψ_1 is correspondingly large. The relevant part of this formula representing the fragment in Fig. 5 is

$$\begin{aligned}
&\mathsf{htin}(z_1, 3, extend(esk, k, pcr(p), n)) \\
&\wedge \mathsf{htin}(z_2, 3, extend(esk, k, pcr(\mathsf{ex}(n, p)), g_1)) \\
&\wedge \mathsf{htin}(z_3, 3, extend(esk, k, pcr(\mathsf{ex}(n, p)), g_2)),
\end{aligned} \tag{3}$$

where $esk, k : \mathsf{S}, p : \top, n : \mathsf{E}, z_1, z_2, z_3 : \mathsf{Z}$. The full formula for $\mathbb{B}_1$ has more conjuncts.

Let the vector $\bar{x}$ contain the variables that appear free in Φ_0, and possibly also in Ψ_1, and let the vector $\bar{y}$ contain the variables that occur free in Ψ_1 only. Summarizing CPSA's analysis for the Envelope Protocol in $T_{bnd}(\Pi)$, we have:

Lemma 2. $\forall \bar{x}. (\Phi_0 \supset \exists \bar{y}. \Psi_1)$, where Φ_0, Ψ_1 are as in formulas 2–3.

However, unlike Lemma 1, this lemma was not derived within PVS. Rather, it is true if CPSA's analysis is correct. We import it into PVS as an axiom.

Lemma 2 is however something capable of direct proof within PVS as a theorem of $T_{bnd}(\Pi)$. Indeed, there is precedent for constructing proofs of this sort. Meier et al. [19] show how to instrument a different protocol analysis tool, called Scyther [7], so that each step it takes generates a lemma in the Isabelle proof system. Then, they use reusable results proved once within Isabelle to discharge these lemmas. Curiously, one of the main lemmas, the authentication test theorem in an earlier form, has already been established within PVS [17]. Thus, it appears possible, although a substantial undertaking, to transform CPSA from a central piece of our analysis infrastructure to a heuristic to guide derivations within PVS.

5   Reasoning about Messages and State

This section presents some details of the theory $T_{annot}(\Pi, \leadsto)$. We then show how the previous lemmas combine allowing us to conclude that the security goal of the Envelope Protcol is achieved.

In $T_{annot}(\Pi, \leadsto)$, the state transitions associated with a protocol are specified by annotating some events in a role of Π with a subset of the transition relation $\leadsto$. The reason for annotating events with a subset of the transition relation, rather than an element, will be explained at the end of this section. We use $\perp$ for an event that is not annotated, and $\uparrow a$ for an event that is annotated with a. The events that are annotated are the transmissions associated with receive-transmit pairs of state-bearing messages.

$$\cdots \Rightarrow -\{\!| \, g_0, pcr(m_0) |\!\}_{\#k} \Rightarrow +\{\!| \, g_0, pcr(m_1) |\!\}_{\#k} \Rightarrow \cdots$$
$$\perp \qquad\qquad \perp \qquad\qquad \uparrow\{(m_0, m_1)\} \cap \leadsto \qquad \perp$$

A node in a bundle inherits its annotation from its role. The set of nodes in Υ that are annotated is $anode(\Upsilon)$, and $anno(\Upsilon, n, a)$ asserts that node n in Υ is annotated with some $a \subseteq \leadsto$. In the Envelope Protocol, a node annotated by a TPM extend role cannot be an instance of any other role.

Our goal is to reason only with bundles that respect state semantics. A bundle Υ with a transition annotating role assignment is *compatible* [14, Def. 11] with transition relation $\leadsto$ if there exists $\ell \in \mathbb{N}$, $f \in anode(\Upsilon) \to \{0, 1, \ldots, \ell - 1\}$, and $\pi \in path$ such that

1. f is bijective;
2. $\forall n_0, n_1 \in anode(\Upsilon). n_0 \prec n_1 \iff f(n_0) < f(n_1)$;
3. $\forall n \in anode(\Upsilon), a \subseteq \leadsto$.
   $anno(\Upsilon, n, a) \supset (\pi(f(n)), \pi(f(n) + 1)) \in a$.

A bundle that satisfies $T_{annot}(\Pi, \leadsto)$ is a compatible bundle.

Because the function f is bijective, all annotated nodes in a compatible bundle are totally ordered. Looking back at Fig. 5, either the nodes in the leftmost strand precede the nodes in the rightmost strand or succeed them.

The compatible bundle assumption allows one to infer the existence of nodes that are not revealed by CPSA. In the case of the Envelope Protocol this is done

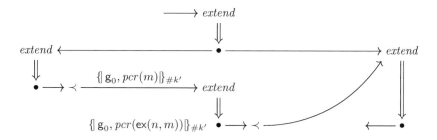

Fig. 7. Inferred Extend Strand

by importing the Prefix Boot Extend Lemma (Lemma 1) from $T_{state}(\leadsto)$ into the strand space world by proving the following lemma (stated here in plain English) within $T_{annot}(\Pi, \leadsto)$ using PVS. Its proof uses the full content of compatibility.

Lemma 3 (Bridge, informally). *Let Υ be a compatible bundle, containing two annotated nodes, $n_0 \prec n_1$, where n_1's state has a value t. Then either n_0's state is a subterm of n_1's state, or else there is an* extend *node between them that incorporates t.*

This Bridge Lemma implies there is another extend strand between the two strands that represent the state split. This theorem is also proved with PVS in $T_{annot}(\Pi, \leadsto)$; however, syntactically it is a sentence of the language of $T_{bnd}(\Pi)$. That is, $T_{annot}(\Pi, \leadsto)$ adds information to $T_{bnd}(\Pi)$, because $T_{annot}(\Pi, \leadsto)$'s models are only the compatible bundles. The theorem is the following.

Theorem 4 (Inferred Extend Strand)

$$\forall z_0, z_1 : \mathsf{Z}, t, t_0, t_1 : \top, m_0, m_1 : \mathsf{M}, esk_0, esk_1, k_0, k_1 : \mathsf{A}.$$
$$\mathsf{htin}(z_0, 2, extend(esk_0, k_0, pcr(m_0), t_0))$$
$$\wedge\ \mathsf{htin}(z_1, 2, extend(esk_1, k_1, pcr(m_1), t_1))$$
$$\wedge\ (z_0, 1) \ll (z_1, 0) \wedge m_1 \text{ has } t$$
$$\supset\ subterm(\mathsf{ex}(t_0, m_0), m_1)$$
$$\vee\ \exists z : \mathsf{Z}, m : \mathsf{M}, esk, k : \mathsf{A}.$$
$$\mathsf{htin}(z, 2, extend(esk, k, pcr(m), t))$$
$$\wedge\ (z_0, 1) \ll (z, 0) \wedge (z, 1) \ll (z_1, 0)$$

Theorem 4 implies that Fig. 5 has an additional *extend* strand, as shown in Fig. 7. Restarting CPSA with $\mathbb{A}_0$ enriched with all of this additional information, we learn that no such execution is possible. This justifies Security Goal 1.

Our Method. We have now completed an illustration of the hybrid method for analyzing a protocol with state. We took the following key steps.

1. We defined states and a transition relation representing a TPM fragment. We proved a key lemma (Lemma 1) in the resulting theory $T_{state}(\leadsto)$.

2. We defined the envelope protocol as a PVS theory $T_{bnd}(\Pi)$. We encoded the states as certain encrypted messages, and used state-passing to represent the actions of the TPM in protocol roles. The encoding function is an injective function g. We connect $\cdots - t_0 \Rightarrow +t_1 \cdots$, as a state-passing representation, with $T_{state}(\leadsto)$ by annotating the role with the annotation:

$$\{(m_0, m_1) \mid t_0 = g(m_0) \wedge t_1 = g(m_1)\} \cap \leadsto.$$

We prove bridge lemmas along the lines of Lemma 3.
3. Independently, we define Π in the CPSA input language, and query CPSA with a starting point $\mathbb{A}_0$ as in our security goal. We translate the results in the form of state analysis sentences such as Lemma 2, which we use within PVS as axioms.
4. From a state analysis sentence and bridge lemmas, we deduce conclusions about all compatible bundles of Π and $\leadsto$. Thm. 4 was an example. These theorems may already establish our security goals.
5. Alternatively, the conclusions about compatible bundles may give us an enriched starting point, which we can bring back into CPSA, as we did here to determine that Security Goal 1 is achieved, and $\mathbb{A}_0$ cannot appear in any compatible bundle.

We have also applied this method to several simple protocols besides the Envelope Protocol. The steps in applying the method are always the same. While the application of these ideas is routine, it is quite time consuming. A goal of future research is to automate much more of the method.

But why annotate events with subsets of the transition relation rather than elements of it? The *extend* role does not guarantee it receives a state-bearing message of the form $\{\! | \, g_0, pcr(m_0) |\!\}_{\#k}$. It says only that the incoming message has the form $\{\! | \, g_0, t_0 |\!\}_{\#k}$. We must eliminate strands in which t_0 is not in the range of the pcr function. That is why we use the annotation shown in Step 2.

A bundle in which a received state encoding message is not in the range of the pcr function will have a node annotated with the empty set. This bundle does not respect state semantics and is eliminated from consideration by the definition of compatibility.

6   Related Work and Conclusion

Related Work. The problem of reasoning about protocols and state has been an increasing focus over the past several years. Protocols using Trusted Platform Modules (TPMs) and other hardware security modules (HSMs) have provided one of the main motivations for this line of work.

A line of work was motivated by HSMs used in the banking industry [16,26]. This work identified the effects of persistent storage as complicating the security analysis of the devices. Much work explored the significance of this problem in the case of PKCS #11 style devices for key management [5,6,12]. These papers, while very informative, exploited specific characteristics of the HSM problem;

in particular, the most important mutable state concerns the *attributes* that determine the usage permitted for keys. These attributes should usually be handled in a monotonic way, so that once an attribute has been set, it will not be removed. This justifies using abstractions that are more typical of standard protocol analysis.

In the TPM-oriented line of work, an early example using an automata-based model was by Gürgens et al. [13]. It identified some protocol failures due to the weak binding between a TPM-resident key and an individual person. Datta et al.'s "A Logic of Secure Systems" [9] presents a dynamic logic in the style of PCL [8] that can be used to reason about programs that both manipulate memory and also transmit and receive cryptographically constructed messages. Because it has a very detailed model of execution, it appears to require a level of effort similar to (multithreaded) program verification, unlike the less demanding forms of protocol analysis.

Mödersheim's set-membership abstraction [20] works by identifying all data values (e.g. keys) that have the same properties; a change in properties for a given key K is represented by translating all facts true for K's old abstraction into new facts true of K's new abstraction. The reasoning is still based on monotonic methods (namely Horn clauses). Thus, it seems not to be a strategy for reasoning about TPM usage, for instance in the envelope protocol.

The paper [14] by one of us developed a theory for protocols (within strand spaces) as constrained by state transitions, and applied that theory to a fair exchange protocol. It introduced the key notion of *compatibility* between a protocol execution ("bundle") and a state history. In the current paper we will also rely on the same notion of compatibility, which was somewhat hidden in [14]. However, the current paper does not separate the protocol behavior from state history as sharply as did [14].

A group of papers by Ryan with Delaune, Kremer, and Steel [10,11], and with Arapinis and Ritter [3] aim broadly to adapt ProVerif for protocols that interact with long-term state. ProVerif [4,1] is a Horn-clause based protocol analyzer with a monotonic method: in its normal mode of usage, it tracks the messages that the adversary can obtain, and assumes that these will always remain available. Ryan et al. address the inherent non-monotonicity of adversary's capabilities by using a two-place predicate $att(u, m)$ meaning that the adversary may possess m at some time when the long-term state is u. In [3], the authors provide a compiler from a process algebra with state-manipulating operators to sets of Horn clauses using this primitive. In [11], the authors analyze protocols with specific syntactic properties that help ensure termination of the analysis. In particular, they bound the state values that may be stored in the TPMs. In this way, the authors verify two protocols using the TPM, including the envelope protocol.

One advantage of the current approach relative to the ProVerif approach is that it works within a single comprehensive framework, namely that of strand spaces. Proofs about state within PVS succeeded only when definitions and lemmas were properly refined, and all essential details represented. As a result, our confidence is high that our proofs about protocols have their intended meaning.

Conclusion. The proof of the Envelope Protocol security goal presented here shows a detailed example of our method for applying CPSA to systems that include a state component. CPSA was coupled with about 2400 lines of PVS specifications to produce a proof of a difficult security goal. The method is sound due to the use of the common foundation of strand space theory for all reasoning.

The approach could be improved in two main ways. First, the proofs within PVS are strenuous. We would like to develop a method in which—apart perhaps from a few key reusable lemmas in the state theory $T_{state}(\rightsquigarrow)$—the remainder of the reasoning concerning both state and protocol behavior occurs automatically in CPSA's automated, enrich-by-need manner. Second, there is some artificiality in the state-threading representation that we have used here. It requires the protocol description to make explicit the details of the full state, and to express each state change in a syntactic, template-based form. Moreover, the state information is also redundantly encoded in the annotations that appear in $T_{annot}(\Pi, \rightsquigarrow)$. Our earlier work [14] instead encapsulated all of the state information in a labeled transition relation. The protocol definitions contain only a type of "neutral node" which are neither transmissions nor receptions. These nodes are associated with the same labels as appear in labeled transitions. This allows us to define "compatibility," and to work with protocol and state definitions as independent modules. We intend also to explore this style of definition.

Acknowledgment. We are grateful to Ed Zieglar for discussions and support.

References

1. Abadi, M., Blanchet, B.: Analyzing security protocols with secrecy types and logic programs. Journal of the ACM 52(1), 102–146 (2005)
2. Ables, K., Ryan, M.D.: Escrowed data and the digital envelope. In: Acquisti, A., Smith, S.W., Sadeghi, A.-R. (eds.) TRUST 2010. LNCS, vol. 6101, pp. 246–256. Springer, Heidelberg (2010)
3. Arapinis, M., Ritter, E., Ryan, M.D.: Statverif: Verification of stateful processes. In: Computer Security Foundations Symposium (CSF), pp. 33–47. IEEE (2011)
4. Blanchet, B.: An efficient protocol verifier based on Prolog rules. In: 14th Computer Security Foundations Workshop, pp. 82–96. IEEE CS Press (June 2001)
5. Cortier, V., Keighren, G., Steel, G.: Automatic analysis of the security of XOR-based key management schemes. In: Grumberg, O., Huth, M. (eds.) TACAS 2007. LNCS, vol. 4424, pp. 538–552. Springer, Heidelberg (2007)
6. Cortier, V., Steel, G.: A generic security API for symmetric key management on cryptographic devices. In: Backes, M., Ning, P. (eds.) ESORICS 2009. LNCS, vol. 5789, pp. 605–620. Springer, Heidelberg (2009)
7. Cremers, C., Mauw, S.: Operational semantics and verification of security protocols. Springer (2012)
8. Datta, A., Derek, A., Mitchell, J.C., Pavlovic, D.: A derivation system and compositional logic for security protocols. Journal of Computer Security 13(3), 423–482 (2005)
9. Datta, A., Franklin, J., Garg, D., Kaynar, D.: A logic of secure systems and its application to trusted computing. In: 30th IEEE Symposium on Security and Privacy, pp. 221–236. IEEE (2009)

10. Delaune, S., Kremer, S., Ryan, M.D., Steel, G.: A formal analysis of authentication in the TPM. In: Degano, P., Etalle, S., Guttman, J. (eds.) FAST 2010. LNCS, vol. 6561, pp. 111–125. Springer, Heidelberg (2011)
11. Delaune, S., Kremer, S., Ryan, M.D., Steel, G.: Formal analysis of protocols based on TPM state registers. In: IEEE Symposium on Computer Security Foundations. IEEE CS Press (June 2011)
12. Fröschle, S., Sommer, N.: Reasoning with past to prove PKCS#11 keys secure. In: Degano, P., Etalle, S., Guttman, J. (eds.) FAST 2010. LNCS, vol. 6561, pp. 96–110. Springer, Heidelberg (2011)
13. Gürgens, S., Rudolph, C., Scheuermann, D., Atts, M., Plaga, R.: Security evaluation of scenarios based on the TCG's TPM specification. In: Biskup, J., López, J. (eds.) ESORICS 2007. LNCS, vol. 4734, pp. 438–453. Springer, Heidelberg (2007)
14. Guttman, J.D.: State and progress in strand spaces: Proving fair exchange. Journal of Automated Reasoning 48(2), 159–195 (2012)
15. Guttman, J.D.: Establishing and preserving protocol security goals. Journal of Computer Security (2014)
16. Herzog, J.: Applying protocol analysis to security device interfaces. IEEE Security & Privacy 4(4), 84–87 (2006)
17. Jacobs, B., Hasuo, I.: Semantics and logic for security protocols. Journal of Computer Security 17(6), 909–944 (2009)
18. Liskov, M.D., Rowe, P.D., Thayer, F.J.: Completeness of CPSA. Technical Report MTR110479, The MITRE Corporation (March 2011), http://www.mitre.org/publications/technical-papers/completeness-of-cpsa
19. Meier, S., Cremers, C., Basin, D.: Efficient construction of machine-checked symbolic protocol security proofs. Journal of Computer Security 21(1), 41–87 (2013)
20. Mödersheim, S.: Abstraction by set-membership: verifying security protocols and web services with databases. In: ACM Conference on Computer and Communications Security, pp. 351–360 (2010)
21. Owre, S., Rushby, J.M., Shankar, N.: PVS: A prototype verification system. In Deepak Kapur, editor, 11th International Conference on Automated Deduction (CADE). In: Kapur, D. (ed.) CADE 1992. LNCS, vol. 607, pp. 748–752. Springer, Heidelberg (1992), http://pvs.csl.sri.com
22. Ramsdell, J.D.: Deducing security goals from shape analysis sentences. The MITRE Corporation (April 2012), http://arxiv.org/abs/1204.0480
23. Ramsdell, J.D.: Proving security goals with shape analysis sentences. Technical Report MTR130488, The MITRE Corporation (September 2013), http://arxiv.org/abs/1403.3563
24. Ramsdell, J.D., Guttman, J.D.: CPSA: A cryptographic protocol shapes analyzer (2009), http://hackage.haskell.org/package/cpsa
25. Thayer, F.J., Herzog, J.C., Guttman, J.D.: Strand spaces: Proving security protocols correct. Journal of Computer Security 7(2/3), 191–230 (1999)
26. Youn, P., Adida, B., Bond, M., Clulow, J., Herzog, J., Lin, A., Rivest, R., Anderson, R.: Robbing the bank with a theorem prover. In: Security Protocols Workshop (2007), http://www.cl.cam.ac.uk/techreports/UCAM-CL-TR-644.pdf

Analysis and Transformation

Towards a Formal Semantics-Based Technique for Interprocedural Slicing*

Irina Măriuca Asăvoae[1], Mihail Asăvoae[1], and Adrián Riesco[2]

[1] VERIMAG/UJF, France
{mariuca.asavoae,mihail.asavoae}@imag.fr
[2] Universidad Complutense de Madrid, Spain
ariesco@fdi.ucm.es

Abstract. Interprocedural slicing is a technique applied on programs with procedures which relies on how the information is passed at procedure call/return sites. Such a technique computes program slices (i.e. program fragments restricted w.r.t. a given criterion). The existing approaches to interprocedural slicing exploit the particularities of the underlying language semantics in order to compute program slices. In this paper we propose a generic technique for interprocedural slicing. More specifically, our approach works with inferred particularities of a language semantics, given as a rewriting-logic specification, and computes program slices using a term slicing-based algorithm.

Keywords: slicing, semantics, Maude, debugging.

1 Introduction

Complex software systems are built in a modular fashion, where modularity is implemented with functions and modules, in declarative-style programming; with classes and interfaces, in object-oriented programming; or with other means of organizing the code. Besides their structural characteristics, the modules also carry semantic information. The modules could be parameterized by types and values (e.g. the generic classes of Java and C#, the template classes of C++, or the parameterized modules of Maude and OCaml) or could have specialized usability (e.g. abstract classes in object-oriented languages).

It is preferable, for efficiency reasons, that the modular characteristics of a system are preserved when new analysis techniques and tool support are developed. One possible solution to integrate both analysis and tool development is to use a formal executable framework such as rewriting logic [13]. For any given program (correctly constructed w.r.t. the language syntax), the formal executable semantics, given as a rewriting logic specification, provides the set of all the concrete executions, for all the possible input data. Furthermore, the notion of a concrete execution extends to an abstract execution—as an execution with an analysis

---

* This research has been partially supported by MICINN Spanish project *StrongSoft* (TIN2012-39391-C04-04).

E. Albert and E. Sekerinski (Eds.): IFM 2014, LNCS 8739, pp. 291–306, 2014.

tool—and we have the set of concrete executions as the basis of any abstraction (and implicitly abstract execution) of a program. One particular abstraction is program slicing [26], which computes safe program fragments (also called slices) w.r.t. a specified set of variables. A complex variant of program slicing, called interprocedural slicing, preserves the modularity of the underlying program and exploits how the program data is passed between these modules.

Interprocedural slicing is the slicing method applied on programs with procedures where the slice is computed for the entire program, taking into account the procedure calls/returns. The main problem that arises in interprocedural slicing is related to the fact that the procedure calls/returns may be analyzed with a too coarse abstraction. Namely, the abstraction relies only on the call graph without taking into account the context changes (i.e., the instantiation of the local variables during a procedure execution) occurring during a procedure call/return. Since we develop a *generic*, formal semantics-based slicing method, we assume that we do not know which language constructs produce these context changes. Hence, we include in our slicing method a phase for inferring these constructs, denoted in the following as *scope-update constructs*.

Now, our proposed technique for interprocedural slicing has two phases which could be described as follows: Given a programming language semantics $\mathcal{S}$, in the first phase we extract scope-update constructs $\mathfrak{c}$ from $\mathcal{S}$ and, in the second phase, we use these constructs for the interprocedural slicing of $\mathcal{S}$-programs (i.e., programs written in the language specified by $\mathcal{S}$ which, in fact, are well-formed terms in $\mathcal{S}$). In this paper we focus on the second phase of the interprocedural program slicing, meaning the term slicing-based algorithm. The first phase, (i.e. the extraction of the scope-update constructs) follows a similar meta-analysis of the language semantics as in [17], where side-effect constructs are extracted. We require $\mathcal{S}$ to be expressed as a rewriting logic theory [13], which is executable and benefits of tool support via the Maude system [3], an implementation of the rewriting logic framework. The technique to obtain the scope-update constructs is, in fact, a meta-analysis of the programming language. The interprocedural program slicing uses $\mathfrak{c}$ to collect and propagate abstract information according to the scope switches from $\mathfrak{c}$. This technique is concretised with an implementation into a generic semantics-based slicing tool developed in Maude.

For presentation purposes, we consider a WHILE language [10] with functions and local variable declarations (which introduce variable scoping); we call this extension WhileF. Then, in order to differentiate two variables based on their scopes, we need to identify scope-update constructs at the level of the semantics. Note that the meta-analysis for scope-updates used in the present work is slightly more complicated than the one for side-effects described in [17], because scope-updates usually work in pairs so now we need to analyze $\mathcal{S}$ targeting pairs of operators (for procedure call and return). Such pairs could be explicitly presented in the language semantics definitions (through different rewrite rules for call and return) or implicitly, as in this work (with an explicit rewrite rule for call and implicit return instruction).

Another interesting difference consists in the fact that the second program slicing step receives as input both scope-update and side-effect information, which implies heavy changes. In this case, it is necessary to address the representability of the derived scope-update constructs w.r.t. the interprocedural program slicing. Namely, a combined representation of scope-update and side-effect constructs could consist in terms representing generic skeletons for procedure summaries (a succinct representation of the procedure behavior w.r.t. its input variables).

The rest of the paper is organized as follows: Section 2 presents related work. Section 3 introduces the basic notions of program slicing and rewriting logic, used throughout the paper, while Section 4 describes the proposed program slicing as term slicing-based algorithm. Finally, Section 5 concludes and presents some lines of future work.

2   Related Work

Program slicing addresses a wide range of applications, from code parallelization [23] to program testing [8], debugging [21], and analysis [12,11]. Since our goal is to design and implement a semantics-based program analysis tool in a rewriting-logic environment, we relate our method to both interprocedural slicing in program analysis and in rewriting logic. With respect to the general problem of program slicing, we refer the reader to the comprehensive survey of slicing techniques, in [24].

The technique of program slicing was introduced in [26], and for a given program with procedures, it computes slices using a limited form of context information (i.e. before each procedure call). The approach resembles an on-demand procedure inlining, using a backward propagation mechanism (thus, producing backward slices). Our approach takes into consideration the context-update constructs (as extracted from the formal semantics) and produces forward slices (via term slicing on the term program). Moreover, the context-update constructs play the role of symbolic procedure summaries, as in [20,11,7,22]. A procedure summary is a compact representation of the procedure behavior, parameterized by its input values, which in our proposed framework is the context-update construct. The interprocedural slicing is explicit in [11,22] and implicit in [20,7], and sets the support for interprocedural program analyses.

The work in [20] uses a data-flow analysis to represent how the information is passed between procedure calls. It is applied on a restricted class of programs— restricted by a finite lattice of data values—, while the underlying program representation is a mix of control-flow and control-call graphs. In comparison, our approach considers richer context information (as in [11]), while working on a similar representation of a program (as a term). The work in [7] keeps the same working structures but addresses the main data limitation of [20]. As such, the procedure summaries are represented as sets of constraints on the input/output variables. The underlying interprocedural slicing algorithm of [7] is more refined than our approach (though not generic), just because of the richer representation of context information. We follow closely the work in [11], which introduces a new program representation for the interprocedural slicing. In comparison, our approach does not require the explicit context representation, but uses term matching to distinguish between different contexts.

In the rewriting logic environment, there are several approaches towards debugging [1], testing [16], and analysis [17]. The dynamic slicing technique in [1] works on execution traces of the Maude model checker. In comparison, we propose a static approach built around a formal semantics and with an emphasis on computing slices for programs and not for given traces (e.g. of model checker runs). The work in [16] presents an approach to generate test cases similar to the one presented here in the sense that both use the semantics of programming languages formally specified to extract specific information. In this case, the semantic rules are used to instantiate the state of the variables used by the given program by using narrowing; in this way, it is possible to compute the values of the variables required to traverse all the statements in the program, the so called coverage. The technique in the current paper follows our previous work on language-independent program slicing in rewriting logic environment [17]. Actually, the implementation of the current work is an extension of the slicing tool we developed in [17]. Both approaches share the methodology steps: (1) the initial meta-analysis of $\mathcal{S}$ and (2) the program analysis conducted over the $\mathcal{S}$-programs. More specifically, in [17] we use the classical WHILE language augmented with side-effect constructs (assignments and read/write statements) to exemplify (1) the inference of the set of side-effect language constructs in $\mathcal{S}$, and (2) the program slicing as term rewriting.

As a semantical framework, Maude has been used to specify the semantics of several languages, such as LOTOS [25], CCS [25], Java [6], or C [4]. These works describe a methodology to represent the semantics of programming languages in Maude, led to the *rewriting logic semantics project* [14] and to the development of the $\mathbb{K}$ [19] framework. We plan to use these semantics to perform program analysis in the future.

3   Preliminaries

Program slicing, as introduced in [26], is a program analysis technique which computes all the program statements that might affect the value of a variable v at a program point of interest, p. It is a common setting to consider p as the last instruction of a procedure or the entire program. Hence, without restricting the proposed methodology, here we consider slices of the entire program.

A classification of program slicing techniques identifies *intraprocedural* slicing when the method is applied on a procedure body and *interprocedural* slicing when the method is applied across procedure boundaries. The key element of a methodology for interprocedural slicing is the notion of context (i.e. the values of the function/procedure parameters). Next, we elaborate on how context-aware program slicing produces better program slices than a context-forgetful one.

Let us consider, in Fig. 1, the program from [11], written as an WhileF program term, upon which we present subtleties of interprocedural slicing. We start the slicing with the set of variables of interest {z}.

The first method, in [26], resembles an on-demand inlining of the necessary procedures. In the example in Fig. 1, the variable {z} is an argument of procedure Add call in Inc, hence, the sliced body of Add is included in the slice of Inc. Note that, when slicing the body of Add, z is replaced by a. Hence, the slicing of Add deems {a} and {b} as relevant. The return statement of procedure Inc is paired with the call to Inc, in the body of A so the variable {y} becomes relevant for the computed slice. When the algorithm traces the source of the variable y, it finds the second call to Add in the body of A (with the arguments x and y) and includes it in the program slice. When tracing the source of x and y, it leads to include the entire body of procedure Main (through the variables sum and i, which are used by the assignments and calls of Main). Using this method, the program slice w.r.t. the set of variables of interest - {z}, is the original program, as in Fig. 1. This particular slice is a safe over-approximation of a more precise one (which we present next) because the method relies on a transitive-closure—fixpoint computation style where all the variables of interest are collected at the level of each procedure body. As such, the body of procedure Add is included twice in the computed slice.

```
function Main (){         function A (x, y) {        function Inc (z) {
   sum := 0;                 Call Add (x, y);           Local i;
   Local i;                  Call Inc (y)               i := 1;
   i := 1;               }                              Call Add (z, i)
   while i < 11 do        function Add (a, b) {      }
      Call A (sum, i)         a := a + b
}                         }
```

Fig. 1. A WhileF program Px with procedures Main, A, Add, and Inc

The second approach in [11] exploits, for each procedure call, the available information w.r.t. the program variables passed as arguments (i.e. the existing context before the procedure call). Again, in the example in Fig. 1, the variable z is an argument of procedure Add. Hence, upon the return of Add, its body is included in the slice. However, because of the data dependencies between variables a and b (with a using an unmodified value of b) only the variable a is collected and further used in slicing. Next, upon the return statements of Add and then Inc, the call of Inc in A (with parameter y) is included in the slice. Note that the call to Add from A (with parameters x and y) is not included in the slice because it does not modify the context (i.e. the variables of interest at the call point in A). As such, the slicing algorithm collects only the second parameter of procedure A, and following the call to A in Main, it discovers i as the variable of interest (and not sum as it was the case of the previous method). Hence, the sliced A with only the second argument is included in the computed slice. Consequently, the variable sum from Main is left outside the slice. The result is presented in Fig. 2.

Any program analysis that computes an interprocedural slice works with the control-flow graph—which captures the program flow at the level of

```
function Main (){          function A (y) {          function Inc (z) {
  Local i;                   Call Inc (y)             Local i;
  i := 1;                  }                          i := 1;
  while i < 11 do          function Add (a,b) {       Call Add (z, i)
    Call A (i)               a := a + b             }
}                          }
                         }
```

Fig. 2. The result of a context-dependent interprocedural analysis for Px

procedures—and the call graph—which represents the program flow between the different procedures—. To improve the precision of the computed program slice, it is necessary for the analysis to use explicit representations of procedure contexts (as special nodes and transitions). This is the case of the second method which relies on a program representation called *system dependence graph*.

4   Semantics-Based Interprocedural Slicing

We present in this section the algorithm for our interprocedural slicing approach, and illustrate it with an example. Then, we describe a Maude prototype executing the algorithm for semantics specified in Maude.

4.1   Program Slicing as Term Slicing

In [17] we described how to extract the set of side-effect instructions SE from the semantics specification S and how to use SE for an *intraprocedural slicing* method. In the current work we focus on describing the *interprocedural slicing method* which is built on top of the intraprocedural slicing result from [17].

The programs written in the programming language specified by S are denoted as $\mathfrak{p}$. By *program variables* we understand subterms of $\mathfrak{p}$ of sort *Var*. If we consider the *subterm* relation as $\preceq$, we have $v \preceq \mathfrak{p}$ where v is a program variable.

We consider a *slicing criterion sc* to be a subset of program variables which are of interest for the slice. We denote by SC the slicing criterion *sc* augmented with *data flow information* that is collected along the slicing method. Hence, SC is a set of pairs of program variables of form $v, \widehat{v'}$, denoting that v depends on v', or just variables v, denoting that v is independent.

We assume as given the set of program functions $\mathfrak{F}_\mathfrak{p}$ defining the program $\mathfrak{p}$. We claim that $\mathfrak{F}_\mathfrak{p}$ can be inferred from the term $\mathfrak{p}$, given the S-sorts defining functions, variables, and instruction sequences. We base this claim on the fact that $\mathfrak{p}$ is formed, in general, as a sequence of function definitions hence its sequence constructor can be automatically identified from S. Also, we use getFnBody($f, \mathfrak{F}_\mathfrak{p}$) to obtain the function identified by f in $\mathfrak{F}_\mathfrak{p}$. Note that getFnBody($f, \mathfrak{F}_\mathfrak{p}$) $\preceq \mathfrak{F}_\mathfrak{p}$.

Furthermore, we denote the method computing the intraprocedural slicing as $\$(B, SC, SE)$, where B is the code, i.e., the body of some function f in $\mathfrak{p}$ (note that $B \preceq \mathfrak{p}$), while SC is a slicing criterion and SE is the set of side-effect constructs. Hence, $\$$ takes the body B of a function f and a slicing criterion

SC (i.e. a set of variables) and keeps only the parts of B that are subterms starting with a side-effect effect construct (from SE) and containing variables from the slicing criterion SC. The result of $\$(B, SC, SE)$ is given as a term $SC :: fn\langle fn(fp^\sharp)\{fs\}\rangle$ where SC is the data flow augmented slicing criterion, $fn \in FunctionName$ is a function identifier, and fs is the slice computed for fn. Meanwhile $fp^\sharp$ is the list of fn's formal parameters fp filtered by SC, i.e., all the formal parameters not appearing in SC are abstracted to a fixed additional variable $\sharp$.

Now we give a brief explanation on how the intraprocedural slicing $\$$ works. We say that a program subterm *modifies* a variable v if the top operator is in SE and v appears as a leaf in a specific part of the subterm, e.g., the variable v appears in the first argument of $\_:=\_$ or in $\texttt{Local\_}$. When such a subterm is discovered by $\$$ for a slicing variable then the slicing criterion is updated by adding the variables producing the side-effects (e.g. all variables v' in the second argument of $\_:=\_$) and the data flow relations $\overset{\frown}{v, v'}$. We call fs a *skeleton subterm* of B and we denote this as $fs \precsim B$.

In Fig. 3 we give the slicing method, **termSlicing**, which receives as input the slicing criterion sc, the set of program functions $\mathfrak{F}_\mathfrak{p}$, and the set of side-effect and context-updates syntactic constructs, SE and CU, respectively. The output is the set of sliced function definitions *slicedFnSet* together with the obtained data flow augmented slicing criterion $dfsc$. Note that $\mathfrak{F}_\mathfrak{p}$, SE, and CU are assumed to be precomputed based on the programming language semantics specification $\mathcal{S}$. The algorithm for inferring SE is given in [17, Section 4]. The algorithm for inferring CU goes along the same lines as the one for SE and it is based on the automatic discovery of stack structures used in $\mathcal{S}$ for defining the programming language commands. For example, in WhileF the only command inducing context-updates is $\texttt{Call\_(\_)}$ instruction. In the current work we assume CU given in order to focus on the interprocedural slicing as term slicing method. However, we claim that **termSlicing** is generic w.r.t. $\mathcal{S}$ since $\mathfrak{F}_\mathfrak{p}$, SE, and CU can be automatically derived from $\mathcal{S}$.

termSlicing is a fixpoint iteration which applies the *current* data-flow-augmented slicing criterion over the function terms in order to discover new skeleton subterms of the program that comply with the slicing criterion. The protocol of each iteration step is to take each currently sliced function and slice down and up in the *call graph*. In other words, the *intraprocedural slicing* is applied on every *called function* (i.e. goes *down* in the call graph) and every *calling function* (i.e. goes *up* in the call graph).

Technically, **termSlicing** relies on incrementally building the program slice, stored in *workingSet*, and the data flow augmented slicing criterion, stored in $dfsc$. This process has two phases: the initialization of *workingSet* and $dfsc$ (lines 0-6) and the loop implementing the fixpoint (lines 7-39).

The initialization part computes the slicing seed for the fixpoint by independently applying the intraprocedural slicing $\$(\_, \_, \_)$ with the slicing criterion sc for each function in the program $\mathfrak{p}$. The notation $A \cup = B$ (line 3) stands for "A becomes $A \cup B$" where $\cup$ is the set union. Similarly, $A \uplus = B$ (line 4)

termSlicing
Input: $sc, \mathfrak{F}_\mathfrak{p}, SE, CU$
Output: $slicedFnSet, dfsc$

```
0   workingSet' := ∅; dfsc := ∅;
1   for all fn(args){fnBody} ∈ 𝔉ₚ do
2     SCinit :: fn⟨fnInitSlice⟩ := $(fnBody, {x ∈ sc | x ≼ fs or x ≼ args}, SE);
3     workingSet' ∪= {SCinit :: fn⟨fnInitSlice⟩};
4     dfsc ⊎= SCinit;
5   od
6   workingSet := ∅;
7   while workingSet ≠ workingSet' do
8     workingSet := workingSet';
9     for all SC :: fn⟨fnSlice⟩ ∈ workingSet do
10      wsFnCalled := ∅;
11      for all Call ∈ CU for all Call fnCalled ≼ fnSlice do
12        fnCldSC := SC ᶠⁿ⌊fnCalled;
13        for all fnCldSCPrev :: fnCalled⟨_⟩ ∈ workingSet do
14          if fnCldSC ⊑ fnCldSCPrev then break;
15        fnCldBd := getFnBody(fnCalled, 𝔉ₚ);
16        fnCldSCNew :: fnCalled⟨fnCldSlice⟩ := $(fnCldBd, fnCldSC, SE);
17        wsFnCalled ∪= {fnCldSCNew :: fnCalled⟨fnCldSlice⟩};
18        SC ⊎= fnCldSCNew fnCalled⌋ᶠⁿ;
19      od
20      wsFnCalling := ∅;
21      for all Call ∈ CU for all fnCalling ∈ 𝔉ₚ s.t. Call fn ≼ fnCalling do
22        fnClgSC := SC fn⌈fnCalling;
23        for all fnCallingSCPrev :: fnCalling⟨_⟩ ∈ workingSet do
24          if fnClgSC ⊒ fnCallingSCPrev then break;
25        fnClgBd := getFnBody(fnCalling, 𝔉ₚ);
26        fnClgSCNew :: fnCalling⟨fnClgSlice⟩ := $(fnClgBd, fnClgSC, SE);
27        wsFnCalling ∪= {fnClgSCNew :: fnCalling⟨fnClgSlice⟩};
28        SC ⊎= fnClgSCNew fnCalling⌉fn;
29      od
30      fnBd := getFnBody(fn, 𝔉ₚ);
31      SCNew :: fn⟨fnSliceNew⟩ := $(fnBd, SC, SE);
32      dfsc ⊎= SCNew;
33      for all Call ∈ CU for all Call fnCalled ≼ fnSliceNew do
34        if _ :: fnCalled⟨_{}⟩ ∈ wSetFnCalled then
35          fnSliceNew := erraseSubterm(Call fnCalled, fnSliceNew)
36      od
37      workingSet' ⊎= {SCNew :: fn⟨fnSliceNew⟩} ⊎ wsFnCalled ⊎ wsFnCalling;
38    od
39  od
40  slicedFnSet := get⟨⟩Content(workingSet)
```

Fig. 3. Program slicing as term slicing algorithm

is the union of two data dependency graphs. Namely, $A \uplus B$ is the set union for graph edges filtered by the criterion that if a variable v is independent in A but dependent in B (i.e. there exists an edge $\curvearrowright$ with v on one of the ends) then the independent variable v is eliminated from $A \uplus B$. For example, the initialization step applied on the program in Fig. 1 produces the following $workingSet'$: z :: Inc$\langle$Inc(z){Call Add(z, $\sharp$)}$\rangle$, $\emptyset$ :: Main$\langle$Main(){}$\rangle$, $\emptyset$ :: A$\langle$A($\sharp$, $\sharp$){}$\rangle$, $\emptyset$ :: Add$\langle$Add($\sharp$, $\sharp$){}$\rangle$.

The fixpoint loop (lines 7-39) discovers the call graph in an on-demand fashion using the context-update set CU, which directs the fixpoint iteration towards applying the slicing on the called/calling function. As such, when a context-update (e.g. Call_(_) in the semantics of WhileF) is encountered in the current slice, we proceed to slice *the called function* (lines 10-19). Next, when a context-update of the currently considered functions is encountered, we proceed again to slice *the calling function* (lines 20-29). Each time we update the current data-flow-augmented slicing criterion and the slice of the current function (lines 30-36). For example, the discovery of the call graph starting with the function Inc(z){Call Add(z, $\sharp$)} in the program from Fig. 1 adds, during the first iteration of the fixpoint-loop, the called function Add(a, b){a := a + b} and the calling function A($\sharp$, y){Call Inc(y)}. We iterate this process until the skeleton subterm of every function is reached, i.e., *workingSet* is stable, e.g., see the result from Fig. 2. Note that the stability of *workingSet* induces the stability of *dfsc*, the data flow augmented slicing criterion.

We now describe in more details each of the three parts of the fixpoint loop: the *called* (lines 10-19), the *calling* (lines 20-29), and the *current* (lines 30-36) functions. The *called* and *calling* parts have a similar flow with slight differences in the operators used. They can be summarized as:

$$SC \uplus= SC \ ^{fn}\lfloor_{fnCalled} \ filtered\$(fnCalled, \sqsubseteq) \ _{fnCalled}\rfloor^{fn}$$

$$SC \uplus= SC \ _{fn}\lceil^{fnCalling} \ filtered\$(fnCalling, \sqsupseteq) \ ^{fnCalling}\rceil_{fn}$$

where fn is the name of the current function, $fnCalled$ is the name of a functions called from fn, and $fnCalling$ is the name of a function which is calling fn.

The operators $^-\lfloor_-$ and $_-\rfloor^-$ stand for the abstraction of the slicing criterion *downwards in the calling graph* from fn into $fnCalled$ and back, respectively. The abstraction $^{fn}\lfloor_{fnCalled}$ pivots on the actual parameters of $fnCalled$ and, based on patterns of function calls, it maps the actual parameters of $fnCalled$ from the current environment $SC :: fn$ into the environment of $fnCalled$. The abstraction $_{fnCalled}\rfloor^{fn}$ renders the reverse mapping from the (sliced) called environment back into the current one. Similarly for the $_-\lceil^-$ and $^-\rceil_-$ operators, which perform the abstraction *upwards in the call graph* from fn to $fnCalling$, pivoting on the parameters of fn. For example, for program Px from Fig. 1 we have $\widehat{z, i}$ $^{Inc}\lfloor_{Add}$ $\widehat{a, b}$ $_{Add}\rfloor^{Inc}$ $\widehat{z, i}$ and $\widehat{z, i}$ $_{Inc}\lceil^A$ $\widehat{y, \sharp}$ $=y$ $^A\rceil^{Inc}$ $\widehat{z, i}$. For the current work, the only pattern of function calls that we have experimented is the *complete list of call-by-reference parameters*.

The operator $filtered\$(fnC, rel)$ (lines 13-17 and 23-27) is a *filtered* slicing of fnC, where the filter is a relation between the current abstraction of SC and previously computed slicing criterions for the called/calling function fnC. We say that $SC \sqsubseteq SCPrev$ if SC is a subgraph of $SCPrev$ such that there is no edge

$\widehat{v, v'}$ in *SCPrev* where v is a node in *SC* and v' is a function parameter which is not in *SC*. This means that *SC* has no additional dependent data v' among the function parameters that should participate to the current slicing criterion. For example, this relation is exploited for the call of function Add in function A from Fig. 1. Namely, the algorithm discovers the relation $\widehat{a, b}$ for Add's parameters upon the call of Add from function Inc. Later, when function Add is called in A only with parameter b, the subgraph relation $b \sqsubseteq \widehat{a, b}$ shows that the already sliced Add(a, b) contains the slice of Add($\sharp$, b) hence, there is nothing else to be done for this function. Meanwhile, $SC \sqsupseteq SCPrev$ is defined as $SCPrev \sqsubseteq SC$ due to the fact that now the sense in the dependency graph is reversed and so the slicing criterion in the calling function (*SCPrev*) is the one to drive the reasoning. Hence, if the filter relation is true then the new slice is not computed anymore (lines 14 and 24) because the current slicing criterion is subsumed by the previous computation.

In lines 30-36 we compute a new slice for the current function fn and in line 37 we collect the slices currently computed for the program functions.

Lines 30-36 are more of a beautification of the slice of the currently sliced function fn. This beautification is made by the elimination from the slice of any context-update subterm *Call fnCalled* having an empty body for the currently computed slice (lines 33-36). For example, the call to function Add from function A, i.e., CallAdd($\sharp$, b), is eliminated from the slice computed for function A due to the emptiness of the sliced body of function Add starting with the slicing criterion b. Note that this fact can be concluded only from the data-flow relation among the parameters of a function, provided that we add a special symbol ℓ for the local variables such that any function parameter v depending on some local variable is going to appear as connected to ℓ, i.e., either $\widehat{v, \ell}$ or $\widehat{\ell, v}$. Namely, in function Inc from Fig. 1 we have $\widehat{z, \ell}$ due to the fact that Add brings $\widehat{z, i}$ in the SC of Inc. However, in what follows we do not insist on the data dependency on local variables in order not to burden the notation.

Finally, in line 37 we collect all the slices computed at the current iteration in *workingSet'*. Note that $\_\Cup\_$ operator from line 37 is an *abstract union* which first computes the equivalence class of slices for each function, based on the graph inclusion of the data-flow-augmented slicing criterion, and then performs the union of the results. Namely, if there is a function with F with three parameters x, y, z such that $\widehat{x, y}$ and z is independent, and if at some iteration of the fixpoint we have the slice $F(x, y, \sharp)\{B_{x,y,\sharp}\}$ in the set *wsFnCalled* and $F(\sharp, \sharp, z)\{B_{\sharp,\sharp,z}\}$ in the set *wsFnCalling*, then in *workingSet'* we have $Fx, y, z\{B_{x,y,z}\}$ where in $B_{x,y,z}$ we put together the two skeletons $B_{x,y,\sharp}$ and $B_{\sharp,\sharp,z}$.

Recall that, in Section 3, we described two interprocedural slicing methods presented in [26] and [11], being the second one more precise than the first one. In our approach the difference is based solely on the data flow relation we use for $. Hence, we can distinguish two types of **termSlicing**: the *naïve* one where the data flow relations are ignored and the *savvy* one which collects and uses data flow relations. Note that the data flow relation is currently assumed as given.

```
Main () {                   A (x, y) {               Add (a, b) {
  sum := 0;                   If x > 1 Then            a := a + b
  Local i, j;                   Call Add(x, y);      }
  i := 1; j := - 1;            Call Inc (y)          Inc (z) {
  While i < 11 Do           }                          Local i, j;
    Call A (sum, i);        B (x, y) {                 i := 1; j := i;
    Call B (sum, j);          If x > 0 Then            Call Add (z, i);
    Call A (j, i)              Call B(x + y, y)        Call Inc (j)
}                           }                        }
```

Fig. 4. PX—the extension of the WhileF program Px

For example, the iterations of the savvy **termSlicing** for the program PX in Fig. 4 and the slicing criterion $\{z\}$ are listed in Fig. 5. Namely, in the first boxed rows the slicing criterion $\{z\}$ is applied on $\mathfrak{F}_{PX}$ to produce the skeleton subterms used as the fixpoint seed. Hence, the fixpoint seed contains one nonempty skeleton as z appears only in Inc. Note that i—the second parameter of Call Add—is abstracted to $\sharp$ as no data dependency is currently determined for it.

In the second box of rows we consider the slicing criterion for Inc—the only one nonempty from the seed—and we iterate the fixpoint for it. The first row deals with the (only) called function appearing in Inc's skeleton, namely $Add(z, \sharp)$. Note that the slicing criterion z is abstracted downwards in the call graph so the slicing criterion becomes a, the first formal parameter of Add. The slice of Add with $\{a\}$ as slicing criterion is showed in the third column while the slicing criterion becomes $\widehat{a, b}$, i.e., a depends on b. Because b is a formal parameter, it gets abstracted back in Inc as Add's actual parameter i. Hence, the updated criterion used in Inc is $\widehat{z, i}$ and it is used for the calling function A, in the second row, and also for the recursive call to Inc itself, in the third row. In these rows, the slicing criterion is abstracted upwards in the call graph and the formal parameter z becomes y in A and j in Inc. Meanwhile i is ruled out (becomes $\sharp$) because it is not a parameter and hence it is not relevant in a calling function. The fourth row shows the computation of Inc's skeleton based on the current slicing criterion $\widehat{z, i}$. Furthermore, upon performing the abstract union $\mathbb{U}$ at the end of the fixpoint iteration, then Inc's skeleton is:

$$Inc(z)\{Local\ i, j;\ i := 1;\ j := i;\ Call\ Add\ (z, i);\ Call\ Inc\ (j)\}$$

The fixpoint iteration continues in the third box by adding to the slice the function Main due to the upward phase (since Main contains a call to A). The upward parameter substitution of y from A is i in Main and the slice of Main is updated in the third row. Note that the $\square$ in all the other rows signifies the reach of the **break** in lines 14 or 24 in **termSlicing** and stands for "nothing to be done." The fourth box contains the final step of the fixpoint when there is nothing else changed in *workingSet'* (i.e. all the rows contain $\square$ in the last column). Hence, for the example in Fig. 4 we obtain the slice in Fig. 2 with the only difference that the sliced Inc is now the entire Inc from Fig. 4 (due to the newly added assignment "j:=i").

Slicing variables	Function contexts	Computed slice (identified subterms)
$z :: \top$	$^\top\lfloor_{\mathtt{Inc}}\, z \to z\, _{\mathtt{Inc}}\rfloor^\top$	$\mathtt{Inc(z)}\ \{\mathtt{Call\ Add(z,\sharp)}\}$
	$^\top\lfloor_{\mathtt{Main}}\, \sharp = \emptyset\, _{\mathtt{Main}}\rfloor^\top, \dots$	$\mathtt{Main()\{\}, A(\sharp,\sharp)\{\}, B(\sharp,\sharp)\{\}, Add(\sharp,\sharp)\{\}}$
$\widehat{z} :: \mathtt{Inc}$	$^{\mathtt{Inc}}\lfloor_{\mathtt{Add}}\, a \to \widehat{a}, b\, _{\mathtt{Add}}\rfloor^{\mathtt{Inc}}\, \widehat{z}, i$	$\mathtt{Add(a,b)}\ \{\mathtt{a := a + b}\}$
$\widehat{z}, i :: \mathtt{Inc}$	$_{\mathtt{Inc}}\lceil^A\, y, \sharp \to \widehat{y}, \sharp\ ^A\rceil_{\mathtt{Inc}}\, \widehat{z}, i$	$\mathtt{A(\sharp, y)}\ \{\mathtt{Call\ Inc(y)}\}$
$\widehat{z}, i :: \mathtt{Inc}$	$_{\mathtt{Inc}}\lceil^{\mathtt{Inc}}\, \widehat{j}, \sharp \to \widehat{j}, i\ ^{\mathtt{Inc}}\rceil_{\mathtt{Inc}}\, \widehat{z}, i$	$\mathtt{Inc(\sharp)\{Local\ i, j; i := 1; j := i; Call\ Add(\sharp, i); Call\ Inc(j)\}}$
$\widehat{z}, i :: \mathtt{Inc}$	$\widehat{z}, i \to z, i$	$\mathtt{Inc(z)\{Local\ i; i := 1; Call\ Add(z, i)\}}$
$y :: A$	$^A\lfloor_{\mathtt{Add}}\, b \sqsubseteq \widehat{a}, b :: \mathtt{Add}\, _{\mathtt{Add}}\rfloor^A\, y$	□
$y :: A$	$^A\lfloor_{\mathtt{Inc}}(z \sqsubseteq \widehat{z}, i :: \mathtt{Inc})\, _{\mathtt{Inc}}\rfloor^A\, y$	□
$y :: A$	$_A\lceil^{\mathtt{Main}}\, i \to \widehat{i}\ ^{\mathtt{Main}}\rceil_A\, y$	$\mathtt{Main()\{Local\ i; i := 1; While\ i < 1\ Do\ Call\ A(\sharp, i)\}}$
$y :: A$	$y = y :: A$	□
$\widehat{a}, b :: \mathtt{Add}$	$_{\mathtt{Add}}\lceil^{\mathtt{Inc}}(\widehat{z}, i \sqsupseteq z, i :: \mathtt{Inc})\ ^{\mathtt{Inc}}\rceil_{\mathtt{Add}}\, y$	□
$\widehat{a}, b :: \mathtt{Add}$	$_{\mathtt{Add}}\lceil^A(x, \widehat{y} \sqsupseteq y :: A)^A\rceil_{\mathtt{Add}}\, y$	□
$\widehat{a}, b :: \mathtt{Add}$	$\widehat{a}, b = a, \widehat{b} :: \mathtt{Add}$	□
$\widehat{z}, i :: \mathtt{Inc}$	$^{\mathtt{Inc}}\lfloor_{\mathtt{Add}}(\widehat{a}, b \sqsubseteq a, \widehat{b} :: \mathtt{Add})\, _{\mathtt{Add}}\rfloor^{\mathtt{Inc}}\, y$	□
$\widehat{z}, i :: \mathtt{Inc}$	$_{\mathtt{Inc}}\lceil^A(\widehat{y}, \sharp \sqsupseteq y :: A)^A\rceil_{\mathtt{Inc}}\, y$	□
$\widehat{z}, i :: \mathtt{Inc}$	$\widehat{z}, i = z, \widehat{i} :: \mathtt{Inc}$	□
$y :: A$	$^A\lfloor_{\mathtt{Add}}(b \sqsubseteq \widehat{a}, b :: \mathtt{Add})\, _{\mathtt{Add}}\rfloor_A\, y$	□
$y :: A$	$^A\lfloor_{\mathtt{Inc}}(z \sqsubseteq \widehat{z}, i :: \mathtt{Inc})\, _{\mathtt{Inc}}\rfloor^A\, y$	□
$y :: A$	$_A\lceil^{\mathtt{Main}}(i \sqsupseteq \widehat{i} :: \mathtt{Main})^{\mathtt{Main}}\rceil_A\, y$	□
$y :: A$	$y = y :: A$	□
$\widehat{a}, b :: \mathtt{Add}$	$_{\mathtt{Add}}\lceil^{\mathtt{Inc}}(\widehat{z}, i \sqsupseteq z, i :: \mathtt{Inc})\ ^{\mathtt{Inc}}\rceil_{\mathtt{Add}}\, y$	□
$\widehat{a}, b :: \mathtt{Add}$	$_{\mathtt{Add}}\lceil^A(x, \widehat{y} \sqsupseteq y :: A)^A\rceil_{\mathtt{Add}}\, y$	□
$\widehat{a}, b :: \mathtt{Add}$	$\widehat{a}, b = a, \widehat{b} :: \mathtt{Add}$	□
$\widehat{z}, i :: \mathtt{Inc}$	$^{\mathtt{Inc}}\lfloor_{\mathtt{Add}}(\widehat{a}, b \sqsubseteq a, \widehat{b} :: \mathtt{Add})\, _{\mathtt{Add}}\rfloor^{\mathtt{Inc}}\, y$	□
$\widehat{z}, i :: \mathtt{Inc}$	$_{\mathtt{Inc}}\lceil^A(\widehat{y}, \sharp \sqsupseteq y :: A)^A\rceil_{\mathtt{Inc}}\, y$	□
$\widehat{z}, i :: \mathtt{Inc}$	$\widehat{z}, i = z, \widehat{i} :: \mathtt{Inc}$	□
$i :: \mathtt{Main}$	$^{\mathtt{Main}}\lfloor_A(y \sqsubseteq y :: A)\, _A\rfloor^{\mathtt{Main}}\, i$	□
$i :: \mathtt{Main}$	$^{\mathtt{Main}}\lfloor_B(\sharp \sqsubseteq \emptyset :: B)\, _B\rfloor^{\mathtt{Main}}\, i$	□
$i :: \mathtt{Main}$	$i = i :: \mathtt{Main}$	□

Fig. 5. Program slicing as term slicing - the fixpoint iterations

termSlicing terminates because there exists a finite set of function skeleton subterms, a finite set of data flow graphs, a finite set of edges in the call graph for each function, and any loop in the call graph is solved based on the data flow graph ordering. Moreover, **termSlicing** produces a valid slice because it exhaustively saturates the slicing criterion. However, the obtained slice is not minimal due to the skeletons union $\mathbb{U}$. Still, there is a consistent difference between the *naïve* and the *savvy* methods. In order to achieve a better degree of minimality we have to apply abstractions on the data-flow-augmented slicing criterion.

4.2   System Description

We briefly present in this section our prototype which is implemented in Maude [3]. The source code is available at http://maude.sip.ucm.es/slicing/. A key distinguishing feature of Maude is its systematic and efficient use of reflection (i.e. Maude's capability of handling and reasoning about terms that represent specifications described in Maude itself) through its predefined META-LEVEL module [3, Chapter 14]. We have used these features to implement a tool that receives a set of definitions, a sort where the computations take place, and a set of slicing variables. Since all these elements can be used as usual data, we can traverse the semantic rules, analyze them, and execute the program using them. Note that the user has to provide the rules responsible for context-update while the parameter passing operators $^-\lfloor$ _ _ $\rfloor^-$ and $^-\lceil$ _ _ $\rceil^-$ are particularized here to an all-parameters-ordered-pass-by-reference pattern.

The tool is started by loading into Maude the slicing.maude file available at the webpage above. It starts an input/output loop where modules and commands can be introduced by enclosing them in parentheses. Once the module with the semantics has been loaded, we have to introduce ESt, the sort for the mapping between variables and values, and RWBUF, the sort for the read/write buffer, as the sorts responsible for the side effects. Similarly, we indicate that CallF is the rule for context-update:

```
Maude> (set side-effect sorts ESt RWBUF .)
ESt RWBUF selected as side effect sorts.
Maude> (set context-update rules CallF .)
CallF selected as context-update rules.
```

We can now start the slicing process by indicating that Statement is the sort for instructions, myFuns is a constant standing for the definition of the functions Main, A, Add, and Inc from Figure 4, and z is the slicing variable. The tool displays the relevant variables and the sliced code for each function as:

```
Maude> (islice Statement with defs myFuns wrt z .)
The variables to slice 'Inc are {i, j, z}
'Inc(z){
    Local i ; Local j ;
    i := _ ; j := _ ;
    Call 'Add(z,i);
    Call 'Inc(j)
}
...
```

We test our proposed method for interprocedural slicing on a set of benchmarks addressing embedded and real-time applications. As such, we use a set of small examples, grouped under the name bundle, from a survey [24] on program slicing techniques, automatically-generated code from typical Scade designs [5], as well as a standard set of real-time benchmarks—called PapaBench [15]. In Figure 6, each program is identified by name, a short description, size parameters (LOC, number of functions, #funs, and function calls, #calls), and the

Name	Program Description	LOC	#funs	#calls	red (%)
bundle	A collection of (extended) examples from [24]	71	7	25	38 %
selector_2	Generated code from SCADE design - 2 SSM	426	6	11	91 %
selector_3	Generated code from SCADE design - 3 SSM	455	7	19	85 %
autopilot	PapaBench - autopilot	1384	95	214	74 %
fbw	PapaBench - fly_by_wire	638	41	110	78 %

Fig. 6. Set of benchmark programs for interprocedural slicing

average reduction in the number of statements, for several runs with different sets of slicing variables. This reduction shows that the methodology works better on bigger programs (the bundle, with very small examples, presents the lowest reduction, because all variables are closely related). The Scade benchmarks, explained below, present the greatest reduction because the variables have very specific behaviors, hence allowing a very efficient use of slicing.

The Scade Suite development platform [5] is a mixed synchronous language, combining variants of Lustre [9] (i.e. data-flow) and Esterel [2] (i.e. control-flow). Scade facilitates the design of embedded and real-time systems in a modular fashion, and the modularity is preserved in the generated C code. The two Scade designs—selector_2 and selector_3—consist of two, and respectively three, parallel state machines (called SSM - Safe State Machines) which embed in their states calls to external functions and constrain (via shared variables) how these state machines communicate among them.

PapaBench is extracted from an actual real-time system for Unmanned Aerial Vehicle (UAV) and consists of two programs fly_by_wire and autopilot, designed to run on different processors. The application consists of a number of tasks which are executed in a control loop. For example, the autopilot program focuses on the UAV airframe and has eight different tasks (e.g. for controlling the navigation, stabilisation, altitude or communication - radio or GPS).

We test our interprocedural slicing at the level of the entire program as well as at the level of each task. Let us consider the function radio_control_task (in autopilot) which manages radio orders based on various operation modes (e.g. PITCH, ROLL, THROTTLE, etc) and sets new values for several flight parameters (e.g. *desired_roll* or *desired_pitch*). This particular function has a call graph of about 21 nodes. We could use, for example, a slicing criterion which consists of all program variables used in radio_control_task in order to investigate the tasks which are depending (i.e. their intraprocedural slice is not empty) or not on the computation of radio_control_task. The interprocedural slice shows a dependence of the radio_control_task with tasks such as `altitude_control_task` and `climb_control_task`, which rely on global flight parameters used by the radio controller. This testing strategy is applied on all benchmarks and, together with the resulting traces and the Scade designs, are available on the tool webpage at `http://maude.sip.ucm.es/slicing/`.

5   Concluding Remarks and Ongoing Work

The formal language definitions based on the rewriting logic framework support program executability and create the premises for further development of program analyzers. In this paper we have presented a generic algorithm for interprocedural slicing based on results of meta-level analysis of the language semantics. In summary, the slicing prerequisites are: side-effect and context-update language constructs with data flow information for the side-effect constructs and parameter passing patterns for the context-update constructs. The actual program slicing computation, presented in the current work, is done through term slicing and is meant to set the aforementioned set of prerequisites. This work complements the recent advances in semantics-constructed tools for debugging [18], automated testing [16], and program analysis [17].

From the prototype point of view, we also plan to investigate the automatic inference of the newly identified slicing prerequisites, i.e., meta-analysis for context-updates deduction and parameter passing pattern inference. This would greatly simplify the user task, since he will just introduce the program and the slicing criterion and the tool would be in charge of computing all the required constructors. We also have to further develop the already existing side-effect extraction with data flow information. Finally, we aim to develop the method for language semantics defined in Maude but also in $\mathbb{K}$ [19].

References

1. Alpuente, M., Ballis, D., Espert, J., Romero, D.: Backward trace slicing for rewriting logic theories. In: Bjørner, N., Sofronie-Stokkermans, V. (eds.) CADE 2011. LNCS, vol. 6803, pp. 34–48. Springer, Heidelberg (2011)
2. Berry, G., Gonthier, G.: The esterel synchronous programming language: Design, semantics, implementation. Sci. Comput. Program (SCP) 19(2), 87–152 (1992)
3. Clavel, M., Durán, F., Eker, S., Lincoln, P., Martí-Oliet, N., Meseguer, J., Talcott, C.: All About Maude - A High-Performance Logical Framework. LNCS, vol. 4350. Springer, Heidelberg (2007)
4. Ellison, C., Rosu, G.: An executable formal semantics of c with applications. In: POPL, pp. 533–544 (2012)
5. Esterel Technologies Scade Language Reference Manual 2011 (2011)
6. Farzan, A., Chen, F., Meseguer, J., Roşu, G.: Formal analysis of java programs in javaFAN. In: Alur, R., Peled, D.A. (eds.) CAV 2004. LNCS, vol. 3114, pp. 501–505. Springer, Heidelberg (2004)
7. Gulwani, S., Tiwari, A.: Computing procedure summaries for interprocedural analysis. In: De Nicola, R. (ed.) ESOP 2007. LNCS, vol. 4421, pp. 253–267. Springer, Heidelberg (2007)

8. Harman, M., Danicic, S.: Using program slicing to simplify testing. Journal of Software Testing, Verification and Reliability 5, 143–162 (1995)
9. Halbwachs, N., Caspi, P., Raymond, P., Pilaud, D.: The synchronous dataflow programming language lustre. In: Proc. of the IEEE, pp. 1305–1320 (1991)
10. Hennessy, M.: The Semantics of Programming Languages: An Elementary Introduction Using Structural Operational Semantics. John Wiley & Sons (1990)
11. Horwitz, S., Reps, T., Binkley, D.: Interprocedural slicing using dependence graphs. In: Conference on Programming Language Design and Implementation, PLDI 1988, pp. 35–46 (1988)
12. Jhala, R., Majumdar, R.: Path slicing. In: Proc. of the 2005 ACM SIGPLAN Conference on Programming Language Design and Implementation, PLDI 2005, pp. 38–47. ACM Press (2005)
13. Martí-Oliet, N., Meseguer, J.: Rewriting logic: roadmap and bibliography. Theor. Comput. Sci. 285(2), 121–154 (2002)
14. Meseguer, J., Roşu, G.: The rewriting logic semantics project. Theoretical Computer Science 373(3), 213–237 (2007)
15. Nemer, F., Cassé, H., Sainrat, P., Bahsoun, J.P., De Michiel, M.: PapaBench: a Free Real-Time Benchmark. In: WCET 2006 (2006)
16. Riesco, A.: Using semantics specified in Maude to generate test cases. In: Roychoudhury, A., D'Souza, M. (eds.) ICTAC 2012. LNCS, vol. 7521, pp. 90–104. Springer, Heidelberg (2012)
17. Riesco, A., Asăvoae, I.M., Asăvoae, M.: A generic program slicing technique based on language definitions. In: Martí-Oliet, N., Palomino, M. (eds.) WADT 2012. LNCS, vol. 7841, pp. 248–264. Springer, Heidelberg (2013)
18. Riesco, A., Verdejo, A., Martí-Oliet, N., Caballero, R.: Declarative debugging of rewriting logic specifications. Journal of Logic and Algebraic Programming (2012)
19. Şerbănuţă, T., Ştefănescu, G., Roşu, G.: Defining and executing P systems with structured data in K. In: Corne, D.W., Frisco, P., Păun, G., Rozenberg, G., Salomaa, A. (eds.) WMC 2008. LNCS, vol. 5391, pp. 374–393. Springer, Heidelberg (2009)
20. Sharir, M., Pnueli, A.: Two approaches to interprocedural data flow analysis. In: Program Flow Analysis, pp. 189–233 (1981)
21. Silva, J., Chitil, O.: Combining algorithmic debugging and program slicing. In: PPDP, pp. 157–166. ACM Press (2006)
22. Sridharan, M., Fink, S.J., Bodík, R.: Thin slicing. In: PLDI, pp. 112–122 (2007)
23. Tian, C., Feng, M., Gupta, R.: Speculative parallelization using state separation and multiple value prediction. In: Proc. of the 2010 International Symposium on Memory Management, ISMM 2010, pp. 63–72. ACM Press (2010)
24. Tip, F.: A survey of program slicing techniques. J. Prog. Lang. 3(3) (1995)
25. Verdejo, A., Martí-Oliet, N.: Executable structural operational semantics in Maude. Journal of Logic and Algebraic Programming 67, 226–293 (2006)
26. Weiser, M.: Program slicing. In: Proc. of the 5th International Conference on Software Engineering, ICSE 1981, pp. 439–449. IEEE Press (1981)

Integrating Software and Hardware Verification[*]

Marie-Christine Jakobs, Marco Platzner,
Heike Wehrheim, and Tobias Wiersema

University of Paderborn, Germany
{marie.christine.jakobs,platzner,wehrheim,tobias.wiersema}@upb.de

Abstract. Verification of hardware and software usually proceeds separately, software analysis relying on the correctness of processors executing instructions. This assumption is valid as long as the software runs on standard CPUs that have been extensively validated and are in wide use. However, for processors exploiting custom instruction set extensions to meet performance and energy constraints the validation might be less extensive, challenging the correctness assumption.

In this paper we present an approach for integrating software analyses with hardware verification, specifically targeting custom instruction set extensions. We propose three different techniques for deriving the properties to be proven for the hardware implementation of a custom instruction in order to support software analyses. The techniques are designed to explore the trade-off between generality and efficiency and span from proving functional equivalence over checking the rules of a particular analysis domain to verifying actual pre and post conditions resulting from program analysis. We demonstrate and compare the three techniques on example programs with custom instructions, using state-of-the-art software and hardware verification techniques.

1 Introduction

Today, software verification has reached industrial size programs, and yearly software verification competitions [1] demonstrate the continuing progress. This success is due to recent advances in the verification techniques themselves, such as lazy abstraction [10], and in the underlying SMT solvers [16]. In general, software analyses rely on the correctness of the processor hardware executing the program. More specifically, strongest postcondition computation used to determine the successor state of a given state for a program statement assumes that the processor correctly implements the statement's semantics.

Assuming correct hardware is certainly valid for standard processors, since they undergo extensive simulation, testing and partly also formal verification processes [22]. However, during the last years processors with so-called custom instruction set extensions became popular [9], which challenge this correctness assumption. Customized instructions map a part of an application's data flow

---

[*] This work was partially supported by the German Research Foundation (DFG) within the Collaborative Research Centre "On-The-Fly Computing" (SFB 901).

E. Albert and E. Sekerinski (Eds.): IFM 2014, LNCS 8739, pp. 307–322, 2014.

graph to specialized functional units in the processor pipeline in order to improve performance and/or energy-efficiency.

In this paper, we present a novel formal technique for integrating software and hardware analyses covering custom instruction set extensions. Existing software-hardware co-verification approaches so far either compute a joint model of software and hardware (or specifically of their interface) [12,13,19,11] or apply some sort of compositional reasoning [23], assuming that components can be either implemented in hardware or in software. Here, we directly combine established software analysis methods for software at the source code level with a set of state-of-the-art model checking procedures for hardware. More specifically, we derive from the software analysis requirements on the hardware which then need to be validated in order for the software analysis to produce trustworthy results. The only other approach aiming at connecting hardware verification with software analysis in this way is [14] who, however, start from the opposite side, namely the application-specific instruction, and from this derive constraints on the software. The disadvantage of this technique is that it might produce overly complex constraints, whose validation is not needed for trustworthiness.

Our three approaches for integrating software and hardware analyses allow for a more precise tailoring and consequently differ in what needs to be verified on the hardware. The first approach proves behavioral equivalence between the specification and the implementation of a custom instruction (e.g., that an adder is really adding integer values). While proving equivalence is potentially the most resource consuming approach it is also the most powerful, as it inherently covers all behavioral properties of the instruction on which software analyses could rely. The second approach ties together software and hardware analysis and makes use of the fact that often software analyses rely on an abstract interpretation of program statements. Consequently, hardware verification is restricted to checking whether the custom instructions obey the rules of the particular abstract domain (e.g., that an adder is faithful w.r.t. to signs of integers). Finally, our third approach features the closest interaction between software and hardware by using the abstract state space of the program generated by the abstract interpretation to see what properties of the program statements the software analysis has actually used during verification (e.g., that a positive integer is returned when adding two positive integers). We then tailor the hardware verification exactly to the needs of the software analysis, hoping to avoid unnecessarily complex and runtime consuming hardware verification. Unlike what could be expected, our three case studies show that the third approach does not always have the lowest effort, since the software analysis might impose so many different properties to check for the custom instruction that even checking full behavioral equivalence becomes simpler.

In summary, our paper makes the following contributions:

– We present three different approaches for integration of software and hardware analyses differing in powerfulness and level of integration.
– We exemplify, discuss and compare our approaches based on three case studies.

2   Background

We start with giving some background information on the type of programs we look at, the program analysis employed and the technique of custom instructions.

2.1   Program Analysis

The programs which we consider in our software analysis technique are written in C, or more precisely in CIL [18]. Following the notation of [2], we model a program as a *control-flow automaton* (CFA). A CFA $P = (L, G, l_0, l_e)$ consists of a set of locations L, a set of control flow edges $G \subseteq L \times Ops \times L$, a program entry location $l_0 \in L$ and an error location $l_e \in L$. The set Ops contains all operations, e.g., assign statements and assume statements such as a (negated) condition of an if or while statement. Furthermore, V denotes the set of program variables – all variables which occur in an operation op of an edge $(\cdot, op, \cdot) \in G$. The error location encodes (non)reachability properties of our program. Alternatively, assert statements could be used.

The left of Figure 1 shows our example program SUM adapted from [21, ex49.c] given in a programming language notation. All variables (sum, i, N) are of type int. The notation $+_{sat}$ stands for saturating addition, an addition that neither overflows nor underflows but saturates at max and min integer values. For the saturating addition we will later employ a custom instruction. The label ERROR marks the error node. We can see this to only be reachable when sum is less than 0 at the end. Thus, our interest is in showing that the sum at the end is non-negative. The right of Figure 1 displays the control-flow automaton of the program. The CFA contains four assignment edges, one for each assignment in the program, and four assume edges, reflecting the two evaluations of the condition of the while statement and the if statement, respectively. Furthermore it contains one blank edge for the goto statement. The rectangular node (node l_6) is the error node, $l_e = l_6$.

The software analyses which we perform on the programs are all based on the idea of *abstract interpretation*. Instead of exploring the complete state space of the programs, we only generate the set of states on a specific level of abstraction, called the abstract domain or *analysis domain*. This level fixes what we are

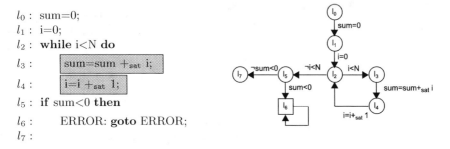

Fig. 1. Example program SUM and its CFA. The two boxes in program SUM highlight the statements replaced by custom instruction saturating addition.

interested in with respect to property checking. All our analyses are specified in the *Configurable Program Analysis* (CPA) framework [2] and are performed using the associated tool CPACHECKER[1] [3]. The framework allows for the definition of arbitrary abstract interpretation based analyses ranging from dataflow analysis to model checking. For this, we – among other parts – need to define the analysis domain and the semantics of program operations on this domain. The latter is given in terms of a *transfer relation*.

In the following, we describe the concepts of a CPA using a sign-dataflow analysis $\mathbb{S}$. In such an analysis, we are only interested in the signs of variables. Consequently, the abstract domain defines abstract states as pairs (l, d), where l is a program location and d is a dataflow fact assigning to every variable $v \in V$ a value $d(v)$ out of the set $\{\bot, -, -0, 0, 0+, +, \top\}$ of abstract values, meaning there is no possible value $(\bot)$, the value of the variable is $< 0, \leq 0, = 0, \geq 0, > 0$ or any value $(\top)$. This set of ab-

Fig. 2. Ordering $\sqsubseteq_V$ of abstract values in sign abstract domain

stract values forms a lattice with ordering $\sqsubseteq_V$ (Fig. 2). This can easily be lifted to the dataflow facts, $d \sqsubseteq_D d'$ iff $\forall v \in V : d(v) \sqsubseteq_V d'(v)$, and abstract states, $(l, d) \sqsubseteq (l', d')$ iff $(l = l')$ and $d \sqsubseteq_D d'$. The CPA framework requires all analysis domains to form a lattice, and the ordering on this lattice needs to be consistent with the set of concrete states represented by the values of the abstract domain. More precisely, if $c(a)$ denotes the set of concrete states represented by a value a in the abstract domain, then $a \sqsubseteq a'$ implies $c(a) \subseteq c(a')$, a, a' being abstract values.

The transfer relation now fixes the semantics of program statements on this abstract domain. As an example, consider the saturating add `sum=sum +sat i`. Abstractly, this statement keeps the value of all variables except for `sum`. Based on the abstract values of `i,sum` a new value is assigned to `sum`. Manually defined transfer rules describe how the value of `sum` changes. Some of these rules are given in Table 1. The table can be read like a function table: the first two rows describe abstract values of the inputs (the arguments to the custom instruction) and the last row the abstract output value. In order to provide a sound analysis, the abstract domain and the transfer relation need to provide an overapproximation of the concrete semantics.

Table 1. Transfer rules for saturating addition `z = x +sat y`

x	-	-0	-0	0	0+	0+	+	...
y	-0	-	-0	0	0+	+	0+	...
z = x +sat y	-	-	-0	0	0+	+	+	...

The abstract domain and the transfer relation are input to the state space exploration algorithm of CPACHECKER. The algorithm builds the abstract state space, usually represented in the form of an abstract reachability graph (ARG). The ARG for our program on executing the sign-dataflow analysis is shown

---

[1] http://cpachecker.sosy-lab.org

in Figure 3. The boxes next to the nodes give us the dataflow facts holding at the particular locations, e.g., in location l_4 we definitely know i and sum to be positive or zero and N to be positive. The latter is due to the CFA edge $i < N$ which, given that i is positive or zero in l_2, guarantees that N is positive in l_3. Dataflow analyses combine abstract states for same locations. For example, state $(l_2, \mathtt{i} :0, \mathtt{N} :\top, \mathtt{sum} :0)$ is combined with $(l_2, \mathtt{i} :+, \mathtt{N} :+, \mathtt{sum} :0)$. Our tool replaces the existing state for $l2$ in the ARG by the combined one, i.e., $(l_2, \mathtt{i} :0+, \mathtt{N} :\top, \mathtt{sum} :0)$ and continues exploration, finally resulting in state $(l_2, \mathtt{i} :0+, \mathtt{N} :\top, \mathtt{sum} :0+)$.

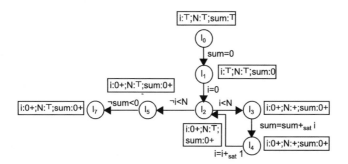

Fig. 3. ARG of program SUM with initial abstract state $(l_0, \mathtt{i} : \top; \mathtt{N} : \top; \mathtt{sum} : \top)$

2.2   Custom Instruction Set Extension

The motivation for customizing instruction sets is to improve processor performance and/or energy-efficiency, while keeping the cost as low as possible [5]. There are several approaches to custom instruction set extension. The original static approach analyzes a set of targeted applications to identify runtime intense portions of the applications' data flow graphs. These subgraphs are then turned into custom instructions and mapped to specialized hardware in form of functional units (FU) accelerating the code. These specialized FUs are then integrated into a processor pipeline and a so-called application-specific instruction set processor (ASIP) is being fabricated.

Since the cost of designing a new processor is immense, the dynamic approach to instruction set extension proposes a flexible interface between the processor pipeline and a runtime reconfigurable fabric added as reconfigurable functional unit (RFU) to a processor pipeline. Runtime reconfigurability helps not only to lower design cost but also to increase flexibility, because the reconfigurable fabric can accommodate different custom instructions that can be switched on demand during runtime. While typically the RFUs are programmed with pre-generated configurations, the most sophisticated approach currently studied in research even shifts the tasks of identifying and generating custom instructions to runtime with the goal to achieve transparent just-in-time acceleration.

Figure 4 displays the design process for custom instruction set extensions. Based on an analysis of application code, potential custom instructions are identified by exploring the design space. In a second step, the most promising custom

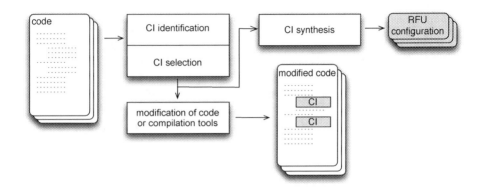

Fig. 4. Design process for custom instruction (CI) set extensions

instructions are selected applying cost functions. Then, custom instruction synthesis is used to generate the configurations for the RFUs and the code is modified to include the custom instructions. The custom instruction set extension problem is well-studied, for a survey see [9].

In this paper we focus on dynamic approaches to custom instruction set extension, for which the effort that can be spent for validation is presumably much lower than for standard processor designs. This issue is particularly emphasized for just-in-time acceleration. It has to be noted that the circuit structures of the underlying reconfigurable fabrics, e.g., the RFUs, are indeed well-tested. What creates the verification challenge is the correctness of the RFU configurations shown in Figure 4. In our example program SUM we use $+_{sat}$ as custom instruction implemented in hardware. This addition, in contrast to the standard addition, uses saturation instead of modular arithmetic, so results do not overflow and wrap around, but instead saturate at the extreme values of the range. Saturating arithmetic is often used in signal or image processing and thus can be found in modern instruction set extensions such as Intel's SSE2 (streaming SIMD extensions).

In the following sections, we present a novel integrated software/hardware verification approach where software analyses such as the one reviewed in Section 2.1 work together with the verification of RFU configurations. We detail three alternatives for the integration of software and hardware analyses designed to explore the trade-off between generality and efficiency.

3   Linking Software and Hardware Analyses

We strive for establishing trust into the correctness of custom instructions, more accurately the configurations for reconfigurable functional units. To this end, we employ formal hardware verification, which we need to properly link to state-of-the-art software analysis. Overall, we introduce three different approaches for integrating software with hardware analyses. While our first approach performs software and hardware verification rather independently, the other two approaches specifically tailor the hardware verification to the requirements of the software analysis. The approaches differ in their generality and also in their complexity of expressing the analysis requirements for hardware verification and of computing the proof. In this section we present the three different approaches using our example program SUM from Fig. 1, where the saturating add should be implemented as a custom instruction. The next section shows how to formally verify these requirements on the hardware. Due to limited space we cannot give all details about the requirements, but we provide them as Verilog sources on our website: http://www.cs.uni-paderborn.de/fachgebiete/computer-engineering-group/people/wiersema/ifm.html.

3.1 Approach #1: Functional Equivalence

The most general requirement on the hardware is full functional equivalence of the implementation I to the desired behavioral specification S. For our example, the custom instruction $+_{sat}$, we thus need to show that it carries out correct addition without overflow or underflow, by comparing the actual low-level hardware description I, e.g., a technology mapped placed and routed netlist, to a high-level behavioral description of the desired saturating addition S, usually given in a hardware description language (HDL) such as Verilog. If functional equivalence can be shown, then all software analysis results will automatically hold for programs running on processor hardware using the custom instruction. For functional equivalence we have to prove for every possible input $\underline{x}$, which is the vector of bits which results from mapping the program variables to the hardware input signals, that the output of the implementation $I(\underline{x})$ must match the output of the behavioral specification $S(\underline{x})$, or short: $\forall \underline{x} : S(\underline{x}) = I(\underline{x})$. Checking for full functional equivalence is done by most of the current hardware verification approaches (see e.g., [15]) and is also the basic strategy of some hardware-software co-verification techniques [6,8]. The downside of this approach is that we actually might verify more than the software analysis needs to know, and thus might have an unnecessarily high effort.

3.2 Approach #2: Requirements of the Analysis Domain

Our second approach provides a closer integration of software analysis and hardware verification. We look at the analysis domain used by the software analysis and only check whether the hardware provides a correct implementation w.r.t. the transfer relation. Therefore, the hardware must follow all (transfer) rules the transfer relation uses for the custom instruction, in case of the sign analysis and the saturating addition, the transfer rules of Table 1. There are significant advantages associated with this approach. First, we might need to check only a part of the circuit implementing the custom instruction, e.g., a single output bit of a binary number in case of sign analysis. Second, we need not even check all different rules. Some rules will be covered by others and some are vacuous. Intuitively, a *covered* rule gives no new information to the transfer relation.

Definition 1. *A rule r_1 is* covered *by a rule r_2 if the inputs to r_1 are less than or equal to the inputs of r_2 and the outputs are equal, both according to the lattice order $\sqsubseteq$.*

The rule assigning the value -0 to z upon inputs $x : 0$ and $y : -0$ is for instance covered by the rule $x : -0$, $y : -0$, $z : -0$ since $0 \sqsubseteq_V -0$. A *vacuous* rule on the other hand provides useless information about the operation as the output value represents the set of all concrete value.

Definition 2. *A rule is* vacuous *if the abstract value given for the output is the top element of the lattice.*

An example for our setting is $x : -$, $y : +$, $z : \top$. Table 1 only gives rules which are neither covered by others nor vacuous and represents the hardware requirements for our abstract domain sign. Compared to functional equivalence, the knowledge about the abstract domain employed in the software analysis simplifies the hardware requirements. However, the results of the hardware verification are now only applicable to software analyses using the same abstract domain.

3.3   Approach #3: Requirements of the Specific Analysis

Our third approach presents an even tighter integration of software analysis and hardware verification. Here, we extract the requirements for the hardware from the specific analysis result represented by the abstract reachability graph. The abstract reachability graph for a program as constructed by CPACHECKER exactly tells us what properties the software analysis has used. These need not necessarily be all the rules encoding the abstract transfer relation, making the hardware verification even simpler than in the second approach. In the extreme case, the behavior of the custom instruction does not influence the validity of the property at all and we need not check anything on the hardware. Furthermore, this approach might be helpful if the knowledge about the rules is not known since the requirement can directly be extracted from the analysis result.

In the following we describe this approach for our sign dataflow analysis for program SUM, for which Figure 3 shows the abstract reachability graph. The graph contains two edges labeled by a saturating addition which we want to realize as custom instruction. The predecessor of each edge is the precondition and the successor the postcondition. Thus, we can extract the following two requirements:

(1) $\mathrm{i} : 0+; \mathrm{N} : +; \mathrm{sum} : 0+ \xrightarrow{\mathrm{sum=sum} +_{\mathrm{sat}} \mathrm{i}} \mathrm{i} : 0+; \mathrm{N} : +; \mathrm{sum} : 0+$

(2) $\mathrm{i} : 0+; \mathrm{N} : +; \mathrm{sum} : 0+ \xrightarrow{\mathrm{i=i} +_{\mathrm{sat}} 1} \mathrm{i} : 0+; \mathrm{N} : \top; \mathrm{sum} : 0+$

So far these requirements are formulated for the program statements but not for the custom instruction $\mathrm{z} = \mathrm{x} +_{\mathrm{sat}} \mathrm{y}$. Especially, the variable names in the extracted requirements are those of the statement and not those of the custom instruction. To transform between software and hardware, we carry out three transformations on the requirements:

1. We replace the program variables' names with names matching the inputs of the custom instruction. Note that the replacement is different for the precondition and the postcondition. For instance, in the first requirement we need to replace i by y and sum by x in the precondition (left part of requirement (1)), but sum by z in the postcondition (right part of requirement (1)).
2. We eliminate irrelevant variables, e.g., variables which do not occur in the custom instruction and which are not related to variables in the precondition or postcondition.[2] As an example, in the second requirement the value of N is irrelevant and thus can be eliminated.
3. We replace constants by their abstract values of the analysis domain. For example, we replace constant 1 in the second requirement by abstract value $+$.

Together, for our example these three transformations give us the following requirements on the hardware, the second already covered by the first.

(1) $\text{y}:0+;\text{x}:0+ \xrightarrow{\text{z=x }+_{\text{sat}}\text{ y}} \text{z}:0+$

(2) $\text{y}:+;\text{x}:0+ \xrightarrow{\text{z=x }+_{\text{sat}}\text{ y}} \text{z}:0+$

Compared to approach #2, only 1 of 7 rules must be checked, possibly with very low effort.

4   Hardware Analysis

As outlined in Section 3, the task of the hardware analysis is to formally verify the validity of certain correctness assumptions for custom instructions. The correctness assumptions are used by the software analysis implicitly or explicitly during the analysis. Figure 5 depicts the general structure of our hardware analysis. As verification input, we expand the implementation of the custom instruction, i.e., its RFU configuration, $I(\underline{in})$ with a property checking circuit $P(\underline{in}, \underline{out})$, where $\underline{in}$ is the set of inputs of the custom instruction and $\underline{out}$ the set of outputs, respectively. The output of the property checker is an error flag $error = P(\underline{in}, \underline{out}) = P(\underline{in}, I(\underline{in}))$, which is set iff the properties encoded in $P(\underline{in}, \underline{out})$ are violated for the given input stimuli $\underline{in}$. To show that the encoded properties for the implementation of the custom instruction actually hold, it is thus sufficient to prove that the error flag is never set under all possible input stimuli. Our main tasks are thus to encode the assumptions and requirements posed by the software analysis into a suitable property checker, i.e., into a circuit description in an HDL such as Verilog, and to prove unsatisfiability. While the details of the property checker change with the used approach from Section 3, the general structure of Figure 5 is always the same.

---

[2] We assume the CI to be side-effect free. Note, if in contrast to our approach irrelevant variables are kept, it will also be proven that the CI has no side-effects.

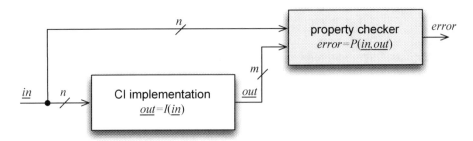

Fig. 5. General structure for the hardware analysis. A property checker encodes the assumptions and requirements posed by software analysis for the implementation of the custom instruction (CI) with n bits input and m bits output.

4.1   Construction of Property Checkers

The design of the property checker is highly dependent on the assumptions and requirements to be verified. Our second and third approach to software/hardware verification, i.e., taking verification requirements from an analysis domain or from a specific analysis, often generates several independent assumptions to be verified. In that case we can devise several property sub-checkers and simply form the error flag as the disjunction of the outputs of these sub-checkers or as the negated conjunction of the underlying assertions, respectively.

As mentioned above, we take the translated software assumptions (cp. Sections 3.2 and 3.3) and encode each of them into a verification input for the hardware verification, i.e., we specify them using a behavioral hardware description in a language such as Verilog. Since the assumptions are already formulated in the terms of the custom instruction at this point, the encoding is most often pretty straight-forward, and using a high level language for property specification enables us to use more complex properties than just boolean formulae. To explore our technique, we performed these steps manually for our case studies, but we are currently looking into methods for automating them.

For example, Figure 6 presents the property checker for the transfer relation of the saturating addition, $z = x +_{\mathsf{sat}} y$, shown in Table 1. The figure displays part of the Verilog code that implements $P(\underline{in}, I(\underline{in}))$, with $\underline{in} = (\underline{x}, \underline{y})$ and $\underline{out} = \underline{z}$. Using the implication rule ($a \rightarrow b \equiv \neg a \vee b$, or in Verilog syntax ~a|b), the shown code is the straight-forward implementation of every implication contained in the table. To enhance readability, the actual signal comparisons have been replaced with auxiliary signals (e.g., x_lt_zero : $x < 0$, x_ge_zero : $x \geq 0$, etc.). The circuitry extracting these auxiliary signals from the input variables is also part of the property checker. If any of the implications impz is violated, the error flag is set. Thus proving that the error flag is never set for any possible input $(\underline{x}, \underline{y})$ proves that all assumptions about the semantics of the abstract domain are adhered to by the custom instruction. This method for constructing the property checker works for all assumptions that argue over the inputs and outputs of the custom instruction in terms of the sign data-flow

```
assign  imp1 = ~( x_lt_zero & y_le_zero ) | z_lt_zero;
assign  imp2 = ~( x_le_zero & y_lt_zero ) | z_lt_zero;
assign  imp3 = ~( x_le_zero & y_le_zero ) | z_le_zero;
assign  imp4 = ~( x_eq_zero & y_eq_zero ) | z_eq_zero;
assign  imp5 = ~( x_ge_zero & y_ge_zero ) | z_ge_zero;
assign  imp6 = ~( x_ge_zero & y_gt_zero ) | z_gt_zero;
assign  imp7 = ~( x_gt_zero & y_ge_zero ) | z_gt_zero;

assign  all_implications_hold =
        imp1 & imp2 & imp3 & imp4 & imp5 & imp6 & imp7;

assign  error = ~all_implications_hold;
```

Fig. 6. Verilog code implementing the property checker for the transfer relation of the saturating addition shown in Table 1 (partial code using auxiliary signals)

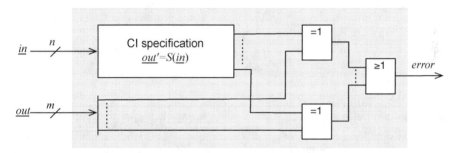

Fig. 7. Property checker for proving functional equivalence between an implementation of a custom instruction and its specification, both with n bits input and m bits output

analysis, whether they are general and cover the complete rules of the abstract domain or concrete as obtained from a specific software analysis.

To prove full functional equivalence between an implementation of a custom instruction and its behavioral specification, we need to construct a circuit that is commonly called miter. A miter is comprised of the implementation $I(in)$ and the specification $S(in)$, both of which receive the same inputs in. The outputs of the implementation, out, and the specification, out', are pairwise XOR-ed, and the disjunction of the results forms the error flag. The specification and implementation are equivalent if the outputs are identical for any input. Figure 7 sketches the resulting property checker for functional equivalence.

4.2   Hardware Verification Tool Flow

To perform the hardware verification we employ the open source academic tool flow VTR [20]. We specify the custom instructions in Verilog and map them to circuits using ODIN II for hardware synthesis, followed by ABC for technology mapping. Both ODIN II and ABC are included in the VTR distribution. The circuits are technology-mapped to an FPGA architecture employing logic blocks with 6-input lookup tables. For a real customizable processor, the resulting circuit netlist would be placed and routed for the reconfigurable fabric of an RFU and the configuration bitstream would be generated. For the sake of simplicity these steps are omitted in our current work. Expanding our tool flow to cover also these steps is part of future work and will allow us to catch not only design errors and errors introduced by hardware synthesis and technology mapping, but also errors due to low-level FPGA implementation tools. We take the circuit netlist for a custom instruction and convert it into an And-Inverter-Graph representation. For the verification input, the property checkers are also specified in Verilog and synthesized into an And-Inverter-Graph representation. When checking for functional equivalence, we can utilize ABC which has the capability to automatically transform two circuits into a miter if they use the same number of inputs and outputs. In all other cases, we use our own tool to combine the representations for the implementation and the property checker into one And-Inverter-Graph, our verification input. Again using ABC, we simplify the graph by removing everything that does not influence the error flag, i.e., is not in its cone-of-influence, and then transform the graph into a large boolean formula in conjunctive normal form (CNF). To prove unsatisfiability of the CNF formula and thus the assumptions posed by software analysis, we leverage the SAT solver picoSAT [4].

The different approaches explained in Section 3 require different amounts of manual interaction and lead to different computation times for the SAT solver. The potential of our method lies within the simplification step before generating the CNF formula: When checking for functional equivalence the circuit will not be reduced by much, but the other two approaches might reveal small and simple rule sets, so that after simplification the formula will be very small. The features and trade-offs involved for the different approaches will be illustrated using case studies in the next section.

5   Experimental Results and Discussion

To demonstrate the feasibility of our method for integrating software and hardware verification and to explore the runtime behavior of the three approaches, we have conducted experiments with three custom instructions as case studies which are summarized in Table 2. The first column lists the custom instructions together with the programs that use them. The second and third column of Table 2 display the abstract analysis domain and the analysis techniques used for the software analysis, the fourth column presents the runtime for the software analysis and the remaining columns present the runtimes for the hardware analyses.

The case study programs are shown in Figure 8, where the program statements that are being replaced by custom instructions are highlighted. The first custom instruction, SATURATING ADD, is the saturating addition. The second custom instruction, CONDITIONAL SET, assigns either 0 or 1 to a variable depending on whether another variable is larger than zero. The last custom instruction

Table 2. Experimental case studies with software and hardware analysis times for 64-bit operands, averaged over 100 runs. Hardware analysis #1 denotes functional equivalence, #2 checking the rules of the analysis domain and #3 checking the rules of the specific analysis.

custom instruction / source code	software analysis			hardware analysis time		
	domain	technique	time [ms]	#1 [ms]	#2 [ms]	#3 [ms]
SATURATING ADD / ex49.c	sign	data flow	30	308	276	121
CONDITIONAL SET / inf6.c	sign	model checking	30	232	122	122
PARALLEL DECREMENT / ex19.c	predicate	model checking	190	374	245	390

is PARALLEL DECREMENT and implements two saturating decrements in parallel. The first two case studies rely on the sign domain, where the first case study performs a dataflow analysis and the second one model checking. The third case study again performs model checking but on the predicate domain. To link software and hardware analyses we have mapped the data type used in the software analysis, which is a signed integer of unspecified bit width, to binary numbers of a pre-defined bit width encoded in two's complement.

Figure 9 shows the runtimes for the hardware verification for varying bit widths of inputs and outputs of the custom instruction. We have implemented the saturating add with a ripple adder structure containing a long path to propagate the carry. Hence, increasing the bit width naturally increases the complexity of the circuit which results in the observed runtimes for checking functional equivalence. Focusing on the assumptions of the abstract analysis domain significantly reduces the effort and checking only the few rules used by the software analysis leads to the smallest runtimes. Since in this case study the software analysis performs a sign analysis, the cone of influence for the error flag only includes a portion of the complete circuit. In summary, this case study supports our expectation that exploiting more knowledge about the specific analysis leads to a more efficient verification.

The conditional assignment results in a rather flat circuit and increasing the bit width does not change the verification complexity too much. As all circuit paths are relatively short, even the check for functional equivalence can roughly compete with the other approaches. The domain knowledge we have applied in this example exploits the fact that we can deduce the correct function of the custom instruction by simply looking at the sign bit of the input conditional variable. The rules deduced from the software analysis form three implications which result in almost the same checks as required when incorporating domain knowledge. This explains why the two approaches perform nearly identically.

The parallel decrement uses two saturating adders in parallel, both of which have one input tied to the constant minus one. We thus have expected this case study to exhibit a behavior similar to that of the saturating adder. However, as the results show, this is only true when comparing functional equivalence with inf6.c using CONDITIONAL SET

```
status=0;
flag=0;
if a>0 then
    status = 0;
else
    status = 1;
if status ! = 0 then
    b=-a+1;
else
    b=-a;
if a>0 then
    as = 0;
else
    as = 1;
if b>0 then
    bs = 0;
else
    bs = 1;
if bs = as then
    flag = 1;
if flag! =0 then
    ERROR: goto ERROR;
```

ex49.c using SATURATING ADD

```
sum=0;
i=0;
while i<N do
    sum=sum +sat i;
    i=i +sat 1;
if sum<0 then
    ERROR: goto ERROR;
```

ex19.c using PARALLEL
DECREMENT

```
x=i;
y=j;
while x≠0 do
    x=x +sat (-1);
    y=y +sat (-1);
if i == j then
    if y! =0 then
        ERROR: goto ERROR;
```

Fig. 8. Case study programs adapted from [21]

the approach using domain knowledge; checking for functional equivalence is always more runtime intense. The absolute runtimes for functional equivalence are also smaller than for the saturating adder since two of the four input operands are constant which allows for some logic optimization beforehand. Surprisingly, the software analysis posed quite complex assumptions to be verified in this case. Rather than checking properties for both adders independently, the analysis tied the adders together by arguing with the invariant difference of both variables before and after execution of the custom instruction. This coupling resulted in a hardware analysis that was more complex than the functional equivalence check. Apparently, knowing about the parallel structure of the custom instruction one could simplify the analysis.

The last case study program pointed to an interesting line of future work that ties together software and hardware analyses even closer. First, reasoning about structural information of an implementation currently is not within the scope of the software analysis tools, but could have helped reduce complexity. Second, sometimes the software analysis makes unrealistic assumptions about the hardware, e.g., when SMT solvers reason about integers they assume unrestricted value ranges. By changing the underlying theory used by the solver from linear arithmetic to bitvectors we could more accurately model the behavior of the hardware.

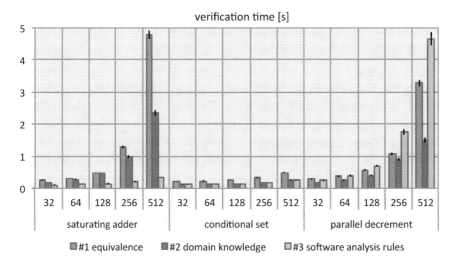

Fig. 9. Runtimes for the hardware analysis in seconds for various bit widths, averaged over 100 runs

6 Conclusion

In this paper, we have proposed a new technique for software-hardware co-verification for the area of custom instruction set extensions. Our technique includes three different approaches, tailoring the hardware verification to the needs of the software analysis to different extents. All of our approaches thereby guarantee trustworthy software analysis, even in the presence of custom instructions. Experimental results show that none of the approaches is superior to all others. However, the approach that extracts requirements from the analysis domain and transfer function seems to be a good compromise, with an average overhead for hardware verification lying in between the other two approaches.

Currently, we are working on further automating the construction of property checkers from the requirements. Moreover, we plan to extend our co-verification approaches to hardware-software-co-certification, integrating proof-carrying code [17] and proof carrying hardware [7].

References

1. Beyer, D.: Status report on software verification. In: Ábrahám, E., Havelund, K. (eds.) TACAS 2014 (ETAPS). LNCS, vol. 8413, pp. 373–388. Springer, Heidelberg (2014)
2. Beyer, D., Henzinger, T., Théoduloz, G.: Configurable software verification: Concretizing the convergence of model checking and program analysis. In: Damm, W., Hermanns, H. (eds.) CAV 2007. LNCS, vol. 4590, pp. 504–518. Springer, Heidelberg (2007)

3. Beyer, D., Keremoglu, M.E.: CPACHECKER: A Tool for Configurable Software Verification. In: Gopalakrishnan, G., Qadeer, S. (eds.) CAV 2011. LNCS, vol. 6806, pp. 184–190. Springer, Heidelberg (2011)
4. Biere, A.: PicoSAT essentials. JSAT 4(2-4), 75–97 (2008)
5. Clark, N., Blome, J., Chu, M., Mahlke, S., Biles, S., Flautner, K.: An architecture framework for transparent instruction set customization in embedded processors. In: ISCA, pp. 272–283. IEEE Computer Society (2005)
6. Clarke, E., Kroening, D.: Hardware verification using ANSI-C programs as a reference. In: ASP-DAC, pp. 308–311. ACM (2003)
7. Drzevitzky, S., Kastens, U., Platzner, M.: Proof-carrying hardware: Towards runtime verification of reconfigurable modules. In: ReConFig, pp. 189–194. IEEE (2009)
8. Erkok, L., Carlsson, M., Wick, A.: Hardware/software co-verification of cryptographic algorithms using Cryptol. In: FMCAD, pp. 188–191. IEEE (2009)
9. Galuzzi, C., Bertels, K.: The instruction-set extension problem: A survey. ACM Trans. Reconfigurable Technol. Syst. 4(2), 18:1–18:28 (2011)
10. Henzinger, T.A., Jhala, R., Majumdar, R., Sutre, G.: Lazy abstraction. In: POPL, pp. 58–70. ACM (2002)
11. Horn, A., Tautschnig, M., Val, C., Liang, L., Melham, T., Grundy, J., Kroening, D.: Formal co-validation of low-level hardware/software interfaces. In: FMCAD, pp. 121–128. IEEE (2013)
12. Kurshan, R., Levin, V., Minea, M., Peled, D., Yenigun, H.: Verifying hardware in its software context. In: CAD, pp. 742–749. IEEE (1997)
13. Li, J., Xie, F., Ball, T., Levin, V., McGarvey, C.: An Automata-Theoretic Approach to Hardware/Software Co-verification. In: Rosenblum, D.S., Taentzer, G. (eds.) FASE 2010. LNCS, vol. 6013, pp. 248–262. Springer, Heidelberg (2010)
14. Loitz, S., Wedler, M., Brehm, C., Vogt, T., Wehn, N., Kunz, W.: Proving functional correctness of weakly programmable IPs - a case study with formal property checking. In: SASP, pp. 48–54. IEEE (2008)
15. Mishchenko, A., Chatterjee, S., Brayton, R.K., Eén, N.: Improvements to combinational equivalence checking. In: ICCAD, pp. 836–843. ACM (2006)
16. de Moura, L.M., Bjørner, N.: Satisfiability modulo theories: introduction and applications. Commun. ACM 54(9), 69–77 (2011)
17. Necula, G.C.: Proof-carrying code. In: POPL, pp. 106–119. ACM (1997)
18. Necula, G., McPeak, S., Rahul, S., Weimer, W.: CIL: Intermediate Language and Tools for Analysis and Transformation of C Programs. In: Nigel Horspool, R. (ed.) CC 2002. LNCS, vol. 2304, pp. 213–228. Springer, Heidelberg (2002)
19. Nguyen, M., Wedler, M., Stoffel, D., Kunz, W.: Formal hardware/software co-verification by interval property checking with abstraction. In: DAC, pp. 510–515. ACM (2011)
20. Rose, J., Luu, J., Yu, C.W., Densmore, O., Goeders, J., Somerville, A., Kent, K.B., Jamieson, P., Anderson, J.: The VTR project: Architecture and CAD for FPGAs from Verilog to Routing. In: FPGA, pp. 77–86. ACM (2012)
21. Sankaranarayanan, S., Ivancic, F.: Necla static analysis benchmarks (necla-static-small) v1.1, http://www.nec-labs.com/research/system/ systems_SAV-website/small_static_bench-v1.1.tar.gz
22. Wagner, I., Bertacco, V.: Post-Silicon and Runtime Verification for Modern Processors. Springer (2011)
23. Xie, F., Yang, G., Song, X.: Component-based hardware/software co-verification for building trustworthy embedded systems. Journal of Systems and Software 80(5), 643–654 (2007)

Code Generation for Event-B

Andreas Fürst[1], Thai Son Hoang[1], David Basin[1], Krishnaji Desai[2],
Naoto Sato[3], and Kunihiko Miyazaki[3]

[1] Institute of Information Security, ETH-Zurich, Switzerland
{fuersta,htson,basin}@inf.ethz.ch
[2] Hitachi India Pvt. Ltd., India
krishnaji@hitachi.co.in
[3] Yokohama Research Lab, Hitachi Ltd., Japan
{naoto.sato.je,kunihiko.miyazaki.zt}@hitachi.com

Abstract. We present an approach to generating program code from Event-B models that is correct-by-construction. Correctness is guaranteed by the combined use of well-definedness restrictions, refinement, and assertions. By enforcing the well-definedness of the translated model, we prevent runtime errors that originate from semantic differences between the target language and Event-B, such as different interpretations of the range of integer values. Using refinement, we show that the generated code correctly implements the original Event-B model. We provide a simple yet powerful scheduling language that allows one to specify an execution sequence of the model's guarded events where assertions are used to express properties established by the event execution sequence, which are necessary for well-definedness and refinement proofs.

Keywords: Event-B, code generation, correct-by-construction.

1 Introduction

The Event-B modelling language [2] is a formal method that is well suited for developing embedded controllers that satisfy strong safety requirements. The advantage of Event-B and its notion of refinement is that we can express and prove safety properties on an abstract model of the system that includes both the controller and its working environment. Details of the system are afterwards gradually introduced into the formal models via refinement. Refinement in Event-B preserves the proved safety properties of the abstract model.

Once the system's model is sufficiently detailed, the controller part of the model can be extracted. This must afterwards be translated into a sequential program that runs on given hardware. We identify three main challenges for this translation. First, the Event-B model must be restricted to a well-defined subset in order to generate code for a particular programming language. Well-definedness for the sublanguage thereby reflects the available data types of the target language. For example, arithmetic operations that are valid in the Event-B model, but not well-defined for a target language, might result in overflows at runtime because of the different domains of the integer type. Second, Event-B's semantics is such that the event that is executed next is chosen non-deterministically from the set of enabled events. This non-determinism must be replaced by a schedule that defines an execution order on the events. As the scheduling

E. Albert and E. Sekerinski (Eds.): IFM 2014, LNCS 8739, pp. 323–338, 2014.

language becomes more sophisticated, one can generate more efficient program code. Finally, it is evident that the translation must preserve the safety properties of the Event-B model.

There has been extensive related work on code generation for Event-B [2, 4–6, 9, 10]. The different approaches have limitations including restricted scheduling languages [6, 9, 10], ignoring the differences between the mathematical notation of Event-B and the target languages [2, 4–6, 10], and missing formal justification of the approach's correctness [6, 9, 10]. More details on the limitations of the existing approaches are provided in Section 5.

To overcome these limitations, we present an approach to generating code from Event-B models that focuses on the translation's correctness. We therefore concentrate on a single target language, namely C. Furthermore, our approach provides a flexible scheduling language that is not only useful for encoding different scheduling strategies but also for proving that the specified schedules are valid, that is, they do not result in programs with behaviours that are not described by the original Event-B model.

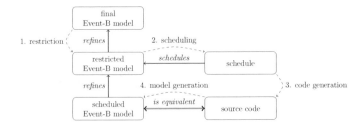

Fig. 1. Overview of our code generation approach

Our code generation approach has four steps. Figure 1 depicts the different entities involved and their relationships together with the corresponding step in which they are provided by the user or the code generator. The "final Event-B model" represents the final refinement step of an Event-B development and is the starting point for our code generation approach. First, we restrict the Event-B model via refinement to ensure that the variables are of suitable types and operations on them are well-defined. Second, we use a special scheduling language to specify a schedule for the restricted Event-B model, that describes the intended execution order on the events. Third, we execute our code generator with the schedule as input. Based on the schedule, the code generator translates the restricted model into a sequential program and thereby generates source code. Finally, our code generator also generates a scheduled Event-B model representing the semantics of the sequential program, and we prove that this scheduled model refines the restricted Event-B model.

The correctness of our translation relies on (i) the use of partial functions and well-definedness to ensure that the operations on the data types provided by the target language are valid, (ii) assertions that are annotated in the schedule and subsequently translated into invariants of the scheduled Event-B model, and (iii) the proof that the scheduled model refines the restricted Event-B model, which relies on the automatically generated invariants.

Overall, our contribution is an approach to code generation from Event-B models that guarantees that generated programs correctly implement their Event-B specifications and therefore will not incur runtime errors such as arithmetic overflows. The novelty of our approach is the use of well-definedness in the restriction step to prevent runtime errors, a flexible scheduling language with assertions for specifying scheduling information during the second step, and the use of refinement in the fourth step of our approach to prove the generated program code's correctness. Based on our approach, we implemented a plug-in for the Rodin platform [3] and successfully generated code for industrial-scale case studies including an elevator control system and a train control system, both with strong safety properties. To make this paper self-contained, we illustrate our approach using a comparatively simple academic example from [2].

Structure. We briefly overview the Event-B modelling method in Section 2.1 and the "cars on a bridge" case study from [2] in Section 2.2. We use this example to illustrate the four steps of our approach to generating code from Event-B models in Section 3. In Section 4, we provide evidence for the general applicability of our approach. In Section 5, we compare our approach with the existing code generation tools for Event-B. We draw conclusions and discuss future work in Section 6.

2 Background

2.1 Event-B

Event-B [2] represents an extension as well as a simplification of the classical B-method [1], which has been focused around the general notion of *events*. Event-B has a semantics based on transition systems and simulation between such systems. We will not describe in detail the semantics of Event-B here; full details are provided in [2]. Instead, we will describe some Event-B modelling concepts that are important for the later presentation.

Event-B models are related by *refinement* and are organized in terms of the two basic constructs: *contexts* and *machines*. *Contexts* specify the static part of a model and may contain *carrier sets*, *constants*, *axioms*, and *theorems*. Carrier sets are similar to types. Axioms constrain carrier sets and constants, whereas theorems express properties derivable from axioms. The role of a context is to isolate the parameters of a formal model (carrier sets and constants) and their properties, which are intended to hold for all instances.

Machines specify behavioral properties of Event-B models. Machines may contain *variables*, *invariants*, *theorems*, and *events*. Variables v define the state of a machine, and are constrained by invariants $I(v)$. Theorems are properties derivable from the invariants. Possible state changes are described by events.

The term $e \mathrel{\widehat{=}} \textbf{any } t \textbf{ where } G(t, v) \textbf{ then } S(t, v) \textbf{ end}$ represents an event e, where t is the event's *parameters*, $G(t, v)$ is the event's *guard* (the conjunction of one or more predicates), and $S(t, v)$ is the event's *action*. The guard states the condition under which an event may occur, and the action describes how the state variables evolve when the event occurs. An event's action is composed of one or more *assignments* of the form $x := E(t, v)$, where x is a variable in v and E (t,v) is an expression of the same type as x. Assignments in Event-B may also be nondeterministic. However, we ignore these assignments in our approach since we only translate deterministic assignments and force the user to first refine non-deterministic assignments into deterministic ones. All assignments of an action $S(t, v)$ occur simultaneously. A dedicated event without any parameter or guard is used for *initialisation*.

Refinement provides a means to gradually introduce details about the system's dynamic behaviour into formal models [2]. A machine **CM** can refine another machine **AM**. We call **AM** the *abstract* machine and **CM** the *concrete* machine. The states of the abstract machine are related to the states of the concrete machine by *gluing invariants* $J(v, w)$, where v are the variables of the abstract machine and w are the variables of the concrete machine. A special case of refinement (called superposition refinement) is when v is kept in the refinement, i.e. $v \subseteq w$. Intuitively, any behaviour of **CM** can be simulated by a behaviour of **AM** with respect to the gluing invariants $J(v, w)$.

Refinement can be reasoned about on a per-event basis. Each event e of the abstract machine is *refined* by one or more concrete events f. Simplifying somewhat, we can say that f refines e if f's guard is stronger than e's guard (*guard strengthening*), and the gluing invariants $J(v, w)$ establish a simulation of f by e (*simulation*).

2.2 Running Example

In this section, we describe the "cars on a bridge" example taken from [2, Chapter 2] that we use as a running example to illustrate our approach to code generation. The system's main functionality is to control the cars on a bridge between an island and the mainland. Due to the bridge's width, only traffic in one direction is allowed at a time. The system is equipped with four sensors to detect the presence of cars entering and leaving the bridge. The system controls the two traffic lights located at both ends of the bridge. Moreover, the maximum number of cars allowed on the island is limited. The Event-B model is gradually developed in four machines. The last refinement includes environment events modelling the movement of cars that triggers the sensors and controller events setting the traffic lights accordingly. For the purpose of illustrating our approach to generating code, we focus on the following events of the last refinement.

ML_out1 :	ML_out2 :	IL_tl_green :	ML_OUT_DEP :
when	**when**	**when**	**when**
$ml\_out\_10 = TRUE$	$ml\_out\_10 = TRUE$	$il\_tl = red$	$ML\_OUT\_SR = on$
$a + b + 1 < d$	$a + b + 1 = d$	$0 < b$	$ml\_tl = green$
then	**then**	$a = 0$	**then**
$a := a + 1$	$a := a + 1$	$ml\_pass = 1$	$ML\_OUT\_SR := off$
$ml\_pass := 1$	$ml\_tl := red$	$ml\_out\_10 = FALSE$	$ml\_out\_10 := TRUE$
$ml\_out\_10 := FALSE$	$ml\_pass := 1$	$IL\_OUT\_SR = on$	$A := A + 1$
end	$ml\_out\_10 := FALSE$	**then**	**end**
	end	$il\_tl := green$	
		$ml\_tl := red$	
		$il\_pass := 0$	
		end	

The events ML_out1, ML_out2, and IL_tl_green are controller events and the event ML_OUT_DEP is an environment event. We omit other events for clarity. The constant d represent the maximum number of cars allowed on the island. The variables a, b, c, ml_pass, il_pass are controller variables and the variable A is an environment variable.

Other variables are shared variables representing the sensors (from the environment to the controller), i.e., ml_out_10, il_out_10, ml_in_10, il_in_10, ML_OUT_SR, and IL_OUT_SR, or the actuators (from the controller to the environment), i.e., ml_tl and il_tl. The interested reader can find the exact meaning of the variables in [2, Chapter 2].

3   A Code Generator for Event-B

In our approach, the code generator translates an Event-B model into C source code. As depicted in Figure 1, prior to generating code we must restrict the Event-B model and provide a schedule. Using the schedule as an input, the code generator then generates two outputs, C source code and an Event-B machine that we use to prove the correctness of the generated source code.

3.1   Well-Definedness Restrictions

The final model of an Event-B development may still include parts that are not well-defined with respect to the target language. Using refinement, we restrict these remaining parts and thereby obtain a restricted model that is well-defined. Our plug-in checks that the model is restricted before generating source code for it. In the following, we describe the semantic differences between Event-B and C and describe our approach to establishing well-definedness.

Basic Types. The two basic types that our code generator supports are 32-bit integers and booleans. While the boolean type in C is equivalent to type BOOL in Event-B, the integer types have different ranges. We therefore define in Event-B the range of the C integer type as a constant C_INT ($C\_INT = -2147483648..2147483647$) and require that every integer variable belongs to this set. C_INT can be seen as a restricted data type in the model and we say that a variable is of type C_INT whenever it belongs to the set described by the constant C_INT, i.e., $variable \in C\_INT$.

Arrays. We support one- and two-dimensional arrays for both basic types. Arrays are represented by total functions in Event-B. If a variable or constant is not of a basic type, then it must be of one of the array types in the table below, where k and l are natural numbers smaller than the maximum value in C_INT. We use $\mathcal{T}(x)$ to represent the translation of a string x that complies with Event-B syntax.

Event-B	C
$f \in 0..k \to C\_INT$	int f[$\mathcal{T}(k)$+1]
$g \in 0..k \to BOOL$	bool g[$\mathcal{T}(k)$+1]
$f \in 0..k \times 0..l \to C\_INT$	int f[$\mathcal{T}(k)$+1][$\mathcal{T}(l)$+1]
$g \in 0..k \times 0..l \to BOOL$	bool g[$\mathcal{T}(k)$+1][$\mathcal{T}(l)$+1]

The restriction on k and l guarantees that the size of a generated array is always positive and at most the maximum number in C_INT. However, the maximal allowed size of an array depends on the target system and its memory management. Hence, we cannot guarantee that the memory allocation at the beginning of the running program will succeed.

Arithmetic Operators. Careless use of arithmetic operators is the source of integer over-flows in software. Since the integer type in Event-B does not have a lower or upper bound, the addition of two positive integer numbers always results in a positive integer number. In a C program, however, this result might be larger than the maximum integer number and cause a runtime error or be mapped to a negative number. Either way, the outcome of the computation is different from that in the Event-B model. Due to the restriction of integer variables to the type C_INT, assignments of the form $x := x + y$ are already checked for well-definedness when proving the preservation of the invariant $x \in C\_INT$. The intermediate results of multiple arithmetic operations and arithmetic operations in predicates, however, are not checked. To enforce the well-definedness of all arithmetic operations, we introduce special operators that are adapted to the integer type C_INT and we restrict the use of each arithmetic operator to just these.

$$c\_plus = \{\lambda a \mapsto b \cdot a \in C\_INT \wedge b \in C\_INT \wedge a + b \in C\_INT \mid a + b\}$$
$$c\_minus = \{\lambda a \mapsto b \cdot a \in C\_INT \wedge b \in C\_INT \wedge a - b \in C\_INT \mid a - b\}$$
$$c\_mul = \{\lambda a \mapsto b \cdot a \in C\_INT \wedge b \in C\_INT \wedge a * b \in C\_INT \mid a * b\}$$
$$c\_div = \{\lambda a \mapsto b \cdot a \in C\_INT \wedge b \in C\_INT \wedge b \neq 0 \wedge a \div b \in C\_INT \mid a \div b\}$$
$$c\_mod = \{\lambda a \mapsto b \cdot a \in C\_INT \wedge b \in C\_INT \wedge 0 \leq a \wedge 0 < b \mid a \bmod b\}$$

The result of an integer division in Event-B is always rounded towards zero as in the C99 standard. In C89 and C90, however, it is implementation dependant whether the result of an integer division is rounded towards zero or towards minus infinity. This difference is important when the integer division results is a negative number. When using a compiler compliant to C89 or C90, the definition of the c_div operation must be adapted to prevent negative results and a possibly inconsistent translation. No such action is required for the modulo operator since the domain of Event-B's modulo operation is already restricted to natural numbers.

Due to the use of lambda expressions in the operator's definition, arithmetic operations change from infix notation to function applications in the model. We keep this style in the translation to source code and define macros to replace the function calls during compilation by the standard operators.

```
#define c_plus(x,y)  (x+y)
#define c_minus(x,y) (x-y)
#define c_mul(x,y)   (x*y)
#define c_div(x,y)   (x/y)
#define c_mod(x,y)   (x%y)
```

Events. For the translation of events to source code, an event's parameters must be fixed to specific values. Theoretically, an event parameter that is fixed to a single value is not that useful as any occurrence of the parameter in guards and actions could just be replaced by its fixed value. For practical reasons, we support event parameters as local storage for computation results. If the result of a computation is used in more than one action, it is more efficient to do the computation only once and store the result.

A core concept of our approach is that the guards of the events are not translated, but their evaluation to true is guaranteed by the flow control structures of the schedule or more precisely by the specified branch conditions, loop conditions, and assertions. The only guards that are translated are those that specify the value of an event parameter. We require in the restricted Event-B model that for every event parameter there is exactly one guard of the form *parameter* $= \ldots$, where the right-hand side of the equation must be an expression of type BOOL or C_INT.

Since an event's actions denote parallel assignments, the order of the actions does not matter in Event-B. This changes when we translate the actions into a sequence of single assignments. As a result, the right-hand side of the assignments in the source code cannot refer to the before-values of the variables. To overcome this issue, we restrict the actions of the event so that the right-hand side of an assignment does not refer to variables that already occurred on the left-hand side of a previous assignment. If this restriction is not guaranteed, the developer must either rearrange the actions where possible or introduce parameters as auxiliary variables to store the before-value of the conflicting variables. This task could be automated in a future version of our plug-in.

Expressions and Predicates. We restrict expressions and predicates to a subset of the Event-B syntax for which we provide the translation mappings presented in Table 2 in Section 3.3. In developments with arrays, there are often events with guards that contain quantifiers to express predicates on arrays. We therefore developed patterns for translating quantified predicates. Due to space restrictions we only present predicates with a single universal quantifier and omit translation patterns for existential quantification and combinations of multiple quantifiers. In our approach, the quantified predicate is translated to a function call of a dedicated function that evaluates the quantified predicate.

Assignments. In Table 3 in Section 3.3 we present the allowed assignments for updating variables in an event's action. The right-hand side of an assignment to a variable of type BOOL or C_INT must be an expression of the corresponding type. The update of arrays is slightly more difficult. We provide different translation rules for updating arrays at one or more positions and for overwriting an array with a set of index-value pairs. The bound variable used in the set comprehension is translated to the iteration variable of a for-loop.

Example. Returning to the "cars on a bridge" example, we first restrict the context of the development, i.e., the values for the constant d to C_INT. There are two options that we can take.

1. We apply generic instantation [7] to give d a concrete value (say $d = 20$) and prove that $d \in C\_INT$ as a theorem.
2. We add an axiom, i.e., $d \in C\_INT$ to further constrain d. In this way, d is left undefined and the user must define its concrete value within the program code. It is then the user's task to ensure that the concrete value satisfies the axioms.

In terms of safety guaranties, the first option is preferable as we prove that the values chosen for the constants imply the specified axioms. Hence, the current version of our plug-in follows this approach. The second option provides more flexibility as the definition of the constants' values can be written into a header file. The constants represent the parameters of the system and can easily be changed without generating new code. However, we have no practical way yet to enforce that the values in the header file are checked with respect to the model's axioms.

We also restrict the variables of the machine of the development. More precisely, integer variables of the machine (e.g., a, b, c) must be restricted to C_INT. This can be done by proving the corresponding condition, i.e., $a \in C\_INT$, $b \in C\_INT$, and $c \in C\_INT$ as invariants or theorems of the machine. In our example, we can prove these conditions as theorems derivable from the restriction of d to C_INT, the fact that all variables are natural numbers, and the invariant $a + b + c \leq d$. Moreover, we replace all occurrences of arithmetic operators in the events' actions by their well-defined version. For example, events ML_out1 and ML_out2 are restricted as follows.

ML_out1 :
when
  $ml\_out\_10 = TRUE$
  $a + b + 1 < d$
then
  $a := c\_plus(a \mapsto 1)$
  $ml\_pass := 1$
  $ml\_out\_10 := FALSE$
end

ML_out2 :
when
  $ml\_out\_10 = TRUE$
  $a + b + 1 = d$
then
  $a := c\_plus(a \mapsto 1)$
  $ml\_tl := red$
  $ml\_pass := 1$
  $ml\_out\_10 := FALSE$
end

Note that arithmetic operations used in event guards need not be restricted, except for those used to define parameters, since only parameter definitions are translated.

3.2   Scheduling the Model

To specify the execution order on the events of the restricted model, we provide the following scheduling language in our plug-in.

```
<schedule>   ::= <sequence>
<sequence>   ::= <sequence> ;{a} <sequence> | <block>
<block>      ::= event | <branch> | <loop>
<branch>     ::= if(c) <body> else <body> fi
<loop>       ::= do(c) <body> od
<body>       ::= "" | <sequence>
```

The symbols a and c represent a list of assertions and a loop or branch condition, respectively. The difference between a body and a sequence is that the body can be empty. For convenience, we can omit {a} if there are no assertions required between two sequentially composed sequences. Furthermore, if there is no else part in the branch, we can just write if(c) <body> fi.

Example. The first part of our schedule is as follows. The numbers are automatically generated in the editor of our plug-in.

```
0:   if(ml_out_10 = TRUE)
1:       if(c_plus(c_plus(a↦b)↦1)<d)
2:           ML_out1
3:       else
4:           ML_out1
         fi
     fi;
     {ml_out_10=FALSE}
5:   if(il_tl=red ∧ 0<b ∧ a=0 ∧ ml_pass=1 ∧ IL_OUT_SR=on)
6:       IL_tl_green
     fi;
```

Note that arithmetic operations used in the branches must be restricted. Moreover, the assertion $\{ml\_out\_10 = FALSE\}$ before the branch at position 5 : allows us to avoid checking this condition in the branch.

3.3 Translation to Source Code

The translation of the schedule is straightforward using if-else statements and while-loops. We omit the translation rules here and just give an example. Event blocks as well as branch and loop conditions are translated according to Tables 1-3. Note that we do not translate assertions, which are only used for the proof of correctness.

Table 1. Translation of Events

Event-B	C
evt-name	{
ANY s, t	int s = $\mathcal{T}(E_i(v, c))$;
WHERE	bool t = $\mathcal{T}(E_b(v, c, s))$;
$\quad s = E_i(v, c)$	
$\quad s \in C\_INT$ (theorem)	vi = $\mathcal{T}(E_i(v, c, s, t))$;
$\quad t = E_b(v, c, s)$	vb = $\mathcal{T}(E_b(v, c, s, t))$;
$\quad t \in BOOL$ (theorem)	}
THEN	
$\quad vi := E_i(v, c, s, t)$	
$\quad vb := E_b(v, c, s, t)$	
END	

The translation of the basic predicates and expressions is straight forward and similar to the translation mappings of the other approaches. Noteworthy is the possibility in our approach to translate quantified predicates, which are useful to express conditions in connection with arrays.

Table 2. Translation of Predicates and Expressions

Event-B	C	Event-B	C
$\neg x$	$!\mathcal{T}(x)$	$x \wedge \cdots \wedge y$	$(\mathcal{T}(x) \ \&\& \ \ldots \ \&\& \ \mathcal{T}(y))$
$\top$	true	$x \vee \cdots \vee y$	$(\mathcal{T}(x) \ || \ \ldots \ || \ \mathcal{T}(y))$
$\bot$	false	$x \Rightarrow y$	$(!\mathcal{T}(x) \ || \ \mathcal{T}(y))$
$a = b$	$(\mathcal{T}(a)==\mathcal{T}(b))$	$x \Leftrightarrow y$	$((!\mathcal{T}(x) \ || \ \mathcal{T}(y)) \ \&\&$
$a \neq b$	$(\mathcal{T}(a)!=\mathcal{T}(b))$		$\quad (!\mathcal{T}(y) \ || \ \mathcal{T}(x)))$
$a < b$	$(\mathcal{T}(a)<\mathcal{T}(b))$		
$a \leq b$	$(\mathcal{T}(a)<=\mathcal{T}(b))$	$f(a)$	f[a]
$a > b$	$(\mathcal{T}(a)>\mathcal{T}(b))$	$f(a \mapsto b)$	f($\mathcal{T}(a), \mathcal{T}(b)$)
$a \geq b$	$(\mathcal{T}(a)>=\mathcal{T}(b))$	$c\_operator(a \mapsto b)$	c_operator($\mathcal{T}(a), \mathcal{T}(b)$)
$identifier$	identifier	$\forall i \cdot i \in c\_upto(j \mapsto k)$	eval_uid()
		$\quad \Rightarrow P(v, c, i)$	
$TRUE$	true		bool eval_uid() {
$FALSE$	false		for(int i=$\mathcal{T}(j)$;i<=$\mathcal{T}(k)$;i++){
			if (!$\mathcal{T}(P(v,c,i))$)
			return false;
			}
			return true;
			}

Noteworthy in our translation of assignments are the different patterns for updating arrays. We can either update an array at one or more fixed positions or we can iterate through the array and use a predicate to evaluate at runtime which positions are updated.

Table 3. Translation of Assignments

Event-B	C
$vi := b$ $vb := r$	`vi = `$\mathcal{T}(b)$`;` `vb = `$\mathcal{T}(r)$`;`
$f(a) := b$ $g(a \mapsto b) := r$	`f[a] = `$\mathcal{T}(b)$`;` `g[a][b] = `$\mathcal{T}(r)$`;`

$f := f \mathbin{\vartriangleleft} \{a1 \mapsto b1\} \mathbin{\vartriangleleft} \ldots \mathbin{\vartriangleleft} \{am \mapsto bm\}$	`f[`$\mathcal{T}(a1)$`] = `$\mathcal{T}(b1)$`;`
	 `...`
	 `f[`$\mathcal{T}(am)$`] = `$\mathcal{T}(bm)$`;`

$f := f \mathbin{\vartriangleleft} \{i \cdot i \in c\_upto(j \mapsto k) \wedge P(v,c,i) \;\|$
 $\qquad\qquad\qquad E_1(v,c,i) \mapsto E_2(v,c,i)\}$
	`for(int i=`$\mathcal{T}(j)$`; i<=`$\mathcal{T}(k)$`; i++){`
	 `  if(`$\mathcal{T}(P(v,c,i))$`)`
	 `    f[`$\mathcal{T}(E_1(v,c,i))$`] = `$\mathcal{T}(E_2(v,c,i))$`;`
	 `}`

Example. The C code generated corresponding to the above snippet of our schedule is as follows.

```
if (ml_out_10 == true){
  if (c_plus(c_plus(a,b),1) < d){
    a = c_plus(a,1);
    ml_pass = 1;
    ml_out_10 = false;
  }
  else{
    a = c_plus(a,1);
    ml_tl = red;
    ml_pass = 1;
    ml_out_10 = false;
  }
}
if ((il_tl == red && (0 < b && (a == 0 && (ml_pass == 1 && IL_OUT_SR == on))))) {
  il_tl = green;
  ml_tl = red;
  il_pass = 0;
}
```

3.4   Proving the Correctness of the Scheduled Model

To prove the correctness of the generated source code, we generate a scheduled model that includes the schedule encoded in the machine as follows. We introduce a new variable pc that represents the program counter and add events that simulate the update of the program counter according to the schedule. The controller events are refined by removing all guards except for parameter initialisations and adding the action $pc := pc+1$ to simulate the increment of the program counter. The additional events for the different blocks are as follows.

Branch. For every branch, we generate a set of events. The events differ slightly depending on whether the branch has an "else" part or not. The symbols s and m represent the block's start and middle position, respectively within the schedule and e is the next valid position in the schedule after the end of the branch. These numbers are automatically computed by the plug-in. The branch condition is represented by bc.

if_true :	if_false (long form) :	if_false (short form) :	if_exit (long form) :
when	**when**	**when**	**when**
$pc = s$	$pc = s$	$pc = s$	$pc = m$
bc	$\neg bc$	$\neg bc$	**then**
then	**then**	**then**	$pc := e$
$pc := pc + 1$	$pc := m + 1$	$pc := e$	**end**
end	**end**	**end**	

Loop. For a loop we generate the following events. The symbols s and e represent the block's start and end position, respectively. Both numbers are automatically computed by the plug-in. The loop condition is represented by lc.

do_true :	do_false :	do_return :
when	when	when
$pc = s$	$pc = s$	$pc = e$
lc	$\neg lc$	then
then	then	$pc := s$
$pc := pc + 1$	$pc := e + 1$	end
end	end	

Example. Based on the (automatically generated) program counter associated with the statements, the scheduled Event-B model corresponding to the above schedule snippet is as follows. Most events are required for modelling the control flow of the schedule determined by the program counter pc.

if_ml_out_10_true :	if_ml_out_10_false :	if_ml_out_true :
when	when	when
$pc = 0$	$pc = 0$	$pc = 1$
$ml\_out\_10 = TRUE$	$ml\_out\_10 = FALSE$	$c\_plus(c\_plus(a \mapsto b) \mapsto 1) < d$
then	then	then
$pc := pc + 1$	$pc := 5$	$pc := pc + 1$
end	end	end

ML_out1 :	if_ml_out_exit :	if_ml_out_false :
when	when	when
$pc = 2$	$pc = 3$	$pc = 1$
then	then	$\neg c\_plus(c\_plus(a \mapsto b) \mapsto 1) < d$
$a := c\_plus(a \mapsto 1)$	$pc := 5$	then
$ml\_pass := 1$	end	$pc := 4$
$ml\_out\_10 := FALSE$		end
$pc := pc + 1$		
end		

ML_out1 :	if_il_tl_green_true :
when	when
$pc = 4$	$pc = 5$
then	$il\_tl = red \wedge 0 < b \wedge a = 0 \wedge ml\_pass = 1 \wedge IL\_OUT\_SR = on$
$a := c\_plus(a \mapsto 1)$	then
$ml\_tl := red$	$pc := pc + 1$
$ml\_pass := 1$	end
$ml\_out\_10 := FALSE$	
$pc := pc + 1$	
end	

IL_tl_green :	if_il_tl_green_false :
when	when
$pc = 6$	$pc = 5$
then	$\neg (il\_tl = red \wedge 0 < b \wedge a = 0 \wedge ml\_pass = 1 \wedge IL\_OUT\_SR = on)$
$il\_tl := green$	then
$ml\_tl := red$	$pc := 7$
$il\_pass := 0$	end
$pc := pc + 1$	
end	

In addition, we generate invariants to capture the effect of the control flow and the user-defined assertions.

invariants :
if_ml_out_Pre :	$pc = 1 \Rightarrow ml\_out\_10 = TRUE$
ml_out1_Pre :	$pc = 2 \Rightarrow ml\_out\_10 = TRUE \wedge c\_plus(c\_plus(a \mapsto b) \mapsto 1) < d$
if_ml_out_Post :	$pc = 3 \Rightarrow ml\_out\_10 = FALSE$
ml_out2_Pre :	$pc = 4 \Rightarrow ml\_out\_10 = TRUE \wedge \neg(c\_plus(c\_plus(a \mapsto b) \mapsto 1) < d)$
if_il_tl_green_Pre :	$pc = 5 \Rightarrow ml\_out\_10 = FALSE$
IL_tl_green_Pre :	$pc = 6 \Rightarrow ml\_out\_10 = FALSE \wedge$
	$\quad (il\_tl = red \wedge 0 < b \wedge a = 0 \wedge ml\_pass = 1 \wedge IL\_OUT\_SR = on)$

Notice how the invariants take into account the effect of the nested branches, e.g. when $pc = 2$, and of assertions, e.g. when $pc = 6$. Proving that the scheduled Event-B model refines the restricted Event-B model is straightforward with these invariants, except for the following problem regarding shared variables.

Shared Variables and Atomicity. Our schedule imposes an atomicity assumption, captured by the scheduled Event-B model, representing the semantics of the program code. The atomicity is indicated by the values of the program counter pc. For example, we assume that the evaluation of conditions in branches and loops are atomic. Moreover, we also assume that the assignments of the original events (which are translated as sequential updates) are executed atomically. However, we break the atomicity assumption between checking the guards and executing the actions of the original events. In particular, the evaluation of the event guards is often distributed to different branch and loop conditions. For example, the guard of IL_tl_green is partially checked by the branch condition at $pc = 5$ and partially guaranteed (assertion $ml\_out\_10 = FALSE$) by the control flow before that. Since this atomicity assumption differs from the atomicity assumption of the restricted Event-B model, where the evaluation of an event's guards and the execution of its actions are assumed to be atomic, inconsistency can arise. This is in particular the case when shared variables are used in the event's guard. Since we schedule only controller events, the environment events in the scheduled Event-B model can updated the shared variable at any time. This is reflected by unprovable invariant preservation proof obligations of the scheduled Event-B model. In our example, variable ml_out_10 is assumed to be shared between the controller and the environment. More specifically, the environment can change the value of ml_out_10 with its event ML_OUT_DEP as follows.

```
ML_OUT_DEP :
when
    ML_OUT_SR = on
    ml_tl = green
then
    ML_OUT_SR := off
    ml_out_10 := TRUE
    A := A + 1
end
```

An attempt to prove that ML_OUT_DEP maintains invariants like IL_tl_green_Pre will fail, since our model does not prevent the occurrence of ML_OUT_DEP between checking the branch condition at $pc = 5$ and executing IL_tl_green's action at $pc = 6$. To remedy the situation, we add a guard, e.g., $pc = 0$ to ML_OUT_DEP to prevent the environment event from occurring during the controller's execution. The meaning of this guard is an *assumption* on the overall system such that when a car leaves the corresponding sensor, then the controller has finished processing the last message and is ready to process the next message. Notice that a similar assumption regarding the speed of the controller has also been made for the original development in [2]. In general, guarding the environment events might give rise to assumptions that are unrealistic. In this case, we must return to the original development and perform further refinement, e.g., to introduce a private copy of the shared variables for the controller. Essentially, we anticipate the possible interference of the environment and account for that earlier in the development.

4 Experience

As stated in the introduction, we applied our approach to different developments. In addition to the "cars on a bridge" example, we generated code for two more sophisticated case studies: an elevator control system and a train control system. While the elevator control system is a simplification of real elevator systems, we developed the core functionality of the train control system from a real specification [7].

Table 4. Statistics

	"cars on a bridge" controller	elevator control system	train control system
controller variables:	5	2	15
shared variables:	8	12	21
controller events:	8	30	34
refinement steps:	3	3	105
schedule lines:	18	88	90
invariants encoding the schedule:	14	67	69
events encoding the schedule:	18	99	92
POs for refinement:	454	9075	8757
lines of C code:	127	312	373

The numbers in Table 4 show that the elevator and train system are comparable in terms of the size of their schedules and the number of proof obligations required to prove refinement. This may be surprising since the train control system is substantially more complex than the elevator control system and required considerably more effort to develop, which is reflected by the large number of refinement steps. This is because the train control system's development includes several refinement steps that already account for the later restriction step and translation to code. Hence, both control systems are refined to a level where they are close to their final implementation and the translation to program code becomes straightforward. With the restriction of a model as the first step of our code generation approach, we force the developer to refine the model to a concrete level and therefore keep the translation effort in check. For this reason our approach works equally well for small academic examples and large, complex industrial systems.

The number of proof obligations generated to prove that the scheduled Event-B model refines the restricted model is rather high. For every invariant/event pair, we have a proof obligation of the form $pc = M \vdash pc = N \Rightarrow \ldots$, where N and M are numbers. However, most of them are trivial as $N \neq M$ holds. The number of relevant proof obligations (i.e. $N = M$) is less than 180 for all three developments and at least 77% are automatically discharged. In fact, our plug-in can generate these relevant proof obligations directly from the schedule rather than having Rodin generating them together with all the irrelevant ones. The remaining task is to prove that this set of proof obligations indeed implies those proof obligations generated to prove the refinement relation. This proof can be done once at the meta-level and is valid for all translations.

5   Related Work

Here we discuss related work in more detail.

Merging Rules. Merging rules are introduced in [2] as a mechanism for synthesising sequential programs from Event-B models. There are two rules for creating branches and loops that constitute patterns for developing sequential programs. As a result, the form of the programs are limited and not every program can be synthesised from its Event-B model. For example, a sequential statement is only possible after a loop.

B2C Tool. The B2C tool [10] was developed to generate code for a specific Event-B model of an instruction set architecture. As a result, the plug-in supports only the translation of the Event-B syntax used in this particular model. The most significant shortcoming is that it does not support contexts and therefore cannot be used when constants and sets are used in a machine.

With the B2C tool, there is no possibility to specify a desired execution order of the events. For every event in the model, a C function is created that checks the guards before the actions are executed. In a function named "iterate", all these event functions are combined in a sequence of function calls equivalent to the event ordering in the Event-B machine. As soon as a function call is successful (the actions were executed) the iterate function returns. In the main function, first the initialisation function is called and then a while loop calls the iterate function as long as there is no deadlock in the system. The disadvantage of leaving the iterate function after a successful action execution of an event is that events at the bottom of the iteration sequence might never be executed.

EB2ALL Tool. EB2ALL [9] is a set of tools for generating code for different target languages. Currently there are four plug-ins included for translations to C, C++,C#, and Java respectively. The EB2ALL tool is based on the B2C tool. The authors of the tool argue that its correctness is justified by an observable equivalence between the Event-B model and the generated code together with some meta-proofs. It is not specified what notion of observational equivalence is intended and no details on the meta-proof are provided. Furthermore, they state that the generated code usually must be altered manually after generation and that correctness is maintained if the manually added code is also verified in some way. Again, formal details are lacking.

In EB2ALL, the default scheduling is the same as in B2C. The tool provides an optimisation by automatically grouping events that have common guards. This is done by analysing the refinement relation of the events. Two events that both refine the same abstract event have the guards of the abstract event in common. Within the iterate function, these common guards are translated into an if-statement surrounding the function calls of the corresponding events. The intention is that if the guards of the abstract event evaluate to false, then there is no need to check the guards of the refining events. Unfortunately, this approach only works if the guards of the abstract event are all deterministic and translatable. Furthermore, this only produces more efficient code when many events refine one single abstract event. Otherwise, the overhead of additional if-statements may outweigh any efficiency gains.

Tasking Event-B. Tasking Event-B [6] is a tool developed for code generation from Event-B models into code with a special focus on concurrent processes. Currently, the tool supports translations to C, Ada and Java. As in EB2ALL, expressions with multiple arithmetic operators are supported. Currently it is not checked whether arithmetic operators maintain the lower and upper bound of the target data type; hence runtime overflows are possible.

Tasking Event-B is the most mature among the existing tools for code generation with respect to scheduling. It is the only tool that provides a scheduling language for user defined scheduling of events. Unfortunately, the language is very restrictive. The bodies of loops and branches are limited to single events. Hence, there is no support for schedules that include structures such as nested branches or a sequence of events within a loop.

Scheduling Patterns. We are unaware of any tool support for the scheduling patterns introduced in [4, 5]. The attractiveness of the work is the proof of correctness for the patterns done using set transformers. However, this reasoning must be done manually. Furthermore, our scheduling language is more expressive than the scheduling language defined in [4]. For example, nested branches are not possible in [4].

Classical B. Our scheduling language has features similar to (classical) B [1], for example conditional statements, sequential statements and loops. In B, the last model of a refinement chain is a special construction, the IMPLEMENTATION, from which program code can be generated. Variables of the IMPLEMENTATION must be either *concrete variables* (i.e., of some implementable datatype) or variables of some predefined libraries. Updates of the variables must be well-defined, which is captured by the preconditions of the corresponding assignments. However, loop and branch conditions do not have preconditions to enforce their well-definedness. As a consequence, they are restricted to predicates over simple expressions (e.g., no arithmetic operations are allowed). In our approach, we check all conditions for well-defineness, hence they can contain any expressions. Furthermore, our approach allows us to state assertions between two sequential blocks. As a result, proof obligations can be generated for each block separately. In B, the effects of the sequentially composed statements are combined together, which often results in complicated proof obligations.

6   Conclusion

We presented our approach to generating program code from Event-B models. Our approach is correct-by-construction and relies on reasoning about well-definedness, assertions, and refinement. Although we presented only the translation to C source code, our approach is also applicable to other languages by adapting the notion of well-definedness and the restriction step to the corresponding target language.

As future work we would like to consider loop termination and liveness properties in general. The challenge here is to integrate standard loop variant reasoning into the scheduled Event-B model. Naturally, this will lead to reasoning about deadlock-freedom and event convergence properties as shown in [8].

Furthermore, as mentioned in Section 4, we have identified the set of relevant proof obligations which can be generated directly from the schedule. We are working on the meta-proof that this set of proof obligations indeed guarantees that the scheduled Event-B model refines the restricted Event-B model. Note that our approach is also correct without the meta-proof, but requires more proof obligations to be proved.

References

1. Abrial, J.R.: The B-book: Assigning Programs to Meanings. Cambridge University Press (1996)
2. Abrial, J.R.: Modeling in Event-B: System and Software Engineering. Cambridge University Press (2010)
3. Abrial, J.R., Butler, M., Hallerstede, S., Hoang, T.S., Mehta, F., Voisin, L.: Rodin: An Open Toolset for Modelling and Reasoning in Event-B. Software Tools for Technology Transfer 12(6), 447–466 (2010)
4. Boström, P.: Creating Sequential Programs from Event-B Models. In: Méry, D., Merz, S. (eds.) IFM 2010. LNCS, vol. 6396, pp. 74–88. Springer, Heidelberg (2010)
5. Boström, P., Degerlund, F., Sere, K., Waldén, M.A.: Derivation of concurrent programs by stepwise scheduling of Event-B models. Formal Asp. Comput. 26(2), 281–303 (2014)
6. Edmunds, A., Butler, M.: Tasking Event-B: An Extension to Event-B for Generating Concurrent Code. In: 4th Workshop on Programming Language Approaches to Concurrency and Communication-cEntric Software (2011)
7. Fürst, A., Hoang, T.S., Basin, D., Sato, N., Miyazaki, K.: Formal System Modelling Using Abstract Data Types in Event-B. In: Ait Ameur, Y., Schewe, K.-D. (eds.) ABZ 2014. LNCS, vol. 8477, pp. 222–237. Springer, Heidelberg (2014)
8. Hoang, T.S., Abrial, J.R.: Reasoning about Liveness Properties in Event-B. In: Qin, S., Qiu, Z. (eds.) ICFEM 2011. LNCS, vol. 6991, pp. 456–471. Springer, Heidelberg (2011)
9. Méry, D., Singh, N.K.: Automatic Code Generation from Event-B Models. In: Proceedings of the Second Symposium on Information and Communication Technology, SoICT 2011, pp. 179–188. ACM, New York (2011)
10. Wright, S.: Automatic Generation of C from Event-B. In: Workshop on Integration of Model-based Formal Methods and Tools (February 2009)

Concurrency and Control

Verifying Linearizability on TSO Architectures

John Derrick[1], Graeme Smith[2], and Brijesh Dongol[1]

[1] Department of Computing, University of Sheffield, Sheffield, UK
[2] School of Information Technology and Electrical Engineering,
The University of Queensland, Australia

Abstract. Linearizability is the standard correctness criterion for fine-grained, non-atomic concurrent algorithms, and a variety of methods for verifying linearizability have been developed. However, most approaches assume a sequentially consistent memory model, which is not always realised in practice. In this paper we define linearizability on a *weak* memory model: the TSO (Total Store Order) memory model, which is implemented in the x86 multicore architecture. We also show how a simulation-based proof method can be adapted to verify linearizability for algorithms running on TSO architectures. We demonstrate our approach on a typical concurrent algorithm, spinlock, and prove it linearizable using our simulation-based approach. Previous approaches to proving linearizabilty on TSO architectures have required a modification to the algorithm's natural abstract specification. Our proof method is the first, to our knowledge, for proving correctness without the need for such modification.

1 Introduction

The correctness of concurrent algorithms has received considerable attention over the last few years. For algorithms that have fine-grained concurrent implementations correctness has focussed on a condition called *linearizability* [12]. This requires that the fine-grained operations (e.g., insertion or removal of an element of a data structure) appear as though they take effect "instantaneously at some point in time within their intervals of execution" [12], thereby achieving the same effect as an atomic operation.

Such fine-grained implementations are becoming increasingly commonplace, and are now standard in libraries such as `java.util.concurrent`. To increase efficiency, these algorithms dispense with locking, or only lock small parts of a shared data structure. Therefore the shared data structure might be concurrently accessed by different processors executing different operations. This complexity makes the correctness of such algorithms, i.e., their proofs of linearizability, a key issue.

Because linearizability is such an important condition, there has been a large amount of interest in proof methods for verifying whether an algorithm is linearizable. However, the vast majority of this work has assumed a particular memory model; in particular a *sequentially consistent* (SC) memory model, whereby program instructions are executed by the hardware in the order specified by the program. This is in contrast to multiprocessor architectures such as x86 [15], Power [1] or ARM [1] that only provide weaker guarantees in order to allow efficient executions.

Processor cores within modern multicore systems often communicate via shared memory and use (local) store buffers to improve performance. Whilst this does give

E. Albert and E. Sekerinski (Eds.): IFM 2014, LNCS 8739, pp. 341–356, 2014.

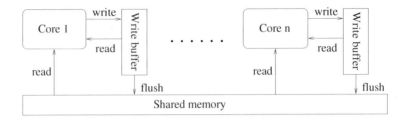

Fig. 1. The TSO architecture

greater scope for optimisation, the order in which instructions are executed by the hardware is no longer the same as that specified by the program. In this paper we focus on one such memory model, the TSO (Total Store Order) model which is implemented in the x86 multicore processor architecture. Rather surprisingly given Intel's and AMD's use of x86, and in contrast to the many different approaches and techniques for linearizability on sequentially consistent architectures, there have only been three approaches to the question of linearizability on a TSO model: [4], [11] and [17].

The proof approaches in both [4] and [11], however, require the natural abstract specification of a concurrent implementation to be modified. Burckhardt et al. [4] define so-called TSO-to-TSO linearizability, which as the name implies compares a concurrent implementation with an abstract specification that executes in TSO memory. Their definition of linearizability thus compares two specifications with local buffers. In our approach, we aim to compare the execution of an implementation in TSO against its natural SC abstraction. In [11] Gotsman et al. define a more sophisticated mapping between the TSO model and a sequentially consistent one (this is called TSO-to-SC linearizability), but to verify the linearizability of an example like spinlock (our running example) they weaken the abstract specification to allow non-deterministic behaviour when one would not naturally expect it. The approach closest to ours is [17] which uses the same principles that we discuss, but does not provide a proof method (rather they use SPIN to model check particular runs of the algorithm, much like testing).

The purpose of this paper is to make two contributions: define linearizability of concurrent algorithms on a TSO memory model which avoids the compromises of [4, 11], and define a proof method for verifying it. We begin in Section 2 by introducing the TSO model as well as our running example, the spinlock algorithm. In Section 3 we introduce linearizability and discuss how we adapt the definition to the TSO model. In Section 4 we explain an existing simulation-based method for verifying linearizability and show how we can adapt this to the TSO model. This method is then applied to the spinlock example in Section 5 before we conclude in Section 6.

2   The TSO Memory Model

In the TSO (Total Store Order) architecture (see [16] for an introduction), each processor core uses a write buffer (as shown in Figure 1), which is a FIFO queue that stores pending writes to memory. A processor core (from this point on referred to as a *process*) performing a *write* to a memory location enqueues the write to the buffer and continues

```
word x=1;

  void acquire()          void release()          int tryacquire()
  {                       {                       {
1   while(1) {          1   x=1;                 1   lock;
2     lock;              }                       2   if (x==1) {
3     if (x==1) {                                3     x=0;
4       x=0;                                     4     unlock;
5       unlock;                                  5     return 1;
6       return;                                  6   }
      }                                          6   unlock;
7     unlock;                                    7   return 0;
8     while(x==0){};                             }
    }
}
```

Fig. 2. Spinlock implementation

computation without waiting for the write to be committed to memory. Pending writes do not become visible to other processes until the buffer is *flushed*, which commits (some or all) pending writes to memory.

The value of a memory location *read* by a process is the most recent in the processor's local buffer. If there is no such value (e.g., initially or when all writes corresponding to the location have been flushed), the value of the location is fetched from memory. The use of local buffers allows a read by one process, occurring after a write by another, to return an older value as if it occurred before the write.

In general, flushes are controlled by the CPU. However, a programmer may explicitly include a *fence*, or *memory barrier*, instruction in a program's code to force a flush to occur. Therefore, although TSO allows non-sequentially consistent executions, it is used in many modern architectures on the basis that these can be prevented, where necessary, by programmers using fence instructions.

A pair of *lock* and *unlock* commands in TSO allows a process to acquire sole access to the memory. Both commands include a memory barrier which forces the store buffer of that process to be flushed completely (via a sequence of atomic flushes).

2.1   Example - Spinlock

Spinlock [3] is a locking mechanism designed to avoid operating system overhead associated with process scheduling and context switching. A typical implementation of spinlock is shown in Fig. 2, where a global variable x represents the lock and is set to 0 when the lock is held by a process, and 1 otherwise. A process trying to acquire the lock x *spins*, i.e., waits in a loop and repeatedly checks the lock for availability. It is particularly efficient when processes only spin for short periods of time and is often used in operating system kernels.

The `acquire` operation only terminates if it successfully acquires the lock. It will lock the global memory[1] so that no other process can write to x. If, however, another

---

[1] Locking the global memory using the TSO `lock` command should not be confused with acquiring the lock of this case study by setting x to 0.

process has already acquired the lock (i.e., x==1) then it will unlock the global memory and spin, i.e., loop in the while-loop until it becomes free, before starting over. Otherwise, it acquires the lock by setting x to 0.

The operation release releases the lock by setting x to 1. We assume that only a process that has acquired the lock will call this operation. The operation tryacquire differs from acquire in that it only makes one attempt to acquire the lock. If this is successful it returns 1, otherwise it returns 0.

The lock and unlock commands act as memory barriers. Hence, writes to x by the acquire and tryacquire operations are not delayed. For efficiency, however, release does not have a memory barrier and so its write to x can be delayed until a flush occurs. This leads to the possibility of a tryacquire operation of a process q returning 0 after the lock has been released by another process p. For example, the following concrete execution is possible, where we write $(q, \text{tryacquire}(0))$ to denote process q performing a tryacquire operation and returning 0, and flush(p) to denote the CPU flushing a value from process p's buffer:

$$\langle (p, \text{acquire}), (p, \text{release}), (q, \text{tryacquire}(0)), \text{flush}(p) \rangle \qquad (1)$$

Thus p performs an acquire, then a release and then q performs a tryacquire that returns 0 even though it occurs immediately after the release. This is because the flush(p), which sets the value of x in memory to 0 has not yet occurred.

At an abstract level, the operations are captured by the following Z specification, which has parameterised operations $Acquire_p$, $Release_p$ and $TryAcquire_p$, the parameter p denoting the identifier of the process performing the operation.

__AS_____
$x : \{0, 1\}$

__Init_____
AS
_____
$x = 1$

__$Acquire_p$_____
ΔAS
_____
$x = 1$
$x' = 0$

__$Release_p$_____
ΔAS
_____
$x = 0$
$x' = 1$

__$TryAcquire_p$_____
ΔAS
$out! : \{0, 1\}$
_____
if $x = 1$
then $x' = 0 \wedge out! = 1$
else $x' = x \wedge out! = 0$

The question is now: "Is the behaviour of spinlock under TSO comparable to this abstract specification?". We answer this question in the subsequent sections by proving that spinlock under TSO is actually linearizable with respect to the specification.

3   Linearizability on TSO

Linearizability [12] is the standard notion of correctness for concurrent algorithms, and allows one to compare a fine-grained implementation against its abstract specification.

The comparison is made at the level of invocations and returns of operations as the fine-grained nature of some operations means that an operation's steps might be interleaved with steps of another operation executed by another process. For example, process p might start a release, but then process q invokes its tryacquire before p's release has returned. The key idea of linearizability is as follows.

> Linearizability provides the illusion that each operation applied by concurrent processes takes effect instantaneously at some point between its invocation and its return. This point is known as the *linearization point*.

In other words, if two operations overlap, then they may take effect in any order from an abstract perspective, but otherwise they must take effect in program order.

The original definition in [12] (for a formalisation, see [7]) is based on the concept of *possibilities*, however there are now a number of different proof strategies which have been applied to a number of algorithms. These range from using shape analysis [2, 5] and separation logic [5] to rely-guarantee reasoning [18] and refinement-based simulation methods [10, 14, 7]. The simulation-based methods, which we will adapt for use in this paper, show that an abstraction (or simulation or refinement) relation exists between the abstract specification of the data structure and its concurrent implementation.

We will return to the proof method in Section 4. In this section we address the question: Is *spinlock* linearizable on TSO? The definition of linearizability is architecture-neutral, so we should be able to answer the question on a TSO memory model. However, the presence of local buffers, and operations under control of the CPU (i.e., the flushes) complicate the answer.

Consider the execution of spinlock in (1). Obviously, such an execution has no corresponding behaviour at the abstract level, since looking at the Z specification, the value of x after *Release* is 1, thus *TryAcquire* returns 1. Hence standard approaches to proving linearizability will fail. There are three alternative approaches to tackling the issue of linearizability on TSO: [4], [11] and [17]. Of these, both [4] and [11] involve changes to the natural abstract specification. For example, in [4] the abstract specification is described with local buffers and flushes. Linearizability, as they define it, (which they call TSO-to-TSO linearizability) then compares two specifications both with local buffers, but this seems to miss the essential nature of the abstract to concrete transformation. On the other hand in [11], Gotsman et al. weaken the abstract specification to allow tryacquire to nondeterministically either fail or succeed when x is 1, i.e.,

$$
\begin{array}{|l}
\_TryAcquire2_p _____ \\
\Delta AS \\
out! : \{0, 1\} \\
\hline
\textbf{if } x = 1 \\
\textbf{then } (x' = 0 \wedge out! = 1) \vee (x' = x \wedge out! = 0) \\
\textbf{else } x' = x \wedge out! = 0 \\
\end{array}
$$

The nondeterminism in the abstract operation models that introduced to the concrete system by hardware-controlled flushes. Since the abstract specification does not have local buffers in it, the authors call it TSO-to-SC linearizability. Again, changing the abstract specification seems to weaken what one has achieved with the proof. The approach closest to ours is [17] which uses the same principles that we use here, but uses model checking to test linearizability. Our aim is to formalise this intuition and provide a refinement-based proof method for it.

Although at first sight it would seem that linearizability simply fails without changing the abstract specification, one needs to take into account the role of the local buffers. Since the flush of a process's buffer is sometimes the point that the effect of an operation's changes to memory become globally visible, the flush can be viewed as being the final part of the operation. For example, the flush of a variable, such as x, after an operation, such as release, can be taken as the return of that operation. Under this interpretation, the release operation extends from its invocation to the flush which writes its change to x to the global memory. The key point is the following principle:

> The return point of an operation on a TSO architecture is not necessarily the point where the operation ceases execution, but can be any point up to the last flush of the variables written by that operation.

Formalisation: We now formalise this intuition. In the standard definition of linearizability, *histories* are sequences of *events* which can be invocations or returns of operations from a set I and performed by a particular process from a set P. Invocations have an associated input from domain In, and returns an output from domain Out (we assume both domains contain an element $\perp$ denoting no input or output, respectively). On TSO, we generalise events so that they can also be flushes which are performed by the CPU and operate on a particular process's buffer:

> $Event ::= inv\langle\!\langle P \times I \times In\rangle\!\rangle \mid ret\langle\!\langle P \times I \times Out\rangle\!\rangle \mid flush\langle\!\langle P\rangle\!\rangle$
> $History == \operatorname{seq} Event$

The TSO history corresponding to the execution (1) is[2]:

$$\langle inv(p, \texttt{acquire},), ret(p, \texttt{acquire},), inv(p, \texttt{release},), ret(p, \texttt{release},)$$
$$inv(q, \texttt{tryaquire},), ret(q, \texttt{tryacquire}, 0), flush(p)\rangle \quad (2)$$

To prove linearizability on a TSO architecture we transform this history to one where the flush on p is the return of the release, since in TSO it is the flush that makes the effect visible. The original return of the release in the history above is removed. That is, the above history is transformed to:

$$\langle inv(p, \texttt{acquire},), ret(p, \texttt{acquire},), inv(p, \texttt{release},),$$
$$inv(q, \texttt{tryaquire},), ret(q, \texttt{tryacquire}, 0), ret(p, \texttt{release}),)\rangle \quad (3)$$

In general, we need to transform a history h consisting of invocations, returns and flushes to a history $Trans(h)$ which replaces flushes by the appropriate returns whilst removing all other flushes and returns that are no longer required. The transformation $Trans(h)$ is formalised below. This new history consists just of invocations and returns, the latter indicating when the effect of an operation is made visible globally.

---

[2] We omit $\perp$ in the events of this and subsequent histories in this section, e.g., $inv(p, \texttt{acquire},)$ denotes $inv(p, \texttt{acquire}, \perp)$.

3.1 Defining the Transformation

We first present a number of preliminary definitions that enable the transformation to be carried out deterministically. Let $mp(p, m, n, h)$ denote matching pairs of invocations and returns by process p in history h as in [7]. Its definition requires that $h(m)$ and $h(n)$ are executed by the same process p and are an invocation and return event, respectively, of the same operation. Additionally, it requires that for all k between m and n, $h(k)$ is not an invocation or return event of p. That is, given $inv?(e)$ and $ret?(e)$ denote that the event e is an invocation and return event, respectively, $e.\pi$ denotes the process executing e, and $e.i$ the operation being executed, $mp(p, m, n, h)$ holds iff

$$0 < m < n \leq \#h \, \wedge$$
$$inv?(h(m)) \wedge ret?(h(n)) \wedge h(m).\pi = h(n).\pi = p \wedge h(m).i = h(n).i \, \wedge$$
$$\forall k \bullet m < k < n \Rightarrow h(k).\pi \neq p$$

Let $bs(p, m, h)$ denote the size of process p's buffer at point m in the history h, and $nf(p, m, n, h)$ denote the number of flushes of process p's buffer between points m and n in h. The number of new items in process p's buffer between two points m and n in a history h is given by

$$bi(p, m, n, h) \, \widehat{=} \, bs(p, n, h) + nf(p, m, n, h) - bs(p, m, h)$$

We use the function mpf below to find indices m, n and l in h such that (m, n) is a matching pair and l corresponds to the point to which the return of the matching pair must be moved.

$$mpf(p, m, n, l, h) \, \widehat{=} \, mp(p, m, n, h) \wedge n \leq l \, \wedge$$
$$\text{if } bi(p, m, n, h) = 0 \text{ then } l = n$$
$$\text{else } h(l) = flush(p) \, \wedge$$
$$nf(p, m, l, h) = bs(p, m, h) + bi(p, n, m, h)$$

The first part of the if states that $l = n$ if no items are put on the buffer by the operation invoked at point m. The second states that l corresponds to a flush of p's buffer and the number of flushes between m and l is precisely the number required to flush the contents of the buffer at m and any items added to the buffer between m and n.

To transform a history h, we do the following two steps.

Step 1. Given $mpf(p, m, n, l, h)$ holds for some p:
  if $n \neq l$
  then $h(l)$ becomes $h(n)$ and $h(n)$ becomes a dummy event δ
  else we do nothing because the return should not be moved.

This results in a history $h' \in seq(Event \cup \{\delta\})$, where all returns have been moved to the return positions of their corresponding flushes.

Step 2. The second step is straightforward: all δ and flushes are removed.

The algorithm described above is deterministic; we let $Trans(h)$ be the function that returns a transformed history by applying the algorithm to history h. For example, history (2) is transformed to the following via Step 1

$\langle inv(p, \texttt{acquire},), ret(p, \texttt{acquire},), inv(p, \texttt{release},), \delta,$
$\quad inv(q, \texttt{tryaquire},), ret(q, \texttt{tryacquire}, 0), ret(p, \texttt{release},)\rangle$

which in turn is transformed to history (3) by Step 2.

3.2 TSO Linearizability

A formal definition of linearizability is given in [7]. We adapt this definition as follows. An incomplete history h is extended with a sequence h_0 of return and flush events, then matched to a sequential history hs by removing the remaining pending invocations using a function *complete*, i.e., *complete*(h) is a subhistory of h formed by removing all pending invocations from h. We say a history h is *legal* iff for each $n : 1..\#h$ such that $ret?(h(n))$, there exists an earlier $m : 1..n-1$ such that $mp(p, m, n, h)$, and for each $n : 1..\#h$ such that $h(n) = flush(p)$, $bs(p, n, h) > 0$.

A key part of adapting the standard definition to TSO is what we mean by a matching pair of invocations and returns. The formal definition of the function mp in [7] (defined above) requires that for all k between m and n, $h(k)$ is not an invocation or return event of p. This is not true for our transformed histories on TSO since operations by the same process may overlap. Therefore, we will use a new version of matching pairs mp_{TSO} defined as follows.

$mp_{TSO}(p, m, n, h)$ iff $mpf(p, x, z, y, h)$
where $m = x - \sum\limits_{p:P} nf(p, 1, x, h)$ and $n = y - \sum\limits_{p:P} nf(p, 1, y, h)$ and $x < z \leq y$

Given RF is the set of all return and flush events, we define TSO linearizability as follows.

Definition 1 (TSO linearizability). *A history h : History is* TSO linearizable *with respect to some sequential history hs iff lin(h, hs) holds, where*

$$lin(h, hs) \mathrel{\widehat{=}} \exists h_0 : seq\, RF \bullet legal(h \frown h_0) \wedge linrel(Trans(complete(h \frown h_0)), hs)$$

where

$linrel(h, hs) \mathrel{\widehat{=}} \exists f : 1..\#h \rightarrowtail 1..\#hs \bullet (\forall n : 1..\#h \bullet h(n) = hs(f(n))) \wedge$
$\quad\quad (\forall p : P; \ m, n : 1..\#h \bullet m < n \wedge mp_{TSO}(p, m, n, h) \Rightarrow f(n) = f(m) + 1) \wedge$
$\quad\quad (\forall p, q : P; \ m, n, m', n' : 1..\#h \bullet$
$\quad\quad\quad n < m' \wedge mp_{TSO}(p, m, n, h) \wedge mp_{TSO}(q, m', n', h) \Rightarrow f(n) < f(m'))$ $\quad\square$

That is, operations in hs do not overlap (each invocation is followed immediately by its matching return) and the order of non-overlapping operations in h is preserved in hs.

Note that history (2) is a complete legal history, and that *Trans* applied to this history gives us history (3). Since `release` and `tryacquire` now overlap in the transformed history (3), a potential linearization in terms of the abstract specification is

$\langle inv(p, Acquire,), ret(p, Acquire,), inv(q, TryAcquire,), ret(q, TryAcquire, 0),$
$\quad inv(p, Release,), ret(p, Release,)\rangle$

Thus, spinlock is TSO linearizable with respect to the abstract specification.

4   A Proof Method for Linearizability on TSO

We do not work directly with this definition of linearizability, but rather use a refinement-based proof method for verifying linearizability as defined in [6–8, 14]. This approach defines simulation rules that form a sound (and complete) proof method for verifying linearizability. Different classes of algorithm use slightly different rules, where the difference depends on how easy it is to identify the linearization points — in some algorithms these can't be identified directly, and depend on the behaviour of other processes [8]. However, for the example in this paper we can use the simplest set of rules found in [7] and described below.

General Approach. The approach is based on proving a concrete specification that has one operation for each line of code is a *non-atomic refinement* [9] of the abstract specification capturing the code's intent. Each allowable sequence of concrete steps must simulate a sequence of abstract operations despite the interleaving of concrete steps performed by different processes[3].

Let P be the set of processes. Let our abstract and concrete specifications be given as $A = (AState, AInit, (AOP_{p,i})_{p \in P, i \in I})$ and $C = (CState, CInit, (COP_{p,j})_{p \in P, j \in J})$ where the sets I and J are used to index the abstract operations and concrete steps, respectively. The function $abs : J \to I$ maps each concrete step to the abstract operation it (together with other steps) implements. We assume the concrete state space $CState$ is composed of a global state GS (the shared memory) and the local state LS of one process (the program counter, local variables and, on TSO, the local buffer). Following [7], linearizability is then shown by:

1. *Defining a status function that identifies the linearization points of operations.*
   Let $STATUS ::= IDLE \mid IN\langle\langle In \rangle\rangle \mid OUT\langle\langle Out \rangle\rangle$ where In and Out are the domains of inputs and outputs, respectively, as defined in Section 3. We define a function $status : GS \times LS \to STATUS$ such that the following hold.
   If a process has no pending operation then the status of the process is $IDLE$. If it is executing an operation and has not passed the linearization point, then the status of the process is $IN(in)$ where in is the input of the operation, if any, and $\bot$ otherwise. If it is executing an operation and has passed the linearization point, the status is $OUT(out)$ where out is the output of the operation if any, and $\bot$ otherwise.

2. *Showing individual concrete runs of a process correctly implement the abstract operations using non-atomic refinement.*
   We find a forward simulation R relating the global state and the local state of a process to the abstract state, i.e., $R \subseteq AState \times (GS \times LS)$, and a set of simulation rules which additionally update the status function appropriately as shown in the example in Fig. 3. In this example, the input in of an invocation step $INVOP(in)$ is used to establish a status of $IN(in)$. After the invocation an internal operation implements $skip$ and leave the status unchanged. Then the linearization point that implements $AOp(in, out)$ is passed and the status changes to $OUT(out)$. Finally the status is used to compute the output of a return step $RETOP(out)$ and the status returns to $IDLE$.

---

[3] We use the term *steps* in this section to distinguish the concrete operations of the specification from the operations of the code (such as `acquire` in our example).

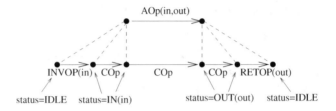

Fig. 3. The status information for non-atomic refinement

There are 5 different simulation rules depending on whether the particular concrete step being considered is an invocation step, a return step, or an internal step before linearization, after linearization or at the linearization point. As an example, the simulation rule for a concrete invocation step is[4]:

$$\forall \, as : AState; \; gs, gs' : GS; \; ls, ls' : LS; \; in : In \bullet$$
$$R(as, gs, ls) \land status(gs, ls) = IDLE \land INVOP_j(in, gs, ls, gs', ls')$$
$$\Rightarrow (status(gs', ls') = IN(in) \land R(as, gs', ls'))$$
$$\lor (\exists \, as' : AState; \; out : Out \bullet$$
$$AOP_{abs(j)}(in, as, as', out) \land status(gs', ls') = OUT(out) \land$$
$$R(as', gs', ls'))$$

where the first and second disjuncts in the consequent capture invocations that do and do not correspond to a linearization, respectively.

3. *Showing interference freedom, i.e., that other processes running in parallel do not destroy this non-atomic refinement.*

   To ensure steps of other processes preserve the local simulation relation R, we define $R(as, gs, ls) \,\widehat{=}\, ABS(as, gs) \land INV(gs, ls)$ where $ABS(as, gs)$ captures how the abstract state is represented by the global state, and $INV(gs, ls)$ provides further constraints between the global and local variables. $ABS(as, gs)$ is preserved by all steps of *all* processes. Hence it is sufficient to prove that $INV(gs, ls)$ is preserved by other processes. The *interference freedom* condition is:

$$\forall \, as : AState; \; gs, gs' : GS; \; ls, ls', lsq : LS \bullet$$
$$ABS(as, gs) \land INV(gs, ls) \land INV(gs, lsq) \land D(ls, lsq) \land COP_j(gs, ls, gs', ls')$$
$$\Rightarrow INV(gs', lsq) \land D(ls', lsq) \land status(gs', lsq) = status(gs, lsq)$$

   where a symmetric predicate $D \subseteq LS \times LS$ is used to constrain the relationship between the local states of any two processes. This predicate must also be preserved by the steps of all processes.

4. *Showing the concrete initialisation satisfies the abstract initialisation.*

$$\forall \, gs : GSInit \bullet \exists \, as : AInit \bullet$$
$$ABS(as, gs) \land (\forall \, ls : LSInit \bullet INV(gs, ls)) \land (\forall \, ls, lsq : LSInit \bullet D(ls, lsq))$$

---

[4] In this paper, we use $R(x, y)$ and $R(x, y, z)$ as shorthands for $(x, y) \in R$ and $(x, (y, z)) \in R$, respectively, for all relations R.

where *GSInit* and *LSInit* are the initial states of the global and local state spaces, respectively.   □

The *status* function captures the status of a single pending operation. Under TSO, however, we may have several pending operations: that operation currently being executed by the process, if any, and those that have completed apart from the flushing of their writes to memory. In our extension to the above approach, we let *status* capture the status of the operation which the process is currently executing. If there is no such process, the status is *IDLE*. All other pending operations, i.e., those completed apart from flushes, will necessarily be before their linearization points.

The other role of the *status* function is to carry the inputs of the operation until they are needed at the linearization point where they, along with the operation's outputs, must match those of the associated abstract operation. To adapt the approach to TSO, we need to be able to keep track of the inputs of completed, but pending, operations. We also need to keep track of the abstract operation associated with each completed, but pending, operation and the completed operation's outputs (since the operation has already completed, its outputs will have already occurred).

To do this we add four auxiliary variables to the local concrete state space *LS*. The first of these $lin : seq((I \cup \{null\}) \times In \times Out)$ records, for each buffer entry, the abstract operation for which its flush is a linearization point (*null* indicates its flush is not a linearization point), the abstract operation's input, and the abstract operation's output. When a flush occurs the values corresponding to the flushed entry are read into the other three auxiliary variables $op : I \cup \{null\}$, $in : In$ and $out : Out$.

We also need to introduce two new simulation rules. The first corresponds to a process with status *IN* returning to *IDLE* without linearizing. This would be the case where the operation is to be linearized by a flush which is yet to occur.

Return without Lin.
$\forall as : AState; \ gs, gs' : GS; \ ls, ls' : LS; \ in : In \bullet$
$\quad R(as, gs, ls) \wedge status(gs, ls) = IN(in) \wedge RETOP_j(gs, ls, gs', ls', out) \Rightarrow$
$\quad\quad status(gs', ls') = IDLE \wedge R(as, gs', ls')$

The second corresponds to the occurrence of a flush. A flush acts as either an internal step or a linearizing step as shown in cases (a) and (b) of Fig. 4, respectively. Case (a) can occur when the process has any status and its status is not changed. When the status is *IN* or *OUT* the internal step may be of the pending operations, and for any status it may be of an operation which has previously completed.

Case (b) also occurs from any status and when the status is *IDLE* or *OUT* it remains unchanged. Such a flush in these statuses corresponds to the linearization of an operation which has already completed. When the status is *IN* the flush may also be linearizing an operation which has already completed, in which case the status is unchanged, or it may be linearizing the pending operation, in which case the status becomes *OUT*.

The rule refers to the post-states of the auxiliary variables *op*, *in* and *out* via $ls'.op$, $ls'.in$ and $ls'.out$, respectively.

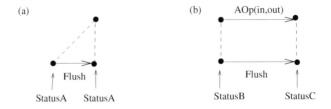

Fig. 4. Simulation rules for flush

Flush.

$\forall as : AState; \; gs, gs' : GS; \; ls, ls' : LS; \; in : In \; \bullet$
   $R(as, gs, ls) \wedge Flush(gs, ls, gs', ls') \Rightarrow$
      $(ls'.op = null \Rightarrow R(as, gs', ls') \wedge status(gs', ls') = status(gs, ls)) \wedge$
      $(ls'.op \neq null \Rightarrow$
          $(\exists as' : AState \bullet AOP_{ls'.op}(ls'.in, as, as', ls'.out) \wedge R(as', gs', ls')) \wedge$
          $(status(gs', ls') = status(gs, ls)$
           $\vee \; (status(gs, ls) = IN(ls'.in) \wedge status(gs', ls') = OUT(ls'.out)))$

5   Spinlock Is Linearizable on TSO

To show that spinlock is linearizable using the approach described in Section 4, we produce a concrete specification of the algorithm. Given P is the set of all process identifiers, the global state of the concrete specification includes the value of the shared variable x which is initially 1, and a variable *lock* denoting which process, if any, currently has the global memory locked.

_GS_____
$x : \{0, 1\}$
$lock : \mathbb{P} \, P$
_____
$\#lock \leq 1$

_GSInit_____
GS
_____
$x = 1$
$lock = \varnothing$

The local state of a given process is specified in terms of its process identifier from P, a program counter indicating which operation (i.e., line of code) can next be performed, and the process's buffer.

Let $PC ::= 1 \mid 2 \mid a1 \mid \ldots \mid a8 \mid ta1 \mid \ldots \mid ta7 \mid r1$ where the value 1 denotes the process is idle when it has not acquired the spinlock, the value 2 denotes the process is idle when it *has* acquired the spinlock, the values ai, for $i \in 1 .. 8$, denote the process is ready to perform the ith line of code of `acquire`, the values tai, for $i \in 1 .. 7$, denote the process is ready to perform the ith line of code of `tryacquire`, and the value $r1$ denotes the process is ready to perform the first line of `release`.

_LS₀_____
$id : P$
$pc : PC$
$buffer : \mathrm{seq}\{0, 1\}$

As detailed in Section 4, we add auxiliary variables to our local state to keep track of information required at linearization points corresponding to a flush. Let $I == \{1, 2, 3\}$ be the indices of the abstract operations such that 1 denotes *Acquire*, 2 denotes *Release* and 3 denotes *TryAcquire*. Let $In == \{\bot\}$ be the set of input values of operations, and $Out == \{0, 1, \bot\}$ be the set of output values.

```
┌─ LS ─────────────────────────
│ LS₀
│ op : I ∪ {null}
│ in : In
│ out : Out
│ lin : seq((I ∪ {null}) × In × Out)
├──────────────────────────────
│ #lin = #buffer
```

```
┌─ LSInit ─────────────────────
│ LS
├──────────────────────────────
│ pc = 1
│ buffer = ⟨⟩
```

Given this specification, the lines of code are formalised as Z operations[5]. For example, for the `acquire` operation we have an operation $A0$ corresponding to the invocation of the operation, an operation $A1$ corresponding to the line of code `while(1)`, and an operation $A2$ corresponding to the line of code `lock`.

```
┌─ A0 ──────────
│ ΞGS
│ ΔLS
├───────────────
│ pc = 1
│ pc' = a1
```

```
┌─ A1 ──────────
│ ΞGS
│ ΔLS
├───────────────
│ pc = a1
│ pc' = a2
```

```
┌─ A2 ──────────────────
│ ΔGS
│ ΔLS
├───────────────────────
│ lock = ∅ ∧ pc = a2
│ lock' = {id} ∧ pc' = a3
```

To model the fact that $A2$ also results in all entries of the process's buffer being flushed, the operation $A3$ corresponding to the following line of code, x=1, is not enabled unless $buffer = \langle\rangle$. It will become enabled after the required number of *Flush* operations have occurred. These remove an entry from the buffer and update the auxiliary variables *op*, *in* and *out* according to the information in *lin*. This information is added to *lin* when the buffer entries are added. For example, the operation $A4$, corresponding to the line x=0, updates *lin* to indicate that the flush of this value will not be a linearization point.

```
┌─ A3 ──────────
│ ΞGS
│ ΔLS
├───────────────
│ buffer = ⟨⟩
│ pc = a3
│ if x = 1
│ then pc' = a4
│ else pc' = a7
```

```
┌─ Flush ───────────────────
│ ΔGS
│ ΔLS
├───────────────────────────
│ lock = ∅ ∨ lock = {id}
│ buffer ≠ ⟨⟩
│ x' = head buffer
│ buffer' = tail buffer
│ head lin = (op', in', out')
│ lin' = tail lin
```

```
┌─ A4 ──────────────────────
│ ΞGS
│ ΔLS
├───────────────────────────
│ pc = a4
│ buffer' = buffer ⌢ ⟨0⟩
│ pc' = a5
│ lin' = lin ⌢ ⟨(null, ⊥, ⊥)⟩
```

---

[5] To simplify the presentation we adopt the convention that the values of variables that are not explicitly changed by an operation remain unchanged.

The other concrete operations are modelled similarly. The operations corresponding to the `unlock` statements are only enabled when $buffer = \langle\rangle$ modelling that the buffer must be completely flushed before the memory is unlocked.

Such a concrete specification is well-formed only if any sequence of operations corresponding to an abstract operation has exactly one linearization point. It is important, therefore, when modelling operations which change *lin* (i.e., those that write to the buffer) to ensure this. If a buffer entry is marked as a linearization point, the sequence of operations in which it occurs should not be linearized by a change in status from *IN* to *OUT*, nor by any other buffer entry.

Linearization can now be proved by defining the function *status* so that the linearization points of *Acquire* and *TryAcquire* are the operations which release the memory lock, and the linearization point of *Release* is the flush that commits the associated value of 1 to the global variable x.

The required relations *ABS*, *INV* and *D* are as follows.

$$ABS : AS \leftrightarrow GS$$

$\forall as : AS;\ gs : GS \mid ABS(as, gs) \bullet$
$\quad (gs.lock = \varnothing \Rightarrow gs.x = as.x) \wedge (gs.lock \neq \varnothing \wedge gs.x = 1 \Rightarrow as.x = 1)$

$$INV : GS \leftrightarrow LS$$

$\forall gs : GS;\ ls : LS \mid INV(gs, ls) \bullet$
$\quad (ls.pc = \{1, a1, a2, a3, ta1, ta2\} \wedge ls.buffer \neq \langle\rangle \Rightarrow gs.x = 0) \wedge$
$\quad (ls.pc \in \{a4, ta3\} \Rightarrow gs.x = 1) \wedge$
$\quad (ls.pc \in \{a5, ta4\} \wedge ls.buffer = \langle\rangle \Rightarrow gs.x = 0) \wedge$
$\quad (ls.pc \in \{a5, ta4\} \wedge ls.buffer \neq \langle\rangle \Rightarrow$
$\quad\quad gs.x = 1 \wedge ls.buffer = \langle 0 \rangle \wedge (head\ ls.lin).1 = null) \wedge$
$\quad (ls.pc \in \{2, a6, ta3, ta6, r1\} \Rightarrow gs.x = 0) \wedge$
$\quad (ls.pc \notin \{a6, ta6\} \wedge ls.buffer \neq \langle\rangle \Rightarrow$
$\quad\quad ls.buffer = \langle 1 \rangle \wedge (head\ ls.lin).1 = 2) \wedge$
$\quad (ls.pc \in \{2, a4, a6, a7, a8, ta3, ta5, ta6, ta7, r1\} \Rightarrow ls.buffer = \langle\rangle) \wedge$
$\quad (ls.pc \in \{a3, a4, ta2, ta3\} \Rightarrow gs.lock = \{ls.id\}) \wedge$
$\quad (gs.x = 1 \wedge ls.buffer \neq \langle\rangle \Rightarrow gs.lock = \{ls.id\})$

$$D : LS \leftrightarrow LS$$

$\forall ls, lsq : LS \mid D(ls, lsq) \bullet$
$\quad ls.buffer \neq \langle\rangle \Rightarrow lsq.buffer = \langle\rangle \wedge$
$\quad lsq.buffer \neq \langle\rangle \Rightarrow ls.buffer = \langle\rangle \wedge$
$\quad ls.pc \in \{2, a4, a6, ta3, ta5, r1\} \Rightarrow ls.buffer = lsq.buffer = \langle\rangle \wedge$
$\quad lsq.pc \in \{2, a4, a6, ta3, ta5, r1\} \Rightarrow ls.buffer = lsq.buffer = \langle\rangle \wedge$
$\quad ls.pc \in \{a5, ta4\} \Rightarrow lsq.buffer = \langle\rangle \wedge$
$\quad lsq.pc \in \{a5, ta4\} \Rightarrow ls.buffer = \langle\rangle$

For example, consider a *Flush* operation occurring when $pc = a5$. For the operation to occur, $buffer \neq \langle\rangle$. Hence, by $INV(gs, ls)$, $gs.x = 1$, $ls.buffer = \langle 0 \rangle$, $(head\ ls.lin).1 = null$ and $gs.lock = \{ls.id\}$.

Consider the **Flush** rule of Section 4. Since $ls'.op = (head\,ls.lin).1 = null$ and $status(gs, ls) = IN(\bot)$, this will hold if both $ABS(as, gs')$ and $INV(gs', ls')$ hold and $status(gs', ls') = IN(\bot)$. The latter follows since the operation does not change $ls.pc$. $ABS(as, gs')$ also holds since the operation does not change $gs.lock$ (i.e., $gs'.lock \neq \varnothing$) and sets $gs'.x = 0$. $INV(gs', ls')$ holds since in addition to setting $gs'.x = 0$ the *Flush* operation sets $ls'.buffer = tail\,ls.buffer = \langle\,\rangle$.

We also need to prove non-interference for this operation. Let ls denote the state of the process on whose buffer the flush is performed. Since $ls.buffer \neq \langle\,\rangle$, when $D(ls, lsq)$ holds for all $lsq \neq ls$, all other process buffers are empty. Since the other process's buffers are not changed by the operation, $DS(ls', lsq)$ holds. Although the operation changes the value of the global variable $gs.x$ to 0, $INV(gs', lsq)$ will remain true since it can only be affected by this change when $lsq.pc \in \{a4, ta3, a5, ta4\}$ and in each of these cases $ls.buffer$ would be equal to $\langle\,\rangle$ by $D(ls, lsq)$, i.e., the *Flush* operation would not be enabled.

Since similar proofs can be carried out for each concrete operation, and the initialisation condition holds (since $as.x = gs.x = 1$ implies $ABS(as, gs)$, $ls.pc = 1$ and $ls.buffer = \langle\,\rangle$ implies $INV(gs, ls)$, and $ls.buffer = lsq.buffer = \langle\,\rangle$ implies $D(ls, lsq)$), spinlock is linearizable on TSO.

6   Conclusions

This paper has presented a definition and simulation-based proof method for linearizability on the TSO memory model. The key to our definition is the treatment of flushes of local buffer entries as part of the operation which made the entries. This enables a proof method which, unlike existing methods, can be used to show implementations of algorithms are linearizable with respect to their natural abstract specifications. This work has applied state-based methods to program verification, and is part of a larger effort on the verification of linearizability on sequentially consistent architectures as well as weaker memory models. This larger effort mechanises the proofs of linearizability by integrating the state-based reasoning into the KIV theorem prover, see [6–8], and in [14] we prove (and mechanise the proof) that our approach is complete, in that all linearizable algorithms can be verified by such simulation-based methods. Given we are using the same simulation-based approach, mechanisation and integration into KIV of the theory in this paper will be relatively straightforward.

One interesting consequence of our approach is that operations on a single process may overlap and hence be reordered under linearizability. This is in contrast to earlier work on sequentially consistent architectures where linearizability implies the additional correctness criterion of *sequential consistency* [13], i.e., that operations on a single process occur in the order that they are called. Sequential consistency will only hold on TSO when, in addition to linearizability, memory barriers are included in all operations which (a) do not write to memory, but (b) occur in a process with other operations which do write to memory. This can be checked by inspection of the code.

Investigating alternative definitions of linearizability on TSO which maintain sequential consistency is an area of future work. Other areas of future work include the reducing the effort needed to apply the proof method. For example, the use of a coarse-grained abstraction as an intermediate layer between the concrete and abstract specifications, and a means to automatically generate the required invariants.

References

1. Alglave, J., Fox, A., Ishtiaq, S., Myreen, M.O., Sarkar, S., Sewell, P., Nardelli, F.Z.: The Semantics of Power and ARM Multiprocessor Machine Code. In: Petersen, L., Chakravarty, M.M.T. (eds.) DAMP 2009, pp. 13–24. ACM (2008)
2. Amit, D., Rinetzky, N., Reps, T.W., Sagiv, M., Yahav, E.: Comparison under abstraction for verifying linearizability. In: Damm, W., Hermanns, H. (eds.) CAV 2007. LNCS, vol. 4590, pp. 477–490. Springer, Heidelberg (2007)
3. Bovet, D., Cesati, M.: Understanding the Linux Kernel, 3rd edn. O'Reilly (2005)
4. Burckhardt, S., Gotsman, A., Musuvathi, M., Yang, H.: Concurrent library correctness on the TSO memory model. In: Seidl, H. (ed.) Programming Languages and Systems. LNCS, vol. 7211, pp. 87–107. Springer, Heidelberg (2012)
5. Calcagno, C., Parkinson, M., Vafeiadis, V.: Modular safety checking for fine-grained concurrency. In: Riis Nielson, H., Filé, G. (eds.) SAS 2007. LNCS, vol. 4634, pp. 233–248. Springer, Heidelberg (2007)
6. Derrick, J., Schellhorn, G., Wehrheim, H.: Proving linearizability via non-atomic refinement. In: Davies, J., Gibbons, J. (eds.) IFM 2007. LNCS, vol. 4591, pp. 195–214. Springer, Heidelberg (2007)
7. Derrick, J., Schellhorn, G., Wehrheim, H.: Mechanically verified proof obligations for linearizability. ACM Trans. Program. Lang. Syst. 33(1), 4 (2011)
8. Derrick, J., Schellhorn, G., Wehrheim, H.: Verifying linearisability with potential linearisation points. In: Butler, M., Schulte, W. (eds.) FM 2011. LNCS, vol. 6664, pp. 323–337. Springer, Heidelberg (2011)
9. Derrick, J., Wehrheim, H.: Non-atomic refinement in Z and CSP. In: Treharne, H., King, S., Henson, M., Schneider, S. (eds.) ZB 2005. LNCS, vol. 3455, pp. 24–44. Springer, Heidelberg (2005)
10. Doherty, S., Groves, L., Luchangco, V., Moir, M.: Formal verification of a practical lock-free queue algorithm. In: de Frutos-Escrig, D., Núñez, M. (eds.) FORTE 2004. LNCS, vol. 3235, pp. 97–114. Springer, Heidelberg (2004)
11. Gotsman, A., Musuvathi, M., Yang, H.: Show no weakness: Sequentially consistent specifications of TSO libraries. In: Aguilera, M.K. (ed.) DISC 2012. LNCS, vol. 7611, pp. 31–45. Springer, Heidelberg (2012)
12. Herlihy, M., Wing, J.M.: Linearizability: A correctness condition for concurrent objects. ACM Trans. Program. Lang. Syst. 12(3), 463–492 (1990)
13. Lamport, L.: How to make a multiprocessor computer that correctly executes multiprocess programs. IEEE Trans. Computers 28(9), 690–691 (1979)
14. Schellhorn, G., Wehrheim, H., Derrick, J.: How to prove algorithms linearisable. In: Madhusudan, P., Seshia, S.A. (eds.) CAV 2012. LNCS, vol. 7358, pp. 243–259. Springer, Heidelberg (2012)
15. Sewell, P., Sarkar, S., Owens, S., Nardelli, F.Z., Myreen, M.O.: x86-TSO: a rigorous and usable programmer's model for x86 multiprocessors. Commun. ACM 53(7), 89–97 (2010)
16. Sorin, D.J., Hill, M.D., Wood, D.A.: A Primer on Memory Consistency and Cache Coherence. Synthesis Lectures on Computer Architecture. Morgan & Claypool Publishers (2011)
17. Travkin, O., Mütze, A., Wehrheim, H.: SPIN as a linearizability checker under weak memory models. In: Bertacco, V., Legay, A. (eds.) HVC 2013. LNCS, vol. 8244, pp. 311–326. Springer, Heidelberg (2013)
18. Vafeiadis, V.: Modular fine-grained concurrency verification. PhD thesis, University of Cambridge (2007)

A Compositional Proof Method for Linearizability Applied to a Wait-Free Multiset

Bogdan Tofan, Gerhard Schellhorn, and Wolfgang Reif

Institute for Software and Systems Engineering
Augsburg University
{tofan,schellhorn,reif}@informatik.uni-augsburg.de

Abstract. We introduce a compositional, complete proof method for linearizability that combines temporal logic, rely-guarantee reasoning and possibilities. The basic idea of our proof method is that each process must preserve possibility steps as an additional guarantee condition for linearizability. To illustrate the expressiveness of our method, we apply it to a wait-free multiset implementation with intricate linearization points. Both the soundness of our method as well as its application to our multiset have been mechanized in the interactive verifier KIV.

Keywords: Temporal Logic, Rely-Guarantee Reasoning, Linearizability, Wait-Freedom, Multiset, Interactive Verification.

1 Introduction

Data structure implementations that offer fast concurrent access on multi-core machines are of particular importance. These implementations use fine-grained locking or non-blocking techniques that apply atomic hardware instructions instead of locks, e.g., compare-and-set (CAS). Thus a higher degree of parallelism can be achieved.

The central safety property of these implementations is linearizability [6]. Roughly speaking, it requires that each concurrent data structure behavior corresponds to some behavior of an abstract data type with atomic operations. Furthermore, linearizability imposes the following constraint on the order of abstract behaviors: It must preserve the order of concrete executions that do not overlap in time. A strong progress condition for non-blocking data structures is wait-freedom: Wait-free operations terminate in a finite number of steps, independent of the behavior of other processes. Wait-free implementations are particularly useful in real-time settings where the number of execution steps of an operation must be known beforehand.

Our proof method for linearizability is based on the well-known (intuitive) technique of identifying linearization points. The key idea behind this approach is that a linearizable operation appears to take effect instantaneously during its execution [6]. This point in time is called a linearization point: In simple cases, linearization points are internal and static, i.e., they coincide with one specific instruction of a running operation, independent from the overall concurrent

E. Albert and E. Sekerinski (Eds.): IFM 2014, LNCS 8739, pp. 357–372, 2014.

system execution. We call linearization points that depend on the concurrent behavior of other processes potential linearization points [1]. In more complex cases, linearization points can be external, i.e., they can happen with an instruction of *another* process. Algorithms with potential external linearization points are particularly challenging for proving linearizability.

Possibilities [6] formalize the intuition of identifying linearization points. Our proof method is based on the key insight [13] that backward simulation with possibilities is a complete proof strategy for linearizability. To reason compositionally about linearizability, we combine a rely-guarantee decomposition rule with possibilities: The basic idea is that each process must preserve possibilities as an additional guarantee condition which performs a step-local backward simulation. We specify and verify our proof method for linearizability in the logic Rely-Guarantee Interval Temporal Logic (RGITL), which offers an expressive framework for the symbolic execution of sequential/interleaved programs with temporal logic [14]. The logic makes it possible to verify safety and liveness properties. It is implemented in the interactive verifier KIV. Both the soundness of our proof method as well as its application to verify the multiset linearizable and wait-free are mechanized in KIV [8].

To illustrate the expressiveness of our proof method, we consider a novel multiset implementation with wait-free operations to insert, lookup and delete an element, respectively. While our multiset operations are pretty simple, they pose intricate linearization problems similar to Herlihy and Wing's queue [6]. In particular, the multiset has potential external linearization points that change the abstract representation and linearize several other running processes.

The structure of the rest of this paper is as follows: Section 2 introduces our wait-free multiset implementation and shows the challenges of proving it linearizable. Section 3 briefly introduces RGITL, in particular rely-guarantee reasoning in the logic. Section 4 then defines our proof method and Section 5 illustrates its application to verify the multiset correct. Finally, Section 6 discusses related work and Section 7 concludes with a brief summary and possible future work.

2   A Simple Wait-Free and Linearizable Multiset

2.1   The Multiset Implementation

We introduce a multiset data structure that can be accessed concurrently by an arbitrary finite number of processes that repeatedly execute one of the algorithms INSERT, DELETE or LOOKUP given in Figure 1. All individual (atomic) steps of these operations are executed in an interleaved manner. First we explain these operations, then we describe our overall concurrent system model.

The implementation stores elements x of the multiset in a shared array Ar of size $N \neq 0$. Each array slot either contains an element or *empty*. All operations get an element x as input parameter (before the semicolon). They sequentially run through the array Ar and compute a boolean output value Out (these two are reference parameters).

```
INSERT(x; Ar, Out) {                      DELETE(x; Ar, Out) {
  let Found = f, Pos = 0 in                 let Found = f, Pos = 0 in
    while ¬ Found ∧ Pos < N do {              while ¬ Found ∧ Pos < N do {
      CAS(empty, x; Ar[Pos], Found);           CAS(x, empty; Ar[Pos], Found);
      if ¬ Found                               if ¬ Found
      then Pos := Pos + 1                       then Pos := Pos + 1
    }; Out := Found}                          }; Out := Found}

LOOKUP(x; Ar, Out) {
  let Found = f, Pos = 0 in
    while ¬ Found ∧ Pos < N do {            CAS(Exp, New; Curr, Out) {
      if Ar[Pos] = x                           if*  Curr = Exp
      then Found := t                          then Curr := New, Out := t
      else Pos := Pos + 1                      else Out := f}
    }; Out := Found}
```

Fig. 1. The Wait-Free Multiset Operations INSERT, LOOKUP and DELETE in RGITL

When operation INSERT finds an empty slot, it atomically replaces *empty* with x using a CAS instruction. CAS atomically compares a current location *Curr* with an expected value *Exp*. If the values are equal it sets *Curr* to a new value *New* and returns true; otherwise it returns false. We specify this using parallel assignments separated by comma, which need one atomic step to execute, and **if***, which (in contrast to using **if**) does not take an extra step to execute its test. Local variables are introduced with **let**. Operation DELETE atomically assigns *empty* to the first slot in *Ar* that it finds to contain x. Operation LOOKUP returns true if it finds the searched element throughout its scan, otherwise it returns false.

In the following, **let** $\underline{V}$ **in** introduces arbitrary initial values for variables $\underline{V}$. For better readability we will write process identifiers $p \colon \mathbb{N}_0$ as subscripts rather than as an input parameter or function argument.

RGITL offers an operator ‖ which interleaves[1] steps of its first and second component. Thus we can specify an overall concurrent system

$$\text{SPAWN}_n(S) \{ \text{ if* } n = 0 \text{ then } \text{PROC}_0(S) \text{ else } \{\text{PROC}_n(S) \parallel \text{SPAWN}_{n-1}(S)\} \}$$

that recursively interleaves $n + 1$ processes $\text{PROC}_p(S)$ with identifiers $p \le n$. The overall system state is $S \colon state$. Each process repeatedly executes an operation $\text{COP}_p(I, In; S, Out)$

$$\text{PROC}_p(S) \{ \{\textbf{let } I, In, Out \textbf{ in } \text{COP}_p(I, In; S, Out)\}\textbf{*} \}$$

with some operation index $I \colon index$, input $In \colon input$ and output $Out \colon output$. The star operator ***** denotes arbitrary iteration.

For the multiset, the operation index is one of $ins \mid del \mid lkp$, the input is an element, the state is Ar, the output is of type *bool*, and we instantiate COP_p as $\{\textbf{if* } I = ins \textbf{ then } \text{INSERT}(In; S, Out) \textbf{ else if* } I = del \textbf{ then } \text{DELETE} \ldots \}$.

---

[1] The version here does not assume (weak) fairness.

2.2 The Abstract and Concrete Specifications for Linearizability

To better understand the challenges of proving our multiset implementation linearizable, we first define its semantics in terms of an abstract specification. Then we briefly explain how to extend the abstract/concrete specifications with execution histories that represent the visible behaviors for linearizability.

Our abstract specification is based on *atomic* operation relations

$$AOP(I)(In, AS, AS', Out)$$

where I is again the operation index, AS/AS' is the abstract state before/after an atomic AOP-transition and In/Out are input and output values, respectively. Initial abstract states are specified according to a predicate $AInit(AS)$.

For the multiset, the abstract state is an algebraic multiset Ms and we define $AOP(lkp) = ALookUp$, $AOP(del) = ADelete$ and $AOP(ins) = AInsert$ as the following atomic relations: The lookup relation $ALookUp$ leaves the multiset unchanged and sets its output to true iff the input element x occurs at least once in the current multiset ($x \in Ms$).

$$ALookUp(x, Ms, Ms', Out) \equiv Ms' = Ms \land (Out \leftrightarrow x \in Ms)$$

The $ADelete$ relation removes one occurrence of its input element x from the current multiset Ms if x occurs in the multiset, otherwise it leaves the multiset unchanged and returns false (where $\{\!|.|\!\}$ denotes a multiset).

$$ADelete(x, Ms, Ms', Out) \equiv Ms' = Ms \setminus \{\!|x|\!\} \land (Out \leftrightarrow x \in Ms)$$

Finally, the insert relation $AInsert$ either adds its input x to the current multiset (this increases the number of occurrences of x by 1) and returns true, or it non-deterministically returns with output false and leaves the multiset unchanged. Restricting $AInsert$ to only return false if the multiset is full w.r.t. a predefined bound on the number of elements (typically the size N of the array) would make the implementation non-linearizable.[2]

$$AInsert(x, Ms, Ms', Out) \equiv Ms' = Ms \cup \{\!|x|\!\} \land Out \lor Ms' = Ms \land \neg\ Out$$

Linearizability defines the behaviors of concrete and abstract operations in terms of execution *histories* which are finite sequences of events. An event $e: event$ models either the invocation $inv_p(I, In)$ or the return $ret_p(I, Out)$ of a particular operation I that is invoked by a process p with some input, possibly returning an output. We use the following simple selectors on events: $e.p/e.i$ selects the process identifier/the operation index and $inv_p.in/ret_p.out$ are the associated input/output values.

Linearizability extends the abstract operation relations with history parameters Hs/Hs' and these extended operations additionally add a pair of an invoke

---

[2] For the same reasons, an atomicity check [4] for our multiset fails, since running the concrete code without interruption as an abstract specification does not offer the possibility to return false non-deterministically.

and return event to Hs with every AOP-transition. Sequences of such operations that are executed by a finite number of processes from an initial state (where $AInit$ holds and Hs is empty), generate the histories of the abstract specification.

Similarly, we extend the state of our concurrent system model SPAWN_n with a history variable H such that each process now first adds an invoke event $inv_p(I, In)$ to H before it executes the internal steps $\text{COP}_p(I, In; S, Out)$ that leave H unchanged.

$$\text{COP}_p(I, In; S, H, Out) \ \{$$
$$H := H + inv_p(I, In); \text{COP}_p(I, In; S, Out); H := H + ret_p(I, Out) \ \}$$

With its return, process p adds a return event $ret_p(I, Out)$ to H. The overall system state is initialized using a predicate $Init(S, H)$ which requires H to be empty. Hence, the visible behaviors H of the extended system $\text{SPAWN}_n(S, H)$ consist of either i) inv_p/ret_p events of a process p that correspond to terminated executions of an operation or ii) pending invoke events where p has added an invoke event to H but not yet returned, i.e., it is still running. Due to preemption, invoke events in H can be followed by events of *other* processes.

Roughly speaking, $\text{SPAWN}_n(S, H)$ is linearizable if every prefix of its histories H corresponds to some history Hs of the abstract specification that preserves the order of non-overlapping executions in H. (Two executions in H are non-overlapping iff the invoke event of one operation occurs *after* the return event of the other one.) However, it is cumbersome to reason about linearizability by searching for a corresponding abstract behavior for each possible concrete behavior [6]. Reasoning in terms of linearization points (possibilities) is more convenient: The basic idea is that the unique order of linearization points in a concurrent execution precisely determines the order of atomic operations in a corresponding abstract execution.

2.3 Challenges of Proving the Multiset Linearizable

This work started by looking at [3] where a *lock-based* multiset *without* a delete operation is shown to be linearizable. We and the authors of [3] first thought that adding a delete operation would violate linearizability. However, our presumed counter-example was flawed as we explain below. Our result here suggests that adding a (blocking) delete operation to their implementation should also be correct. Thus it solves an open challenge from [17].

The presumed counter example was based on the following concrete execution. A lookup and a delete operation concurrently search for an element x that lies ahead of their current positions but they have not reached x's position yet:

Next, both operations are preempted and a concurrent insert operation successfully inserts x below the current search indices of lookup and delete:

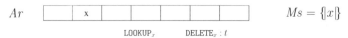

Then the delete operation runs to completion and removes x from the upper part of the array:

Finally, the lookup operation completes and returns false.

This concurrent behavior seems to contradict linearizability: At least one occurrence of x is always in the multiset while lookup returns false. It is however wrong to think that if some x is always in the *array*, then it must also be in the *multiset*. Indeed, according to linearizability, the order of the abstract insert and delete operations may be changed here, since the respective concrete executions do *overlap* in time. That is, the concrete history

$$inv_p(lkp, x),\ inv_q(del, x),\ inv_r(ins, x),\ ret_r(ins, t),\ ret_q(del, t), ret_p(lkp, f)$$

can be correctly reordered to the abstract history

$$inv_q(del, x),\ ret_q(del, t),\ inv_p(lkp, x),\ ret_p(lkp, f),\ inv_r(ins, x), ret_r(ins, t)$$

where first the delete operation takes effect, deleting the initial occurrence of x in the multiset, and thus making a lookup with false possible.

The concurrent execution above already motivates a central idea of our linearizability proof in terms of linearization points: Successful delete operations must potentially linearize *early* during their execution, before they actually delete their element from the array. Consequently, the abstract representation becomes a *collection of multisets*, since potentially linearizing a delete operation does not leave the abstract state unchanged and the linearization must be possibly revised due to future executions of other processes. To illustrate this effect, we consider the previous concurrent execution again:

Initially, no process is running and the abstract representation is merely $\{\{x\}\}$. In general, when no running delete operation exists, the abstract multiset is uniquely given by the elements in the array. As soon as a delete operation starts, it might have already linearized which gives possible multisets $\{\{\}, \{x\}\}$ where the empty multiset $\{\}$ results from deleting x from the initial multiset $\{x\}$. After the insert operation succeeds, the abstract representation is either $\{x, x\}$, or $\{x\}$ if the delete has potentially linearized. Finally, as soon as the delete operation succeeds, $\{x\}$ becomes the only possible multiset again.

Thus we compute possible abstract multisets by executing running operations to the end, then abstracting the array content to a multiset. This corresponds to the general approach of [13] to compute observation trees.

Note that in the execution above, the lookup operation must linearize to false *with* the potential linearization of the delete operation that removes the *last* occurrence of x from the multiset. If there were any delay between these two linearizations, then a concurrent INSERT might insert x below the current position of the lookup operation and linearizing to false would no longer be possible, since any possible abstract multiset would contain x. In this case, the linearization point of the delete operation is also an external potential linearization point for all running lookup/delete operations that can now complete with false.

The linearizability proof poses a further challenge for lookup/delete operations that return false: These operations must potentially linearize with false before they pass the first slot of the array. Starting with an empty array, after passing the first slot, a concurrent insert at the first slot makes linearizing these operations to false impossible. Together, successful delete operations, plus lookup/delete operations that return false, must potentially linearize *early* during their execution. Intuitively speaking, this allows us to move their linearization point towards the time of their invocation. We will formalize this intuition when we instantiate the abstraction relation of our proof method (see properties *DELt/DELf/LKPf* in Section 5.1).

3   RGITL

We specify and verify our proof method and the multiset case study in the logic RGITL that we briefly introduce next. For a detailed exposition refer to [14].

3.1   Syntax and Semantics

The semantics of RGITL is based on intervals which are finite or infinite sequences of the form $I = (I(0), I'(0), I(1), I'(1), I(2), \ldots)$ where every $I(k)$ and $I'(k)$ is a state function that maps variables to values. The state transition from $I(k)$ to $I'(k)$ is called a program transition, whereas the transition $I'(k)$ to $I(k+1)$ from a primed to the subsequent unprimed state is an environment transition. Thus intervals alternate between program and environment transitions, similar to reactive sequences [12].

The logic discerns static variables v (written lowercase) that do not change in any transition of an interval, from dynamic variables V (written uppercase) that can change arbitrarily. Primed and double primed variables V' and V'' are evaluated over $I'(0)$ and $I(1)$, respectively, if I is not empty. (For an empty interval, both V' and V'' are evaluated over $I(0)$.) Formulas φ are higher-order/temporal logic expressions of boolean type: For instance, the temporal logic operator φ_1 **until** φ_2 states that φ_2 holds in some state of a given interval and up to that state φ_1 holds. From this operator, the standard temporal logic operators eventually $\diamond$ and always $\square$ can be easily derived. For instance, formulas $\square\ V = V'$ and $\square\ V' = V''$ state that variable V does not change in any program/environment transition of an interval.

Assertions in RGITL are based on the well-known sequent calculus where a sequent $\Gamma \vdash \Delta$ is valid if the conjunction of all formulas from the antecedent Γ implies the disjunction of all formulas from the succedent Δ. Programs in RGITL are formulas: A program restricts the program transitions of an interval only. A typical program assertion $Init, \alpha, E \vdash \varphi$ states that program α satisfies property φ, starting in an initial state that satisfies predicate logic formula $Init$, given that the environment behaves according to formula E.

3.2 RG Reasoning

Rely-Guarantee (RG) reasoning [7] extends Hoare's well-known approach to reason about sequential programs with pre-/post-conditions to a concurrent setting: Assumptions of a process p about possible environment transitions are specified using a two-state predicate R_p: $state \times state \to bool$ over the entire program state. These are called rely conditions. In return, each process p must specify guarantees for its steps using a further two-state predicate G_p: $state \times state \to bool$, called guarantee conditions.

RGITL offers native support for RG assertions which are a special type of temporal formulas: An RG assertion for partial correctness

$$Pre(S), Inv(S) \vdash [R(S', S''), G(S, S'), Inv(S), \alpha(S)] \; Post(S)$$

requires that final states of a program α satisfy the post condition $Post$: $state \to bool$ if the program starts in a state where the precondition Pre: $state \to bool$ holds; program transitions preserve G and propagate the invariant Inv: $state \to bool$ if previous environment transitions satisfy R and propagate Inv, respectively. This semantics can be easily formalized in the logic using the **until** operator, see [17].

Similarly, an RG assertion for total correctness (using $\langle \, . \, \rangle$ instead of $[\, . \,]$) strengthens partial correctness by additionally requiring that α terminates if the environment always preserves the rely conditions and propagates the invariant. (We verify such liveness properties by induction over a given variant term.)

RGITL offers a Hoare-style calculus for the symbolic execution of RG assertions for partial and total correctness of sequential programs. For instance, we execute an assignment $(S := e); \alpha$ according to the following rule

$$\frac{Pre(s_0), Inv(s_0), s_1 = e \vdash G(s_0, s_1) \\ Pre(s_0), Inv(s_0), s_1 = e \vdash Inv(s_1) \\ Pre(s_0), s_1 = e, R(s_1, S), Inv(S) \vdash \langle R, G, Inv, \alpha \rangle \; Post(S)}{Pre(S), Inv(S) \vdash \langle R(S', S''), G(S, S'), Inv(S), (S := e); \alpha \rangle \; Post(S)} \quad (1)$$

where the static variables s_0/s_1 denote the state vector S before/after the assignment. In its first/second premise, the rule requires proving the guarantee/invariant propagation for the assignment transition. In the third premise, the RG assertion must be shown for the rest program α: The antecedent is typically simplified to the stable part of $Pre(s_0)$ over the assignment and the subsequent rely, i.e., to a formula $Pre_{new}(S)$ with $Pre(s_0) \wedge s_1 = e \wedge R(s_1, S) \to Pre_{new}(S)$.

Symbolic execution is practical for sequential but not for interleaved programs. Therefore, we apply RG decomposition rules for interleaved programs that reduce the verification to the constituent (sequential) sub-programs. Here we use the following RG decomposition rule for $\texttt{SPAWN}_n(S)$ (ignoring operation indices, inputs/outputs and histories for a moment):

1) $reflexive(G_p)$, $transitive(R_p)$, $G_p(S, S') \to R_q(S, S')$
2) $Pre_p(S') \land R_p(S', S'') \to Pre_p(S'')$, $Post_p(S') \land R_p(S', S'') \to Post_p(S'')$
3) $Inv(S), Pre_p(S) \vdash [R_p, G_p, Inv(S), \texttt{COP}_p(S)] \; Post_p(S)$
4) $(\exists\, S.\, Init(S)) \land (Init(S) \to Inv(S) \land \bigwedge_{p \leq n} Pre_p(S))$

$$\overline{Init(S) \vdash [\; \bigwedge_{p \leq n} R_p, \; \bigvee_{p \leq n} G_p, Inv(S), \texttt{SPAWN}_n(S)] \bigwedge_{p \leq n} Post_p(S)}$$

(2)

The conclusion of the rule states that each transition of the interleaved system preserves some guarantee G_p and propagates the invariant as long as the previous environment transitions satisfy all rely conditions R_p and propagate the invariant. (Note that we can not prove total correctness for $\texttt{SPAWN}_n$, since the system can invoke infinitely many operations.) Premises 1), 2) and 4) are simple predicate logic conditions on the used RG conditions: Guarantees must be reflexive, relies transitive, and a guarantee step of a process p must be a rely step for each other process q. Moreover, pre-/post-conditions must be stable over rely steps, since a process might start after/terminate before another process. Finally, there must exist an initial overall system state where predicate $Init$, the invariant and all pre-conditions hold. The central premise 3) requires proving an RG assertion for partial correctness of an individual operation $\texttt{COP}_p(S)$.

4 Proof Method: RG Reasoning with Possibilities

Our proof method for linearizability combines RG reasoning with possibilities as we explain next. The underlying system model is $\texttt{SPAWN}_n(S, H)$, Section 2.2.

4.1 Possibilities

Possibilities characterize linearizability in terms of linearization points (see Theorems 9 and 10 in [6]). Intuitively, our possibilities predicate $Poss(H, R, AS)$[3] holds if H, R, AS has been reached by a finite sequence of invocation, linearization and return steps as defined below. Parameter set R stores the return events for those running operations that have already linearized but not yet returned.

Formally, we define possibilities

$$Poss(H, R, AS) \equiv \exists\, AS_0.\; AInit(AS_0) \land \Delta Poss(([\;], \emptyset, AS_0), (H, R, AS))$$

as possibility steps $\Delta Poss$ on triples (H, R, AS) that start with an empty history, an empty set R and an initial abstract state AS_0. A possibility step is either an

---
[3] See [13], p. 248 for a comparison with the original syntax in [6].

invocation step *Invoke*, an abstract atomic operation step *Linearize*, or a return step *Return*

$$\Delta Poss \equiv (Invoke \lor Linearize \lor Return)^*$$

where * denotes the reflexive and transitive closure of the underlying relation.

In an invocation step, the executing process p must not have a pending invocation event in H ($nopi_p(H)$). The step adds an invoke event to H but changes neither the return set R nor the abstract state AS.

$$Invoke((H, R, AS), (H', R', AS')) \equiv \exists\, p, I, In.$$
$$H' = H + inv_p(I, In) \land nopi_p(H) \land R = R' \land AS = AS'$$

The execution of a linearization step requires a pending invoke in H (denoted $pi(n, H)$ where $n < \#H$) for a process that has not yet linearized (no corresponding event in R). It executes an abstract atomic transition AOP and adds the corresponding return event to R.

$$Linearize((H, R, AS), (H', R', AS')) \equiv H = H' \land \exists\, n, Out.$$
$$pi(n, H) \land (\forall\, e.\ e \in R \rightarrow e.p \neq H(n).p)$$
$$\land\ AOP(H(n).i)(H(n).in, AS, AS', Out) \land R' = R + ret_{H(n).p}(H(n).i, Out)$$

We write $Lin_{I,Out}$ for a linearization step of operation I with output Out.

Finally, a return step completes a running operation that has already linearized by removing its return event e from R and adding it to the history.

$$Return((H, R, AS), (H', R', AS')) \equiv$$
$$AS = AS' \land \exists\, e.\ e \in R \land H' = H + e \land R' = R \setminus \{e\}$$

To illustrate possibilities, we reconsider the concurrent multiset execution from Section 2.3 where the abstract multiset is $\{\!|x|\!\}$ initially and a lookup and a delete operation are invoked by processes p/q: Executing the *Invoke* steps for processes p and q we get a history $H = inv_p(lkp, x), inv_q(del, x)$. Now we have three possible continuations which yield possible values (R, Ms) as follows: Either i) no *Linearize* transition is executed $(\emptyset, \{\!|x|\!\})$, or ii) the delete operation linearizes with true $(\{ret_q(del, t)\}, \{\!||\!\})$, or iii) the delete operation linearizes with true and then the lookup linearizes with false $(\{ret_q(del, t), ret_p(lkp, f)\}, \{\!||\!\})$.

4.2   Proof Method

Our proof method is a linearizability-specific instance of rule (2). Similar to premise 3) of the rule, our method essentially requires to show the following RG assertion for partial correctness of an individual process p

$$nopi_p(H), Inv(S, H), \square\ Out' = Out''$$
$$\vdash [R_p(S', H', S'', H'') \land R_p^{poss}(H', H''), G_p(S, H, S', H') \land G^{poss}(S, H, S', H'),$$
$$Inv(S, H), \mathtt{COP}_p(I, In; S, H, Out)]\ \mathbf{t} \tag{3}$$

Fig. 2. Step-Local Backward Simulation

In (3), the rely/guarantee predicates R_p/G_p can be chosen freely for each case study whereas predicates R_p^{poss}/G^{poss} have linearizability-specific definitions that we introduce next. Predicate

$$G^{poss}(S, H, S', H') \equiv \forall R', AS'. \; Abs(S', H', R', AS') \rightarrow$$
$$\exists R, AS. \; Abs(S, H, R, AS) \wedge \Delta Poss(H, R, AS, H', R', AS')$$

ensures linearizability by propagating possibility steps backwards over each program transition as Figure 2 shows: For each transition of COP_p from S, H to S', H', we must show that each abstract state R', AS' that is related to S', H' according to an abstraction relation Abs, has been reached by a finite number of possibility steps starting from some abstract state R, AS that Abs relates to S, H.

The main idea of the abstraction relation is to restrict the number of possible abstract states that must be propagated backwards in concrete proofs, by taking the concrete state into account. The abstraction relation must be *total* over invariant states $Inv(S, H) \rightarrow \exists R, AS. \; Abs(S, H, R, AS)$.

Furthermore, proof obligation (3) uses the following rely properties

$$R_p^{poss}(H', H'') \equiv \;\; (nopi_p(H') \rightarrow nopi_p(H''))$$
$$\wedge \forall n. \; pi(n, H') \wedge H'(n).p = p \rightarrow pi(n, H'') \wedge H'(n) = H''(n)$$

which ensure that after adding an invoke event inv_p to H, this event remains pending and unchanged in H throughout the entire execution of p. These properties obviously hold for an individual process of the concurrent system. They are required to propagate possibility steps during p's execution, e.g., the linearization step *Linearize* requires a pending invocation in H for the respective process.

In (3), the output variable Out is local, so the output that is computed by the internal steps in COP_p corresponds to the output that is added to H in the final return transition. The post-condition is trivial for simplicity, but using an extra predicate to allow more complex post-conditions is possible.

Finally, there must exist an initial concrete system state. All concrete initial states must correspond to abstract initial states where no process has linearized.

$$Init_H(S) \wedge Abs(S, H, R, AS) \rightarrow AInit(AS) \wedge R = \emptyset$$

Theorem 1 (Compositional Proof Method for Linearizability).
With the predicate logic side conditions above, proof obligation (3) is a compositional proof method for linearizability:

$$Init_H(S), \text{SPAWN}_n(S, H), \Box \ (S' = S'' \land H' = H'')$$
$$\vdash \Box \ ((\exists \ r, as. \ Poss(H, r, as)) \land (\exists \ r, as. \ Poss(H', r, as)))$$

Intuitively, the theorem states that each prefix of H has a possibility (which implies linearizability). Further details and a mechanized soundness proof are described at [8]. Our method is compositional as it ensures the overall system property of linearizability based on the process-local RG proof obligation (3). Completeness of the method follows from the completeness of the step-local backward simulation technique in [13] (based on Owicki/Gries reasoning [11]) and the completeness of RG reasoning w.r.t. the Owicki/Gries method [12].

Since we typically want to talk about local states in concrete RG specifications, procedure COP_p in (3) can initialize local variables $S.LSf_p$ of process p with the invocation transition using an initialization function $init(I)$. (Directly using a **let** for the initialization would hide relevant local state information from specifications. We leave locality properties for LSf_p implicit in (3).)

5   Verifying the Multiset

To talk about local states in the multiset specifications, we introduce a function LSf as part of the program state $S = LSf, Ar$ which stores the following local information for each process p: I_p is the operation index, In_p is the input element, $Found_p$ is the boolean flag that determines whether the operation has found the searched element and Pos_p is the current index position of the running operation.

5.1   Instantiating the Abstraction Relation

The abstraction relation Abs of our proof method formalizes the intuitive considerations from Section 2.3 by relating a concrete state S, H to possible abstract states R, Ms as $Abs(S, H, R, Ms) \equiv BASE \lor DELt \lor DELf \lor LKPf$. In the base case $BASE \equiv Ms = Absf(Ar) \land R = Linsf(LSf, Ar)$ the abstract multiset Ms consists of all elements in Ar, computed by function $Absf$. Set R corresponds to precisely those running processes which have either not found their searched element and are at the end of their scan or which have found it and set their found-flag to true. Function $Linsf$ computes the return events of these processes.

The second disjunct in the definition of Abs describes the early linearization of a running delete operation (of process p) that *potentially* deletes the searched element that lies ahead of its current position at $Ar[n]$.

$$DELt(S, H, R, Ms) \equiv \exists \ p, n.$$
$$I_p = del \land \neg \ Found_p \land Pos_p \leq n < \#Ar \land Ar[n] = In_p$$
$$\land \ (\forall \ n_0. \ Pos_p \leq n_0 < n \rightarrow Ar[n_0] \neq In_p) \land ret_p(del, t) \in R$$
$$\land \ Abs(LSf, Ar[n]:=empty, H + ret_p(del, t), R \setminus \{ret_p(del, t)\}, Ms)$$

The definition can be viewed to consist of three steps. First a possible future state (S', H') from current state (S, H) is computed by running the remaining steps of p. This deletes input element $In_p = Ar[n]$ (the resulting array Ar' is written $Ar[n]:=empty$) and adds the return event $ret_p(del, t)$ to H. Second, Abs is called recursively to compute a possible abstract state (R', Ms') for state (S', H'). If the recursive call chooses the base case then Ms' is just the content of Ar'. Finally the effect of linearizing the delete early is to add the return event $ret_p(del, t)$ to the set R'. The final result of Abs therefore is $(R, Ms) = (R' \cup ret_p(del, t), Ms')$.

The third disjunct of Abs similarly considers a running delete process that potentially linearizes to false as it does not see its searched element ahead

$$DELf \equiv \exists\, p.$$
$$I_p = del \wedge \neg\ Found_p \wedge Pos_p < \#Ar \wedge (\forall\ n.\ Pos_p \leq n < \#Ar \rightarrow Ar[n] \neq In_p)$$
$$\wedge\, ret_p(del, f) \in R \wedge Abs(LSf, Ar, H + ret_p(del, f), R \setminus \{ret_p(del, f)\}, Ms)$$

The last disjunct $LKPf$ for a lookup operation that returns false is symmetric to $DELf$. It is easy to see that the recursion in Abs is well-founded, since it decreases the number of running processes.

5.2   The Main Proofs

Instantiating the RG parameters of our proof method is straight-forward: In the overall initial system state the array is empty. The invariant states that for each running process, the pending invocations in H correspond to the respective local state information in LSf. The rely condition R_p states that the length of the array is not concurrently changed and the guarantee G_p is defined as the rely conditions of all other processes.

With these instances, the predicate logic premises of our proof method hold trivially. Therefore, we only focus on the central proof obligation (3) which requires to prove an RG assertion for partial correctness for each individual multiset operation run by a process p. To also prove wait-freedom of each multiset operation, we show its stronger version for total correctness by induction over the variant $\#Ar - Pos_p$. Symbolic execution of the algorithms leads to proof goals for each transition (first premise of rule (1) for an assignment) where the guarantee must be shown. In particular, G^{poss} must hold for the transition, so a sequence of suitable abstract steps $\Delta Poss$ has to be chosen which makes the diagram of Fig. 2 commute. The choice is easy — usually the empty sequence since the step does not linearize any running algorihm — for all steps except for one step in each algorithm as detailed below. All proofs then are by well-founded induction over the number of running processes. They unfold the definition of Abs for both states (S, H) and (S', H'). The base case is usually trivial, each of the three recursive cases gives two states (S_0, H_0) and (S'_0, H'_0) shown in Fig. 3 that are reached by executing one pending operation to the end (indicated by the dashed line). Often the COP_p-transition commutes, i.e., it also modifies (S_0, H_0) to (S'_0, H'_0). Then the induction hypothesis (the dotted lines in the figure) closes the premise immediately. Otherwise, the state (S''_0, H''_0) reached by executing the transition from (S_0, H_0) must be

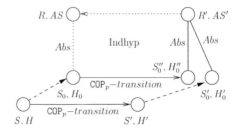

Fig. 3. Inductive proof scheme for backward simulation

shown to represent the same possible abstract states as (S'_0, H'_0), which is usually proved as a lemma using the same proof principle again.

The complex case for the DELETE$_x$ operation is the invocation transition. The proof discerns three cases. First, the delete may not have linearized, i.e., the set R' in Fig. 2 does not contain a return event for the process p executing the operation. Then $\Delta Poss$ is empty. Otherwise, when the multiset after the invoke (AS' in Fig. 2) still contains x, then just the delete linearizes, i.e., $\Delta Poss = Lin_{del,t}$. Otherwise, the linearization of the delete triggers some linearizations of lookups and deletes to false, i.e. $\Delta Poss = Lin_{del,t}; (Lin_{lkp,f} \vee Lin_{del,f})^*$. The exact sequence is determined by the difference between R' and R.

The critical transition for LOOKUP$_x$ is finding x. In particular, if we consider a multiset (after this transition) that does not contain x, there must be a running delete process q that (potentially) removes the last occurrence of x right *after* p linearizes with true. As a consequence, the transition then linearizes the current lookup process with true, the running delete process q with true, plus again a sequence $(Lin_{lkp,f} \vee Lin_{del,f})^*$ of currently running lookup/delete processes that can now return with false.

The critical transition of INSERT$_x$ is when it puts x in an empty array slot. This step can additionally linearize a running delete operation that now potentially deletes the element that has just been inserted. In this case the effects of the abstract insert and delete operations cancel each other (such behavior is typically found for data structures that use elimination [10]).

6   Related Work

The basic idea of our guarantee condition G^{poss} is based on [13] where backward simulation is shown to be sound and complete for linearizability. The approach uses predicate logic and non-compositional Owicki/Gries reasoning [11]. The adaptation to our temporal logic setting with RG reasoning has the following benefits: Verified programs can be specified in an abstract programming language rather than as transition systems with program counters. More importantly, it avoids the manual encoding of *local* state information that merely reflects the control flow of a program. Such properties are automatically computed and propagated by the symbolic execution of RG assertions (see also [17] for a comparison of our two local proof methods for linearizability for a restricted class of linearizable algorithms where potential linearization points do not modify the abstract state). Finally, we can verify liveness properties within one framework, here wait-freedom (total correctness) of the multiset operations. (For more challenging liveness proofs in RGITL see [15,14].)

Doherty et al. [2] use forward/backward simulations in a non-compositional approach to verify linearizability based on IO-automata. They also report on model checking linearizability. In general, model checking linearizability can quickly find bugs, however, it does not consider all possible executions [19].

Recent work [9] describes an RG-based approach for proving linearizability which annotates potential linearizations in the concrete specifications using abstract auxiliary code that works on a state that roughly corresponds to our R, AS. In contrast, we separate concrete and abstract code using a step-local simulation. The approach is manual and only considers partial correctness, while we mechanically verify the soundness of our method as well as its application.

The proof obligations in [18] are restricted to "pure" linearization points that leave the abstract state unchanged (as in [1]) and thus cannot prove our multiset. In more recent work [5], a complete approach for proving linearizability for a specific type of purely blocking queue algorithms is introduced. (An operation is purely blocking if its infinite blocked executions never modify the shared state.) Proof obligations are not based on linearization points, but rather on a characterization of queue-specific behaviors. They mechanize a proof for Herlihy Wing's queue, but only give a manual soundness proof of their reduction. Nevertheless, as our wait-free multiset is purely blocking, it would be interesting to find such characterizations for multisets and to analyse how their proofs would relate to ours.

7 Conclusion

We have introduced a general proof method for linearizability based on possibilities. It improves the complete proof strategy of [13] by using RG reasoning and symbolic execution with temporal logic. We have illustrated the expressiveness of our method by verifying a novel wait-free multiset implementation with potential external linearization points that change the representation and linearize several other processes. We leave it for future work to investigate whether the multiset can be verified with only a fixed small number of local states instead of the full function LSf, by exploiting the symmetry of the underlying operations (similar to [16]). Another option for future work is to apply our techniques to further algorithms such as the elimination queue [10] that can be verified based on similar ideas.

Acknowledgement. We thank Stefan Schödel for verifying various lemmas of the case study in KIV.

References

1. Derrick, J., Schellhorn, G., Wehrheim, H.: Verifying linearisability with potential linearisation points. In: Butler, M., Schulte, W. (eds.) FM 2011. LNCS, vol. 6664, pp. 323–337. Springer, Heidelberg (2011)

2. Doherty, S., Groves, L., Luchangco, V., Moir, M.: Formal verification of a practical lock-free queue algorithm. In: de Frutos-Escrig, D., Núñez, M. (eds.) FORTE 2004. LNCS, vol. 3235, pp. 97–114. Springer, Heidelberg (2004)
3. Elmas, T., Qadeer, S., Sezgin, A., Subasi, O., Tasiran, S.: Simplifying linearizability proofs with reduction and abstraction. In: Esparza, J., Majumdar, R. (eds.) TACAS 2010. LNCS, vol. 6015, pp. 296–311. Springer, Heidelberg (2010)
4. Flanagan, C., Freund, S.N.: Atomizer: A dynamic atomicity checker for multi-threaded programs. In: Proceedings of the 31st ACM SIGPLAN-SIGACT Symposium on Principles of Programming Languages, POPL 2004, pp. 256–267. ACM, New York (2004)
5. Henzinger, T., Sezgin, A., Vafeiadis, V.: Aspect-oriented linearizability proofs. In: D'Argenio, P.R., Melgratti, H. (eds.) CONCUR 2013. LNCS, vol. 8052, pp. 242–256. Springer, Heidelberg (2013)
6. Herlihy, M., Wing, J.: Linearizability: A correctness condition for concurrent objects. ACM Trans. on Prog. Languages and Systems 12(3), 463–492 (1990)
7. Jones, C.B.: Specification and design of (parallel) programs. In: Proceedings of IFIP 1983, pp. 321–332. North-Holland (1983)
8. KIV: Presentation of KIV proofs for wait-free multiset (2014) (2013), https://swt.informatik.uni-augsburg.de/swt/projects/ifm14.html
9. Liang, H., Feng, X.: Modular verification of linearizability with non-fixed linearization points. In: Proceedings of the 34th ACM SIGPLAN Conference on Programming Language Design and Implementation, PLDI 2013, pp. 459–470. ACM (2013)
10. Moir, M., Nussbaum, D., Shalev, O., Shavit, N.: Using elimination to implement scalable and lock-free fifo queues. In: SPAA, pp. 253–262. ACM (2005)
11. Owicki, S.S., Gries, D.: An Axiomatic Proof Technique for Parallel Programs I. Acta Inf. 6, 319–340 (1976)
12. de Roever, W.P., de Boer, F., Hannemann, U., Hooman, J., Lakhnech, Y., Poel, M., Zwiers, J.: Concurrency Verification: Introduction to Compositional and Noncompositional Methods. Cambridge Tracts in Theoretical Computer Science, vol. 54. Cambridge University Press (2001)
13. Schellhorn, G., Derrick, J., Wehrheim, H.: How to prove algorithms linearisable. In: Madhusudan, P., Seshia, S.A. (eds.) CAV 2012. LNCS, vol. 7358, pp. 243–259. Springer, Heidelberg (2012)
14. Schellhorn, G., Tofan, B., Ernst, G., Pfähler, J., Reif, W.: RGITL: A temporal logic framework for compositional reasoning about interleaved programs. Annals of Mathematics and Artificial Intelligence (AMAI) (2014)
15. Tofan, B., Bäumler, S., Schellhorn, G., Reif, W.: Temporal logic verification of lock-freedom. In: Bolduc, C., Desharnais, J., Ktari, B. (eds.) MPC 2010. LNCS, vol. 6120, pp. 377–396. Springer, Heidelberg (2010)
16. Tofan, B., Schellhorn, G., Reif, W.: Formal verification of a lock-free stack with hazard pointers. In: Cerone, A., Pihlajasaari, P. (eds.) ICTAC 2011. LNCS, vol. 6916, pp. 239–255. Springer, Heidelberg (2011)
17. Tofan, B., Travkin, O., Schellhorn, G., Wehrheim, H.: Two approaches for proving linearizability of multiset. Science of Computer Programming Journal (to appear, 2014)
18. Vafeiadis, V.: Automatically proving linearizability. In: Touili, T., Cook, B., Jackson, P. (eds.) CAV 2010. LNCS, vol. 6174, pp. 450–464. Springer, Heidelberg (2010)
19. Vechev, M., Yahav, E., Yorsh, G.: Experience with model checking linearizability. In: Păsăreanu, C.S. (ed.) Model Checking Software. LNCS, vol. 5578, pp. 261–278. Springer, Heidelberg (2009)

A Separation Principle for Embedded System Interfacing

Lucian M. Patcas, Mark Lawford, and Tom Maibaum

Department of Computing and Software
McMaster University, Hamilton, Ontario, Canada L8S 4K1
{patcaslm,lawford,maibaum}@mcmaster.ca

Abstract. In designing systems, engineers decompose the problem into smaller, more manageable tasks. A classic example of this is the *separation principle* from control systems which allows one to decompose the design of an optimal feedback control system into two independent tasks by designing (a) an observer, and (b) a controller. We investigate an analogous result for embedded system interfacing that will allow separation of the design of the input and output hardware interfaces while still guaranteeing the ability of the software to meet the system requirements. We define the notions of observability (controllability) of the system requirements with respect to the input (output) interface. We show that for a system that can be modeled by a functional four-variable model, observability and controllability allow for the separation of the design of the input and output interfaces. We also show that this separation is not always possible for systems that need the general, relational four-variable model. By strengthening either observability or controllability, we restrict the choice of input or output interfaces, but ensure separability of their designs.

1 Introduction

In designing systems, engineers like to decompose system design into smaller, more manageable tasks. A classic example of this is a conjecture by Kalman [7] that became known as the "separation principle" or "separation theorem" for linear control systems which states that one can decompose the physical realization of a state feedback controller into two stages: (a) an observer that computes a "best approximation" of the physical plant's state based upon the observations of the physical plant's outputs (monitored quantities), and (b) computation of the control signals to the plant (the control outputs) assuming access to perfect state information from the plant. When the actual plant's state is replaced in (b) by the approximation computed in (a), it can be shown that an optimal control results [5].

For reasons of flexibility and cost, the designs produced by control engineers are usually implemented as software-controlled embedded systems. A general view of an embedded system based upon [13] is depicted by the inner loop of Fig. 1. Based on the measured values of plant parameters obtained from the

E. Albert and E. Sekerinski (Eds.): IFM 2014, LNCS 8739, pp. 373–388, 2014.
© Springer International Publishing Switzerland 2014

sensors, the software controller commands the actuators with the purpose of maintaining certain properties in the plant. Parnas and Madey's four-variable model [11] (outside square of Fig. 1) helps to clarify the behaviour of, and the boundaries between, the plant, sensors, actuators, and control software. The model has been used successfully for the past five decades in the development of safety-critical embedded systems in various industries [14,3,8,15]. The four-variable model was also used extensively in the *Requirements Engineering Handbook* [9] that was put together at the request of the U.S. Federal Aviation Administration.

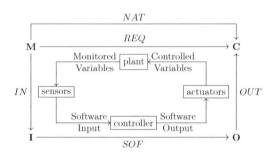

Fig. 1. The four-variable model

In the four-variable model there are four types of "variables" (hence the name): *monitored variables* (physical parameters of interest in the plant such as temperatures, voltages, aileron angle in a plane wing etc.); *controlled variables* (the physical parameters the system attempts to control); *input variables* (the digital representations of the monitored variables available to the software); and *output variables* (the variables set by the software in order to modify controlled variables). The sets of the possible values of the monitored and controlled variables are denoted by **M** and **C**, respectively; the sets of the possible values of the input and output variables are denoted by **I** and **O**, respectively. The *system requirements REQ* relate values of monitored variables to values of controlled variables. The environmental constraints on the system are described by the relation *NAT* (from "nature"), which restricts the possible values of the monitored and controlled variables. An environmental constraint might be, for instance, the maximum rate of climb of an aircraft in the case of an avionics system. The possible *system implementations* (system designs) are modelled by a sequential composition of *IN*, *SOF*, and *OUT*. Here, *IN* models the *input hardware interface* (sensors and analog-to-digital converters) and relates values of monitored variables to values of input variables. The *output hardware interface* (digital-to-analog converters and actuators) is modelled by *OUT*, which relates values of output variables to values of controlled variables. Relating values of input variables to values of output variables is *SOF*, which models the *control software*.

To account for the inaccuracies introduced by the hardware interfaces, *IN* and *OUT* are in general relations, not functions. For example, assume that *IN* models an A/D converter that converts analog voltages in the range 0–5V with an accuracy of ±0.5V; then, for an actual monitored voltage of 2.5V, the value of the corresponding input variable in the software can be any of the digital representations that correspond to 2V, 2.5V, and 3V. A typical engineering practice is to allow tolerances on requirements (i.e., more outputs acceptable for the same input), in which case *REQ* is a relation as well [8]. If we want to capture all the possible implementations of the control software (i.e., the software requirements), then *SOF* will typically have to be a relation. An actual implementation of *SOF* is a deterministic program that runs on a computer and can be modeled by a function.

The relations *NAT* and *REQ* are described by application domain experts and control engineers. The system designers allocate the system requirements between hardware and software, and describe *IN* and *OUT*. The software engineers must determine *SOF* and verify whether it is acceptable with respect to *NAT*, *REQ*, *IN*, and *OUT*. A difficult part in designing a system is to come up with the right triple *IN*, *SOF*, and *OUT* such that their integration produces an acceptable system design. For complex projects that require numerous subcontractors, communication and agreement between the various teams tend to be challenging, especially when the teams are large and geographically dispersed. Being able to design the input and output interfaces separately would:

- help designers manage with system design complexity;
- reduce the interaction required between the various teams;
- allow changes to the input (output) interface without requiring changes to the output (input) interface, an idea similar to Parnas' information hiding principle [10] that prevents local changes from propagating throughout other parts of the system.

At the same time, it would also be highly desirable for the pair of input/output interfacing to not prevent acceptable software implementations from being possible. The control software must be able to observe specific changes in the monitored variables via the input interface and react to these changes by modifying the values of the controlled variables via the output interface, as specified in the requirements. Thus in our attempt at a separation principle for embedded systems interfacing, *IN* plays a role similar to Kalman's observer and *OUT* plays a role similar to Kalman's controller.

To address the deficiencies of the software acceptability notion presented in [11], we proposed in [12] a new semantics for the four-variable model based on the demonic calculus of relations. Using this semantics, we formalized software acceptability and proved a necessary and sufficient condition for an acceptable software implementation to exist. In the current paper we revisit this condition in Section 3 and present it from a different angle by introducing the notions of observability and controllability of requirements with respect to the input, and, respectively, output interfaces. As it turns out, this necessary and sufficient condition has a surprising practical implication: if functions are used, the input and output interfaces can always be designed independently and an acceptable software implementation will still be possible as long as the observability and controllability conditions both hold; in the relational case, however, the input and output hardware interfaces are, in general, mutually dependent. Since relational specifications are more realistic in practice because they can model the nondeterminism induced by hardware inaccuracies and tolerances on requirements, in Section 4 we prove two stronger conditions that allow the input and output interfaces to be designed independently while still guaranteeing the ability of the software to meet the system requirements. In Section 5 we discuss some of the practical and theoretical implications of our results as well as limitations and future research directions.

2 Mathematical Preliminaries

The mathematics presented in this section will be applied to the four-variable model in the subsequent sections of the paper. We take a semantic view and consider that relations are models of specifications as well as of actual implementations.

2.1 Relations and Covers

A relation R from a set A to a set B is a subset of the cartesian product $A \times B$. In other words, R is a subset of the set of all ordered pairs (a, b), where $a \in A$ and $b \in B$. Some operations involving a relation $R \subseteq A \times B$ are:

- *domain* of R: $\mathsf{dom}\,(R) = \{a \in A \mid \exists b \in B.\ (a, b) \in R\}$;
- *range* of R: $\mathsf{ran}\,(R) = \{b \in B \mid \exists a \in A.\ (a, b) \in R\}$;
- *converse* of R: $R^\smile = \{(b, a) \in B \times A \mid (a, b) \in R\}$;
- *image set* of $a \in A$ under R: $R(a) = \{b \in B \mid (a, b) \in R\}$.

The image set of an element in the domain of a relation denotes the inaccuracy or tolerance acceptable for that input.

A relation $R \subseteq A \times B$ is *univalent* if it maps every element in its domain to exactly one element in its range. Univalent relations also go by the name *functional relations* or *partial functions*. Relation R is *total* if and only if $\mathsf{dom}\,(R) = A$. The relations that are both univalent and total are called *mappings* or *total functions*.

A *cover* of a set A is a family $\mathcal{C} = \{C_\alpha \subseteq A \mid \alpha \in \mathcal{I}\}$ where α is an index in some index set $\mathcal{I}$, $A = \bigcup_{\alpha \in \mathcal{I}} C_\alpha$, and the subsets C_α of A, called the *cells* of $\mathcal{C}$, are not necessarily pairwise disjoint. A particular case of a cover is the Wonham cover induced by a relation on its domain [16]. The Wonham cover induced by $R \subseteq A \times B$ on $\mathsf{dom}\,(R)$ is:

$$\mathsf{cov}\,(R) = \left\{A' \subseteq A \mid \exists b \in \mathsf{ran}\,(R).\ A' = R^\smile(b)\right\}. \tag{1}$$

The cells of $\mathsf{cov}\,(R)$, indexed by $\mathsf{ran}\,(R)$, are the image sets of the elements in the range of R under the converse of R. In the sequel, when we use the word cover we will mean a Wonham cover.

2.2   Demonic Factorization of Relations

For the goals set in Section 1, we are interested in existence conditions for the dotted arrows in the commutative diagram depicted in Fig. 2. This diagram is isomorphic to the four-variable model diagram.

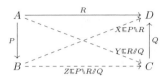

Fig. 2. Demonic factorization

The *composition* of two relations $P \subseteq A \times B$ and $Q \subseteq B \times C$ is the relation

$$P \,\mathbf{;}\, Q = \{(a,c) \in A \times C \mid \exists b \in B. \ (a,b) \in P \wedge (b,c) \in Q\}. \tag{2}$$

The problem with this notion of composition is that specifications P and Q are allowed where some points in the range of P are not in the domain of Q. In practice, this means that an implementation of $P \,\mathbf{;}\, Q$ will not always produce a result when expected to. Consider, for instance, the relations $P = \{(a_1, b_1), (a_1, b_2)\}$ and $Q = \{(b_1, c_1)\}$, depicted in Fig. 3. In this example, $P \,\mathbf{;}\, Q$ allows the dead end (a_1, b_2) because a_1 can still reach c_1 via b_1. Semantics that allow such behaviours are called *angelic*. In angelic semantics, specifications that allow "bad" behaviours for some inputs are permitted as long as they also allow "good" behaviours for those inputs. In contrast, a *demonic semantics* rejects any specification that allows "bad" behaviours. Considering that many embedded systems are used in safety-critical applications, it is always wise to plan for the worst, hence we find a demonic semantics more adequate.

(a) Angelic composition   (b) Demonic composition

Fig. 3. Composition of relations

The *demonic composition* of P with Q is the relation

$$P \square Q = \{(a,c) \in A \times C \mid (a,c) \in P \,\mathbf{;}\, Q \wedge P(a) \subseteq \mathsf{dom}\,(Q)\}. \tag{3}$$

As can be seen in Fig. 3, $P \square Q$ is empty for those inputs for which there is a chance of not producing expected results, thus it is our choice of sequential composition in the four-variable model. Demonic and angelic compositions are the same when P is univalent or Q is total.

The following subrelation of a relation $P \subseteq A \times B$ is obtained by restricting the domain of P to the domain of another relation $R \subseteq A \times C$:

$$P\big|_{\mathsf{dom}(R)} = \{(a, b) \in P \mid a \in \mathsf{dom}(R)\}. \tag{4}$$

This construction is helpful when working with partial relations. The rationale for allowing partial relations is that, in practice, in the early stages of system development it is more likely that incomplete specifications are produced rather than total specifications. More detail is added as the system becomes better understood and, eventually, the specifications will cover all the possible cases that can arise. Before getting to that point, however, many useful analyses can be performed, such as the implementability checks described in Sections 3 and 4.

A relation $P \subseteq A \times B$ is a *demonic refinement* of a relation $R \subseteq A \times B$, written $P \sqsubseteq R$, if and only if $\mathsf{dom}(R) \subseteq \mathsf{dom}(P)$ and $P\big|_{\mathsf{dom}(R)} \subseteq R$. Demonic refinement is also known as total correctness in [2,6]. The intuition for demonic refinement is as follows:

- for every input in the domain of R, P must produce only outputs allowed by R (i.e., an implementation is at least as deterministic as its specification);
- for the inputs outside the domain of R, P is allowed to produce any output or no output at all.

Demonic refinement is a partial order on relations. As an example, consider the relations in Fig. 4: $R = \{(a_1, b_1), (a_1, b_2), (a_2, b_2)\}$, $P = \{(a_1, b_1), (a_2, b_2), (a_3, b_2), (a_3, b_3)\}$, and $Q = \{(a_1, b_1), (a_2, b_1), (a_3, b_2), (a_3, b_3)\}$. Here, P refines R, but Q does not refine R because $(a_2, b_1) \notin R$.

Fig. 4. Examples of demonic refinement

Demonic composition and demonic refinement induce two residuation operations, the demonic left and right residuals. If composition is seen as a multiplicative operation, then the residuation operations play the role of division and their results are quotients. The demonic left and right residuals are useful when a relation is refined by a demonic composition of two relations and one of these relations is not known, as in triangles $\triangle A, B, D$ and $\triangle A, C, D$ in Fig. 2. The *demonic left residual* of R by Q, denoted $R /\!\!/ Q$, is defined as the largest solution, with respect to $\sqsubseteq$, of the inequation $Y \square Q \sqsubseteq R$, where Y is the unknown:

$$Y \square Q \sqsubseteq R \Leftrightarrow Y \sqsubseteq R /\!\!/ Q. \tag{5}$$

A solution Y, called a *demonic left factor* of R through Q, does not always exist. In [12], we proved the following necessary and sufficient condition for the existence of a demonic left factor:

$$(\exists Y.\ Y \square Q \sqsubseteq R) \Leftrightarrow \forall a \in \mathsf{dom}\,(R).\ \exists c \in \mathsf{dom}\,(Q).\ Q(c) \subseteq R(a). \tag{6}$$

According to (5), the demonic left residual $R \mathbin{/\!\!/} Q$ is defined only when a demonic left factor exists. If $R \mathbin{/\!\!/} Q$ is defined, then its value is:

$$R \mathbin{/\!\!/} Q \mathrel{\doteq} \{(a,c) \in A \times C \mid c \in \mathsf{dom}\,(Q) \wedge Q(c) \subseteq R(a)\}. \tag{7}$$

The symbol $\doteq$, called "venturi tube" [6], has the following meaning: for any two expressions ϕ and ψ, if $\phi \doteq \psi$, then ψ is defined and equal to ϕ if and only if ϕ is defined.

Similarly to the demonic left residual, the *demonic right residual* of R by P, denoted $P \mathbin{\backslash\!\backslash} R$, is defined as the largest solution, with respect to $\sqsubseteq$, of the inequation $P \square X \sqsubseteq R$, where X is the unknown:

$$P \square X \sqsubseteq R \Leftrightarrow X \sqsubseteq P \mathbin{\backslash\!\backslash} R. \tag{8}$$

A solution X, called a *demonic right factor* of R through P, does not always exist. Therefore, by (8), the demonic right residual $P \mathbin{\backslash\!\backslash} R$ is not always defined. We proved in [12] that the following condition is necessary and sufficient for the existence of a demonic right factor and for the definedness of the demonic right residual:

$$(\exists X.\ P \square X \sqsubseteq R) \Leftrightarrow$$

$$\mathsf{dom}\,(R) \subseteq \mathsf{dom}\,(P) \wedge \forall b \in \mathsf{ran}\left(P|_{\mathsf{dom}(R)}\right).\ \exists d \in D.\ \left(P|_{\mathsf{dom}(R)}\right)^{\smile}(b) \subseteq R^{\smile}(d). \tag{9}$$

If $P \mathbin{\backslash\!\backslash} R$ is defined, then its value is:

$$P \mathbin{\backslash\!\backslash} R \mathrel{\doteq} \left\{(b,d) \in B \times D \;\middle|\; b \in \mathsf{ran}\left(P|_{\mathsf{dom}(R)}\right) \wedge \left(P|_{\mathsf{dom}(R)}\right)^{\smile}(b) \subseteq R^{\smile}(d)\right\}. \tag{10}$$

The demonic left and right residuals are also useful when we wish to decompose a relation into a demonic composition of three relations and the relation in the middle is not known. This situation is depicted in Fig. 2, where we are interested in solving the inequality $P \square Z \square Q \sqsubseteq R$ for Z. A solution Z, which we call a *demonic mid factor* of R through P and Q, does not always exist. In [12] we showed that:

$$(\exists Z.\ P \square Z \square Q \sqsubseteq R) \Leftrightarrow$$

$$\mathsf{dom}\,(R) \subseteq \mathsf{dom}\,(P) \wedge \forall b \in \mathsf{ran}\left(P|_{\mathsf{dom}(R)}\right).\ \exists c \in \mathsf{dom}\,(Q).$$

$$Q(c) \subseteq \left\{d \in D \;\middle|\; \left(P|_{\mathsf{dom}(R)}\right)^{\smile}(b) \subseteq R^{\smile}(d)\right\}. \tag{11}$$

We also proved that any demonic mid factor is a demonic refinement of the residual $P \setminus R \mathbin{/\!/} Q$, which we call the *demonic mid residual* of R by P and Q. In other words, this residual is the largest solution, with respect to $\sqsubseteq$, of the inequality $P \square Z \square Q \sqsubseteq R$:

$$P \square Z \square Q \sqsubseteq R \Leftrightarrow Z \sqsubseteq P \setminus R \mathbin{/\!/} Q. \tag{12}$$

If a demonic mid factor exists, then the value of $P \setminus R \mathbin{/\!/} Q$ is well defined and is given by:

$$P \setminus R \mathbin{/\!/} Q = \left\{ (b,c) \in B \times C \,\middle|\, b \in \mathsf{ran}\left(P|_{\mathsf{dom}(R)} \right) \wedge c \in \mathsf{dom}\,(Q) \wedge \right.$$
$$\left. Q(c) \subseteq \left\{ d \in D \,\middle|\, \left(P|_{\mathsf{dom}(R)} \right)^{\smallsmile}(b) \subseteq R^{\smallsmile}(d) \right\} \right\}. \tag{13}$$

More details on the demonic calculus of relations can be found in [4,1,2,6,12].

3   Implementability

In this section we ask the question of implementability of system requirements: is an acceptable implementation of the system requirements possible given a particular choice of hardware interfacing between the system and the physical environment? We present necessary and sufficient implementability conditions in both the functional and relational cases of the four-variable model. For the reasons mentioned in the introduction, we would like to be able to design the input and output interfaces independently of each other, while ensuring that an acceptable implementation is still possible. As it turns out, this separation is always possible in the functional setting, but not always when relational specifications are used.

To not overcomplicate the presentation, in this paper we do not use the relation NAT explicitly; instead, we assume that the system requirements specify only physically meaningful outputs for the inputs that are possible from the environment. More details about how NAT affects implementability can be found in [12].

We now return to the question of implementability of system requirements and give the following definition for implementability.

Definition 1. *System requirements REQ are implementable if an input interface IN, an output interface OUT and software SOF exist such that $IN \square SOF \square OUT \sqsubseteq REQ$.*

In Definition 1, a system implementation is given by the demonic composition of IN, SOF, and OUT. As explained in Section 2.2, the demonic composition ensures that there are no dead ends when integrating IN, SOF, and OUT. As a satisfaction criterion, we use the demonic refinement of relations, which ensures that for every input in the domain of the requirements an implementation will produce only results allowed by the requirements. The demonic refinement

allows arbitrary system behaviour for the inputs outside the domain of the requirements, but this should present no danger as it is assumed that for a final
product hazard analyzes have been conducted and all the inputs that could
lead to hazardous system behaviour have been added to the domain of REQ
as additional safety requirements. We call *acceptable* a system implementation
$IN \square SOF \square OUT$ such that $IN \square SOF \square OUT \sqsubseteq REQ$. Definition 1 implies that
the system requirements are implementable only if an acceptable system imple-
mentation exists. A software implementation is *acceptable* if and only if it is
part of an acceptable system implementation. Therefore, the implementability
of system requirements reduces to the existence of an acceptable software implementation, which is relative to the choices made by the system designers for
the input and output hardware.

The question now is when does an acceptable software implementation exist?
The software must be able to observe specific changes in the monitored variables
via the input interface and react to these changes by modifying the values of the
controlled variables via the output interface, as specified in the requirements. We
introduce the notions of observability and controllability of system requirements
with respect to the input and, respectively, output hardware interfaces.

Definition 2. *System requirements REQ are* observable *with respect to an input
interface IN if there exists a demonic right factor of REQ through IN.*

For system requirements REQ to be observable, Definition 2 requires that there
exists a relation $X \subseteq \mathbf{I} \times \mathbf{C}$ such that $IN \square X \sqsubseteq REQ$. Observability is a necessary
condition for implementability since if $IN \square SOF \square OUT \sqsubseteq REQ$ we can take
$X = SOF \square OUT$. Intuitively, observability says that in the worst case IN always
retains at least as much information about the monitored variables as REQ.

Definition 3. *System requirements REQ are* controllable *with respect to an
output interface OUT if there exists a demonic left factor of REQ through OUT.*

For system requirements REQ to be controllable, Definition 3 requires that there
exists a relation $Y \subseteq \mathbf{M} \times \mathbf{O}$ such that $Y \square OUT \sqsubseteq REQ$. Clearly controllability
is also necessary for implementability since if $IN \square SOF \square OUT \sqsubseteq REQ$ we can
always take $Y = IN \square SOF$. The intuition for controllability is that in the worst
case OUT must be at least as precise as REQ.

In the remainder of the section, we will discuss how observability and controllability affect implementability of system requirements in both the functional
and relational cases of the four-variable model.

3.1 Functional Case

Here we assume the extreme case where the specifications in the four-variable
model are all total functions.

Proposition 1. *System requirements REQ are observable with respect to an
input interface IN if and only if $\forall M' \in \text{cov}(IN). \ \exists M'' \in \text{cov}(REQ). \ M' \subseteq M''$.*

Proof. By (1) and specializing (9) to total functions.   □

Proposition 2. *System requirements REQ are controllable with respect to an output interface OUT if and only if* $\mathrm{ran}\,(REQ) \subseteq \mathrm{ran}\,(OUT)$.

Proof. By specializing (6) to total functions.   □

Proposition 3. *System requirements REQ are implementable with respect to an input interface IN and an output interface OUT if and only if REQ is observable with respect to IN and controllable with respect to OUT.*

Proof. By specializing (11) to total functions.   □

Because observability is defined only in terms of *REQ* and *IN*, and controllability only in terms of *REQ* and *OUT*, a corollary of Prop. 3 is that for an acceptable *SOF* to exist, *IN* and *OUT* are always separable. The practical implication is that the input and output interfaces of a system modeled using a functional four-variable model can always be designed independently and an acceptable software implementation is guaranteed to exist.

3.2 Relational Case

We now consider the most general case where the specifications in the four-variable model are partial relations.

Proposition 4. *System requirements REQ are observable with respect to an input interface IN if and only if the following conditions are both satisfied:*

(i) $\mathrm{dom}\,(REQ) \subseteq \mathrm{dom}\,(IN)$;
(ii) $\forall M' \in \mathrm{cov}\left(IN\big|_{\mathrm{dom}(REQ)}\right).\ \exists M'' \in \mathrm{cov}\,(REQ).\ M' \subseteq M''.$

Proof. Follows from (1) and (9).   □

Proposition 4(i) requires an input interface to "see" every input for which the requirements specify system behaviour. Proposition 4(ii), also known as refinement of covers in mathematical topology, requires the accuracy of the input interface to be the same or of finer granularity than what the requirements imply. For example, in Fig. 5a, $\mathrm{cov}\left(IN\big|_{\mathrm{dom}(REQ)}\right) = \{\{m_1, m_2, m_3\}\}$ and $\mathrm{cov}\,(REQ) = \{\{m_1, m_2\}, \{m_3\}\}$. The cell $IN^{\smile}(i_1) = \{m_1, m_2, m_3\}$ in $\mathrm{cov}\left(IN\big|_{\mathrm{dom}(REQ)}\right)$ corresponds to i_1 and represents the accuracy with which *IN* produces i_1; in other words, the software is not able to distinguish between m_1, m_2, or m_3 when it receives the input i_1. The requirements in this example, on the other hand, require the system to make a distinction in how it treats m_3 compared to m_1 and m_2, reflected by the two distinct cells $REQ^{\smile}(c_2) = \{m_3\}$ and, respectively, $REQ^{\smile}(c_1) = \{m_1, m_2\}$ in $\mathrm{cov}\,(REQ)$. The software will not be able to make this distinction because the cell $\{m_1, m_2, m_3\}$ in $\mathrm{cov}\left(IN\big|_{\mathrm{dom}(REQ)}\right)$ is not contained in any of the cells of $\mathsf{cov}\,(REQ)$. Consequently, the accuracy of IN is coarser than required and REQ is not observable with respect to IN. In the example depicted in Fig. 5b, $\mathsf{cov}\left(IN|_{\mathsf{dom}(REQ)}\right) = \{\{m_1, m_2\}, \{m_2\}\}$ and $\mathsf{cov}\,(REQ) = \{\{m_1\}, \{m_1, m_2\}, \{m_2\}\}$ satisfy Prop. 4(ii). Because $\mathsf{dom}\,(REQ) = \mathsf{dom}\,(IN)$, Prop. 4(i) is also satisfied, hence REQ is observable with respect to IN, ensuring that there is a way to relate the software inputs to values of controlled variables via a demonic right factor of REQ through IN. Note that $IN \setminus REQ$ is the largest, with respect to $\sqsubseteq$, such factor (i.e., the least restrictive specification).

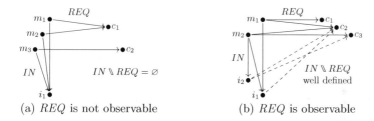

(a) REQ is not observable   (b) REQ is observable

Fig. 5. Observability

Proposition 5. *System requirements REQ are controllable with respect to an output interface OUT if and only if $\forall C' \in \mathsf{cov}\left(REQ^\smile\right). \exists C'' \in \mathsf{cov}\left(OUT^\smile\right). C'' \subseteq C'$.*

Proof. Follows from (1) and (6).   □

The intuition for Prop. 5 is that for the system requirements to be controllable the output hardware should allow for the same or finer control over the controlled variables than what is implied by the requirements. The cells in the covers of $REQ^\smile$ or $OUT^\smile$ are measures of the amount of control: the smaller the cell, the more precise the control. For example, in Fig. 6a the cell $REQ(m_1) = \{c_1, c_2\}$ in $\mathsf{cov}\left(REQ^\smile\right)$ does not contain any of the cells of $\mathsf{cov}\left(OUT^\smile\right)$. As such, OUT does not have the right amount of control over the controlled variables and REQ is not controllable with respect to OUT. Figure 6b depicts an example where there is a way to relate the monitored values to software outputs via a demonic left factor of REQ through OUT and, consequently, REQ is controllable. Note that $REQ \,/\!/\, OUT$ is the largest, with respect to $\sqsubseteq$, such factor (i.e., the least restrictive specification).

In contrast to the functional case, in the relational case observability and controllability are not sufficient for implementability. A counterexample to the sufficiency of their conjunction is given in Fig. 7a, which combines the examples from Figs. 5b and 6b. In this example, REQ is observable and controllable even though there is no acceptable software. By (12), any acceptable software implementation is a demonic refinement of $IN \setminus REQ \,/\!/\, OUT$, which is not well defined here. The reason for this is that i_1 cannot be connected with either

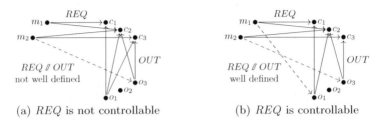

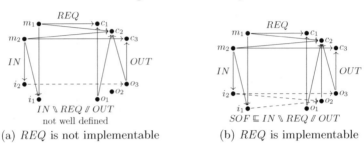

Fig. 6. Controllability

(a) REQ is not implementable

(b) REQ is implementable

Fig. 7. Implementability

o_1 or o_2 without breaking demonic refinement. For example, if we connect i_1 with o_1, then m_2 will be connected with c_1 via $IN \square SOF \square OUT$, something not allowed by REQ. If we extend OUT with the pair (o_2, c_2) as in Fig. 7b, then $IN \setminus REQ \mathbin{/\mkern-6mu/} OUT$ becomes well defined, hence an acceptable SOF is possible. The demonic mid residual $IN \setminus REQ \mathbin{/\mkern-6mu/} OUT$ is the least restrictive specification for acceptable software.

Proposition 6. *System requirements REQ are implementable with respect to an input interface IN and an output interface OUT if and only if the following two conditions are both satisfied:*

(i) $\mathrm{dom}\,(REQ) \subseteq \mathrm{dom}\,(IN)$;

(ii) $\forall M' \in \mathrm{cov}\left(IN\big|_{\mathrm{dom}(REQ)}\right).\ \exists C' \in \mathrm{cov}\,(OUT^{\smallsmile}).\ C' \subseteq \bigcap_{m \in M'} REQ(m).$

Proof. Follows from (1) and (11).   □

The conditions in Prop. 6 imply both observability and controllability. However, the requirements are implementable if and only if a certain balance exists between observability and controllability. In Fig. 7b, REQ is implementable because if we consider the cell $IN^{\smallsmile}(i_1) = \{m_1, m_2\}$ in $\mathrm{cov}\left(IN\big|_{\mathrm{dom}(REQ)}\right)$, then there is the cell $OUT^{\smallsmile}(o_2) = \{c_2\} = REQ(m_1) \cap REQ(m_2)$ in $\mathrm{cov}\,(OUT^{\smallsmile})$; similarly, for $IN^{\smallsmile}(i_2) = \{m_2\}$ in $\mathrm{cov}\left(IN\big|_{\mathrm{dom}(REQ)}\right)$, there is $OUT^{\smallsmile}(o_3) = \{c_2, c_3\} = REQ(m_2)$ in $\mathrm{cov}\,(OUT^{\smallsmile})$, hence Prop. 6(ii) is satisfied.

As can be seen in Prop. 6(ii), IN and OUT are coupled. In practice, this means that for the requirements to be implementable, the input and output hardware cannot be, in general, designed independently of each other.

4   Separability

In this section, we present two stronger implementability conditions for the relational setting that allow the input and output hardware to be designed independently of each other.

We obtain the first stronger implementability condition by strengthening controllability as follows.

Proposition 7. *System requirements REQ are implementable with respect to an input interface IN and an output interface OUT if the following two conditions are both satisfied:*

(i) *REQ is observable with respect to IN;*
(ii) $\forall M' \in \mathsf{cov}\,(REQ).\ \exists C' \in \mathsf{cov}\,(OUT^{\smile}).\ C' \subseteq \bigcap_{m \in M'} REQ(m).$

Proof. To prove the implementability of REQ we have to show that Prop. 6 is satisfied. Proposition 6(i) follows easily from Prop. 7(i). Also from Prop. 7(i), we have that for any $M' \in \mathsf{cov}\left(IN|_{\mathsf{dom}(REQ)}\right)$ there is a $M'' \in \mathsf{cov}\,(REQ)$ such that $M' \subseteq M''$. If we substitute M'' for M' in Prop. 7(ii), we get that there exists a $C' \in \mathsf{cov}\,(OUT^{\smile})$ such that $C' \subseteq \bigcap_{m \in M''} REQ(m)$. Because $M' \subseteq M''$, we also have that $C' \subseteq \bigcap_{m \in M'} REQ(m)$. In conclusion, we have proved that for any $M' \in \mathsf{cov}\left(IN|_{\mathsf{dom}(REQ)}\right)$ there is a $C' \in \mathsf{cov}\,(OUT^{\smile})$ such that $C' \subseteq \bigcap_{m \in M'} REQ(m)$, which is exactly Prop. 6(ii).   □

We call a relation REQ that satisfies Prop. 7(ii) *strongly controllable* with respect to OUT. An example of strongly controllable requirements is in Fig. 7b. Strong controllability is not necessary for implementability, as shown in Fig. 8a. Here, the requirements are implementable and, consequently, controllable with respect to OUT, although they are not strongly controllable. As such, strong controllability reduces the number of output hardware choices when compared with controllability. On the other hand, strong controllability ensures that IN and OUT can be chosen independently of each other as long as they satisfy their respective constraints in Prop. 7.

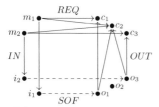
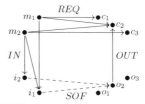

(a) *REQ* is implementable, but not strongly controllable
(b) *REQ* is implementable, but not strongly observable

Fig. 8. Strong observability and controllability not necessary for implementability

In the second stronger implementability condition, we strengthen observability as follows.

Proposition 8. *System requirements REQ are implementable with respect to an input interface IN and an output interface OUT if the following conditions are all satisfied:*

(i) $\operatorname{dom}(REQ) \subseteq \operatorname{dom}(IN)$*;*
(ii) $\forall M' \in \operatorname{cov}\left(IN|_{\operatorname{dom}(REQ)}\right)$*.* $\exists C' \in \operatorname{cov}\left(REQ^{\smile}\right)$*.* $M' \subseteq \bigcap_{c \in C'} REQ^{\smile}(c)$*;*
(iii) *REQ is controllable with respect to OUT.*

Proof. Similar to the proof for Prop. 7. $\square$

We call *REQ strongly observable* with respect to *IN* if *REQ* and *IN* satisfy Props. 8(i) and 8(ii). An example of strongly observable requirements is in Fig. 8a. Strong observability is not necessary for implementability (Fig. 8b). In this example, the requirements are implementable without Prop. 8(ii) being satisfied. As such, strong observability restricts the acceptable choices of input hardware compared with observability, but at the same time it allows the separation of *IN* and *OUT* as long as they satisfy the constraints of Prop. 8.

5   Discussion

In this paper, we presented one necessary and sufficient (Prop. 6) and two sufficient (Props. 7 and 8) implementability conditions that allow the system designers to choose a pair of input and output hardware interfaces such that an acceptable software implementation is guaranteed to exist. Implementability does not imply that implementing the SOF relation is practical. Nevertheless, it gives software engineers the confidence that their efforts are not destined to fail from the beginning. If implementability is not satisfied, then no acceptable implementation will be possible.

From a system development perspective, an important question is which implementability condition to use and when. If separating *IN* and *OUT* at design time is important, then one of the stronger implementability conditions should be used as follows:

- if the input hardware is more difficult to design than the output hardware, then it is desirable to have as many options as possible for the input hardware. In such cases, Prop. 7 is more suitable because the implied strong controllability limits only the choices of output hardware without overly-restricting the input hardware. If for observability the necessary and sufficient condition of Prop. 4 is used, then this will allow the widest possible range of acceptable input hardware;
- similarly, Prop. 8 together with Prop. 5 should be used if having more design options for the output hardware is more important than for the input hardware.

If the system designers need as many acceptable options as possible for both the input and output interfaces, and separability of *IN* and *OUT* is not as important, then the necessary and sufficient implementability conditions in Prop. 6 should be used.

The stronger implementability conditions in Props. 7 and 8 can be viewed as a "separation principle" for embedded systems interfacing similar to the well known separation principle for linear control systems design [7]. The analogy is not perfect, however. An observer in the control engineering sense would be constructed in the four-variable model as a simulation of a linear system inside *SOF*. The relation *IN* represents the input hardware that obtains the samples that would be used as input to the observer simulation. Similarly, a state feedback controller in the control engineering sense would be computed as a matrix multiplication inside *SOF*, the results of which would then be sent to the physical plant via the output hardware represented by *OUT*. Also, in control engineering observability and controllability of a plant are sufficient for separability of observers and controllers, while in the relational four-variable model either observability or controllability of *REQ* needs to be strengthened in order for the designs of the input and output interfaces to be separable.

The results presented in this paper are very general. The relations *REQ*, *IN*, *OUT*, and *SOF* model input-output behaviours without internal states. Also, we did not assume any structure on the sets **M**, **C**, **I**, and **O**. Because of this generality, our implementability conditions do not explicitly consider constraints that a practical implementation has to deal with, such as timing. In our current formalization, the sets **M**, **C**, **I**, and **O** contain all the possible values for every, respectively, monitored, controlled, input, and output variable. Time can be added explicitly to the four-variable model by treating the elements of **M**, **C**, **I**, and **O** as functions of time [11,8]. A useful research direction would be to specialize our implementability conditions to their timed versions.

The results also have applicability beyond embedded systems. They can be applied to essentially any system that can be modeled using a commutative diagram similar to the one of the four-variable model (Figs. 1 and 2). Such commutative diagrams also appear in stepwise refinement techniques where mappings between behaviours at different levels of abstraction are rather frequent.

To be useful in practice, our implementability checks need to be supported by tools. For a completely automated check, SMT solving may be a fruitful direction, although many SMT solvers do not cope well with formulas that have existential quantifiers within the scope of universal quantifiers. Another approach would be to develop heuristic algorithms for the problem at hand. When SMT solving and heuristics do not work, or in the case of very large or infinite relations, verifying implementability will still be possible in an higher-order proof assistant such as Coq, Isabelle, PVS etc., paying the price of having to do tedious and, more than often, hard proofs.

We have formalized and checked the mathematics presented in the paper with the proof assistant Coq. The files are available at www.cas.mcmaster.ca/~patcaslm/papers/2014-iFM/coq.

References

1. Brink, C., Kahl, W., Schmidt, G. (eds.): Relational Methods in Computer Science. Advances in Computing. Springer (1997)
2. Desharnais, J., Mili, A., Nguyen, T.: Refinement and Demonic Semantics. In: Brink, et al. (eds.) [1], ch. 11, pp. 166–183 (1997)
3. Faulk, S., Finneran, J., Kirby, J., Shash, S., Sutton, J.: Experience applying the CoRE method to the Lockhead C-130J software requirements. In: Ninth Annual Conference on Computer Assurance, Gaithersburg, Maryland (June 1994)
4. Frappier, M.: A Relational Basis for Program Construction by Parts. Ph.D. thesis, Computer Science Department, University of Ottawa (1995)
5. Joseph, D.P., Tou, T.J.: On linear control theory. Transactions of the American Institute of Electrical Engineers. Part II: Applications and Industry 80(4), 193–196 (1961)
6. Kahl, W.: Refinement and development of programs from relational specifications. Electronic Notes in Theoretical Computer Science (ENTCS) 44(3), 51–93 (2003)
7. Kalman, R.E.: Contributions to the theory of optimal control. Bol. Soc. Mat. Mexicana 5(2), 102–119 (1960)
8. Lawford, M., McDougall, J., Froebel, P., Moum, G.: Practical application of functional and relational methods for the specification and verification of safety critical software. In: Rus, T. (ed.) AMAST 2000. LNCS, vol. 1816, pp. 73–88. Springer, Heidelberg (2000)
9. Lempia, D.L., Miller, S.P.: Requirements engineering management handbook. Tech. Rep. DOT/FAA/AR-08/32, U.S. Department of Transportation, Federal Aviation Administration (June 2009)
10. Parnas, D.L.: On the criteria to be used in decomposing systems into modules. Communications of the ACM 15(12), 1053–1058 (1972)
11. Parnas, D.L., Madey, J.: Functional documents for computer systems. Science of Computer Programming 25(1), 41–61 (1995)
12. Patcas, L.M., Lawford, M., Maibaum, T.: From system requirements to software requirements in the four-variable model. In: Schneider, S., Treharne, H., Margaria, T., Padberg, J., Taentzer, G. (eds.) Proceedings of the Automated Verification of Critical Systems (AVoCS 2013). Electronic Communications of the EASST, vol. 66 (2014)
13. Thompson, J., Heimdahl, M., Miller, S.P.: Specification-based prototyping for embedded systems. In: Nierstrasz, O., Lemoine, M. (eds.) ESEC/FSE 1999. LNCS, vol. 1687, pp. 163–179. Springer, Heidelberg (1999)
14. Van Schouwen, A.: The A-7 requirements model: Re-examination for real-time systems and an application to monitoring systems. Tech. Rep. 90-276, Queens University, Ontario, Canada (1990)
15. Wassyng, A., Lawford, M.: Lessons learned from a successful implementation of formal methods in an industrial project. In: Araki, K., Gnesi, S., Mandrioli, D. (eds.) FME 2003. LNCS, vol. 2805, pp. 133–153. Springer, Heidelberg (2003)
16. Wonham, W.M.: Lecture notes on supervisory control of discrete-event systems. Systems Control Group, Department of Electrical & Computer Engineering, University of Toronto (July 2013), http://www.control.toronto.edu/DES/

Author Index